THE PSYCHOLOGY OF RELIGION

An Empirical Approach

BERNARD SPILKA
University of Denver

RALPH W. HOOD, JR.
University of Tennessee at Chattanooga

RICHARD L. GORSUCH
Graduate School of Psychology,
Fuller Theological Seminary

PRENTICE-HALL, INC., Englewood Cliffs, New Jersey 07632

Library of Congress Cataloging in Publication Data

Spilka, Bernard.
    The psychology of religion.

    Bibliography: p.
    Includes index.
    1. Psychology, Religious. I. Hood, Ralph W.
II. Gorsuch, Richard L. III. Title.
BL53.S625 1985   200'.1'9   85-597
ISBN 0-13-736398-2

Editorial/production supervision and interior design: *Marjorie Borden*
Cover design: *George Cornell*
Manufacturing buyer: *Harry Baisley*

Printed in the United States of America

10 9 8 7 6 5 4 3 2 1

ISBN 0-13-736398-2 01

Prentice-Hall International, (UK) Limited, *London*
Prentice-Hall of Australia Pty. Limited, *Sydney*
Editora Prentice-Hall do Brasil, Ltda., *Rio de Janeiro*
Prentice-Hall Canada Inc., *Toronto*
Prentice-Hall Hispanoamericana, S.A., *Mexico*
Prentice-Hall of India Private Limited, *New Delhi*
Prentice-Hall of Japan, Inc., *Tokyo*
Prentice-Hall of Southeast Asia Pte. Ltd., *Singapore*
Whitehall Books Limited, *Wellington, New Zealand*

To very significant people in our lives—

Ellen	*Laura*	*Sylvia*
Ed	*Linda*	*Eric*
Joan		*Kay*
Dave		

CONTENTS

six   Religion and Death   *125*

PART III   RELIGIOUS CHANGE, ORGANIZATION, AND
EXPERIENCE

seven   Religious Experience   *153*

eight   Mysticism   *175*

twelve   Religion and Mental Disorder   *287*

PART V   EPILOGUE

thirteen   Psychology, Psychologists, and Religion: Present Realities and Future Trends   *319*

PREFACE

Twenty years ago, religion was considered a taboo topic in psychology (Douglas, 1962). A half century earlier, it was a highly respected area of study, dignified by such notables as William James, G. Stanley Hall, and Carl Jung. Unhappily, a rapidly developing behaviorism that had no place for religion, and an early psychoanalytic bias that relegated faith to the realm of the childish and neurotic, forced work on religion to the periphery of scientific respectability.

Following an extended period of incubation, the empirical psychology of religion appeared to undergo a renaissance in the mid-1950s. In rapid succession, new journals appeared that were exclusively devoted to social scientific research in religion. Among these were the *Journal for the Scientific Study of Religion, Journal of Religion and Health, Review of Religious Research,* and *Journal for Psychology and Theology.* In addition, the mainstream publications of the American Psychological Association began to offer rigorous empirical research in the psychology of religion, something that had not been seen for many years. This burgeoning of literature has seen the inclusion of a chapter on the psychology of religion in *The Handbook of Social Psychology* (Lindzey and Aronson, 1969), a central psychological reference. This was soon followed by the appearance of Strommen's (1971) definitive source, *Research on Religious Development: A Comprehensive Handbook.* In an almost sudden burst of pent-up energy, recent years have witnessed the publication of a number of texts and collections of readings in the psychology of religion (Argyle and Beit-Hallahmi, 1975; Batson, 1982; Brown, 1973; Scobie, 1975; and Tisdale, 1980). Nonempirical, interpretive psychological and philosophical discourse, however, may still dominate this area (Faber, 1975; Homans, 1968; Pruyser, 1968, 1974). One also must recognize the appearance of a number of massive research bibliographies in the psychology of religion (Capps, Rambo, and Ransohoff, 1976; Meissner, 1960; Menges and Dittes, 1965; and Summerlin, 1980). Movement into the mainstream of psychology is in process. In the mid 1970s, a great step in this direction was taken when the American Psychological Association formed its Division 36, Psychologists Interested in Religious Issues. The division has flourished, now having a membership of 1,000 professionals.

Although the last two decades have seen more empirical research published than in the preceding three-quarters of a century, the overwhelming majority of these efforts still tend to be known primarily to specialists in the area. The present volume represents one effort to rectify this situation. The psychology of religion is developing at a breakneck pace. This trend will undoubtedly continue, and with it our knowledge of one of the most truly human of life's ventures—religious faith.

CHAPTER ONE
THE PSYCHOLOGICAL NATURE AND FUNCTION OF RELIGION

"My religion is to do good" (Paine, 1897, p. 406).

". . . dogma has been the fundamental principle of my religion" (Newman in Benham, 1927, p. 238b).

"Religion. n. A daughter of Hope and Fear, explaining to ignorance the nature of the Unknowable" (Bierce, 1967, p. 241).

1

WHY STUDY RELIGION?

These "definitions" suggest that people view religion in many different ways. Each person makes an individual interpretation of what religion is or should be. Frequently the meaning of faith, if not church allegiance and affiliation, is changed. Finally, one decides what religious practices should be observed and under what circumstances. History tells us of holy wars, the deaths of martyrs, religious conflict and bigotry as well as ecumenism, and a commitment to the highest human ideals. Yet we cannot confront the definition and meaning of faith without psychologically comprehending its many roles within the individual and the community. This is our purpose here.

The ease with which notions of religiosity or religiousness, of piety, and of a "deep and abiding faith" are discussed in today's world does not mean these things are to be taken lightly. Few human concerns are more seriously regarded than religion. We surround ourselves with spiritual reference, making it a context in which the birth of a baby is celebrated by means of christening, baptism, or circumcision. Marriages are solemnized by the clergy, and the sacred is continually invoked to convey the significance of almost every major life event. Finally, death is circumscribed by theologies. Images of an afterlife, of "going to meet one's God," and of resurrection alleviate to some degree the burden on both the living and the dying.

Why do we expend so much energy on religion? Simply because it is an extremely important aspect of social and psychological reality. Our goal is to find an entrance into this most personal and socially significant complex of facts, values, feelings, experiences, wishes, dreams, and behavior. Individual expression in contemporary western civilization has been chosen as our primary focus, because most empirical psychological research has been undertaken within the Judeo-Christian realm. Given this setting, our role is to search in mind, society, and culture the nature of religious belief, behavior, and experience. We want to understand what religion is *psychologically*. What is religion's character and position in the efforts humans make to cope with their everyday worlds?

Before undertaking this immense task, a disclaimer is in order. Let us recognize that it is *not* the place of psychologists to challenge religious institutions and their theologies. God is not our domain; neither is the world vision of churches. We will not enter into debates of faith versus reason or religion versus science; nor will we question revelation or scripture. Psychology, a social and behavioral science, is our resource, and we will begin and conclude our task on this level of understanding. Because religion is such a sensitive issue, this caution will be restated in various contexts in later chapters. As scholars, it is an emphasis and consideration that must always be kept before us.

BASIC PURPOSES AND DIRECTIONS

In this chapter, our purpose is to introduce some of the most basic questions that confront workers in the psychology of religion. Just what is meant when we speak of religion? Can a definition be provided on which virtually all agree? We may be forced to say, "I don't really know how to define it, but when I come across it, I know it is religion." In other words, where does one find religion?

The second issue is, how do we view religion? From the perspective of our culture with its institutions and their formal structures, or from the stance of the individual? Both levels need to be understood.

Our third issue is the complexity of personal faith. To many people, religion is one word—therefore, it must mean one thing. However, research and observation tell us that there are many different ways people express their spiritual inclinations. We will discuss some of these frameworks and will try to show the elaborate and highly involved nature of religious belief, expression, and behavior.

Fourth, the sources of religious impulses, needs, and responses must be addressed. Here we will examine the roles of theorized "instincts," learning, and habits, but on a higher plane we will see how religion defends and protects us while also possibly stimulating growth and self-realization.

Finally, we will introduce in broad outline a point of view regarding how people relate to their faith. We intend to show how religiosity is associated with perspectives and behavior relative to oneself, others, and the world—the stress is on personal meaning, control, and the maintenance and enhancement of self-esteem.

We raise the foregoing issues in an effort to clarify how psychologists empirically study religion. The word *empirical* is crucial, and we will use it repeatedly. It means (1) reliance on observation, and (2) the acquisition of knowledge and information that is objective and easily understood. It further demands utilization of scientific methods. We want data that are *public* (understandable by all) and *reproducible* (the same findings should result from approaching the problem in the same way). This is the way of science, and it is capable of conveying an exciting and fascinating awareness of the nature and place of religion in our lives. Chapter 2, which deals with some of the most demanding features of a scientific and empirical orientation to religion, shows that this path is not an easy one to tread.

This is the orientation with which you will become acquainted in the following pages. Emphasizing an empirical approach does not mean that observations are made in an intellectual, value-free vacuum. Psychologist Kurt Lewin is reported to have said that "there is nothing as practical as a good theory." We must have theories, ways of organizing our thoughts and ideas, so that the data we collect make sense. The theories we hold are "open," always amenable to new information. To close our minds is the most impractical thing we can do. Our approach is therefore both theoretical and empirical, because neither aspect is meaningful without the other.

DEFINING RELIGION THEORETICALLY—IS IT POSSIBLE?

Noted theologian Paul Tillich (1957) harshly calls upon us to clarify our muddled thinking about religion when he observes that:

> There is hardly a word in the religious language, both theological and popular, which is subject to more misunderstandings, distortions and questionable definitions than the word "faith." It belongs to those terms which need healing before they can be used for the healing of man. Today the term "faith" is more productive of disease than of health. It confuses, misleads, creates alternatively skepticism and fanaticism, intellectual resistance and emotional surrender, rejection of genuine religion and subjection to substitutes (p. ix).

Although Tillich further points out that he could not find a substitute for "the reality to which the term 'faith' '' (p. ix) refers, he devoted a volume to its exposition. We are confronted with a similar task, but our method and approach are different and we hope they will help clarify this basic issue.

Social scientists and religionists have teased out every abstraction, nuance, and implication in each word in any definition of religion that has probably ever been offered or is likely to be constructed. We therefore agree with Yinger (1967) that "any definition of religion is likely to be satisfactory only to its author" (p. 18). It may have been a similar awareness that earlier caused George Coe (1916), a noted psychologist of religion, to state:

> I purposely refrain from giving a formal definition of religion . . . partly because definitions convey so little information as to facts; partly because the history of definitions of religion makes it almost certain that any fresh attempts at definition would unnecessarily complicate these introductory chapters (p. 13).

We might also recognize the view of another scholar who claimed that "Religion, like poetry and most other living things, cannot be defined. But . . . some characteristic marks may be given" (Dresser, 1929, p. 441). Let us therefore accept this wisdom and avoid the pitfalls of unproductive, general, theoretical definitions. Other definitions, about which there is little or no argument, will be employed (see Chapter 2). They are termed *operational definitions* and will be only briefly alluded to in this chapter.

Where Do We Find Religion?

Since we are not going to define religion theoretically, we might consider the "place" or "location" of religion. This should provide some focus in terms of where to look to enhance our understanding of individual and collective faith. Simply put, one finds religion either "inside" a person or "out there" in a social order. But this is too pat, too simple an answer, for the person and social order are inseparably related. There is no individual independent of the environment, and the environment presupposes a person. The environment with which we deal is social, cultural, and historical. The spiritual environment in western civilization invariably refers to some transcendent—"ultimate reality," God, the Divine, the Infinite—and, to repeat, this is not what the psychologist of religion studies.

The "Outside" Perspective

Individuals with the "outside" kind of orientation look to religion in an institution, a religious grouping of some sort, a church, sect, or cult—a collective organization—"the faithful," "the believers," "the chosen." Reference is to a history, theological doctrine, the Bible, and other sacred writings, including church dogma, liturgy, ritual, and whatever practices and beliefs the group considers spiritually meaningful.

From the psychological point of view, this is usually the context for individual religious expression. It is the basis for adherence to a belief; the reference for deviation and acceptance or for assessing knowledge, feelings, attitudes, beliefs; and finally for behavior relative to the dos and don'ts that every religious system advocates in order to live the "good life." Psychologists of religion are not, as a rule, involved in the study of faith from this "outside" perspective—this is primarily the sphere of the sociologist or anthropologist of religion. However, it is a significant and indispensable aspect of any understanding of religion.

The "Inside" Perspective

This orientation focuses on the individual. Here we find the personal nature and subjectivity of religious faith. Phrases such as "inner experience" and "the perception of the infinite," as well as religious beliefs, religious behavior, religious attitudes, and religious experiences, become important. To illustrate, nineteenth-century philosopher-ethnologist Max Müller saw religion as ". . . the *perception* of the infinite under such manifestations as are able to *influence* the moral character of man" (Müller, 1889, p. 188; emphasis added). Walter Houston Clark (1958), one of the giants of the contemporary psychology of religion, claims that "religion can be *most characteristically* described as the *inner experience of the individual* when he senses a Beyond, especially as evidenced by the effect of this experience on his behavior when he actively attempts to harmonize his life with the Beyond" (p. 22).

These views probably represent the dominant view of religion in our culture. "Inner experience" or "perception" is anchored in something external and independent of us—"an infinite" or "the beyond." Some approaches talk of "the Divine" (Clark, 1958, p. 23) or "the Ultimate" (Williams, 1962, p. 8), both of which connote some fundamental transcendent referent. Invariably, this is a being, the deity, in whom resides universal absolute truth; it is the object of adoration by people whose moral character and relationship to the world is believed to be constructively transformed in the religious process.

Cultural Locations for Individual Faith

In a number of instances, the transcendent concept—God, the Infinite, the Divine—is replaced by some sociocultural concept. Edward Scribner Ames (1910) offers the hypothesis that "religion is the consciousness of the highest *social* values" (p. viii; emphasis added). Wieman and Westcott-Wieman (1935) simply cite "the highest values" (p. 29). Although the word *highest* has a strong subjective quality, the significant feature of this approach is its focus on a social and/or personal framework as the essence of religion itself. We will see shortly that objective methods can be applied to the subjective character of such definitions, permitting them to be measured by psychologists.

Erich Fromm (1950) more fully accepted a social scientific outlook when he perceived religion as "any system of thought and action *shared by the group* which gives the individual a frame of orientation and an object of devotion" (p. 21; emphasis added). The individual is thus placed in an explicit social context, and although "an object of devotion" is invoked, there is no limitation to such being of a traditional religious nature. One could include popular heroes or political, economic, or social ideologies. We are probably familiar with people who believe some doctrine to such a degree that its pervasive effect on their lives is hardly different than what we would view as religious.

The great theologians of the past and present have always contended that no aspect of living, including the most commonplace and mundane of activities, can be divorced from a truly religious perspective. Poet Kahlil Gibran claimed, "your daily life is your temple and your religion" (Gibran, 1923, p.

88). Religion thus becomes life as lived, but existence is charged with values, and the origins of these values comprise a significant part of religion.

Our search for religion still necessitates some criteria of where to look, and it is doubtful that anyone has pointed more effectively in the right direction than Yinger (1970) when he suggested:

> . . . where one finds awareness of and interest in the continuing, recurrent *permanent* problems of human existence—the human condition itself, as contrasted with specific problems; where one finds rites and shared beliefs relevant to that awareness, which define the strategy of an ultimate victory; and where one has groups organized to heighten that awareness and to teach and maintain those rites and beliefs—there one has religion (p. 33).

Given some "outside" system, religion becomes the knowledge, beliefs, feelings, actions, and experiences of the individual as they are manifested in relation to that system. Studying this "inside" perspective is the task of the psychologist of religion.

Operational Definitions

Although operational definitions will be discussed in depth in Chapter 2, these are essential for our empirical, scientific work to have any validity. Operational definitions are anchored in tangible religious indicators, which may be as obvious as church attendance or stated beliefs about the importance of faith in one's life. When we identify some index or measure that we have used or intend to employ, we are providing an operational definition. A concept—for example, religiosity—is denoted in terms of specific "operations"—e.g., certain procedures and instruments such as responses to a questionnaire, frequency of participation in church services, etc. We must, however, never come to believe that religion or religiosity is completely circumscribed by these simple indicators or "facts" about the religious life of the individual. They may be only superficial signs, yet they are operationally definable, and everyone agrees on what they are in themselves. They might also show us the way to other empirical techniques that explore religiousness in much greater depth.

BEING RELIGIOUS: ONE THING OR MANY?

Our passion to be efficient, to summarize the complex, to wrap it all up in "twenty-five words or less" is often an enemy to real understanding. As H. L. Mencken put it, "There's a solution to every problem—simple, neat and wrong." To many people, religion must mean only one thing—whatever they believe it to be. But words are symbols that place many things under one heading or label, and the term *religion* is an excellent example of this tendency. It seems to have many facets and dimensions.

Long ago sophisticated thinkers put aside notions that people simply range from those who claim to have no religion or who are antireligious to those who manifest different degrees of orthodoxy or commitment to a faith. A little experience with religiously inclined persons is enough to convince even a casual observer that people embrace religion for a variety of reasons and express their spirituality and religious concerns in many different ways.

When we examine the schemes various scholars have proposed, we conclude that some stress the purpose of faith: others attend to the possible personal and social origins of religion. Most psychological researchers emphasize religious expression in belief, experience, and behavior. There is obviously great overlap among the various proposals, but all agree on one thing: Even though there may be only one word for religion, there may be a hundred possible ways of being religious. Wilson (1978) thus notes that "Religion is clearly not a homogenous whole. Individuals who are religious in one respect might not be in another . . . religion is multidimensional" (p. 442).

Personal to International Faith: Levels of Religion

Taking the broadest perspective, Williams (1962) focuses on religion as varying from the individual level to one encompassing all humanity. The former starts with what Williams identifies as *secret religiousness.* We keep this faith exclusively to ourselves. It consists of that concealed set of beliefs and images which, for whatever reason, we would rather not let others know.

Expanding from these most personal formulations, we encounter *private religiosity.* This is the faith we share with our intimates. Further social enlargement brings us to a *denominational* framework—for example, Presbyterianism or Reform Judaism. Here one's religion partakes of things in common with many others. Under an even broader canopy, faith attains a *societal* form that expresses many of the basic values of a culture, such as might be evidenced in Protestantism or Christianity. Finally, since all such categories describe potential divisions among humans, Williams suggests that an *international* religious outlook may be appropriate.

A scheme such as this provides the empiricist with a framework for structuring religion on many levels and with far more than the psychologist of religion would usually be called upon to handle empirically.

Some Multidimensional Schemes

The concept of religious multidimensionality means that personal or social religion has many facets, and participation in or expression of one aspect does not necessarily imply involvement in others. This is well illustrated by the very complex scheme proposed by Verbit (1970). He suggested that there are six *components* of religion, and four *dimensions* within each of these components. These components and dimensions are best comprehended within the framework of Verbit's definition of religion as "man's relationship to whatever he conceives as meaningful ultimacy" (p. 24).

The *components* he denotes are:

1. *Ritual*—private and/or public ceremonial behavior.
2. *Doctrine*—affirmations about the relationship of the individual to the ultimate.
3. *Emotion*—the presence of feelings (awe, love, fear, etc.)
4. *Knowledge*—intellectual familiarity with sacred writings and principles.
5. *Ethics*—rules for the guidance of interpersonal behavior, connoting right and wrong, good and bad.
6. *Community*—involvement in a community of the faithful, psychologically, socially and/or physically.

Each of these components subsumes or varies along four *dimensions*:

1. *Content*—the essential nature of the component—e.g. specific rituals, ideas, knowledge, principles, etc.
2. *Frequency*—how often the content elements are encountered or acted upon.
3. *Intensity*—the degree of commitment to any of the components.
4. *Centrality*—the importance or salience of the components.

Obviously, there must be some overlap among both the components and the dimensions. Any component is likely to show different degrees of dependence among, for example, frequency, intensity, and centrality. This is, however, a question that can be assessed empirically. Unfortunately, this potentially useful system has never been operationalized and evaluated through research.

Other scholars, many prior to Verbit, had already advanced similar conceptions, and a number attempted to realize the significance of their ideas through research. Since the measurement and operational aspects of these systems are of considerable importance, they will be discussed further in Chapter Two. For illustrative purposes, Table 1-1 presents a sampling of these schemes, and Table 1-2 compares the very popular framework suggested by Glock (1962) (see Table 1) with those of Davidson (1975), Fukuyama (1961), and Verbit (1970). The interested reader may want to study further some of these formulations by locating the references cited; however, for our purposes, additional detailed discussion and evaluation of these frameworks are not necessary.

Some of the forms of individual religion listed in Tables 1-1 and 1-2 are based on theory while others are based on statistical analyses of data. A number have been developed with certain religious groups, but not checked on with others. Many of these schemes remain isolated within the literature marking potentially useful approaches which, to date, have been largely overlooked. Some stress the motives and traits of people in their relationship to religion, and in the following pages we will refer to research using measures of these characteristics as we attempt to understand the psychological foundations for various religious expressions.

Even though religion is highly complex, we should recognize one of those "behind-the-scenes" variables that may be of fundamental significance. This has been called *salience,* or "the importance an individual attaches to being religious" (Roof and Perkins, 1975, p. 111). There is reason to believe that the connection between religious belief and religious and nonreligious behavior may, in part, be a function of salience. For example, the more important religion is to a person, the greater the likelihood that religion will influence how that person responds and thinks in everyday life.

WHY ARE PEOPLE RELIGIOUS?

This is probably the most fundamental question of all concerning faith. Some of us find answers that totally cancel doubt; others live in uncertainty and turmoil. To many, faith is proof of the activity of a deity and the search ends with this awareness. In contrast, there are those whose religion drives them on an unending search for truth and knowledge. When we phrase the question "Why reli-

TABLE 1-1.   Some Conceptual and/or Empirically Demonstrated Multidimensional Approaches to the Study of Individual Religion

Allen and Spilka (1967)

Committed religion

"utilizes an abstract, philosophical perspective: multiplex religious ideas are relatively clear in meaning and an open and flexible framework of commitment relates religion to daily activities" (p. 205).

Consensual religion

"vague, non-differentiated, bifurcated, neutralized" (p. 205). A cognitively simplified and personally convenient faith.

Allport (1966)

Intrinsic religion

"faith as a supreme value in its own right . . . oriented toward a unification of being, takes seriously the commandment of brotherhood, and strives to transcend all self-centered needs" (p. 455).

Extrinsic religion

"religion that is strictly utilitarian; useful for the self in granting safety, social standing, solace, and endorsement of one's chosen way of life" (p. 455).

Broen (1957)

Nearness to God—God is

"very real and constantly near and accessible . . . emphasizing the Deity's loving presence and guidance rather than His judgment function" (p. 17).

Fundamentalism—
Humanitarianism

a dimension with one end defining "man as essentially sinful, and emphasiz(ing) his need for, and rightful fear of, a punishing God. The other extreme sees "man as containing the potential for good and . . . little need for much outside intervention in the form of some Deity" (p. 178).

Clark (1958)

Primary religious behavior

"an authentic inner experience of the divine combined with whatever efforts the individual may make to harmonize his life with the divine" (p. 23).

Secondary religious
behavior

may have a primary source, but its essence is in a "routine and uninspired carrying out . . . of an obligation" (p. 24).

Tertiary religious behavior

"a matter of religious routine or convention accepted on the authority of someone else" (p. 25).

Fromm (1950)

Authoritarian religion

"Man is controlled by a higher power . . . *entitled* to 'obedience, reverence and worship' . . . The main virtue of this type of religion is obedience, its cardinal sin is disobedience" (p. 35).

Humanistic religion

". . . is centered around man and his strength . . . virtue is self-realization, not obedience . . . God is a symbol of *man's own power* . . . not, of force and domination, having *power over man*" (p. 37).

Glock (1962)

Experiential Dimension

"religious people will . . . achieve direct knowledge of ultimate reality or will experience religious emotion" (p. S-99).

(continued)

TABLE 1-1 *(continued)*

Ideological Dimension	"the religious person will hold to certain beliefs" (p. S-99).
Ritualistic Dimension	"the specifically religious practices expected of religious adherents" (p. S-99).
Intellectual Dimension	"the religious person will be informed and knowledgeable about the basic tenets of his faith and its sacred scriptures" (p. S-99).
Consequential Dimension	"the secular effects of religious belief, practice, experience and knowledge . . . what people ought to do and the attitudes they ought to hold as a consequence of their religion" (p. S-99).
Literal religion	stresses language of a literal sort, taking "at face value any religious statement without in any way questioning it" (p. 43).
Antiliteral religion	stresses a simple summary rejection of literalist religious statements.
Mythological religion	"a reinterpretation of religious statements to seek their deeper symbolic meanings which lie beyond their literal wording . . . more complex . . . capable of assimilating both the intention of religious orthodoxy and the realities of the contemporary world" (p. 43).
James (1902)	
Healthy-mindedness	an optimistic, happy, extroverted, social faith: "the tendency which looks on all things and sees that they are good" (p. 87).
Sick souls	"the way that takes all this experience of evil as something essential" (p. 162). A faith of pessimism, sorrow suffering, and introvertive reflection.
Lenski (1961)	
Doctrinal Orthodoxy	"stresses intellectual assent to prescribed doctrines" (p. 23).
Devotionalism	"emphasizes the importance of private, or personal communion with God" (p. 23).
McConahay and Hough (1973)	
Guilt-oriented, Extrapunitive	"religious belief . . .centered on the wrath of God as it is related to other people . . . emphasizes punishment for wrong doers" (p. 55).
Guilt-oriented, Intropunitive	"A sense of one's own unworthiness and badness . . . a manifest need for punishment and a conviction that it will inevitably come" (p. 56).
Love-oriented, self-centered	"oriented toward the forgiveness of one's own sins . . . God as . . . benevolent" (p. 56).
Love-oriented, other-centered	"emphasizes on the common humanity of all persons as creatures of God, and God's love . . . related to the redemption of the whole world" (p. 56).
Culture-oriented, conventional	"values which are more culturally than theologically oriented" (p. 56).

TABLE 1-2. A Comparison of Some Multidimensional Schemes for Studying Religion.

VERBIT(1970)	GLOCK(1962)	FUKUYAMA(1961)	DAVIDSON(1975)
Ritual	Ritualistic Ritual Commitment Devotionalism	Cultic	Practice Public(Conservative) Private(Liberal)
Doctrine	Ideological Orthodoxy Particularism Ethicalism	Creedal	Belief Vertical(Conservative) Horizontal(Liberal)
Emotion	Experiential	Devotional	Experiential Desirability(Conservative) Frequency(Liberal)
Knowledge	Intellectual	Cognitive	Intellectual Religious Knowledge(Conservative) Intellectual Scrutiny(Liberal)
Ethics			
Community	Consequential		Consequential Personal(Conservative) Social(Liberal)

gion?'', it is to determine the psychological foundations for (1) religion in general, wherever it exists and regardless of the form it takes: and (2) the development in, and expression of faith by, the individual. It is also obvious that these goals are closely related. Our immediate concern is with the first of these issues, and we will see that there are no simple answers.

The Instinct Tradition

Early in the development of psychology as a science, most scholars tried to explain much human behavior by postulating *instincts*. L. L. Bernard's (1924) massive review of this literature reported that some 5,684 instincts were offered by some 323 authors in 388 books. Of these, 83 religious instincts were theorized. In other words, religion was innate, unlearned, and biological in origin. For example, Le Bon (1903) claimed the existence of such an instinct, which he termed a "religious sentiment." This was vaguely referred to as natural and unconscious. In a related claim, Trotter (1919) felt that religion was an expression of a more basic "herd instinct."

The difficulty of dealing with a specifically religious instinct prompted some social scientists to see faith as a product of a number of instincts. William McDougall (1909), one of the classic figures of early psychology, perceived religion to be an outgrowth of what he called the instincts of curiosity, fear, and subjection plus three religious emotions—admiration, awe, and reverence. Bernard (1924) showed that those who looked toward an instinctual basis for religion were naive with respect to heredity and often did not know that religion, as they conceived it, was not a universal phenomenon. Dresser (1929) placed all of these attempts in perspective by observing:

> When a group of instincts is substituted for the alleged religious instinct as the origin of religious experience, the objection is that psychologists have not even been able to agree on the list of instincts and their corresponding emotions as attributed to life in general (p. 185).

Today, except in very well-defined situations involving animals, the term *instinct* has fallen into disfavor. However, it lurks in the background in some conceptions, although the word remains unspoken. For example, Ostow and Scharfstein (1954) speak of "the need to believe," which they affirm "is almost as necessary to humans as eating . . . belief is essential to the efficient functioning of a human organism" (p. 155). They look to an inner source for faith that borders on what their forerunners might have taken for instinct. Thus, we read that "religious and moral conceptions must have a primal source in the deep, often unconscious drives that lie behind our beliefs and practices" (p. 37). Such vagueness, which is unsatisfactory to the scientific mind, is still acceptable to many people. This entire approach offers the appearance of knowledge, not its substance.

THE DEFENSIVE-PROTECTIVE TRADITION

The Need for Meaning and Control

Probably the most widespread view is that human weakness and inadequacy create the need for religion. Once present, our faith protects us from the storms of life that rage about us. Those who subscribe to this view proclaim life to be a massive uncertainty. The shifting foundations of each moment place us under ever-present stress. And, to complete the tale, the final outcome of this existential drama poses the grimmest of possibilities—simple complete termination, death.

It is therefore not surprising that humans struggle to make the ambiguous clear, the doubtful certain, and the indeterminate sure. We search for clues to make sense out of life, to give us a feeling of control, and to make what happens predictable. Religion offers us such possibilities through scripture, theologies, prayer, liturgy, and ceremony. These are themes to which we will return later when we present our own theoretical orientation. John Dewey (1929) captures the essence of this perspective thus:

> Man who lives in a world of hazards is compelled to seek for security . . . One . . . attempt (is) to propitiate the powers which environ him and determine his destiny. It expressed itself in supplication, sacrifice, ceremonial rite and magical cult. In time these crude methods were largely displaced. The sacrifice of a contrite heart was esteemed more pleasing than that of bulls and oxen; the inner attitude of reverence and devotion more desirable than external ceremonies. If a man could not conquer destiny he could willingly ally himself with it; putting his will, even in sore affliction, on the side of the powers which dispense fortune, he could escape defeat and might triumph in the midst of destruction (p. 3).

Philosopher Josiah Royce (1912) refers to "this natural chaos" (p. 44) as a prime source of spiritual motivation, while noted psychologist of religion Paul Johnson (1959) sees faith as "the opposite of fear, anxiety and uncertainty" (p. 200). In the last analysis, Bergson (1935) suggests that "religion is a defensive reaction of nature against . . . the inevitability of death" (p. 131).

Our frailty and vulnerability thus become origins for religion offering us continuing life. We are saved and successful; we have hope.

An alternative version of human shortcoming focuses on the weakness of the child. According to Freud (1957), the child confers upon the father a mantle of omnipotence. With age and experience, growing awareness of paternal limitation leads to the view that "God is the exalted father, and the longing for the father is the root of the need for religion" (p. 36).

Catholic theologian Hans Kung (1979) perceives this as a defective religion. "Religious questions . . . become a form of self-deception and escapism . . . religion relies solely on wish-fulfillment and . . . is reduced to pure satisfaction of needs . . . a religion (of) infantile structures, a regression to childhood wishing" (p. 97). Religion is again "a daughter of hope and fear" (Bierce, 1967, p. 241). Contemporary life introduces new sources of doubt, as W. T. Stace notes:

> . . . there has been growing up in men's minds, dominated as they are by science, a new imaginative picture of the world. The world, according to this new picture, is purposeless, senseless, meaningless. Nature is nothing but matter in motion. . . . . If the scheme of things is purposeless and meaningless, then the life of man is purposeless and meaningless too (Stace in Muscatine and Griffith, 1966, p. 543).

He then infers that "the essence of the (religious) spirit itself (is) belief in a meaningful and purposeful world" (p. 547). Many scholars claim that the basic motivation of humans is to derive meaning from chaos, and this effort may be the tap root from which much religion springs.

The Role of Anxiety

Defense of the personality involves anxiety, and Freud (Hall and Lindzey, 1978) recognized three forms: reality, moral, and neurotic. Reality-based anxiety may be hypothesized as a feature of the kind of faith we have discussed above. There is uncertainty in life; there are real, objective, independent sources of danger in the world, and the reality anxiety these arouse are likely to be powerful sources of religion.

For many people, moral anxiety based on guilt and guilt feelings may be an extremely potent basis for religion. Right and wrong are concepts that are present when we are born and follow us throughout life. In the course of development, we learn these ideas and they become part of us. Whether or not they are part of the criminal law, the Ten Commandments, the Golden Rule, or simply those social regulations, fashions, fads, or folkways by which we order social life, their violation is likely to result in guilt and feelings of distress. Our self-esteem suffers; we have not lived up to the standards we have set for ourselves, standards which may have even been acquired in a home where powerless parents formed a "coalition with God" (Nunn, 1964) to enforce discipline.

"Straying from the fold" can arouse considerable guilt, but this can be resolved by a return to religion. Conversions, religious mystical experiences, and other signs of apparent strengthening of faith have been reported in response to such motivation (Argyle and Beit-Hallahmi, 1975; Clark, 1929; Starbuck, 1899). There is another side to this coin. Mowrer (1961) and others (for example, Fairchild, 1971) further point out the role of religion in enhancing feelings of guilt. We are taught that if we are sinful, God will punish us; some version of "hellfire and damnation" will follow us both in this life and that to come.

In many ways, the problem of guilt and guilt feelings is also basic to Freud's third form of anxiety—neurotic anxiety. The difference lies in the degree to which the person seems able to control impulses. Religion may, however, provide that additional self-justification, that extra source of outside power to buttress inner doubt and weakness. Too often a rigid, unbending, tyrannical faith results. Images of a threatening, demanding, punitive God to suppress unacceptable desires is also a common feature of such neurotically based religion. Simply put, whether it be moral or neurotic anxiety, the fundamental need is that "Religion must remain an outlet for people who say to themselves, "I am not the kind of person I want to be" (Herbert, 1965, p. 506).

Human shortcoming, weakness, and deficiency take many forms that a spiritual system may help resolve. Walters and Bradley (1971) suggest that a lack of friends can stimulate religious activity. They also claim evidence that social and economic deprivation parallels the development of strong religious feelings and commitments. It therefore appears that wherever we observe conflict, frustration, distress, and inadequacy, there is a likelihood of faith entering the picture to resolve the dilemma. Anthropologist F.L.K. Hsu (1952) captures the central theme of this approach to religion thus:

> Man will always love and be in need of love. Man will always aspire to heights which he cannot reach; Man will always be fallible; Man will always die and be in distress; and Man will always have a seemingly ever-expanding universe before him even if he has conquered all earth. As long as man is subject to these and other circumstances, religion will have a place in human culture (p. 133).

THE GROWTH-REALIZATION TRADITION

In our society, we learn in one form or another the principle that "No one does something for nothing." We therefore look for reasons based on human imperfection to explain why people engage in good and noble acts. The common question is, "What do they get out of behaving that way?" Somehow an unresolved conflict or unfulfilled need is thought to underly the best of which humanity is capable.

Religion as Overall Growth and Realization

It may not always be true that "belief in God is a sign of man's alienation from himself, his projection onto God of that which is an unrealized possibility for men" (Browning, 1975, p. 132). Bertocci (1958) writes of "Religion as creative insecurity" and seems to be moving from a deficiency view to one in which religion produces something very positive. Faith becomes a struggle to attain a higher plane, increased self-realization, and enhanced regard and respect for others. Johnson (1959) thus writes of the "productive functions of faith" such as the integration of personality, the potential of betterment, the uniting of believers, etc. In like manner, Gardner (1978) claims that "all true religion is a path out of the quicksands of self-preoccupation and self-worship" (p. 33).

The theme of general uplift and enlightenment is widely accepted. We read that "religion . . . is a process of organizing the self around and toward the highest values" (Wieman and Wescott-Wieman, 1935, p. 29) or that it is "man's attitude toward the universe regarded as a social and ethical force" (Ellwood, 1922, p. 47). Religion is self-enhancement, growth, realization, actualization, the broadening of experiential horizons, the attainment of the greatest love, freedom, and experiences of which humans are capable. This is Tillich's perception that "faith as ultimate concern is an act of the total personality" (Tillich, 1957, p. 4).

Religion as Cognitive Growth

On the cognitive side, the idea of intellectual expansion and intelligence is foremost. This idea is seen in Einstein's "cosmic religion," "the strongest and noblest driving force behind scientific research" (Einstein, 1930, p. 357). Ultimate meaning is stressed (Polanyi and Prosch, 1975, p. 153). O'Dea (1961) states this position impressively when he claims:

> . . . religion gives answers to questions that arise at the point of ultimacy, at those points in human experience that go beyond the everyday attitude toward life . . . because men are cognitively capable of going to the "limit-situation," of proceeding through and transcending the conventional answers to the problem of meaning and of raising fundamental existential questions in terms of their human relevance (1961, p. 30).

From a developmental-psychological point of view, David Elkind (1970) sees religion as a normal and natural result of cognitive growth. Utilizing the theories of the noted Swiss psychologist, Jean Piaget, Elkind picks on four basic components of intelligence: *conservation, representation, search for relations,* and *search for comprehension.*

Conservation is a "life-long quest for permanence amidst a world of change" (Elkind, 1970, p. 37). "Permanence" implies that something still exists even if it is not immediately present. A mother may leave her child; however, when the concept of object permanence is present, there is assurance that she continues to exist and will return. The greatest threat to such permanence is death, and religion conserves life through images of a hereafter. The natural product of conservation becomes a God that ensures immortality. By the age of two, object permanence is established in an individual; refinement and application of such permanence in religion follows as a matter of course.

Human thought is very much a process of representing reality in symbols. The growth of language is central in this *search for representation* because it encapsulates the most complex aspects of reality in a single word. So it is that religion and God represent the most elaborate, intricate, and involved of our innermost thoughts and images plus formulations of a transcendental spiritual reality, and the resolution of basic contradictions (e.g., virgin birth, immaculate conception, etc.). Representation is a powerful cognitive tool which, it is claimed, intrinsically leads to a religious perspective.

The *search for relations* also appears to be a basic component of intellectual growth. Understanding entails knowing how one is linked to others and to the world at large. The child gains personal meaning from knowing his/her connections to family members, friends, school, neighborhood, and other immediate objects of reference. With increasing age and the likelihood of exposure to more and more of the world through the media and education among other influences, we find ourselves pressed to comprehend new relationships. Cognitive vistas expand from those of the family to community, nation, world, and universe. The search for relations does not end, for we need to locate and understand who we are in "the scheme of things." Religion comes to satisfy this associational urge as it ties us to ever broader horizons, indeed to those which are best known as ultimate.

Finally, as one grows from childhood into adolescence, intelligence increasingly embraces abstract generalizations. The goal is to cope with existence, and individuality enters the picture. Reasoning and intellect reach out to integrate our widening perspectives. Religion serves this *search for comprehension* well for many people, and churches with their theologies offer guidelines to resolve these struggles.

Elkind (1970) takes the position that religion is a normal, natural outcome of mental development. We are, however, not born into a spiritual vacuum and, as representatives of society, our parents and others offer us their religious solutions. The problems of permanence, representation, relationship, and comprehension thus come to be resolved or, at least, approximated satisfactorily for most people.

Just as religion may be founded on human weakness and deficiency, it is possible to look at it in a positive sense as an "attitude of participation in a meaningful cosmic order" (Angyal, 1972, p. 225). Possibility and realization are manifested in an even more general sense when we read that "the idea of God . . . best corresponds to the obscure yearnings of human beings to reach perfection" (Adler, 1964, p. 272–73). These views primarily represent the modern humanistic tradition in psychology and lead to an awareness of human promise and potential.

Religion as Habit

When William James claimed that "Habit is . . . . the enormous fly-wheel of society, its most precious conservative agent" (James, 1890, p. 51), he might have had in mind the way most people acquire their religion. They are simply taught it in their homes and these teachings are generally reinforced by society. Births, marriages, and deaths are solemnized by religious institutions, language, and concepts. No political figure would think of not including in speeches what Franklin Roosevelt called "God stuff" (Lerner, 1957, p. 704).

Robert Bellah (1967) states that, outside of the churches, there exists in American society a generalized religious atmosphere, a "civil religion" that infuses all aspects of social and political life. Our milieu from early childhood tells us that it is simply un-American not to believe in God, to deny this "object-less obsession with faith as faith" (Marty, 1959, p. 31). We believe; we obey; we usually know enough not to think too deeply about it. It is habitual religion, mechanical religion, convenient religion. It is the faith to which we expect all to give assent, but which will otherwise not interfere with our personal life. This concept may be rather widespread in modern-day America. It is a religion of unthinking, automatic habit.

AN INTEGRATING FRAMEWORK FOR THE PSYCHOLOGY OF RELIGION

We must now return to our original question, "Why religion?" At this point, we are able to offer some psychological focus. Social scientists, as part of the scientific venture, desire to organize their ideas and research under the direction of a theory. We have seen some broad formulations that attempted to coordinate all aspects of the psychology of religion. The likelihood is that no one theory will ever suffice for this complex realm. Many theories may be necessary to explain religious expression, belief, motivation, cognition, development, etc. However, we can suggest some guidelines for psychological thinking in the area of religion.

The Ever-present Social Context

We must recognize the fact that historically and contemporaneously religious institutions and ideas are pervasive in our social order as they also appear to be in every known culture. Although understanding of this context is left to historians, anthropologists, and sociologists, it means that religion is taught—intentionally, actively, formally, and just as influentially—passively and informally, and infuses virtually every human setting and activity. People are born into environments in which religion is present. Although we may reject the "faith of our fathers," more commonly we accept it with variation that reflects individual experience, choice, and the social context.

Parents and significant others provide models for us throughout childhood and these continue to be important throughout life. We see in their example how religion functions. They may teach that it is something negative, to be used for personal problem solving, especially during crisis. It may be an agency of control employed by parents to keep children in line. God might be viewed primarily with fear. Church going may be an inconvenience or a rigid, demanding weekly requirement.

In contrast, religious practice might stress the positive aspects of faith. The deity can be viewed as loving and forgiving. There may be a striving for the kind of religious experience that opens the mind and spirit and enhances the richness of life. Faith becomes a search for the truth, a way of living rather than an external appendage or an unyielding limitation.

Basic Forms of Personal Faith

What is being said here also relates to our discussion of religious multidimensionality. To date, the most fruitful conception suggests two major ways of expressing one's faith. Allport and his students (Allport, 1959; 1966; Allport and Ross, 1967) have termed these *intrinsic and extrinsic religion.* The cognitive-personality variation developed by Allen and Spilka (1967) of committed and consensual faith seems to describe, from a different vantage point, the same approaches to personal religion (Dittes, 1969). For our purposes, we will often refer to *intrinsic-committed* and *extrinsic-consensual* forms of faith, but the terminology "intrinsic and extrinsic religion" is more firmly established in the literature, and will also be employed to identify these two broad religious perspectives.

These two kinds of religion represent cognitive, motive, and behavioral patterns (Hunt and King, 1971). Extrinsic religion is described as "strictly utilitarian: useful for the self in granting safety, social standing, solace and endorsement for one's chosen way of life" (Allport, 1966, p. 455). Intrinsic religion "regards faith as a supreme value in its own right. It is oriented toward a unification of being, takes seriously the commandment of brotherhood, and strives to transcend all self-centered needs. " . . . A religious sentiment of this sort floods the whole life with motivation and meaning" (Allport, 1966, p. 455).

Our work has shown that there are cognitive correlates to these motivational factors. These were originally termed "committed" and "consensual" religion. The former kind of faith could be described as candid, open, personally relevant, abstract and relational, discerning, and differentiated. Consensual religion reveals a number of intellectual shortcomings and is viewed as restrictive, detached to the point of irrelevance, concrete, vague, and simplistic (Allen and Spilka, 1967). Table 1-3 summarizes and defines the characteristics of this intrinsic-committed and extrinsic-consensual dichotomy.

Although much evidence has accumulated regarding the nature of these forms of personal faith, we can say little about how they develop. There is apparently no research on the early home life and childhood behavioral tendencies of adults who manifest these religious orientations.

Our measures tell us that all religious people reveal both intrinsic-committed and extrinsic-consensual dispositions. Granted that there are those in whom one form or the other dominates, the problem is largely the extent to which a person is inclined in one direction or the other. It has also been shown that there are people who are indiscriminately pro- or antireligious, who simply assent to or reject any religious proposition regardless of its implications (Allport and Ross, 1967; Hood, 1978; Thompson, 1974). Despite these leanings, it is our contention that this religious dichotomy reflects some very basic ways in which individuals relate to their faith. In other words, it describes fundamental social-psycho-

Table 1-3.   Characteristics of Intrinsic-Committed and Extrinsic-Consensual Faith[1]

INTRINSIC-COMMITTED	EXTRINSIC-CONSENSUAL
Devout, strong personal commitment	"Follows the rules," convenient, called on in crisis
Universalistic, strongly ethical, holds to brotherhood ideals, stresses love of one's neighbor	Exclusionist, ethnocentric, restricted to in-group, chauvinistic, provincial
Unselfish, transcends self-centered needs, altruistic, humanitarian	Selfish, self-serving, defensive, protective
A guide to living, general framework for daily life, provides life with meaning	Expedient, used when needed, not integrated into daily life
Faith is of primary importance, accepted without reservations, creed is fully followed	Faith and belief is superficial, beliefs selectively held
Faith is of ultimate significance, a final good, supreme value, the ultimate answer	Utilitarian, means to other ends, is in the service of other personal wants and desires
Sees people as individuals	Views people in terms of social categories-sex, age, status
High self-esteem	Low or confused self-esteem
Loving, forgiving, positive God	Stern, vindictive, punitive God
Open to intense religious experience	Tends to be closed to religious experience
Views death positively	Negative orientation toward death
Associated with feelings of power and competence, internal control	Ties to powerlessness and feelings of external control

COGNITIVE CHARACTERISTICS	
Uses abstract principles and sees relationships among things	Concrete and literal in outlook and judgment
Discerning, orderly, exact in meaning, clear	Vague, mechanical, routine answers, use of cliches, obscure in meaning
Complex, differentiated, uses multiple categories, ideas, sees things as on a continuum	Uses few categories, polarized in thinking (e.g., good or bad), simple ideas
Open, flexible, creative in thinking, thoughtful, tolerant of different ideas and positions	Closed, restrictive, intolerant of different viewpoints, rigid, mechanical in thought

[1]These characteristics are derived from many sources, chiefly Hunt and King (1971), but also the research of many others

logical-religious patterns that can aid us in understanding much about the psychology of individual religious expression.

AN ATTRIBUTIONAL APPROACH TO THE PSYCHOLOGY OF RELIGION

If there is a basic human propensity, it is the need to seek explanations about what goes on both within and outside of ourselves. Ever since Aristotle (McKeon, 1941) postulated a "desire to know" (p. 688), many philosophers and psychologists have suggested similar fundamental human needs. John Dewey (1929) theorized a need for knowledge as the basis of his "quest for certainty." Frankl (1963) wrote movingly of a "search for meaning"; Maslow (1970) described a "desire to know and to understand" (p. 48). Motivational theorists have posited and researched exploratory and curiosity drives (Berlyne, 1960; Bindra, 1959). The list of those holding these ideas is extremely long and clearly stretches from ancient times until today. We have treated such tendencies as part of the growth-realization tradition, and though we do not always seek to comprehend the causes of what occurs in ultimate terms, the general urge to know, to acquire meaning, may be hypothesized to be universally present.

Psychologists term this tendency *attribution,* and attribution theory occupies a central place in the field of social psychology. As a coordinating theme, it has been slowly entering the psychology of religion (Proudfoot and Shaver, 1975; Ritzema, 1979) and may provide a fruitful avenue for organizing much of our specialty.

MOTIVATIONAL BASES OF ATTRIBUTIONS

The basic premise of attribution theory is that the fundamental motivation of people is to make sense out of their world. We thus make attributions—inferences about the sources or causes of events. Valins and Nisbett (1971) therefore claim that "Attribution is a process whereby the individual 'explains' his world" (p. 1). Kruglanski, Hamel, Maides, and Schwartz (1978) further view the attributional process as an effort to acquire new knowledge.

In addition to being motivated by a "need to know," to make the world meaningful, the attributional process appears to be activated by a "need to control" one's life. Harold Kelley (1967) adds this dimension when he remarks, "The theory describes processes that operate *as if* the individual were motivated to attain a *cognitive mastery* of the causal structure of his environment" (p. 193; emphasis added). Especially when threatened with harm or pain, all higher organisms seek to predict and control the events that are about to befall them (Seligman, 1975). This fact has been linked by attribution theorists with particularly strong tendencies to seek explanations and make attributions following encounters with novelty (Berlyne, 1960), frustration or failure (Wong, 1979, Wong and Weiner, 1981), and restriction of control and personal freedom (Worchel and Andreoli, 1976; Wortman, 1976).

A third motivational source of attributions, also buttressed by much research, suggests that "people assign causality in order to maintain or enhance their self-esteem" (Bulman and Wortman, 1977, p. 351). Like the question of control, this has the ring of what we called the *defensive-protective tradition.*

In sum, attributions are triggered when meanings are unclear, control is in doubt, and self-esteem appears to be challenged (Bulman and Wortman, 1977; Kelley, 1971; Taylor, 1983; and Thompson, 1981). The research further indicates that these three factors are interrelated. Extensive literature on the concept of alienation—of which meaningless and powerlessness are major components—strongly affirms that feelings of control and capability go with perceptions of life and the world as being understood and making sense (Dean, 1961; Elmore, 1963; Spilka, 1970). Likewise, self-esteem is tied to perceptions of meaningfulness and control (Becker, 1973; Davids, 1955; Oken, 1973; Seeman, 1959).

Given these three sources of attribution motivation, the individual may attribute the causes of events to a wide variety of possible referents—oneself, others, chance, God, etc. A massive amount of research testifies that the attributed cause selected is a function of a wide range of factors—personal characteristics, the nature of the event that occurs, the setting in which it takes place, whether it has a positive or negative outcome, plus a host of other possibilities (Harvey and Weary, 1981; Jones et al., 1971; Shaver, 1975). Our concern is to comprehend those influences that relate to the making of religious attributions.

In our view, this is the key role for the psychology of religion. It must come to grips with the sources of religious attributions and how they help people cope with life. Different personal approaches to religion may result in attributions to enhance self-esteem, exercise environmental control, or seek meaning. For example, there are many for whom "Things go better with Jesus." In like manner, effectiveness is attributed to prayer, and various characteristics are attributed to the deity and its role in the world. Religion is thus a source of meaning, an agency of control for people through worship and prayer, and, through the provision of meaning and capability, self-esteem is maintained and enhanced in the face of threat and insecurity.

Slowly but surely research is being conducted on these issues and is rapidly gaining a prominent place in the psychology of religion. For example, Gorsuch and Smith (1983a, 1983b) are looking at the nature of attributions to God and the determinants of these attributions. Spilka and Schmidt (1983) are also focusing on the factors that stimulate attributions. Hunsberger (1983) has looked at biases that enter this process. The theoretical position being advanced here has been developed by Spilka, Shaver, and Kirkpatrick (1985) with a view toward the provision of a comprehensive program for research on the attributional aspects of religion.

In addition to assessing the motivational bases of attributions, it is our contention that this process is the product of interactions between external *situational factors* and internal *dispositional influences* (Magnusson, 1981). In other words, all behavior takes place in an interpersonal, institutional, or sociocultural situational context. Relative to religious attributions and actions based on such cognitions, it is imperative that we examine these factors. Hence we now distinguish, somewhat expediently, situational and dispositional influences on the making of religious attributions. Throughout this text, we will continue this process, suggesting the place of attributions for the topic under discussion.

SITUATIONAL INFLUENCES

The dominant theme in attribution research has been an emphasis on immediate situational and environmental factors as determiners of thought and behavior (Jones et al., 1971; Shaver, 1975). This could imply that most of what we observe in the way of religious belief, experience, and behavior might result from the circumstances in which these phenomena occur and are studied. Consider, for example, intense religious experiences. Something has happened to an individual in terms of his/her perceptions, emotions, and feelings (Proudfoot and Shaver, 1975). Schachter (1964) suggests that the affected individual "will label his feelings in terms of his knowledge of the immediate situation" (p. 54). Berkowitz (1969) claims that "persons who do not know the nature of their intense sensations will label their feelings in accord with the action of the other people around them" (p. 93). Dienstbier (1979) has referred to this labelling as *emotion-attribution theory*. Here the task is to define the causes of emotional states when ambiguity exists relative to its possible causes. Since we are seeking to understand causal attributions in a broader sense, not necessarily just involving emotion or even much ambiguity, we will term our approach *general attribution theory*.

We perceive situational influences as falling into two broad categories: *contextual* and *event character*. The first category alludes to the degree to which situations and circumstances are religiously structured, while the latter stresses the nature of the occurrence being explained.

Contextual Factors

Religious structure may be conveyed by the locale in which the activity in question or its assessment is conducted (e.g., church versus nonchurch surroundings, the presence of religiously defined others, or involvement in religious activities). This implies that religious attributions should occur in religious settings, not just anywhere, and this is what has been found. About two-thirds to three-quarters of religious mystical experiences take place when the person is engaged in a religious activity such as a church service, Bible reading, prayer, etc. (Bourque, 1969; Pahnke, 1963; Spilka, 1980). As Berkowitz (1969) notes, if others are present, their similar actions and involvements should aid the selection of a religious interpretation. The work of Hood (1977) also demonstrates the significance of immediate situational influences in the motivation and definition of nature and spiritual experiences. Contextual factors apparently work to have those affected attribute their state to the intervention of God. The salience of religion is heightened in these circumstances. The more salient, important, noticeable, or conspicuous religion is in a situation, the more likely it is that religious attributions will be made.

Event Character Factors

A second consideration for understanding religious attributions lies in the *nature* or *character* of the event being explained. A number of influences are possible here: (1) the importance of the event; (2) whether the event is a positive or negative happening; (3) whether the event occurs to the experiencing person or to another individual; and (4) the domain or content of the event—social, political, economic, medical, etc. In recent research, these factors have been shown to affect the intensity and frequency of making religious attributions (Spilka and Schmidt, 1983).

Event Importance

Considering the awe with which the power of God is regarded, we might reserve for the deity happenings of the greatest significance while perceiving the commonplace to result from the actions of people or chance. A disaster takes place, and the insurance company defines it as an "act of God." A young person dies and this tragedy may be viewed as "God's will." Unexpected great successes may occasion perceptions of the "hand of God." At other times one is told "God works in mysterious ways." An alternate possibility is that divine explanation is invoked when something major takes place and we know very little about the factors that produce such effects. Death, the destruction wreaked by a tornado, and the birth of a child may be explainable by scientific means, but to many persons there still remains a "miraculous," extraordinary quality to the event. Science and common sense are not seen as answering such questions as: "Why now?", "Why here?", "Why me?" If someone is suffering from a severe illness or a terminal condition, allusions and attributions to God do not seem farfetched. The afflicted person might also see alleviation of his/her state as only possible through divine intervention, and instances of remission when all seemed hopeless are frequently viewed as "God's mercy."

Positive-Negative Influences

Implicit in these examples is another possible influence on the attribution process—namely, the positive-negative quality of what takes place.

An interesting study by Bulman and Wortman (1977) illustrates this point. They were concerned with the attributions offered by victims of serious accidents, clearly an extremely important concern since the result was a major, permanent handicap such as severe paralysis. Since this was a truly critical happening for which a satisfactory meaning is difficult to come by, attributions to God should have been common and they were. Variations on the theme that "God has a reason" were the most frequently offered of all explanations. Most of those seeing "God's hand" in their suffering also felt that their disabling injury was predetermined. The inevitability of a God-ordained accident also meant that the victims tended to see a benevolent purpose in what took place. One respondent stated, "God's trying to put me in situations, help me learn about Him and myself and also how I can help other people" (p. 358). In such explanations there is the attribution that God is "just" and that even tragedy has a constructive meaning.

Personal-Impersonal Events

There is reason to believe that we might be more ready to explain certain things that happen to us by religious attributions than when these things occur to others. We are likely to lament the tragedies we hear about, but when we are the victims, the question "Why me?" is suddenly of the greatest importance, and attributions to God may appear especially appropriate. If something exceptionally good happens to someone else, such as the winning of a large amount of money in a sweepstakes, we might say "That's luck for you." If we are so benefited, we might claim that "God was looking out for us."

Event Domain

Finally, the domain of the event might be expected to influence the likelihood of making religious attributions. Reference to God might be offered for political, economic, social, medical, or other events, but chances are that the often intensely personal and fearful nature of medical conditions may elicit more religious attributions than would result from occurrences in any of these other areas. In these circumstances, meanings may be most unclear and control is often less than for the other domains.

Situational Complexity and Event Significance

Reality tells us that any particular event will include all of these dimensions—importance, positive-negative quality, personal-impersonal nature, and domain—and contexts may also vary in relation to the event itself. In other words, these factors *interact* to such a degree that any unraveling of this web will constitute a very significant research task.

Although events may vary along four dimensions, one may ask why these are of such importance. They have already been shown to be influential in research (Spilka and Schmidt, 1983), but the reason for their effects needs to be clarified. It is our view that the considerations of meaning, control, and self-esteem loom in the background. For example, the more important an event, the greater the likelihood that it will arouse questions of meaning, control, and self-esteem. Similarly, personal events should elicit these concerns more than impersonal ones. Though we might theorize similarly about negative occurrences relative to positive ones, and for certain domains rather than others, all of these dimensions will have to be assessed by research. This theory is in the process of development, and though much has already been conceptualized, still more needs to be done.

DISPOSITIONAL INFLUENCES

A third set of factors leading to religious attributions might be termed *dispositional.* These factors fall under three overlapping headings: background factors, cognitive-linguistic readiness, and personality traits and characteristics.

A number of scholars have used the concept of *attributional styles,* which seems to be derived from the more well-established notion of *cognitive style* (Ickes and Layden, 1978; Metalsky and Abramson, 1980). This appears to be a redefinition of the position that traits and attitudes are, in part, generalized tendencies to interpret the world in certain ways. Emphasis is placed, therefore, on the cognitive aspects of personal characteristics. Our framework stresses the importance of cognitions and their relationship to motivations and emotions. In addition, we are extending the style concept to include dispositions based on one's background and linguistic skills and knowledge. It is our position that people are disposed to pattern their attributions regarding the causes of events so that some explanations are much more congenial to them than are other possibilities. For example, some individuals may perceive the causes of positive or negative outcomes as a result of their own actions; others may define these same occurrences as due to the action of God, while still others may chalk it all up to fate or luck. The literature in this area is not as strong as it might be, largely because of the emphasis of workers on situational effects; however, it appears to be gaining strength (Metalsky and Abramson, 1980; Metalsky, Abramson, Seligman, Semmel, and Peterson, 1982).

Background Factors

Most people in our culture are exposed early in life to religious teachings in their homes, churches, communities, and generally by their peers. Childhood experience with these influences usually carries considerable weight in later years. One's motivations and perceptions could reveal inclinations to employ religious concepts in situations where others might utilize different possibilities. Much research confirms this likelihood. A common observation suggests that the stronger a person's spiritual background, the greater the chance that that individual may report intense religious experiences and undergo conversion (Coe, 1900; Clark, 1929; Starbuck, 1899). Frequency of church attendance, knowledge of one's faith, and strength of spiritual beliefs are also correlates of religious socialization when young (Wilson, 1978). In sum, religious attributions are to be expected from persons whose lives included early and strong references to the sacred plus membership in a home that could be called orthodox.

Cognitive-Linguistic Factors

Attributions depend on having available a language that both permits and supports thinking along certain lines. On an elemental level, the more familiar we are with certain words, the more rapidly we recognize them visually and auditorially (Howes, 1957; Howes and Solomon, 1951). On a higher plane, Bernstein (1964) tells us that "Language marks out what is relevant, affectively, cognitively and socially, and experience is transformed by what is made relevant" (p. 117). Laski (1961) and Bourque and Back (1971) show that religious persons possess a religious language with which they describe their experiences. Those who lack such a vehicle will undoubtedly explain their feelings and perceptions in the words available to them. This might involve the terminology of esthetics or nature or whatever seems of personal significance at the time. Meaning to the experiencing individual is therefore a function of the language and vocabulary available to that person and this relates to one's background and interests. Thought is very much a slave of language (Carroll, 1956).

Personality-Attitudinal Factors

Attributions are influenced by a third set of dispositional factors, which may be subsumed under the broad rubric of personality. A number of these factors have been examined relative to religion. These are self-esteem, locus of control, the concept of a "just world," and form of personal faith.

Self-Esteem

Persons with high self-esteem seem to attribute their failures to outside factors and their successes to themselves (Ickes and Layden, 1978; Miller and Ross, 1975; Snyder, Stephan, and Rosenfield, 1978). Could this imply that religious individuals with high self-esteem view their defeats and tragedies as due to God or the Devil, while still claiming credit for personal triumph and prosperity? Since self-esteem relates positively to intrinsic-committed faith and negatively to extrinsic-consensual religion (Spilka and Mullin, 1977), the former might associate with God attributions for favorable outcomes and the latter more with negative occurrences. Evidence supporting this contention has been reported (Spilka, Schmidt, and Loffredo, 1982). In other words, self-esteem seems to interact with form of personal faith.

Other traits that tend to overlap, often greatly, with self-esteem show similar tendencies (Ickes and Layden, 1978; Miller and Ross, 1975). On the other hand, Benson and Spilka (1973) showed that positive images of God were held by religious adolescents with high self-esteem. This could suggest that religious youth see God as playing a considerable role in both their successes and failures. More research is needed to resolve this question.

Locus of Control

This concept has been studied primarily as a general tendency to see events as either internally determined by the person or externally determined by factors outside the individual (Lefcourt, 1966; Phares, 1976; Rotter, 1966). Levenson (1973a; 1973b; 1974) expanded this notion to include control by oneself (internal) or by powerful others or chance (both external). Kopplin (1976) added the idea of "God control" to these last referents. We have found that these general interpretive propensities tie fairly closely to definitions of control in specific situations (Spilka, Schmidt, and Loffredo, 1982).

Researching this area, Randall and Desrosiers (1980) observed a tendency for belief in supernaturalism to associate with external control. Other work has shown that "people who are more involved in religious activities perceive themselves as having more control over what happens to them" (Shrauger and Silverman, 1971, p. 15). A number of studies have supported this finding, and it should be noted that this relationship may be strongest among religious fundamentalists (Furnham, 1982; Silvestri, 1979; Tipton, Harrison, and Mahoney, 1980). One wonders if this finding is a variation on the theme that "God helps them who help themselves." It could imply that people who feel they are under the protection of God believe strongly in the doctrine of free will, and hence also consider themselves to be determiners of their own destinies. That is, of course, as long as they live up to their spiritual obligations. The suggestion and, to some degree, the evidence is that those who see much control vested in God make more attributions to God, and further that intrinsics are more likely than extrinsics to make religious attributions.

"A Just World"

In the words of poet Robert Browning, the Judeo-Christian tradition holds dear the perspective that "God's in his heaven, all's right with the world." Stated differently, this implies that many, if not most, people feel there is justice in life even if much appears tragic and unfair. Apparently we are reluctant to accept the notion that there are chance occurrences. There must be a reason for everything, and that reason must make sense even if, like Job, we are unable to fathom it.

Psychologist Melvin Lerner (1975) and his students have conducted much research on the idea that we need to believe that what happens to us and others is based on a justice principle—we must live in a "just world." This implies that good people will gain eventual rewards, if not in this life then in the next, and, of course, that bad people will get their just desserts, too. Trust that the world is "just" increases as God-belief grows, and the more that image is of an active God, the stronger one affirms themes of justice. This outlook is also correlated with frequency of church attendance and self-rated religiosity (Rubin and Peplau, 1973).

Attribution and Form of Personal Faith

At least two kinds of individual religiosity, intrinsic-committed and extrinsic-consensual, are suggested by the literature. The research is quite conclusive that these inclinations represent very different ways of viewing and responding to the world (Hunt and King, 1971). They clearly relate to different attributional patterns on many levels. In other words, these inclinations suggest varying interpretations for the role of oneself, others, and religion.

The attributions of the intrinsic-committed religionist revolve around a benevolent God who is involved in human affairs, a loving being upon whom one can rely at all times (Spilka and Mullin, 1977). A God who is good fits in with self-perceptions that are likewise positive (Kahoe, 1976; Spilka, 1976). Here we see an intrinsic-committed faith negating feelings of powerlessness and supporting self-esteem. One feels more the determiner of life's vicissitudes than the victim or plaything of fate, luck, and chance.

Attributions of trust in the deity are further reinforced by findings that relate personal faith to attitudes toward death. The intrinsic-committed person tends to show a low fear of death (Kahoe and Dunn, 1975); Magni, 1972) and views this ultimate threat in terms of courage and final reward (Minton and Spilka, 1976; Spilka et al., 1977).

We know that high self-rated religiosity, high frequency of church attendance, and belief in an active deity are features of intrinsic-committed religion. These are also characteristics of belief in a just world, hence we can expect the latter to be a correlate of the conviction that justice will prevail in life, that the ideal of justice is a cornerstone of the universe.

The development of these concepts of personal faith were originally founded on research relating religion and prejudice (Allen and Spilka, 1967; Allport, 1959, 1966; Allport and Ross, 1967). Work on prejudice shows that persons with these outlooks are likely to blame their shortcomings and failures on others; they attribute blame to external forces over which they have little or no control. Conspiracies and threats abound and involve minorities who are vested with power plus all manner of undesirable personal qualities (Adorno, Frenkel-Brunswik, Levinson, and Sanford, 1950; Allport, 1954; Bettelheim and Janowitz, 1950; Neumann, 1960). The picture is one of insecurity and peril due to others who are different.

Intrinsic-committed religion counters these views and negates prejudice (Allen and Spilka, 1967; Allport and Ross, 1967). Individuals with this approach see themselves as like, rather than unlike, others and are not inclined to make distinctions on the basis of race, status, sex, or age (Spilka and Mullin, 1977).

In general, an intrinsic-committed orientation is associated with interpretations (attributions) of self, God, and the world as nonthreatening and positive. Personal capability parallels a sense of trust in others and the deity.

Extrinsic-consensual faith contrasts sharply with its intrinsic-committed counterpart. This framework is tied to attributions of relative helplessness, low intrinsic motivation, and the feeling that one is often a victim of circumstance and external powers (Kahoe, 1974; Minton and Spilka, 1976; Strickland and Shaffer, 1971).

The deity is attributed to be a punitive, wrathful, unloving God (Spilka, 1976; Spilka et al., 1977), but also one who is not usually involved in human affairs. This God is an impersonal, distant, deistic being who started it all but then left it up to humans to make their own way. Where God might be perceived as softening the blow of death, the opposite seems true as death is viewed in terms of pain, loneliness, forsaking dependents, failure, and as a simple, natural termination of life (Spilka et al., 1977).

The extrinsic-consensual religionist is also on the other side of the prejudice issue, treating people as dissimilar from oneself on the basis of race, status, sex, or age (Allport, 1966; Allport and Ross, 1967; Feagin, 1964; Spilka, 1976).

Since religion may be viewed as a means to other goals, the person who embraces an extrinsic-consensual outlook seeks materialistic considerations—namely, money, prestige, and power (Spilka, 1977).

Attributionally, we have pictured opposites in their extreme form. Extrinsic-consensual faith is tied to a perspective of oneself as a relatively helpless individual. The world is a dangerous, threatening place and one must look out for oneself. God is sought mainly in crisis and tragedy, but otherwise the deity is seen as uninvolved in living. These people are therefore likely to trumpet the platitude that "God helps those who help themselves," especially if things are going well and success is attributed to the self. When times are bad, the cry is for help from God, as if catastrophe and failure must come from the outside, if not from the deity itself. The very negative persectives on death held by extrinsic-consensual persons might further suggest, at least in these circumstances, that aid from the divine is also seen as doubtful and tenuous.

Once again, a reminder is in order. Religious people are, as a rule, neither intrinsic-committed nor extrinsic-consensual; they usually share and express both orientations, and may do so equally or be inclined toward one approach more than the other. We have been speaking of "pure types" when, in reality, trends are meant. Of most significance is the fact that these tendencies can be interpreted as attributional patterns relative to oneself, others, and many aspects of life. We act upon such attributions and they associate religious thinking and behavior with our cognitions, motivations, and expressions in other areas. Religion and prejudice, religion and altruism, religion and personal adjustment, religion and political, economic, and social views and actions are affiliated through the "causes" we believe to be true. Our task is to understand the sources of these attributions and their operation in the lives of persons whose attributions are to God, the church, the supernatural, to whatever is defined as spiritual in nature. This is one of the major tasks of the psychologist of religion.

SUMMARY AND CONCLUSIONS

In this chapter we have attempted to look at the problem of defining religion, and unhappily must admit that we have avoided direct confrontation with the issue. Where so many brilliant scholars have failed, we had to ask if we could point in some undeniable directions and accomplish more than foundering on the sharp edges of a concrete definition. The history of such attempts is more a tale of restriction and limitation than of success in opening minds to fresh ideas.

Our hope was to indicate where religion may be found, the location of the "inside" personal perspective within the context of the "outside" institutional-cultural framework. Given such a focus, the seemingly simple word *religion* was shown to be a very complex, multidimensional phenomenon. Unfortunately, a wide variety of schemes exists—some more helpful than others, and most theorized but not researched—and too many that suggest promise remain stillborn.

Our search for the motivational basis of religion then took us to four broad psychological traditions. The classical instinct heritage of psychology was shown to be a dead end. Explaining one unknown in terms of another does not tell us anything about the psychological roots of spiritual faith. Much more fruitful is the defensive-protective tradition that claims religion grows from weakness, deficiency, and shortcoming. People turn to deities to gain solace, security, and the illusion of safety and certainty. For others, maybe only a minority, religion sponsors growth and personal enrichment. The goal seems to be the gaining of an even deeper and broader perspective; a reaching out toward truth, perfection, integration into the scheme of things; a struggle to understand one's place in the universe.

Something much more prosaic and mundane may be involved in becoming "religious." Here we have simple, basic, unadorned habit. Religion is learned in a social order that has kept churches and their doctrines as central social, political, and moral forces throughout history. The outcome has been religion as an integral part of family life and childrearing. For most it is a mechanical, occasional church going need plus a set of beliefs and ideas that should not be questioned or, in most instances, should not be afforded much thought. It becomes an inviolate absolute that is *simply there.*

Finally, we offered an attributional approach to religion, suggesting a multiform approach through what is termed intrinsic-committed and extrinsic-consensual types of faith. We skimmed the surface, but observed two broad patterns of religious motivation, and responsiveness. For religious persons, these relate to virtually all other areas of life—how one deals with oneself, others, and the religious system itself. What we hope we may have accomplished is a way of organizing one's thoughts about religion and showing how a psychology of religion can relate the complexities of human mental life to the context of a religious outlook. Concurrently, the task is also to understand that one's personal religious orientation is simultaneously a reflection of one's history, motivations, cognitions and behavior.

CHAPTER TWO
THE OPERATIONAL
DEFINITION OF RELIGION

Religion is said to be knowledge, and it is said to be ignorance. Religion is said to be freedom, and it is said to be dependence. Religion is said to be desire, and it's said to be freedom from all desires. Religion is said to be silent contemplation, and it is said to be splendid and stately worship of God. People take every kind of liberty with this old word. (Müller, 1889, p. 44)

THE NATURE OF OPERATIONAL DEFINITIONS

In Chapter One, we tried to avoid defining religion because, as Max Müller observed almost a century ago, it seems like an exercise in futility. Still, questions about the definition and nature of religion are indispensable if we want to investigate and understand religious phenomena from a psychological perspective. What we require are not abstract, theoretical definitions, but *operational* ones.

According to physicist and philosopher of science Henry Margenau, *operational definitions* mean "recourse, wherever feasible, to instrumental procedures when meanings are to be established" (Margenau, 1954, p. 209)—that is, to the procedures by which it is measured in a study. We will, therefore, consider religion in terms of its measurable aspects and qualities. Keep in mind, however, that no operational definition can describe or explain the total concept from which it is derived, and this is certainly true when we study religion. We will thus treat religion, or rather different facets of it, through the measures we use to illustrate its many features. For example, one operational definition could conceive of religious expression in behavior such as church attendance; another in terms of a questionnaire on religious beliefs; a third through a personal report of a religious mystical experience. Whatever is chosen, the definition might serve as a window to provide us with a little more insight into what religion is psychologically.[1]

Operational Definitions for the Psychology of Religion: Needs and Problems

The almost unbelievable breadth and variety of religious phenomena and expressions is the most obvious reason for operational definitions in the psychology of religion. They define the boundaries of the area, and such boundaries are necessary for focused discussion. The complexity of religion makes such limitation essential for both research and understanding.

A second reason for using operational definitions arises from differences between personal approaches to religious questions and a social science perspective on these same issues. Usually the former are of a theological and philosophical nature. As a rule, we are personally less interested in how religion might be defined than we are in evaluating ideas and practices that we make part of our own spiritual outlook. The institutions concerned with religious phenomena reveal similar concerns, because they are interested in the search for the "true" faith. History shows that personal and institutional definitions of "true" faith vary widely, and discussions of religion contain numerous direct and indirect judgments about philosophical and theological truth in an attempt to eliminate what are conceived as false definitions.

In contrast to the personal approach of seeking the "true" faith, the psychologist desires to understand all religious approaches without regard for their

---

[1]Psychology strives to be a rigorous empirical science, and operational definitions are central to realizing this aim. This is also the goal of the psychology of religion. Operational definitions rely on measurement, and this entails the use of a variety of terms that may be unfamiliar to many readers. These will be introduced here, and are utilized throughout this volume. In order to enhance understanding, these concepts, many of which are based on statistics, are defined in an elementary way in an appendix at the end of this chapter. Make liberal use of this aid to ensure that you fully comprehend what the authors mean when discussing research studies.

philosophical or theological correctness. A study of how "invalid" religion arises is just as important psychologically as a study of how "valid" religion develops. The distinction between valid and invalid religion is not a part of the psychological task. Evaluating the truth of religion is, as already noted, outside of the realm of psychology and beyond the professional expertise of psychologists and social scientists. An understanding of how social scientists define religion should, however, help to develop further understanding of the social scientific role in general.[2]

Another problem found in the psychology of religion arises from the translation of general definitions of religion into operational definitions—that is, into *operations* by which religiousness can be measured. Since the definitions of religion formulated by most psychologists have evolved not only from their psychological view of religion but also from their philosophical stance, it is easy for personal biases to influence the translation. When the resulting operational definitions are explicitly set out, such biases can be identified. Since operational definitions do not always closely follow theoretical definitions, the measuring instruments representing the former in a research study may actually measure a different facet of religious faith than implied by the theoretical definition. This can create serious problems of interpretation. For this reason, it is very important to examine operational definitions closely—namely, the way religion is measured and not just how it is verbally defined.

To illustrate, let us consider the Allport-Vernon-Lindzey Scale (see this chapter's appendix) for measuring religion (Allport, Vernon, and Lindzey, 1960). Their *R* or *Religion Scale* was an attempt to operationalize a definition of the truly religious person advanced by Spranger (1928). This definition claims that "a religious man is he whose whole mental structure is permanently directed to the creation of the highest absolutely satisfying value experience" (Spranger, 1928, p. 213). Hunt (1968), however, noted that "the R scale is primarily measuring individual's active involvement in traditional religious institutions as a means of making life meaningful" (Hunt, 1968, p. 70). In addition, elements of the Christian tradition are prominent in the items of the scale. It can be argued that in our culture some Christians possess mental structures in keeping with Spranger's definitions, but is every Christian so committed? And what about the people of other faiths in our country? It is apparent that the measurement operation utilized here—namely, the items selected—provides a different operational definition than the theoretical one.

When we see what the operational meaning is, we know *functionally* what the nature of the religious phenomenon being studied must be. Then, by relating that operational definition to a host of other variables, as is done throughout this text, the character of religion as viewed from this particular operational stance becomes even more explicit. For this reason, instead of listing numerous definitions of religion which may or may not have been empirically studied, we shall examine operational definitions to evaluate how they specify the nature of religion.

[2]This is not to say that a psychologist is always a psychologist. In our many individual roles, we, as everyone else, make implicit and explicit decisions about the validity of religious positions. Such personal judgments may well be influenced by empirical data. In addition, the values and personal commitments and interests of individual psychologists often lead them to study one or more particular aspects of religious phenomena. It is therefore not a question of religious values and psychology being totally unrelated, but rather that *psychology's task is a scientific one.*

In this chapter, we survey operational approaches to the definition of religion. First, we begin with *typologies*. Next *trait formulations* are discussed, and compared with typologies. We also consider whether religion is to be defined broadly or narrowly, plus the issue raised in the first chapter: Is religion a unitary phenomenon or is it composed of several independent dimensions? Attempts to integrate different traits into a multitrait system for defining religion form the next section. Since both typological and trait approaches commonly employ questionnaires, a fourth section of the chapter discusses the implications of definition by questionnaire and refers to some possible alternative procedures. The concluding section confronts the issue of the best definition of religion for psychological purposes.

Religious Typologies

A typology is a system that classifies individuals. Each person is placed in one and only one category in the system. For example, an individual might be considered a member of the category "Born-again Christian," or be designated a "convert" as opposed to the category "nonconvert." The simplest typology is that of being classified as "religious" or "nonreligious." Another obvious typological distinction is religious affiliation, such as Protestant, Catholic, or Jew. These could be further typed in terms of denomination, sect, or other meaningful classification. Differences among typological categories are generally assumed to be qualitative rather than quantitative. The crucial operational question concerns how the decision is made to place a person in one category or another. Research Box 2-1 gives an example of a typology.

Hunt (1972) developed a typology when he felt that too much of the psychology of religion had been influenced by a "conservative-liberal" dimension that people were confusing with a "literal-symbolic" dimension. The popular tendency was to equate conservative with literal and liberal with symbolic. Hunt proposed to overcome this limitation by classifying individuals according to their orientation toward religious phenomena. This could be *literal* or *antiliteral*, respectively, whether all religion was accepted or rejected. Alternatively, a *mythological* approach might be employed. Here myth is used in the technical sense of being symbolic.

Hunt developed a set of items where a person chooses between one of the three possible interpretations of a statement similar to those used by Broen (1957). The Hunt instrument was labeled the *LAM scale* (Literal—Antiliteral—Mythological). The number of times a respondent selects each interpretation can then be counted, thereby permitting the person to be placed in the most frequently chosen category.

But Hunt's LAM is seldom used typologically. Hunt actually reports three scores for a person, one for each of the categories. In later work, Polythress (1975) developed a more complex typology by applying a different scoring method to the LAM scale.

Limits and Possibilities for Religious Typologies

It is evident from the work of Hunt that a number of characteristics are necessary for determining who goes into what category. When scores indicating the degree of the various characteristics are computed, it is usually more con-

RESEARCH BOX 2-1.   *Harrell, S. "Modes of Belief in Chinese Folk Religion." Journal* for the Scientific Study of Religion, *1977, 16, 55–65.*

To determine the types of believers in a primitive or folk religion, Harrell (1977) interviewed sixty-six residents of a Taiwanese village where a traditional religion still prevailed. This included such elements as ancestor worship and the use of magic charms.

Each person was questioned regarding three aspects of folk religious belief: (1) auspicious days or events; (2) interaction with supernatural beings in response to calls for help, and as a cause of illness; and (3) the fate of the dead. The discussion centered on which of these tenets of the folk religion were true and why. Four categories of believers were identified from both the interviews and casual observation data:

Intellectual Believers

These are people who base their beliefs on an effort to make the world intellectually coherent and orderly. The prototype was a retired coal miner with six years of education. He conceived of the world as cosmologically and morally ordered. This led him to reject some religious folk doctrines such as a purely economic relationship between humans and supernatural beings.

True Believers

A true believer was identified as a totally credulous person. A mother and son demonstrated this particular belief style. The son had a long list of food taboos and the consequences of ignoring them. Illnesses were attributed to violations of these taboos, and no data could ever challenge these convictions.

Practical Believers

These people rely on the empirical evidence of their senses and the practical utility of their beliefs and practices. They believe in folk religion because it is perceived as helping them achieve what they want from life. A typical case in this study was a chemical salesman who carefully distinguished between physically based illnesses requiring treatment by a doctor because of their physical basis, and recovery from a wound following prayers to a temple god. This convinced him of the validity of that aspect of his religion.

Nonbelievers

These people have closed their minds to the possible validity or utility of folk religious tenets. These tenets have then been replaced with scientific ideas or competing folk medicines and psychologies. A pharmaceutical salesman, who dismissed religion out-of-hand, was nevertheless willing to admit that some folk religious ideas might be related to outcomes. Still he felt there would be a naturalistic explanation for the relationships. Religious activity on his part occurred only as an aspect of participating in the general culture, not because of any religious meaning per se.

Harrell reports that the great majority of Taiwanese are practical believers followed by a sizable number of nonbelievers. True believers were rare (only three of the sixty-six formally interviewed), and intellectual believers were rarer still, with only one good example observed. This analysis of Taiwanese folk religion suggests that religion is primarily of interest because of the benefits it offers the individual, while only a very few are interested in religion for its ability to provide cosmological answers.

venient to work with these refined data rather than to establish a cutoff point beyond which all persons are simply described as a type. This last approach adds an unnecessary step, and as we must recognize, may lose some significant information.

Another problem concerning typologies is the many people who do not readily fit into the "pigeonholes" that typologies become. Few people are categorically religious or nonreligious. Instead, they will manifest some of the characteristics of those considered religious, and some of the features of persons regarded as nonreligious. It therefore seems much more worthwhile to examine how those particular characteristics develop and are expressed rather than to force a person into a category.

TRAIT APPROACHES IN THE PSYCHOLOGY OF RELIGION

As opposed to typologies, where a person is placed in a unique category, one might receive a score on one or more dimensions. For example, the number of times an individual worships could be counted and be a score for a dimension of religious activity. Technically, a trait is an ordered scale. People are ranged along some dimension to the degree to which they possess the characteristic or trait the scale is supposed to measure.

A continuing problem with trait approaches is the question of the breadth of their definition. With respect to religion, should it be defined across several religious traditions and secular movements that seem to perform similar functions? Or should it be formulated more narrowly in order to describe each person in terms of religious traditions within our culture? In other words, does religion—for example, Protestantism, Communism, Capitalism, Vegetarianism—include an all-consuming love for opera, football, or needlepoint, or, in our culture, should it be restricted to the Judeo-Christian tradition?

General Trait Definition of Religion

Probably the broadest and most widely used operational definition of religion is based on its personally conceived importance to the individual. People frequently implicitly rate themselves on a scale, with 1 meaning that "religion is not at all important" to 9 indicating that "religion is the most important aspect of their lives." Scores of 2 through 8 refer to increasing degrees of importance. It is both an advantage and disadvantage of this question that no particular definition of religion is given. The advantage is that it can cover many different facets of religiousness—for example, permitting its use with college students in many different countries. The disadvantage is that it assumes that all respondents in a study possess a more or less similar understanding of religion.

The Functional, Nondoctrinal Approach

This general trait orientation defines religion in terms of those basic questions with which we are all concerned. Yinger (1969), a proponent of this perspective, suggests that the critical question is not "How religious is a person?" but "How is a person religious?" To answer this query, he proposed a set of seven items that relate to what he views as the major and permanent problems of human existence including suffering, injustice, and death. Although several of the items use the term *religion* as a response to such needs, the scale is apparently not as general as the initial question. Perhaps it is for this reason that studies have found Yinger's measure to be composed of a number of characteristics rather than only the one he hypothesized (Roof, Hadaway, Hewitt, McGaw, and Morse, 1977; Nelsen, Everett, Nader, and Hanby, 1976).

Yinger has continued to develop his concept using open-ended questions to discover what people see as life's fundamental problems. This is presented in Research Box 2-2. It is interesting to note that religion is mentioned in only a small percentage of responses to this basic question, suggesting further that, from a psychology of religion perspective, the functional approach is very broad indeed.

RESEARCH BOX 2-2.   *Yinger, J.M. "A Comparative Study of the Substructures of Religion."* Journal for the Scientific Study of Religion, *1977, 16, 67–86.*

Yinger (1977) begins with the assumption that religion is a response to the deepest problems of meaninglessness, suffering, and injustice. To determine if these are the basic questions with which people are concerned, he asked 751 college and university students in Japan, Korea, Thailand, New Zealand, and Australia the open-ended question, "What do you consider the one most fundamental or important issue for the human race; that is, what do you see as a basic and permanent question for mankind, the question of which all others are only parts?" (Yinger, 1977, p. 72).

Analyses of the responses indicated that ninety-two percent of the students referred to the themes of meaning, suffering, and its reduction, or the problem of injustice. Sixty percent were concerned with meaninglessness, fifty-four percent with suffering, and thirty-eight percent with injustice. (These percentages add up to more than 100 because many respondents indicated a combination of these problems.)

Yinger also sought reactions to statements reflecting these three issues. He defined religious responses as seeing suffering and injustice as growth experiences, being interested in talking about basic human problems, and belief in an order and pattern to existence. The percentage of those who responded in a religious direction averaged in the seventies across the items. He thus concluded that most people are interested in religion even when it is defined from a nondoctrinal perspective.

Yinger's nondoctrinal definition of religion may be of limited usefulness to the psychology of religion because it assumes that everyone asks questions and seeks explanations for inconsistencies. Since raters judge the responses, this assumption may influence the results through the response-coding methods used. As Wright and D'Antonio (1980) note, Yinger's codebook defines categories such as "love" in the meaninglessness, injustice, and suffering category. While arguments do exist for such a combining technique (Fletcher, 1966), the average college student interprets love more in what Kohlberg (1969) terms a conventional way than in the postconventional mode employed by Yinger's formulations. When Wright and D'Antonio added a love category to national data, it was the most popular of all thirty-five percent, with the category of meaninglessness, injustice, and suffering accounting for only twenty percent of the responses.

In contrast to Yinger, Harrell (see Research Box 2-1) found that only a very small proportion of his sample viewed religion as providing explanations for any question. Instead, religion met a host of other needs. This suggests that a single-function approach may be appropriate only for select groups. The reason Yinger was even partially successful may be that, to date, his research has been limited to college-level groups, which would probably contain many "intellectual believers."

RELIGION IN TERMS OF NONDOCTRINAL BELIEFS AND ATTITUDES

There are numerous broad operationalizations in which religiosity is defined by means of *beliefs and attitudes*. To the degree that the propositions represent opinions about the truth of a particular position, they are regarded as *beliefs*. If they are presented as evaluations, such as liking the church, they would be considered *attitudes*. Belief and attitude items may be indiscriminately mixed with one another to form a scale. McLean (1952) has produced a *Religious World View Scale,* which is composed of many such items concerned with Christianity.

It is not at all unusual to find research in which investigators constructed their own belief and attitude scales, and to use these in only one study. Many such scales are referred to as "orthodoxy" scales. Although such instruments represent what their authors believe may be orthodox for large numbers of people, they seldom represent orthodoxy in an exacting sense. The label *orthodoxy* is unsatisfactory since it is technically defined relative to a particular religious standard. There is thus an orthodox Jew, an orthodox Catholic, an orthodox Mennonite, Buddhist, Quaker, and so on, but there is no single scale that would identify all of these people as orthodox. Instead, orthodoxy needs to be measured in terms of the similarity of a person's beliefs to those of the official creed of a particular institution.

In a much more rigorous manner, Scott (1965) constructed a general religiousness scale utilizing attitude items. Details of this instrument are given in Research Box 2-3. The scale possesses good psychometric characteristics and avoids language that might limit its usefulness to only one Christian tradition. For this reason, it is a good example of a fairly broad definition of religion as attitude and value.

RESEARCH BOX 2-3.   *Scott, W. A.* Measuring Religious Beliefs as Values. *Unpublished manuscript, 1969.*

Scott suggests that *"a person may be said to entertain a value to the extent that he (sic) conceives a particular state of affairs to be an ultimate end, an absolute good under all circumstances, and a universal 'ought' towards which all people should strive"* (Scott, 1965, p. 15). Given this definition, he did not assume that he was able to select all of the values that people might have. Instead, he utilized it to generate responses to open-ended questions in order to search out the values of college students. He asked respondents to cite the type of person that was admired, and what they found admirable about that individual. A series of questions about the desirable traits concluded the study. This approach was designed to evaluate the degree to which the traits met the three-fold criteria of being an ultimate end, an absolute good, and a universal ought. Only about half those questioned seemed to possess any sense of value by this definition.

The answers were then examined and value categories were developed from both the responses and from general knowledge of college-student culture. Typical values for this group included intellectualism, kindness, social skills, loyalty, academic achievement, physical development, status, honesty, self-control, creativity, independence, and religiousness.

Items were generated for each of the values, including religiousness, and then administered to several samples, permitting revisions to be made. This resulted in a scale of twenty religious items (Scott, 1965, pp. 254–55). Ten of these items are scored directly; typical ones are "being devout in one's religious faith" and "saying one's prayers regularly." The remaining ten items were reverse scored. Examples of these are "denying the existence of God" and "seeking scientific explanations for religious miracles." A high score thus denotes religiousness. These statements tend to be oriented toward Christianity, but most are appropriate for anyone in the Judeo-Christian tradition. In keeping with his definition of value, Scott asked persons to rate each item by checking *"whether it is something you always admire* in other people, or something that *depends upon the situation whether you admire it or not"* (Scott, 1965, p. 245).

The Role of Religious Knowledge

Another way of operationalizing religion is to define it through one's knowledge of religious topics. This is a seldom-used approach because the Western religious tradition has always clearly affirmed that there is more to religion than knowledge. Hence, religious information generally has been viewed as only one aspect of religion or as an indirect measure of it at best. Even so, there is another major problem with this view. As Johnson (1974) noted, religious knowledge is correlated with I.Q. and academic achievement. General intellectual and academic ability is very pervasive in psychological data, and any religious knowledge scale may be expected to reflect these factors rather than religion.

The authors know of no measure of religious knowledge that has been constructed to be specifically independent of general knowledge of our culture and intelligence. For this reason, operational definitions of religion in terms of knowledge are not currently practical.

Operationalizing Religious Experience

Instead of asking for agreement or disagreement with various belief and attitudinal statements, one may focus on whether or not certain events have been experienced. William James (1902), in his famous *Varieties of Religious Experience,* offered numerous case histories that underscore the proposition that certain experiences are considered intrinsic to religion. Otto (1923) further suggested that it is the encounter with the "holy" that is unique in religion. This emphasis has constituted an important tradition of research into mystical or intense religious experiences for almost a century, and is discussed in depth in a later chapter. We will now simply note that there have been many studies identifying mystical experiences. For example, Hood (1975) developed a *mystical experience scale* aimed specifically at determining the extent to which an individual had experienced mystical states as such have been defined in the literature. Included are sets of items reflecting (1) a felt loss of identity; (2) a sense of being absorbed into a greater whole; (3) perception of an inner subjectivity of life; (4) a sense of timelessness and spacelessness; (5) belief in the experience as a source of new and valid knowledge; (6) elements of mystery, awe, and reverence; and (7) great difficulty in representing the experience in words. This scale involves no particular religion, thus one would expect the mystics of most spiritual traditions to score quite high on it.

Operationalizing Private Religious Behavior

Another avenue to the operational understanding of religion is to ask questions regarding religious behavior. Such activity can vary from that which is private and can only be stated by the involved person to highly institutionalized expressions that are reportable by almost anyone who knows the individual. For example, devotionalism scales usually include questions about personal spiritual responsivity such as saying prayers in times of difficulty, on awakening, or before going to sleep. This is one way of assessing private religious behavior. Seldom have these measures been used as general definitions of religiousness.

Operationalizing Institutional Religious Behavior

Measures of public institutional religious activity are also available, and are frequently used as operational definitions of religiosity. The most widely employed of these, and probably the poorest, is to ask about religious membership. If someone belongs to a religious group, it is assumed that person is religious. An obvious shortcoming of this approach is that many people are affiliated with religious bodies as children, but are nonreligious by almost any other criterion of religiousness principally in nonreligiously oriented research, and interesting findings have sometimes occurred. There is no doubt that more useful data would have resulted from better questions, but even a bad operational definition may be better than none at all.

Part of the problem with defining religiosity by membership can be mitigated by requesting religious preference rather than affiliation. This allows individuals to identify their orientation, and if "no preference" is included as one response category, the respondents can also indicate if they are not religious in the institutional sense of the term.

It is both an advantage and a disadvantage that religious membership and preference consider everyone regardless of tradition. Under a very broad but institutionally oriented definition of being religious, this approach would be advantageous. However, if some variation among the religious is of concern, membership or preference is too broad to be useful.

Another very widely accepted institutionally relevant operational definition is attendance at religious functions. Usually the question that has been phrased is "How often do you attend religious services?" Possible responses are: "Never to once a year," "Once a year to several times a year," "Several times a year to once a month," "Two or three times a month," "Once a week," "More than once a week." These scales can be elaborated to include not only religious services, but other church activities as well. A second item is often added to attendance to indicate committee meetings and other similar involvement.

Institutional participation may also be suggested by asking the amount of money contributed in the last month or year. Constructing good items to measure financial contributions is somewhat more difficult than writing most religious items because of the need to control several confounding variables. A given time needs to be designated so that all can respond for the same period. The total amount of disposable income also needs to be taken into account. It is usually easiest to ask for a percent of income contributed over a given time period. This will obviously have a different meaning for college students who have no income but are on allowances compared to those earning their own living. Some people are also sensitive about being asked about their financial affairs. Such problems may be why contribution items have been used much less frequently than participation items.

Defining a Consequential Dimension

It has been argued that religiosity can be determined by the consequences that derive from religious faith, and that can be seen in a person's life. Among such consequences could be peace of mind, personal satisfaction in living, and the belief that experienced success and happiness are a result of religious participation. This procedure is generally found in approaches that utilize a number of traits (*multitrait approaches*). As a separate measure of religiousness, it appears to be of dubious benefit. It is difficult to know if people perform a specific behavior because of their religious faith or in spite of it. The relationship of religious beliefs to consequences can be better viewed as a means of determining if religion relates to nonreligious behavior as various theological or psychological systems hypothesize.

A Priori Content-Oriented Approaches

Numerous scales have been constructed to measure some previously (i.e., a priori) conceptualized facet of religiousness. The authors of these instruments invariably make no claim that their particular scale represents all religion, as is true of most of the measures already introduced. Rather, the interest is in one specific aspect of faith for its own sake, or as a supplement to other scales. As a rule, these specialized definitions are operationalized through belief and attitude items. While a behavior such as religious friendships is included occasionally, other manifestations of religion, such as knowledge and experience, are rarely used to assess these rather focused content areas.

Probably the broadest of these topics is the *liberal-to-conservative dimension.* It may be operationalized with a simple item that requests people to indicate which term most accurately describes their religious stance. Referent terms that have been employed are: fundamentalist, conservative, orthodox, neoorthodox, liberal, and humanist. Multi-item scales are also used in this area.

Lee (1965) produced a fundamentalism scale, the other end of this measure being implicitly a humanistic or very liberal religious position. We have noted previously that measuring fundamentalism has an advantage in that it is better defined theologically than many other concepts in the psychology of religion. Miscommunication is therefore less likely to occur than when labels are not as clearly understood.

Note that we are recommending the term *fundamentalist,* be reserved for a particular theological content within the Christian tradition. It is uniquely identified with *The Fundamentals: A Testimony to the Truth* pamphlets (Stewart and Stewart, 1910). Be forewarned, however, that fundamentalism is often loosely used in the social science literature to refer to conservative authoritarian religion. Whether theological fundamentalism is related to an authoritarian emphasis is still a question for empirical analysis and not something to be automatically assumed (for further discussion, see Etheridge and Feagin, 1979; and Hood, 1980).

Religious Preferences

There is an alternative to measuring fundamentalism-liberalism exclusively with belief and attitude scales—namely, through rating religious preferences. People are asked to indicate their denominational preference, and those making a particular choice are considered to be like the model person of the denomination selected. For example, persons with a Southern Baptist preference would automatically be judged as more conservative than members of the United Methodist Church. One difficulty with this approach is that there are vast individual differences within each denomination, especially among mainline religious bodies that have existed for many generations. Such variation is lost when this technique is used.

Unfortunately there is not always agreement on the exact ordering of denominations from fundamentalist to liberal. Hodge (1979) had twenty-five nationally known experts grade denominations on this dimension, and produced the following ordered list (p. 185): Assemblies of God, Seventh-Day Adventist, Latter-Day Saints, Missouri Synod Lutheran, Nazarene, Southern Baptist, Churches of Christ, Presbyterian U.S., American Baptist, Lutheran Church in America, Disciples of Christ, United Presbyterian, United Methodist and Episcopal (tied), and United Church of Christ. Maranell (1974) gave his *fundamentalism scale* to clergy, and on the basis of their responses ranked the religious bodies thus: Seventh-Day Adventist, Missouri Synod Lutheran, Roman Catholic, Church of Christ, Baptist, Presbyterian, Disciples of Christ, Episcopal, Methodist, and Unitarian-Universalist.

These two orderings are reasonably consistent since they used national samplings. Variability among these and other orderings may be a function of differences in opinions over our country plus the influence of other demographic variables such as sex, age, socioeconomic status, and whether clergy or laity are studied. Since variation occurs even within local congregations, it is apparent that religious preferences are best used to identify theological position when there is no other way of obtaining such information.

Still, denominational choice could be employed to represent other aspects of faith (Hoge, 1979). Russell (1975) found that most people judged world religions as similar or different according to several criteria, only one of which was a godless to fundamentalism dimension that resembles liberalism-conservatism. Again, because of great differences among congregations in some denominations, these findings appear most useful for understanding the perceptions of group members than for converting religious preferences into measures of religiosity.

Religious Values

Rokeach (1973) developed a widely known scale to measure a broad set of values including religiousness. Participants rank-order eighteen value terms, one of which is "salvation (saved, eternal life)." The result is the relative position of religion among the ordered set of values. The ranking procedure itself encounters some statistical problems; otherwise, it appears adequate for many Christian groups. It is, however, felt that the particular definition used, salvation, is more narrow than Scott's scale, which was discussed earlier and which seems more appropriate for moderate to conservative Christian denominations.

Specifying Religious Content

Scales measuring beliefs and attitudes toward a specific concept within Christianity are also available. Thurstone and Chave (1929) developed a number of sound measures of such characteristics. Their most popular ones measure *Attitude toward God* and *Attitude toward the Church*. Research Box 2-4 describes the research base of the latter instrument. In later work, Chave (1939) published some fifty-two experimental scales on different aspects of institutional religion. A set of three measures of *Scriptural Literalism* has also been reported (Hogge and Friedman, 1967). In addition, the degree to which a person views *Jesus as the Christ* is readily evaluated by both single-item and scale procedures (Gorsuch and McFarland, 1968).

Individualized Religious Orientations

A few attempts have been made to distinguish operationally among people who score high on measures of religiosity because they only see their institutional tradition as valid, and those who score high who view other traditions as equally meaningful. Jeeves (1957) developed a *Religious Individualism Scale* that was adapted and published by Brown (1962). It distinguishes between those with individualized-personal and institutional orientations to religion. Kelly (1970) handles this problem by constructing a three-item scale of *Religious Relativism* to identify those who believe that the importance of religion lies in the process of belief rather than its content. Interestingly, the evidence originally presented suggests that both of these scales are fairly independent of specific, content-focused measures. This means that people may be highly religious by a particular content-

RESEARCH BOX 2-4.   *Thurstone, L. L. and Chave, E. J.* The Measurement of Attitude. *Chicago: University of Chicago Press, 1929.*

L. L. Thurstone and E. J. Chave (1929) constructed a scale to measure attitudes toward the church that used a new method developed by Thurstone. Initially, a set of 130 statements were written, each of which gave a favorable, neutral, or unfavorable view of the church. These were then submitted to a panel of judges who sorted the items into eleven categories indicating the degree of positivity, neutrality, or negativity of each statement. The first analysis checked the consistency of the judges' ratings. Items on which judges disagreed—that is, where some ratings were considerably different than those of other judges—were dropped. Second, the remaining items were then examined to determine their scale values. This was based on the eleven-point, positive-to-negative scale categories into which the items were sorted. The scale value of an item was the median (see this chapter's appendix) of the categories the judges used. For example, if judge A placed an item in category 4, judge B put the same item in category 5, and judge C used category 6, the median would be 5 (this is a simplification for illustrative purposes).

The items were also given to 300 people who checked those with which they agreed. An analysis was then conducted to see if checking one item meant that the person checked other items with similar scale scores. If this was not generally true for an item, it was deemed irrelevant and dropped. The best 45 items formed the final scale. Note that the project required 130 items, a panel of judges, and 300 respondents to end up with a 45-item scale. Developing a good scale is never easy!

In using the scale, the respondent's scores were the mean-scale value (see this chapter's appendix) of the items they checked to specify their agreement. A high score on the original scale indicates a *negative* attitude toward the church. A few sample items with their scale scores are:

I enjoy my church because there is a spirit of friendliness there (scale value 3.3; note: low and positive).

I like the ceremonies in my church, but do not miss them much when I stay away (5.1).

I think the church is a parasite on society (11.0, the highest possible scale value, indicating the most negative item).

oriented definition of religion, and yet hold that it is the process of belief in which they individually engage that is important rather than beliefs per se.

Interpersonal Considerations

Another a priori method of measuring one aspect of religiousness is to evaluate the extent of interpersonal involvement the individual has with other religious people. Lenski (1961) found such an approach useful in his research. He distinguished between two types of personal religious involvement that denote somewhat different perspectives on religion. On the one hand, there is *communal* involvement. People are asked how many of their five closest friends belong to the same religious group they do. If religion is communal, most or all of their friends will be similarly involved, thus providing a religious community in which the person participates. On the other hand, one may take part in religious institutions, attend services, and so on, without any of their close friends being involved. This kind of religion is termed *associational,* because these people only associate with those outside of the religious community while remaining religiously active. Such association is generally measured by questions concerning how often the individual engages in various institutional rituals.

Scientifically Functional Distinctions: Intrinsic-Committed and Extrinsic-Consensual Religion

The scales we have discussed were primarily recommended for their intuitive appeal or because they offered an additional and significant construct that had not been included in measuring religiousness, but that some investigators felt should be. The *scientific functional* approach differs by emphasizing that the new instrument clarifies a previously puzzling relationship. It is thus needed because of its functional utility for scientific theories of religious phenomena. This phenomenon is illustrated by Allport's research on religion and prejudice.

Allport was long concerned with faith and bigotry (Allport and Kramer, 1946). As discussed in greater detail later in this book, a repeatedly confirmed finding puzzled him—namely, members of traditional Christian groups showed more prejudice than nonmembers despite Christianity's emphasis on love and brotherhood. Allport hypothesized that two different motivations lead to being religious. *Extrinsically* motivated people seem activated by what they can get out of religion, while *intrinsically* motivated individuals are concerned about religion for religion's sake. In other words, extrinsics are utilitarian, asking the question, "What's in it for me?" Intrinsics are searching for truth and living the tenets of their faith. Allport suggested that the former are the prejudiced ones. Several attempts have been made to operationalize the intrinsic-extrinsic distinction to test this hypothesis (Wilson, 1960; Feagin, 1964). In his last work in this area, Allport and Ross (1967) measured intrinsic and extrinsic orientations with separate scales. In combination, these scales helped to explain previous findings by supporting Allport's expectations. Intrinsics appeared to be less prejudiced than extrinsics, and those who scored high on both scales, and were designated indiscriminately pro-religious, seemed to be the most prejudiced of all.

Allen and Spilka (1967) worked along the same lines as Allport and for the same reasons. In their analyses, they identified what they termed *committed* and *consensual* orientations, with the former being a vague, cognitively closed religious system to which a person clings without question. In contrast, committed religion is based on a cognitively open faith of abstract, differentiated principles of relevance to life. As hypothesized, the consensualists are prejudiced; the committed are not.

Both the Allport and Ross and the Allen and Spilka conceptualizations were in response to the seemingly unexpected relationship between religiosity and prejudice, and both methods serve the scientific function of explaining this troubling relationship. This does not mean that their results are identical. At the present time, measures of extrinsic religiousness are not the same as those of consensual religion, and further work is necessary to identify the most effective constructs.

MULTITRAIT SYSTEMS

Theory Based Approaches

Specifying religion by a single operational definition imposes some rather severe limits. First, religion is a highly complex phenomenon, and a single scale by its very nature denies this complexity. Second, the basic character of religion for one scholar is likely not to be the basic character for another. Unfortunately, psychology, as a social science, has no method for resolving such disputes since they are essentially philosophical and theological. Any one definition is therefore usually critiqued by those with varying conceptual positions.

The Dimensional System of Charles Glock

To respond to these problems, it has been proposed that religion be defined by a number of scales. A prominent set of such instruments was developed by Glock and his associates (Glock, 1962; Stark and Glock, 1968), who proposed that all world religions have five aspects. You will remember from Chapter One that these are: the *ideological* or belief aspect; the *intellectual* aspect, consisting of knowledge and cognitive concepts; the *ritualistic* aspect, made up of the overt, institutional behavior traditionally defined within that culture as religious; the *experiential* aspect, which includes those experiences that arouse religious feelings; and the *consequential* aspect, which details the impact of the first four dimensions upon life in the secular world. In essence, Glock was saying that each of these manifestations of faith should be measured separately.

While Glock's formulation is broad, and probably applicable to all of the major world faiths, operationalization of these constructs has generally been within the Western religious tradition—in specific, within Christianity. For example, Faulkner and DeJong (1966) operationally defined the ideological dimension in terms of beliefs about God and the Bible; the intellectual dimension through statements regarding creation, knowledge of the gospels, and miracles; the ritualistic dimension by reference to church attendance, prayer, and Bible reading; the experiential dimension by emphasizing purpose in life and mystical experience; and the consequential dimension in terms of sabbath observance, premarital sex, and lying about church contributions.

Unhappily, the Faulkner-DeJong work exhibits a problem often found in a priori multitrait scales: high intercorrelations (see this chapter's appendix) among the scales. As this study demonstrates, and others show (Clayton, 1971), Glock-type instruments are interrelated to such a degree that a person who scores high on one of the scales generally scores high on the others. This means that if the score on one scale is known, the scores on the other scales can be reasonably well estimated by use of the appropriate statistical formulas. In this instance, additional scales provide little new information and may be unnecessary. Ideally, each scale should be distinct, and thus independent, of every other scale, so that each provides new and unique information. When this is not true, as in the present case, the same people tend to be identified as religious, supposedly in different ways, but the only difference is in the labels used.

One of the more sophisticated analyses utilizing the Glock approach is that of Wimberly (1978). He selectively picked items from previous investigations, and developed new ones to represent the Glock dimensions; however, he included both religious and political statements. Glock had suggested that these dimensions were relevant to all faiths, and while politics may not be viewed by everyone as a religion, there are arguments, particularly from a functional viewpoint, that some people treat it as one. Another argument is that Glock's dimensions are logical ones, and therefore, should apply to almost any area, not just religion. Wimberly's use of political items would therefore seem justified.

Factor analysis (see this chapter's appendix) was used to examine the data. Several factor dimensions appeared, which were patterns of belief, knowledge, experience, private behavior, institutional behavior, and social interaction (i.e., associations and friendships with others). Similar factors were found in the political realm. Once again, the factor dimensions were highly intercorrelated, and this resulted in one broad, general dimension consisting of conservative belief, positive experience of the presence of God, private devotional behavior, institutional participation, and, to a lesser degree, friends from the same religious tradition. Think of these as if they constitute a single scale, and together these elements might be considered to reflect a form of religious conservatism.

Interestingly, measures of knowledge, such as knowing the Ten Commandments, related poorly to the other dimensions. As discussed earlier, this is probably true, because it possesses a major component of intelligence and academic achievement that is independent of religious belief.

A Self-Other Approach

Other *a priori* trait systems have been theorized, but they too tend to have similar relational problems. Whereas the Glock approach dealt with traditional religious content, McConahay and Hough (1973) were less concerned with beliefs than the self and other orientations these portend. They also hypothesized four perspectives: (1) *guilt-oriented, love-oriented;* (2) *self-centered, love-oriented;* (3) *other-centered;* and (4) *conventional religious.* As with the Glock scales, these too show high intercorrelations.

The Unidimensional-Multidimensional Debate

The difficulty of building several, statistically independent scales that are not functionally redundant has led to an ongoing debate. The question is whether religion is unidimensional and can be measured by one scale, or whether it is multidimensional and requires several scales with each dimension assessed by a separate instrument. It is apparent that there is a general dimension of religiousness underlying most of the a priori attempts within the mainstream Christian tradition. To some degree, the majority of scales seems to tap this fundamental substrate. It is also evident that a priori scales contain more than just general religiousness. Extrinsic faith, religious individualism, and religious relativism appear, on the basis of analyses relating them to other a priori scales, to demonstrate the lowest correlations with these measures—hence, they provide more unique information

Empirical Multitrait Systems: Factor Analysis

In addition to *a priori* scale development, the statistical technique of factor analysis provides another way of constructing multitrait systems. This was the explicit purpose of the Broen (1957) and Wimberly (1978) studies discussed earlier.

Factor analysis identifies qualitative differences among items or scales by analyzing their empirical relationships. For example, if two items always identify the same people as religious, these items are grouped as a single factor. If, in the same analysis, there are other items that consistently identify a different subset of people as religious, those two items are believed to indicate another factor or dimension of religiosity. The goal is to take a number of items and develop from the interrelationships among these the minimum number of factors that adequately reflect how the data might be used to group people as religious. Statistically and functionally, the result is a set of relatively independent scales. They would thus represent qualitative differences in how people might be defined as religious. The several items that constitute a factor classify individuals on a quantitative basis indicating the degree to which they meet the definition of ''religious'' suggested by that particular scale.

Factor analysis is a very complex statistical procedure with many subtleties, and for this reason, factor analytic studies seldom give identical results. This problem may be a function of a number of influences, not the least of which are the items and the people studied. Unless sampling of both items and respondents is similar, the results of factor analytic studies are unlikely to match.

Interested readers easily will find an immense and fascinating literature in which factor analysis has been applied in research in the psychology of religion.

Item Factor Analysis and The Concept of God

Some factor analyses have been conducted within explicitly defined religious content areas, one of which has been the concept of God. Spilka, Armatas, and Nussbaum (1964) began by collecting adjectives that churchgoers used to describe their images of God. These were then objectively presented to similar samples, and factor analysis was applied to see how many different ways the adjectives were used. Although a large number of factor dimensions were observed, Gorsuch (1968) suggests that the dimensions could be evaluated at several different levels depending on the degree of specificity needed. Table 2-1 summarizes the results of the latter work. At the most general level, there was a very broad *traditional Christian* concept of God. One might use this rather extensive definition, but it would not give a very accurate description of how each person views the deity. Greater specificity could be gained by breaking down the overall Christian image into scales measuring the degree to which individuals evaluate God as com-

TABLE 2-1   Levels of Factor Analyzed God Concepts (with Sample Associated Adjectives)

I. Traditional Christian ("Glorious," "Majestic," "Redeeming")
    A. Companionable ("Fair," "Faithful," "Moving," "Warm")
        1. Evaluative ("Timely," "Valuable")
        2. Kindliness ("Forgiving," "Gentle," "Merciful")
        3. Relevancy (not "Feeble," not "Weak")
    B. Benevolent Deity ("All-Wise," "Loving," "Forgiving")
        1. Lack of deisticness (not "Impersonal or Inaccessible")
        2. Eternality ("Eternal," "Everlasting")
        3. Kindliness ("Forgiving," "Gentle," "Merciful")
II. Wrathfulness ("Avenging," "Hard," "Severe," "Wrathful")

panionable and/or benevolent. Still further detail results by using scales assessing concepts of evaluation, kindliness, relevancy, etc. A wrathfulness God concept, which is unrelated to the traditional view, was also found in this study. These various God concepts can be measured by having individuals check off those adjectives that they feel best describe the deity.

Factor Analyzing "General Religion"

An even broader approach to factor analyzing the religious domain was carried out by Strommen, Brekke, Underwager, and Johnson (1972). They interviewed some 5,000 Lutheran young people, and had them respond to a very wide-ranging set of religious items. These were then factor-analyzed to determine the various manifestations of religiousness that might exist among young Lutherans. We do not know if these same dimensions would result from similar treatment of data from other religious groups. Among the factors found was one defined as "the heart of Lutheran piety." This included transcendental meaning in life; the existence of a personal, caring God; an emotional certainty of faith; a fundamentalist position; and seeing Christian practice as important for life. A second factor found among this group was considered a "law orientation," because it consisted of needs for unchanging structure and religious absolutism plus several scales representing social distance from and prejudice toward other groups. Strommen et al. suggest that these needs are more highly developed forms of intrinsic-committed and extrinsic-consensual religion. A third factor showed an acceptance of responsibility for the church, and a desire for it to be involved in social issues. Other factors represented organizational participation, moral commitment, and reactions to the church and clergy.

Another important set of factor analyses of "general" religion were carried out by King and Hunt (King, 1967; King and Hunt, 1969, 1972a, 1972b, 1975). These studies are significant for several reasons. First, they include a wide range of items selected from many of the previously cited a priori scales, as also was true of the work of Strommen et al. Second, their samples consisted of religiously active people in several denominations. This means that the factors may be able to distinguish among these religious bodies as well as between these people and their nonreligious counterparts. Even though a few of the latter were present in the samples, the results still would be of greater relevance for the former than the latter. Third, King and Hunt conducted not just one factor analysis, but a number, thus replicating their results and showing that they are more than just the happenstance of one study.

The factors King and Hunt observed were of several types. The first were "basic religion scales": These were (1) a major dimension of *creedal assent,* including belief in God, the Scriptures, and Christ; (2) *devotionalism,* meaning how often one prays; (3) *church attendance;* (4) *organizational activity* outside of worship services; (5) *financial support;* (6) *religious despair;* and (7) *orientation to growth and striving,* including trying to understand and grow in one's faith. Second were a number of "composite" religious factors, such as (1) *salience: behavior,* where a person reports trying to convert others plus reading the Bible; (2) *salience: cognition,* indicating a feeling of closeness to God, and a belief that religion provides meaning in life; and (3) *active regulars,* which consist of items showing both high attendance and contributions. A third set of factors, which appeared to represent cognitive style, were: (1) *intolerance of ambiguity,* where people want a simple, complete answer to their questions; (2) *purpose in life: positive;* and (3) *purpose in life: negative.* The first factor in this set indicates that life is fulfilling, while the second suggests the opposite. These last two factors show the responsiveness of factor analysis to item sampling. They are virtually the opposite of each other and appear as two separate factors rather than as the two ends of one dimension. This occurred because so many items reflecting life's purpose were included. In addition, for technical reasons only, positive items correlate more highly with each other than they do with negative items. Factor analysis is a very sensitive tool!

An examination of the correlations among the factors demonstrates that most are relatively independent of each other, at least more so than are some a priori scales. Still, there is overlap, usually involving similar concepts and items. Furthermore, relationships among the scales are definitely positive, suggesting that a broad and somewhat diffuse general perspective on religion underlies the correlations. That is, those who score high on one religious measure have some tendency to score high on all positive religious indices. One suspects that the strength of this general outlook would be increased if a sample were taken that included nonreligious as well as religious people.

It could be argued that some of the King and Hunt factors resulted from sampling areas that few have deemed religious, such as cognitive style. Other factors represent different manifestations of religion, as in the distinction between beliefs and attitudes and reports on various behaviors. These two domains usually are not directly related, but evidence varying degrees of association through intervening variables. It is therefore not surprising they form separate factors.

Factor analyses of items suggest that highly specialized scales can be developed and used, whether they be eleven concepts of God, the dozen King and Hunt factors, or the seventy-eight separate scales of Strommen and his coworkers. Such instruments do interrelate, at times substantially, so that broader, more basic dimensions are apparent. The major one appears to be a traditional, Christian Gospel orientation centering in creedal assent, which is independent of law-oriented, intolerant approaches.

Scale Factor Analyses

There is much to be said for factoring scales instead of items as individual items are subject to many idiosyncratic interpretations. Combining several items into scales creates greater accuracy because the various interpretations are, in a sense, averaged out, leaving a more clearly defined product. Factoring scales also allows one to begin with a priori constructs, and then to determine how these are organized. The results of such analyses help identify when a number of a priori scales form the same factor or where discrepant findings indicate empirically different definitions of religion.

Spilka, Read, Allen, and Dailey (1968) conducted two factor-analytic studies of thirty-eight scales using religiously diverse college students plus many of the a priori religious measurement devices discussed above. Strong evidence for distinguishing between intrinsic commitment to traditional Christianity and a consensual, extrinsic approach to one's faith was obtained. These factors appeared in both studies, and at several levels in the second one. There is also data suggesting another dimension concerned with formal, institutional approaches as opposed to religious individualism. Contributing to the traditional Christianity factor was a more general dimension oriented toward orthodoxy and fundamentalism.

The results of Spilka and his associates are compatible with those of Gorsuch and McFarland (1972). Using a more limited set of scales, they found two factors, one of which was labeled *intrinsically pro-religious,* and the other, *Christian orthodoxy* (a bad choice of names; "conservative Christianity" would have been better). Neither a religious individualism nor an extrinsic factor occurred because there were insufficient variables of this sort present. The one individualism variable that was included did not load on either of the two factors, while the single extrinsic scale was negatively related to both. The two factors were strongly interrelated, and, if desired, could be combined into a broader, although somewhat less clearly defined, general Christianity dimension.

Factor analyses of scales, like items, suggest a general Christianity factor, inclusive of both classical, conservative belief, and an intrinsically committed stance, although these two are not identical. Extrinsic, consensual approaches are distinct from these, as is religious individualism.

Factor Analyses of Religious and Nonreligious Items

The foregoing factor analyses were concerned only with religious items or scales. If such content were included with other data with which they do not correlate, separate factors should result, and there would be a strong tendency for broader dimensions of religiousness to stand out. These findings of a general single religiousness dimension are also compatible with research by Lurie (1937) and Brown (1962, 1966).

With few exceptions, this expectation of a clearly defined general religious factor does occur. Ferguson (1939, 1941, 1944, 1946) carried out a number of studies that consistently produced a single religious factor. Cline and Richards (1965) used questionnaires, projective tests (see this chapter's appendix), and in-depth interviews for a host of items, and also found one religious factor.[3]

General Conclusions for a Multitrait System

In our culture, it appears that religious and nonreligious Christians are distinguished by being intrinsically committed to a basically traditional, Gospel-oriented interpretation of Christianity, which is, however, not identical to fundamentalism. This dimension can be assessed with reasonable consistency by numerous scales of creedal assent and similar beliefs and attitudes.

It is also apparent that further breakdowns and refinements can be made among persons identified as religious. Within the intrinsic dimension is a subdimension of conservatism-fundamentalism. In addition, a distinct collection of items and scales represents a separate extrinsic-consensual, law-oriented approach to Christian faith. There may also be dimensions of religious individualism and relativism, but these have not yet been as clearly distinguished because so few

---

[3]Sometimes, however, the results are slightly more variable, as when Kawamura and Wrightsman (1979) factored religiosity and other variables, and obtained two religiosity factors, one representing religious beliefs and attitudes, the other religious behavior. However, numerous measures of religious activity were associated with the first factor as well. It appears that the second factor occurred because two unique items of religious behavior were included.

scales currently exist that can be included in these kinds of analyses. For technical reasons, unless there are three or four factorially similar instruments in these studies, such factors are unlikely to be observed.

These dimensions are primarily of beliefs and values. Religious behavior, as already noted, is generally separate. Belief does not automatically imply behavior, and vice versa.

It should be recognized that more discrete and unique factors can be found in analyses of people from a single religious body. Although they are likely to score similarly on the more fundamental, broad dimensions, there would still be variation on questions being debated within that group, and these would be the basis of the factors. Examples of such specific factors related to a well-defined religious tradition are found in analyses of the Bahai faith (Keene, 1967) and the Unitarian-Universalists (Tapp, 1971). In both cases, unique dimensions resulted that seemed interpretable given the religious histories of the groups. This does not mean that such singular factors are more or less "real" than those from more general studies, but that people within these well-demarcated churches are alike on the more general dimensions.

ARE QUESTIONNAIRES THE ONLY MEANS OF MEASURING RELIGION?

The measurement and operational definition of religion has almost universally been through questionnaires. While an occasional study (e.g., Cline and Richards, 1965) has included projective tests and interviews, this has been more the exception than the rule. The overwhelming majority of our conclusions about the nature of religion result from questionnaire approaches.

Several different questionnaire approaches exist, but all produce essentially identical results, provided the questions cover the same area. Self-ratings on single-item scales also correlate highly with full scales, but are only appropriate if the single item is carefully developed on a topic that has been widely discussed so that there will be few idiosyncratic interpretations about it (Gorsuch and McFarland, 1968).

Questionnaires definitely have limitations, and the degree to which the definition and nature of religion will be viewed differently when a broader range of assessment devices is used to operationalize the concepts under study is not known. It is, however, apparent that the results obtained by other procedures may differ greatly from those from questionnaires. Vernon (1962) asked people directly how they would rate their feelings about religion, and found that this question produced expected results. He also asked people to list twenty different statements in response to the query "Who am I?" The statements were then rated on the degree to which they demonstrated religious identification. Both of Vernon's techniques indicated that sixty to seventy-five percent of the respondents possessed some kind of religious orientation. There was, however, *no* relationship between those identified as religious by the twenty questions and by the self-rating approaches.

Currently, we do not know to what extent nonquestionnaire measures might be useful.

WHAT IS THE BEST OPERATIONAL DEFINITION OF RELIGION?

The Relativity of Definition

We have seen that there has been considerable work on the operational definition and nature of religious phenomena. Numerous empirically based definitions have been proposed, and many of these have been interrelated. While these efforts reveal a number of similarities, the latter are based, for the most part, upon contemporary expressions of American Christianity. Empirical research is, of course, subject to change as the culture changes. For example, one of Ferguson's (1944) measures of general religousness assessed the degree to which a person took a stand against birth control when that was characteristic of many religious traditions through World War II. It is obvious that times have changed, and along with them views of birth control.

Cultural relativity within American society must make us aware how the emphasis on Christianity in the psychology of religion has submerged work on other religious heritages in our nation. Although such heritages are much less known, there has been a fair amount of work on the religious identification of Jews (Dashefsky and Shapiro, 1974; Goldstein and Goldscheider, 1968; Rosen, 1965). Since this is a significant part of the Judeo-Christian heritage, it needs to be integrated with the work on American Christians.

Essentially forgotten in this enterprise are the Asian traditions of Buddhism, Confucianism, and Shintoism that have existed in the Chinese and Japanese ghettos of various urban areas for at least a century. A smaller Moslem-American community has similarly been bypassed. In addition, the past two decades have witnessed both the revival of old religious traditions, such as those of various American Indian groups, and the growth of new cult-type organizations outside of the Judeo-Christian mainstream, the best known of which are probably the Unification Church of Sun Myung Moon, the Hare Krishna, and Scientology (Fichter, 1983; Wilson, 1981). Most efforts to understand these groups from a social science viewpoint have been undertaken by anthropologists and sociologists. A true psychological understanding of religion cannot take place without substantive work on members of these bodies. They provide the potential of a kind of cross-cultural psychology of religion within the American milieu. Indeed, conclusions about religion must be tempered by the fact that our work has largely been of a particular aspect of our culture at a particular point in time.

Operational Definitions and Theological Considerations

There is little in operational definitions of the nature of religion to decide whether people are ''truly'' religious in a theological or philosophical sense. It is often possible to understand what particular authors see as basic to religious faith from the definitions they use, or from the results of those definitions. This, however, is ''grist for the theological mill'' for they do not lead to any definite conclusions. For example, we know that Biblical literalism is currently associated with a general religious orientation as well as with a special conservative dimension. Does this mean that the Bible should be interpreted in a literal manner, or that it is an historical accident or phase that Christians should move beyond?

The answer to this question will not be found in psychology or in measurement, but rather in one's theology and the role of the Bible in it.

It is also clear that many theologies possess stricter criteria for identifying the truly religious person than a psychologist is likely to have for defining religiosity. The latter might hold that the religious person should be high on several independent dimensions. Perhaps psychological data will serve as a warning that differences important to theologians may be unimportant to laity, just as Harrell (1977) found that only a small percentage of those he studied maintained a cognitive, intellectual type of religious belief.

Do We Need New Scales?

From a practical viewpoint, a large number of adequate scales are indeed available, not only the seventy-eight published by Strommen and his associates (Strommen, Brekke, Underwager, and Johnson, 1972), but, among many others, the dozen or so referenced in this chapter. Technically, these instruments show excellent reliability and validity (see this chapter's appendix), as good or better than any other kind of attitude or belief measured in psychology (Gorsuch, 1984). As Scott (1969) notes:

> Judging by the usual standards of reliability and validity, tests of religious dispositions come close to meeting the psychologists' most optimistic aspirations. It is common to find such tests with reliability coefficients in the middle .90's, and validities in the .50's—far above the level psychologists are accustomed to. This is probably due to the highly institutional nature of religious manifestations in the society and to the inclusion in tests of items describing those manifestations (p. 15).

An important conclusion to be drawn is that few new scales are needed and certainly no new ones are necessary in most of the areas described here. Instead, we should extend our use of the currently available instruments to build up further knowledge about them, and more importantly, to press forward the other frontiers of the psychology of religion. The definitional realm is probably that which has been most developed, and further progress in it may not be as significant as advances in other domains. In fact, progress of the latter type ought to alert us to the scientific limitations of current scales so that needed improvements can be made.

Two conditions must be met before consideration is given to developing a new scale to assess some facet of religion. First, a detailed review of the literature is essential to ensure that no similar instrument exists. The scales cited here are only a sample. Hundreds more like them have been published. William Silverman (1983) has recently produced an extensive bibliography of these materials. Indeed, it is unlikely that any new scale will do better than one that is presently available, especially one that is well buttressed by supportive and confirming research. Second, a new scale should only be constructed if it can be substantively argued that a new concept has been created that is theoretically predicted to be unrelated to factors already found. In other words, tests should be in the service of a guiding theory, and not produced in a hypothetical void. There are more than enough indices of general religiousness and traditional Christianity. A new scale should only be recommended when it has been empirically demonstrated to add unique information over and above measures currently known. This means that every new scale must be immediately included in research with a number of standard devices in order to demonstrate whether or not it adds to these other measures.

Finally, the development of a new scale should only be undertaken if there are adequate resources available for its evaluation and refinement. Even a simple measure requires a considerable amount of time and empirical analysis to have any possibility of competing with instruments that have already proven themselves.

This means that scale development in the psychology of religion has progressed to a level requiring advanced training in both the psychology of religion and complex multivariate statistical techniques such as factor analysis. For most investigators, the best operational definition of religion is therefore one already in use, and which has been included in a number of studies so that considerable background information on it is already available.

Operational Definition and Research Purpose

From a scientific point of view, it is impossible to identify the best operational definition of religion without knowing the scientific context in which that definition will play a role. As Machalek (1977) notes, "There is little analytical gain in advancing 'definitions for all purposes' " (p. 401). For some situations, the best definition might be a scale such as Scott's, which was discussed earlier. This would be particularly true if one were working with a general population, and for example, simply needed to know how to look further into the possibility of bringing religious resources to bear upon someone's problem. It might also be an excellent scale in a study in which the major focus of research was nonreligious, but religion was to be considered as a background variable. It would, however, not be appropriate for religious institutions that desired to investigate the views of their parishioners, for consideration should be afforded constructs and issues crucial to that institution at that point in time. Many of these views could possibly be measured by instruments already in the literature, such as the Hogge and Friedman (1967) *Biblical Literalism Scale*, Hood's *Religious Mysticism Experience Scale*, or a measure of consensual religiousness.

Other studies may require more specificity in measurement. Gray (1970) observed that broad attitudes toward the church scales are not suitable when one is interested in evaluating a specific group. Such attitudes simply do not address the essentials for well-defined religious bodies. In his literature analysis of the United Presbyterian Church, Gray located six themes central to the nature of the church: origin and constituency, mission, relation to culture, worship and the means of grace, Christian education, and ecumenicity. Selecting a unique set of scales to assess any one of these topics would be appropriate. The scales of Strommen et al. and King and Hunt might cover many relevant areas. A general measure of church attitudes should still be included so that it can be seen whether the specialized scales do indeed add something of significance. Research Box 2-5 illustrates this principle by showing the utility of both general and specific definitions of religion.

The reader may feel that it is somewhat odd to insist continually upon looking first at the broader scales and to ask if more specialized ones add new information. This approach is recommended because it meets best the criteria of science.

RESEARCH BOX 2-5.   *Maranell, G. M.* Responses to Religion. *Lawrence: University Press of Kansas, 1974.*

Maranell (1974) developed eight a priori scales and related them to denominational membership of clergy and a host of other variables in samples from eight populations. Some of the scales are highly intercorrelated, especially with Fundamentalism. This scale is really concerned with the utility of the Bible, but seldom asks about biblical fundamentalism such as inerrancy and theism. The more religiously oriented of the eight scales consistently forms a "general Christian" factor similar to what has been seen in many other studies.

In analyzing denominational differences, Unitarian-Universalists were lowest on the general factor, a pervasive finding for all of the scales except *Ritualism*, where this group tied for second lowest. Age differences were also similar for all of the measures, with older respondents being more religious. The individual scales, however, add no new information in these areas. It is therefore certainly better to say that religiousness is higher among older people than to report the same result for each of the eight scales. The broad definition of religion operates quite well here.

The religiosity scales are also correlated with a number of political attitudes, and again no differences among these instruments were observed. When strong results were found, all the scales related in the same direction. The simple conclusion is that the more religious are the more politically conservative.

Yet, each scale measures more than the general Christian factor. That "moreness" occasionally produces significant variation in the findings. For example, correlations with indices of bigotry are positive for the extrinsically oriented scales of ritualism and church orientation, but generally negative for theism and altruism (Christian) scales.

The results for both general religiousness and the individual scales are useful in understanding Maranell's data. The broad definition of religion allows wide-ranging phenomena to be summarized without becoming lost in detail. When complex relationships exist, the more specific definitions permit exceptions to the general trends. Religion is thus *both* unidimensional and multidimensional.

The purpose of scientific investigation is to develop the most parsimonious descriptions with the greatest generalizability. Broad measures of religiosity and their dimensions provide the highest likelihood of obtaining such brief, efficient, and widely applicable explanations.

Definition and Attribution Theory

Since the themes of attribution theory are employed throughout this work, religion might be operationally defined by finding out the probability and frequency with which people make religious attributions. In other words, what is the likelihood of religious explanations being sought for occurrences in everyday life? Are supernatural understandings present; is God perceived as involved in daily affairs; is prayer effective? We must also consider the nature of religious attributions as suggesting different forms of personal faith. For example, is the deity loving and forgiving, or punitive and threatening? Are sin and evil or positive qualities imputed to humans? Under what conditions are these various attributions made? Work of this nature is in its infancy. Gorsuch and Smith (1983a, 1983b) have been studying causal and sanctioning attributions to God. Situational factors affecting religious attributions to self and God are being examined by Spilka and Schmidt (1983). Operational definitions of religion from an attributional perspective may hopefully introduce new psychological dimensions for building a theory for understanding religion.

SUMMARY AND CONCLUSIONS

Social scientists are concerned with understanding the nature of religious phenomena but not the theological correctness of what they observe. While psychologists occasionally offer abstract discussions of religion, those that are important for both practice and theory are the actual operations by which religious people are identified. The operations "rewrite" the abstract definition.

A religious *typology* occurs when each individual is placed into only one category—such as being classified as either an intellectual believer, a true believer, or a nonbeliever. Typologies are, however, seldom used for long since people do not fit readily into these "pigeon holes." Instead, the characteristics of particular types tend to evolve into separate scales that describe the religious propensities of individuals. Therefore, typologies rather quickly become *trait definitions*.

A trait approach operationalizes religiosity as the degree to which a person possesses a certain feature or characteristic. Trait definitions vary widely. Sometimes religion is perceived as concern with basic questions about the meaning of life. Other times it ranges from measurement of religious attitudes to assessments of institutional behavior. Definitions of limited aspects of religion have also been suggested, such as a liberal-conservative dimension, attitudes toward the church or Bible and so on. Because the relationship between some of these variables and phenomena—such as prejudice—was unclear, the distinction between intrinsic-committed and extrinsic-consensual religion was made.

Religion is highly complex; hence, single trait definitions are neither adequate nor appropriate. More and more, investigators have tended to define religion as a *multiple trait* set of characteristics. These can either result from a priori thinking or from empirical analyses that employ the techniques of factor analysis. Considerable research suggests that intrinsic commitment to a basically traditional, Gospel-oriented interpretation of Christian faith is a central component of religiosity in our culture. Liberal-conservative and extrinsic dimensions also have appeared and seem to be useful. Additionally, factor dimensions of religious individualism and relativism may be replicable. All of these, however, form only the broader scope of variations in religiousness, and can be more finely analyzed. Where such has taken place, the resulting distinctions are not yet well established.

The question also has been raised as to whether religiosity—which in the research mainstream has meant American Christianity—is basically unidimensional—namely, consists of one trait—or multidimensional. Many different answers have been made to this query, and the findings seem to be a function of how broadly the area is examined. Most religious expressions are intercorrelated sufficiently to justify a broad definition that considers the above dimensions as subcategories. This permits religious and nonreligious people to be distinguished on a global level.

Within samples of religious people, however, there are numerous possible distinctions, and the foregoing dimensions provide for even finer informational categories. The latter are especially useful when detailed analyses are required or when only religious persons are being studied.

The operationalization of religiousness by contemporary psychologists has, overwhelmingly, utilized questionnaires. Moreover, a sufficient number of religiosity scales have been developed so that almost every possible definitional approach is already available. Frequently, these scales are of high psychometric quality. Current researchers are strongly discouraged from developing new instruments unless they can demonstrate that they are uniquely different from any previous scale. This requires both theoretical and empirical findings over and beyond currently existing scales. The psychology of religion is continuing to grow in both scientific sophistication and research productivity—hence, operational definitions are becoming more and more rigorous and demanding.

TECHNICAL APPENDIX

Correlation

This is a statistical procedure that determines the strength of a relationship between two variables. The procedure results in a number called a *correlation coefficient*. This number can range from − 1.00 through .00 or zero to + 1.00. If the coefficients are in the .00 to + 1.00 range, they are said to be *positive*. This means that the numerical values of the two variables increase and decrease together. In other words, for example, if intrinsic religion and perceptions of a loving God are positively related, the higher the score a person obtains on a measure of intrinsic religion, the higher the score that individual should get on a measure of belief in a loving God. In like manner, a low score on one of these scales should be accompanied by a low score on the other scale.

If the correlation coefficient is in the .00 to − 1.00 range, the relationship is said to be *negative*. Now, the scores on the two variables are related in opposite directions. We know that self-esteem and extrinsic religion tend to be negatively correlated. This means that a high score on a self-esteem scale is associated with a low score on extrinsic faith, and vice versa. One thus reads of two or more variable being positively or negatively correlated, associated, or related.

The higher the coefficient observed—meaning the closer it is to either + or − 1.00, the stronger the relationship between the two variables; however, the importance of the coefficient is a function of the size of the sample from which the correlation is computed. The larger the sample, the smaller the coefficient that is said to be *statistically significant*. One looks these up in a table, but all you need to know now is that *when a correlation is said to be statistically significant, even if it is low, meaning close to .00, it indicates an association, a relationship, that has a very low probability of arising on the basis of chance alone.* Since there is a low probability of this happening, we are inclined to infer that the relationship is real, and that the two variables, whatever they are, are meaningfully associated. To illustrate, if intrinsic religion and the likelihood of having a religious mystical experience are correlated—e.g., .40—and the sample is large enough for the researcher to claim that this is a statistically significant relationship, we would assume that the two variables are positively associated.

Correlation implies prediction. Using the appropriate formulas, the statistically sophisticated scientist can use correlation and other related statistics to predict one variable based on information on the other. The higher the correlation coefficient, the more accurate the prediction that is possible.

Finally, we must mention the fact that if a correlation is not statistically significant, the two variables are to be considered *independent of each other*. No meaningful association or relationship is said to exist.

Factor Analysis

In this chapter, an effort has been made to give some insight into the nature of this highly complex statistical procedure. It is a way of simplifying correlational data, a means of explaining a table of correlations with a much smaller pattern of factors or dimensions. Consider for a moment that you have three scales. Scale A may be correlated with scales B and C, and scale B with C. There are three intercorrelations. Let N = the number of variables, here 3. Then we know that the total number of intercorrelations equals $N(N - 1)/2$, or here $3(3 - 1)/2$ or $3(2)/2 = 3$. But suppose we had fifty variables, a number that is not unknown in this kind of work. There then would be a large number of relationships to explain, actually, 1,225 such relationships.

Factor analysis is a technique of analyzing this large matrix of correlation coefficients and, depending on the pattern of interrelations present, it is possible to simplify it, using various criteria, into five, ten, or twenty factors. A factor consists of a subset of the original variables that sometimes can be made into a scale, such as you read about—for example, in the work of Broen, Gorsuch, or Wimberly. Table 2-1 consists of a complex pattern of different levels of factors. Factor analysis is a very high-level set of methods, and we will not discuss these further here. If you are mathematically and/or statistically sophisticated, you might want to read Gorsuch (1983) to gain more understanding of this form of multivariate analysis.

Mean and Median

One of the most obvious ways of describing data is to report how "it is grouped." We are asking for a measure of "central tendency." The one with which you are most familiar is a *mean* or *average* of a set of numbers or scores. You might have intrinsic religion scores for three people: 25, 30, 35. To compute the mean, you would simply add the scores and divide by the number of scores, here $(25 + 30 + 35)/3 = 90/3 = 30$, and 30 is the mean or average score. The size or weight of the scores is taken into account. The *median* is more a measure of position. It is the score that divides all of the other scores in half. Half fall on each side of the median. In our simple example, 30 is also the median. When there are more numbers and they are not equally spaced, recourse is made to a formula for computing the median. This was what Thurstone and Chave did, and which is reported in Box 2-4. It is a measure that is much less affected by extreme scores than is the mean.

Psychometric

This is a term used to describe the different aspects of psychological measurement. Under the term *scale*, discussed below, some of the psychometric characteristics of such instruments are very briefly mentioned—for example, *reliability* and *validity*. Basically, these are based on correlational techniques (see *correlation*), and one speaks in terms of reliability and validity coefficients. As a matter of convention, we would like to have reliability coefficients above .70 or .75, but some useful information may still be gained with coefficients as low as .6. We get into a very debatable range when we use measures with such low reliabilities. Where validity is concerned, the situation becomes more complex. If correlations between a scale and another measure are said to be indicative of validity, the correlation coefficient must minimally and obviously be statistically significant (see *correlation*), and hopefully be quite high.

Reliability

This psychometric characteristic is mentioned under the terms *psychometric* and *scale,* As noted, it refers to the consistency of a measure or scale. Consistency may be over time or at one time. In the former case, a scale may be given twice, and the reliability consists of correlating the test scores from the two administrations. If the correlation coefficient is high, usually meaning above .75, the measure is said to have good *test-retest reliability*. When a test is given only once, we speak of *internal consistency reliability*. The reliability coefficient is in a sense an average correlation among the items in the scale, meaning that if the coefficient is high, all of the items are essentially measuring the same thing. Another way of looking at reliability is to consider the test and item scores as having two components, a "true" one and an "error" one. The higher the reliability, the smaller the error component relative to the true component. A variety of sophisticated statistical procedures may be used to compute reliability coefficients.

Scale

The term *scale* has a number of meanings in both mathematics and social science. Here we will use it to designate a measuring instrument, usually a questionnaire, the items of which form a unified whole. This means that the items are supposed to measure one thing only. A scale is also assumed to demonstrate certain psychometric characteristics. Chief among these are reliability or consistency in measurement, and validity or evidence that the items measure what they are supposed to measure. This is a simplification of a very complex set of issues, and the interested reader should consult a good book on psychological measurement for additional understanding.

Validity

This term was also discussed in the above section on *psychometric* and *scale*. It asks whether the scale measures what it is supposed to measure. The "supposed to measure" aspect is usually based on a theory that says the instrument should predict some other psychological phenomenon—for example, a belief or a behavior. If it does, we say it possesses *predictive validity*. Other possibilities are that the scale in question correlates very highly with a criterion measure—hence, it has *criterion validity*. Suppose we have a very long and valid scale of general religiousness, and because it is inconvenient to use, we decide to construct a brief instrument. The validity of the latter might be indicated by the strength of the correlation coefficient with the longer scale—the higher the coefficient, the more valid the short scale. *Construct validity* is explicitly premised on confirmation of a theory by findings with the measure. All of these forms of validity basically state that the measure is doing what it should be doing.

CHAPTER THREE
CHILDHOOD: STAGES IN RELIGIOUS DEVELOPMENT

"Mummy, in the Bible, there is a story about a flood and God promised that there would never be another flood. How come there was a flood in Texas then?" (Madge, 1965, p. 14).

"If God was there before the world was made, what did he walk on?" (Madge, 1965, p. 14).

"If Jesus is born every Christmas and crucified every Good Friday, how does he grow so quickly?" (Madge, 1965, p. 14).

"Where do prayers go?" "An invisible microphone comes down and takes the prayers up to God." "Stars carry them up to God" (Long, 1965, p. 92).

David Elkind (1970) claims that religion is natural in children. Whether or not it is, its expression is striking and impressive. There is a refreshing insight in the way a child approaches faith, but as one ages, more formal ways of religious thinking come to the fore; one form of individuality is lost and another takes its place. Still, the religious life of a child is fascinating, and psychologists of religion are attempting to learn about it.

Understanding religious concepts such as love, forgiveness, God, salvation, and justice is an important part of Western religions. The many forms of Christianity, for example, often express their faith in creeds that are meaningless unless the words make sense—that is, unless the participants have the mental capacity to understand them. For this reason, we describe the cognitive development of the child with implications noted for religious development.

The primary feature of a child's religious development is that it takes place in a changing organism. Children begin life quite limited in their physical skills and mental capacities. In most religions—and certainly in the Judeo-Christian tradition—this limited mental capacity is of importance for religious development. It means that a young child cannot grasp religious concepts in the same way as an older child. And the latter has limited cognitive capacity compared to that of an adolescent.

Cognitive development per se does not assure religious understanding or commitment. Religious understanding is missing in many adults of obvious high cognitive development, and religious commitment can be found at all levels of cognitive development.

Cognitive development places limits on one aspect of religious growth: It limits the understanding of words used and their interrelationships as seen in concepts. Expecting a young child to be able to expound upon the Christian concept of the trinity as would a seminary professor is asking too much. The child's view of the nature of a trinitarian God could only be expected to be a child's approximation of an adult view because of the child's limited cognitive development.

STAGES OF COGNITIVE DEVELOPMENT AND THEIR IMPLICATIONS FOR RELIGIOUS DEVELOPMENT

Developmental psychologists use two paradigms to describe the cognitive development of children. Historically, the first is that of intellectual development as observed in "intelligence" tests. The intelligence score reflects the ability of the child to understand and utilize academic materials.

The results of an intelligence test are generally given as I.Q. scores, which indicate how well the child is doing *relative to other children of the same age.* Unfortunately, that says little about the capabilities of children of a particular age. To obtain that information, it is necessary to examine the raw scores and items to determine what each level of child is capable of understanding. Thus, the intelligence testing paradigm gives the levels of religious cognitive development only as a derivative.

Generally, cognitive development as described by I.Q. test materials starts with the simple, widely occurring names of things at the youngest ages. With an increase in age and cognitive ability, the child is expected to know not only material objects but also names of abstract concepts. Higher abilities are then shown by knowing uncommon names, abstractions, and being able to interrelate the abstractions. These increases in cognitive ability are known intuitively by most parents and teachers. We expect the same advances in religious cognitive development—namely, moving from names of things interrelated in the simplest of ways to abstract concepts and then to the ability to interrelate abstract concepts.

The second paradigm of cognitive development is built upon the work of Piaget (e.g., Piaget, 1972). By posing problems for children to solve and then identifying the mechanisms by which the child approaches the problem, the cognitive processes are identified. Unlike the I.Q. test approach, the "errors" a child makes are often as important as the "correct" answers, for *how* the decision is reached is the critical question.

Piaget's Stages of Cognitive Development

Piaget and his disciples generally identify several stages of development. Each stage consists of a general set of abilities that the child has which form a consistent, integrated whole (or gestalt). As the child grows up, new abilities are added to the old ones and a new gestalt forms. The new gestalt not only handles all of the problems solvable by the earlier gestalt but also those the older methods cannot solve.

For example, a child first learns addition and subtraction, and thereby can treat a set of mathematical problems. If given a situation in which multiplication might be the best tool, the child may use it but only by doing a set of additions (e.g., three times three is solved by transforming it into three plus three plus three). Adding the ability to multiply and divide takes nothing away from the earlier skills. Identifying a child's current stage of mathematical understanding indicates the mathematical capabilities of the child.

Piaget identifies three major stages of cognitive development, each a distinct gestalt. These stages form a sequence with the child passing through each one. Each new stage integrates the thinking of the earlier stage(s) into a new gestalt. The first stage is *preconcrete operations,* or pre-operational; the second is *concrete operations,* and the third is *formal operations.*

A child at the preconcrete operations stage cannot relate to logical, abstract deductions but needs limited, direct examples. Learning occurs basically by direct conditioning. This is the stage at which most religious education materials concentrate on Biblical stories. Only later are the abstract concepts of the religion addressed.

The concrete operations stage, which is generally typical of the elementary school years, adds to a child's ability to learn the meaning of specific objects, the skills of classification, and the principle of reversibility. With classifications, similar objects and behaviors can be grouped and then generalized from one to another within a category. At this stage, children also are able to reverse operations. Whereas in the pre-concrete operational stage learning that "Jane" is sister" and "I am Jane's sister" required two separate steps—one to learn each relationship—now learning that "Mary is Virginia's sister" means that the child also knows that "Virginia is Mary's sister." Concepts such as fairness begin to have meaning because they use reversible operations. However, the thought processes are still concerned with concrete objects and behaviors.

A child at the formal operations stage is able to use logic and reasoning as adults generally think of such. Abstract concepts may be introduced and then interrelated to draw high-level conclusions. While formal operations begin about the age of twelve and have completed their development by age fourteen or fifteen, cognitive growth in the I.Q. sense continues until sixteen or eighteen.

Several general characteristics of cognitive stages are particularly important for our task:

1. A child can understand and use all of the preceding stages as well as the current stage he or she is in. When children learn multiplication, we still expect them to be able to add and subtract.

2. Children cannot understand or use materials at a higher stage than their own. If they could, they would be at the higher stage.

3. Changes from one stage to the next are preceded by the neurological growth necessary for the reasoning at that stage but changes also require appropriate experiences. Adolescents capable of learning calculus will not do so unless they take the appropriate prerequisite courses.

4. The experiences necessary to move to a higher stage are those that show the limits of the current stage. As long as the current stage provides an adequate basis for decision making, there is no need to develop further.

5. Moving from one stage to the next stage requires a certain amount of time. The shift may be gradual for some children and faster for others.

Implications for Religious Development

The cognitive stage indicates the level at which children may be approached. If it occurs at a lower level than a child is at and at which the problem might ideally be solved, the child will consider the rationale to be childish. For example, when children already know how to multiply a set of numbers, having them solve a multiplication problem by a series of additions will generally make the presenter seem rather foolish.

If the presentation is at a higher level than a child can understand, he or she either will not comprehend it at all or will reconceptualize it into a rationale at his or her level. To continue the example, a child presented with a multiplication problem will be confused or may redefine it into a set of addition problems. The result is more likely to be confusion than redefinition.

Because the level of understanding is different at each cognitive stage, children need to be confronted with the higher stage approach to a given area when they are ready for it. For example, if a concept only is presented at the concrete operations stage and not reintroduced at the formal operations stage, the conceptualization may remain rather primitive. This may be a major problem for religious groups whose children participate as part of the family until adolescence and then stop practicing. Since their last contact with their faith was before they were fully functional in formal operations, they will continue to conceptualize religion concretely. It is not surprising that such people feel that religion is childish since their only contact with it was during their childhood.

Conceptualizing a religion one has left before understanding it at the formal operations stage is sometimes difficult to overcome. The words and concepts for such a person have meaning only within a preformal operations frame of reference. When religious leaders use such words, such a person will assume that the leader employs them in the preformal operations sense, and often will not really hear what the person is saying.

The cognitive development of children forms the limits for religious conceptualization. Regardless of how the concepts are presented, children can comprehend them only in terms of the cognitive level they are at, or if they are in the process of developing, possibly at one higher stage. More complex materials will be understood, if at all, by analogous thinking at the earlier stage.

Generalizing Cognitive Stages to Religion and Related Areas

Piaget (1972) implies that the stages of cognitive development are basic structures of thinking and apply to any area of thought. But that does not mean that one automatically thinks at a given level in all areas. Actual thought processes of a particular area are contingent upon the experiences in that area after the child is capable of that type of thought. Thus, a child might be at the preconcrete operations level for verbal reasoning but at a higher level in the mathematical thinking area, or vice versa. In this case, the actual level of thinking in the two areas would probably be a function of the school curriculum.

Because the stage of thought for a particular substantive area is contingent upon experiences with that domain, there is no intrinsic reason for stages in one domain to be identical to those of another domain. The experiences natural to one subarea may be insufficient to move the people to a stage commonly found in another subarea. *For that reason, there need not be any necessary relationship between stages of several content areas.* The stage of development of mathematical thinking may well be different than the stage of moral development thinking, and both of these stages may be unrelated to the stage of religious conceptualization. Attempting to translate stages directly from one content area to another is only fruitful for those subcultures that provide equal stimulation in both areas.

SUBSTANTIVE STAGES OF POSSIBLE RELEVANCE TO RELIGIOUS DEVELOPMENT

Moral Development

Stages of moral development have been long identified. Hobhouse (1906) and McDougall (1908) set out four to five stages that are surprisingly similar to contemporary stages. Peck and Havighurst (1960) identified and presented data on the stages as generally now conceptualized. Kohlberg (e.g., 1969), who trained at the University of Chicago while Havighurst was working with Peck on the stages, has been an able popularizer of the notion of stages of moral development. (While Piaget's first book [1932] was on moral development, it is not a topic to which he returned in any depth. Indeed, he did not define clear stages of moral development in that book—and presents at least three different versions of possible stages—nor do his discussions of stages of cognitive development [e.g., 1972] usually include discussion of moral development. It has been his stages of cognitive development with their implications for thinking in all areas that have been important as a background for stages of moral development.)

Bull (1969) and Kohlberg (1969) discuss basically similar stages and form the basis of this discussion. Four stages are relatively clear among these and other writers. These stages are, with Bull's labels, Anomy, Heteronomy, Socionomy, and Autonomy, derived from the Greek *nomos* meaning "law." Note that, as in Piaget's states of cognitive development, the stages are defined by the method of reasoning—i.e., that which is seen as a critical issue in reaching a decision (Gorsuch, O'Connor, and Shamsavari, 1973). The content of the decision reached is independent of the process (Gorsuch and Barnes, 1973), because it involves the sources of information that are trusted about the situation, the expectations of the reactions of others given a particular course of action, and so on.

The first stage of moral development is *Anomy,* meaning without law. Others refer to this stage as premoral, instinctive, or amoral. It is the moral development reflection of the early preconcrete operations stage of cognitive development, and is dominated by the simple learning process–conditioning. For example, a child learns not to touch forbidden objects because of direct and immediate consequences.

The second stage is *Heteronomy,* which is law imposed by others through physical or social sanctions. At this stage, the child seeks to maximize rewards while avoiding punishments. They believe that if a person is not punished, the act was not wrong.

The third stage is *Socionomy,* during which the laws are those that stress social relations. Kohlberg has described this as the "good boy-good girl" stage, for reputation among significant others is the primary concern.

Bull's fourth stage is *Autonomy,* during which laws come from within oneself. Peck and Havighurst (1960) broke this stage into two substages: an "irrational-conscientious" to reflect straight legalistic approaches to morality and a "rational-altruistic" stage. Kohlberg further subdivides the latter into a lower phase concerned with social utilitarianism and a higher phase that emphasizes justice. It should be noted that there is little evidence that these further breakdowns beyond Bull's may be stages per se; they may be different ways of being autonomous based on alternative value systems. The research basis of Bull's moral development scheme is presented in Research Box 3-1.

Research on stages of moral development is consistent with the theory that they are the application of cognitive stages within the area of morality. The literature suggests that people progress through the stages as a function of problems that their current level cannot resolve provided that they are cognitively capable of doing so, but do not progress beyond a stage that allows adequate resolution of the moral problems of their culture (Gorsuch and Barnes, 1974; Gorsuch and Malony, 1974; Chapter 1). Table 3-1 summarizes cognitive and moral developmental stages.

Change is a function of two factors. First, a neurological basis is required for the cognitive elements necessary. Second, experience with moral and ethical dilemmas is necessary. Experimental studies show that children with the appropriate cognitive capabilities shift upwards in stages of moral judgment when they participate in discussion groups considering moral dilemmas. Note that the answers are not taught deliberately; instead, the children are exposed to many stages of thinking and, according to moral development theory, the logical advantages of the higher stages naturally draw the children to the next stage (another theory that the research designs have difficulty in eliminating is that Kohlberg's

RESEARCH BOX 3-1.   *Bull, N. J.* Moral Judgment from Childhood to Adolescence. *Beverly Hills, Calif.: Sage, 1969.*

In order to determine various stages in the development of moral judgment, the author conducted a large-scale investigation of 360 children and youth ranging in age from seven to seventeen. The methods used were written tests, projective tests, and interviews. These methods were all scored in terms of the four theorized levels of moral judgment (anomy to autonomy). The five visual projection tests used—namely, pictures of moral situations, were counterbalanced so that both sexes and four ages ranging from eight to eighteen years were pictured. The moral themes for these events dealt with (1) the value of life (murder and physical cruelty), stealing, cruelty to animals, lying, and lastly, cheating. The results were studied in relation to intelligence (I.Q.), age, socioeconomic class, and church attendance and religious attitudes.

Although relationships with religion were not strong and there was some inconsistency relative to age, generally moral judgments were associated with church attendance and positivity of attitudes toward religion. Specifically, the strongest correlations were found between religion, value of life, and lying. It was felt that religion was part of the broader aspect of family learning and perspective.

"higher" stages are just the preferred stages of our culture; when children hear and try out several stages, the people around them reinforce the culturally defined higher stages).

There is little direct evidence that the stages are intrinsically related to religious development. For example, Gorsuch and McFarland (1972; personal

TABLE 3-1   Cognitive and Moral Stages of Development

AGE OF FIRST OCCURRENCE	STAGES OF COGNITIVE DEVELOPMENT	STAGES OF MORAL DEVELOPMENT
—	Preconcrete Operations	Anomy: premorality. Morality from simple conditioning.
Early elementary school	Concrete Operations	Heteronomy: external morality. Reward and punishment oriented.
Early adolescence	Formal Operations	Socionomy: external-internal morality. Oriented toward approval by others.
		Autonomy: internal morality. Oriented to internalized authority, rules, or principles.

communication) found no relationship between stages of moral development and religious positions as classically measured.

For our purposes, the stages of moral development are important for two reasons. First, the extensive research can serve as a model for further identifying religious stages. Second, morality is often seen as an important area to which religion speaks, and for such speech to be meaningful the stage of moral development must be taken into account.

Stages of Understanding History

Most religions have a significant conceptual basis in history. A particular historical event may be crucial in the formation of the religion. The history of the religion may also be important to understanding that faith. Thus, the stages of how a child comes to understand history may be important to developing an understanding of one's religion. (Godin [1971] reviews this area.)

Following Piaget's cognitive stages, the levels of historical consciousness can be divided into three stages. The first stage, typical of children up to eight or nine years of age, is one of rote learning. Little understanding of the differences between reality and fantasy or present and past is observed. Instead, this stage simply identifies present versus absent, with both fantasy and history placed in the latter category. The child often needs to check whether something is currently present—as with the child who asks upon seeing a cave if there might be a dragon within.

Upon reaching the concrete operations stage of cognitive development at about eight or nine years old, historical understanding adds the capability of classification. The major classification for religious development is that of true and false. Differentiating between fantasy stories and past events that the religion believes is an important task here.

With the new ability of reversibility comes an understanding of historical sequences. Children can now see shifts in civilizations and in religious understandings, linking them to their historical area.

When the formal operations stage is reached, the full historical perspective is possible. One can follow the historical progress of a time period or a people. Interpretation and comparison of the historical situation for a particular event with a current event are now possible. Historically based motivation is meaningful now also. It is only at this stage that understanding how and why the events occurred and their relevance for contemporary thinking is possible.

The stage of historical understanding conditions the understanding children have of past events and so conditions how they view the stories of their religious faith. This kind of understanding has been investigated for several biblical reports of events. Goldman (1964), for example, obtained a stratified sample of children with twenty at each age (ten boys and ten girls) from six through sixteen matched for I.Q. Three Biblical stories—Moses and the burning bush, crossing of the Red Sea, and temptations of Jesus—were included with the children's responses being scaled by the Guttman technique. Another major study is by Van Bunnen (1964), who interviewed 192 Belgian children about the story of the burning bush.

The results of such research are compatible with the proposition that understanding of historical events is primarily a function of the cognitive stage of development. The ages vary somewhat for the transition from one approach to another for different samples and stories, which is consistent with the expectation that personal experiences and the complexities of each story will influence the exact age at which a transition in understanding takes place.

For all three stories, the first stage of cognitive and historical understanding lasted up to eight to eleven years of age and centered on specific aspects of the story. These might be concern with why the bush did not burn, what kind of chariots the Egyptians were driving, or why Jesus did not just go to the store to get his bread. They reflect the preconcrete operations stage of learning each separate element.

The concrete operations stage was found to be characteristic of a child's approach to these stories from ages eight to thirteen. The Red Sea story is seen as an adventure story but the religious constructs, being more abstract, are missed. The events are viewed in a historical context of "long ago."

It is only with the reaching of an age typical for formal operations thinking—eleven to thirteen—that the stories are related across time with implications for contemporary life. The story of Moses now can be related to the ways in which God today calls people, with the religious significance of fire also having meaning if taught. The Exodus can now become an example of God's continuing concern for his people across all time. And the children are now able to identify with Jesus's being tempted and find religious meaning in the options Jesus confronted.

THE DEVELOPMENT OF SPECIFIC RELIGIOUS CONSTRUCTS

Based on this analysis, the development of religious concepts can also be theorized as age-linked. James Fowler (1981) has advanced such a framework; however, its considerable abstruseness and complexity combined with a lack of empirical research does not recommend its inclusion here. It is premised upon the work of Piaget and parallels Kohlberg's stage theory of moral development. The psychology of religion would welcome a rigorous treatment of these theoretically productive views.

There are a number of extensive studies of the meaning of specific religious ideas and concepts relative to cognitive stage formulations. We will look briefly at these for concepts of God and prayer plus intrinsic and extrinsic religious orientations.

Concepts of God

Early research on the concept of God found few age differences because of a methodological problem: the use of structured materials (Elkind, 1971). Structured questions, such as picking the multiple-choice alternative that best fits one's concept of God, are inappropriate for identifying the impact of a stage of cognitive development for at least two reasons. First, children have been around adults enough to know the preferred choice even though they cannot utilize that information in their own thinking. Second, modes of thinking can be researched only by examining thinking processes, not the conclusions of these processes.

Harms (1944) was concerned with such an approach to understanding the development of concepts of God but wanted to avoid a verbal question approach. Hence, he asked children to draw pictures of God and arrived at the following three stages:

1. *Fairy-tale stage.* Children between ages three and six see God as they would any character from a fantasy.

2. *Realistic stage.* Children from six to eleven see God in concrete terms, such as a human figure in the act of helping someone.

3. *Individualistic stage.* In adolescence, youth seem to have a more individualized view of the nature of God with the result being considerable variety. Harms identified three approaches taken by the adolescents. The first group drew conventional religious symbols to represent God. The second used unique, imaginative drawings with considerable abstraction. The third group made drawings that Harms felt represented religious motifs which could not have been personally experienced either directly or through teachings from their religion.

Another major study of the development of religious concepts was by Deconchy (1967). He asked children from eight to sixteen to free associate to words, including "God," and then divided the responses into three levels:

1. *Attributive themes.* From the ages of eight to ten, God is seen as a set of attributes, many of which are anthropomorphic with overtones of animism. The concept of God is unrelated to other constructs, such as the historical events of Jesus.

2. *Personalization themes.* Children from eleven to thirteen or fourteen view God from a perspective that emphasizes nonphysical anthropomorphic characteristics.

3. *Interiorization themes.* From fourteen or fifteen on, the concepts of God are more abstract than at younger ages. Concepts that reflect one's relationship with God—such as doubt—also appear.

Both of the above studies have definite value, but neither was established to test the developmental stages of conceptualization of God from a contemporary perspective. Such a study would need to investigate the reasoning leading to certain concepts and would need to take the Piaget stages into account. Given the vital nature of the concept of God to most religions, such a study would be worthwhile.

Concept of Prayer

Children's concepts of prayer appear to follow Piagetian cognitive development, but little research has been done in this area. The most relevant study is that of Long, Elkind, and Spilka (1967). This is presented in Research Box 3-2.

Children were interviewed by using open-ended and incomplete questions. Three major stages were identified. These were:

1. Ages up to seven respond with learned formulas based on memorized prayers. However, they have difficulty going beyond this point, even to linking the prayers to God.

2. Ages seven to nine identify prayer as a set of activities that are concrete in nature, occurring at a given time and place. The purpose is also concrete and is centered on self-oriented prayer requests.

3. Ages ten to twelve identify prayer abstractly and consider it more of a sharing conversation rather than a request. The significance is not in what material objects one might gain from it but, rather, in more abstract goals.

RESEARCH BOX 3-2.   *Long, D.; Elkind, D.; and Spilka, B. "The Child's Conception of Prayer."* Journal for the Scientific Study of Religion. *1967, 6, 101–109.*

Based on the ideas of Piaget and later Elkind's research on the child's conception of religious denomination, interviews were carried out with eighty girls and eighty boys ranging in age from five to twelve. Twenty of the children participated at each age level. Six open-ended questions were employed to determine possible changes in the concept of prayer (e.g., "What is a prayer?" "Can you pray for more than one thing?"). To get at fantasy content and feeling-tone, four incomplete sentences and two open-ended questions were used (e.g., "I usually pray when . . .", "Where do prayers go?"). The children were individually interviewed, and their responses were analyzed for degree of differentiation and abstraction. This resulted in "prayer conception scores." Three judges independently analyzed the children's responses according to a scoring manual that designated different levels of differentiation and degree of concretization-abstraction.

A clearly age-related pattern was demonstrated. Stage 1 (ages five to seven) revealed a pattern of global and undifferentiated responses in which the replies tended to be unclear, inconsistent, and sometimes unrelated to the questions. Stage 2 (ages seven to nine) evidenced a clear, differentiated, but very concrete concept of prayer. The object of prayer was always for something specific. Stage 3 (ages nine to twelve) showed a growth of individuality and an abstract, differentiated set of ideas about prayer.

The content of prayer changed from an initial stress on personal gratification to thanking God to prayers with humanitarian and altruistic sentiments. At the earliest ages, prayer tended to be emotionally neutral and associated with fixed times (eating, going to bed, etc.). It then developed to be used when one felt unhappy, and finally expressed empathy and identification with others and the deity. Fantasy shifted from mythical to historical personages as go-betweens, to direct communication with God.

This study suggests a partial identification of stages that parallel Piaget's cognitive stages. The first two stages appear to parallel the preconcrete operations and the concrete operations stages. The last stage may be a transitional one, because the oldest of the children are still too young to be at the formal operations stage of cognitive development. The results of Brown's (1966) study of adolescents adds to the findings in that the older the child, the less the orientation toward material consequences from prayer.

Concept of Religious Identity

Another conceptual task in religious development is the development of one's concept of religious identity. What meaning is given to one's religious heritage? In a series of studies, Elkind (1962, 1962, 1963) followed Piagetian methods to interview children. The results suggest that three stages are appropriate for Catholic, Jewish, and Protestant children. These stages are:

1. Ages up to seven, for whom the meaning of their religious group was based on limited conceptualization. The answers were global and undifferentiated to such a degree that it is difficult to consider their responses as reflecting understanding. These appeared to be based on verbal conditioning to the religious group's label.

2. Ages seven to nine, who were reported as a classification process typical of the concrete operations stage of cognitive development. Here were used specific, concrete characteristics, such as where a person worships. The classification system was applied across religious groups.

3. Ages ten to twelve, who showed a more abstract approach to religious identity. A member of this group was more likely to classify others religiously by their beliefs and other abstract characteristics than by concrete behaviors.

Elkind's stages appear to reflect Piagetian stages of cognitive development, particularly for the first two stages. It is unclear whether the last stage is transitional between concrete and formal operations because of the heavy reliance on classification. It seems that the questions asked were not aimed at formal operations but were better suited for concrete operations. This was appropriate given the maximum age in the studies.

EXTRINSIC-INTRINSIC RELIGIOUS ORIENTATIONS

Extrinsic and intrinsic orientations have already been described in earlier chapters. The nature of the constructs has been such that they may imply a sequence. Since intrinsic religion is motivated internally with extrinsic religion being externally and concretely motivated, most religious groups would hope for their members to move from an extrinsic motivation to a more internal autonomous motivation—namely, intrinsicness.

If extrinsic and intrinsic religious motivations form a developmental sequence, then, Venable and Gorsuch (1983) reasoned, they should show characteristics commonly found among developmental stages. These characteristics would include shifts across age groups, preferences for higher stages rather than lower, and the ability to comprehend up to one's own stage but not much beyond.

Administering an "age universal" form of the Allport Ross I and E scales to fifth, seventh, ninth, and eleventh graders, only partial evidence, at best, was found for a stage conceptualization. Children did prefer the reasoning typical of an intrinsic religious position over that of an extrinsic position, and the intrinsics were able to reproduce both intrinsic and extrinsic thinking better than the extrinsics. However, the age changes necessary for traditional developmental stages was missing. Figure 3-1 shows a plot of the scores. At all grades, the means on the intrinsic and extrinsic scales were the same across ages. Hence, it is difficult at this time to say that E and I form stages. A social psychological model may be preferable to a cognitive developmental model.

Abstract Religious Thinking

In similar research, Goldman (1964) introduced the concept of abstract religious thinking as a specific variable. Peatling (1974; Peatling and Laabs, 1975) operationalized the construct in a scale that was further validated in research by

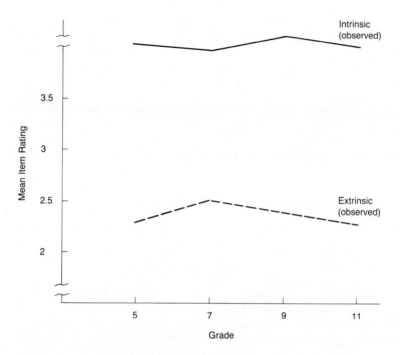

FIGURE 3-1.   Intrinsic and extrinsic scores for children in different grades. *Note:* If these were developmental stages, extrinsic scores should decrease with age and intrinsic scores should increase with age (Venable and Gorsuch, 1983).

Hoge and Petrillo (1978). The scale presents four responses to Biblical stories used by Goldman, responses that vary in their degree of abstractness.

Peatling (1974) found appropriate age changes in abstract thinking. The total score increased two to four points between ages nine, twelve, and fifteen, but less than one point between ages fifteen and eighteen. This is consistent with both Piagetian stages and I.Q. research. In the former, formal operations begin in early adolescence but take a few years to spread through a variety of cognitive areas. In the latter, mental age increases till about age sixteen, when it then levels off.

Investigators of abstract religious thinking have been concerned with how it develops. It is accepted that general cognitive development is a necessary prerequisite for cognitive development in a specified area such as religion. Peatling (1974) found the latter correlated a strong 0.62 with intelligence test scores.

Appropriate interactions with religious materials would also be expected to increase abstract religious thinking. Goldman appropriately found positive correlations of 0.2 to 0.3 for religious activities correlating with his scale of religious thinking. But when Hoge and Petrillo (1978) used Peatling's measure, the results were not as clear. Number of years in a Catholic school correlated positively, as hypothesized, but some measures of religious attendance and involvement correlated negatively with abstract religious thinking. These researchers agree with Peatling and Labbs (1975) that more conservative religious training is associated with more concrete thinking.

Perhaps, at this point, a distinction needs to be made between abstraction and abstract reasoning. The former is possible with any biblical story at any level, for a child can be taught that an abstract interpretation is "correct" even if it cannot be understood. The latter is the ability to interrelate religious concepts using abstract thought processes involving formal operations and can only appear at the formal operations stage. Abstract interpretations are undoubtedly related to liberal Christian and syncretistic religious systems, but is abstract reasoning so related? It is the ability to interrelate constructs with formal operations that is critical to a Piagetian formal operation stage, and it is doubtful that reasoning has been researched when the Peatling scale is used.

ATTRIBUTION THEORY AND STAGES OF CHILDHOOD RELIGION

To date, little research has been done on the attributions children make, and even less relative to religious attributions. One can note the images children employed in the Long, Elkind, and Spilka (1967) study of prayer, and attributions of omnipotence with God answering prayers to set things right or to provide gifts. Here is the powerful parental image that is frequently inferred by psychoanalysts, and parallels can be drawn easily. God is good and in the earliest years tends not to be associated with discomfort, pain, or punishment. With increasing age, God might be a punisher or a confidant who is totally trustworthy. Benevolence dominates, but as more and more abstract individual views enter the picture, the nature of the deity in human terms becomes more and more difficult to maintain. Relative to prayer, the attributions are that it is first an effective way of bringing about change, and second, a way of increasing one's understanding and control of life. Here we see evidences of the motivation for making attributions—namely, the need to establish meaning and control, and to enhance one's esteem through prayerful communication with ultimate power. Madge (1966) focuses on the meanings children obtain via religion, but all of these motives can be seen in Marshall and Hample's (1966, 1967) compilations of children's letters to God.

Stages of cognitive development potentially imply levels or forms of attribution, but the content of these levels is probably learned in the home, and here we have little or no information. The interaction of cognitive level and experience content in producing attributional patterns is truly unresearched. In light of Elkind's (1970) theory on the cognitive origin of religion in the child, it may prove to be one of the more significant areas for study in the future.

SUMMARY AND CONCLUSIONS

Cognitive Stages

The existence of cognitive stages that create differences between a child's conceptualization and utilization of religious concepts and those of an adult is clearly established. The usefulness of Piagetian stages is also apparent. The way children understand concepts of God, prayer, and religious identity, for example, are strongly influenced by the Piagetian stage at which the child functions. It is not that general cognitive development causes religious cognitive development, but rather that religious cognitive development is limited by cognitive development. Children must be able to think in abstractions before abstract religious ideas are introduced.

Unfortunately, little is known about the environmental factors that influence the stage of religious cognitive development. Numerous studies of changes in Piagetian cognitive tasks exist, but no parallel experimental work has been conducted on religious cognitive development. Likewise, studies indicate that the stage of moral development can be increased by intervention (assuming that the necessary cognitive development has occurred) but the models provided by that research have likewise not been applied in research on religious cognitive development.

Content, Gnosticism, Faith, and the "Age of Accountability"

It is important to be clear that religious cognitive development is only one aspect of religious development. The relationship of religious cognitive development to acceptance of a particular religious content has not been investigated but, as in the case of moral development, is theoretically unrelated. Religious material can be found at any level of cognitive development, and a child or person limited to a particular stage of cognitive development may be just as committed to a specific faith as someone at the highest stage of cognitive development. For example, it is well established that Bible knowledge has little if any correlation to being a Christian. And the Christian faith has never limited itself to a particular stage of cognitive development. The mentally retarded, Ph.D.s, and little children can all exhibit Christian faith.

In an academic environment, it is tempting to equate the highest level of understanding of a topic with the highest "good" regarding that topic. But religions seldom view understanding as the primary goal. To do so is to commit what Christians would call agnostic heresy since salvation would be from knowledge rather than faith. Instead, the primary goal is embodied in terms such as faith.

While the contents of this chapter do not relate directly to questions of faith, they do relate to the "age of accountability." In the Judeo-Christian world, children generally are expected to study their faith and indicate their acceptance of it after they have reached the age of accountability, a final step that results in full church membership. Various traditions label the ceremony the Bar Mitzvah, Confirmation, or Baptism. It was suggested in this chapter that the age for such ceremonies needs to be set no earlier than early adolescence. Only then do youth have the necessary cognitive tools—formal operations—to allow an adult-type examination of their faith. And for some youth it may need to be middle to late adolescence to allow time for a normal but slower cognitive development or for the cognitive development to generalize into the religious domain.

CHAPTER FOUR
IMPACT OF FAMILY AND SCHOOLS ON RELIGIOUS DEVELOPMENT

Train up a child in the way he should go, and when he is old he will not depart from it. (Proverbs 22:6, RSV)

Education and admonition commence in the first years of childhood, and last to the very end of life. (Plato, 1952, p. 45.)

If obedience to the will of God is necessary to happiness, and knowledge of him will be necessary to obedience, I know not how he that withholds this knowledge, or delays it, can be said to love his neighbor as himself. (Samuel Johnson in Boswell, 1952. p. 151)

In childhood, the major factors influencing development are the family and the school. From a child's perspective, both family and school have a major salient characteristic in common: They are dominated by adult figures. The adult figures of home and school are not only bigger physically but also both further along in cognitive development and obviously more experienced. And when adults cannot directly oversee the child, they generally appoint an agent to act on their behalf, whether that agent be babysitter, day care center, or recess monitor. Agents such as a babysitter or an older sibling are still considered parenting figures because they take a dominant role over the child. Hence, the child's world is dominated by parenting and teaching figures.

In the first major section of this chapter, the impact of the family on the religious development of the child is examined. This discussion centers on parents, but possible impact of siblings and other family members is also noted. In the second major section, the impact of schools with some specific religious teaching is examined. This includes parochial schools and religious classes auxiliary to public schools.

The situation of youth is somewhat different than that of children. Adult dominance is less and peer interaction is more prominent. The final section of this chapter consists of the impact of peers and others on the religion of adolescents. In particular, the role of colleges is discussed.

IMPACT OF THE FAMILY

Parental Impact

Correlation of parent and child religiosity. Argyle and Beit-Hallahmi (1975) summarize their review of the parent-child correlations well: "There can be no doubt that the attitudes of parents are among the most important factors in the formation of religious attitudes" (p. 30). The correlations are indeed high, suggesting a strong relationship.

Just how high the correlations are depends on a number of factors. Denomination is an important variable. The studies suggest that the percentage of children affiliating with their parents' religious group varies from forty to ninety percent (Argyle and Beit-Hallahmi, 1975). The lower figure is typical of more liberal denominations, which do not stress participation in their group as highly important, and the latter of groups that emphasize the uniqueness of their denomination. Table 4-1 gives figures for some American denominations.

Several cautions are needed to properly interpret children affiliating with their parent's denomination. First, some groups define membership as a rite of infancy, such as the Roman Catholic infant baptism. In these cases, a person remains a member unless they decide to become active in another religion. As a result, most of the people who are so indifferent that they do not even bother to drop out officially are counted as members. Some would say such people are not members since they, for example, have not gone through confirmation; however, most studies ask the persons themselves for their affiliation and we suspect many nonconfirmed people consider themselves members. In other groups, such as the Baptists, membership occurs at the time of baptism in early adolescence.

TABLE 4-1 Percentages of Children Staying in Their Parents' Religious Denomination or Belonging to None

				DENOMINATIONS					
	Bapt.	Cath.	Disc.	Epis.	Luth.	Meth.	Pres.	Sects	U.C.C.
Same	74	85	54	62	76	62	59	62	58
None	5	7	6	12	4	6	8	5	6

Notes: Percentages are the averages from two national studies collected in the 1970s (Hadaway, 1970; Kluegel, 1980). *N*'s per group varied from 89 to 1766; the largest percentage difference between the two studies was 6 percent.
Abbreviations: Bapt. = Baptist, Cath. = Catholic, Disc. = Disciples of Christ, Epis. = Episcopalian, Luth. = Lutheran, Meth. = Methodist, Pres. = Presbyterian, U.C.C. = United Church of Christ.

When asked about membership, the latter's ''yes'' would be expected to contain less of these ''indifferent members'' than the former.

It is also of interest to examine the total number of religious traditions that are active within *any* branch of Christianity. This is particularly important for a religious group such as the Disciples of Christ. They stress the underlying unity of all Christendom, and so children of this group can ally with another denomination without feeling that they have completely left the religion of their parents. The number of children raised in a denomination who are not affiliated with any other Christian group are given in Table 4-1. The figure is generally quite low, suggesting that most children raised in a Christian home of any denomination are, as young adults, affiliated with some Christian group.

Table 4-1 is convincing evidence that the religious culture of the parents is usually passed on to the children. The children are primarily affiliated with the denomination of their parents, or are affiliated with another similar Christian group.

The correlation of parents' religiousness and that of their children is less if some other measure than just affiliation is involved. Hoge and Petrillo (1978) report typical data. Mother's church attendance and father's church attendance correlated 0.6 and 0.5, respectively, with the church attendance of their adolescent offspring. Acock and Bengtson (1978) also give correlations in this range, with a multiple correlation when both parents are given separate but equal weights (and the sex of the child is also a predictor) of 0.67. Combining this with the cited affiliation data suggests that a sizable number of those who stay affiliated with their parents' faith also attend, but that others are affiliated only nominally.

Less is known about how specific religious attitudes are correlated between parent and child. The necessary studies would need to measure both the parents' and child's current religious positions and then determine their similarity. Measuring only the degree of religious commitment of the child is insufficient. Any theory that proposes that parents teach their children their own religious beliefs and values would necessarily hold that parents likewise teach nonreligious (and even antireligious) beliefs and values also. Hence, the religious attitudes of the parents need to be taken into account.

We expect specific religious content to correlate less between parent and child than religious affiliation. The reasons for this expectation are several. First, religious affiliation is communicable at all ages and at many different levels. The youngest child can be taught that the religious group identity is positive and good. Numerous other reinforcements can be found in the religious membership besides theologically based ones, including friendships and group activities. Second, religious affiliation is a broader definition of religiousness than specific doctrine. Others in the group may communicate to the child beliefs that the parents do not hold. And since the group theology always includes a wider variety of positions than is likely to be found in one family, the child can adopt positions somewhat divergent from the parents and still be active in the same religious group. Therefore, the child is more likely to have the same group membership than to have the same beliefs as the parents.

The possibility that religious affiliation is more likely to be that of the parents than is religious content per se leads to the "mellowing" of most religious movements over time, a phenomenon described by Niebuhr (1929). The first generation is attracted to the group for theological reasons. A large percentage can therefore be expected to hold the central beliefs of that group. But later generations remain affiliated as long as they are within the tolerances of the group. As time passes and the group shifts from primarily converts to primarily those raised within the group, the percentage of those strongly holding the core beliefs diminishes. So a religious group becomes theologically broader with each generation. The long-term result is a moderating of the core beliefs.

Is one parent more important in the religious development than another? Argyle and Beit-Hallahmi (1975) note that several studies in the 1930's concluded that the mother was more important. But times have changed, with mothers no longer working in the home and supervising children to the degree that they did in the 1930s. Hoge and Petrillo (1978) found mother and father correlations of the same size as did Cornwall, Olsen, and Weed (1979) and Hoge and Keeter (1976). It appears that both are equal in this respect, but more sophisticated research might be needed. Researchers could, for instance, include a measure of how much time each parent spends with each child. And in single parent homes, we would expect the parent living in the home to have the most effect.

We can conclude that parent's religiousness is indeed *associated* with that of their children. However, the research to date cannot prove a causal relationship. Data in each study collected at one point in time and other causal factors were not held constant. The effect of parents could be direct, as we suspect, or it might be indirect. It would be indirect if, for example, the parents had no impact outside of exposing the child to a religious organization.

The research that exists is consistent with the hypothesis that parents have a direct impact. For example, Hoge and Petrillo (1978) did examine peer groups and the type and quality of church programs along with family factors; the correlations for the family factors were twice as high as for the other factors, thus providing support for a true parent effect. This study needs further confirmation for a strong conclusion that the parents are responsible. The Hoge and Petrillo (1978) work is an excellent example of an attempt to investigate this area in a comprehensive manner; hence, it is presented in Research Box 4-1.

It is surprising that an experimental study of parenting effect has yet to be published. Certainly many quasi-experiments are conducted informally. Every attempt by a church group to help parents be more effective is a quasi-experiment on this topic. We need some serious evaluations of parent education. Not

RESEARCH BOX 4-1.   *Hoge, D. R. and Petrillo, G. H. "Determinants of Church Participation and Attitudes among High School Youth."* Journal for the Scientific Study of Religion, 1978, 17, *359–79.*

The issue of the loss of youth from the churches raises the question of the sources of positive attitudes and involvement by adolescents. To understand these, the researchers examined four major possible influences: family, peer group, church programs, and religious beliefs.

Working with 10 Methodist and 20 Baptist churches plus 5 Catholic parishes, 148 Methodist, 151 Baptist, and 152 Catholic youth and their parents were studied. From the latter, data were gathered from 315 mothers and 284 fathers. In addition, church personnel working with the youth were interviewed. Four measures of involvement and attitudes were constructed: (1) church attendance, (2) a youth program participation index, (3) an approval of organized religion index, and (4) the degree of liking for participation in youth church programs.

Parental church attendance was strongly and positively related to youth attendance, whether this information came from the adolescents or their parents. Parental church and youth participation also relate positively, but neither parental attendance or organizational involvement associates with youth approval of religion or liking for church programs. In like manner, religious socialization ties, but rather weakly, to youth attendance but not their program participation, approval of religion, or liking of church programs. Parental control, support, or disagreement with parents does not affiliate with any of the youth religious activities or measures. Apparently the latter's involvement is often motivated independently of parents.

Peer group influences are quite important. When close friends participate in church activities and peers who are active treat the youth well, he or she is also likely to be active and favorable toward religion and church programs. Programmatic factors were not strong predictors of attitude and involvement, although some favorable influence comes from youth liking such programs and what looks like the ability of pastors to communicate with these adolescents. Relative to belief, creedal assent is the strongest indicator of positive attitudes and church and program participation and liking.

Overall, family factors are the major predictor of youth church attendance; peer group influences youth program participation and liking most, but program factors also greatly influence liking of religion and program involvement. Religious interest and belief are noteworthy, but not powerful influences on attendance and participation, but are especially significant in approval of organized religion.

only would it unambiguously resolve the question of causation, it would also evaluate methods of effective religious parenting.

Identification of projection theories. These theories suggest that the image of God comes from the parental figure(s). Freud proposed a projection theory in which one, as it were, builds a parental figure to replace the actual parent. One then "projects" it to the outside world—just as a slide projector throws an internal image onto a screen—and calls the projected image "God."

There are major problems with such projection theories. First, these theories are difficult if not impossible to test. There is no accepted operational measure of, for example, projection. The empirical tests that have been conducted are, as shown below, inconclusive even if the operational definitions of the investigators were widely accepted.

Second, the theories are often interpreted as philosophical statements that go beyond what psychology can test. It seems that many—college students included—assume that a projection theory means there could be "nothing but" the projected image and that all God images are such projections. A projection theory, because it is close to a philosophical position, may be reassuring to people who want to believe there is no God. Despite the limited nature of the projection theories, they seem to encourage the genetic fallacy.

A philosophical interpretation of projection theories is not required by the psychological theory. The theory could be psychologically valid if only some people project such an image. It could also be valid if the images people project only slightly distort the image that reality presents.

Third, another limitation of the parental theory is that it is at best applicable to only a limited set of religions—namely, those arising from Judaism (including Christianity and Islam). It is difficult to generalize it to polytheistic and oriental religions despite the fact that most theorists treat it as arising from universal conditions affecting all our species—namely, our own finitude in combination wth parental figures.

Studies of the relationship of the concept of God to concepts of parents are reviewed by Nicholson and Edwards (1979) and typified by Spilka, Addison, and Rosensohn (1975). While, as Nicholson and Edwards (1979) show, the results do vary somewhat according to methods used, the general trend of results is clear. There are some small, positive relationships between concepts of God and concepts of most admired or same-sexed parent. For example, in Spilka et al. (1976) many of the correlations are insignificant while the significant ones are no larger than 0.3. Hence, even if no critique of the empirical studies were possible, the results for the projection theory could only be viewed, at this point, as weak. Spilka (1979) suggests that this line of research is at its end, with researchers becoming disenchanted with it. Still, it continues. Vergote and Tamayo (1980) employed fairly rigorous procedures in a extensive program of research on a large number of samples of normals, delinquents, and mentally disordered individuals from many different countries. They were not able to support Freudian views, and felt that their findings were explained by no psychological theory.

The methods used to test the projection theory primarily show the difficulty in testing it. The procedure has been to compare the image of God on, for example, a semantic differential checklist against the same checklist used with parental figures. If the two profiles match, that is assumed to be evidence for a projection theory. But such a conclusion is wrong. It fails to consider a major alternative hypothesis: any two living objects highly valued will have similar profiles and so will correlate. An example of this approach is provided in Table 4-2.

It would be possible to improve this research by introducing several controls. To control for the effects of similarities between highly valued living objects, the profile of several such ratings (not including parents) could be statistically removed from the profile. To control for the effects of religious teachings (i.e.,

TABLE 4-2   Semantic Differential Similarities with God

In projection research, each participant is asked to rate several people on a series of pairs of adjectives. Here are several such pairs:

Loving   --- Hateful
Kind   --- Cruel
Like   --- Dislike
Friendly --- Distant

Place the letter *P* on each line to show the degree to which one or the other adjective of each pair describes your most preferred parent. Next, place an *F* on each line to describe the best friend that you have ever had. Next, place an *A* on each line to describe the person you most admire. If you have had a favorite dog (or cat), place a *D* (or *C*) on each line for it. Finally, place a *G* on each line to describe the best Christian view of God.

Do your letters fall close together? For many of us, the letters become very crowded because they are at almost the same places on the scales. Projection theory would have us conclude that our friends are projections from our parents, our views of our favorite pet are projections from our parents, and soon, if the same logic is applied, that is suggested for the image of God ("Poor Fido; he/she doesn't really have a personality but is just a figment of my projection").

Or can we conclude that in our culture highly valued personalities are viewed the same because these characteristics are valued? Then God and parents are alike not because of any projection but because they are both valued personalities.

for the fact that any personal projection is likely to be onto an image already provided by a religious group), the view of God seen in the religious heritage also would have to be removed. Then the person's projection of parents, if any, could be identified.

But both of these controls would probably be futile. The existing data suggest that the correlations between parental and God images are sufficiently small so that the first control would eliminate them completely. And the second control would be rejected by some proponents of a projection theory on the grounds that it would also remove the impact of the religious projection that the projection theory assumes we all make. Hence, there is not yet an established procedure by which the theory can be tested. A good illustration of this kind of research is provided by Nicholson and Edwards (1979), and is presented in Research Box 4-2.

Although there is obvious disagreement, as a serious scientific venture, projection theories may not be worth further work. The most useful realm for them appears to be more philosophical than psychological.

Impact of Methods of Childrearing

Since it is well established that the family has a definite impact on the religious development of children, the next question is how the impact is made. Also included here is the vital question of why some parents are more effective in this task than others.

The research in this area is associational, and so, regardless of what statis-

RESEARCH BOX 4-2   *Nicholson, H.C. and Edwards, K. "A Comparison of Four Statistical Methods for Assessing Similarity of God Concept to Parental Images." Paper presented at the Annual Meeting of the Scientific Study of Religion, San Antonio, Texas, October 1979.*

Noting that a variety of statistical procedures have been employed in comparing images of God with those of one's mother and father, the authors distinguished four methods. These fell into two categories: the correlational approach which measures the degree to which high or low scores assigned to God or parents seem to parallel each other—namely, the higher one is, the higher the other, and vice versa. The Difference Approach attempts to assess similarity by noting the "distance" or difference between the scores assigned to God and mother or father. Since these procedures are fairly sophisticated statistically, we will not try to detail them here, but rather emphasize their degree of agreement or disagreement.

Two sets of rating data for images of mother, father, and God were gathered from samples of 105 and 131 persons ranging in age from thirteen to seventy-three years and including normal and abnormal adults, college students and sunday school attenders. It was shown that all of the methods are consistent with one another, but still leave room for much variation among them in findings. God-father and God-mother variations among the methods were observed in the two different samples suggesting different results are a function not only of the use of various statistical procedures, but also the nature of the samples studied and the measures used. The ranges of the computed scores and their reliability are factors that enter the picture. It is also clear that God-mother and God-father scores are not independent of each other as is assumed by some of the methods.

Generally, God image was more similar to mother than father images, but for one of the procedures, the image of the preferred parent was more similar to the God concept than that of the nonpreferred parent. The Freudian view was not supported, but the complexity of the results and variation among the methods suggests the presence of a wide variety of influencing factors. The authors note, for example, developmental, personality, and social possibilities along with religious affiliation and background, age of conversion, etc. In contrast to what they regard as the pessimistic view of other researchers working on these problems, these workers feel the issue might be more fruitfully handled with more rigorous and appropriate statistical procedures plus consideration of a wide variety of confounding factors.

tical techniques are used, causation cannot be evaluated. Such procedures do provide the necessary background for laying out a possible change program however, to increase parental effectiveness, and then compare such a treated group against appropriate control groups to see if the impact of the experimental group was greater.

Research in this area has no general theoretical basis. Instead, the studies typically identify several elements that anyone would suspect as good parenting in our culture. With only a few exceptions, the parenting literature from child development has been untapped.

The first conclusion is that emphasis on religion within the home is important. Hunsberger (1976) grouped students of three denominations by degree of religious emphasis in the home. He found that the degree to which the college students felt they currently agreed with the religion they were taught when they were growing up varied meaningfully. Students reporting the greatest perceived agreement were from homes in which religion had been stressed; students reporting a lower level of agreement stated their homes did not stress religion. Hunsberger's further work (1980) has confirmed this result: Stressing religion in the home during childhood is seen by college students as being associated with greater commitment on their part. It appears that religious parents are more successful at communicating their commitment than nonreligious parents are in conveying their lack of religiousness, probably because religious parents place more emphasis on their perspective.

Both parental behavior and teachings are important. Church participation by the parents is one of the stronger correlates of the older child's participation. Hoge and Petrillo (1978) found this for high-school students and Hoge and Keeter (1976) found the same result for college teachers' recall of their parents' activities and their own activity. Hoge and Petrillo (1978) also found that youths who reported both that their parents carried their beliefs over into actions and that their parents talked to them about religion participated more in religious activities.

One expectation for effective communication of parents' religion to children would be that the parents agree on what is to be communicated. Two lines of research suggest that this is a significant variable. First are studies on mixed marriages. When the husband and wife are from different religous traditions, the impact on the child is less. Hoge and Petrillo (1978) report a correlation of 0.3 between agreement and impact; it is a factor but not a major one. We suspect it would be more important if a more sensitive measure of religious beliefs were used than just whether parents belong to the same church.

Lack of agreement in a marriage has been investigated by Nelson (1981). He found that parents who fought more had less effect on their children. This may be both because of a lack of agreement on what is to be taught children and because the children have a model for disagreeing with one parent in the other parent's behavior.

Recent studies have examined the relationship of different styles of child rearing to a child's religious commitment. Studies such as Dudley (1978), Erickson (1962; reanalyzed by Greeley and Gockel, 1971), Hoge and Petrillo (1978), and Hoge and Keeter (1976) suggest that many variables commonly assumed to relate to effective parenting actually do relate. These include the parents talking with the children about religion, being sincere, being personally interested in the child, and the existence of family harmony. Less anticipated is that attempts to control religion are unrelated while the perception of emancipation from parents is positively related.

Since these studies are associational and based on reports from youth, they are primarily concerned with how parents are perceived. The behaviors that will best communicate, for example, religious sincerity are not yet identified. And it may be, for example, that family harmony comes from the children's acceptance of the family faith rather than vice versa.

At the current time, the advice to parents is clear: be in agreement on the religious faith you wish to impart, sincerely model that faith in both words and deeds, and strive toward a relationship with your children that will encourage discussion of religion and its implications. But remember that it is also important that the child feel free to take his or her own position.

Siblings and Other Family Members

Families consist of more than just parents and a child, but the impact of other children in the family is still open for investigation. MacDonald (1969) found that firstborn children are closer to parents and more religious than later born, but one study is not enough for conclusions. Neither has the effect of a particularly religious or nonreligious older or younger sibling been investigated (the effect may vary depending on the number of years between the siblings, the degree to which they liked and felt they were liked by their siblings, etc.). Studies of family dynamics that include siblings are needed.

IMPACT OF SCHOOLS

The general feeling is that families are of greater importance in religious development than any other factor. The greater possibility of parental impact—as compared to schools—may exist for several reasons. These reasons include the parents being involved with a child for at least some eighteen years, the more varied interactions across settings that parents have, and the deeper emotional relationships between parent and child as compared to teacher and child. Another factor arises from the variety of teachers in contemporary education who have contact with any particular child. It is not unusual for a student to go through a high school without ever knowing any teacher on a personal basis. And now even in elementary schools it is common for the child to be taught by several teachers without anyone having a real responsibility to know the child. Peck and Havighurst (1960) state the conclusion of many psychologists: "School and church personnel should not expect to work many 'miracles' of character reformation—and certainly not by dealing with children in mass" (p. 190).

Schools come in several forms. The impact of religious schools meeting only an hour each week—such as Sunday schools—is not evaluated here. That is because the length of time is probably too brief to achieve the impact necessary to be identifiable by the commonly used methodologies. Also there have been few studies of the impact of religious schools meeting for an hour or less a week, although the Shoemaker and Gorsuch 1982 experimental program suggests that the schools could have a definite effect.

We will review schools meeting for one hour a day for several days a week or more, including released time programs and parochial schools, but most of the studies have been of parochial schools.

Who Goes to Religious Schools?

The type of child who goes to a religious school is clear: one with religious parents. Johnstone (1966) divided Lutheran families by their religious involvement. The "ideal" family consisted of two Lutheran parents who had not been divorced, were living at home, attended church each Sunday, and had family devotions. "Marginal" Lutheran families were defined as those scoring considerably lower on each of the variables by which "ideal" Lutheran families were defined. Of the people raised in the "ideal" families, 63 percent had extensive parochial school education and only 19 percent had extensive public school education. The "marginal" Lutheran families showed the opposite trend: Only 27 percent had extensive Lutheran school experience while 60 percent attended public schools extensively.

The same high relationship between the religiousness of the family and attendance at parochial schools has been found in most other studies. It has been observed for Catholic schools (Greeley and Rossi, 1966), Christian "fundamentalist" day schools (Erickson, 1964), and for Jewish schools (Himmelfarb, 1977; but not by Shapiro and Dashefsky, 1974).

The relationship of family religiousness and sending a child to a parochial school is expected and is another way in which the religiousness of parents affects their child's behavior. But this strong relationship causes a methodological problem. Generally, only religious parents send their children to religious schools. So when their children grow up religious, do we give the "credit" to the family or to the school? Since the parents' religiousness leads to the use of religious schooling, it seems only fair to give them credit. On the other hand, the schools may indeed make the parents' task easier, and so should not the school be able to claim that it influences the child's development? Certainly we should be able to say both, but methodological limitations often mean that we can be methodologically sure of only one or the other influence.

Impact of Schooling

Major studies on the impact of religious schooling have arrived at different conclusions. Johnstone (1966) and Erickson (1964) see little direct effect on religiousness besides religious knowledge. Johnstone (1966) did conclude that parochial students know more about Biblical characters and events than students with public schooling; but when variables concerning personal religious belief and behaviors were examined, they found little influence after family effects had been statistically removed. The notable differences in religiosity that were found in both studies could, according to these authors, be attributed solely to the high religiousness of the families that send children to parochial schools.

Investigations of Jewish and Catholic schooling have generally concluded that there is an effect of schooling over and above what the family contributes (Greeley and Rossi, 1966; Greeley and Gockel, 1971; Shapiro and Dashefsky, 1974; Bock; 1977; Himmelfarb, 1977). Shapiro and Dashefsky (1974) also found Jewish family religiousness to be uncorrelated with Jewish education, possibly because Jewish ethnic identity leads to Jewish education in addition to Jewish religiousness. When the schooling was divided according to the Jewish tradition it represented, little effect was found for any except the conservative schools.

Greeley and Rossi (1966) noted definite ethnic effects. People with Irish and German backgrounds were more influenced by Catholic schooling than other groups.

Note that studies suggesting a definite schooling effect are associated with distinctive ethnic groups for whom religious identity is generally related to ethnic identity—such as Jewish and Irish Catholic groups. It may be that parochial schools are most effective when they can reinforce the feeling of being different from others and that the difference is partly religious. Such schooling then would be effective but it would be implicitly broader than just religion.

Greeley and his associates (Greeley and Rossi, 1966; Greeley and Gockel, 1971) have attempted to draw some reasonably consistent conclusions across the studies. First, Greeley and Rossi (1966) suggest the existence of a "multiplier effect" from having both a religious family and religious schooling. They note that long-term behavior is most influenced when all the child's life is oriented in the same direction, as in the ethnic minorities. This is in opposition to Johnstone's conclusion that the only children for whom some religious schooling effect might be found were those from homes with marginal family religiousness.

Second, Greeley and Gockel (1971) thoroughly discuss both Johnstone and Erickson. They note that Erickson's conclusion is for *elementary* school children, whereas the studies finding an effect are for *high school* youth. They have probably identified an important variable, for other reasoning would suggest that adolescence rather than childhood is the most likely time for a parochial school effect. As noted in Chapter Three, the development of the necessary cognitive abilities to grasp and utilize many of the abstract concepts essential to most religions only occurs in adolescence. Other research on value development (Gorsuch, 1973) has suggested that the task of childhood is becoming sufficiently socialized to be able to participate in *any* group, but the task of adolescence is deciding *which* group one wants to be a part of. The latter task is traditionally at the heart of accepting a religion.

When investigating adolescents, Greeley and Gockel (1971) suggest that the Greeley and Rossi (1966) adolescent data are sufficiently similar to the other studies so that the differences in results are probably a function of regional variation, identity, and methods of research. Indeed, in checking Johnstone's data and results, they conclude that Johnstone may have "undersold" the conclusions by using too high a significance level ($p = 0.01$), as Erickson (1962) also suggested.

The "multiplier effect" was found for adults, and so Greeley and Gockel (1971) suggest that long-term effects of schools are most likely when all the social influences are in the same direction. This is in keeping with the Jewish studies which, while not analyzing for a multiplier effect, conducted their research with post-high school men. Shapiro and Dashefsky (1974) and Bock (1977) found that both home and schooling added to later Jewish identity.

Bock (1977) makes one additional point that further research may find to be highly important: the number of hours of religious schooling. There seems to be a minimum level of instruction necessary for any effect to occur. Bock identified this level in his sample to be 1,000 classroom hours. This shows why it is difficult to find Sunday school effects; it would take twenty years of attending one hour each Sunday to produce the effect (or thirty years with the forty-five-minute classes many churches now hold). And all those hours in a classroom would need to be spent after a minimum age so that religious material could be understood. Further, the classes would need to be taken just as seriously as classes in which grades are given.

An extended number of hours of instruction may be necessary for a clear, long-term educational effect. But sending children to Sunday school may also be important because it shows the child how serious the parent is about religion, or because it gives social support for and guidance to living one's faith at that time. These issues have not been investigated.

Based on this research, we suggest:

1. Religious schooling is most likely to be effective when conducted with adolescents and in depth (e.g., for more than 250 class hours per year for four or more years).
2. It may have more impact on children from less religious families since those from religious families are already consistently religious (and so cannot show any change).
3. Long-term religiousness is likely to be a function of all the religious training a person is given. So the most religious person is likely to be one who both has a religious family and religious schooling.
4. Because religious parents are the ones who send their children to religious schools, it will continue to be difficult to separate the effects of religious homes and religious schools. Special research methodologies need to be used for this task.

Still unaddressed is the question of whether religious schooling is more effective than religious training in the home. This is unaddressed because none of the studies examined whether, for example, two hours of home training is more effective than two hours of religious schooling. And yet most parental decisions about parochial schools are made in part on the basis of cost-effectiveness. Assuming that the parents can make their desired impact on the religious upbringing of their child, would it be easier for them to turn that task over to a parochial school? If the answer is "yes," they may wish to do so to increase the time for other activities valued in their religious setting.

PEER AND COLLEGE IMPACT

The older the child, the more time is spent with peers of the same age. Post-high school youth are often in a unique situation: college. It is at this point in their life that most of their interpersonal experiences are with age peers. While classes are under the control of parental-type authorities, the interaction of a professor and a student seldom occurs outside the classroom.

Peer Impact

Our cultural folklore suggests that peers have a major impact in adolescence. Indeed, that folklore states the case so emphatically that some find the strong relationship between parent and youth religiousness hard to believe. This may be because youth clearly see the differences between themselves and their parents from disagreements, and the agreements—which are never discussed because they are agreements—are often overlooked.

Little research has investigated the relative effect of parents and peers on youth, but the results so far suggest that both are often important. Hoge and Petrillo (1978) found them to be significant predictors of both church attendance and church youth group participation.

The impact of parents and peers may differ depending on the dependent variable. When it is church attendance, parents are more important than peers. For youth group participation, peers are more important than parents. And for liking of youth programs, parents are unimportant while peers (and the programs themselves) are important influences (Hoge and Petrillo, 1978).

Note that peer group influence is not solely an adolescent phenomena. With adulthood, people relate almost exclusively in age peer groups outside of the work setting. Adulthood is the most peer-dominated period of life and, as expected, having a spouse and friends of the same religious faith increases one's own involvement in it (Lenski, 1963).

IMPACT OF COLLEGE

The literature on the impact of college in general and studying within a discipline in particular is extensive (Feldman, 1969; Hoge, 1974).

The possibilities for colleges to impact religion are intriguing. Students are cognitively developed and yet still too young (one hopes!) to be "set in their ways." The professors are sophisticated and extensively educated in their areas. Perhaps most important is the minimizing of other influences. Students generally live away from their parents and do not work, so all authority figures are on campus. Peer groups are structured and influenced by the campus. The student population completely changes every four years so that variations in tradition may occur quickly, compared to other institutions.

Perhaps most important of the reasons for examining college impact is that colleges see themselves as instruments of change. Religious organizations have always sponsored colleges with the explicit reason of providing an opportunity for religious growth.

Feldman's (1969) review is still appropriate. He notes that some students shift across the college years but that the nature of the shifts are difficult to predict. The type of college and its emphasis influence who attend; religiously sponsored institutions attract more religious students than do other colleges. Many students report religious changes during college, but within most colleges those decreasing in religion cancel out those increasing so that the group mean remains much the same.

Comparing Feldman's review with later studies suggests that the era during which the research was conducted may influence the results. First, most of the studies reported by Feldman were conducted in the 1950s and 1960s. They reported a decrease in religiousness from freshman to senior years and that students from more conservative denominations were more likely to change. More recently, Hunsberger (1976) noted that conservative Christians were more likely to keep their faith unchanged than were liberal Christian students. He has replicated this and also notes that only a few students now report religious change during college (Hunsberger, 1978).

The general impression that education leads people to question their beliefs seems to be dated. It is now apparent that the changes are complex and depend on the student and the school. The general proposition that higher education always leads to less religion is negated by a study at Brigham Young University (Christensen and Cannon, 1978). Students there have consistently reported that they have become more conservative during their college years.

To the degree that college does have an impact, that impact should be maxi-

RESEARCH BOX 4-3.   *Madsen, G. E. and Vernon, G. M. "Maintaining the Faith during College: A Study of Campus Religious Group Participation,"* Review of Religious Research, *1983, 25, 127–41.*

The question of whether college increases or decreases traditional Christian faith continues to be a question. However, the research is now becoming more sophisticated and recognizes that it is not college per se but that which happens at college that is the prime factor of psychological importance.

Madsen and Vernon (1983) mailed questionnaires to high school graduates just before they entered college and during the spring of their senior year. Then the degree to which these students changed on religious measures was compared. The students were principally Mormons and principally attended the University of Utah.

It was found that religious attitudes were related to participation in campus religious activities at the beginning of college and at the end of college, a finding that would only be surprising if it did not occur. The more interesting results are what happened to the religious attitudes of those who participated in campus religious organizations and those who did not. Those results are:

RELIGIOUS PARTICIPATION WHILE ON CAMPUS	CHANGE IN RELIGIOUS ATTITUDES
Yes	Increased 0.7
No	Decreased 2.3

Does college influence religiousness? Perhaps that is not the question. Perhaps it is the question of what happens to the individual in the particular college setting that impacts that person or predicts the direction in which he or she is changing. College provides the opportunities, but the person must take advantage of the opportunities for them to have an effect.

---

mal among those who have spent the most time in college settings—namely, college teachers. But when Hoge and Keeter (1976) examined college training and discipline with home and background partialed out, little effect from college and discipline remained. The primary impact on creedal assent and church commitment was from home and background.

The literature on college impact is unclear because, except for the Brigham Young study, it seldom takes the goals of the college personnel into account. College impact can occur only as someone impacts the student. Theoretically, the impact can range from liberal to conservative, depending on who influences the student. The type of impact will vary within one campus as well as across campuses. What those most in contact with a particular student are actually communicating is a critical but as yet unexamined variable.

ATTRIBUTION THEORY, AND THE ROLES OF FAMILY
AND SCHOOLS IN RELIGIOUS DEVELOPMENT

Primarily, we have been trying to understand the roles of the family and schools in the maintenance or loss of religion on the part of adolescents. This is an attributional problem, for we are seeking to comprehend the causes of what we observe—for example, how do one's parents influence the degree and nature of the faith that is held? Are God images generalizations from those of mother? Of father? Who or what is to take credit or take the blame? In other words to whom do we attribute what we observe?

If we ask others to explain why they are religious or not, they will make attributions to personal considerations, past experience, the nature of religion as they see it, their parents, friends, etc. Hoge and Petrillo's (1978) work looks at parents, peers, beliefs, and liking as factors. Youth and parents participated, and it was possible to see both correspondences and differences in their attributional frameworks. The need is not merely to make these comparisons and general inferences, but rather to define the specific variables that might be functioning. Once the attributions are denoted, experimental or investigative methods may be applied with families to determine if what has been referred to in the past by youth and parents is actually operative in families with younger children. Longitudinal studies would result and the findings could be definitive.

In like manner, the role of peers in high school and college plus exposure to various kinds of information might be assessed from the perspectives of youth to obtain their attributions regarding what has influenced their faith one way or the other. These inferences could then be checked out. In this way, we are observing the interaction of situational and dispositional determinants of religious attitudes and behavior. At this time, however our knowledge is rather general. Much more research is necessary to fill in the details.

Projection theories are clear instances of attribution. The origins of the God concepts of children and youth are being sought in images of the father, the mother, the preferred parent, or even in one's self-precepts (Spilka, Addison, and Rosensohn, 1975). Although we have been pessimistic regarding the future of this kind of research, it might be fruitful to group individuals who pattern their parental and God attributions certain ways and then seek the determinants of, say, father-God versus mother-God correspondences.

We are asking what different attributions signify. Certain ones relative to family might imply the development of an intrinsic orientation, others an extrinsic faith. Since adolescence in our society is often described as a time of turmoil, and various researchers have pointed to the resolution of religious matters through conversion to or rejection of religion, the motivations for various attributions need examination. Are the problems ones of meaning, control, or self-esteem? Both a popular and a professional psychological literature claims that all of these are significant issues during the period of youth. The explanatory attributions employed at this time provide leads that merit intensive examination, and should help fill the many gaps in our knowledge of what occurs in religious development during the adolescent years.

SUMMARY AND CONCLUSIONS

1. Our first conclusion must be a methodological one, because it conditions all other conclusions. Without experimental and longitudinal data, it is difficult to separate out the impact of home so that other influences can be identified.

2. The more religious the parents, the more religious the children. Religious affiliation may be more effectively passed on than religious beliefs, but parents are a definite factor in both cases.

3. There is little evidence to support projective theories.

4. Preliminary evidence suggests that good parenting for communicating religious commitment consists of the parents modeling religion in both word and deed. A close, positive relationship between parent and child that still allows the children sufficient freedom to make their own religious choices is associated with parental impact, but it is unknown if this is cause or effect.

5. Religious schools have a long-term impact, provided they are attended during the high-school years. They may need to involve 1,000 or so classroom hours.

6. Peer groups have some impact, particularly when the peer group is the prime group involved (e.g., youth programs). Peer group impact is probably less overall than cultural folklore suggests.

7. While considerable research exists on the impact of colleges, few clear and consistent trends occur. Perhaps the belief and practices of those with whom each student has the most contact during college need to be taken explicitly into account.

CHAPTER FIVE
RELIGION IN ADULT LIFE

"Things are coming to a pretty pass . . . when religion is allowed to invade private life" (Melbourne quoted in Cecil, 1939, p. 181).

"That man is not contented with believing the Bible, but he fairly resolves, I think, to believe nothing *but* the Bible" (Hogarth on Samuel Johnson quoted in Krutch, 1944, p. 250).

"I consider myself a Hindu, Christian, Moslem, Jew, Buddhist, and Confucian" (Gandhi quoted in Peter, 1977, p. 450).

My own discovery, not original with me, but still my own, was that man has never at any time had faith in anything but his dreams, or in the dreams of his ancestors which he learned in a church (Goodenough, 1955, p. 176).

The best preacher is the heart
say the Jews of faith
The best teacher is time
The best book is the world
The best friend is God
(Carl Sandburg quoted by Golden, 1961, p. 46).

In the individuality of adulthood, there are many ways religion can be viewed. In these comments, we see such variety. They may specifically refer to faith, but they represent much broader perspectives on one's place in the world. As we will continue to see, personal religion is thus integrated with the rest of existence.

Alfred Adler (1969) defined "the three great basic problems of life [as] work and occupation, friends and social relations, love and marriage" (p. 97). Increasing age usually means more encounters with personal crisis; therefore, other tasks also enter the picture. In addition, there is always the continuing burden of clarifying one's values and maintaining a sense of worth and dignity. Although Adler's motives are central, they do not encompass all of life. People continually relate themselves to the larger sociocultural context as they try to locate themselves in the "scheme of things." We will therefore organize our understanding of religion in adult life around these broad personal, interpersonal, and sociocultural issues.

Despite the current surge of interest in life-span psychology, work on the middle years of life still lags. However, a few noteworthy remedying efforts have appeared (Allman and Jaffe, 1977; Levinson, Darrow, Klein, Levinson and McKee, 1978; Neugarten, 1968). The idea that religion may play an important role during this period is barely recognized. For example, the highly significant effort by Levinson and his colleagues (1978) ignores it completely. The backbone of church and synagogue life in the United States is certainly neither the young or the old—it is the great mass of the middle-aged. Nevertheless, psychologists usually study their problems without regard for the age of those involved in these matters, and unhappily the legacy left to us is a literature that fails to integrate time of life with the problems of this period.

We face one more basic issue. What are the age limits of adulthood? When does it begin? End? Levinson et al. (1978) suggest that early adulthood takes in the age range from seventeen to forty-five with middle adulthood extending this up to sixty-five years and late adulthood continuing past this time. To deal with the age range of seventeen to forty-five as a unit probably means engaging in research dealing largely with samples of college students under the age of twenty-two. Our focus is, of course, on adulthood, and we will make ours a problem-centered approach spanning the entire gamut of age from approximately twenty years onward.

RELIGIOUS BELIEF AND BEHAVIOR AMONG ADULTS

The Background and Meaning of Religious Beliefs

Before examining the functions of faith in adult life, we need to understand the nature and significance of religion to the average person. Tables 5-1 and 5-2 provide some basic information on the characteristics of religious people that form the backdrop of faith for the average American adult.

Many national samples of persons over eighteen years of age suggest there are both complex and changing views on the place of religion in our national life. Probably most graphic are polls that show that 94 to 98 percent of the populace affirm a belief in God (Princeton Religion Research Center, 1980; Rosten, 1975). When the United States was recently compared with eleven European countries, it demonstrated the highest incidence of God-belief, suggesting that a rather firm

TABLE 5-1. Selected Characteristics of Religiously Identified Christian Adults (3360 Protestants; 1449 Catholics)

	PROTESTANT	CATHOLIC
Sex: Male	42%	45%
Female	58	55
Race: White	81	96
Nonwhite	19	4
Age: 18–24	11	14
25–34	19	22
35–54	34	37
55 and over	37	28
Education: Less than		
High school graduate	39	32
High school graduate	17	53
At least some college	14	15
Occupation: Professional-business	21	21
Clerical and sales	22	30
Service	15	11
Manual workers	27	28
Farm workers	4	2
Not in labor force	11	8
Self-appraised strength of religious identification:		
Strong	55	52
Somewhat strong	13	13
Not very strong	33	35

Adapted from Roozen, D. A. *The Churched and the Unchurched in America.* Washington DC: Glenmary Research Center, 1978, pp. 16–25.

bedrock of faith exists in our nation. Still, acknowledgement of this basic position tells us little about other religious outlooks.

More pertinent than simply assuming the existence of a deity is the importance of religion in one's life. Surveys report that 72 percent of eighteen to twenty-four year olds claim that their faith is either "very" or "fairly" important in their lives. Among older samples, these numbers increase until they reach 91 percent for those of fifty years or more (Princeton Religion Research Center, 1980). Although these findings are similar for older persons on data gathered almost two decades ago, at that time 89 percent of the younger group felt this way. This suggests that religion may be lessening in importance among the more youthful segments of our society. A more current study by the Gallup organization, in which young adults were asked "Independently of whether you go to church or not, would you say you are a religious person?" revealed that 73 percent believed they were, while 22 percent considered themselves nonreligious. Only two percent claimed to be atheist. For the population as a whole, 81 percent affirmed their religiousness (Anderson, 1982).

In 1957, when national samples were asked if religion can answer today's

TABLE 5-2.   Selected Religious Attitudes and Activities and Life Satisfaction of Religious Adults[1, 2]

98 percent have at least one Bible in their home.
94 percent of those eighteen and older believe in God.
92 percent claim a religious preference
89 percent claim they engage in prayer.
69 percent claim they are church members.
57 percent state their beliefs are very important to them.
41 percent attend church weekly.

TRENDS WITH AGE	18 to 24	25 to 29	30 to 49	50 +
Average weekly church attendance (1978).	28%	31%	42%	48%
Report a "great deal" of confidence in the church or organized religion.	29	35	37	48
Religious belief is "very important."	38	51	55	71

Life Satisfaction of Churched and Unchurched Christians

	PROTESTANT		CATHOLIC	
	CHURCHED	UNCHURCHED	CHURCHED	UNCHURCHED
General happiness				
Very happy	39%	31%	34%	28%
Pretty happy	50	52	53	56
Not too happy	11	17	14	16
Marital happiness				
Very happy	71	61	71	67
Pretty happy	27	35	27	30
Not too happy	2	4	2	3
Work satisfaction				
Very satisfied	54	48	52	42
Moderately satisfied	34	38	36	38
A little dissatisfied	8	10	9	14
Very dissatisfied	3	5	3	6
Other satisfactions "a great deal"				
Where one lives	55	43	49	43
Family life	80	72	79	74
Friendships	76	65	71	61
Health	62	56	63	63

[1]Princeton Religion Research Center, *Religion in America 1979–1980.* Princeton, New Jersey.
[2]Roozen, D.A. *The Churched and the Unchurched in America.* Washington, DC: Glenmary Research Center, 1978.

problems, 81 percent felt it could. In 1981, those agreeing reduced to 65 percent (Gallup, 1981). It is, however, noteworthy that this problem-solving perspective for faith is connected to personal happiness. Only eight percent of those who consider themselves "not very happy" accept this position, but it is present in 49 percent of people who regard themselves as "very happy" (Gallup, 1981). We should further point out that the 65 percent of Americans who trust the churches represent a greater portion of the population than those affirming like confidence in any of our other institutions, whether it be the military, business, or even the Supreme Court (Princeton Religion Research Center, 1980).

These observations tell us that it is probably much easier to state a belief in God than to translate it into either personal spirituality or a sense that one can rely on religious institutions. Still cited research tells us that among adult Americans there is a fairly solid substrate of religious sentiment that may have great significance not only in their own personal lives, but also for their national life.

Religious Behavior

The truth of this last assertion is quite apparent when one surveys the religious behavior of Americans. For example, George Gallup tells us that 98 percent of homes have at least one Bible, 69 of every hundred adults claim to be church members, and 41 percent attend Sunday services weekly (see Table 5-2).

Even though church attendance declined from a 1958 high of 49 percent to its present level of 41 percent, this number is not uniform for all churches. There is evidence that the more conservative churches have been growing while their liberal conterparts seem to be declining slowly or maintaining a stable holding pattern (Chalfant, Beckley, and Palmer, 1981; Kelley, 1972). Churchgoing behavior is age-related with only 28 percent of eighteen to twenty-four year olds attending during an average week in 1978; however, about half (48 percent) of those fifty years and older are present at services (Princeton Religion Research Center, 1980).

We seem to be observing a core of about 40 to 50 percent of the population who identify very strongly with their faith. A much larger group whose spiritual inclinations are expressed less in formal religious behavior surround this "saving remnant." Such religious dispositions appear to increase with age.

Some people have viewed the charismatic movement as a youthful phenomenon in which much commitment and emotion are expressed. The facts indicate otherwise as more middle-aged and older persons affiliate with these groups than eighteen to twenty-four year olds (Princeton Religion Research Center, 1980).

A very significant personal religious activity that tells us much about how people respond spiritually is prayer. Table 5-2 indicates that 89 percent of our populace admit to private prayer (Princeton Religion Research Center, 1980). Estimates vary widely regarding the frequency of prayer, probably because most studies are not always clear as to the proportion of church members assessed. Locality, religious group, ethnic heritage, and class level may also be influencing factors. Given these considerations, it is not surprising that Moberg (1971) summarizes evidence suggesting that anywhere from 58 to 92 percent of church members claim they pray frequently. Argyle and Beit-Hallahmi (1975) cite research by Gorer to the effect that these propensities also grow stronger with age. There was an orderly increase in those reporting private prayer from 32 percent among thirty year olds to 72 percent by age seventy. This observation has been confirmed in other work (Marty, Rosenberg, and Greeley, 1968). Regardless of age, more women pray regularly than men (Argyle and Beit-Hallahmi, 1975).

The variety of religious behavior in which one can engage is surprisingly great. For example, only 16 percent of Americans are willing to state that they never read the Bible, but about 40 percent claim that they read it at least once a week (Marty, Rosenberg, and Greeley, 1968). These activities show no orderly relationship to age.

In another realm, by 1980 Americans were contributing over $80 billion annually to organized religion, and per capita donations ranged from approximately $80 in some churches to well over $700 in others (Bureau of the Census, 1981). Sums of this magnitude indicate a considerable formal religious involvement.

Scattered data are also available for other activities such as saying grace at meals, reading religious publications other than the Bible, obeying prescribed food and dietary rules, observing birth-control prohibitions, etc. Apparently, those behaviors requiring the least time, effort, and money are often the most practiced. The extent of their observance, however, still indicates a fairly solid religious commitment by the majority of adults. Our principal question, however, concerns the meaning and significance of these signs of religious adherence and devotion in other aspects of living. This is our task as we first examine religion in relation to Adler's "tasks of life."

WORK, JOB, AND OCCUPATION

For many centuries, work and economic progress have been blessed by the Judeo-Christian tradition. Even today individual worth remains associated with the idea of hard, honest, and dedicated labor. Historically, from its beginnings, Protestantism, justified individualism and capitalism in the same breath (Tawney, 1926), and Max Weber (1958) stressed work and achievement striving as moral and spiritual imperatives. Similar notions, however, existed much earlier among both Jews and Catholics (Green, 1959).

Achievement Motivation and the "Protestant Work Ethic"

Because Protestantism and work valuation are theoretically affiliated, sociologists of religion have implied that Protestants differ from Catholics and Jews in their economic outlooks and interpretations of work. Inclinations for the members of one religious group to be more positive or negative to their work situation or labor in general have been contradicted by other investigations. Ethnic and class differences appear of greater significance. There is thus no evidence that the so-called Protestant work ethic is restricted to Protestants (Blackwood, 1979; Greeley, 1963; Kim, 1977; Schuman, 1971).

The motivation to achieve has been posited as a major contributor to occupational success (McClelland, Atkinson, Clark, and Lowell, 1953; McClelland, 1961). Initial results suggested that Jews and Protestants were more motivated to achieve than Catholics; however, this was due to earlier independence training of children plus other factors such as culture and social class (McClelland,

1955; McClelland, Rindlisbacher, and deCharms, 1955). Bressler and Westoff (1963) also hypothesized that Catholics would reject achievement values and actually attain less financial success to the extent they had experienced a Catholic education. However, it was concluded that "the Catholic breadwinner, like other Americans, derives his orientations to worldly success from the norms of his several subcultures and the broader society" (p. 233).

Andrew Greeley (1963) also attempted to assess achievement strivings of Catholics relative to Protestants and Jews by studying the career plans and occupational values of college graduates. Again, no evidence was found to suggest less "economic rationality" on the part of Catholics than these other groups. Protestants and Catholics possessed similar aspirations. Where group differences were manifested, these often distinguished between Jews and Christians. Similar results are also reported by Christenson (1976).

Jewish-Christian Differences

Jewish-Christian distinctions have been well substantiated in regard to economic accomplishment (McClelland, 1961). For example, Jews tend to be over-represented in higher income and status occupations (professionals, managers, and proprieters) and underrepresented in lower job classifications (clerical, skilled, and unskilled workers) both for the population in general and for different cities (see Table 5-3) (Goldstein and Goldscheider, 1968; Sklare, 1971). When major religious bodies are compared in income and occupational prestige, Jews once again score higher along both of these dimensions than Catholics and a variety

TABLE 5-3.   Occupational Distribution for Jewish and Total Populations of the United States by Sex and for Various Religious Groups by Income and Occupational Prestige[1]

OCCUPATION	MALES		FEMALES	
	JEWISH POP.	TOTAL POP.	JEWISH POP.	TOTAL POP.
Professionals	20.7%	9.2%	17.9%	10.5%
Managers and proprietors	40.7	10.5	12.7	2.4
Clerical workers	4.5	8.1	41.5	27.2
Sales workers	20.9	7.4	18.3	6.2
Blue collar	13.2	64.8	9.5	53.7

DENOMINATION	OCCUPATIONAL PRESTIGE SCORES	INCOME
Protestant		
Baptist	37.21	8,693
Episcopalian	48.19	11,032
Lutheran	38.90	9,072
Methodist	41.23	10,103
Other denominations	38.33	Not available
Catholic	40.40	11,374
Jewish	48.89	13,340

[1]Adapted from Goldstein and Goldscheider (1968) and Wilson (1978).

of Protestant denominations; however, Episcopalians and Presbyterians are comparable to Jews (Wilson, 1978). Although McClelland (1961) feels that this phenomenon is not totally explainable on the basis of religion alone, he claims that American Jews manifest higher levels of achievement motivation than either Catholics or Protestants in general, and this may be due in part to Judaism's stress on individual self-reliance and personal responsibility in striving for "perfection in conduct for everyone" (p. 364).

It has been known for some time that Jews are disproportionately present among noted scientists and Nobel Prize winners (Levitan, 1960). This association of Jews with science has a long history (Roback, 1951) and could result from Judaism's emphasis on learning (Feuer, 1963) plus a troubled past of encounters with prejudice and discrimination (Rosen, 1959). Intellectual endeavors of a scholarly nature could not be banned as easily as had been the ownership of land and property, nor are they readily put aside when poverty dominates. This tradition might lead to greater scientific creativity and propensities among Jews than their Christian peers. Such was found by Lois-Ellin Datta (1967) when she studied applicants for the Westinghouse Science Talent Search. This study is presented in Research Box 5-1.

Religiosity Correlates of Economic Achievement

Since middle-class values extol the virtue of a strong work ethic, Russell Dynes (1955) examined the relationship between socioeconomic status and the church-sect typology. Those who affiliate with sects usually stand in opposition to established cultural values and may, by rejecting economic achievement, find themselves lower in socioeconomic status than church-oriented persons who fit the social order much better. This view gained some support, but we still do not know if those who embraced a sect-like faith and ideas did so because of less education and related background factors. In this instance, religion could be a salve to the economically deprived. A personally involved, sect-like faith may meet their needs much better than the formalized perspective of the churches that is more in harmony with the work-success values of the middle and upper classes in our society.

A somewhat different tack was taken by Blackwood (1979), who found God belief to be unrelated to the traditional work ethic. He concluded that there is "little religious basis for the work ethic and a corresponding insignificant role for religion in effecting change in commitment to the work ethic over time" (p. 249)

Another research avenue concerns the "professional self-concept," or how a people regard themselves relative to the occupation to which they aspire. Walberg (1967) suggested that those entering the teaching profession need to identify with the authoritarian requirements of the teaching role and that such control components are found in the established religions. This led to the hypothesis that persons affiliated with religious groups would possess more positive professional self-concepts than atheists or agnostics, whose ideologies might conflict with authoritarian teaching motifs. Support was found for this view, but may reflect a broad tendency for religiously involved persons to be generally more comfortable with themselves since they are in the American cultural mainstream. Those embracing agnostic and atheistic views are likely to be at variance with conformist themes in our culture, and thus show a quality of tension that could lower their self-concepts.

RESEARCH BOX 5-1.   *Datta, Lois-Ellin. "Family Religious Background and Early Scientific Creativity."* American Sociological Review, *1967, 32, 626–35.*

The author suggests that there are three hypotheses associating religion and science. The first is based on the ideas of Max Weber and suggests that asceticism and the questioning of authority are associated with Calvinism and should support an affiliation of religion with science. Baptists, Lutherans, and Methodists are regarded as illustrating this form of religion. This grouping was designated Protestant I. The second hypothesis claims that the crucial element is liberality of thought, and it is felt this tendency is found among Congregationalists, Friends, Episcopalians, Presbyterians, and Unitarians; this grouping was designated Protestant II. The third hypothesis infers the critical values to be liberality and hedonism, characteristics said to be basic to Judaism.

After noting many shortcomings and problems in research on religion and scientific creativity, 573 youth who participated in the 1963 Westinghouse Science Talent Search and who scored above the eightieth percentile on a science aptitude test were selected for study. On the basis of ratings by judges of the scientific creativity suggested by science projects, the youth were divided into three groups: Group I—high potential creativity; Group II—moderate potential creativity; and Group III—low potential creativity.

The two Protestant groups were essentially equivalent in scientific creativity, though the percentages for Protestant I increased as one went from the highest to the lowest creativity category; no similar tendency was found for the Protestant II group. The Jewish sample revealed markedly higher percentages than both Protestant groups for all categories of creativity. In the highest creativity category the percentage of Jews was three times that for the Protestants, and was successively lower in the middle and low potential creativity categories. This suggests support for the third hypothesis. These findings were maintained when controls were introduced for socioeconomic status and size of home town. Comparisons with the religious backgrounds of college seniors showed no correlation between choosing science and religion; hence, it is felt that the findings of this study may at best be generalized to other samples of high scholastically achieving adolescents.

Work and Form of Personal Faith

It is clear that economic and occupational orientations are not associated with religion in general. However, another alternative is possible. Looking at forms of personal faith, the intrinsic-committed and extrinsic-consensual differentiation becomes relevant to our discussion. It will be remembered that extrinsic-consensual religion has been described as utilitarian and self-serving in nature. Such tendencies may carry over into the realm of job and career achievement. In other words, intrinsic-committed individuals ought to value signs of economic success less and humanistic goals more than their extrinsic-consensual peers. In one study, concern with status, achievement, materialism, income, and security affiliate with extrinsic-consensual leanings. In contrast, instrinsic-committed leanings associate most with social, altruistic, and religious values (Spilka, 1977).

Studying a large sample of middle-aged persons, Kivett, Watson, and Busch (1977) also focused on intrinsic religion but did not include measures of its extrinsic counterpart. Their main concern was the perception by persons forty-five to sixty-five years old of the degree to which they control their own lives (internal control) as opposed to feeling they are victims of circumstance (external control). They found intrinsic faith and perceptions of personal, internal control were associated. Those who had occupations in which they had power over others or machines and equipment also had high levels of internal control, so a complex of internal control, intrinsic faith, and environmental occupational control went together.

SUMMARY

Unhappily, research on Adler's first great task of life, job and occupation, is sparse relative to religion. Nevertheless, Campbell (1981) points out, among other things, that "standard of living, and work (have) the greatest influence in accounting for the level of satisfaction people feel with their life in general" (p. 49). Gutmann (1977) cites a study of sixty-two cultures by Abarbanel in which older people replace their decreasing economic role with increased involvement in religion. Other investigations also claim that religion grows in importance as one ages, but most agree that this primarily affects blacks and women (Britton and Britton, 1972; Jackson, 1970; Orbach, 1961). That religion may be a substitute for lessened meaningful work and job involvement is an idea worthy of more investigation.

SOCIAL RELATIONSHIPS

According to Adler, the second major task of adult life concerns interpersonal relationships. The overall picture of social interaction and friendships in contemporary life is not what most would consider ideal. Levinson and his associates (1978) claim that a "close friendship with a man or woman is rarely experienced by American men" (p. 335). They suggest that middle life involves a turning inward, a concern with the "balance between the needs of the self and the needs of society" (p. 242). The possible role of religious doctrine and spirituality is noted, but not analyzed, and we remain in limbo regarding what looks like adult social isolation.

There is a strong element of potential social involvement in simply associating oneself with a church. Attendance at religious functions usually puts one into contact with others of similar outlook and characteristics (Gans, 1967; Warner, Meeker, and Eells, 1960). We have observed in Chapter 12 that connections to a church can act to socialize a person into the community with regular churchgoers appearing to be better off psychologically than nonattenders.

Social Interest and Trust

One indicator of good interpersonal outlooks and behavior is degree of positive social interest and trust in others. There is some contradiction among the studies examining these variables. In a study over thirty years old, Kirkpatrick

(1949) found that the more religiously conservative churchgoers claim to be, the less humanitarian are their social sentiments. When religion is distinguished in terms of intrinsic-committed and extrinsic-consensual forms of faith plus other spiritual expressions, social interest, among adults twenty-two to fifty-six years of age, is associated with the first orientation (Edwards and Wessels, 1980). In contrast, social interest declines as extrinsic tendencies increase. A similar pattern was noted with empathy, or understanding of others. The concept of social interest employed in this work was based on that of Alfred Adler, which stresses interpersonal feeling, insight, and social understanding.

Turning to a related concept—namely, trust and faith in people—Pargament, Steele, and Tyler (1979) used a measure of expected favorableness of interactions with others and observed no ties with either intrinsic faith or frequency of church attendance. Spilka and Mullin (1977) also employed a questionnaire dealing with "faith in people" and, at best, found it weakly related to intrinsic religion.

The foregoing research also examined a variable called "comfortable interpersonal distance"; namely, how close a person is willing to let another approach before becoming uncomfortable. Here it was found that the more extrinsic and consensual individuals are, the greater the distance placed between themselves and others. The opposite tendency was noted for intrinsic-committed persons. A significant influencing factor is the similarity or difference of the referent individual in relation to the person making the distance judgments. Extrinsic-consensual inclinations affiliate with increasing interpersonal distance from others who were older and lower in status than the judge. No such trends were found with intrinsic-committed persons. These findings could mean that those possessing the latter kind of faith treat others as individuals and do not tend to define people in terms of status and age categories. In opposition, perceptions of others as individuals are less likely to be present when an extrinsic-consensual orientation dominates. Another possibility is that those embracing an intrinsic-committed perspective attribute positive characteristics to people in general, while those with an extrinsic-consensual orientation see positive traits primarily in people who are extrinsically useful.

There is a lack of direct research evaluating religion and interpersonal outlooks and behavior; however, a great many studies have been directed at the closely related phenomena of religious and racial prejudice and how one's spiritual orientation affects such attitudes. In addition, more recently another dimension of social responsivity has come under scrutiny—namely, altruistic and helping behavior. Both of these areas possess a strong moral quality and are discussed in Chapter Eleven.

LOVE AND MARRIAGE

We now come to the third of Adler's three great tasks of life, that of establishing a life-long love, sexual, and marital relationship. Psychological research on love has only recently begun, and has to date primarily been confined to the nonreligious realm, often being restricted to questions of emotional arousal in physiological terms. Although such research is developing rapidly as a legitimate field for research in social psychology, its application to the psychology of religion seems premature (Rubin, 1973; Walster and Walster, 1978). We must therefore confine ourselves to a literature concerned with sexual behavior and marital relationships.

Sexual Behavior: The Religious View

Not many years ago a book was written titled *The Intimate Enemy* (Bach and Wyden, 1969). This title describes well the long and troubled association of religion and sexual behavior. Indeed, their bond has been intimate with theologies and religious institutions restricting sexual activity at every turn. In the simplest terms, sexual responses, including thoughts, are supposed to be curtailed, if not prohibited, until one's faith bestows its blessing on the marriage covenant. Circumscription frequently follows the couple into the marriage bed, especially among the more orthodox religious bodies. The purpose of sexual contact as well as its method and frequency may be defined. This is a terribly important business surrounded by threats of sin, guilt, and punishment. Still, biological nature is with us and nowhere is reality harsher to the classical religious image than where sex is concerned. It was apparently always so, but churches never ceased to impose their will in this realm.

Religion and Sex in Marriage

The establishment of a mutually satisfying, life-long marital relationship is probably the best test of how people confront Adler's third great task of life. Marriage as an ideal state and the only one in which procreation should occur has always been extolled by the Judeo-Christian tradition. Some conflict existed in medieval Catholicism regarding the evaluation of the sexual act even among spouses, but this seemed to be put aside fairly quickly, and silence about such relations was preferred (Hunt, 1974). The modern religious mood has been one of growing liberalism in which sexual pleasure without intention of producing offspring has become acceptable (Tavris and Sadd, 1975).

Sexual activity   Despite religious liberalization regarding sexual behavior, it has usually been theorized that the effect of religion should be both negative and restrictive. Some studies suggest this might be true, but others contradict such an eventuality. Kinsey et al. (1948) point out that religiously active males of all groups engage in intercourse less frequently than nonreligious men. Hunt (1974) claims the latter reveal coital rates 20 to 30 percent higher than those of the most religiously involved. In Kinsey's work on females, it is therefore unclear why religion seems unrelated to frequency of sexual activity. There are some indications that by the time one is over thirty the rates for the devout and nondevout are the same, with about one-third of the first group peferring sexual relations more often. Approximately one-half of the nondevout desire more frequent sex; however, this difference does not seem associated with marital happiness.

The hypothesis has existed for a long time that religion might relate to a lower incidence of orgasm among religious than nonreligious women. To date, however, no researcher has found differences in orgastic frequency either among women of different religious groups or of differing levels of devoutness (Hunt, 1974; Kinsey et al., 1953; Tavris and Sadd, 1975).

The search for variations in sexual behavior that are related to religiosity has not resulted in any noteworthy findings. Some data suggest restriction in alternative sexual behavior on the part of more religiously active marrieds, meaning less sexual experimentation in these relationships, but again this limitation is not of fundamental significance (Tavris and Sadd, 1975).

Sexual behavior and marital satisfaction   The connection between sexual activity and marital satisfaction has also never been fully clear. Wallin and Clark (1964) observed that religiosity might reduce the impact of a woman's lack of sexual gratification on her general assessment of marital happiness. The *Redbook Report on Female Sexuality* (Tavris and Sadd, 1975), however, claims that very religious women report greater happiness and satisfaction with marital sex than either moderately religious or nonreligous women. Higher proportions also state their contentment with frequency of sexual activity and claim to be orgasmic more often than their less devout peers. Frankness in sexual communication with their husbands also appears greater, and in summary, they feel that they are happier personally and more of them affirm that their marriage is good or very good.

Considering the usually hypothesized repressive role of religion relative to sex, these finding were initially surprising. Suggestions that the most religious women might "not know what they are missing," or are responding to the questionnaire in a socially desirable way, do not seem convincing. Tavris and Sadd (1975) suggest that these women may have lower sexual expectations and thus be more realistic and less willing to believe widely advertised fantasies about sexual gratification.

Whatever the reason for the apparently greater marital satisfaction of more religious persons, it is a finding that has been around for some time (Burgess and Cottrell, 1939). Although Dyer and Luckey (1961) found no differences in happiness ratings among religious groups, Chalfant, Beckley, and Palmer (1981) report satisfaction was highest for Jews and those affiliated with liberal churches. To resolve these questions, more needs to be known about the samples in these different studies and the role of rapidly changing attitudes and feelings in the last two decades. For example, Landis (1960) observed a tie between the marital happiness of parents and one's own marriage. The perceived happiness of the marriage of parents might have provided a model for the marriage into which one has entered. Since it is fairly likely that the religious feelings of spouses tend to be similar, among the more religious, who probably come from religious homes, there may be a supportive complex of perceptions leading to increased marital satisfaction.

RELIGION AND DIVORCE

The picture presented above suggests a positive association between religiosity and marital harmony. A more exacting assessment of this relationship might come from examination of divorce statistics. Here, again, religion seems to have beneficial results in that marital stability goes with increasing religious activity and identification. Generally, the supportive function of a church is found in traditional rules that glorify the marriage state as a permanent union. McGuire (1981) further points out that the various faiths pretty much agree on gender roles—namely, the what, who, and how of male and female behavior, outlooks, responsibilities, and correct relations with members of the opposite sex. These functions of institutionalized religion take place within an economic and social context and under daily stresses that usually take precedence over spiritual aspirations when it comes to marriage. The unfortunately all-too-common reaction is divorce.

Today, one in two marriages ends in divorce, but religion does exercise a restraining influence on such drastic action. Surveys of research reveal religiously identified persons have a divorce rate about one-third that of unaffiliated peers (Benson, 1960; Vernon, 1968). Despite the strong Catholic position against divorce, the Catholic rate is slightly above those for Protestants and Jews. The latter apparently possess the most stable marriages, a tendency probably related to the emphasis placed on family solidarity in Judaism (Wilson, 1978). The situation with regard to Catholicism, which also surrounds family life with strong theological supports, has been changing rapidly. By 1971, a majority of Catholics expressed strong disagreement with the church's position on divorce and remarriage, and this trend has undoubtedly grown during the 1970s.

The data are in conflict when it comes to understanding how religious conservatism affects divorce rates, for though traditional Catholics and orthodox Jews show a low likelihood of divorce, Catholics manifest higher separation rates than Protestants (Chalfant, Beckley, and Palmer, 1981; Goldstein and Goldscheider, 1968). It is also known that the most conservative Protestant groups—Baptists and the sects—have the highest incidence of divorce. Lutherans, a fairly moderate body, evidenced the lowest incidence of divorce in one major national study (Chalfant, Beckley, and Palmer, 1981). One must infer from this literature that class and ethnic factors greatly confound the issue. When these influences are joined with rapidly increasing signs of marital instability and breakup across all religious groups, it is difficult to offer any definitive conclusions. However, the trends are still there, although not as strong as religionists desire, for marital happiness and stability to be associated with church involvement and commitment.

A related and interesting problem is that persons who claim no religious affiliation are between two and three times more likely to have never been married than those who are church affiliated (Chalfant, Beckley and Palmer, 1981). A number of possible explanations merit exploration. For example, the nonaffiliated may be among the youngest persons in the samples, those least likely to have established a church attachment or to be married. They could be the most educated who usually marry later, factors that also relate to separation from religious institutions and ideas.

Religiously defined groups are an integral part of the social structure within which people interact, hence a person probably has a much greater chance of meeting peers of similar religious background and outlook than others who differ along these lines. This is probably most true in early life and it is possible that when one is ready to marry he/she may first look toward traditional sources of mates as one avenue to establish a harmonious and lasting marital relationship. In this regard, parents and their religious friends could serve as models for their children.

The foregoing implies that those with no religious preference are unlikely to utilize these channels. Since most Americans are church affiliated, those outside of the system would have a lower probability of relating to members of the opposite sex in such a way as to further marriage prospects. There is also the possibility, as was shown in Chapter Twelve, that persons who are not religiously affiliated are less conforming, even to the point of being psychosocially disturbed. These characteristics, in themselves, are impediments to marriage. As we can see, the situation is far more complex than appears at first glance.

Interfaith Marriage: The Definitional Problem

On the surface, it would seem simple to define interfaith marriages by labeling the religious identification or preference of spouses. This does not consider either the degree of commitment of the individual parties to their own faith or discrepancies in intensity of personal religious involvement. In addition, religious labels may also reflect great or small theological differences relative to cultural variations among the churches themselves. One of the authors knows a Korean Missouri Synod Lutheran who lived most of his early life in Korea and who has married an American Methodist woman. We could also observe a like distance between two spouses with mainstream American upbringing, one of whom is Southern Baptist and the other United Presbyterian, who may or may not vary much in their church attachment. How do these possibilities compare to Catholic-Jewish or Protestant-Jewish marriages?

Considering the variety of Protestant groups and their potentially immense differences in theological conservatism, when does a mixed marriage really merit consideration as truly of an interfaith nature? Finally, a marriage could be defined as statistically interreligious, yet one of the parties may have converted to the other's faith either nominally—as is frequently done for purposes of marriage—or possibly with the deep commitment of the true convert. Again, one of the authors is familiar with a young couple representing two different Protestant backgrounds, yet both spouses have made an extremely strong commitment through conversion to a Pentacostal sect. These are only some of the complexities that are frequently overlooked by researchers in this area, so the data to which we refer is very open to challenge (Yinger, 1968a; 1968b).

INTERMARRIAGE TRENDS AND POSSIBLE BASES

Intermarriage Among Jews

There has been a steady increase in rates of intermarriage over the last fifty years. In general, by the 1960s for all religious groups there were, percentage-wise, about twice as many interfaith marriages as occurred in the 1930s (Bumpass, 1970). Much has been made of the observation that intermarriage has occurred least between Jews and Christians, yet by the late 1960s and early 1970s the percent of Jews intermarrying was fifteen times higher than in the first decade of the twentieth century (Reiss, 1976). Yinger (1968a), however, points out that only 3.7 percent of Jews had intermarried as opposed to 12.1 percent of Catholics and 4.5 percent of Protestants.

The prohibition against intermarriage by Jews seems to be breaking down, yet it still functions as a strong force within Jewish communities. Among the factors influencing interfaith liaisons by Jews are sex, education, parentage, orthodoxy, and the proportion of Jews relative to the larger community (Berman, 1968; Rosenthal, 1963).

More Jewish males than females marry outside of their faith, a finding that might reflect stronger familial and religious ties among Jewish women. Data generally suggest a weakening of spiritual attachments with increasing education and this correlates with increasing intermarriage yielding rates for college-educated Jews three to four times higher than among those with a high school education (Goldstein and Goldscheider, 1968; Rosenthal, 1963; Yaffe, 1968). This tendency also holds with regard to parental education, which undoubtedly correlates with that of the child. It probably also represents a home in which religion counts for less than might be true where parents have less schooling.

If one considers Jewish religious education as opposed to its secular form, the intermarriage situation is reversed as those exposed most to these influences are least likely to contract interfaith marriages. More Jewish education ties to stronger religious identification, and, especially among Jews aged forty and older, the incidence of intermarriage declines sharply as one goes from a reform to an orthodox orientation (Goldstein and Goldscheider, 1968).

Another influential factor is whether the person and his/her parents are native or foreign born, with native-born offspring of native-born parents showing the highest likelihood of intermarrying (Rosenthal, 1963). Finally, although there is some controversy about this issue, the smaller the available pool of Jews in an area from which to select one's mate, the more intermarriage will take place (Berman, 1968; Rosenthal, 1963).

The Jewish intermarriage situation probably well illustrates what can occur when social and cultural circumstances combine to break down the walls created by discrimination and a history of exclusiveness often generated more by fear than by positive group identification.

Intermarriage Among Christians

Many of the factors that lead to intermarriage by Jews are also found among Catholics and Protestants (Wilson, 1978). The smaller one's own religious group relative to other faiths in the social milieu, the more mixed marriages take place. These tendencies also increase with acculturation to general American society (e.g., native versus foreign born for self and parents), and with increased education among Catholics, but not Protestants. In contrast, as with Jews, the greater exposure one receives to religious education from a parent church, the less one will go outside of his/her group for a mate. Although Jewish men are more likely to enter mixed marriages than Jewish women, sex appears inconsequential among Protestants; however, Catholic women seem more vulnerable to intermarriage than their male counterparts (Wilson, 1978). One study of Catholic university students indicates a greater willingness to marry outside of their faith than Protestants or Jews, yet less readiness to change their faith (Landis and Landis, quoted in Rosten, 1975). Catholic women who enter such mixed marriages may still feel that they remain Catholics and follow their religion because they may sign a traditional antenuptial agreement that affirms that their children will be brought up as Catholics. It is evident that mixed marriages are increasing in frequency, and this must mean a growing breakdown in religio-ethnic community solidarity; however, all the motives and circumstances underlying these developments are not apparent.

Correlates of interfaith marriage   If there is one finding about mixed marriages that has been repeatedly confirmed, it is the relative instability of these unions. In a series of studies on Catholic-Protestant marriages, divorce rates ranged from two to five times greater than was true of marriages within these separate faiths (Reiss, 1976). When Catholics marry others who possess no religious affiliation, the probability of divorce is greatest among all mixed marriages (Wilson, 1978). However, much variation exists in the stability of Protestant interdenominational liaisons, suggesting that one cannot infer that these unions are consistently less stable than intradenominational marriages (Bumpass and Sweet, 1972).

The outcome of mixed marriages involving Jews is similar to that cited for Catholics and Protestants. When one partner is Jewish, divorce rates are five to six times higher than when both partners are Jewish (Ellman, 1971). As might have been expected, Jews who intermarry are those with least commitment to their faith (Goldstein and Goldscheider, 1968), yet their high rate of divorce still implies a divisive influence, although a latent one, for religion.

A caution ought to be introduced at this point. Religion may not be the main element leading to family instability. One major factor is the age of those marrying. A larger number of younger people enter interfaith marriages, and marital breakdown is most frequent among this group regardless of religious considerations. This also relates to less income, more reliance on parents, and even residence in a parental home, all of which lead to divorce (Kenkel, 1966).

Variations in religious background and commitment between spouses mean different expectations about marriage, sex roles, economic and social relationships, and the place and treatment of children. Landis and Landis (Rosten, 1975) claim that a major, if not the most important, source of conflict is the role of religion in childhood education. This seems to be of special significance if one of the parents is Catholic. It is, however, found in all mixed marital combinations, and may be a contributor to the fact that interfaith marriages have a high probability of remaining childless (Berman, 1968).

The best solution for a lasting mixed marriage seems to be conversion of one of the members to the faith of the other (Rosten, 1975). When this takes place, the evidence is that many, if not most, converting members were not very committed to their original faith and are unlikely to increase in adherence to the new religion (Gordon, 1964). Franzblau (1965) claims that 95 percent of contemporary conversions to Judaism take place for marital reasons, and such converts will probably not change their ways.

Although intermarriage is increasing among all groups, it still appears to be a source of conflict. In a time of growing marital discord, religious differences make their contribution even when age and other influences are controlled (Reiss, 1976).

RELIGION, MARRIAGE AND CHILDREN

Religiously and culturally, one of the main, if not the prime purpose of marriage, is considered to be procreation. The Judeo-Christian tradition stresses the scriptural commandment, "Be fruitful and multiply." In 1968, Pope Paul VI reaffirmed the Catholic church's stand against artificial means of birth control. Hirsch

(1925) states the classic Jewish position that "nature and God had ordained the human family should be maintained by the birth of a new generation" (p. 179). Furthermore, "a marriage that was not blessed by children, according to the old Jewish law, could be dissolved" (p. 185). Most Protestant bodies also strongly support the family as a child-bearing and rearing institution, but leave the issue of having children up to the parents. There is little doubt, however, that Judaism and Christianity see the parental role as essential to adult self-realization.

Birth Control

Despite the position of Catholicism on birth control, Catholic couples, including those who adhere to many formal practices, continue to deviate in increasing numbers from church birth-control teachings (Rosten, 1975). By 1970, approximately 70 percent of Catholic women were employing disapproved forms of birth control, and this number was growing at a rapid rate. Between 1955 and 1970, those using the accepted rhythm method had reduced by 50 percent, and utilization of no birth control means had dropped even more (Rosten, 1975).

Paralleling these trends, despite the Pope's 1968 stand, are indications of growing disagreement by priests on birth control. In 1971, 41 percent dissented from the church's position, and this tendency increased the younger the priest was, reaching 64 percent for those under thirty-nine years of age (Rosten, 1975). Almost a third of all priests (31 percent) had personally given permission for the use of artificial means of birth control. For the youngest groups, this percentage reached 45, and 52 percent of these felt the church would "someday officially approve the use of artificial methods of birth control" (Rosten, 1975, p. 371). Regarding the use of the birth-control pill, which had recently come into vogue, 80 percent of Catholics under the age of thirty-five favored its use (Rosten, 1975).

Family Size and Planning

Even with liberalization, Catholics are still more averse to family planning and birth control than Protestants and Jews. Differences are narrowing as 83 percent of Catholics approve making birth-control information available to married persons who desire such. For Protestants and Jews, the percentages were 88 and 98, respectively about a decade ago (Rosten, 1975). The birth control issue is thus essentially dead.

If we examine family statistics by rel: gous group, the traditional Catholic attitude is still evidenced in larger families than exist among Protestants and Jews, the latter having the fewest children (Janssen and Hauser, 1980; Wilson, 1978). The differences are not great, and the average size of the Catholic family continues to decrease. These data are affected by other considerations such as education, class level, and religious commitment. Generally in the population, as one goes down the class ladder, larger families are found, but this is reversed among Catholics. Family size also reduces for all faiths, with increasing education of the spouses; this further demonstrates the often-found conflict between religious teachings and secular education (Wilson, 1978). As expected, this trend is also reversed with religious education and orthodoxy among Catholics (Walters and Bradley, 1971).

Overviewing this research on Adler's third great task of life, love and marriage, the problem is, as we have so frequently mentioned, extremely complex and involved. This is, unfortunately, a weak excuse for treating faith in shallow terms. Essentially nowhere do we find form of personal faith considered relative to sexual behavior, marital satisfaction and harmony, parent-child relations, and the concept of love. No research on love per se appears to have been undertaken. This is an area needing sophisticated research, particularly because of the significance of marriage and family life in the Western religious tradition.

RELIGION AND THE QUALITY OF LIFE

Adler's formulation of the major responsibilities of living leads individually, and in concert, to a further all-encompassing consideration—namely, the quality of one's life. We know that job satisfaction, good interpersonal relationships, and a happy marriage and love relationship are central components of a sense of well-being (Campbell, Converse, and Rodgers, 1976). The role of religion in creating or maintaining a similar personal perspective is much less well documented, yet it is often taken for granted.

Life Satisfaction and Happiness

In a national sample of persons ranging from eighteen to over seventy-five years old, Campbell and his co-workers (1976) examined some seventeen areas contributing to life satisfaction. Religion seemed to stand by itself, surprisingly independent of work, marriage, and social life. Still about a quarter of the respondents chose religion as "one of the two most important domains of life" (p. 83). Despite this, it was handled in a cursory manner, with the implication that it is of significance to many people, but not of enough note for these researchers to have paid much attention to it. This trend continues in a later work (Campbell, 1981), where it is claimed without research evidence that religion may have important implications for many aspects of living, but probably has "no influence on a person's satisfaction with family life" (p. 103). We are thus left with some assent to the significance of religion for life satisfaction, but little more.

The research literature is both unclear and contradictory regarding religion in middle and later life. Many studies suggest increasing religious interest and activity as one ages, but by no means is this a general finding (Maves, 1971; Palmore, 1968). If there were a clear trend indicating growing spiritual inclinations, we could infer their potential for maintaining or increasing personal contentment and happiness. The available data suggest that it would be risky to draw such a conclusion.

One survey of research on faith in the middle years claims that those with clearly established religious frameworks reveal greater personal satisfaction than their peers who lack a well-defined faith. In addition, the former also look forward to retirement with less apprehension (Miller, 1962 cited in Maves, 1971). Indirect positive evidence about the association of religious involvement with happiness also comes from national studies by George Gallup and his polling organization. Apparently, the church-affiliated feel rather good about their attachments. One can read further into these observations a connection between such affiliations and self-esteem (Gallup and Poling, 1980).

RESEARCH BOX 5-2   Pargament, K. I.; Steele, R. E.; and Tyler, F. B. "Religious Participation, Religious Motivation, and Psychosocial Competence." *Journal for the Scientific Study of Religion*, 1979, 18, 412–19.

Theorizing that religion would be a significant factor in the psychosocial functioning of adults, these researchers administered a variety of psychological tests to 133 church and synagogue members from four mainline Protestant churches, four conservative synagogues, and four Catholic churches. There were forty-four Catholics, thirty-nine Jews, and fifty Protestants ranging in age from twenty-four to sixty-three in the sample. Measures of intrinsic religious orientation were combined with scales assessing a variety of attitudes toward oneself, others, and sources or loci of control in life. Four groups varying in religious activity and motivation were created by combining church attendance and the intrinsic motivation scores. These were high church attenders scoring either high or low on intrinsic motivation and infrequent church attenders scoring similarly on the intrinsic scale. Comparison of these groups revealed that:

1. Frequent attenders are both more satisfied with their congregations and perceive God as exerting more control in life than do infrequent attenders.

2. Similar findings were observed for those high in intrinsic religious motivation; however, it should be noted that church attendance and an intrinsic orientation are positively related.

3. High intrinsic religious motivation is associated with indicators of greater psychosocial competence, more of a sense of personal and God control, and less of a feeling of control by powerful others and chance.

4. Those low in intrinsic motivation show most feelings of control by others and chance, and further reveal the least positive views of themselves and others.

It was concluded that church participation and an intrinsic religious perspective have similar significance among Catholics, Jews, and Protestants. In addition, these factors are associated with increased personal satisfaction and psychosocial competence.

Another major research effort with like conclusions was conducted among women. Working through the popular magazine *Redbook*, Shaver, Lenauer, and Sadd (1980) obtained a sample of 65,000 women who responded to a 97-item questionnaire regarding the place of religion in their lives. A sample of 2,500 women similar to the American female population demonstrated that those who were either most or least religious reported the greatest degree of happiness and the fewest physical and mental-health symptoms. Women who considered themselves "slightly religious" manifested the highest levels of unhappiness and symptom presence. These may also be the women who are in most doubt regarding their faith, and, if so, it may not be religion per se that ties to happiness but rather assurance and confidence in their spiritual belief system.

One of the factors mediating happiness may be a sense of having power or the ability to influence events and persons in significant positions. Cardwell (1980) studied such feelings in relation to church attendance among Mormons and observed that powerlessness declined as church attendance increased. This implies that perceived competence grows with involvement in church and religious activities. Powerlessness is a central component of alienation, and other work confirms reductions in both of these tendencies with strong religious commitments (Minton and Spilka, 1976). An illustration of similar findings has been provided by Pargament, Steele, and Tyler (1979). This research is discussed in Research Box 5-2.

These studies tell us that commitment to religion seems to relate to the making of favorable attributions to oneself and to others. Self-esteem is positively affected as is a sense of personal control over life.

A controversial finding that definitely needs additional verification has been obtained by Reynolds and Nelson (1981). Exploring social and psychological factors that relate to survival among institutionalized elderly, chronically ill patients, these researchers found religion and life satisfaction associated with longevity. Those who died within a year after the initial data were gathered tended to be less religious and, among other factors, showed a lower degree of personal satisfaction. In any event, the importance of religion to the elderly has been repeatedly affirmed (Moberg, 1965), and Research Box 5-3 demonstrates some special problems in measuring this commitment.

RESEARCH BOX 5-3.   Mindell, C. H., and Vaughan, C. E. "A Multidimensional Approach to Religiosity and Disengagement." *Journal of Gerontology, 1978, 33,* 103–108.

In some studies, church attendance among the elderly is less than among their middle-aged and younger cohorts. Although this might suggest less religiosity, it has been interpreted as indicative of a growing physical limitation due to poor health. In this work, 106 elderly persons living with their children or grandchildren were studied with respect to two aspects of religion: (1) organizational activity as indicated by church attendance, and (2) nonorganizational behavior that includes personal religious feeling, listening to religious programs on radio or television, and personal prayer plus the belief that their faith has helped them understand life.

Most of the sample did not attend church frequently, and although low to moderate in organizational religiosity, they were highly religious in the nonorganizational sense. When the sample was divided into those who showed high and low levels of health impairment, the groups did not differ in degree of organizational involvement. This was explained on the basis of their residing with close relatives who could provide transportation to and from church. Both groups, however, showed high levels of nonorganizational religiosity, with the high-level impaired group showing more such activity than the low-level impaired group.

Religion and Coping with Life Crisis

This last study points up another fact of life—namely, that increasing age is likely to bring with it more and more experience with personal crisis and tragedy. In the chapter on Religion and Death, we observed that religion often serves as a resource for the bereaved and those expecting death. Among younger, severely and permanently injured individuals it can also offer satisfactory interpretations regarding what has been or is occurring (Bulman and Wortman, 1977). In like manner, O'Brien (1982) found that patients on long-term hemodialysis with positive religious outlooks adjusted best to their distressing circumstances.

Argyle and Beit-Hallahmi (1975) claim that religion is helpful to the disabled in at least three ways: (1) it aids acceptance of physical handicap; (2) it provides support in the face of pain; and (3) it buttresses an individual through the long and frustrating process of rehabilitation. Behind these roles seems to be the fundamental religious motives of achieving meaning, a sense of control over life, plus support for one's self-esteem. What has happened to the person is seen as part of a larger persepctive, a spiritual one, which offers understanding and justifies constructive action (Jackson, 1967). In the last analysis, this translates into hope.

Crisis can be a spur to religion because, as Fichter (1981) notes, "religious reality (may be) the only way to make sense out of pain and suffering" (p. 20). This could be one avenue through which the nonreligious person gains a religious outlook. Still, the inclination to use one's faith when confronted by tragedy comes more easily to those who turned to religion in similar past circumstances. There is also the suggestion that this is most true for the intrinsically religious (Fichter, 1981).

An interesting question concerns the possible influence of faith on the basic physiological responses people make when stressed. King and Funkenstein (1957) claim that more conventionally religious persons manifest norepinephrine-like cardiovascular reactions under stress. Such bodily responses have been associated with the outward expression of anger. In contrast, less religious individuals reveal a tendency to demonstrate an epinephrine-like reaction, or one said to be commonly found in states of fear and anxiety. Implied is the possibility that religion is a support for arousal of control motivation where its lack might result in a turning into oneself and a more passive response pattern.

The meaning of these findings is unclear, for religion is not supposed to sponsor the overt expression of anger, but rather its suppression in instructions to "turn the other cheek" (Bateman and Jensen, 1958). Some might argue that outletting rather than turning in rage is psychosomatically better and therefore healthier. It is also possible that religion, by providing a framework for meaning, denies or reduces fear and anxiety? These are ideas for future research to assess. We are also unable to state which pattern of body response is best for the person in the long run.

A final consideration relating to the elderly is worthy of theoretical note—namely, that the tendency of older people to be more religious than their younger counterparts might result from their being reared in a different world in which religion was valued more. Those were also times when less was known about many kinds of crises, hence meaning and control from naturalistic sources was often lacking. Esteem must have suffered correspondingly, and a greater need probably existed for the development and maintenance of a religious world-view in which pain and suffering became comprehensible and possibly controllable through the expression of one's faith in a just and merciful God.

Once again, the research has been neither prolific nor definitive in determining the role of religion in either establishing the quality of life or dealing with crisis. With minor contradiction, the evidence suggests that meaning and hope involving religion contributes to life satisfaction and happiness. In the face of death and severe personal tragedy, its role is clearly positive and helpful.

RELIGION AND POLITICS

Going beyond Adler's three great problems of life to the broader context cited at the beginning of this chapter, we will now examine how religion relates to political outlooks and behavior. The domain for politics is selected because it constitutes one of the most important responsibilities of adult life.

Benson (1981) points out that, in the popular mind, religion is a private matter. It is therefore supposed to be independent of the collective and mundane, such as politics. This view may also be reinforced by the historical separation of church and state. However, one does not have to look far into either history or contemporary life to find strong and intimate connections between religion and politics.

As might be expected, the factors that associate these two realms are complex and frequently indirect. For example, church pronouncements are often affected by community and regional traditions, and may further involve rural-urban distinctions and class and ethnic influences. Needless to say, these also shape the political process.

Civil Religion

Relative to the political milieu, it is necessary to recognize a pervasive and often not so subtle infusion of religious ideas throughout our culture. Robert Bellah (1967) adopted Rousseau's term *Civil Religion* to describe this phenomenon. Greeley (1972) claims that despite the formal separation of church and state in American society, "there is an official religion if not an official church in the American republic. This religion has its solemn ceremonials, such as the inauguration, its feast days, such as Thanksgiving, Memorial Day, the Fourth of July, and Christmas" (pp. 156–57). In addition, invocations to God are plentiful on such occasions. These may also be found on coins, in patriotic songs, and through the presence of religious representatives at public functions. Civil religion goes beyond the formal churches. It is much of Herberg's (1960) "American Way of Life" religion, surrounding us so that we take it for granted.

Benson (1981) observes that "Civil religion provides a kind of divine stamp of approval of the social order as it now exists" (p. 50). He adds that "the God of civil religion has a special concern for America, guiding it to play a special role in the world" (p. 50). This is the kind of faith that probably prompted President Lyndon Johnson to suggest at a Presidential Prayer Breakfast that "the capital erect a 'monument to God,' alongside those of Washington, Lincoln, Jefferson and Robert A. Taft" (Demerath and Hammond, 1969, p. 207). We must not lose sight of this context, for it conditions much of the way we think about religion in American life.

A Conceptual Framework for Understanding Religion and Politics

In the insightful work *Piety and Politics,* Alan Geyer (1963) offered a theory of how religion and politics may be related. Although he applied his perspective to foreign policy and primarily to interactions on the institutional level, he recognized that "It is in the individual that tensions between religious and political loyalties become existential reality" (Geyer, 1963, p. 101). The problem is how to "accommodate both the religious and political dimensions of experience" (p. 99).

Religion performs a number of political functions for the person. It may, according to Geyer (1963), be both a source or sanction for political loyalty or political conflict. Here it serves to justify or rationalize the positions that people take. In other instances, religion can be a sanctuary from political conflict, or even operate to reconcile political differences. There is likely to be overlap among these roles as encouraging political loyalties could exacerbate interpersonal differences and polarize groups even more than before religion entered the arena.

Religion as a source or sanction for political loyalty   Spiritual systems are based on certain core doctrines that may be identical to, or spring from, the same sources as political tenets. Political institutions often legitimize, or culturally rationalize, their existence by utilizing religious themes. Here again is civil religion. Parallels are drawn from sacred writings "to unite . . . believers with a supreme center of loyalties" (Geyer, 1963, p. 30). The force of political ideology and action is strengthened when it becomes religious. There is nothing like a testimonial from God to back one's stance. Few political figures would dare to eschew in their speeches what Franklin Roosevelt maybe too candidly referred to as "God stuff" (Lerner, 1957, p. 704). This advice seemed to have been taken by President Reagan who referred to God ten times in one speech and twenty-four times in another (Cannon, 1984).

Additional spiritual supports buttress loyalty to the existing political order, as in scriptural prescriptions that tell us "Obey them that have the rule over you, and submit yourselves: for they watch for your souls . . . " (Hebrews 13:17).

Possible indications of religion as a source or sanction for various political positions are all about us. The tendency for Catholics to embrace liberal causes may, in part, be a result of more than a century of papal encyclicals espousing what has come to be known as "welfare state ideology." An antimaterialistic stance coupled with pro-labor sympathies on the part of American Catholic spokespersons also could have contributed to Democratic loyalties (Lipset, 1964).

Church pronouncements against birth control were instrumental in putting laws on the books in Massachusetts and Connecticut prohibiting the dispensing of information on contraception (Lipset, 1964). In like manner, Richardson and Fox (1972) showed that Mormon and Catholic legislators prevented the passage of abortion reform bills as counseled by their churches. The recent opposition of the Mormons to the proposed constitutional amendment on equal rights for women also stems from their theology (*BYU Today,* 1980; Kimball, 1975).

Sunday sermons, religious publications, and public statements by significant clergy that are carried by the media may reinforce church and theological identifications on the part of the laity. Mass mailings of letters to government figures and/or visits to these policymakers could influence political stands. Churches are interest groups; they do affect elections by the way they establish themselves and their doctrines as both sources and sanctions for political loyalty.

Religion as a sanction for political conflict   Political and religious loyalties are often the basis for separation and conflict in these same areas. In wartime, the theme "God is on our side" is heard frequently by the military of all contestants. The antagonism of Christians for communism was well expressed by Cardinal Mindszenty during the Hungarian uprising when he blessed the weapons of the rebels (Vernon, 1962). "Onward Christian Soldiers" is both a call for unity and battle.

When religion supports political conflict, challenge and opposition become religious obligations. God, scripture, cross, and star are invoked along with other religious symbols to call the faithful to the colors. These actions demonstrate that religion "accepts the realities of hostility and violence and announces the will of God as active in and through such realities" (Geyer, 1963, p. 59).

Religion interprets one's response as a moral imperative, intensifying confrontation and reducing the likelihood of compromise and negotiation (Bell, 1963). Lane (1969) terms this "primitive moralism." It resolves lingering doubts by phrasing issues in dogmatic, polarizing language. Conflict within the person is minimized through identification with spiritual authority. The matter is stated in the context of good and bad and right and wrong; it is no longer personal but universal in import. "True believers" must be created (Hoffer, 1951).

We see such sanctioning of righteous conflict in the position of the "moral majority" against what they define as "pornography" and "humanism" (Woodward and Salholz, 1981). Needs to protect the young against secularism and evolutionary theory are voiced. These accompany appeals to introduce "creation science" into the schools. Concurrently, there are efforts within the Congress for a constitutional amendment in behalf of "voluntary prayer." Religion thus becomes a source and a sanction for many kinds of conflict, not the least of which are political.

Religion as a sanctuary from political conflict   There are those who feel that their faith is demeaned when it is concerned with public affairs, especially when the morality of politics is open to question. For them, religion is a sanctuary, a bulwark against the baseness of the world. Lipset (1964) suggests that such opposition to political action is found among those whose religion stresses other-worldy, transcendental doctrines.

Many who are alienated and powerless because of poverty, little education, chronic illness, minority status, and other forms of deprivation and frustration find a haven in this kind of religion. It avers that they may suffer in this life, but they are sure to be rewarded in the next world for their trust and faith in God.

Here we have a religion that is wildly accepted in America. One study of 1,580 California clergy revealed that over one-third had never given a sermon on a political issue. The more traditional the cleric, the less likely social and political matters would be discussed from the pulpit. Because of a bias toward young preachers in this study, the researchers concluded that their work underestimated the aversion of ministers to involve themselves and their churches in things political (Stark, Foster, Glock, and Quinley, 1970).

Although many clergy and their followers employ religion as a shield against the trials of life, and by doing so reject politics, we also find the opposite to be true. In some countries, religious conservatism seems to be supplanted by radical politics (Glock and Stark, 1965; Stark, 1964). Here the political system offers an alternative value framework that competes with religion. As one of these orientations strengthens, the other weakens. Apparently this is most likely to occur among those at the bottom of the socioeconomic ladder.

Religion as a reconciler of political conflict   If there is a basic, idealistic theme in the Judeo-Christian tradition, it is well summarized in the often-expressed hope for "peace on earth, good will toward men." Whether it be the Golden Rule or church pronouncements for harmony and understanding, motives for reconciliation lie at the heart of spirituality. Tying one's faith to partisan goals may sanction political loyalty, but it also stimulates separatism and conflict. Recognizing that this clashes with unifying religious principles, many churchgoers find themselves at odds with "religion as usual." Such efforts are primarily designed to improve life, enhance peace, and keep the message of reconciliation alive in an often lukewarm institutional religious context.

One group active in reducing racial separation were the "freedom riders" of the 1960s, many of whom were religiously motivated. Politically, they allied themselves with either democratic or socialistic positions. Only two percent were Republicans (Gerner, 1965).

In like manner, religionists stressing the "right of conscience" (Pontier, 1971) protested against the Vietnam war, nuclear arms, apartheid in South Africa, segregation in the United States, and a host of inequities and social evils. Allport (1959; 1966) suggests that those who embrace a universalistic faith are likely to possess an intrinsic perspective. Much research on churchgoers who take liberal, anti-prejudice stands has already been cited in this volume and demonstrates that an intrinsic-committed faith parallels constructive social, economic, and political outlooks. Unhappily, as central as the motif of reconciliation is in religious teachings, the how, when, and where of its expression is a source of much controversy, not only among the laity, but also with clergy and church authorities (Hadden, 1969; Quinley, 1974).

We have seen that religion and political orientations and actions are related in a complex manner. Individuals may look to their faith for ways to authenticate their political views, thus strengthening political loyalties. Lipset (1964) quotes Alexis de Tocqueville to the effect that " 'political doctrine' is inherent in every religion." Whatever religious position adults take, it is likely to have political implications.

Religion and Politics: The Research Scene

Most of the research conducted on politics and religion tells us little about the dynamics of these collective interactions. To be informed that Jews and Catholics are inclined to vote Democratic, while Republicans are largely Protestant is not very enlightening (Chalfant, Beckley, and Palmer, 1981). We lack information on individual factors that affiliate specific people with specific sides of political issues. One truly outstanding scholarly piece of work that goes far toward answering this question has recently been reported by Benson and Williams (1982), Research Box 5-4 details this very significant effort.

This very impressive research project seems to relate to the theory on religion and politics presented earlier. In an initial and rough manner, we could hypothesize that each type of religionist uses his/her faith as a source or sanction for actions that enhance their political loyalties. By taking some of the more extreme stands, political conflict is likely to be exacerbated. Faith appears to be differentially invoked depending on the issue before the Congress. The centrist position usually taken by Integrated and Nominalist religionists could represent the use of religion as a sanctuary or reconciler. These motives, however, may be applied to all

RESEARCH BOX 5-4.   Benson, P. L. and Williams, D. L. *Religion on Capitol Hill: Myths and Realities.* New York: Harper and Row, 1982.

The purpose of this investigation was "to chronicle the religious beliefs and values held by members of the United States Congress, and to track how they connect with the legislative decisions of the Congress" (p. 2). To accomplish this goal, a random sample of 112 senators and representatives (a 20 percent sampling of the Congress) was selected for study. It was possible to interview eighty of these. This group closely matched the characteristics of both those not interviewed and the Congress in toto in sex, age, educational level, party affiliation, Senate-House distribution, conservatism-liberalism, and voting inclinations on a wide variety of political issues.

The beliefs assessed were organized into seven categories: beliefs about (1) "the nature of religious reality"; (2) "religious reality's relationship to the world"; (3) "means of apprehending religious reality"; (4) "salvation and paths to salvation"; (5) "about the last things (eschatology)"; (6) "people and society"; and (7) "values and ethical principles" (p. 24).

Eighty-six percent of the participants affirmed a belief in God, and overwhelmingly images of a transcendent, loving deity were described. The major human problem with which religion is said to deal is lack of meaning and purpose in life, and the path to salvation is through works, faith, and living a virtuous life. A broad spectrum of beliefs about people, societal values, and ethical principles and responsibilities were verbalized. Many stressed self-control, the significance of the home, family, and nation, and social justice.

In terms of religious affiliation and activity, 90 percent of the respondents are members of churches and synagogues, and 74 percent attend services once a month or more. Seventy-four percent acknowledge praying at least once a week and 37 percent read scripture minimally once during this same period. One-third consider religion very important in their lives, and another 60 percent regard it as moderately important.

Since many people consider the Congress to be less religious than the American people, it may come as a surprise to find that the authors of this research conclude: "Congress well reflects the dominant religious beliefs and behaviors present among the American public. It is not true, as some contend, that the members of Congress are less religious than the people they serve" (p. 82).

After carrying out extensive statistical analyses of the data, Benson and Williams denote six types of religionists in the Congress.

Legalistic religionists.   Fifteen percent of the sample evidenced this form of faith that places "very high value on rules, boundaries, limits, guidelines, direction, and purpose" (p. 126). These people also stress discipline and self-restraint.

Self-concerned religionists.   Constituting 29 percent of the respondents, their faith is "visible, articulate, enthusiastically shared, regularly practiced, apparently genuine—and almost entirely concerned with the relationship between the believer and God . . . little impetus toward concern for fellow creatures" (p. 128).

Integrated religionists.   "These people's beliefs work to liberate, to free them to speak and act . . . God not humankind is their audience" (p. 129). They balance pressures to vote in certain ways and may respond in terms of religious principle. These comprised 14 percent of the sample.

People-concerned religionists.   Stressing the connection between faith and action, they possess complex God images and well-examined religious concepts. This 10 percent group focuses on constructive national change.

Nontraditional religionists.   Making up only nine percent of the respondents, these intellectually perceptive members of Congress hold abstract concepts of God plus many individualized religious ideas. They might also be viewed to have a secular-humanist orientation.

Nominal religionists.   Twenty-two percent of the participants reject most traditional religious ideas. Their church attachments appear superficial. Spirituality seems most concerned with providing solace as religion is basically unanalyzed and vague. It is restricted in that it is unlikely to affect daily life and thought.

One of the central goals of this work was to determine ties between religion and voting behavior in the Congress. Only one percent of the sample felt there was no connection between the two, while almost one-quarter (24 percent) saw a strong affiliation.

Political conservatives differ from their liberal colleagues by maintaining images of God as omnipotent, strict, guiding, protective of social institutions, and as playing an active role in one's life. Life after death is assured, and the path to salvation is personal and accomplished by doing good. Liberals stress social justice, love, and the social nature of salvation.

Taking eight political issues on which there were votes in Congress, Benson and Williams show the existence of noteworthy associations between the form of religion held by members of Congress and their voting records. These data were summarized in Table 5-4. It may be seen that the most liberal actions were taken by people-concerned and nontraditional religionists. Most conservative voting was carried out by the legalistic and self-concerned religionists. Middle-of-the-road positions were maintained by nominal and integrated religionists.

TABLE 5-4. Religious Types and Voting Patterns

VOTING BEHAVIOR	TYPES OF RELIGIONISTS					
	LEGALISTIC	SELF-CONCERNED	INTEGRATED	PEOPLE-CONCERNED	NONTRADITIONAL	NOMINAL
Pro						
Civil liberties	32%	30%	60%	80%	81%	51%
Foreign aid	21	26	63	97	88	55
Hunger relief	30	29	78	90	83	60
Abortion funding	23	28	71	87	86	44
Anti						
Government spending	47	45	25	23	22	34
Pro						
Strong military	84	78	44	19	26	58
Private ownership	50	54	29	19	18	37
Free enterprise	65	61	35	23	20	42

Adapted from Benson and Williams (1982), p. 161.

121

of the religionists depending on the matter up for action. Obviously, much more study is needed before we are able to comprehend the tie between the specifics of religion and politics within the individual lawmaker. In addition, we must not forget the role of a large number of other factors which influence voting behavior. Still, Benson and Williams' research constitutes a major step forward in this most significant area.

FORM OF PERSONAL FAITH AND RELIGION IN ADULT LIFE

With the exception of relatively few studies, primarily in the domain of inter-personal relations, the possible differential involvement and expression of intrinsic-committed and extrinsic-consensual forms of personal faith have been ignored. In part, the lack of pertinent research is a function of a more basic avoidance of research in the area of adult life per se. This is being corrected, it would ap-pear, at an ever-increasing rate. It would be our fundamental hypothesis that the more promising and favorable expressions in regard to job and occupation, social relationships, love and marriage, and life quality in and/or out crisis are likely to be found in conjunction with intrinsic-committed religion. In contrast, less de-sirable outcomes are expected to attend extrinsic-consensual outlooks.

RELIGIOUS ATTRIBUTIONS IN ADULT LIFE

One cannot reasonably expect any distinctive pattern of religious attributions as a function of being an adult. Certain special considerations might, however, be examined, such as the situation of the elderly, particularly the impaired aged, and, of course, the place of these explanations in crisis situations. We need to comprehend to what degree, under what circumstances, and the manner in which causal attributions are invoked relative to Adler's tasks of life—work, love and marriage, and interpersonal relations. When such attributions are made or not made tells us when cause is referred to natural or supernatural determinants. To date, we know little about such possibilities.

Thus far, studies of adult images of God have given us the range of these concepts, but not when different ones become causal referents. The recent work of Gorsuch and Smith (1983) on attributions of responsibility to God suggest that certain influences such as religious orientation and event outcomes are involved in these explanations.

In another realm, for example, we know that Christian Scientist college students utilize standard health services less than their non-Christian Science peers, but both groups seem to employ medical supports when under stress (Nudelman, 1980). The function of religious attributions for exacerbating or reconciling such actions with Christian Science theology is worthy of understanding. Paralleling this in the realm of sexual attitudes and behavior, recent work (Wulf, Prentice, Hansum, Ferrar, and Spilka, 1984) shows that single evangelical Christians are sexually active in violation of the proscriptions of their faith. The nature of the attributions that accommodate these apparently conflicting domains should add to our insights regarding religion in life.

In these instances, and for the various realms of adult life, we are asking for information on how religious interpretations provide a sense of meaning, personal control, and support for one's self-esteem. Initial work directed toward attaining such knowledge has begun, but it is still in its infancy (Ritzema, 1979; Spilka and Schmidt, 1983) and it is too inconclusive to recommend that more than additional specifying research be carried out. In other words, that religion is a significant aspect of adult life for most Americans cannot be doubted; however, its full import has yet to be assessed and understood.

SUMMARY AND CONCLUSIONS

We have tried to organize religion in adult life around Adler's three great problems of life, work, social relations, and love and marriage. To these we added two other significant aspects of adulthood—namely, life satisfaction and participation in the political process. Although a scattered literature is available relating religion to each of these areas, comprehensive, current treatments of these topics are lacking. This is probably a function of the fact that psychology in general has not dealt with the middle years of life until recently. With new talk of "life-span developmental psychology," hopefully this shortcoming will be rectified. Still, there is little doubt that American adults tend to be religious, although their beliefs and activities are often tempered by utilitarian motives.

When religion is related to achievement motivation and Protestant ethic notions, no consistent, meaningful findings are evident. Religion seems to have little or no influence on work attitudes and actions. Although most of this research has not defined religiosity in a rigorous manner, different perspectives in this area may relate to the holding of different faith orientations. One must, however, recognize that work and occupation were more closely associated with religion in centuries past, and today, with increasing secularization throughout our culture, the two realms tend to be quite independent of each other.

In the realm of social relations, some research suggests an association of positive social attitudes with intrinsic-committed as opposed to extrinsic-consensual outlooks. Much more needs to be done to find out if this actually carries over to behavior. The scarcity of relevant research on these topics is surprising in itself though the work reported in Chapter Eleven on prejudice, altruism, and compassion may be pertinent here.

More work has been done on religion in relation to love and marriage than appears to be true of any other aspect of adulthood. In the main, religion is positively associated with marital happiness and the presence of loving relationships. Although differences in religious affiliation and outlook are correlated with marital disruption, interfaith marriages are on the increase, a tendency that does not bode well for the future of the institution of marriage. It is evident that the influence of religion relative to love and marriage has been reducing at a rapid rate while other sociocultural forces are gaining in importance.

Despite the above suggestions that religion is becoming less and less significant in modern life, there is considerable evidence that many subjectively regard their faith as a source of personal strength and satisfaction. Religious commitment often provides a sense of meaning to a life that too frequently conveys a feeling of absurdity. In addition, religion implies that one might exert some control over life events especially in times of crisis. Identification with religious institutions and symbols may thus also endow individuals with heightened security and self-esteem.

Religion seems to have always been involved in the political process. Although we have shown how it may be manipulatively employed through the concept of "civil religion," religion and politics are related in many ways to enhance political loyalties, and create, avoid, or reconcile political conflicts. The very significant research of Benson and Williams (1982) shows many of the subtle ways religion can affect political decisions and actions, suggesting that, even if it has receded somewhat into our cultural background, it is still a force to be reckoned with.

Unfortunately, research on religion in adult life has barely looked at the influence of different forms of faith and virtually left the realm of attribution theory untouched. The role of religion in the forty or so years of adulthood is an area begging for research understanding.

CHAPTER SIX
RELIGION AND DEATH

Then shall the dust return to the earth as it was: and the spirit shall return to God who gave it (Ecclesiastes 12:7).

This is the meaning of death: the ultimate self-dedication to the divine (Heschel, 1951, p. 296).

" 'I shall arise.' For centuries
Upon the grey old churchyard stone
These words have stood; no more is said" (Hill, 1924, p. 662).

)DUCTION

These poignant comments tell us that religion and death are the most inseparable of companions. We can hardly think of one without the other. To some scholars, if there were no death, there would be no religion (Becker, 1973; Weisman, 1972). On the other side of the coin, for many, death minus faith signifies no meaning for life and the end of the human adventure. It would be nature without hope.

As discussed earlier, there are many reasons for the existence of religion. From the individual side, it has been inferred that religion is a way of coping with the unpredictable. It offers both explanations and means of potentially controlling the unknown, unexpected and especially the undesired. Since death meets all of these criteria in an extreme way, it is not surprising that the great religions of the world make it a central part of their belief system and theology. Yinger (1970) thus proposes that "the most significant of the tendencies with which religion everywhere grapples is fear of death" (p. 123). The noted anthropologist, Malinowski (1965), claimed, "Death, which of all human events is the most upsetting and disorganizing to man's calculations, is perhaps the main source of religious belief" (p. 71). Following this one step further, the philosopher, Unamuno (1954), felt that the ubiquitous spiritual theme "of immortality originates and preserves religions" (p. 41). Ducasse (1961) generalizes that "most religions have taught in one form or another that the 'soul' or 'spirit' of the individual does not perish when his body dies, but goes on living in another world" (p. 14). Empirically, it becomes quite understandable why two-thirds of a large sample of clergy agree that fear and anxiety about death is a motivator of religious activity (Spilka, Spangler, Rea, and Nelson, 1981). Only two percent felt that death concern was not a factor in religious involvement.

Those who claim all religion results from fear of death seem to be inferring well beyond the data, because religion performs many functions in life. Still, as Tillich (1952) notes, "The anxiety of fate and death is most basic, most universal, and inescapable" (p. 40). It would therefore seem quite reasonable to accept the premise that much of religion seems to have developed in response to the threat and reality of death. This should be kept in mind as we examine how religion complexly ties to death-related attitudes and behavior.

If death by itself is not enough of a problem for the individual, its burden may be enhanced by the way it is treated by the society in which one lives. The teachings of our culture may work to make things worse. In some societies, death defines new roles for the deceased and may confer on them a higher status in their spiritual domain (Keesing and Keesing, 1971); however, in the American social order, the situation is quite different. Historian Arnold Toynbee saw death as "un-American—an affront to every citizen's inalienable right to life, liberty and the pursuit of happiness" (Woodward, 1970, p. 81). Our stress on achievement and success within an individualistic heritage thus makes death even more of a threat, if not a sign of personal failure. As Wheeler (1971) perceived, "Death is not only unacceptable, it is insulting. It makes life absurd. Because death exists God must also exist in order to eliminate the absurdity of life" (p. 11). Although these comments may seem rather strong and one-sided, they rather accurately reflect the dominant view of death in America.

RELIGION, DEATH AND THE INDIVIDUAL

Religion As a Source of Meaning and Control

Death is an ever-present fact of life that cannot be denied, and religion offers believers much solace and support in the face of such a personal crisis. When we consider the individual and social functions faith performs, its role relative to death becomes evident. Religion has a ready set of explanations about the meaning of death and also offers a sense of control through prayer and adherence to religious precepts. The expectation is that if one holds the right beliefs and obeys the behavioral prescriptions of the faith, one should live a long and happy life and furthermore should be assured of a sympathetic godly ear when a need for such exists as when death threatens.

Psychologically, fear and anxiety would seem to be reduced and security enhanced by religious understandings (Keesing and Keesing, 1971). Weisman (1972) touches on this fundamental theme by observing, "Religion recognizes man's yearning for survival and depends on man's inability to imagine anything else" (p. 101). Finally, death is a disruption in our lives, and both religious ideology and ritual work to restore stability to the survivors (Honigmann, 1959).

Death and Afterlife

Among the religious meanings associated with death is the concept of an afterlife, and few formulations seem as personally gratifying as the continuation of life following death. Few conceptions are as gratifying as life after death. We may be severed from our bodily existence with all its stresses and strains but still maintain the hope that the next world will bring a contrasting bliss. The essence of the issue is that we and our loved ones are preserved for eternity in a happy, everlasting reunion.

As indicated in Table 6-1, national polls tell us that belief in life after death is quite prevalent among Americans. Variation among the studies is probably due to the asking of somewhat different questions with different answer possibilities. The sampling procedures used to obtain the respondents also might have varied considering that these polls were carried out over approximately a ten-year period. The one investigation that presented information on church members plus a national sample reveals stronger belief in an afterlife among the former, who, of course, should be more religious than the unselected national group. It is also evident that the more conservatively Christian a church is, the greater the proportion of its adherents who affirm the existence of a life beyond death.

When we examine belief in heaven and hell as presented in Table 6-2, the same association holds with church strictness. Believers in an afterlife show considerable confidence in the existence of heaven and hell. Still, more of the faithful attest to the reality of the former than the latter. It may also be that the vision of hell is too discomforting not to be denied. Although some research suggests that religious persons may be concerned with the possibility of punishment in the hereafter (Florian and Har-even, 1983–84), one major study concluded "Virtually all respondents expressing belief in a personal life after death also believed that it would be at least a good life for them" (Dixon and Kinlaw, 1982–83, p. 290).

TABLE 6-1   Belief in the Existence of a Life after Death

RELIGIOUS GROUP	CHURCH MEMBERS[1]	NATIONAL SAMPLE[1]	NATIONAL SAMPLE[2]
Total, all respondents	—	—	75%
Total Protestants	65%	50%	78
Roman Catholics	75	48	83
Jews	—	—	17
Other or no religion	—	—	26
Baptists	—	—	81
American	72	41	—
Southern	97	65	—
Christian Church	—	42	—
Congregational	36	26	65
Episcopal	53	35	68
Evangelical Reformed	—	50	—
Lutheran	—	—	78
Amer. Luth. Church	70	52	—
Missouri Synod	84	50	—
Methodist	49	42	75
Presbyterian	69	—	70
United	—	36	—
U.S.	—	43	—
Sects[3]	—	67	83
Unitarian	—	0	—

[1]Data in Stark, R. and Glock, C.Y., *American Piety*, 1968. Appear to have been collected in the early 1960s. Responses presented "completely true" to the statement, "There is a life beyond death."

[2]Data taken from Marty, M. E., Rosenberg, S. E., and Greeley, A. M. *What Do We Believe?* 1968. Question was "Do you think your soul will live on after death?"

[3]In National Sample 2, this is labeled "other denominations." There appears to be considerable overlap from the descriptions.

Regardless of affiliation, research demonstrates that the more religious people are—that is, within the Christian tradition—the greater the likelihood that they believe in an afterlife (Berman, 1974; Cerny and Carter, 1977; Clark and Carter, 1978; Minton and Spilka, 1976).

Some Cautions and Qualifications

Before continuing further to show how religion and death are affiliated, it is important to keep in mind that these are complex issues, and that just as religiosity is associated with a number of social variables, so is belief in life after death. A few observations will suffice—the role of age, education, and income. Table 6-3 illustrates a slight tendency for belief in an afterlife to move upward with increasing age. Another more recent national poll suggests a like trend from 69 percent of twenty to twenty-nine year olds believing this way to some 76 percent of those seventy years of age and older affirming such a view (Greeley, 1976, pp. 64–65). Older persons may hold these outlooks for a number of reasons. When

TABLE 6-2   **Believe in Heaven and Hell and Personal Outcome by Believers and Nonbelievers.**[1]

> **Question A:** To believers in an afterlife. "Do you think there is a Heaven where people who have led good lives are eternally rewarded?"
>
> **Question B:** To same group as Question A. "Do you believe there is a Hell to which people who have led bad lives and die without being sorry are eternally damned?"
>
> **Question C:** To believers in Hell. "Do you think there is any real possibility of your going there?"

	AGREEMENT WITH QUESTIONS		
RELIGIOUS GROUP	BELIEVERS (A)	BELIEVERS (B)	BELIEVERS (C)
Total, all respondents	68%	54%	17%
Protestants	71	54	15
Roman Catholics	80	70	27
Jews	6	3	2
Other or no religion	26	20	6
Baptists	78	68	17
Congregational	58	25	5
Episcopal	54	17	5
Lutheran	66	49	17
Methodist	66	44	10
Presbyterian	61	39	15

[1]Source is Marty, M. E., Rosenberg, S. E. and Greeley, A. M. *What Do We Believe?*

they were young, such beliefs were probably more widespread and stronger in general and, hence, were possibly better learned by these people. Getting closer to death could also be a stimulus for increasing concern, and notions of a benevolent afterlife might counter such feelings. Belief in heaven or hell is apparently quite stable throughout life. The fact that more people affirm the existence of heaven than hell may reflect the fact that one doesn't want to think of something worse after life, when death itself is hardly greeted with enthusiasm.

The trend is particularly clear with education and income, for beliefs in a life beyond death and the existence of heaven. In both instances, higher education and economic status go with less belief. The two variables are probably positively correlated, and the dominant influence is likely to be more education and knowledge among those who are financially better off.

In other words, it appears that not only are beliefs in an afterlife—heaven and hell—a function of religion, but of other demographic factors as well. It is necessary to keep such complexities in mind when conceptualizing problems such as we are examining here.

Personal considerations also cloud this picture. Although we employ the terms afterlife, heaven, and hell, we have little idea of their meaning to those who hold these beliefs (Hertel, 1980). Some coloring undoubtedly comes from views that are prevalent in our culture or are held over from childhood. Different religious

TABLE 6-3.   Belief in an Afterlife, Heaven and Hell in Relation to Age, Education, and Income (1965)[1,2]

	PERCENT BELIEVING IN		
AGE	AFTERLIFE	HEAVEN	HELL
18 to 24	73	68	56
25 to 34	74	66	54
35 to 44	73	67	55
45 to 54	73	67	51
55 to 64	76	71	56
65 and over	79	70	55
EDUCATION			
0 to 8 grades	78	74	65
1 to 3 yrs. H.S.	74	72	65
H.S. Grad.	75	68	52
1 to 3 yrs. Coll.	77	67	47
Coll. Grad.	66	51	38
INCOME			
Upper	73	62	19
Middle	74	68	12
Lower	76	71	10

[1]These data are taken from Marty, Rosenberg, and Greeley (1968), and are from a 1965 national survey.

[2]See table 6-2 for the questions asked.

systems probably add other images. The same may be true of the kind of education to which various people have been subject. All of these influences are, however, mediated through one's own idiosyncratic life experiences, necessitating an understanding of each personality and the manner in which it responds to the world. In sum, then, the problem is both individual and social.

Religion and the Near-Death Experience

During the 1970s, the idea of "near-death experiences" (NDEs) achieved great popularity. Although usually publicized as a "post-death experience," and frequently viewed as evidence for life after death, a careful reading of this work leads to a more conservative interpretation. It is clearly much more accurate to view these phenomena in terms of a potential response pattern when one perceives death as inevitable. This often appears as an altered state of consciousness in anticipation of death during a life-threatening episode. Among the many reactions that have been reported, those most noted are out-of-body experiences, perceptual alterations of space and time, and a wide variety of emotional states, of which the most common are fear and concern about others (Kalish, 1969).

The initial popularizing work in this area was by psychiatrist Raymond Moody (1976), whose book *Life After Life* tended to be taken uncritically by many as proof of an afterlife. A follow-up investigation by Osis and Haraldson (1977) opened the door further to similar interpretations, but more rigorous thinking and research has questioned these views. Kastenbaum (1981) proposed criteria for conceptualizing these events while Ring (1980) has reported a fairly exacting study of the nature of these experiences. This work permits us to examine the role of religion in these phenomena.

There is little doubt that a fair proportion of NDEs possess religious content. Hardt (1979) suggests that this is true to the extent that the participant is religiously oriented, but Ring (1980) failed to support this infererence. Still, he reports that some of those he studied claimed that they talked to God, and in rare instances visions of religious figures such as Jesus occurred. The influence of culture was apparent in Osis and Haraldson's (1977) work on American & Indian experiencers. Neither group reported seeing the religious figures perceived by members of the other group, only those of which they had knowledge from their own spiritual tradition.

The aftereffects of NDEs are quite significant religiously. Rosen (cited in Kalish, 1969) studied persons who attempted to commit suicide by jumping off bridges in the San Francisco Bay area and reported that the majority felt they were reborn into a new and happy life. A general increase in religiousness was found by Ring (1980), but this was expressed more in terms of inner spiritual feeling than by adherence to formal church practices. Rejection of the latter was still accompanied by a heightened religious openness and tolerance. Despite the finding that NDEs resulted in a great increase in belief in a life after death, no corresponding changes were observed for belief in God or the existence of heaven or hell. Ring suggested that these views tend to be quite stable and resistant to change.

There is still much to be learned about the reasons for and results of near-death experiences, especially as they relate to religious expressions. It does appear that we can reasonably rule them out as confirmation of an afterlife.

Religion and Fear of Death

Research Problems.   Probably more research has been conducted on how religion and death fear or *thanatophobia* are associated than other possible relationships between the terribly complex realms of religion and death. One can piece together a steady and orderly development in this work until today when it does seem to have been successfully examined. In many instances, the measures of religion contain within them questions dealing with belief in an afterlife as this is often considered a central component of traditional Christianity and hence Western religion. One researcher, Berman (1974), found in his work that "the major influence on the maintenance of a (belief in an afterlife) appears to be religious" (p. 131).

Before examining this research, some questions must be raised as there is some apparent contradiction among these studies. Surveying this literature, a total of thirty-six research investigations were located tying religion and/or belief in an afterlife to death fear and anxiety. Of these, the great majority, twenty-four, reported that stronger faith or afterlife views were affiliated with less death concern and fear. Seven failed to show any relationship; three revealed the opposite—more faith, more anxiety; and two demonstrated two of these possibilities by assessing different levels of death fear, such as conscious and unconscious expressions.

Martin and Wrightsman (1964) and Lester (1967; 1972) cite a host of short-comings in this work; poor experimental designs, weak measurement, inadequate controls, and inappropriate statistical analyses, among others. The samples also vary widely; most workers use college students, but others have studied elderly persons, psychiatric patients, student nurses, medical students, the terminally ill, seminarians and, of course, regular churchgoing community members.

There is always the problem of defining the critical variables as in any research. Here, it has been undertaken usually two ways: (1) designating the religious group to which a respondent belongs; and (2) employing some instrument or measure to indicate the religiousness of a participant. Relative to the former, Diggory and Rothman (1961) categorized the members of their sample as Protestants, Catholics, Jews, and other and/or none. Degree of religious commitment or involvement was unspecified. No information was provided regarding sex, age, or ethnic considerations for the various groups. Were the Catholics largely Irish, Italian, Slavic; the Jews first, second or third generation or of German, Polish or Russian origin? We can always ask the question of the denominational affiliation of the Protestants, for they can range from conservative to liberal groups. In like manner, were the Jews Orthodox, Conservative or Reform? Finally, there is that mystery of what "other" includes, and why it is matched with "none."

Techniques of measuring religion and death outlooks vary widely. Templer and Dotson (1970) used eight religious questions and analyzed these individually; Leming (1980) used the Faulkner-DeJong scales (1966) that were claimed to measure different aspects of personal faith, but seem to measure one largely undefined form (Weigert and Thomas, 1969). Leming (1980) also developed a series of death fear and concern scales that clearly need further refinement—a never-ending process. Templer (1970) and Templer and Dotson (1970) used Templer's death anxiety scale, while Cerny (1975) adopted the scale of Boyar (1964). Both of these devices have been shown to be multidimensional in character (Spilka, Stout, Minton, and Sizemore, 1977), making it difficult to ascertain what is really being evaluated. Dickstein (1972) has done a service by indicating many of the deficiencies of measurement in the area of death fear and concern. It is no wonder that contradiction exists among the various studies summarized by Lester (1967; 1972).

Conceptually, there is another serious problem. We have seen already that people do not simply vary along a single dimension of religiosity, easily anchored at one end by atheism and the other by orthodoxy. There are a number of different forms of personal faith, so researchers need to consider the multidimensionality of the religious sphere. The evidence now also suggests that the realm of death attitudes is similarly complex (Hoelter and Epley, 1979; Hooper and Spilka, 1970; Leming, 1980; Spilka et al., 1977). Still, most of the work undertaken over the past two decades has tended to treat both religion and death as unidimensional. That this is a serious problem is easily demonstrated by the finding of Magni (1972) that the Lester scale for measuring attitudes toward death is unrelated to the Kalish instrument, which seems to be dealing with the same favorable-unfavorable dimensional outlook. A similar observation comes from the work of Berman and Hays (1973), who show Templer's death anxiety scale to correlate weakly with Lester's fear-of-death instrument. Obviously, these questionnaires are not assessing the same phenomena, and therefore may not provide comparable results when related to religious variables that themselves might be dealing with different features of that realm.

Religious group differences in fear of death   Most studies involving different religious groups denote their samples as Catholic, Protestant, and Jewish, and other and/or none. Catholic-Protestant differences in death fear are sometimes present in favor of the former (Faunce and Fulton 1958), but more often similarity prevails (Lester, 1967; 1972). Where Jews fit into these comparisons is unclear. Direct studies with sizable samples are lacking. If death fear relates to belief in an afterlife, Jews should show much less of the latter, but there is no evidence to suggest that this might be true for Jews.

Templer and Ruff (1975) offer an interesting alternative emphasis in their investigation of a large sample of psychiatric patients. They found that those who changed their religious affiliation from that in which they were reared displayed greater anxiety about death. Although these are deviant participants for such work, there is always the probability that religious inconsistency may exacerbate various basic personality concerns.

Religiousness and fear of death   Lack of information on differences among religious bodies in fear of death is unfortunate; however, such variation might relate to the way death and dying are treated in a group's theology. To date, no researcher appears to have undertaken this kind of study. Within traditional Christianity, it is commonly believed that death is followed by a new life with God. Immortality is assured the faithful. As Table 6-1 and 6-2 indicate, persons affiliated with the more conservative Christian churches hold these views more than do liberal Christians. Discrepancies between the positions espoused in theology and those held by churchgoers seem to differ greatly. Distinguished psychologist of religion Paul Pruyser (1968) aptly comments that popular images "about immortality are a far departure from the tenets of corporate faith and contradict them grossly." (p. 96)

Regardless of church affiliation, those who participate more in religious activities should hold a more orthodox Christian view about immortality and afterlife. This has been demonstrated in national samples (Gallup, 1982; Stark and Glock, 1968). It could be further theorized that this dimension of conservatism in personal theology may be a major influence in one's attitude toward death. In other words, greater church attendance and stronger traditional beliefs among Methodists, for example, as well as Baptists will tend to emphasize ideas about immortality and life beyond death. To the extent that this is true, anxiety about death should be relatively low. Even though we know that personal religion is more complex than this, most research in this area was carried out thinking of both death concern and religion as single, simple dimensions. In the previous section, reference was made to work of this sort and some of the contradictions found, yet two-thirds of all the studies do report low death fear, concern and anxiety go with high church attendance and orthodox and fundamentalistic beliefs. Representative is the work of Kalish and Reynolds (1976) and Stewart (1975). As part of a much larger investigation, Kalish and Reynolds had their respondents rate themselves in devoutness. They later asserted that "the more devout definitely claim to be more accepting of death and dying and show less fear" (p. 90). Stewart used college students, and found that fear of death was inversely related to strong religious beliefs and a high frequency of engaging in religious activity. Other studies of a similar nature usually obtained like results (Cerny, 1975; Kalish, 1963; Martin and Wrightsman, 1965).

In 1972, Magni introduced an innovation into this research. Taking advantage of investigations showing that intrinsic and extrinsic religion reflect different individual approaches to faith, he administered three questionnaires said to assess death fear and anxiety to a small sample of Swedish nurses along with the intrinsic and extrinsic religion scales used by Feagin (1964). Consistently, extrinsic faith related to death concern, and in one instance, intrinsic religion countered these feelings. Kahoe and Dunn (1975) selected one of the death-fear instruments and with better defined religious groups confirmed Magni's observation with intrinsic faith. Rather, small samples may have negated similar findings with extrinsic religion. In these studies, the multidimensionality of the religious realm was finally recognized.

By this time, there were hints in the literature that the death concern area was not as simple as first believed (Hooper and Spilka, 1970). Minton and Spilka (1976) were able to create a number of reliable subscales. This work revealed that at least five different components were present. These were defined as (1) lack of death fear, (2) sensitivity to death, (3) fear of the dying process, (4) awareness of the content of death, and (5) loss of experience and control. Clark and Carter (1978) indicated that these might distinguish among persons varying in commitment to Christianity. Recently, Leming (1979) reported some eight overlapping aspects of death fear.

There is reason to believe that all of these scales may be ordered along a positive-negative continuum with regard to feelings about death. In three separate studies, both the religion and death attitude domains have been treated multidimensionally, and confirm and extend the work of Magni (1972) and Kahoe and Dunn (1974). Research Box 6-1 provides the definitions of these perspectives and illustrates the patterns of relationships found by Spilka et al. (1977) and Cerny and Carter (1977). Summarizing these, in the main, positive views of death, or at least not negative ones, tend to be associated with intrinsic and committed forms of faith, while unfavorable outlooks tie to extrinsic and consensual expressions of religion.

More recent work by Hoelter and Epley (1979) has explicitly focused on the dimensionality of the fear of death. They constructed eight reliable measures similar to those of Leming (1979). These are termed (1) fear of the dying process, (2) fear of premature death, (3) fear for significant others, (4) fear of conscious death, (5) fear of being destroyed, (6) fear for the body after death, (7) fear of the unknown, and (8) fear of the dead. Although overlapping slightly with the instruments developed by Spilka et al. (1977), these scholars introduce some new ways of conceptualizing this realm, and have related their scales to five aspects of religious belief and behavior. A number of the religion measures suggest that the more religious show greater concern for significant others relative to death, implying a meaningful relationship with what would be expected of intrinsic-committed religionists.

RESEARCH BOX 6-1.   *Spilka, B., Stout, L., Minton, B. and Sizemore, D. "Death and Personal Faith: A Psychometric Investigation."* Journal for the Scientific Study of Religion, *1973, 16, 169–178.*

Beginning in 1962 with the work of Hooper and later with Hooper and Spilka (1970) and Minton and Spilka (1976), it became apparent that people think about death in a complex manner. The use of a single and simple negative to positive continuum along which people could be distributed in degrees of anxiety or fearfulness about death had to give way to the various subtleties of human cognition so that we could understand better what there was about death that made people dread it or even look forward to it in an expectant, hopeful way. The original research conducted was based on ten conceptually different ways of perceiving death. One could see it as (1) a natural end, (2) in terms of pain, (3) loneliness, (4) an unknown, (5) forsaking dependents, (6) failure, (7) punishment, (8) an afterlife of reward, (9) courage, or (10) with indifference. Because of problems associated with the early instruments designed to assess these outlooks, Spilka, Stout, Minton, and Sizemore (1977) undertook a very rigorous analysis of statements that might tap these views, and it was possible to construct scales to assess the following eight death perspectives.

Death as Pain and Loneliness:	Death is viewed as painful, associated with loss of mastery and consciousness plus isolation.
Death as Afterlife of Reward:	Death leads to reward, justification, a benevolent eternity.
Indifference toward Death:	Death is of no consequence, an unimportant occurrence in the scheme of things.
Death às Unknown:	Life's termination is mysterious, unfathomable, and ambiguous.
Death as Forsaking Dependents:	Guilt over leaving one's dependents.
Death as Courage:	Death is an opportunity to show character and strength, the final realization of one's highest values.
Death as Failure:	Death is personal failure and defeat, the ultimate in frustration and helplessness.
Death as Natural End:	Death is merely the natural conclusion of life, a terminal point with nothing beyond it.

The above measures were now related to two overlapping multidimensional formulations of the nature of religion: intrinsic and extrinsic forms (Allport and Ross, 1967); and objective versions of the committed and consensual types (Allen and Spilka, 1967; Spilka, Read, Allen and Dailey, 1968). The differential associations of the death and religion measures for two studies (Cerny and Carter, 1977; Spilka, Stout, Minton and Sizemore, 1977) are given in Table 6-4. Clark and Carter (1978) have further confirmed these results.

TABLE 6-4. Correlations between death perspective scales and forms of personal religion from the studies of Spilka et al (1977) and Cerny and Carter (1977)

DEATH PERSPECTIVE SCALES	PERSONAL RELIGION							
	COMMITTED		CONSENSUAL		INTRINSIC		EXTRINSIC	
	SPILKA	CERNY¹	SPILKA	CERNY	SPILKA	CERNY	SPILKA	CERNY
Loneliness and pain	−.08	−.19**	.13	.18**	−.26**	.21**	.36**	.41**
Afterlife of reward	.35**	.77**	.20*	.51**	.37**	.72**	−.07	.05
Indifference	−.09	−.38**	.18*	−.14*	−.25**	−.38**	.39**	.14*
Unknown	−.24**	−.41**	.12	−.23**	−.18*	−.47**	.21**	.14*
Forsaking dependents plus guilt	−.11	−.07	.14	.12	−.13	−.13*	.31**	.31**
Courage	.20*	.45**	.14	.35**	.12	.41**	−.01	.10
Failure	−.18*	−.15*	.17*	.25**	−.23**	−.17**	.49**	.41**
Natural end	.04	.11	.19*	−.03	−.13	.04	.29**	.04

*Indicates statistical significance at or beyond the .05 level.

**Indicates statistical significance at or beyond the .01 level.

¹The higher coefficients are probably a function of the broader range of religious activity and belief in Cerny and Carter's larger sample.

There can be little question that both the death attitude and religion domains are complex and multidimensional, and it appears that more and more work reflects such an awareness.

Fear of death and belief in an afterlife   In a creative experimental investigation, Osarchuk and Tatz (1973) theorized that intensifying one's fear of death should strengthen belief in an afterlife. Their results suggest that raising concern about death may indeed cause one's beliefs in an afterlife to become stronger. They further suggest that these views may help people cope better with death. The details of this work may be seen in Research Box 6-2.

Using the same measures that Osarchuk and Tatz developed, Berman (1974) was unable to demonstrate that persons who recently had a life-threatening experience had their afterlife beliefs similarly affected. He did show that the main influence supporting these views was religious affiliation and degree of religious activity.

Religion and the Terminally Ill

The true test of faith probably comes in the final confrontation with death. Over two decades ago, in a slightly more traditional time, one of the authors attended a symposium in which three clergy discussed their encounters with the dying. A liberal Protestant minister expressed his own anguish when dealing with terminality. He listened sympathetically but often felt unable to provide the desired solace. The frequently simplistic consoling theology of the patients was not that which he embraced, but it was not a time for lecturing or disputation. In contrast, a Catholic priest claimed that he felt quite able to convey the promise of eternal fulfillment to terminally ill patients of his faith and that when he left their bedsides, they had gained renewed confidence in God. Lastly, an Orthodox rabbi offered his succinct and poignant theological statement, "The only thing you can do for the Jew who is dying is to get him better." In these few words, he established the lack of a detailed eschatology within Judaism. These positions represent the full range of spiritual possibilities and reactions even if they adumbrate a much greater variety of subtleties and nuances that both laypeople and clerics might offer.

Anecdotal reports abound of the effectiveness of religious supports to the dying, yet such supports may still be questioned. Kubler-Ross (1970) points to the "bargaining with God" in which many terminally ill engage. Here, the theme is for the patient to "make a deal" with God: "Make me better" or "Let me live and I'll be good, go to church regularly, and take my place with the faithful, as I should have done all these years." The theme of death as punishment for wrongdoing may also be present and distress the patient further.

Religion for the terminally ill can be consoling and encouraging; it may also bring additional discomfort. For most people, we would hypothesize that it is more likely to have positive effects. It has already been claimed that the majority of Americans believe in life after death. This may, of course, be positive or negative; however, Kalish and Reynolds (1976) indicate that two-thirds of their multi-ethnic sample describe the future life in terms "of heavenly paradise" (p. 86). A similar inference might be drawn from the already demonstrated tenden-

RESEARCH BOX 6-2.   *Osarchuk, M. and Tatz, S. J. "Effect of Induced Fear of Death on Belief in an Afterlife."* Journal of Personality and Social Psychology, *1973, 27, 256-60.*

To test their hypothesis that raising one's fear of death should strengthen belief in an afterlife, Osarchuk and Tatz (1973) constructed two equivalent and reliable ten-item scales of belief in an afterlife (forms A and B). High- and low-afterlife belief groups were formed. Half of the people in each group received form A first; the other half received form B first. From each of these groups, ten members were assigned to a death-threat subgroup; ten to a shock-threat group, and ten were designated a control group. Six subgroups were thus formed, three with high belief in an afterlife and three with low belief. To the death-threat subgroups

A taped communication was played, giving an exaggerated estimate of the probability of an early death for individuals aged 18 to 22 due to accident or disease related to food contamination. The tape contained a background of dirgelike music. A series of 42 death-related slides was coordinated with the communication, including scenes of auto wrecks, realistically feigned murder and suicide victims and corpses in a funeral home setting (p. 257).

The members of the shock-threat groups, with appropriate cautions and communications, were informed they would get a series of painful electric shocks. They never received such. The control groups simply engaged in innocent play for the same amount of time that the other groups either underwent the death or shock threats. All took the alternate form of the belief in afterlife scale that they had not taken earlier. The results were partially as predicted. The three subgroups of those with low afterlife beliefs showed the same degree of belief in an afterlife before and after their experience (death or shock threat or nothing). In contrast, the participants with a high belief in an afterlife demonstrated a meaningful increase in these views, but only those exposed to the death threat. It appears that death threats of the sort utilized here can influence one's belief in a life beyond death. It would have been interesting to see if other religious views, such as belief in the existence of God, were also influenced, but this was not done.

cy of more people to affirm the existence of heaven than hell. Religiousness, especially of an intrinsic-committed form, is positively related to those views (Cerny and Carter, 1977; Spilka, Stout, Minton, and Sizemore, 1977).

Taking our cue from the work of Osarchuk and Tatz (1973), we would expect the terminally ill, on the average, to be more religious than healthy persons, because the ill would reap the additional benefits of spiritual support. They might even show less fear of death. Unfortunately, empirical work in this area is at a premium, and that which is available is equivocal. Feifel (1974) failed to show any differences in his conscious and unconscious indicators of death fear between healthy or terminally ill respondents who were religious or nonreligious. In another study (Feifel and Branscomb, 1973), also involving the terminally ill, it was concluded that those "who responded with positive imagery (about death) rated themselves as significantly more religious than those giving either ambivalent or negative answers" (p. 285). Again, the dying were not found to be more religious than other patients or healthy participants.

The above observation is further elaborated in the work of Gibbs and Achterberg-Lawlis (1978) and Duke (1977). The former compared terminal cancer patients and a group of outpatients with minor difficulties. They found that a strong religious commitment was affiliated with low conscious death fear and positive death imagery. This also correlates with denial, meaning emotional rejection of various aspects of one's illness and death. In other words, less death fear by religious persons might have been, in part, a product of simply avoiding recognition of the nature and significance of death. It was also reported that "half of the patients . . . volunteered their visions of God or of other religious figures or deceased family members" (p. 568). Such explicit religious experience during terminality is worthy of more research and understanding. Gibbs and Achterberg-Lawlis point out the need for spiritual counselors who appreciate the fact that "for these dying patients (religion) is a powerful sustaining source and one that those in the helping professions . . . must be able to appreciate and implement to the patient's greatest benefit" (p. 568).

Duke (1977) also studied terminally ill cancer patients and explicitly notes that lessened death fear, high meaning of life, and a strong religious faith apparently go together.

Religion and Death Concern among the Elderly

Nothing is more true than the assertion that "we are all born terminally ill"; however, terminality for most people occurs in old age. In fact, the older we get, the more we become aware of our own inevitable death. More and more, friends and family members die. Our own health is likely to show signs of deterioration and physicians increasingly recommend circumscription of activities, limit our intake of various foods, and explain many physical and psychological occurrences as "just getting old." Society's glorification of youth may accentuate rejection and isolation, and before we are really prepared for it, retirement may be upon us. Without friends, job, health, and too frequently an immediate supportive family, many are relegated to a "golden age" manor to await departure from this "mortal coil." This is the reality a very large number of the elderly confront every day. Therefore, one should not be surprised that the void is often filled by religion. Cavan (1949) has shown a steady growth of religious involvement and viewpoint from the sixties through the nineties. In her work, by the latter ages, 100 percent of the sample expressed full certainty in the existence of an afterlife. Moberg (1965) and others (Argyle and Beit-Hallahmi, 1975; Kalish and Reynolds, 1976) confirm these tendencies. Kalish and Reynolds further express the view that death attitudes may be more a function of age than religiousness.

Research findings on the relationship of religion and death attitudes among the elderly are generally consistent. These results suggest that older religious individuals show little or no fear of death. In line with bible reading and church involvement, they usually possess spiritual and scriptural perspectives about death that include an afterlife (Jeffers, Nichols, and Eisdorfer, 1961; Swenson, 1961). Using a multidimensional approach, Wittkowski and Baumgartner (1977) and Kiely and Dudek (1977) further confirmed a positive relationship between religious commitment and a calm accepting and understanding orientation toward death and dying.

Religion, the Elderly, and Predicting Death

Recent years have witnessed the development of a literature dealing with social and behavioral influences that predict the likelihood of death (Botwinick, West and Storandt, 1978; Lieberman, 1965; Palmore and Jeffers, 1971). Life satisfaction and social participation seem to be the biggest predictors of a long life. A number of studies also demonstrate the association of happiness and satisfaction among the elderly with religious involvement (Bortner and Hultsch, 1970; Edwards and Klemmack, 1973; Graney, 1975; Leonard, 1977). The final test of these relationships might be in assessing the hypothesis that religion and longevity go together. Richardson (1973) carried out a study with a large sample of octogenarians (80 + year olds) but failed to find one-year survival had anything to do with faith.

Religion and Euthanasia

Among the topics brought to the public's attention by the current interest in death is euthanasia. This is a complex issue that is badly simplified by phrases such as "mercy killing," "death with dignity," or "the right to die." Distinctions have been made between "passive" and "active" euthanasia. The former refers to a state in which the quality of life is extremely low, death is imminent, pain may be severe, and the question is whether "heroic" measures to prolong life are to be withheld. This permits the individual to succumb sooner in a more natural manner than would otherwise be true. Active euthanasia suggests an "active" terminating of a life that has been seemingly rendered unliveable because of severe and prolonged suffering. Frequently, requests for death are made by the patient and a close family member complies with the patient's wish despite great personal anguish. The passive form of euthanasia seems to be widely practiced among physcians, often with the tacit approval of the family. Anywhere from two-thirds to over 90 percent of health professionals apparently are in favor of this procedure (Carey and Posavac, 1978; Hoggatt and Spilka, 1978; Rea, Greenspoon, and Spilka, 1975). Active euthanasia also seems to have its advocates, with one study (Carey and Posavac, 1978) reporting 17 percent of physicians and 36 percent of nurses positive toward such a practice.

Clergy apparently share these sentiments. Carey and Posavac (1978) found 96 percent of their sample of clerics advocating passive euthanasia and 21 percent espousing its active form. Nagi, Pugh, and Lazerine (1977–78) showed with larger samples that clergy accepted passive euthanasia with widely varying percentages depending on the reason given for such action. Their data revealed percentages among Protestants ranging from thirty-four to seventy-three in favor of this practice. The comparable numbers for Catholic priests were thirty to sixty-nine, which do not seem to be markedly different. Support for active euthanasia is similar to what Carey and Posavac observed. The range for Protestant clergy approving this extreme measure varied from thirteen to twenty-five percent, depending on circumstances. Catholic priests were much less accepting, with only one to three percent countenancing such action. Unfortunately, no information was provided by Nagi et al. regarding the Protestant denominations sampled. We suspect that the majority may have been from the liberal end of the spectrum. Other work relating to passive euthanasia showed that to the extent clergy hold theologically conservative positions, they reject passive euthanasia (Spilka, Spangler, and Rea, 1981). This finding may be associated with views such as man's taking into his own hands what is perceived of as God's prerogatives. It could also relate to a general philosophic conservatism relative to the value of life and individualism. In contrast, Klopfer and Price (1978) report that a favorable view of euthanasia is positively associated with belief in an afterlife. The more conservative clergy in the Spilka, et al work manifested stronger beliefs in a rewarding life beyond death, but still opposed euthanasia more than their liberal clerical counterparts. Such contradictions require research resolution.

Euthanasia, Religion, and the Elderly

Surprisingly, little is known about variables that relate to the approval of euthanasia, but one recent investigation (Cutler, 1979) suggests that the elderly are both less afraid of death than their younger peers, and less approving of euthanasia. In this work, religiosity was also negatively associated with a favorable view of this position. The latter seems to be a very significant factor here. Since the age relationship disappeared when religion was controlled, it was concluded that religion accounted for the opposition of the elderly to euthanasia.

Unfortunately, we know little about the relationship between religion and euthanasia. National samples tell us that Protestants and Catholics believe similarly about euthanasia, with around 30 to 40 percent favoring it (Gallup, 1975); however, religionists and theologians have lined up on both sides of the issue. The moral and spiritual arguments advanced are complex and controversial, and interested readers might want to examine some of these by reading such works as Oden's *Should Treatment Be Terminated?* (1976), Ramsey's *The Patient as Person* (1970), and Russell's *Freedom to Die* (1975). Euthanasia is an emotional matter of the most basic religious import and raises questions of the greatest significance to the Judeo-Christian tradition and Western society as a whole.

Religion and Bereavement

In life as well as scripture, there must always come that time when "man goeth to his long home, and the mourners go about the streets" (Ecclesiastes 12:5). These mourners must now return to a life without a loved one. We are not restricted here to the elderly; people of all ages die, and the experience for those who remain is often shattering. Even at a distance we all feel a special pain when we think of the death of a child or a young adult. Neither is it possible to cast off the demise of a spouse with whom one has lived for decades. The death of a parent also terminates a life-long relationship. We must all cope with such losses, and religion may play a special role in these difficult times.

Death is rarely suddenly thrust upon us. It is frequently expected and preceded by chronic illness. Terminal cancer can imply a long period of declining health; heart disease might also portend a definite mortality, but sometimes such patients survive for decades. When terminal health problems occur, the survivors-to-be may begin a process of anticipatory grief (Schoenberg et al., 1974). Here, the normal grief process begins prior to the death. Religion is likely to play a number of roles in this development. Nolan (1974) points out that anticipatory grievers practice a "bargaining with God." The mourner pledges all manner of proper religious commitment if the loved one is permitted to live. By engaging in prayer and ritual, it is sometime felt that extra time is being bought. Such ceremonial actions, whether undertaken prior to or after the death of a loved one, appear therapeutic in nature, and may assuage guilt and pacify troubled emotions.

Many scholars have tried to analyze the grief process in terms of possible stages though which the bereaved pass. A brief review of such schemes by the first author revealed thirteen such efforts in which the number of stages varies from three to ten. The assumption that people pass through such a sequence has never been verified by research, and, in fact, what are discussed are expressions of grief rather than phases. In addition, for our purposes, these have not been related to religion and will not be discussed here. A popular self-help attempt along these lines has been proposed by Westberg (1962), and this utilizes faith as an aid to overcoming grief. A more professional approach has been advanced by Spiegel (1977), but again research support is lacking.

We are most familiar with grief and bereavement following the death of a significant person in our lives. Research evidence affirms that once again the function of faith is benign. Loveland (1968) points out that bereaved persons feel more religious and engage in more prayer than they did prior to the death, yet basic beliefs do not appear to be affected. These activities still appear to exert a favorable psychological influence on the survivors. Haun (1977) further shows that adjustment problems are greatest among the bereaved when religious orientation is weak. Those with strong religious commitments apparently cope best with their loss.

Studies of widows reveal further spiritual benefits. Subjectively, almost three-quarters of a group of religious widows stated that their faith aided them (Parkes, 1972). Other work confirmed that devout widows "turned to the formal doctrine of their religions for explanation" (Glick, Weiss, Parkes, 1974, p. 133). Three out of five saw their faith as a significant source of consolation. In neither of the above investigations did basic religious beliefs change. Some may have been accentuated to operate selectively as it was observed that "ideas of resurrection and afterlife did not seem to reduce the initial intensity of grief . . . but did seem to help sustain morale once grief began subsiding" (Glick, Weiss, Parkes, 1974, p. 133).

A number of scholars have pointed out the salutary effects of religious ceremony and ritual during grief (Gorer,1965; Jackson, 1957). Structure is introduced, social support provided, and a formal set of occasions permit the working through of the pain of loss. The Jewish practice of shiva has been distinguished as a seven-day, repetitive set of mourning rituals that both utilize spiritual and community support and also serve "as a distraction from grief rather than as an occasion for its expression" (Parkes, 1972, p. 160). It has been analogized also to group therapy (Kidorf, 1966). Gerson (1977) describes in depth the highly defined mourning process in Judaism and how it is designed to thwart the development of pathological grief by formally prescribing degrees of return for the mourners to normal society interaction.

Death and the Clergy

Clergy are usually the prime bearers of the meaning conveyed to believers of how a spiritual system conceives of death. During terminal illness, the cleric's pastoral role can be of utmost significance, both to the sufferer and his/her family. Ritual often enters this picture with some version of "last rites" being performed. Later, clergy continue to play important roles in funerals, mourning ceremonies, and grief work with the survivors.

Despite the significance of clergy in all activities in which death may be symbolically or actually present, it is surprising that there has been so little research in this area. This has not prevented experienced clerics from offering much advice to their fellows suggesting the complexity of the issues and problems with which they find themselves dealing (Bailey, 1976; Bane, Kutscher, Neale, and Reeves, 1975; Kutscher and Kutscher, 1972).

Unhappily, where research exists we again encounter severe shortcomings in much of this work, but it is all we have. For example, Preston and Horton (1972) lost 35 percent of their potential sample. Fulton and Geis (1968) lost 65 percent of their hoped-for respondents. Garrity and Wyss (1976) were only able to get information from 49 percent of the clergy they approached. Another common problem is illustrated by this latter work and that of Kutscher and Kutscher (1972)—namely, failure to define the religious groups from which the samples were taken in addition to a similar lack of material on other possibly very pertinent demographic characteristics of their participants. Finally, it is to be noted that most of this work was undertaken ten to twenty-five years ago.

Clerical feelings about death   The few studies (Magni, 1970; Meissner, 1958) conducted on seminarians to determine their orientations and reactions to death symbols appear neither definitive, consistent, or useful. The true test must come among those on the firing line of death confrontation in actual life. Where we have data on the death perspectives of clergy, the dominant outlook conceives a positive afterlife. This view is most strongly held by conservative clergy (Spilka, Spangler, Rea, and Nelson, 1981; Spilka, Spangler, and Rea, 1981). There is also a great inclination to see death as a natural terminus to life or as a mystery. These conceptions tend to be more widely maintained among liberal clerics. Finally, death anxiety is high enough to suggest that a considerable degree of such concern is present among clergy.

Training clergy to deal with death   The recent emphasis on death and dying has had considerable impact on seminaries with the development of workshops and other formal training for clergy (Bendiksen, Hewitt, and Vinge, 1979; Kalish and Dunn, 1976).

One study of 276 priests, ministers, and rabbis (Spilka et al., 1981) revealed that only 15 percent felt they had educational experiences that prepared them very well to deal with death. Another 45 percent thought that they were moderately well trained, while the rest considered themselves rather poorly prepared to do death work when they entered their profession. As expected, the majority ordained within the past two decades felt moderately or well educated for death work (64 percent). The greatest weaknesses existed among the older clergy, who acquired their skills in the pastorate. This kind of invaluable experience is now often made available to seminarians via internships prior to their formal ordination.

Clerical involvement with death   Objective determination of the effectiveness of clergy when working with the terminally ill or their families is simply not available. Approximations to this ideal scientific state may be made by questioning the clergy themselves and the people to whom they offer their services. First, it is important to determine just what clergy do in this kind of work.

In two studies of over four hundred clergy (Spilka, Spangler, and Rea, 1981; Spilka et al., 1981), it was found that about 60 percent claimed to deal often or very often with the dying and their families. Only ten to twelve percent are rarely involved, and about one percent are not at all engaged in these efforts.

Clergy may actively participate in a number of functions relating to death such as pastoral visits to the dying and their families. These contacts, whether by home pastor or hospital chaplain, have considerable latitude in terms of content, and it is instructive to know just what goes on at these times. More than half of one clerical sample (91 percent) state they make two or more calls to the home of bereaved parishioners in the year following a death. About 10 percent make no visits (Spilka, Spangler, and Rea, 1981).

Table 6-5 tells us what pastors actually seem to do when they make visits either to homes or to the hospital. These are according to the perceptions of the recipients of the ministrations. Prayer-related behavior along with talk about daily matters clearly prevails, although there is also some attention to church matters, scriptural reference, the future, and unfortunately, irrelevancies. Evident counseling also occurs.

The dynamics of these interactions need to be understood in great detail, but again we have only the anecdotal and experiential wisdom of pastors to fall back on (Bruder, 1962; Hulme, 1970; Johnson, 1967). Empirical data are lacking, although knowledgeable inferences are unquestionably made. We can only guess how many critical interactive subleties are part of this process. A skill in listening must necessarily be cultivated. Studies of the personality and manner of successful pastors also need to be undertaken. On another level, these are psychotherapeutic encounters and may need insights from that realm.

Theology, personal faith, and clergy effectiveness   The strength imparted by one's faith especially to the clergy often comes from their church's theology. This appears true with two-thirds of pastors claiming that their theology is "very helpful," while only two to three percent feel it is of little or no help (Spilka et al., 1981). Contrary to expectations, such aid is not greater among those of more conservative than liberal persuasion (Spilka, Spangler, and Rea, 1981).

The cleric's own religious faith is even more important than theology in providing support in death work. Eighty-three percent consider this of prime importance when working with the dying. Only two percent were dissatisfied with its role. It is thus abundantly evident that clergy draw much strength for death work from their church's theological conceptualization of death. In addition, their

TABLE 6-5. Activities of Home Clergy and Hospital Chaplains with Cancer Patients and the Families of Children with Cancer[1] (Percentages Engaging in the Activity[2])

	CANCER PATIENTS		FAMILIES OF CHILDREN WITH CANCER	
ACTIVITY	HOME CLERGY	HOSPITAL CHAPLAIN	HOME CLERGY	HOSPITAL CLERGY
Offering to pray for	43%	47%	42%	44%
Offering to pray with	42	35	51	44
Actually praying with	46	22	56	48
Reading religious material	17	14	20	20
Counseling	21	16	20	24
Talking irrelevancies	21	18	34	36
Seeming to understand	44	28	44	44
Talking church matters	15	6	7	12
Talking about family	47	12	46	40
Discussing the future	15	8	15	12
Other	9	22	17	8

[1]These data are taken from Spilka and Spangler (1979).

[2]The percentages add up to more than 100 as clergy engage in more than one activity at any time.

own individual spiritual commitment seems to be a noteworthy source of support.

The strong backing of theology and faith contribute to the belief of clergy which 64 percent express that they are "very helpful" to the dying patient or his/her family. Still, it may be the strain of these efforts and the doubts they arouse that make almost 70 percent also feel less than "very satisfied" with their exertions. None are "completely dissatisfied," but 11 to 14 percent are quite unhappy. The general ambivalence of pastors was illustrated by 43 percent who used such qualifying adjectives to describe themselves as "frustrated, inadequate, apprehensive," etc. At least, with families of the dying, church conservatism implies more personal satisfaction, possibly a concomitant of stronger beliefs in an afterlife that seem to be better and more forcefully defined.

Happily, it is possible to look at the obverse side of these impressions by examining what cancer patients and the families of children with cancer think about their encounters with clergy. Research Box 6-3 provides information on a study that looked at the consumer's side of clergy-client relationships.

Work with the bereaved reports similar findings of the helpfulness of clergy at this troubled time (Carey, 1979–80; Haun, 1977). Carey (1979–80) compared perceived satisfaction with physicians, nurses, chaplains, social workers, and the family by widows and widowers. Although the family is viewed as most helpful, the widows identified the hospital chaplain as a close second (71 percent). Forty-four percent of the widowers confirmed this view, the difference possibly being a function of greater religious commitment on the part of the widows.

In most ways, clergy are like everyone else when death is involved. They become anxious, confused, desirous of helping but want to withdraw from this

RESEARCH BOX 6-3.   *Spilka, B., Spangler, J. D., and Nelson, C. B. "Spiritual support in life-threatening illness."* Journal of Religion and Health, *1983, 22, 98–104.*

The final criterion of pastoral effectiveness resides in those to whom clergy bring their capabilities. We have seen what they do, and even though there is great individuality in these associations, there is reason to believe that the clergy are important to terminal patients and their families. In this study, 101 cancer patients and 45 parents of children with cancer were questioned about their interactions with home pastors and hospital chaplains. On the average, these participants were quite religious. All responded to a questionnaire of fifty-five items, of which six were open-ended, permitting a free response.

Twenty-nine percent of the patients received visits by their pastors in their homes, while 66 percent were also visited in the hospital. The corresponding data for the families of children with cancer were 42 percent home visits and 56 percent for hospital visits. About 55 percent of both the patients and parents saw hospital chaplains. Seventy-eight to 87 percent of the patients and parents expressed satisfaction with these visits whether they were to the home or hospital. Table 6-5 indicates what goes on in these interactions. Although family talk and counseling is clearly of substantive utility and desired, this seems to be a time for the spiritual. Most satisfaction attends situations where home clergy actually pray with patients and the family. Engaging in religious reading is also positively regarded. In the hospital, the families favorably regard discussions of the future by the chaplain. Finally, the willingness of a home pastor or chaplain to be present, to lend him/herself to this troubled situation is considered most desirable.

As is so frequently true, clarity attends the undesirable more than the favorable. Most that is displeasing can be broadly subsumed as poor communication and lack of understanding by the pastor—impersonality, appearing to visit out of duty alone, failure to appreciate the pain of the situation.

Insensitivity is part of this picture. Extremely distressing are efforts to effect apparent "deathbed conversions." For example, one pastor harangued a patient to "change his pagan ways." Much more common are indications of the pastor's own discomfort—looking at his/her watch, acting "nervous," verbalizing shallow clichés, standing at a distance from patients, being painfully silent and unresponsive, and finally revealing haste to leave.

A final comment on pastoral identity might be offered. A fair number of patients reported difficulty knowing a visitor was a hospital chaplain. Wearing informal sports clothes, lacking a badge stating position or possessing a badge too small to read at any distance, plus failing to identify oneself verbally—all fall under this heading.

The many things pastors do and may represent can bring comfort, solace, and satisfaction to those greatly in need of such. They may also convey a lack of feeling and compassion without intending to do so. We already have initial insights into this area, but future research clearly is needed to provide more.

harsh reality. Parkes (1972) observed they "are often embarrassed and ineffectual when face-to-face with those who have been or are about to be bereaved" (p. 169). Nevertheless, probably with mixed feelings, they have entered a profession and taken on duties that must involve death and dying. Experience may make for some additional comfort in the face of tragedy and more effective denial of the meanings implicit in this situation for themselves and those they love. The clergy never become immune to the feelings engendered by death; it is an ever-present source of concern for which they, as well as those to whom they minister, gain strength and support from their faith.

Religion and Suicide

As upsetting as death itself is, it is rarely ever more distressing than when it comes about by one's own hand. Although it has been employed, and apparently approved, under very special conditions, the Judeo-Christian tradition takes a very dim view of suicide. Witness the mass suicide of the almost 1,000 Jewish defenders of Masada approximately two millenia ago or the voluntary martyrdom of many early Christians (Rosen, 1975). Historically, established religion has been on both sides of the issue, both as prescriber and proscriber of suicide depending on time, place, and circumstance. The dominant position is, however, overwhelmingly negative. Stigma and disgrace have been the lot of both the suicide and his/her family in Western society for many centuries. Jackson (1972) points out that suicide is so regarded because it represents an attack upon society, the self, and God. It is a serious threat to a theology that sees life and death in the hands of an omnipotent and benevolent creator. Formal theological anti-suicide statements may be obtained easily from the classic writings of Judaism, Catholicism, and Protestantism, but suffice it to say that suicide is regarded with the utmost of contempt, fear, and opprobrium.

Among early researchers, Durkheim (1951) saw suicide resulting from a lack of identification with a cohesive group. Examining suicide rates of Catholics, Protestants, and Jews in Europe during the last century, he explained the higher incidence of Protestant than Catholic suicide by referring to the former as "a less strongly integrated church than the Catholic church" (p. 159). In addition, he claimed the ". . . proclivity of Protestantism for suicide must relate to the spirit of free inquiry that animates this religion" (p. 158). The even lower rates for Jews were viewed as due ". . . to the hostility surrounding them . . . (which) . . . obliges them to live in greater union" (p. 160).

The group integration hypothesis may hold, but other workers have noted great inconsistencies in Catholic, Protestant, and Jewish suicide rates (Argyle and Beit-Hallahmi, 1975; Dublin, 1963). These may be a function of the fact that religion is tied to socioeconomic status, political power, education, and other demographic factors which themselves relate to suicide. Stengel (1964) further asserts that the odium with which suicide is viewed may mean suppression of such a recorded cause of death particularly in places where feelings might run extremely high as would be true of Catholic countries.

Going beyond Durkheim to see if religion outside of its social integrating role might suppress suicide directly, Stark, Doyle, and Rushing (1983) examined American data on church affiliation and suicide among Catholics and Protestants.

Noting some severe critiques of Durkheim's work and conclusions that may invalidate it, these researchers found that low suicide rates go with strong church membership per se. Templer and Veleber (1980) follow the Durkheimian thesis further with American data to the effect that they claim the higher the suicide rate in individual states, the lower the proportion of Catholics in the population. In a somewhat peripherally related investigation of college students with accepting attitudes toward their own possible suicide, Minear and Brush (1980-81) noted that these individuals were less religiously oriented than other students who rejected the idea of their own suicide.

Group comparisons, especially when they are as broad and uncontrolled as in the above research, obscure much more potent religious factors—namely, degree of commitment and involvement. Hole (1971) observed that religion was an inhibitor of suicide among depressed patients when it was of importance to the person. Comstock and Partridge (1972) also found that suicide reduced as church attendance increased. Hoelter (1979) showed highly consistent and negative associations between the acceptability of suicide and a variety of religious variables such as current and childhood church attendance, self-perceived religiosity, religious orthodoxy, and strength of belief in a supreme being. All of these measures are undoubtedly highly intercorrelated, but the point is clearly made.

Focusing on the elderly, Nelson (1977) suggested that "a high level of religiosity could serve to insulate the individual against feelings of isolation and despair" (p. 67). Utilizing the more subtle concept of indirect life-threatening behavior—such as refusing medication, pulling out intravenous needles, and acting in a medically self-destructive manner—it was revealed that this behavior lessened as the elderly patient's devoutness increased.

Current explanations of suicide stress the role of serious personality disturbance, usually of a depressive nature (Dublin, 1963; Hole, 1971). Argyle and Beit-Hallahmi (1975) suggest that to the extent that one's faith supports personal and social integration, the acceptability and likelihood of suicidal behavior should be low. If, as has been frequently claimed, depression is a precursor to suicide, religion may both counter these tendencies and exacerbate them. Chapter Twelve discusses these possibilities in greater detail.

Suicide is a very difficult area to research properly, and we have, as is so often true, better theories than data in this troubled realm. It does appear that suicide and religion are most likely to be negatively affiliated, implying another constructive role for religious faith; however, the issue is far more complex than this. Since attention is turned toward the suicide after the fact, the accuracy and reliability of much of the information gathered must be called into question. A strong aversion to classifying a death as suicide must also enter this picture with its great potential for selectively biasing any research. It is reasonable to expect suicide and religion to be associated as theory suggests, but it is likely to be some time before any truly solid conclusions may be drawn about these relationships.

DEATH IN THE RELIGIO-SOCIAL CONTEXT

Religion can obviously be quite compelling in our everyday secular social environment. When cultural settings and religious settings are coordinated, their combined power is likely to be strongly directive. There are at least two excellent illustrations of this influence relative to death—namely, the Mormons and the Amish.

The Mormon Case: Religion, Health, and Death

Vernon and Waddell (1974) demonstrate, from a variety of sources, how the Church of Jesus Christ of the Latter-Day Saints (Mormon) propounds doctrines relating to food practices which in themselves affect health and mortality. Among the states, Utah, which has the highest proportion of Mormon residents, also has the lowest rates for death (6.0/1,000) (Dolmatch, 1981), and various degenerative diseases (Vernon and Waddell, 1974).

Mormon theology shows a high valuation of the way one treats his/her body and thus stresses abstinence from alcohol, caffeine-stimulated beverages, and tobacco. Nutritional counsel focuses on "wholesome" foods (Vernon and Waddell, 1974, p. 201). Those who have traveled in Utah and/or associated with religiously committed Mormons know the seriousness with which they identify with these ideals. It is therefore no surprise that mortality rates from diseases in which the prohibited substances have been involved tend to be quite low. Using data from infancy deaths and those resulting from accidents that should not necessarily be tied to drinking and smoking, Vernon and Waddell (1974) demonstrate that in the latter, Utah is representative of our nation. The evidence suggests that a strong religious system that is integrated with the sociocultural context may influence nutrition and health practices, eventuating in mortality rates different from those that prevail elsewhere.

The Amish: Religion and Family Support

To a considerable degree, the Amish, like the Mormons, have been able to maintain settings in which their religious ideology is minimally distinguished from the social framework in which they live. As a rule, the Amish have been highly successful in religiously and culturally preserving their unity by creating relatively "isolated" communities.

As with the Mormons, Amish spiritual ideology is well integrated into social life. Bryer (1979) shows how death has therefore come to be regarded as a joint religious-familial concern. Where the dead or dying are segregated in hospitals or mortuaries in our larger culture, the tendency among the Amish is in the opposite direction—back to the home, family, and community. Neighbors and relatives are informally, if not formally, organized to perform various ceremonial functions such as preparing the dead for burial and providing mutual support via reinforcing the Amish view of "death as a spiritual victory over temporal life" (Bryer, 1979, p. 259). Other families who have had similar experiences visit and collectively work through the grieving process with the newly bereaved. Death is not denied, but openly accepted as a part of life explicitly involving families and the community.

This socioreligous support, it is felt, permits grief to be worked through relatively quickly with a very low likelihood of undesirable psychological aftereffects developing. Death, therefore, does not weaken or diminish the community, but seems to strengthen the ties that keep it integrated.

Sociologists and anthropologists always have shown that death is as much a cultural matter as an individual concern. The way a people structures life may hasten death or extend longevity, or once death has occurred bring people together or separate them further. Religion can contribute to either development; thus, we need to understand much about the role and meaning of faith in the individual and his/her context.

RELIGION, DEATH, AND ATTRIBUTION THEORY

At the core of attribution theory is the need for meaning, and this need is greatest when death is confronted. The idea of ceasing to exist without understanding why such occurs and what will follow the cessation of life is also the ultimate threat to personal control and self-esteem. Religion, however, offers an attributional framework to ameliorate, if possible, the trauma of nonexistence, and also exacerbate it. In the Judeo-Christian tradition, death is affiliated with wrongdoing. However, both sides of the coin are included as we also read "For the wages of sin is death; but the gift of God is eternal life . . ." (Romans 6:23). Attributions are thus made to the self and the deity. Death is seen as caused by wrongdoing, which means that the attribution implies one is not a good person. The further implication is that one not only dies but that life is terminated for all time. If one is good and does the right thing, God will bestow the best of all possibilities on the individual—namely, everlasting life.

We have seen that attitudes toward death and religion are multidimensional in nature. Relative to the scriptural basis for attributions about death, different religious and death perspectives suggest different attributional patterns. We know that intrinsic-committed (IC) and extrinsic-consensual (EC) orientations demonstrate different attributional tendencies (see Chapter One). A more basic positive-negative continuum seems to exist. When these are combined as shown in a number of studies (Minton and Spilka, 1976; Spilka et al., 1977), radically different attributions seem to result. We know IC persons view themselves more positively than do their EC peers, hence the form of personal faith they embrace seems to be associated with self-perceptions of being spiritually good. The evidence further tells us that they do not make negative attributions to death, but associate it with a rewarding afterlife and the actions of a benevolent deity. In contrast, EC individuals view themselves and death in more unfavorable terms.

With regard to the motivational basis of attributions, IC and EC people vary in the meaning death has for them, the former embracing positive conceptions, the latter undesired, negative ones. The utilitarian orientation of the EC person connotes a lack of control relative to death that is not a concern of the IC view. EC individuals would thus be expected to perceive death as an unwanted interference with their ambitions and practices. A God that would do that could not be the object of favorable attributions, and there is evidence to suggest this is true (Spilka and Mullin, 1977). Given the foregoing, and data on the self-esteem of IC and EC persons, we can see how meaning and control attributions are consonant with those to the self.

Images regarding an afterlife, particularly in relation to conceptions of heaven and hell suggest some fruitful avenues for studying the meaning, control, and esteem aspects of attributions relative to self and deity. We have seen the notable effects of near-death experiences on afterlife conception, but more work needs to be done from an attributional framework to understand the significance of these for the individual.

The fact that virtually no research has been conducted in this realm utilizing an attributional stance means, among other possibilities, that we do not know the influence of situational factors on the nature of the explanations people employ at any given time. The pioneering work of Osarchuk and Tatz (1973) opens the door to comprehending the attributional foundations of attitude shifts with regard to religion, afterlife, and death. In like manner, what does it mean when we conduct our studies on adolescents who are likely to respond in terms of death-at-a-distance as opposed to working with the elderly, the terminally ill, the bereaved, the person with high potential for suicide, the suicide attempter, or even the caregiver who frequently encounters death—the cleric, physician, nurse, etc.?

Situational influence clearly affects religious and death attributions, but these are likely to interact with dispositional influences. In the chapter on Religion and Mental Disorder, much of relevance with respect to death is present, for example, in the religious perspective of the depressed. Just as form of personal faith represents a dispositional characteristic of considerable attributional import relative to death, so may many other factors of a similar nature enter the picture. Clearly this is a fertile topic for study, from an attributional framework. To date it remains largely unexplored.

SUMMARY AND CONCLUSIONS

Death and religion are indeed intimate companions. The evidence is quite convincing that one's faith may be a source of strength for the individual confronting death. The form of personal faith adopted is, however, an important variable influencing the manner with which one conceptualizes and probably handles death and dying. Still, we cannot lose sight of the complex matrix of associations among demographic and social factors such as sex, age, ethnic group, socioeconomic status etc. that influence both religion and death perspectives.

Technically, much of the available research on religion and death is questionable because of failure to appreciate the intricacies of how humans link their feelings about death to the personal theology they hold, and how the latter is further connected to the religio-social order. The pattern of these affiliations still appears of sufficient basic potency that general inferences may be made. Whether those who participate in this research are college students, the elderly, terminally ill, the bereaved or clergy, religious commitments are likely to counter fear and negative perspectives on death and dying. The cornerstone of support appears to come from beliefs in a benevolent afterlife which is at the heart of most Western faiths and many others around the world.

Personal and institutional religions perform many functions relative to death. They provide explanations as to the meaning of death which are avenues to consolation and solace for many people. Of utmost importance is that the internal support that faith provides is buttressed by the ability of churches to maintain social relationships and keep people integrated with each other in the face of death.

In other words, they focus on the future and are directed toward the living. Death becomes by necessity reluctantly accepted as a fact of life, and the latter must continue until it ends for all involved.

We must not lose sight of the fact that religion offers a sense of control to the person relative to death. Prayer, observance and holding the right beliefs are probably most often taken as offering security and protection in a world that continually threatens life. Those who meet these institutional criteria for being defined as a "good" person can also benefit in terms of self-esteem. Meaning, control, and positive self-views become this world's positive concomitants of an intrinsic-committed faith.

Another facet of religion of great import is its emphasis on moral issues which are a significant aspect of how we deal with death. Psychological study brings to the fore many human considerations of euthanasia and suicide for religionists to ponder. In addition the role of clergy and the community have been, in part, explicated, revealing ways in which the human encounter with death may be eased. Religion may thus be a constructive or destructive force in regard to death; most often it seems to play the first role. We nevertheless need to know more about how it functions. This constitutes a noteworthy problem for the psychology of religion.

CHAPTER SEVEN
RELIGIOUS EXPERIENCE

"Where is God? I have myself sought to find my God so that if I could, I might not only believe but somehow see. For I see the things which my God has made and God Himself I do not see." (O'Brien, 1964, p. 61).

"The very beginning, the intrinsic core, the essence, the universal nucleus of every known high religion . . . has been the private, lonely, personal illumination, revelation, or ecstasy of some acutely sensitive prophet or seer." (Maslow, 1964, p. 19).

"A father said to his double-seeing son, 'Son, you see two instead of one' 'How can that be?' the boy replied. 'If I were, there would seem to be four moons up there in place of two.'" (Shah, 1972, p. 172).

INTRODUCTION

The study of religious experience is perplexing partly because so much time and effort can be wasted on defining precisely what is meant by *experience*. At a common-sense level, we are aware that experience is something other than action or behavior. Yet we experience our actions and our behaviors, and it is quite strange to think of experience without any action involved—for even to do nothing is to do something. Similarly, experience is not only thought or belief, but clearly involves *what* we think and *how* we believe. Finally, many people try to reduce experience to feelings or emotions, yet while these are part of what we mean by experience, experience is certainly not only emotions or feelings. Indeed, in some sense experience is a total way of reacting or being and is reduced to something else only with grave risk. Perhaps, as St. Augustine said of time, we know what it is unless we are asked to *say* what it is! Hence, initially we shall not clearly define religious experience in this chapter, but rather we shall look at other kinds of phenomena psychologists have studied when religious experience has been foremost in their mind. And it was foremost in the mind of the psychology of religion's most respected investigator, William James.

PAST AND PRESENT CONCEPTUALIZATIONS AND RESEARCH

James and the Varieties of Religious Experience

James' classic work, *The Varieties of Religious Experience,* has continued to be in print since initially delivered as the Gifford lectures in 1902. While one can speculate as to varying reasons for the persistence of this fine work, the simple fact remains that James continues to set the tone for much empirical work in the psychology of religious experience. We shall use James' conclusions to his work to suggest the framework for a theory of religious experience that is both simple enough to be useful and suggestive enough not to be used too simply.

James' definition of religion for purposes of the Gifford lectures clearly revealed his own explicit commitment to understanding intense religious experiences as rather extreme and hence pure examples of religiosity found in an infinite variety of more diluted forms throughout all religions. For James, religion was "The feelings, acts, and experiences of individual men in their solitude, so far as they stand in relation to whatever they may consider the divine." (p. 31). James further clarified this definition in defining the divine as ". . . a primal reality as the individual feels impelled to respond to solemnly and gravely, neither by a curse nor a jest" (p. 38). Thus, James squarely places solitary individuals seeking and confronting their God at the forefront of concern for the psychology of religion. And the totality of their response is for James the infinite material for the varieties of religious experience. Culling from a wide variety of written and personal testimonies, James' Gifford lectures weave a pattern of complexity across a wide warp and warf of reported religious experiences. Yet in his conclusion to these justly famous lectures, he is most parsimonious indeed. The infinite varieties of religious experience are seen to represent simply an initial discontent and its favorable resolution. The discontent and its resolution are the essence of religious experience. For James, God, however acknowledged, does intervene in particular lives. James' major conclusions from his study of religious experience entail three broadly conceived scientific claims and two more narrowly acknowledged psychological consequences. We shall not now list these conclusions. Instead, we turn to a major study in progress. It is over seven decades later, the investigator's name has changed, the material is more systematically collected, but, as we shall see, the conclusions are the same.

The Religious Experience Research Unit of Manchester College, Oxford

Alister Hardy (1979) recently published data collected from the first eight years of an ongoing project of the Religious Experience Research Unit at Manchester College, Oxford. Initiated in 1969, this project, is an effort to study contemporary religious experiences of persons voluntarily responding to requests printed in newspapers and elsewhere to report their religious experiences. Hardy's request was not merely for experiences of the extreme type typical in James' self-chosen examples, but for those of the more temperate variety as well. In *The Spiritual Nature of Man,* Hardy published an extensive classification of the major defining characteristics of these religious experiences from an initial pool of 3,000 reported experiences. This scheme is structured on three levels with some twelve major, seven middle-level, and ninety lower-level categories. Hardy's significant effort to classify religious experiences would not have appealed to James who preferred to let the experiences speak for themselves unfettered by what he would probably claim was a tyranny of classification schemes. Hardy's conclusions, reached ostensibly independently of James, are interesting as they are precisely what James concluded much earlier. Both Hardy and James affirm a transcendental reality, and a sense of presence and personalization relative to a "higher" universe. As for psychological consequences, the power of prayer is acknowledged, early childhood experiences are considered very significant, and feelings of safety, security, love, and happiness are regarded as concomitants of religious experience.

Other studies of voluntarily submitted documents of religious experience are not inconsistent with either James' or Hardy's claims (Laski, 1961). It would appear that from a purely methodological perspective persons interested in studying personal testimonies of religious experience are perhaps biased in favor of interpretating such experiences favorably and receive from persons only experiences congruent with a rather simple if not naive view of religion. Simple and naive, perhaps. But could it nevertheless be true? If we look at more sophisticated studies of religious experience, collected in more experimental or quasi-experimental settings, we can have a firmer base upon which to formulate conclusions. Yet in order to do this, we shall once again turn to James' most simple summary of religious experience: discontent and its resolution. We do so, however, not just in terms of James, but updated in light of contemporary critical commentary. We do so in order to have a framework within which to organize the empirical literature on religious experience.

Limits and Their Transcendence

Before looking at particular studies of religious experience, we are going to suggest the wisdom of James' earlier formulation of religious experience. For while James is most often noted for his insistence of the richness and diversity of religious experience, he also insisted that what all religious experiences share in common is a resolution to a previously experienced uneasiness. James is not alone in this.

In his classic work on the study of religious experience and mental illness, Boisen (1936) noted that what distinguished religious experience from otherwise intense and indeed often pathological experiences was the fact that religious experiences are victorious resolutions of what would otherwise be devastating defeats. He spoke of inner conflict and inner resolution. Religious experiences, like some pathological experiences, confront great personal disharmony. But there is a difference—and as Boisen insisted the difference is in the outcome. A religious experience marks the successful resolution of an inner conflict.

Boisen's perspective meshes nicely with both theological and nontheological perspectives in which the concepts of limits and transcendence are related (Corssan, 1975; Johnson, 1974). In the simplest sense, a total involvement and awareness of limits produces the discontent and disharmony (James' uneasiness) which if successfully overcome are transcended. Hence, limits point to the possibility of transcendence and the integrated experience of both are what we can call religious experience. This is the sense in which Bowker (1973) has recently emphasized that the psychological origin of the sense of God must be rooted not in the particulars of experience, but rather in terms of content that meaningfully points to a limitation to be overcome. In this sense, God is always "beyond" and the psychology of religious experiencing is in the experience of this "beyondness" through the mode of transcendence of previously experienced limits.

We have then a rather basic perspective within which to organize the empirical literature on religious experience. It can be followed back to James' notion of discontent and resolution, but only if we keep in mind the fact that such discontent and resolution is in an interpretation that is religiously rooted precisely in the sense that James defined religion. In a fundamental sense, religious experience is the meaningful transcendence or resolution of limits or discontents within the perspective of whatever is considered divine. Not surprisingly then, religious experience is almost infinite in its particular varieties, as James insisted. We shall now look at some of this variation in terms of the most general categories within which contemporary psychologists confront religious experience. In so doing, we traverse a broad terrain indeed—from recent discoveries of the physiology of the brain to psychedelic drugs; from altered states of consciousness to speaking in tongues; from the handling of snakes to healing; from simply sitting to immersing oneself in an isolation tank. And in so doing, we shall see the potential for religious experience in all of these experiences.

A Physiology of God?

Perhaps one of the most shortsighted views of religious experience is to assume that such experiences are merely emotional. The "merely" here implies a negative overtone and asserts that since what is perceived as religious is physiological in origin it can be discounted. Such a view was noted by James (1902) as "medical materialism" and its insufficiency was well noted:

> Medical materialism finishes up Saint Paul by calling his vision on the road to Damascus a discharging lesion of the occipital cortex, he being an epileptic. It snuffs out Saint Teresa as an hysteric, Saint Francis of Assisi as an hereditary degenerate. George Fox's discontent with the shams of his age, and his pining for spiritual veracity, it treats as a symptom of a disordered colon.(p. 13).

The point, of course, is not that physiological processes may not be involved in religious experience, but that some think the identification of the physiology involved in religious experience "reduces it away." Ironically, this conceptual error is precisely one advanced by earlier religionists who attempted to validate an experience because it came from supernatural and not merely natural sources. Of course, the problem is that one cannot draw either a firm conceptual nor even a tentative scientific distinction between such terms as *natural* and *supernatural*. As fourteenth-century mystic Meister Ekhart said, "Never mind therefore what the nature of anybody's God-given knack may be . . . Do not worry about whether it is natural or supernatural; for both nature and grace are his" (Blackney, 1941, p. 41).

However, this is not to say that physiological arousal might not be involved in some aspects of religious experiencing. What is crucial is that such arousal be appropriately identified as part of a broader context that is identified as religious because of other than merely physiological processes. One recent study has attempted to demonstrate the usefulness of this view with specifically religious persons. However, before presenting this study let us briefly note what is known as a cognitive-arousal theory of emotions in general psychological theory.

COGNITIVE-PHYSIOLOGICAL AROUSAL AND ITS RELEVANCE TO RELIGIOUS EXPERIENCING

It has long been noted that when persons describe their emotional states, they usually do so by initially describing the set and setting within which they became aware of rather diffusely identified internal physiological processes. In other words, persons tend to assess how they feel in terms of two different processes: (1) what the arousing circumstances were—external, perceptual factors; and (2) what internal physiological processes they became aware of. Hence, the labeling of physiological arousal is due not just to physiological arousal but to the specific circumstances in which physiological arousal occurs. In this view, physiological arousal might be differentially labeled as "fear," "awe," or "anger," depending upon the circumstances in which it occurs. This theory of emotions is largely associated with the psychologist Schachter (1971) who has done some intriguing experimental work to test his theory.

In the now-classic study, Schachter and Singer (1962) injected a drug, epinephrine (adrenalin), into persons participating in an experiment they thought was to test the effects of a vitamin compound on vision. In fact, half the persons received an injection of epinephrine, which usually produces increased respiration and heart rate, "edgy" feelings, and slight muscle tremors. The others received a placebo injection (saline solution) that produces no identifiable physiological effects. Hence, the experimenters could be reasonably assured of physiological arousal only in the experimental group. These experimental persons were then divided into three groups and provided differing information as to the effects of their injection. One group was told truthfully what physiological arousal to expect. Of the remaining two groups, one was given no information while the other was given misinformation to the effect that they would experience—numbness, itching, and maybe even a headache.

Environmental cues were then provided for all persons in the experiment and were either euphoric or angry in nature. The cues were provided by "stooges" of the experimenter who were in the room with the participants, presumably as another participant in the study. The "euphoric stooge" acted appropriately playful in the euphoric condition and the "angry stooge" acted appropriately angry in the anger condition. The experimenters watched all participants through a one-way mirror.

Results of the experiment were generally as predicted from this cognitive-arousal theory. Persons either having no physiological arousal (saline placebo group) or given correct information as to expectations did not use environmental cues to label their arousal. However, other participants, either without information as to what arousal to expect or with misinformation as to what arousal to expect, tended to interpret their arousal in emotional terms appropriate to the stooges' behavior—euphoric or angry. Hence, Schachter argues that given a situation of unanticipated physiological arousal, external cues (in this case, stooges' behavior) influence the labeling of what emotion is occurring.

Schachter's work is important because it suggests that even if one takes an arousal view of emotion and of some experiences, the fact of the physiological arousal is only one component in a complex labeling process that takes external factors into account to assess what meaning such arousal has. (Plutchik and Ax, 1967). In our own view of limits and transcendence, Schachter's work suggests that physiological arousal may be a factor in initiating feelings that become meaningfully religious only if other appropriate conditions are met. Hence, as James (1902) notes, religious experience cannot be exhausted by an appeal merely to physiological origins. The question now becomes under what conditions will physiological arousal be interpreted religiously? One suggestive clue is contained in a footnote in James' work: "The plain truth is that to interpret religion one must in the end look at the immediate content of the religious consciousness." One recent study does just that.

The Return of the Ostracized

It has been over two decades since a renowned psychologist prophesized the "return of the ostracized" to psychology (Holt, 1964). The ostracized was imagery, and its return was correctly predicted as part of the reemergence of concern with experience rather than merely behavior (Bergin, 1964). One might have expected that psychologists would have looked to religious variables as part of their new concern with imagery given the unquestioned centrality of imagery within the world's great religious traditions (Holmes, 1980). Indeed as both Shepard (1978) and Lilly (1977) have argued, it is precisely in situations of solitude, isolation, and focused concentration that imagery is likely to be elicited. Yet it became of concern to social scientists, largely because such imagery when *unanticipated* and *undesired* interferes with ongoing activities. This proves obviously disrupting when the activity is attending to a radar scope, surviving during periods of forced isolation, or managing one's duties on a space flight!

On the other hand, many religious practices encourage persons to turn away from the typical perceptual environment to an alternate environment in which it is both desired and anticipated that imagery will occur. Furthermore, such imagery, rather than being dysfunctional to some other activity, is infused with meaning in and of itself. Indeed, one extreme position advocated by LaBarre (1972) is that the origin of all religions is ultimately rooted in such imagery.

Obviously, LaBarre's claim is extreme and too psychologically reductive, yet one only needs compare it to a very similar claim in James (1902) to appreciate the important role of imagery in the origin if not maintenance of religions. If this is true, imagery is a central fact of the content of religious experiencing and one ought to anticipate studies of the elicitation of this imagery by psychologists interested in religion. Furthermore, such studies are directly relevant to physiological theories of religious experiencing since it is seldom that mere physiological arousal is of major importance in religiously defined experience. Rather, it is the physiological elicitation of imagery that is of greater importance and more typically of central concern in religion.

Isolation Tanks

The most impressive attempts to elicit imagery in a general sense have occurred in sensory isolation studies. Initial studies occurred at McGill University where sensory stimulation was minimized through the use of goggles, constant noise, and devices to minimize tactile sensations. With sensory participation minimized in the "external" world, concern centered around presumably self-generated processes and experiences. As the research advanced, more sophisticated isolation techniques were devised, culminating in the isolation tank pioneered by Lilly (1956, 1977; Lilly and Lilly, 1976).

Early isolation-tank studies gave exaggerated results eventually discovered to be artifacts of the experimental situation. The very uniqueness of the isolation environment combined with excessive experimental forewarnings and precautions produced panic and bizarre experiences in some participants. Most impressive were claims to "hallucinations" variously reported. Yet as studies progressed, it was discovered that if potential participants were knowledgeable-initiated into the tank situation, they could experience a wide variety of positive effects and that all negative phenomena could be eliminated (Suedfeld, 1975; Zubeck, 1969). Among the more positive effects likely to be experienced is imagery.

Imagery is readily elicited in the isolation-tank situation if participants are relaxed and unfearful, and given specific instructions to attend to internal states, contents, and processes. Unstructured phenomena such as either focused or diffuse white light or various geometric forms and colors occur in almost all participants. These are readily attributable to such things as spontaneous neural firing in the retina which are attended to in isolation situations. Some of these processes may be given meaningful status in religious traditions. More detailed instructions and time in the tank can lead to more meaningful imagery, particularly meaningful figures, not unlike dream and hypnogogic imagery (Jackson and Kelley, 1962; Rossi, Sturrock, and Solomon, 1963; Suedfeld and Vernon, 1964). Notice that we do not call such imagery, hallucinations, since this term has a loaded meaning. Indeed, whether or not hallucinations are elicited in the isolation-tank situation depends upon the way the term is defined. Certainly, if the definition is such that a person must "see" an image that is mistakenly taken for a "real, external object," hallucinations are rare if not nonexistent in isolation-tank experiences.

An Aside on "Hallucinations"

Recent studies seriously question the existence of "hallucinations" as a unique phenomenon and certainly do not define them, as is commonly assumed, as a misperception involving pathological processes. Instead, one can best conceive of processes involved common to both imagery and hallucination and in the social and cultural processes that encourage and facilitate the experience and report of such phenomena (Al-Issa, 1977). In this sense at least, religious variables are of immense relevance. In particular, religions have fostered acitivities such as prayer and meditation that are either aimed at or have as an anticipated consequence, the elicitation of imagery (Coleman, 1977; Larsen, 1976; Pelletier and Garfield, 1976). Similarly, apparently spontaneously experienced imagery possesses great religious significance in some religious traditions. Catholicism makes a distinction between a "vision" and an "apparition" that parallels contemporary discussions of "image" and "hallucination." Apparitions are perceived as "exterior" and are a special case of visions. (Volken, 1961, p. 10). A purely secular psychologist would be tempted to call an apparition an hallucination.

Yet what is crucial in our discussion is the fact that the meaningful status of imagery varies with the context within which it is interpreted and with the nature of the ontological status it is given (Bettelheim, 1976; Klinger, 1971; Singer, 1966; Watkins, 1976). Indeed, within meditative traditions one can distinguish two major orientations toward religious imagery. On the one hand are traditions emphasizing that imagery, while likely to occur, is to be ignored in favor of higher states of perfection. On the other hand are traditions that insist upon the elicitation of imagery and its importance as a valid religious experience in and of itself. In the former case, it is recognized that prayer and meditative practices may elicit *unintended* and *unwanted* imagery, while in the latter case we have the implication that one must be appropriately set to facilitate *desired* and *intended* imagery. In part, these differences parallel an important distinction between introvertive (imageless) and extrovertive (imagery) mysticism discussed in Chapter Eight.

Isolation Tanks and Religious Imagery

While this discussion may seem like a long detour, its relevance to isolation-tank experiments should be immediately obvious (it will also be important to our discussion of presumably "psychedelic" drugs later in this chapter). Despite the long tradition of isolation-tank studies, efforts have not been directed toward producing *particular* categories of imagery. This is due largely to ignoring set conditions likely to elicit such imagery and to the failure to seek participants with prior experiences favorable to the elicitation of particular categories of meaningful imagery. Of course, in light of what we have already discussed, such people ought to be readily available among the religiously devout.

In the only effort to specifically use religious participants to elicit religious-ly meaningful imagery in an isolation tank, a recent study selected intrinsic and extrinsic religiously oriented persons to participate in an isolation-tank study (Hood and Morris, 1981). Since participants were selected from a class of almost four hundred psychology students tested much earlier for their religious orientation (on the Allport and Ross scales discussed in Chapters One and Two) they did not know why they were selected for this study.

Each participant was introduced to the tank situation, forewarned about what to expect, including the possibility of imagery, and then given one of two explicit sets: One set was to think specifically about and try to imagine cartoon figures; the other set was to think specifically about and try to imagine religious figures. Half the intrinsic and half the extrinsic participants received each set.

Results were as predicted. All participants experienced a variety of mean-ingful and nonmeaningful imagery. There was no difference in amount of imagery between intrinsic or extrinsic persons. However, the category of image was af-fected by set—with more cartoon imagery produced for all persons under the car-toon set and more religious imagery produced for all persons under the religious set. However, the intrinsic participants produced more religious imagery under the religious set than the extrinsic persons, and even under the cartoon set the intrinsic persons produced more religious imagery than the extrinsic persons did under the religious set!

This study suggests that intrinsically oriented persons, placed in a facilita-tive environment, *whether given a set or not,* tend to experience religious imagery. Extrinsic persons tend to do so only when set. In terms of the arousal theory of Schachter, it is reasonable to assume that intrinsic persons spontaneously are "set" to respond to imagery elicited under appropriate arousal conditions while extrin-sic persons are not spontaneously set. However, both intrinsic and extrinsic per-sons can be externally "set" to experience imagery that is religiously meaningful under appropriate arousal conditions. (Controls in this study ruled out the mere report of religious imagery under conditions having no arousal probabilities.)

If we now concern ourselves with the circumstances and conditions under which arousal of imagery can be anticipated, the solitude and isolation of either prayer or meditation as encouraged within religious traditions or that of the iso-lation tank constructed for less noble purposes are by no means exhaustive. Of relevance are a variety of circumstances and substances. One controversial cate-gory of arousal substances of immense current interest is that of "psychedelic drugs."

"Psychedelics" and Religious Experience

It has long been recognized that religious traditions have employed various naturally occurring and synthetic substances in their religious rituals. How-ever, until recently it was rather arrogantly assumed that such concerns were more the domain of the anthropologist dealing with less "advanced" religious tradi-tions (Furst, 1972, 1976; Harner, 1973, LaBarre, 1974; Lewis, 1971). While speculation occasionally erupts with widely reductionistic claims (such as Allegro's 1971) assertion that the Christ of the Judeo-Christian tradition is a personifica-tion of a fertility cult whose primitive origins are rooted in the use of the "psychedelic" mushroom *amanita muscaria*), such claims have been of concern primarily to historians and theologians, not psychologists. Yet with the re-emergence of concern with religious experience among psychologists, the issue of the relationship between drug-induced experiences and presumably spontaneously occurring experiences has become of immense importance. The literature on psychedelic drugs is immense, easily running into many thousands of studies (Aarson and Osmond, 1970); Barber, 1970; Masters and Houston, 1966). Curiously, very few studies have been conducted using religious variables or directly assessing the religous importance of drug-induced experiences. Indeed, it is unfortunate that some of the elaborate and sophisticated studies using both pre- and post-measures to assess changes reliably as well as control groups to assure that validity claims make no effort to assess variables directly or indirectly related to religious concerns (Barr et al, 1972). This is true despite the fact that the religious importance of psychedelics has continually been debated since Leuba argued that intense experience is "higher" religious traditions were to be invalidated since they were similar to be drug-induced experienes of less advanced religions (Leuba, 1925). Yet if physiological arousal can lead to evaluation in religous terms, clearly any physiological arousal is of potential religious importance. The issue is not physiological arousal per se but rather why it is that a particular type of physiological arousal, "psychedelic" drug-induced arousal, has been and continues to be of such immense religious concern. Indeed, it this not part of what is implied in the entire debate concerning the "psychedelic revolution"?

Our discussion of the immense literature surrounding psychedelic drugs obviously should focus upon their possible religious import. We are less concerned with the little understood and much debated possible mechanisms of their functioning, but rather with their effects in experiential terms. Our discussion is also in general terms, including under the rubric "psychedelic" such drugs as LSD, mescalin, and psilocybin, since users in both scientific studies and in street use report similar effects from these drugs (Huxley, 1963; Smith, 1964, 1976; Zaehner, 1961). And, surprisingly, the effects are quite minimal.

Meaningful images that occur under these drugs are not typically attributed to objects to be expected to exist in the world in the sense that if one opened one's eyes, the object would be "there." Such images are interpreted in terms of the psychological and, indeed, religious commitments, of the person. And as we shall see shortly, such differences are the very strong concern of a newly yet rapidly emerging area of psychology of relevance to religion—the psychology of altered states. However, before discussing this area, let us look briefly at the only experimental study with psychedelics attempting to elicit religious experiences among persons strongly committed to a religious interpretation of the world. The study occurred on Good Friday and is appropriately known as the "Good Friday Experiment" (Pahnke, 1963, 1966). This is detailed in Research Box 7-1.

What is of interest in the Good Friday experiment is the conscious effort to select participants committed to religious values to participate in a study that would maximize set and setting factors to elicit a religious interpretation of a drug-induced experience. Ironically, the experiment did not assess the elicitation of either imagery or perceptual variations despite its deliberate selection of a psychedelic substance, psilocybin. This is even more curious given the fact that the studies of elicited imagery under psychedelics indicate that virtually all persons report religious imagery as at least part of the experience, even if such imagery is not

RESEARCH BOX 7-1.   Pahnke, W. N. *Drugs and Mysticism: An Analysis of the Relationship between Psychedelic Drugs and the Mystical Consciousness.* Unpublished Ph.D. Dissertation. Harvard University, 1963.

To help understand the relationship between religious experience and psychedelic drug experience, the author carried out what came to be known as the "Good Friday experiment." Twenty volunteer seminary students were selected after undergoing five hours of medical and psychological screening. None had ever taken a psychedelic drug. The participants were divided into five groups of four persons each on the basis of friendship and compatibility. Leaders who had used the drug were assigned to each group to instill trust and alleviate the fears of the subjects.

This was a double-blind study in which none of the participants—the experimenter, the leaders, or the students—knew what drug was administered to them. Two members of each group received 30 milligrams of psilocybin; the other two members received identical-appearing capsules of 200 milligrams of nicotinic acid. One of the leaders in each group received 15 milligrams of psilocybin. There were thus twenty experimental participants and ten control ones. About an hour and a half before a Good Friday service, the pills were ingested. Then all sat through the two-and-a-half-hour service in a lounge adjacent to a private chapel in which the service was held. The service was broadcast into the chapel.

Following the service, each volunteer described his experience into a tape recorder, and then on the next day wrote a description of it. A week later, he responded to a 147-item questionnaire about the characteristics of the experience. This procedure was repeated six months later. Judges content analyzed the descriptions of the experience, and after the six-month repeat of the questionnaire, the group was broken down into the experimental and control subjects. Nineteen of these in the experimental group and only one of the control's showed any degree of having had a mystical religious experience. Evidence of the positive effects of the experience were present after six months.

---

self-defined as "religious experience" (Masters and Houston, 1966). What was assessed were a variety of mystical phenomena that are discussed in Chapter Eight as well as a variety of both short-term and long-term consequences of the experiment.

The author's own conclusion regarding the data meshes nicely with what we have said about physiological arousal and its interpretation:

> The fact that the experience took place in the context of a religious service, with the use of symbols which were familiar and meaningful to the participants, appeared to provide a useful framework within which to derive meaning and integration from the experience, both now and later (Pahnke, 1966, p. 307).

While this study is not without its serious methodological flaws (Dittes, 1969), it remains the only study attempting to elicit religious experience within a mainline Christian tradition in a normal religious service on an appropriately meaningful day with the addition of a psychedelic substance! Yet it does suggest the obvious—the *meaningfulness* of a physiological arousal substance or of any substance that modifies or alters one's typical way of experiencing the world is a question of ideological commitments, not merely of physiology. To be religious is at least partly to have a framework within which to interpret experience, and the interpretation will be part of the experience. Early studies (Downing and Wygant, 1964) unfortunately not followed up, suggest that among religious persons taking psychedelic drugs, the effect was to deepen one's commitment to *already established religious views*. In this sense, as Roszak (1969) notes, part of the protest against the psychedelic movement stems from its genuine religious threat to our existing cultural form. Indeed, it is not surprising that associated with the psychedelic street movement was the seeking of religious literature, largely from Eastern sources, from a youth alienated from certain contemporary church traditions. Yet it is clear that such movements are not antireligious but rather an aspect of religious rebellion and renewal that is part and parcel of the history of religions as we will see in Chapter Ten. As might be expected, much of this debate is rooted in "mystical religion," a topic we discuss in detail in Chapter Eight.

Hence, the issue here is not whether a substance can elicit "genuine" or "counterfeit" religious experiences (Leary, 1964; Watts, 1962; Zaehner, 1961). For if the distinction between natural and supernatural is difficult, so is the distinction between "natural" and "artificial." The differential utilization of substances by varying religious and cultural traditions is of immense scientific interest. The bottom line appears to be not whether religious traditions attempt to elicit experiences, but rather *how*. As for the question of evaluation of experiences elicited by specified or unspecified conditions and substances, throughout this book much can be gleaned that is relevant. Yet, most relevant now is the controversial emergence of an area in psychology known as "altered-states research."

ALTERED STATES: RELIGION THROUGH THE BACK DOOR?

The catchall phrase *altered states* is rapidly becoming the accepted term for a loosely knit area in which the focus is upon the empirical study of what had previously been assumed to be either novel or pathological experiences. Included in this area are such phenomena as creativity, hypnosis, dreaming, meditation, psychedelic drugs, paranormal claims, and any number of other "fringe" topics. Yet what is shared in common by altered-states investigators is an insistence upon the normalcy and validity of these experiences in and of themselves. Not surprising then is the curious fact that such investigators have been forced to confront "religious themes" given their explicit recognition that many experiences of interest to them have been, and for many still are, identified as religious in nature. Perhaps the greatest impetus to this area was the early work of Maslow (1970) and his perhaps presumptious claim to have discovered the naturalistic basis of the "universal" or "core religious" experience. Indeed, as we shall soon see, investigators typically claim a simple empirical resolution to the complex problem of religious experiences. However, despite such naive claims, the intriguing fact remains that investigators are busy empirically studying phenomena of immense relevance to religious experience. Indeed, as we shall soon see, the ostracized image has returned to haunt the pyschology of religion with a vengeance.

What Is an "Altered State"?

Tart (1960) has done most to attempt some theoretical clarification of the concept of "altered states." Basically, altered states of consciousness are defined as a self-recognized different mode of experiencing the world. Loosely speaking, Tart's distinction would allow dreaming to be a recognized altered state of consciousness relative to normal, waking consciousness. What is important in Tart's notion of altered states is that each altered state of consciousness has a typical pattern of functioning, recognized as such by the person. Hence, things that might seem strange, even bizarre, are not really so when recognized that they are normal for that particular state of consciousness. Furthermore, persons move in and out of various states of consciousness. (Berger and Luckmann, 1967)

It is fruitful to note the empirical recognition of various modes of consciousness and their "contents" in light of the psychology of religious experiencing. In so doing, we shall appeal to the notion of arousal and its recognition once again—but now in terms of arousal recognized in conscious modes of experiencing the world. When arousal is specifically instigated by religious practices, we have perhaps the least controversial example of a religious experience—prayer.

RELIGION, BRAIN AND CONSCIOUSNESS

Prayer and Meditation: A New "Physiological Respectability"

It is only recently that psychologists have become interested in what many presume to be a uniquely religious activity—prayer. And while full-scale theoretical treatments of prayer have yet to emerge in contemporary psychology, the study of prayer is in process although psychologists seem to feel most comfortable in discussing "meditation" and its infinite varieties (Goleman, 1977; Naranjo and Ornstein, 1971). The activities of prayer and meditation share in common an apparent withdrawal from normal waking consciousness and a concern with a passive receptivity "withdrawn" from normal daily activities. Of course, we must be careful with language here, for to the devout prayer and meditation has always been affirmed as a meaningful, indeed often difficult confrontation with reality—a reality legitimated and made meaningful in terms of religious interpretations. What the contemporary psychologist is discovering is that such activities have interesting correlates in terms of brain activity. Let us note but one major example.

Brain Waves and Prayer

There is little doubt that part of the scientific concern with prayer and meditation is traceable to the work of a German scientist Hans Berger, whose pioneering work demonstrated a relationship between brain waves and patterns of consciousness. The current literature in this area is immense and no doubt suffers from a premature and often uncritical popularization (Goleman and Davidson, 1969; Teyler, 1972) On the positive side, the discovery that electrodes attached to the human scalp can record varying brain waves is of relevance to the reemergence of concern with religious experience for a very simple reason: There is at least one physiological index indicating that prayer or meditation is a "different mode of consciousness" than, say, normal waking consciousness or sleep.

We can make four major classifications of brain waves that are at present conceptually meaningful. Keep in mind that their meaningfulness comes not from the brain waves per se, but from the fact that descriptions of modes of consciousness recognized to be normal yet different from one another are associated with different identifiable brain-wave frequencies. Consider the following gross definitions of consciousness and their related brain-wave frequencies (Johnston, 1974).

BRAIN WAVE FREQUENCY	MODE OF CONSCIOUSNESS
Beta (above 13 cps*)	Active thought; focused attention with eyes open. Oriented toward the "external world."
Alpha (8 to 12 cps*)	Relaxed yet aware. Probably eyes closed. Oriented toward the "internal world"
Theta (4 to 7 cps*)	Drowsiness. Fluid dream like images likely to occur (hypnogogic imagery).
Delta (to 4 cps*)	Deep sleep. Person has consciousness, yet is "unaware."

*Cycles per second

From the above chart, it becomes readily apparent that the activities of prayer and meditation are likely to be theta/alpha in orientation rather than either delta or beta. None of this is really surprising since persons who pray and meditate clearly recognize that they are "turned inward" in what for them is a meaningful activity involving a mode of awareness they themselves recognize. What is new is that brain-wave patterns have been identified correlating prayer and meditation with external indices that permit scientific investigation of such states. The literature in this area is rapidly evolving, but for our purposes we need only note that its direct relevance to the psychology of religion is at this point minimal; minimal because most investigators have taken a decidedly reductionistic approach to hard physiological data, correlated with religious modes of consciousness, almost as if the religious awareness or experience were "explained" by the physiological correlate. Perhaps the most recent and provocative of these claims has been the "bicameral mind" theory of the origin of human consciousness (Jaynes, 1976). Its claim is really quite simple: Religion has a single source in a dual brain.

The Split Brain Hypothesis

Closely related to the discovery of brain waves and their utilization in the study of consciousness is the perplexing duality of the human brain. It has long been noted that the human brain is apparently doubled, with two apparently identical cortical halves connected by the structure known as the corpus callosum (Ornstein, 1977; Springer and Deutsch, 1981). Now what is of interest about this fact of brain anatomy is the claim that a dual mode of normal human consciousness is associated with this apparently duplicated normal human cortex. The evidence for this claim comes largely from a literal splitting of the human brain.

It has long been noted that for purely physiological reasons the right half of the body is controlled largely by the left half of the brain, and vice versa. Hence, the right hand is controlled by the left side of the brain. Of most interest, however, is language ability. In most persons, language ability resides in the left side of the brain. And if one adopts a "verbal access" view of consciousness that argues that conscious understanding is possible precisely because of language, a most interesting experiment becomes possible. What if the brain was split at the corpus callosum so that the two halves of the brain could not directly interrelate? When the study has been done in humans (Gazzaniga and Le Doux, 1978), the results have been most stimulating.

The fact of hemispherical specialization is largely undetected in normal persons because of the interconditioning that occurs via the corpus callosum. Yet when the corpus callosum is severed, special tests can affirm the specialization. The most interesting tests occur when language tasks are involved. For instance, if an object is placed in the left hand of a split brain patient, information goes to the right hemisphere, which lacks verbal specialization. Hence, the person cannot say what it is that is being handled. However, the person could pick up the identical object from a group of objects with the use of the right hand. Many other notable examples could be given, but what has this to do with religious experience? According to the bicameral theory, almost everything.

Science and Religion: Left and Right Brains?

The existence of dualities has long been noted. We tend to contrast intuitive with rational; religion with science; verbal with nonverbal. For some, these dualities are rooted in the fact that consciousness is largely a hemispherical brain process. Hence, dual terms such as intuitive/rational imply different dominant cognitive styles and these occur because of the differing dominance of hemispheres. A dominant left hemisphere (verbal) is associated with a verbal, rational cognitive style; a dominant right hemisphere (nonverbal) is associated with a dominant nonverbal, intuitive cognitive style. The list of dichotomies is endless, causing at least one investigator to bemoan the emergence of "dichotomania" among contemporary scientists (Gardner, 1978). More relevant, however, is the claim that religious consciousness is a "right hemispheric phenomenon." It is as if modern physiological psychology has achieved what Descartes failed to do—locate the soul, but this time in the cortex, not the pineal gland. The bicameral theory, however, is a bit more sophisticated. This perspective suggests that God relates to persons as the left hemisphere relates to the right. The theory is decidedly evolutionary—and in the beginning was God.

The Death of God and the Origin of Human Consciousness

Jaynes' bicameral theory is provocative in that it links modes of human consciousness with historical forms within an evolutionary context. Jaynes speculates that consciousness in the sense of a self-reflexive awareness is a recent evolutionary phenomenon rooted in the earlier failure of bicameral consciousness. And bicameral consciousness was a God-consciousness.

Jaynes argues that early men were "bicameral" in that their right and left hemispheres were separated in the same way that a split brain patient's might be today. The effect was that men were "unconscious" in that they did not reflexively decide what to do or contemplate action, but simply did what they were told. What they were told occurred "inside" their heads via the left hemisphere. Left hemispheric visions and voices dictated socially acceptable behaviors to the right hemisphere, which controlled action. Persons confronted with novel, problematic situations obeyed their left hemisphere, which provided a solution to be carried out via the right hemisphere. The solution was dictated largely by voices and to a lesser extent by visions. These "voice-visions" hallucinations were perceived as gods by persons whose otherwise unconscious actions were always thusly initiated in problematic situations. In Jaynes' (1976) own terms:

> The bicameral man was ruled in trivial circumstances of everyday life by unconscious habit, and in his encounters with anything new or out of the ordinary in his own behavior or others' by his voice visions (p. 213).

Jaynes further speculates that when the stable world order broke down, bicameral consciousness was evolutionarily ineffective and reflexive, self-awareness emerged. This awareness was the "death of the gods, and the emergence of what we now view as normal consciousness. Voice-visions of the bicameral mind now occur only in isolated experiences and in those of the mentally ill.

The merit of Jaynes' admittedly speculative theory is that it represents but one of the more recent reductionistic efforts to equate religious experiencing to physiological processes. Jaynes' theory is more sophisticated than most in that it requires consideration of external initiating factors—in his case, historical patterns of authoritarian social control that are maintained by left hemispheric voice-visions. Yet it remains pitifully true that his theory leaves little to comfort the religiously devout in that there is no room for religious experiencing that is veridical with respect to particular religious commitments. Indeed, there is little comfort in having the mentally ill as the only vestiges of religious experiencing persons in the modern world! Hence, Jaynes' conceptual shortsightedness becomes evident—if one acknowledges physiological and anatomical considerations that permit an understanding of how particular experiences could occur, the meaningfulness and value of those experiences remains an open question. It would appear then that physiological and anatomical data will forever remain incomplete in terms of explaining religious experience. Roszack (1975) has recently given a most helpful warning regarding merely physiologically oriented research:

> . . .the very nature of the research works to reduce and distort what it studies. For one thing, the hard focus on measurable, empirical effects isolates what may well be the least important aspect of religious experience, leaving behind the total life discipline which is both its root and its blossom. What remains is a collection of data points; statistical series, pointer readings, computer printouts, graphs and charts. The temptation, then, is to believe that the behavior which has thus been objectively verified is what religious experience is *really* all about, and - further - that it can be appropriated as an end in itself, plucked like a rare flower from the soil that feeds it. The result is a narrow emphasis on special effects and sensations: "peak experiences," "highs," "flashes," and such. Yet even if one wishes to regard ecstasy

as the "peak" of religious experience, that summit does not float in mid-air. It rests upon a tradition and a way of life; one ascends such heights and appreciates their grandeur by a process of initiation that demands learning, commitment, devotion, service, sacrifice. To approach it in any more hasty way is like "scaling" Mount Everest by being landed on its top from a helicopter.

If Roszack's warning is heeded, our simple framework of integrating religious experience derived from James and others becomes even more viable. We can simply note that if any type is likely to occur in problematic or novel situations, the resolution of the problematic situation will likely reduce the arousal. Furthermore, when this resolution is successful in meaningful religious terms, a religious experience has occurred. It is in this sense that much of what is called attribution theory (Proudfoot and Shaver, 1975), is relevant to the psychology of religious experience. For persons attribute meaning to processes that they perceive in themselves, and religions provide terms for identifying experiences that are by this very process meaningful. It is a vacuous move to wonder what an experience would be outside of such interpretations, for the interpretations are part and parcel of the experience. While we can talk about mere physiological arousal or the occurrence of particular states of consciousness, only when such phenomena are incorporated into meaningful frames of reference are they truly and fully "experiences." In this sense, it is obvious why research with psychedelic drugs that elicits religious imagery under nonreligious set and setting conditions only produces reports of religious imagery and not of a religious experience (Masters and Houston, 1966). On the other hand, we can also see why psychedelic elicited experiences that are incorporated into religious beliefs are considered to be most meaningful religious experience (Masters and Houston, 1966). In fact, a strong case can be made that much of the interest in non-Christian religion in recent times is related to persons seeking meaningful systems within which to confront a wide variety of drug-elicited experiences. (Roszack, 1969).

We can see now why much of the physiological data on religious experience is limited in its explanatory power. It is almost as if many investigators were trying to explain religious experience outside the context of religion—as if one could somehow see the "real" television picture if they could just manage to view the electrons in the circuits of the set.

If what we have said is correct, religious beliefs are essential for religiously experiencing the world. And while such experiences will entail bodily processes, the bodily processes can never simply be equated with the experience (Penfield, 1975; Pratt, 1922). A good example is glossolalia.

SPEAKING IN TONGUES: GLOSSOLALIA

Glossolalia, or speaking in tongues, is a universal phenomenon (May, 1956). Early psychologists easily attributed it to mental illness, with one investigator calling glossolalia a "stigmata of degeneration" (Mackie, 1921). However, there are strong conceptual arguments for distinguishing glossolalia from what are only apparently pathological parallels (Kelsey, 1964, Kildahl, 1972). Consistent with this is the fact that studies have generally failed to find empirical evidence indicating that glossolalia groups differ psychologically from equivalent but non-glossolalia controls. (Goodman, 1972; Hine, 1969; Richardson, 1973). Some of the difficulty of research in this area is that looseness in definition of glossolalia prevails. One finds claims that it is a meaningless but phonologically structured human sound (Samarin, 1972), to assertions that it has identifiable semantic content to claims that its basic form depends on the linguistic competence of the speaker (Laffal, Monahan, and Richman, 1974; Samarin, 1972). The intriguing fact is its reemergence in contemporary mainline religious bodies. Many of these groups appeal to scriptural sources such as in Acts and Corinthians for an interpretation and even mandate for glossolalia. To some, the emergence of tongue speaking among apparently well-adjusted, normal middle-class Americans has been, to say the least, a surprise. What makes glossolalia of interest here is the debate on whether or not it occurs in an "altered state" and what this means for our perspective on religious experience.

Is Glossolalia Produced in an Altered State of Consciousness?

Cutten (1927) was one of the earliest investigators of glossolalia to argue that it occurred in and was presumably caused by a trance state. Most recently, this view has been echoed by an anthropologist, Goodman (1969, 1972). She argues that similarities in glossolalic utterances across cultures can best be explained by the theory that glossolalia results from an induced trance state. Her view is challenged by Samarin (1972) who has argued that Goodman's data are not ruly cross-cultural since it was all collected within similar Pentecostal settings. Samarin also points out that patterns identified in typical southern Virginia mountain preaching are similar to those found in glossolalia, and hence mountain preaching without glossolalia (and hence without trance) has similar patterns that are presumed to be caused by a trance state when exhibited in glossolalia. Likewise, Hine (1969) has noted that glossolalia is not always accompanied by trance. On the other hand, several investigators have given criteria by which one can both recognize and induce a trance state resulting in a high probability of glossolalia occurring.

Obviously, the outcome of this debate requires additional research. Yet the conceptual confusion must be noted. As with our previous discussion of altered-states research, one can recognize a pattern or mode of experiencing the world by differing criteria. One could seek to define glossolalia clearly and then obtain physiological data indicative of some "trance state." However, such data, even if obtained, would not go far in terms of causally explaining glossolalia, as Jaquith has noted. Similarly, one can identify glossolalia via behavioral and self-report criteria and note both its occurrence and what meanings are attributed to it. These meanings may or may not relate to identifiable physiological ("trance") criteria. They will certainly not be illuminated by the physiological criteria, whatever they might be.

As we already know, various meanings can be attributed to glossolalia even if at some other level all such utterances are identical. In this sense, Lovekin and Malony (1977) (see Research Box 7-2) show that glossolalia can be a positive influence as has also been shown with sensory isolation and psychedelic studies conducted in a religious context. Experience becomes religiously meaningful within a religious context. One can also have an experience for which a religious in-

RESEARCH BOX 7-2   *Lovekin, A. and Malony, H. N. "Religious Glossolalia: A Longitudinal Study of Personality Changes." Journal for the Scientific Study of Religion, 1977, 16, 383-393.*

A conflicted literature on the personality characteristics of glossolalics and the question of personality changes paralleling the transformation to a glossolalic state prompted the researchers to conduct an in-depth study of the glossolalia process. Fifty-one nonglossolalic participants in a Catholic church program that encouraged glossolalia were administered a variety of religion and personality measures.

During the seven-week program, twelve of the people became fully glossolalic (new tongues group). Thirteen had been glossolalic prior to entering the seminar (old tongues group), and fourteen demonstrated no such behavior at any time (no tongues group). The three groups were compared on the measures that were administered again at the end of the program, and also three months later.

On measures involving anxiety, depression, and hostility, the glossolalics scored lower than the no tongues group. Still, the last group scored higher on ego strength and evidenced less extrinsic religiosity than the two glossolalic groups.

The hypothesis that becoming glossolalic aided personality integration was not supported. There was some suggestion that those who do not become glossolalic may be more troubled than those that do.

terpretation is sought, or that is meaningfully recognized relative to a prior religious commitment, but in all cases the religious commitments provide the meaning. Of course, other meaning systems could yield nonreligious meanings. (Hutch, 1980).

A SUGGESTIVE RESEARCH MODEL FOR RELIGIOUS EXPERIENCE

From what we have reviewed in this chapter, it is clearly premature to claim an all-inclusive "theory" of religious experience. But we can, however, suggest a model—a way of organizing experience within the confines of religious interpretations. Religious experience may be best conceived as successfully resolving or coming to terms with some discontent, some problematic situation, some novelty. Both the problem and its resolution are part and parcel of the experience. Neither alone suffices. Yet we can now add some suggestive distinctions rooted in Maslow's (1955, 1962) notions of deficiency and growth motivations.

Deficiency and Growth Motives Conducive to Religious Experience

It would appear that initial discontents, setting the stage for religious experience, can come from two major sources. One we can call deficiencies, meaning by this personal recognition of a lack relative to some group norm or standard. This would encompass not having what others have, whether it be in a material, physical, or psychological sense. Persons so deprived are likely to seek out situations or circumstances in which they could achieve what is normative for their group. Importantly, such experiences are likely to be confirmatory in that the experience itself will confirm or solidify the person as one of the group. Perhaps most typical here would be "born-again" experiences common in Western Christianity.

On the other hand, some experiences are sought for what might be called "growth" reasons. Here the lack is not with respect to some group norm, but rather with respect to an ideal. Such persons may be motivated to seek situations or circumstances in which experiences will occur that might even alienate them from an already established group. In this sense, motivation for religious experience provides a double-edged sword so to speak. Sometimes religious experiences solidify and further integrate existing groups; in other instances, they can produce disunion and perhaps a lonely outcast's uncertainty as to whether or not one's experience was genuine. The issue resides, of course, in the eventual support of the interpretation within which the experience is both recognized and occurs. If it is true that we judge experience by its fruit, it is less certain whether this is the solution to a problem or simply moves the problem one step further back. For instance, since the ultimate validity of religious practices cannot be ascertained by science whether or not a particular religious practice or experience is functional to some group, even cultural norm cannot be the sole religiouis criterion for its validity. Hence, as religious experiences deviate from those acceptable to researchers studying religion, one might anticipate that biases might lead to negative evaluations. This has been well documented in scientific studies of religious fundamentalism. (Hoop, 1983) Examples from research on snake handlers, distantly related to glossolalia in their common origin in the holiness movement, are available (Gerrald and Gerrald, 1966).

The problem of ultimate validity of religious experiences is itself a theological issue. From the handling of snakes in the backwoods of the South to the quiet contemplative diary of a modern statesman (Hammarskjold, 1964; LaBarre, 1969), religious experience shows an almost endless variety, and as we demonstrate throughout this text, experience cannot be understood in isolation. To focus upon one aspect of experience, be it the most obvious proximate initiating situation or a supposedly atypical state of consciousness within which it occurred, is to not have a proper perspective that permits one to come to terms with experience. What we have demonstrated in this chapter is an expression of recent scientific efforts to confront experience, largely through its apparently physiological substrates.

It is obviously clear that no experience can be reduced to its physiology, and certainly religious experience is not simply a state of physiological arousal, or an altered mode of awareness. It may be these, but certainly not simply these. The religiously devout claim for themselves a rich life, rooted in a religious experience of the world. Religion without such experiences remains lifeless, or as Kierkegaard noted,

> . . . just about as genuine as tea made from a bit of paper which once lay in a drawer beside another bit of paper which had once been used to wrap us a few dried tea leaves from which tea had already been made three times (Muggeridge, 1976, p. 138).

And while it would be a mistake to reduce religion merely to experience, it would be equally mistaken to judge hastily by nonreligious criteria any mode of experiencing the world. As for the claim to a single, universal religious mode of experiencing the world, what we have noted in this chapter makes it obvious that such claims are to be met with suspicion. If there is an exception, it is in that realm loosely defined as "mystical." Accordingly, we devote the entirety of our next chapter to it.

ATTRIBUTION THEORY AND RELIGIOUS EXPERIENCE

When Proudfoot and Shaver (1975) introduced attribution theory to the psychology of religion, its focus was on religious experience. The issue became the perceived causes of religious experiences, and, as indicated in Chapter Eight what may hold true for one is likely to be pertinent for the other. We have to understand the bases of those attributions that denote one experience as religious as opposed to what may be similar to others that are not considered religious. Boisen (1936) and James (1902) suggest a consistently positive aspect to these spiritual encounters. Their meanings are therefore favorable and desired and must be self-enhancing. A sense of heightened control is also implicit in the idea of transcending limits. Religious experiences thus meet our criteria for the motivational activation of attributions.

Earlier we discussed the arousal of emotional states as part and parcel of the religious experience. The model proposed by Proudfoot and Shaver took this as their starting point and suggested that context and setting provided the basis of such arousal being defined as religious. Related work by Schachter and Singer (1962) and Hood and Morris (1981) were cited as demonstrating how imagery could be directed by setting manipulation. At the same time, dispositional factors, primarily in terms of form of personal faith, were shown to exert a significant influence. The Good Friday experiment illustrates well the interaction of context and probable dispositional inclinations to produce religious attributions when stimulated by drugs. Physiological arousal is not enough; setting and disposition provide the necessary direction for creating religious attributions. Glossolalia, as both experience and behavior, conforms to the same attributional guidelines.

More potential has been demonstrated for the application of attribution concepts to religious experience than for any other aspect of faith. Still, there is not only a continuing need for further specification of the motives and conditions that relate to such experience, but the considerable variety of these episodes suggests the appropriateness of attending to interactions among predisposing factors. The research of Hood demonstrates the fruitfulness of research directed toward such ends.

SUMMARY AND CONCLUSIONS

In this and the next few chapters, we deal with one of the most central and significant areas in the psychology of religion and also one of the most difficult to define and understand. In large part, this is due to the subjective nature of the topic—namely, religious experience. Nevertheless, we note that for almost a century scholars have attempted to interpret and classify these personal encounters. Recent efforts to discover a physiological basis for religious experience have made noteworthy contributions to the research literature, but drawing correlations between the experiential level and that of underlying physiology still leaves much to be desired. This confronts a basic problem of general psychology, one with a long conceptual and research history that is currently far from being resolved. This concerns how to draw parallels between cognition and physiology. The realm of religious experience is important for such study, but has largely been ignored by the psychological mainstream.

We have observed that students of religious experience first have to stimulate these occurrences, and to this end, experiments have been conducted with drugs, isolation tanks, and various means of inducing sensory deprivation. Studies of split brain phenomena and brain waves also are among the topics being explored for their relevance to the religious domain. This work is fascinating, and although its association with religious experience is still more suggestive than demonstrated, labors along these lines are opening doors to our understanding of experiential phenomena.

Another research channel has been suggested by the fact that religious experience is related to other facets of religion such as form of personal faith, glossolalia, and conversion. Work also is proceeding along these lines, and some progress has resulted from this research.

A fundamental issue that faces both the researcher and the person having a religious experience focuses on the causes of these events. Here, attribution theory enters the picture and appears to be among the most productive research avenues to pursue. However, work along these lines has just begun and points not only to the importance of the setting in which religious experience takes place but the characteristics of the experiencing person. Relative to the latter, the evidence suggests two possible sources of motivation: (1) shortcomings, deficiencies, and problems that result in personal discontent and distress, and (2) a need to grow, actualize, expand one's horizons. These suggest an individual basis in competence, adequacy, and well-being. Both motivational considerations have gained support, but much more research is necessary to comprehend fully how these bases for experience function both in the individual personality and the sociocultural context.

CHAPTER EIGHT
MYSTICISM

"In spite of such rebellion, and the tortures to which it has subjected them, the mystics oddly enough are a long-lived race: an awkward fact for critics of the psychological school" (Underhill, 1955, p. 62).

"And it is true that the mystics are not for everyone" (Merton, 1961, p. vii).

"Certainly one of the fundamental Kabbalistic premises to assist in guiding the emergent psychology is that everything in the cosmos is a unity—that we cannot study persons as separate entities, apart from the rest of the world" (Hoffman, 1981, p. 208).

" 'Since we cannot change reality, let us change the eyes which see reality," says one of my favorite Byzantine mystics" (Kazantzakis, 1961, p. 45).

Mysticism remains the perennial topic of concern for those interested in religious experience. Its claim to a contact or union with ultimate reality, with the divine, produces obvious ambivalence. For some, the claim holds the hope that they might actually confront God in this life. For others, there is a mysticism without God. Many feel that such claims seem absurd, and naturalistic efforts are made to explain these perceived fallacious interpretations of what must nevertheless remain a profound human experience. Religionists have used appeals to mysticism to legitimate claims of their founders as well as to delegitimate claims of others. Mystics have used their experiences to both challenge and support institutions and societies. Whatever one's final view of mysticism, its centrality and importance for the study of religion is undisputed.

THE EARLY PSYCHOLOGISTS AND MYSTICISM

Early psychological concern with the scientific study of religion was heavily focused on mysticism (James, 1902; Leuba, 1925; Pratt, 1920; Starbuck, 1899). Typically, the dominant view, explicit or implicit, was one of demystification. The principal argument was that mystics misinterpreted their experience of union or confrontation with the divine. The nature of this misinterpretation varied with investigators, but most agreed that mystical experience was either pathological itself, or tinged with pathological characteristics. Freud (1961) claimed that it was a regressive experience, an "oceanic experience," typical of the earliest infantile encounters with the world. There were exceptions to this trend. James (1902) was the most notable. He devoted major portions of his classic work to a nonreductionistic, indeed immensely positive evaluation of mysticism.

Following initial concern with mysticism by the early psychologists of religion, the subject lay dormant. In the "middle years" of the psychology of religion, Clark (1958, 1969) paved the way for its reemergence by insisting on the centrality of mysticism to any psychology of religion in a wide variety of publications. With the 1970s, the psychology of religion came full circle. Mysticism once again is a central topic of concern (Spilka, 1977). This time, however, emphasis is on empirical studies of mysticism largely made possible by the work of the philosopher W. T. Stace (1961).

CONCEPTUALIZING MYSTICISM

A major problem in the study of mysticism has been the issue of definition. While James had long ago provided criteria to define mysticism, these did not lead to operational measures facilitating empirical research. On the other hand, Stace's work did.

In a now seminal work, Stace (1960) identified two related types of mysticism, the *introvertive* and the *extrovertive*. However, both forms share common criteria. These are:

1. The mystical experience is *noetic*. It is not perceived as a mere "subjective" experience nor an "emotional" experience. Rather it is a valid source of knowledge.

2. The mystical experience is *ineffable*. It cannot be adequately described in words.
3. The mystical experience is *holy*. This is the "religious" aspect of the experience, but not necessarily in any particular theological terms.
4. The mystical experience is characterized by *positive affect*. It is a profound yet pleasant experience.
5. The mystical experience is *paradoxical*. It defies logic.

In addition to the five common criteria of mysticism, Stace provides additional criteria uniquely identifying extrovertive and introvertive mysticisms. For *extrovertive* mysticism, these are:

a. The mystical experience is characterized by an *inner subjectivity* to all things. In some sense, all things are "alive."
b. There is a *unity* to the diversity of things perceived. Everything is seen as distinct, yet somehow perceived simultaneously as part of a whole, as one thing.

For *introvertive* mysticism,

a. The mystical experience is *timeless* and *spaceless*.
b. The mystical experience is one of a "void"; a perfect unity of consciousness devoid of any content; a dissolution of sense of self.

Stace hedges a bit, suggesting that extrovertive mysticism may be a lower or preliminary form of the more fully developed introvertive mysticism. In addition, he suggests a separate category of a "nature mysticism" for which explicit criteria are not developed. For now, it is important to emphasize that Stace's criteria are important, not because others could not or have not been offered, but rather because Stace's criteria have been operationalized by those concerned with the empirical study of mysticism. This is an obviously important move since once operationalized, like any other concept, mysticism becomes susceptible to empirical treatment. Of course, given the fact as Hood and Morris (1981) have shown that most empirical studies of mysticism rely either directly or indirectly on Stace's criteria, conceptual criticisms of Stace's work are relevant to the evaluation of the adequacy of these operational indicators. For now, however, we must confront the operationalization of mysticism.

HOW IS MYSTICISM ASSESSED?

There are four major ways mysticism is measured in the contemporary psychology of religion. The first is through the utilization of scales derived directly or indirectly from Stace's criteria. Most typical is the directly derived mysticism scale (M-scale) developed by Hood (1975). Initial psychometric work with this scale indicates a blurring of Stace's distinction between *introvertive* and *extrovertive* mysticisms. Instead, two major factors are noted. These are (1) items dealing with minimal phenomenological criteria of mysticism (such as unity, timelessness and spacelessness, ineffability, and pure consciousness); (2) a religious interpretation factor that includes items dealing with criteria such as holiness, positive affect, and noetic quality). In terms of attribution theory, this makes sense; a distinction is made between minimal experience and its interpretation.

The following are representative items used across several investigators to help assess the report of mystical experience:

Have you ever had an experience . . .

_____ in which all things seemed to be unified into a single whole?

_____ of tremendous personal expansion, either psychological or physical?

_____ in which time place and distance are meaningless?

_____ in which you realized your oneness with all things?

_____ of holiness?

_____ of deep and profound peace?

_____ which could not be put adequately into words?

_____ in which a new view of reality was revealed to you?

_____ in which all is felt to be perfection at that time?

_____ in which everything seemed to disappear from your mind until you were conscious only of a void?

Items like these have been used by a wide variety of investigators to indicate mystical and mystical type experiences (Hood and Morris, 1981).

A second way in which mysticism has been measured is by using actual descriptions of mystical experiences and having persons indicate whether or not they have ever had an experience similar to the one described. This scale, the Religious Experience Episodes Measure (REEM) was initially developed by Hood (1970) from samples culled from James' work and has recently been updated by Rosegrant. (1976) Importantly, James' criteria for mysticism overlap Stace's including noetic ineffability criteria, but are not as extensive. However, the REEM includes descriptions clearly mystical both in terms of James' more limited and Stace's more extensive criteria. As an example, consider whether or not you have ever had an experience like this one from the REEM:

> I remember the night and almost the very spot on the hilltop where my soul opened out and the inner and outer worlds rushed together. My own deep struggle was being answered by the unfathomable deep without, reaching beyond the stars. I stood alone with him who had made me, and all the beauty, love, and sorrow of the world. I felt the union of my spirit with his. The ordinary sense of things around me faded, and for the moment nothing remained but an indescribable joy.

A third way in which mysticism has been measured is to have persons describe experiences by either responding directly to each of Stace's criteria or having raters judge a person's experience in terms of the extent to which it fits each of Stace's criteria. These approaches have the advantage of allowing interviews that can then be assessed for mysticism at a later date.

A fourth way in which mysticism has been measured is simply to ask persons if they have ever had a mystical experience or if they have ever had an experience as described by Stace's criteria (e.g., "Have you ever had an experience that you cannot put into words?"). This approach is most typically used in survey research where a limited number of questions can be asked. The advantage is that it provides data concerning the frequency of mystical experience among various social groups.

One of the best measures of mystical experience was developed by Hood. This is discussed in Research Box 8-1.

RESEARCH BOX 8-1   *Hood, R. W. Jr. "The Construction and Preliminary Validation of a Measure of Reported Mystical Experience."* Journal for the Scientific Study of Religion, *1975, 14, 29–41.*

Utilizing the conceptual categories for mysticism postulated by Stace, the author developed a pool of 108 items which, after a number of revisions, was reduced to thirty-two core statements. These were administered to three hundred college students, primarily Protestants, and the results were subjected to a factor analysis. This suggested that the items consisted of two factor scales. Scale 1 seems to measure "general mysticism"—namely, an experience of unity, temporal and spatial changes, inner subjectivity, and ineffability. This scale was not restricted to religion and thus refers to a broad type of mysticism. Scale 2 is religion-bound and may be regarded as mysticism, religiously interpreted, for it stresses the acquisition of new, objective knowledge associated with positive feelings of joy. Since the two factors tend to be highly intercorrelated, they are considered two aspects of an overall conception of mysticism, and three scores are derived for the mysticism or m-scale. These are separate factor scale scores and a combined total-scale score.

Both forms of mysticism relate highly and positively to an intrinsic religious orientation and to religious experience as defined by the Hood Religious Experience Episodes Scale. Another sample of eighty-three students permitted assessment of the relationship between the m-scale and an index of ego permissiveness or openness to experiences of all types. Again, a strong positive association was observed. A third sample of twenty-nine students were administered the Minnesota Multiphasic Personality Inventory, probably the most widely employed measure of many aspects of personality. This inventory demonstrated modest positive correlations between the M scale and hypochondriacal and hysterical tendencies. Respectively, these may be interpreted as strong sensitivity to both internal body stimulation and what goes on outside of oneself, something to be reasonably expected of persons who have mystical experiences. Although further research is necessary with the M scale, initial work with it seems quite promising.

INTERRELATIONSHIPS AMONG MEASURES

It is apparent that different ways of measuring mysticism can lead to different outcomes. To date, few studies have directly concerned themselves with interrelating independently developed scales or questionnaires. However, despite the development of additional scales to measure mysticism, it appears reasonable to conclude that current ways of measuring mysticism do tap the same category of experiences—experiences of unity with something other than one's self (Brown, Spilka and Cassidy, 1978; Uerbersax, 1979). All measures of mysticism developed have produced at least one factor identified as an experience of unity factor. Importantly, Stace's extrovertive and introvertive classifications are merely different ways of experiencing unity—extrovertive mysticism is a perceptual experience of unity in diversity, while introvertive mysticism is an experience of unity devoid of content. Yet, an experience of unity is essential to mysticism, however assessed (Hood, 1976; Morris and Hood, 1980).

SOME ATTRIBUTIONAL CONSIDERATIONS IN ASSESSING MYSTICISM

Before we consider the relatively large contemporary literature of mysticism, we must at least briefly confront some important attributional considerations. Specifically, we refer to a problem well noted in both the conceptual and the empirical literature of mysticism—that of distinguishing between experience and its interpretation.

The general attributional problem of distinguishing the minimal properties of experience from its higher order interpretations raises particularly unique problems in mysticism for at least two reasons. First, the debate over the *religious* nature of mystical experience, at least, partly hinges upon whether or not nontheological descriptions of mystical experience are possible, and if possible, necessary. Second, among proponents of various religious mysticisms, the debate is focused two ways: Theologically committed investigators tend to find their own mysticisms "superior" to others, while nevertheless recognizing similarities. For instance, both Otto (1932) and Zaehner (1961) provide meaningful conceptual analyses of various mysticisms and conclude in favor of the superiority of Christian mysticism, while Suzuki (1957) does a similar favor, acknowledging the superiority of Zen Buddhism. To the psychologist, the obvious but interesting point is that Otto and Zaehner are Christians, while Suzuki is a Buddhist (and a Zen Buddhist at that!).

In more secular terms, focusing upon philosophical rather than theological issues, Bertrand Russel (1921) erroneously we think, sees mysticism as more of a profound emotion, yet in terms of interpretation he rejects the validity of any metaphysical claim based upon mystical experience. Perhaps even more blunt is Scharfstein's (1973) recent assertion that any claim to metaphysical truth put forth by mystics on the basis of their mystical experiences are but "ontological fairy tales." Similarly, Melchert (1977) has recently argued the philosophical case that no ontological claims can legitimately follow from any mystical experience. Nevertheless, it is readily apparent that in the history of mysticism one can find diverse ontological claims proffered by mystics—dualistic and monistic; atheistic and theistic. All this belies an immense area of theological, philosophical, and psychological concern (Betty, 1977; Robertson, 1975).

While we readily grant that mystical experience is essentially always situated, and that mystical experience is recognized, recalled, and interpreted as any other human experience, recent philosophers such as Katz go too far when they claim that the distinction between relatively pure experience and the interpretation of experience is a fallacious distinction. Clearly, one can have an experience, even though it is isolated by a variety of psychological factors from the "stream of consciousness" (to use James' phrase) that can be organized and interpreted in a variety of ways and expressed in many linguistic forms. Hence, the distinction between experience and the interpretation of experience is especially empirically fruitful in that linguistically different descriptions may in fact mask fundamentally similar experiences at the minimal phenomenological level. While in a significant sense Katz is correct in that there are no unmediated experiences, experiences need not be mediated the same way.

As Moore (1978) has recently emphasized, conceptual analyses of mystical experiences are dependent upon basic data provided by reports of mystical experience, and these may be of four distinct types, of varying theoretical importance. Using Moore's terms, we can distinguish between first-person reports of experiences, more or less spontaneously formulated (*reflexive interpretation*) and first-person reports of experiences doctrinally interpreted (*retrospective interpretations*). Also, we can note first-person reports of mystical experiences interpreted in terms of prior sets, conditioning, and intentions (*incorporated interpretations*). Finally, features of the experience may be unaffected by prior beliefs and intentions as in Moore's *raw experience*. Significantly then, the discussion of experience versus interpretation provides much material to guide empirical investigation, especially in attributional terms. The important point for now is simply to note that neither does the investigator of mysticism have to have mystical experiences, as Staal (1975) seems to suggest; nor does the linguistic relativism of a person's existential life situation imply the impossibility of a uniformity to mystical experiences diversely described, as Katz (1978) seems to suggest. We can look to the meaning behind diverse descriptions as at least an open possibility, both conceptually and empirically. Furthermore, as Buber noted within the context of his own experience, variations in interpretation of an experience can occur with a single person over time, while the nature of the experience in its minimal raw form remains recognized as a constant. Buber, (1965) speaking of his own mystical experience, notes that:

> Now from my own unforgettable experience I know well that there is a state in which the bonds of the personal nature of life seem to have fallen away from us and we experience an undivided unity. But I do not know what the soul willingly imagines and indeed is bound to imagine (mine too once did it)—that in this I had attained a union with the primal being or godhead. That is an exaggeration no longer permitted to the responsible understanding (p. 24).

In attributional terms, one is likely to appreciate Buber's comments and interpret Buber's latter rejection of his earlier interpretation of merging with the "primal being" as theologically rooted in his commitment to Judaism, whose mysticism is fiercely insistent upon maintaining a distance from God. Yet, what is important is that we have, in Moore's terms, a *raw experience* maintained constantly (experience of unity) with a *retrospective interpretation* used to correct a previous spontaneously offered *reflexive interpretation*.

As with the conceptual research on mysticism, in which the issue of experience and the interpretation of experience is not without some concern, the empirical literature on mysticism is confounded with the distinction between mystical experience *qua* experience, and the report of mystical experience. Investigators studying mystical experiences are caught with studying persons' attributional reports of mystical experience, and not the experience itself. Hence, in all cases we will note that "reported mystical experience" is being studied, not "mystical experience *per se*," and as we shall see, the distinction is both conceptually and empirically warranted.

The conceptual issue has already been discussed above, and for now it is sufficient to note that the empirical issue is simply put: Factors accounting for the differential *occurrence* of mystical experience are not precisely the same factors accounting for the differential *report* of mystical experience. Furthermore, reporting mystical experience is heavily influenced by attributional factors. Hence, we shall briefly introduce empirical data concerning at least the frequency of reported mystical experience. These data shall serve as the backdrop for a scrutiny of empirical studies of the report of mystical experience that we shall then discuss in terms of three major groupings: (1) religious orientation and the report of mystical experience; (2) reported mystical experience and psychological well-being; and (3) triggering conditions of reported mystical experience. While these categories are neither exhaustive nor mutually exclusive, they are reasonably characteristic of the major research on the empirical study of mysticism current in the psychology of religion. Let us first, however, address ourselves to the relatively simple empirical question, "How common is the report of mystical experience?"

REPORTED MYSTICAL EXPERIENCE: SAMPLING FOR EMPIRICAL STUDIES AND SURVEY DATA

It is interesting that the major writers on the purely conceptual nature of mysticism have insisted that while the true mystic is perhaps a rare individual, few individuals pass through life without some aspect of mystical experiences. Scharfstein (1973) goes so far as to speak of "everyday mysticism," and survey data suggests that to go so far is perhaps not unreasonable.

Investigators have seldom found it difficult to identify significant percentages of persons reporting either mystical or fragmented aspects of mystical experiences. For instance, Kuhre (1971) found that 48 percent of his sample of college students affirmed having experienced "union with the Divine," while Maslow (1964) emphasized that "peak experiences" were the norm rather than the exception.

Similarly, Bourque and Back (1968) found that 66 percent of their sample of general college students affirmed having experienced being "somehow in the presence of God," while Vernon (1968) found that even among persons denying any religious affiliations 26 percent were either sure or thought they had this same experience. Likewise, Laski (1961) indicated no problem in finding overwhelming positive reports of "transcendent ecstasy" among her admittedly highly selective convenience sample. Hence, investigators wanting to study intense, mystical, or mystical-related experiences have not reported a lack of subjects. A review of our own samples over the last ten years indicates approximately 35 percent of our subjects overall indicate a positive response to questions regarding the occurrence of mystical experiences.

While these data vary in terms of the precise wording of experiences, these percentage figures are remarkably consistent with systematic survey data collected in direct query to the incidence of reported mystical experience.

Survey Data

In a series of Gallup polls, Back and Bourque (1974) attemped to tap the incidence of reported mystical experience. The specific question asked was as follows: "Would you say that you have ever had a 'religious or mystical experience'—that is, a moment of sudden religious awakening or insight?" The question was included in three separate Gallup polls in 1962, 1966, and 1967. Overall, slightly more than 31 percent of persons polled answered affirmatively, with a progressive increase in affirmative responses from 1962 (20.5 percent) through 1966 (31.8 percent) to 1967 (41.2 percent). While Back and Bourque are cautious in interpreting these changes and have done excellent work in attempting to determine sociological factors influencing the report of mystical experience (Back and Bourque, 1974; Borque and Back, 1968, 1974), the intriguing fact is that their percentage figures are quite consistent with others obtained from sampling for empirical studies.

The efforts of Back and Bourque (1974) also can be directly compared to recent work by Greeley (1974). Using a national sample of 1,468 persons, Greeley found in response to the specific question of whether or not a person ever "felt as though you were very close to a powerful, spiritual force that seemed to lift you out of yourself" that approximately 35 percent answered affirmatively, and approximately half experienced this at least several times. An illustration of some of this survey work is presented below in Research Box 8-2.

RESEARCH BOX 8-2.   *Bourque, L. B. "Social Correlates of Transcendental Experiences." Sociological Analysis, 1969, 30, 151–63*

Concern with the prevalence, nature, and activating conditions (triggers) for mystical experiences stimulated this research. Gallup poll data on 3,518 persons were collected regarding intense, ecstatic religious and aesthetic experiences. Thirty-two percent acknowledged moments of "sudden religious insight or awakening," while 47 percent reported what were regarded as similar aesthetic occurrences. The latter seem to be triggered largely by art or music in a secular context. They often produce positive, expansive feelings of peace and a sense of truth revelation. Religious mystical experiences tend to occur in religious environments and to consist of a single episode that was life-changing. This was usually accompanied by feelings of revelation and a sense of supernatural power being present. Great overlap was noted between the religious and the aesthetic experiences suggesting that they are not qualitatively different, but may be the result of the characteristic inclinations of the respondent and the triggering situation. Relative to the former, aesthetic experiences tended to be found among white, middle-class, educated persons, while the religious episodes were more frequent among the lower class, southerners, the poorly educated, the elderly, Protestants and Baptists, and rural blacks. Those having both aesthetic and religious experiences were most like those who had just the aesthetic ones.

Greeley's data have cross-cultural support from a study by Hay and Morisy. (1978). In a regular omnibus survey in Great Britain at the end of 1976, they asked whether persons had been, "aware of, or influenced by a presence or power, whether referred to as God or not, which is different from their everyday selves." In addition, this survey included the specific question used in the Greeley survey. Again, these data are encouragingly consistent. Overall, slightly more than 36 percent of persons affirmed that they had experienced such a presence or power, and again, approximately half of these had this experience at least several times. Likewise, in terms of the Greeley question, "Have you ever felt that you were very close to a powerful spiritual force that seemed to lift you out of yourself?" Hay and Morisy found 30.4 percent positive reports as compared to Greeley's 35 percent. This is an impressive similarity across national samples and, again, is consistent with convenience samples reported in empirical studies.

Finally, in a sample of 1,000 persons adjusted to represent the population of the San Francisco Bay area, Wuthnow (1978) found that 39 percent of persons overall affirmed an experience of "feeling that you were in harmony with the universe," while 34 percent who denied having such an experience nevertheless stated that they would *like* to have such an experience.

Survey data appear remarkably consistent in finding that between 30 percent and 40 percent of persons in America and Britain have experienced mystical-type phenomena. Of course, survey data are limited in terms of the sophistication of questions asked, and we readily agree that such questions add little to the empirical validity of the claim that a third of the populations of America and Britain actually have mystical experiences. Yet the commonality of the report of mystical experiences is clearly supported by varying samples and questioning procedures.

As an adjunct to these data, we add two cautions. First, precisely what is measured by survey questions is in need of serious empirical clarification, as the work of Back and Bourque (1970) has demonstrated. For our purposes, it is sufficient to note that while approximately a third of all sample types report mystical encounters, differing percentages report experiencing specific criteria of mystical involvement. For instance, Greeley's (1974) data indicates that 55 percent affirm an experience of great peace or joy, while only 25 percent claim a sense that all the universe is alive. Similarly, Bourque and Back (1968) report that 66 perent of their sample of college students reported a feeling of timelessness, while 86 percent affirmed an ineffable experience. Similarly, Wuthnow's (1978) data indicated that 50 percent of his sample had an episode that they believed to be sacred or profound. Hence, wide variations exist in affirmation of what we would accept as component criteria of mystical experiences, despite the rather constant percentage reported to questions not unreasonably held to be at least grossly indicative of the report of mystical experience.

Second, persons agreeing in the affirmation of mystical incidents nevertheless may vary widely in what criteria they utilize to make such attributions personally. For instance, in a recent study of 302 persons selected from students and members of religious and civic organizations, Thomas and Cooper (1978) found that 34 percent affirmatively answered the Greeley question cited earlier. This percentage corresponds both to the findings of Greeley (1974) and answered the specific Greeley question "Have you ever had the feeling of being close to a powerful, spiritual force that seemed to lift you out of yourself?'' This percentage corresponds to both Greeley's and Hay and Morisy's (1978). However, when content analyses were performed on persons' open-ended descriptions of the precise nature of this experience, it was found that wide variations occurred. Only 2 percent of these responses were found to be specifically mystical in the sense of criteria of mysticism closely aligned with the work of Stace. Twelve percent of these events were psychic experiences and 12 percent were simply examples of faith and consolation. The remaining 8 percent were uncodable, including irrelevant incidents. Hence, the obvious point: Persons affirming any linguistically described experience (and how else can they be described?) vary widely in what they use as criteria for such affirmations. What is important about these type data is that they remind us that the linguistic frameworks within which encounters are described are significant factors determining both their recognition and report.

Overall, these survey data are intriguing. Significant percentages of mystical and mystical-related experiences are affirmed among widely diverse samples and sampling procedures. Furthermore, a rough figure of 35 percent seems to occur constantly with respect to the more mystically worded experiential items. Hence, studies of persons reporting mystical experiences are embedded within a context of the normalcy of the report of such experiences. It is to these empirical studies that we now turn our attention.

Religious Orientation and the Report of Mystical Experience

A major concern in the empirical study of mysticism has been its relationship to indices of religiosity. On the one hand are investigators suggesting a hostile relationship between mystics and religious institutions. To these investigators, mysticism is a direct confrontation with the Divine. It does not need institutions or dogmas for its success, and may be even hampered or hindered by such "worldly trappings." At the other extreme are those investigators that insist upon the containment and even cultivation of mysticism within religious organizations— as if this fragile flower could not bloom without the care and concern of those organizations that can most effectively nourish it. Perhaps we overstate these extremes a bit, and indeed we must also note the claims of those who find a thoroughly "secular mysticism." A mysticism in which the criteria of holiness is little more than a sacredness for which nothing "religious" (in the institutional sense) is relevant.

Given these considerations, it is surprising that empirical research has found some rather consistent patterns in relating religiosity and mysticism, despite a wide use of assessment means to identify mystics. Let us first note studies relating mystical experience to institutional and personal forms of religious commitment.

Several studies have noted that less institutionally oriented individuals are more likely to report mystical experiences than institutionally oriented persons. For instance, Hood (1973) had persons identify themselves as either primarily personally religious, primarily institutionally religious, or equally personally and institutionally religious. Persons were then interviewed regarding their most personally significant life experiences. Later coding of these experiences for mystical quality, using Stace's criteria indicated that personally religiously oriented persons reportedly had more mystical experiences than institutionally oriented persons with equally oriented persons in between. Furthermore, institutional orientation negatively correlated with reports of mysticism while personal religious orientation positively correlated with reports of mysticism. While a developmental hypothesis was not directly tested in this study (e.g., persons were not individually followed over time), these data suggest one interpretation common to researchers in mysticism—namely, that religious institutions tend to inhibit if not eradicate mystical experiences among their members. As James (1902) noted long ago,

> A genuine first hand religious experience . . . is bound to be a heterodoxy to its witnesses, the prophet appearing as a mere lonely madman. If his doctrine prove contagious enough to spread to any others, it becomes a definite and labeled heresy. But, if it then still proves contagious enough to triumph over persecution, it becomes itself an orthodoxy; and when a religion has become an orthodoxy, its day of inwardness is over: the spring is dry: the faithful live at second hand exclusively and stone the prophets in their turn. The new church, in spite of whatever human goodness it may foster, can be henceforth counted on as a staunch ally in every attempt to stifle the spontaneous religious spirit, and to stop all later bubblings of the fountain from which in purer days it drew its own supply of inspiration (p. 337).

Viewing these data in light of James' speculations suggests that intense religious experiences, such as mysticism, are more characteristic of solitary individuals outside churches than of members of congregations. While this perspective has some merits, it needs empirical qualification in several senses. First, many churches simply do not facilitate intense religious experiences as normative demands as Dittes (1969) has noted, and hence such organizations are unlikely to have members reporting such encounters for this simple reason. Second, insofar as mystical experiences are profound episodes of unity characterized by ineffability, they may not be regarded as meaningful (Rosegrant, 1976). If so, religious persons who have an attributional system for meaningful religious experiences may not identify ''contentless'' mystical experiences precisely because they lack meaning within a particular religious attributional system. Third, religious organizations contain many persons who are extrinsically rather than intrinsically religious, and thus can be expected to be involved in religion for functional motives unrelated to more profound personal experiences. These alternatives suggest that the relationship between religious commitment and mysticism is rather complex, and not simply linear. If anything, one might anticipate two hypothesized relationshps between religiosity and reported mystical involvement. First, indices relating religious participation and reported mystical experience ought to be curvilinear as with religiosity and prejudice focused on in the chapter on religion and morality. Therefore, both nonattenders and frequent attenders can be expected to have high frequencies of reported religious experiences, including mystical confrontations, with relatively infrequent attenders in between. This hypothesized relationship has at least some empirical support. For instance, Hood (1976) found that more frequent church attenders have higher rates of mystical experience than less frequent attenders, but not higher than nonattenders. Similarly, Hood (1972, 1973a) has shown in several studies that regardless of the nature of their religious commitment, intrinsically religiously committed persons report more mystical experiences than their extrinsic peers. It is thus reasonable to conclude that the truly devout, characterized by intrinsic commitments, differ remarkably from their extrinsic and less consistent brethren but not from the religiously non-committed. What Hood's studies suggest is that nonreligious mysticism, reported by nonchurch attenders, may focus more upon the minimal properties of mystical experience, whereas mysticism within church contexts is perhaps more focused upon its religious interpretation in terms of a specific (e.g., theological) attributional meaning system. In any case, the relationship between mysticism and church attendance as an indicator of religious commitment appears to be curvilinear as noted in the figure below.

High

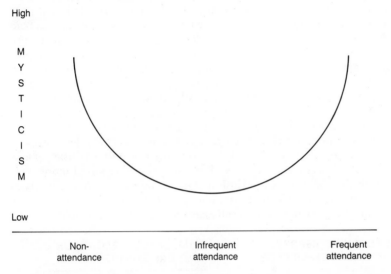

M
Y
S
T
I
C
I
S
M

Low

| Non-
attendance | Infrequent
attendance | Frequent
attendance |

If there is a differing motivational basis for reported mystical experience among frequent church attenders and nonattenders, one might also anticipate differing consequences for persons reporting mystical experience based upon whether or not they have an attributional system within which to explain mysticism. For instance, if mysticism is experienced outside an attributional system that gives it meaning, it should have little consequence for the person. It would appear that mystical incidents are significant, life-transforming experiences *only for those who religiously interpret them* (Hood and Hall, 1977; Rosegrant, 1976; Swartz and Seginer, 1981). Otherwise, they are apparently only (ironically!) experiences of "nothingness"!

Mystical Experiences and Conflictual Religious Orientation

If mysticism is confronted most effectively within attributional systems that establish its meaning, one might anticipate that persons uncertain of their religious orientation ought to have conflicts with respect to at least the interpretation of what are otherwise merely minimal experiential "components" of mysticism. This is precisely what Maslow hypothesized and what empirical data suggest are reasonable.

Maslow (1964) suggested that many persons have religious and mystical experiences but fail to understand them precisely because they lack a meaningfully felt religious system within which to acknowledge these experiences. In fact, Maslow argued that such persons may fail to admit these events because of their unease with the religious language that most typically has been the legitimating language for such experiences. Interestingly, Allport's treatment of intrinsic and extrinsic religious orientation permitted a relevant, if indirect, test of Maslow's assertion.

Allport's subscales to measure religious orientation can be combined to produce four categories of persons. Intrinsic persons are those who score relatively high on the intrinsic subscale and relatively low on the extrinsic subscale. Extrinsic persons are those who score just the reverse. Each of these are relatively "pure types" representing differing orientations to religion. Persons scoring high on both the intrinsic and extrinsic subscales are identified as "indiscriminately pro religious" (Allport and Ross, 1967). One modification of Allport's scoring prodiscriminate general pro response to anything religious. Similarly, persons scoring low on both the intrinsic and extrinsic subscales represent a pervasive negative religious orientation, and are identified by Allport as "indiscriminately antireligious." (Allport and Ross, 1967). One modification of Allport's scoring procedures uses median splits to create these four categories (Hood, 1971).

Given these four categories of religious types, Hood (1970) demonstrated that one could distinguish, as expected, between intrinsic and extrinsic persons in terms of reported mystical experience: Intrinsic persons reported more. Yet, one could not distinguish between intrinsic and indiscriminately pro persons (both high) or between extrinsic and indiscriminately anti persons (both low) on the report of mystical experience. The results can be summarized as follows:

EQUALLY HIGH REPORTS OF MYSTICAL EXPERIENCE	EQUALLY LOW REPORTS OF MYSTICAL EXPERIENCE
Intrinsic persons and Indiscriminately Pro-Religious Persons	Extrinsic persons and Indiscriminately Anti-Religious Persons

In terms of attribution theory and both Allport's and Maslow's independent theorizing, these data make sense. Intrinsic persons report mystical experiences that they can identify through a meaningful attributional system. Extrinsic persons have a meaningful attributional system to identify mystical experiences but simply don't experience them as frequently. On the other hand, what about the indiscriminately pro and anti categories? The difficulties in distinguishing these types from their respective pure intrinsic or extrinsic counterparts suggest an intriguing possibility consistent with both Allport's and Maslow's theorizing.

The methodological difficulty of differentiating between intrinsic and indiscriminately pro-religious persons is important in that it suggests the possibility that intrinsic persons report mystical experiences that in fact they have had, while indiscriminately pro-religious persons simply endorse REEM items as part of their general tendency to acquiesce in the face of any religiously worded items and hence are "false positives" with respect to having actually *experienced* anything mystical.

Similarly, it was suggested that the failure to distinguish between extrinsic and indiscriminately anti-religious oriented persons may not reflect simply a real difference in the lack of mystical experiences, but rather the possibility that the indiscriminately anti-religious persons are "false negatives" in that they have mystical experiences but fail to identify them in these terms. This suggestion is consistent with Maslow's contention that many persons have religious experiences but resist identifying them as such, as well as with suggestions by Bourque and Back (1968, 1974) regarding the role of language in the differential identification and report of intense experiences.

In order to extend the suggestive findings of this study, an additional study was undertaken to further explore the conceptual fruitfulness of Allport's four-fold classification scheme, despite problems with the purely psychometric validity of this classification scheme (Kahoe, 1976).

Our view is that while the psychometric wisdom of creating categories from the combined use of Allport's scales is perhaps minimal, both indiscriminate categories are empirically identifiable. Specifically, it would appear that persons denoted as indiscriminately pro- or indiscriminately anti-religious are in fact motivated by conflicting stances with respect to religious orientations. We suspect that the indiscriminately pro-religious category represents many persons overly sensitive to religious issues, suggesting a more fundamental failure to integrate successfully *either* an intrinsic or extrinsic religious orientation. Similarly, we suspect that the indiscriminately anti-religious category represents at least some persons overly sensitive to the suppression or repression of religious attitudes and experiences and who have not successfully integrated a nonreligious orientation to life.

While these inferences are admittedly speculative, they are not inconsistent with Allport's (1967) formulation in which he identifies the problematic nature of the "inconsistent" indiscriminately pro- and anti-religious categories and notes ". . . that for some purpose these categories will be of central significance" (Allport and Ross, 1977, p. 442). While a wide variety of measures were used to test the hypothesized inconsistency of the indiscriminate categories, in this second study we focused only upon indices of anxiety or stress that we assume to characterize persons in the indiscriminate categories based upon the assumption that these persons have a conflictual stance with respect to their religious orientation.

Two different indices were employed in this additional study by Hood (1978). One was Byrne's (1964) *Repression-sensitization scale* (RS scale), which is essentially empirically equivalent to the paper/pencil test of anxiety.

The second measure was a physiological measure of stress, a voice stress analyzer. The basic theory underlying the use of such devices is that muscle micro tremors in speech can be electronically recorded and assessed for indications of stress, or perhaps general physiological arousal. (Podlesny, and Raskin, 1977). The use of this device was to detemine if persons indicated stress when either affirming or denying that they had a mystical experience.

Importantly, this study replicated the original study with respect to reported mystical experience and religious orientation; intrinsic and indiscriminately pro-religious persons both scored high on mysticism while extrinsic and indiscriminately anti-religious persons both scored low.

Results of analyses based upon the assumption of a conflictual religious orientation for the indiscriminate categories were generally supportive of this hypothesis.

In particular, on both the RS scale and the stress analyzer the indiscriminate pro-religious persons indicated stress, suggesting that their religious orientation is conflict-ridden and accompanied by anxiety or stress, especially when affirming mystical experiences. The data were less conclusive for the indiscriminate anti-religious categories. However, it is important to note that neither the intrinsic nor the extrinsic categories indicated stress, suggesting their differing but nonconflictual religious orientations.

The complementary nature of these two studies suggests that the indiscriminate categories are both conceptually and empirically useful. The fact that they may not be "pure" and represent a conflictual stance toward religion can be explored in a variety of ways, and perhaps help clarify distinctions between healthy and unhealthy religious orientations.

Empirical measures that more adequately identify these categories are clearly needed. The indiscriminate anti-religious category may reflect persons who appear nonreligious, but ambivalently so. Maslow's claim that such persons deny significant personal experiences because of their "religious" implications remains an intriguing possibility not refuted by these studies. Furthermore, it suggests the necessity noted by Vernon (1968) of not neglecting the "religious none" in any studies of religiosity. Similarly, Dittes' (1969) claim that the indiscriminate pro-religious category represents a general pro-religious institutional factor may need qualification. As one example, it may be that the apparently high rates of mystical experience commonly revealed in surveys may contain a significant number of conflicting reports due to apparently greater contemporary social pressure to affirm such experiences by persons who identify themselves as religious. If we summarize these two studies following our initial chart on page 188, we can add stress data as follows:

Reported Mysticism

		High	Low
	High	Indiscriminately Pro-Religious	Indiscriminately Anti-Religious
Stress	Low	Intrinsic	Extrinsic

In terms of attribution theory, these tentative findings make sense. In particular, the distinction between experience and its interpretation allows us to identify persons varying in the actual experience of mysticism. Intrinsic persons experience mysticism and have an attributional system to interpret it nonstressfully as meaningful. Extrinsic persons have similar meaning systems but simply do not experience mysticism as frequently. However, the indiscriminately religious types are perhaps stressed: The indiscriminately pro-religious are stressed because they feel pressured to report experiences they may not have had, and the indiscriminately anti-religious are stressed because they may have experiences for which they lack a legitimating meaning system to acknowledge them. These possibilities are further supported by research indicating that persons do distinguish between criteria for identifying mystical experiences and the actual report or failure to report such experiences (Hood and Morris, 1981). Thus, attributions are as important as actual experiences in the study of mysticism.

PSYCHOLOGICAL WELL-BEING AND THE REPORT OF MYSTICAL EXPERIENCE

We now turn to an area of research of immense importance but one in which research has really just begun. This is the entire area of the relationship between psychopathology and the report of mystical experience. However, the very bias of this formulation is evident, and we shall prefer to speak of relationships between psychological well-being and the report of mystical experience if for no other reason than to balance biases.

The survey data already discussed provide ample evidence for Tisdale's (1975) claim that mysticism is both normal and normative. Likewise, Stark's (1971) review of the relationship between psychopathology and religious commitment is instructive here. As Stark noted, we had always *assumed* that such a relationship existed, and yet as noted in Chapter Twelve the empirical literature at a minimum demonstrates that the relationship between religiosity and psychopathology is not nearly so simple.

With respect to the report of intense experiences, especially religiously interpreted ones, the problems of contemporary psychology are immediately evident. In the past, such experiences simply have been declared pathological via a brute nominalism. Only with the rise of a concern with experience rather than mere behavior, "Eastern" modes of thought, and "anti-psychiatry" perspectives has modern psychology begun to confront intense experiences as a topic of concern in and of themselves. Hence, we are just beginning to see studies as positive psychological correlates of reported mystical experience. While what has appeared so far is of minimal conceptual and empirical sophistication, the studies are nevertheless not without merit.

For instance, Hood (1976) has provided purely conceptual arguments against hypothesizing mysticism to be a regressive experience. In addition, he has provided empirical evidence that reported mystical experience is associated with strong, not weak, ego strength. In one study (Hood, 1974), an apparent relationship between weak ego strength and mysticism was shown to be due only to a bias in the scoring of religiously worded items from standardized psychological test items. An example of some of these items and the bias inherent in their scoring is indicated in Box 8-3. Consider the following paraphrased items from a widely used subscale of a very popular measure of personality.

> Do you believe that your sins are unpardonable?
> Have you ever had unusual religious experiences?
> Do you believe Christ performed miracles?
> Do you pray?

A "yes" response to any of these items is scored to contribute to your total pathology score! For further understanding of such biases, see Hood (1974).

RESEARCH BOX 8-3   *Hood, R. W. Jr. "Differential Triggering of Mystical Experience as a Function of Self-actualization.* Review of Religious Research, *1977, 18, 264–70*

The question of whether mystical experience is most likely to be found among persons who are mentally disordered or manifest a high level of mental well-being has never been conclusively established. Because work on the latter possibility was essentially nonexistent, the author tested Abraham Maslow's hypothesis that "peak" or mystical experiences would be found among exceptional persons who could be considered self-actualized. It was also theorized that such individuals would be likely to have had their experiences triggered more by deviant means and situations than by traditional ones.

A total of 187 undergraduate students participated. Eighty-seven took measures of Hood's mysticism scale and a measure of self-actualization. The remaining 100 respondents had taken the Mysticism scale and scored at the high extreme. Of these, fifty who scored high on the self-actualization measure and fifty who scored low were selected for further study. These groups were, however, equivalent on the Mysticism scale. These 100 respondents were later contacted and were asked to fill out an open-ended questionnaire on the setting that triggered their mystical experience(s).

Mystical experience, but not necessarily religious mystical experience, was shown to correlate positively with self-actualization. Highly self-actualized persons tended to report less traditional triggers for these episodes than low self-actualized persons. This is seen in the following table. The hypotheses were thus supported.

Frequency of Triggers for Mystical Experiences among High and Low Self-actualized Persons

	SELF-ACTUALIZATION GROUPS	
TRIGGERS	HIGH (N = 50)	LOW (N = 50)
Nature	4	16
Sex	12	2
Religion	4	15
Drugs	15	1
Introspection	10	12
Miscellaneous	5	4

However, using other indices of psychological strength, uncontaminated by religious biases, reported mystical experience has been shown to correlate positively with measures of health and psychological strength. This makes sense in terms of the conceptual literature on mysticism in which the dominant view is of a healthy person's relinquishing their "ego" or "surrendering themselves to God." Such a view is only narrowly interpreted as weakness!

This claim is supported by additional empirical data using other indices of psychological well-being. For instance, Taft (1969, 1970) has developed a scale to measure what he terms "ego permissiveness." This concept is basically related to the psychoanalytic notion of "regression in the service of the ego" and is meant to refer to a process whereby the ego can constructively utilize preconscious and unconscious potentialities (Kris, 1952). In less psychoanalytic language, this concept is termed "openness to experience" (Schachtel, 1959), and is specifically indicated by belief in the supernatural, ecstatic emotions, and alteration of consciousness, among other factors (Taft, 1970). Using Taft's ego permissiveness scale, it was demonstrated that mysticism significantly correlated with this measure (Hood, 1975). While much of this correlation is perhaps due to a positive bias inherent in Taft's scale in favor of intense experiential states, religious and otherwise, it is still reasonable to suppose that persons open to experience of all types are also likely to be open and receptive to mystical experience.

This latter claim is supported by studies indicating that persons reporting "deeper" hypnotic experiences on a standardized scale also scored higher on mysticism (Hood, 1973). While these data are limited in depth, they are consistent with the belief that persons reporting mystical experience and those indicating hypnotic suggestibility are persons capable of an openness to "wider" and "deeper" aspects of reality, and hence one might expect both hypnotic suggestibility and mysticism to be related.

TRIGGERING CONDITIONS FOR THE REPORT OF MYSTICAL EXPERIENCE

We now consider a final major area of research on the report of mystical experience: the conditions that trigger the experience. The phrase *trigger* comes from Laski's (1961) provocative work and is characterized by the notion that no "causes" of mysticism are postulated. Rather, certain conditions seem to facilitate the experience while not in fact producing it. The conceptual issue here is of immense importance and suggests fine interplays between psychology and theology that we shall ignore here in favor of a more simple focus upon relevant empirical data.

First, survey studies (Greeley, 1974; Laski, 1961; Wuthnow, 1978) are consistent in finding that the mystical experiences are triggered by a wide variety of settings and circumstances among which are many social situations, especially the availability of appropriate linguistic contexts within which to express the experience (Back and Bourque, 1970; Bourque and Back, 1968, 1974; Hood and Hall, 1977).

Second, correlational studies also suggest the differential triggering of mystical experiences according to reasonable "attributional contexts" within which such experiences can be expected. For instance, in one study it was shown that more traditionally religious persons who have mystical experiences attributed them to normative triggers such as prayer and nature, while less traditionally religious persons attributed their mystical experiences to drugs or sex (Hood, 1977). Similarly, evaluations of mystical experiences have been shown to be attributed at least partly to the perceived social legitimacy of their triggers—with drug-induced experiences less positively evaluated than those attributed to prayer. (Hood, 1980). The issue of drug-induced mystical experiences is controversial, but it must be noted that drugs have often been cited in the conceptual literature on mysticism, and in at least one study have been used in quasi-experimental tests to elicit mystical experience (Pahnke and Richards, 1966). However, the *spontaneous* report of mystical experience under psychedelic drugs is apparently no more than under other circumstances and conditions. (Masters and Houston, 1966). Similarly, where erotic activities elicit mystical responses is partly a function of the context and religious importance attributed to erotic activities. (Hood and Hall, 1980). Hence, the issue is largely an attributional one in which the context is crucial in determining the meaning of otherwise triggered mystical experiences. It would thus appear empirically fruitless to try to identify specific triggers of mystical experience given the almost endless variety of possible triggers. Efforts at higher level integrations are needed. One such effort is the set/setting stress incongruity hypothesis. Before reading about that, Research Box 8-3 demonstrates some interesting findings about personality and triggers for mystical experience.

Set/Setting Stress Incongruities and Mysticism

In two closely related quasi-experimental nature studies, Hood (1977b, 1978b) has provided data consistent with a set/setting incongruity hypothesis for the elicitation of mystical experience. In particular, while Hood argues against stress being a trigger of mystical experience, he does propose a way in which stress in terms of set and setting incongruities may serve to elicit mystical experience. The reasoning for this hypothesis is related to the concepts of "limits" and "transcendence."

Theoretically, the concept of "limit" is seen as entailing a related concept— "transcendence"—and in fact it is the awareness of limits that makes possible and facilitates transcendence. Perhaps it is the case that a sudden contrast in ground (setting), produced by an incongruent anticipatory set, forces an acute awareness of self into relief, and hence any factor that indicates to a person a limit simultaneously provides a possibility of transcendence. In this context, insofar as stress suggests a limit, it also potentially suggests transcendence of which mysticism is an example. However, stress is unlikely to serve this function and can be, especially if anticipated, merely a disruptive and threatening factor serving to elicit more negative, regressive experiences. Only when we speak of stress both in terms of setting and set does the notion of limit seem relevant to positive experiences. Specifically, we suggest that when anticipatory set and setting stress are *incongruent*, a sudden awareness of limits is likely to be produced that facilitates transcendence or positive mystical experiences.

In this context, much of what is termed "nature mysticism" is relevant since mystical experiences in nature are generally recognized as quite common and likely to occur suddenly given appropriate, nonstressful situations. However, upon closer inspection the nature of these nonstressful situations is only apparent since it appears to be the case that a nonstressful personal set is interrupted suddenly by a natural, stressful event. This clash between anticipatory set stress and sudden setting stress appears to be a trigger of mystical experience. This impression is also consistent with certain Zen techniques in which, at the appropriate moment, the teacher suddenly and profoundly presents the unaware student with a stressful stimulus that then triggers the appropriate experience of "enlightenment"

(Elwood, 1980). This is also consistent with research by Rosegrant (1976) indicating that mysticism scores seemed to be greatest in a nature situation where set and setting clashed.

Given the above considerations, two independent studies manipulating both anticipatory set and setting stress conditions were undertaken so that all possibilities of set and setting congruencies occurred. The results of these studies can be schematically represented as follows:

Setting Stress

		HIGH	LOW
Anticipatory Set	*High*	Low Mysticism	High Mysticism
Stress	*Low*	High Mysticism	Low Mysticism

These studies seem particularly important insofar as they represent at least preliminary efforts to provide some type of theoretical explanation for the occurrence of mystical experience that can serve to integrate much of the existing empirical literature in at least two senses.

First, insofar as it is reasonable to argue that set/setting stress incongruencies suddenly make one aware of "limits" and hence in so doing make "transcendent" experiences possible, there is a broader theoretical context within which this specific interaction is meaningful. This interpretation not only suggests similarities between psychopathology and mysticism in terms of a common background in stress, but perhaps more importantly suggests differences as well. Certainly psychopathological reactions are likely to occur when set and setting stress cumulatively become overwhelming, and the person simply succumbs to these stresses. Reactions to these stresses are thus not only likely to be negatively experienced, but also to be unfruitful to the person and society as well. However, mystical experiences are perhaps more likely to occur when an incongruity between set and setting stress suddenly makes a person aware of limits to growth that can in fact now be transcended. Hence, the reaction itself is likely to be positively experienced and to be fruitful to the person and society. As Boisen (1936) argues, it is when insights achieved in mystical experience are integrated into a new and valuable social self that a truly religious basis for positive psychological growth occurs.

Second, as Greeley (1974) has argued, these data indicate that mystical experiences are in fact relatively common and easily researched. Scharfstein (1973) even goes so far as to speak of "everyday mysticism," and certainly in the context of nature mysticism this phrase may be more legitimate than previously suspected. Again, to use the concept of "limits," it appears that anything that suddenly illuminates or makes one aware of a supposedly limiting situation simultaneously may trigger mysticism, at least at its lower levels. Here Laski's (1961) concept of "anti-trigger" is relevant in that anything that simply reminds one of or is inalienably associated with everyday occurrences is unlikely to trigger mysticism. However, any factor that suddenly emerges or is recognized to point to the limits of everyday reality may suddenly serve as a trigger to mysticism.

Second, higher order abstractions concerning triggering conditions are beginning to be isolated. Hood's efforts with respect to set and setting stress incongruities is one such example. The direction for further research lies this way through theory guided research seeking higher order classifications of triggering conditions that can be empirically investigated.

A COORDINATING TYPOLOGY

This overview of research on reported mystical experience strongly indicates that it would be premature to claim any established "facts" in this area. It is, however, obvious that reported mysticism can be empirically investigated and that conceptually guided work promises to provide much for theory across disciplines—theology, philosophy, and the behavioral and social sciences.

Much of the conceptual literature on mysticism is centered on criticisms of existing typologies. For instance, Zaehner (1961) has insisted that the distinction between theistic and nontheistic mysticisms were minimized in Stace's (1960) work. To date psychological research on mysticism is heavily influenced by Stace's criteria as discussed in this chapter. Yet we propose a typology of mysticism using a theistic/nontheistic and image/imageless dimension to create four types of mysticism that can be investigated empirically. Our typology assumes an experience of unity common to all mysticisms, but clearly distinguishes between whether or not there is a content to the experience and whether or not it is a theistic or nontheistic experience. This typology is presented below, along with a dominant representative of each mysticism type (Hood, 1981). This typology is not exhaustive, but does serve to link major debates on mysticism types. It is compatible with Stace's criteria but emphasizes Zaehner's criticisms as well. It also distinguishes introvertive (imageless) and extrovertive (image) mysticism as "types" rather than as continuums.

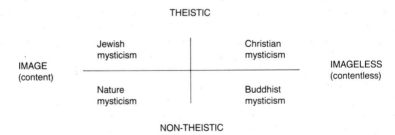

ATTRIBUTION THEORY AND MYSTICAL EXPERIENCE

Since mystical experience is a variant of religious experience, it is very much an attributional phenomenon. Throughout the chapter, attributional allusions have been offered. We theorize that the basis for attributions relative to mystical experience are needs or desires for meaning, control, and self-esteem. Assertions that the causes of such confrontations lie with the divine provide the mystic with possibly the most important meaning in his/her life, often having significance that is totally life-transforming. A sense of control over one's destiny seems part of the picture, and, although such experiences seem quite widespread, those having these encounters reveal the positive kind of personal uplift found among persons who feel they have been specially "chosen."

Dispositional and situational factors are clearly involved in denoting the who and when of mystical episodes. Intrinsic-committed persons are more disposed in this direction than their extrinsic-consensual colleagues. It is also evident that religious contexts and events are more likely to stimulate and/or shape these incidents than nonspiritual surroundings and activities. The issue for attribution theory is in the defining of these experiences, since similar happenings probably occur under esthetic or nature conditions among other possibilities, but the likelihood they will be designated religious mystical experiences appears to be low. Bourque and Back's indications of linguistic factors influencing reports of these events also testifies to their being dispositionally influenced.

Although mystical experiences have most often been considered relative to psychopathology and inadequacy, a strong case has been made that those offering these attributions are frequently in very good shape psychologically. Distinctions between the mystical attributions of those who are mentally in difficulty and others who demonstrate good ego strength and a high level of well-being need to be researched.

The task for the future is likely to be further specification of the nature of mystical episodes, but in their interaction with dispositional and setting characteristics. They may be expressions of human potential that are sensitive to a wide variety of factors as some research suggests. Their meaning for religion cannot be underestimated, nor their role within the individual personality. Research and theory may remove the veil of the romantic and exotic from these phenomena, but they are unlikely to reduce their significance in the eyes of those involved in mystical encounters.

SUMMARY AND CONCLUSIONS

Despite considerable difficulty conceptualizing mystical experience, a number of operational approaches to this area have been introduced. Utilizing these methods, the empirical research suggests that a wide variety of circumstances, situations, and substances apparently elicit mystical experiences. Specific triggering conditions, however, elicit mystical experiences differentially according to a wide variety of social, cultural, and personal variables, only some of which have been identified. Survey research does indicate that thirty to forty percent of the population do have such experiences, implying them to be normal rather than pathological phenomena.

This raises questions about what stimulates these events, and theory-guided research to discover higher order abstractions concerning triggering conditions is only now beginning to be constructed. Hood's (1978b) efforts with respect to set and setting stress incongruities is one such example.

The research on mystical experience relative to religious orientation and psychological state suggests that:

1. Personal religious commitment may be more indicative of the report of mystical experience than church commitment, even though a significant minority of church-goers reports such incidents. Mysticism can be a disconcerting force insofar as modern religious institutions may fail to provide meaningful forums for this kind of experience.

2. It seems clearly established that intrinsically religious persons are more likely to report mystical experiences than their extrinsically religious peers.

3. It remains an important empirical task to identify what appear to be false positives and false negatives in the report of mystical experience. This kind of research promises to link psychological and sociological perspectives, particularly in the interface where normatively legitimated language contexts may encourage the report of intense religious experience.

4. The persistent assumption that mysticism is "pathological" is clearly unwarranted conceptually. Though the data are not yet definitive, mysticism and psychological well-being do appear to be closely associated (Hood, Hall, Watson, and Biderman, 1979).

With this survey of empirical research on reported mystical experience it would be premature to claim any established "facts" in this area. If anything, we have but indicated a beginning. It is obvious, however, that reported mysticism can be empirically investigated and that conceptually guided research promises to provide much for theory across disciplines—theology, philosophy, and psychology. While one can wonder at what depth mysticism is being investigated when so many persons are identified as "mystical," one cannot doubt the value of establishing empirically rooted data with respect to this topic that has been—and continues to be—of such immense importance.

CHAPTER NINE
CONVERSION

"If I had not destroyed myself completely, I should not have been able to rebuild and shape myself again" (Ward, 1975, p. 35).

". . . and Priests in black gowns were walking their rounds, and binding with briars my joys and desires" (Blake, 1967, p. 44).

". . . I heard for the first time (consciously at least) what it meant to be a Christian. I can remember going out in a daze to my own rooms saying to myself, If this is true something in my life has to change" (Hardy, 1979, p. 71).

INTRODUCTION

In the early months of 1881, G. Stanley Hall (1904) delivered a series of public lectures at Harvard. The young science of psychology was courageous enough to tackle some of the most profound and meaningful religious phenomena of the times. Hall's topic was religious conversion.

At the turn of the century, religious revivals were common in America, especially in American Protestantism. Methodists and Baptists as well as a variety of evangelical Protestants preached religious revivalism and argued for what has become known as "born-again" experiences. James' (1902) distinction was between those "once born," who are cultivated within and socialized to accept their faith, and the "twice born," who with a more melancholy temperament are literally compelled through crises to accept or realize a faith within an instant. Not surprisingly, American psychology of religion was fascinated by this religious phenomenon, and conversion became perhaps the earliest major focus of the psychology of religion.

Hall's students at Clark University continued and expanded the interest of their mentor. Most notable were Leuba, (1896, 1912) who published the first psychological journal article on conversion in 1896; and Starbuck, who published the first full book-length treatment of conversion in 1899. Their methods paralleled Hall, including the use of personal documents, but were extended to include interviews and questionnaire data. Likewise, other early investigators such as Coe (1916) added quasi-experimental techniques to the investigation of converts. This early period in the psychology of religion provided a framework for understanding religious conversion that remains fruitful even today. If this early research can be faulted on methodological and other grounds, its richness in terms of its extensive individual focus has been largely lost in contemporary psychological concerns. Today, as we shall see later in this chapter, conversion is likely to be less positively evaluated, and certainly studied with less personal depth. In the late 1950s, Clark (1958) bemoaned the lack of attention of modern psychology to conversion, noting:

> For students of religion and religious psychology there is no subject that has held more fascination than the phenomenon called conversion. Yet of recent years a kind of shamefacedness becomes apparent among those scholars who mention it . . . among the more conventional psychologists of the present day, who infrequently concern themselves with the study of religion and practically never with the subject of conversion. It is quite obvious that the latter is regarded as a kind of psychological slum to be avoided by any really respectable scholar (p. 188).

Clark's point is well stated and provides an initial framework for this chapter. Quite naturally, we can focus upon two major periods in the study of conversion that we shall term the classic and the contemporary periods, respectively. In the classic period, we have extensive psychological study of conversion, relying heavily upon a wide diversity of techniques and data, but always with a primary emphasis upon individual psychological processes. In the contemporary period, we have two major concerns. First, the retreat from primary psychological concern with conversion and the dominance of more sociologically oriented explanations. Second, the reemergence of intense psychological concerns with sudden, crises-precipitated conversions but within a context of suspicion and delegitimation. These major distinctions are not exclusive and may overlap, but as we shall see, they provide major differing, and to some extent, even contradictory views of conversion.

The Classic Research on Conversion

What we have chosen to call the classic research on conversion is of interest not merely as history, but as excellent descriptive psychology. The early investigators focused upon a variety of procedures. These included personal documents such as private letters, confessions, and autobiographical and biographical summaries. Questionnaires, interviews, and public confessions were also employed. While contemporary psychology tends to minimize the use of many of these sources, especially personal documents, their value can be immense—not in terms of identifying the causal determinants of conversion, but as rich descriptions of the process of conversion. James (1902) notes the value of what he has called "sporadic adult cases" to illustrate in rich, concrete detail almost "ideal types" of conversion. Such a view was common to the early investigators of conversion—a search for particular cases that illustrate precisely the investigator's conceptualization of conversion. How then did the early investigators conceive of conversion?

Early Conceptualizations of Conversion

Three major considerations most typically appear to have occupied a central concern in the early studies of conversion. Basically, these had to do with the role of time in identifying types of conversions, the age at which conversion is most typical, and the issue of explanatory processes in accounting for conversion. Surprisingly, despite variations across investigators, a rather impressive consensus can be detected within each of these emphases.

The Question of Time

Early investigators did not fail to classify conversion types into simple dichotomies based primarily upon the obvious dimension of time. Some persons converted quickly, suddenly adopting a faith perspective previously unknown or of peripheral concern to them. Others seemed to mature and blossom gradually within a faith perspective that in some sense had always been theirs. We have already noted James' reference to the "once" and "twice" born, with the latter likely to be associated with a sudden religious conversion. James acknowledges the possibility of gradual conversions, but his focus and fascination is clearly with conversions of a sudden nature, likely precipitated by crises.

In this concern and fascination, James is not alone. Starbuck (1899) focuses upon conversions initiated by a sense of escape from sin and those elicited by a struggle toward a positive religious ideal. He called the former "self-surrender conversions" and the latter "voluntary conversions," with the clear implication that only the former would likely be crisis-initiated and sudden. Ames (1910) favors restricting the use of the term *conversion* only for sudden instances of religious change associated with intense emotional experiences. Similarly, Coe (1916) carefully notes at least six "senses" of the term conversion, but prefers its limitation to experiences that were both intense and sudden. Johnson (1959) later echoed these views succinctly when he stated, "A genuine religious conversion is the outcome of a crisis." (p. 117).

While sudden, crisis-initiated conversions did indeed occupy the major fascination of many early investigators, others warned against such a premature and narrow focus. For instance, Pratt (1920) suggests that the fascination of investigators with sudden crisis-stimulated conversions favored its overrepresentation in texts concerned with the psychology of religion. In addition, he notes appropriately that most cases of sudden conversion were socially elicited. In his own words,

> I venture to estimate that at least nine out of every ten "conversion cases" reported in recent questionnaires would have no violent or depressing experience to report had not the individuals in question been brought up in a church or community which taught them to look for it if not to cultivate it (p. 153).

Similarly, Cutten (1908) notes that investigators had focused heavily upon Paul's conversion as reported in the New Testament as the ideal model of genuine religious conversion and had simply unwittingly reduced Paul's unique experience to a general formula.

The early concern with sudden versus gradual conversions was not simply a debate over the time factor in conversion. The time factor was seen as an indicator of two types of conversion that in all likelihood utilized differing psychological processes. Hence, interest focused upon divergent explanations of the process of conversion in sudden and gradual converts. This shall concern us shortly. Yet, before we go too much further we need to confront a more fundamental issue. Simply put, regardless of the time span within which conversion occurs, how was conversion defined by these early investigators? Here, fortunately, almost unanimity reigns supreme.

Defining Conversion

For almost all investigators, conversion was conceptualized as a reorientation of self. In most general terms, one self was replaced by another. Hence, conversion in its religious sense was seen only as part of the general phenomena of personality change. One could have "unreligious conversions," as most investigators realized. As Coe (1916) succinctly put it, "Conversion is by no means co-extensive with religion." (p. 54). In addition, most investigators agreed that interpersonal processes paralleled conversion. As an example, James (1902) notes that falling in love paralleled the conversion process. Pratt (1920) goes so far as to state that "In many cases getting converted means falling in love with Jesus." (p. 160). Yet, what made conversion of interest to the psychology of religion was precisely its *religious* nature. What then is religious conversion? Contemporary views are rooted in fundamental considerations established by the classic researchers.

A Definition of Conversion

Among the early investigators, perhaps Coe (1916) did most to clarify conversions. He insisted upon four major criteria that remain useful today. First, conversion is a profound change in self. Second, this change is not simply a matter of maturation, but most typically is identified with a decision, sudden or gradual, to accept another perspective within which the new self is to be identified. Third, this change in self constitutes a change in the entire mode of one's life—a new centering of concern, interest, and action. Fourth, and finally, this new change is seen as "higher" or as an emancipation from a previous dilemma or less valuable life. In simple summary terms, Coe (1916) speaks of "self-realization with a social medium" (p. 152). There is *self-realization* because a new self is actualized from the old; there must be a *social medium* since one adopts a religious framework within which the realization of the self is recognized.

Coe's view meshes nicely with James' (1902) assertion that "To say a man is 'converted' means . . . that religious ideas, peripheral in his consciousness, now take a central place, and that religious aims form the habitual center of his energy." (p. 196). The fact that conversion must result in a new *habitual* mode of action and interpretation of the world led investigators such as Strickland (1924) to argue against James' twice-born view and to say that any person who consciously adopts a religious life is "twice born" regardless of whether the process of arriving at that life was sudden or gradual. Yet, while investigators differed as to the importance of a sudden versus gradual distinction in the process of religious conversion, all agreed that the study of age in relationship to conversion was important.

THE AGE AT WHICH CONVERSION TYPICALLY OCCURS

Given the fact that religious conversion is the adoption of a religious perspective as a major determining factor of one's life, early investigators could not help but notice that conversion was apparently an age-related phenomena. The major focus was upon adolescence.

While most early investigators agreed that conversions could occur at any time in the life span, most agreed that conversion was typically an adolescent phenomena. Johnson (1959) surveyed five major studies on conversion that totally included over 15,000 persons, and the average age of conversion was 15.2 years with a range of from 12.7 to 16.6 years.

These data do not permit distinctions between sudden and gradual conversions; however, the questionnaire data of Clark (1929) does permit such a breakdown. Clark further divides sudden conversions into those elicited by a definite crisis and those linked to specific emotional concerns, not necessarily of major crisis proportion. Based upon his 2,174 cases, Clark (1929) was able to classify them as to what percent were sudden, either crisis or emotional, and what percent were gradual. He found one-third of the cases to be crisis or emotionally elicited, and the remaining two-thirds to be a function of gradual growth. These results suggested that while crisis-initiated conversions may be most interesting and indeed are heavily discussed by investigators, less intense emotional and gradual growth processes account for most cases of conversion. These data are not inconsistent with Starbuck's (1899) analyses of adolescent conversion in which he found that even though two-thirds of all conversion cases were at least partly initiated by a deep sense of sin or guilt, many cases of conversion were also functions of more gradual and progressive efforts toward an integrated life. Starbuck suggests that while sin and guilt likely trigger sudden conversions, especially in middle adolescence, in late adolescence conversion, if it occurs, is likely to be more gradual, and less concerned with depreciating feelings of guilt or deep sense of sin.

While developmental views of religious growth have been discussed extensively in Chapter Three, the importance of considering age in relation to conversion is in terms of the implication for theories of the differing process of conversion. Granted that early investigators were almost unanimous in asserting that adolescence was the developmental span most typical for conversion, whether sudden or gradual, interesting conceptual issues emerged: Why adolescence?

EXPLANATORY EFFORTS TO CONFRONT CONVERSION

The early investigators agreed that conversion (1) was a life changing process that (2) typically occurred in adolescence. Furthermore, the process itself could be sudden or gradual. It was these simple, most basic facts that needed explanation.

Perhaps Starbuck (1899) more than any investigator most forcefully argued for a natural linkage between adolescence and the necessity for some type of conversion. His argument, while certainly not unique, emphasized two basic facts concerning human development. First, humans need to have an organized framework within which their life takes on meaning and purpose. Adolescence is precisely that period within which persons must begin to orient themselves within some meaning system—one chosen from alternatives made available from the culture within which they mature. Hence, religious systems exist precisely as one type of meaning system within which individuals can orient themselves, understand, interpret, and direct their lives. Adolescence takes on particularly crucial importance precisely because adolescents are forced to come to grips consciously and reflexively with their life for a variety of developmental and maturational factors, including puberty. As but one example, emerging sexual impulses require some system of interpretation as to purpose and meaning, and all adolescents must come to grips in some fashion with these natural tendencies. Hence, in Starbuck's own words:

> Theology takes these adolescent tendencies and builds upon them; it seems that the essential thing in adolescent growth is bringing the person out of childhood into the new life of mature and personal insight (p. 224).

Starbuck's view links the two essential factors in Coe's definition of conversion—self-realization within a social medium. Religiousness provides possible systems of meaning, supported by appropriate social institutions within which the necessary task of self-realization can occur. We suggest that this is the dominant and most useful model of conversion implicit in the classical psychological literature on conversion. It is far from dated and, as we shall soon see, meshes nicely with what we have argued throughout this text concerning the role of attributions in religions. In order to develop these views, we focus upon some other wisdom contained in the classic psychological literature on sudden versus gradual conversions.

The importance of distinguishing conversion types in terms of time, whether sudden or gradual, is linked with suggestions as to different psychological *processes* involved in these two types of conversions. In our view, this basic assumption is most fruitful and can be used to formulate a reasonable model of conversion.

Characteristics of Sudden Conversion

Sudden conversions apparently are characterized by three major distinguishing criteria. First, they are apparently *passive;* the convert suddenly feels in the grip of forces beyond him/herself. This "otherness" that confronts the person simply suddenly presents itself, often in a moment of crisis. An explanation of the "otherness" must be part of any explanation of sudden conversion.

Second, and closely related to this "otherness" quality, is the act of "surrendering" or giving into this otherness. Conversion occurs when the person gives in or accepts this "otherness" rather than simply confronting or rebelling from it. Without such acceptance, conversion does not occur.

Third, sudden conversions tend to be characterized by intense feelings of unworthiness, of sin, and of guilt. What Pratt (1920) terms the James-Starbuck thesis is the concept that the twice-born, prior to their conversions, wallow in extreme feelings of unworthiness, self-doubt, and depreciation that are released or overcome via the conversion process. In this sense, at least, conversion is a solution to the burdens of guilt and sin found unbearable prior to conversion.

Characteristics of Gradual Conversion

Similar to sudden conversions, gradual conversions result in a changed self. Yet, they occur almost imperceptibly and probably cannot be typically related to a single "turning point in life." As Coe (1916) notes, Paul's sudden conversion must be understood within the context of the more typical gradual conversions such that Paul's conversion is the exception rather than the rule even in New Testament examples. Similarly, as Strickland (1924) notes, the more typical model of conversion in the New Testament is that of Peter and Andrew on the shore of the Lake of Galilee converted without associated crises or dramatic emotional turmoil. Such gradual conversions can best be illuminated in contrast to the perhaps more dramatic sudden conversion typified by Paul.

First, as Starbuck (1899) notes, they are characterized by an active search for meaning and purpose. The emphasis is upon a conscious striving toward a solution to personal or collective problems. Typically, the potential convert had been striving to find "something more" to life. He or she is unlikely to experience an awareness of a force or otherness that initiates the conversion process at a precise moment.

Second, there is an absence of emotional crises or feelings of guilt and sin. The approach is more purely cognitive and entails purposive goal directed efforts to find a meaning or to create a new self.

Third, rather than a sudden moment of surrender and acceptance of a new life, gradual converts continually and progressively deepen in a faith that they have cognitively assented to accept. The precise moment of acceptance cannot be identified, but rather there is an awareness, gradually acknowledged, that one has become and is becoming a different person.

The classic work of E. T. Clark (1829) relating to this discussion is summarized in Research Box 9-1, as follows:

RESEARCH BOX 9-1.   *Clark, E. T.* The Psychology of Religious Awakening. *New York: Macmillan, 1929.*

The participants in this extremely significant study consisted of 2,174 persons who had conversion experiences. Three kinds of conversions were denoted: (1) *the definite crisis awakening,* in which a personal crisis fairly suddenly results in a religious change; (2) *the emotional stimulus awakening,* where a gradual religious growth is accelerated by an emotional event that results in religious change; and (3) *the gradual awakening,* which refers to a steady, progressive, slow growth of religious feeling. These three forms accounted for 6.7, 27.2, and 66.1 percent of the conversion experiences respectively. Proportionately, the men showed about six times as many definite crisis awakenings as did the women who were slightly higher with gradual awakenings. The groups were equivalent in emotional stimulus conversions. The average age for these conversions ranged from twelve to fourteen years.

A stern theology was associated primarily with definite crisis awakenings, suggesting that fear and anxiety were large components in these conversions. In addition, 41 percent of these experiences occurred during revivals, which must have been highly emotional settings. The dominant emotional states reported at these times were primarily joyful reactions. This appeared to result from alleviation of a sense of sin and/or depression that were the main feelings prior to the conversion. This work suggests that psychological disturbance seems to be associated primarily with the definite crisis awakening that is a sudden conversion experience.

SUMMARY OF CRITERIA DISTINGUISHING GRADUAL AND SUDDEN CONVERSIONS

If we summarize the distinctions most typical from the classical literature on sudden and gradual conversions, we have the following:

SUDDEN CONVERSIONS		GRADUAL CONVERSIONS
Sudden awareness of "other"	versus	Gradual and increasing search for meaning or purpose
Predominance of negative emotions and feelings of sin and guilt	versus	Absence of emotions, especially intense feelings of sin and guilt
Passive act of surrendering to a faith perspective	versus	Active assent to a faith perspective

It would be foolish to make these distinctions hard and fast. Rather, we have differences in extremes that have and continue to play a crucial role in identifying two major types of conversions. Most useful would be a model to integrate these two types and to illuminate the process involved in each as complementary rather than contradictory. Such a model can be developed from the classical literature.

A Model for Conversion Processes

We accept the importance of distinguishing between sudden and gradual conversions as "ideal types." Our model interprets the classical literature on conversion and represents a standard against which contemporary explanatory efforts may be measured. It also recognizes that what makes religious conversion unique is that persons realize themselves within a religious matrix—they become, suddenly or gradually, the kind of persons normatively acknowledged within varying religious groups. Hence, of necessity, the personal process of conversion hints at and is embedded in the social matrix of religious groups. Thus, our model for religious conversion is quite similar to our model for religious movements discussed in Chapter Ten.

We can summarize our conversion model as follows:

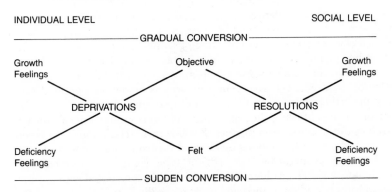

In the above diagram, we have continued our purely conceptual use of the concept of deprivation, linked as before with growth and deficiency orientations borrowed from Maslow's conceptualizations. By definition, feelings of sin and guilt produce low self-esteem that can be resolved by religious conversions within which such sins and guilts are resolved. Hence, as with our discussion of the relationship between individuals and social movements in Chapter Ten, religious groups help to create and resolve deficiency feelings. Whether these feelings are objective or felt is not resolvable simply by psychology alone. Broader theological issues become relevant here and must be acknowledged. For instance, as several early investigators note, many forms of fundamental Protestant theology insist upon the sinful and woefully inadequate nature of persons apart from God and provide a theological framework for the objectivity of intense feelings of sin and guilt that make one ripe for a sudden conversion. Instead, revivalist activities of such groups as the early Baptists and Methodists in many rural parts of America were designed precisely to instill in and to take advantage of crisis release from sin and guilt that revivalist set and settings prompted. Such revivalistic activities are still common in many parts of America, especially with fundamental or evangelical Protestant sects. Strickland (1924) offers the following summary of some reasons for the revivalist's success in eliciting sudden religious conversions.

1. Theological beliefs dictate the valued form of entering Christian faith—Paul's conversion sets a norm.

2. Revivalist theologies focus upon sinful and depraved nature of persons who are in need of "saving grace."

3. Emerging Protestant sects such as Baptists and Methodists in America in the eighteenth-century attract converts from outside established faiths and hence elicit intense feelings on the part of participants in new movements.

4. New religious movements appeal to the masses with special appeals to the uneducated and lower classes. The approach has to be more emotional than intellectual.

5. Sudden and strange nature of conversion lent appeal to insistence that supernatural factors are operating. This adds to emotional intensity.

6. Failure of normative religious education left many ripe for alternative religions. Hence, appeal of the revivalists.

On the other hand, a more gradual conversion process operates when meaning and purpose for life is sought outside a crisis-precipitated emotional conflict. Nevertheless, we still speak of deprivation and resolution here insofar as persons who seek for and find alternative meaning systems are released from the now-perceived deficiencies of previous systems. Such gradual conversions may be initiated by crises but, being more cognitive in orientation, require prolonged time to become integrated into a new sense of self and purpose in life. Yet, as most early investigators insisted, such divergent processes as sudden and gradual conversions may nevertheless result in identical faith commitments.

Not surprisingly, differing theologies and religious groups appeal to each of these extremes in the conversion process. For instance, Clark notes that when it was possible to identify the previous theological confrontations of a portion of his converted sample, as might be expected, the type of conversion varied with theological orientations. Persons identified as previously confronted with a stern, sin-insisting and guilt-producing theology were more likely to have had sudden conversions than persons identified as previously confronted with theologies that emphasized compassion and mercy. These results are presented in Table 9-1.

Given that theologies and religious groups exist that support both sudden and gradual conversions, it is clear that immense difficulties occur in attempting to differentiate the validity of either deprivations or resolutions. Hence, the issue of subjective and objective must be noted again and left hanging. Clearly, one's

TABLE 9-1   Brief Conversion Related to Previous Theological Orientation

THEOLOGICAL ORIENTATION	NO. OF CASES	SUDDEN CONVERSION		GRADUAL CONVERSION
		DEFINITE CRISIS	EMOTIONAL STIMULUS	
Stern—emphasizing sin and guilt	176	34.6%	34.7%	30.7%
Compassionate—emphasizing love and forgiveness	133	2.2	5.5	92.3

[1]After Clark (1929).

personal religious resolution may be another's madness. Just as many refuse to "feel" the necessity of salvation from sin yet are seen as objectively deprived by fundamentalist groups, so are many fundamentalist groups seen to be encased objectively within a rigid, outmoded religious framework. Interested readers might want to read a theological statement presented by James (1902, p. 244–245). He found Luther's viewpoint to be psychologically perceptive in legitimating intense feelings of guilt and sin among persons of a "melancholy temperament." James' example also offers a resolution most likely to occur in a crisis-instigated, sudden conversion.

The recognition that theological orientations appeal to differing predispositions was accepted by most early investigators. Some efforts were made to suggest such proclivities. For instance, most agreed that temperamental factors inclined one to accept the theological appeal rooted in the emotionalism of sudden conversions and almost all investigators appealed to the then-recent discovery of the "unconscious" to explain the unique characteristics of sudden conversion. However, few conducted empirical investigation of these claims. An exception was Coe, (1922) who attempted some quasi-experimental studies of the reasonable claim that temperamental differences were involved in becoming either suddenly or gradually converted. In his own widely cited research, Coe studied two groups of converts. One was a group of seventeen persons who anticipated striking transformations and experienced them, and another was a group of twelve persons who anticipated similar changes, but who did not experience them. As expected, Coe found that emotional factors were dominant in the former group while cognitive factors dominated in the latter group. In addition, persons who experienced the striking transformation were shown to be susceptible to hypnotic and similar phenomena, while persons who did not have these experiences were less susceptible to such influence.

Coe's research was the exception in the classical period, and most investigators were content with less data-based speculations concerning reasons for differences in conversion types. If temperamental differences were widely assumed to account for differences in conversion types, almost all of the early workers believed that "unconscious" or "subconscious" factors would account for the remaining differences. The new discipline of psychoanalysis was just emerging, and most felt it held the key to ultimate psychological explanations of the distinction between sudden and gradual conversion.

In our view, psychoanalysis has proved less to be an empirical science than a particular mode of description. Suffice it to say that the "unconscious" held out more promise as an explanatory system than has been demonstrated (Ulanov and Ulanov, 1975; White, 1961). One need only compare the radically different psychologies of religion provided by Freud and Jung to see the lack of empirical support for differences in psychoanalytic interpretations and, perhaps more appropriately, psychoanalytic speculations on the origins and functions of religion (Freud, 1964, June, 1938). Whatever the hope of the classical psychologists of religion with respect to psychological explanations of conversions, most would agree with Strickland's (1924) claim that whatever physiological or psychological mechanism is presumably involved in either sudden or gradual conversion, the final test was in its fruits as a total life commitment. In Strickland's still appropriate words:

. . . the mere acceptance of a suggested idea and the relaxation of nerve tensions will not of themselves produce action for new ideals, nor changed habits of life. And if action from new ideals and changed habits of life do *not* follow, there has been no conversion (p. 123).

The classical research on conversion is summarized in Table 9-2.

CONTEMPORARY RESEARCH ON CONVERSION

Present-day research on conversion is heavily focused upon more sociologically oriented variables accounting for conversion than upon psychological processes. Rambo's (1982) recent bibliography on conversion studies list only twenty-five psychological studies since 1970, with the majority of these clinical descriptive studies. On the other hand, over a hundred sociologically oriented studies are cited for the same time period. In terms of our previous discussion of conversion as self-realization within a social matrix, clearly the move has been to emphasize this latter aspect. As we shall soon see, this shift in emphasis has created some unnecessary confusion in reconceptualizing classical definitions of conversion.

Reconceptualizing Conversion

There is little consensus in the contemporary literature regarding definitions of conversion. For instance, Parrucci (1968) defines it as " . . . a reorientation of the personality system involving a change in the constellation of religious beliefs and/or practices." Such a definition is consistent with classical views of conversion but makes it a nonempirical issue of whether or not converts have radical personality changes—such changes are part of the definition. On the other hand, investigators (Down, 1980; Greil, 1977; Lofland and Skonoud, 1981) have argued that some converts do not have radical shifts in personality, self, or even religious beliefs. Usually these researchers have essentially redefined conversion to mean the joining of a new religious group with obvious differences in definitional consequences. Clearly, characteristics related to joining new religious groups need not precisely parallel those defining conversion in the more classic sense. Still, what seems most common to contemporary definitions of conversion is a more or less explicit commitment typically involving a new or renewed religious group membership. Conversion can be either intrafaith or interfaith (Parucci, 1968; Singer, 1980). Intrafaith conversion involves explicit commitment to the group within which one has been socialized; interfaith conversion is to a faith within which one has not been previously socialized, either because of socialization within another religion or because of no prior religious socialization.

Some contemporary investigators have attempted to use a time dimension to categorize conversion types. For instance, Scobie (1973, 1975) adds an "unconscious" type to the classical sudden and gradual conversion types. By unconscious conversion, Scobie refers to the inability of a person to recognize any period in life when he or she was not religious. This is more appropriately referred to as religious socialization without any of the characteristics of gradual or sudden religious *conversion*. Despite Scobie's reintroduction of classical distinctions, no additional empirical research has been done to illuminate further the psychological variables involved in each of these conversion types.

TABLE 9-2 Summary of Classical Research on Conversion

DEFINITION	TYPE	AGE	PREDISPOSING FACTORS		MOTIVATION	RESULTS
			PERSONAL	SOCIAL		
Radical change in religious sense of self	Sudden	Middle or late adolescence	Emotional; Suggestive	Raised with Stern theology	Passive	Release from sin, guilt; new life
	Gradual	Late adolescence; early adulthood	Intellectual; Rational	Raised with compassionate theologies	Active	Search for meaning; purpose; new life

Other recent workers have suggested that conversions must be identified by their effects ranging from personality changes to alterations in life style. For instance, Lofland and Stark (1965) distinguish between merely verbal converts and those they term total converts. Travisano (1970) separates mere alterations in faith commitment from true conversion. Again we note that contemporary investigators appeal to what the classical literature previously resolved—conversion must be identified in terms of a radical shift in personality associated with an awareness of a new or renewed faith commitment. Travisano illustrates this nicely in comparing the responses of two different Jews to the opening query, "Since you became a Unitarian . . . " Despite the fact that both Jews are new Unitarians, only one was a convert in Travisano's sense. The example of mere alterations is as follows:

> One thing that bothers me is your phrases. I would say I'm Jewish, and you keep identifying me as a Unitarian. I'm Jewish. There is a Unitarian Society in (another city) where they have candles and robes and crap like that. If that were the case here, you wouldn't be interviewing me (p. 599).

The converted Jew's response is qualitatively different:

> I was born a Jew, and now I have accepted the promised Messiah of Israel who came in fulfillment of the Scripture. Christ came to the Jews. The first Christians were Jews. As a Hebrew Christian I am a completed Jew. (p. 598).

These examples emphasize the classic notion that conversion be restricted to radical shifts in belief, behavior, or values linked with the adoption of a new faith commitment or with the explicit commitment to one's faith for the first time. Given this conceptualization of conversion, contemporary literature has tended to focus once again upon the process of conversion.

Conversion Processes

Contemporary studies of conversion are becoming increasingly complex through recognition of the fact that conversion is a multidetermined process. Furthermore, theories rooted largely in passive explanations in which the converted has little if any active role in his or her conversion are giving way to activist oriented theories. While it is premature to expect a theory of conversion to be empirically adequate across diverse groups, one theory has clearly dominated the field. This was proposed by Lofland and Stark (1965) based upon Lofland's (1977) perceptive study of what eventually developed into the increasingly successful Unification Church of Reverend Moon.

Lofland and Stark provided a model to describe the process by which conversion to the particular group they studied could be explained. They did not contend that their model was appropriate to all religious conversion or to other types of religious groups. As Lofland has recently emphasized, their model was an effort at qualitative theorizing and was not presented as a causal, testable model to guide empirical investigation (Lofland, 1966; Lofland and Skonoud, 1981). Overall, their model entailed a process of several identifiable but interrelated phenomena. It denotes seven factors contributing to conversion, some of which are predisposing while others are identified merely as situational contingencies.

The predisposing factors include (1) an experience of tension or dissatisfaction that (2) is interpreted within a religion's perspective (3) by persons who perceive themselves as active religious seekers. These factors may precipitate a conversion if four situational contingencies operate. They include (1) encountering the cult at a crisis point in life (2) with strong affective attachments established with one or more committed believers (3) combined with minimal nonbeliever contact. If (4) intensive interaction among the seeker and believers is continued, conversion is likely.

Obviously, this model applies to gradual conversions and has value in emphasizing social processes long ignored by classic investigators. However it must be remembered that classic investigators mainly focused upon sudden religious conversions, within which more purely psychological processes can be assumed to play a more dominant role.

The Lofland and Stark formulation has been applied to various other groups both descriptively and as an empirical, testable model (Baer, 1978; Richardson and Stewart, 1977). As noted, this was neither the intent nor the value of the model. It is thus not suprising when Seggar and Kunz (1972) note that the model accounted for only one of seventy-seven cases of conversion to the Mormon faith. The intent of the model was to capture adequately the process of conversion to a *particular* religious group, something that Lofland (1977) argues remains validly descriptive today. Yet this does not mean that the model can be applied uncritically to other groups and, as Seggar and Kunz (1972) and Snow and Phillips (1980) argue, may not apply to the majority of other groups. Yet the value of the model is in suggesting that studies of conversion must be multifaceted, taking into account a wide variety of psychological (e.g., felt tension) and social (e.g., social isolation) factors. Few contemporary empirical studies have been directed at such a multifaceted look at conversion. An exception is the work of Heirich (1977) with Catholic Pentecostals.

Heirich's study is particularly impressive because it utilizes a comparison group of persons who did not convert to assess the differential effect of commonly believed determinants of conversion. Numerous studies indicating the presence of a particular factor, such as stress or maladjustment prior to conversion, are of little value in explaining conversion without knowledge of their presence in similar groups of persons who did not convert.

Using an initial sample of 275 persons, Heirich employed sophisticated statistical procedures to categorize the major factors contributing to their conversion. A summary of his findings are in Table 9-3. A "tree" has been constructed that lists each major factor, the number of persons in each group, and a y value. The y value can range from 0, meaning no persons in the group converted, to 2.0, meaning all persons in the group converted.

Scrutiny of this "conversion tree" indicates the importance of less dramatic factors accounting for the slightly less than half of all persons converting in this study. For instance, the completed converted group (19) consists of those who had not attended Mass frequently, were introduced to the Pentecostal group by a teacher or spiritual advisor, were not an eldest child, and who had Pentecostal friends. Hence, conversion was influenced largely by interpersonal factors of a rather mundane nature. On the other hand, among those least likely to convert

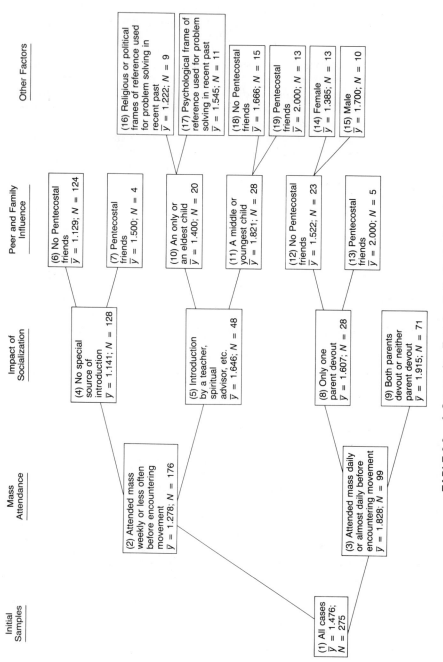

TABLE 9-3　A Conversion Tree for Catholic Pentecostals

(group 6) were those who had no Pentecostal friends and were not introduced to the movement by a teacher or spiritual advisor. Also, comparing persons with political or psychological meaning systems to those with religious ones indicates the obvious importance of attributions in the process of gradual conversion.

Heirich's study remains the most sophisticated empirical effort to confront what we identify as a gradual conversion process upon a highly select group of Catholic Pentecostals. While it may not illuminate gradual conversions among other groups or suggest much that is applicable to sudden conversions, its importance is in identifying the role of less dramatic factors in conversions. Apparently, especially in gradual conversions, interpersonal and situational factors play a dominant role in determining conversion. Such data must be taken into account by investigators who have perhaps overemphasized the role of stress and "maladjustment" in precipitating religious conversions.

Numerous studies have focused upon a wide variety of stress factors presumably predisposing one to conversion. Many of these theories explicitly or implicitly imply psychological deficiencies that are resolved via conversion. Such theories are extremely limited for both conceptual and empirical reasons. On the conceptual side is the obvious problem that all persons can be identified as exhibiting some degree of stress or maladjustment, and in this sense any of life's collective activities can be seen as efforts at resolving these problems. Religious conversion is not unique in this respect even if the argument is true. On the other hand, empirical studies indicating "maladjustment" among contemporary religious sect and cult members are of minimal importance since the criteria by which such members are identified as maladjusted are likely to be precisely those criteria the religious group opposes. As has been pointed out by more than one investigator, functioning members of deviant religious groups are adjusted to those groups by definition even though they appear as "maladjusted" by tests based upon other norms. (Simmonds, 1977; Simmonds, Richardson and Harder, 1976).

Not only is it apparent that conversion to even more extreme groups is not exhaustively explained by appeals to either explicit or implicit psychopathological factors, but numerous empirical studies have begun to illuminate the positive problem-solving value of almost all conversions at both the individual and social level. For instance, independent studies of the Catholic Pentecostal movement have shown its appeal to middle-class, well-educated adults who find the movement supportive of a common problem-solving perspective that may legitimate what would otherwise be a deviant definition of reality (Harrison, 1974; McGuire, 1975). As such, the Catholic Pentecostal movement promises to be a socially approved movement within the church and one in which members can participate with less resistance as the movement gains social and theological acceptability. (Harrison and Maniha, 1978; Johnson and Weigert, 1978). Likewise, similar arguments can be made for conversion to various forms of Protestant fundamentalism (Richardson, Stewart, and Simmonds, 1979; Stones, 1978). As is typical of successful social movements in general (Cantril, 1941; Toch, 1965; Truner and Killian, 1957) resolution of problems—not simply personally perceived but interpersonally shared problems—is both a reason for and an outcome of religious conversion. One contemporary study adds support to this thesis.

Conversion and Purpose in Life

The classical literature suggests that gradual conversions involve more cognitive struggles with issues of meaning and purpose. As such, more gradual converts can be anticipated to have found purpose and meaning through their conversion. Paloutzian (1981) has recently demonstrated this with a group of Protestant converts. This work is presented in Research Box 9-2.

Paloutzian's data indicate that overall conversion does provide a meaning or purpose, that even at its lowest ebb it exceeds that of the definitely nonconverted group (see Research Box 9-2). Furthermore, perhaps an initial enthusiasm following conversion wanes over time and then reaches a plateau at an intermediate level. Of course, such a view assumes an individual process not directly interpretable by these data collected across differing groups. Overall, the classical claim that conversions, especially gradual ones, lead to a new meaning and purpose in life seems at least not inconsistent with these findings. Of course, the evaluation of claims to meaning and purpose can be made most problematic, especially when conversion is to religious groups that themselves are in tension with their environment. The fact that persons find meaning and purpose in life within the matrix of religious groups varying in tension with their environment necessarily links the conversion literature with our concerns in Chapter Ten.

RESEARCH BOX 9-2.   *Paloutzian, R. F. "Purpose in Life and Value Changes Following Conversion," Journal of Personality and Social Psychology, 1981, 41, 1153–60.*

Working with his "cognitive need" theory, which assumes people seek to bring meaning into their lives, the author hypothesized that religious conversion would accomplish such a goal. Ninety-one undergraduates participated in this study; fifty-one Christian believers constituted an experimental group, with the remaining forty respondents designated as controls. Six subgroups were constructed: The two control groups were: (1) those denying they had converted (N = 24), and (2) persons not sure if they had converted (N = 16). The other groups were: (3) believers for 1 week or less (N = 11), (4) believers for 1 week to 1 month (N = 10), (5) believers for 1 to 6 months (N = 8), and (6) believers for 6 or more months (N = 22).

The participants were administered psychological tests to indicate purpose in life (Crumbaugh and Maholick, 1969), patterns of values, plus items to verify conversion. Purpose in life was significantly higher for the converts than the nonconverts; however, the convert group who had adopted Christianity from one week to one month showed a drop in purpose in life, but this increased for the two longer-time groups. It is suggested that the one week to one month group may have been in a period of reassessment, after which the sense of meaning achieved immediately following conversion reappeared (see Table 9-4). The findings on values were mixed, suggesting a need for further research on conversion relative to this area.

TABLE 9-4   Purpose in Life Scores as a Function of Time from Conversion

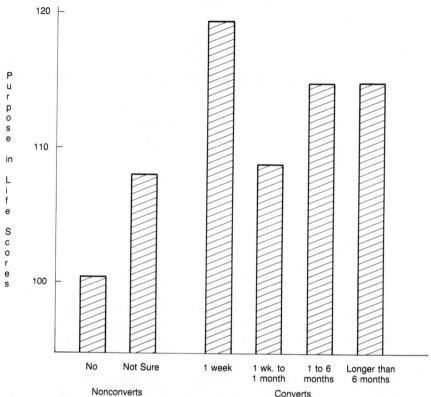

Conversion and the Nature of Religious Groups

As a personal change in self, conversion is typically embedded within the legitimating context of a religious group. As indicated in Chapter Ten groups are by definition in tension with their environment; hence, their members, especially their new converts, are likely to experience this tension. This is likely to occur when a sect emerges within a religious denomination in opposition to it or when a new cult emerges upon the religious scene to compete for religious commitments among the community of faithful. Furthermore, converts often come from more established denominations and churches that are not in tension with their environment. Thus, converts may move in two directions: either from social acceptability to social unacceptability, or vice versa. In the former case, we ought to expect great turmoil and concern, especially if the youth of parents from a respectable denomination convert to a sect or cult. In the latter case, we ought to expect social relief and gratification among parents whose youth have "returned" from the influence of a sect or a cult deemed unacceptable. This can be diagramed as follows:

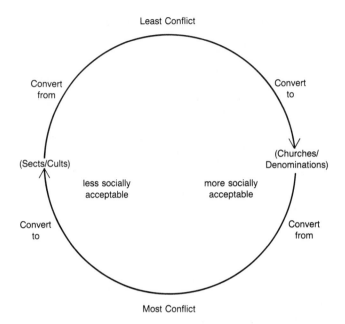

Conversion to sects or cults is socially controversial especially if the new converts come from established denominations. This has become the focus of much contemporary debate both in the popular press and in scientific journals. To clarify what empirical research can contribute to the issue, we must first note two major categories of theories of religious conversion.

Strauss (1979) has emphasized that despite the variety of theories of conversion, such theories can be succinctly categorized into two groups: *active* and *passive*. *Active theories* emphasize the positive and independent role of converts in acting responsibly to commit themselves to a new faith perspective. *Passive theories* emphasize the often negative and dependent role of the convert as a victim of forces eventuating in their commitment to a new faith. The latter theories tend to be reductionistic, focusing upon variously conceived psychological and social forces that necessitate a conversion without confronting the possible validity of the faith commitment to which the person was converted. On the other hand, active theories necessitate confrontation, with the faith perspective of the convert as a viable alternative within which persons can orient their identities and interpret the world. It should be obvious that passive theories tend to delegitimate the claims of the convert, however subtly, while activist claims tend to legitimate the claims of the convert. Nowhere has this become more evident than in current arguments centering around claims to ''brainwashing'' of cult or sect converts and of the ''deprogramming'' activities of their opponents.

BRAINWASHING AND CONVERSION

The term *brainwashing* has entered the popular language as a summary term for some loosely defined techniques of coercive persuasion that presumably can make a person adopt a set of beliefs they would not otherwise accept. Historically, the term became popular through the writings of Hunter (1951), who used it to refer to Chinese Communist techniques. Another phrase associated with similar popularizations by American psychiatrist Lifton (1961) is "thought reform." Neither concept can be precisely defined, but both are related to what Schein (1971) in more neutral terms has called *coercive persuasion*. While an inadequate polemical literature abounds concerning coercive techniques, responsible scientific writing summarizing such techniques is quite consistent in agreeing that they (1) can produce limited, situational attitude change that (2) is highly unstable when techniques or controls are eliminated. We shall briefly look at the history of these techniques in order to provide the context for their relevance to our primary concern, religious conversion.

Historical Considerations

Two major varieties of coercive persuasion have been utilized in recent history, the Chinese and the European. While both forms overlap, their distinctions in the extreme are quite clear (Somit, 1968).

European-oriented techniques primarily emphasize the obtaining of confessions of guilt from presumably innocent persons. In addition, typically the techniques are forced upon single persons treated in isolation. In contrast, the Chinese-oriented techniques mainly attempt to change a person's ideological commitments rather than merely to produce confessions of guilt. In addition, the technique is often applied to small groups of individuals, many of which are solicited as *volunteers* (Somit, 1968).

While claims have been made that brainwashing is rooted in specific social psychological principles and is a highly specific and effective technique, this is clearly not the case. These coercive methods were apparently developed independently by the Europeans and the Chinese, and never followed a systematic theoretical development. However, in the broadest sense, such procedures follow a fairly easily reconstructable process.

Processes of Coercive Persuasion

While several summaries of coercive techniques of persuasion have been offered, we shall focus only upon what is shared across several responsible efforts to reconstruct from historical and personal accounts the process of this kind of influence (Hunter, 1951; Lifton, 1961; Summit, 1968). Basically, these include five major factors:

1. *Total control and isolation:* Persons are individually or in small groups isolated under the absolute control of authorities.

2. *Physical debilitation and exhaustion:* Persons are physically exhausted and debilitated. Extreme means such as torture and starvation may be used to achieve this. More typically, less extreme means are used. These include continual forced discussions, minimal sleep, and minimal food.

3. *Confusion and uncertainty:* Personal belief systems are challenged and attacked. Personal uncertainty of one's own fate is linked to uncertainty concerning their beliefs and values.

4. *Guilt and humiliation:* A sense of guilt and personal humiliation is induced by a variety of techniques. All are directed at making the potential convert feel unworthy or humiliated if he or she persists in present commitments.

5. *Release and resolution:* A single "out" is provided. Persons who "voluntarily" convert are relieved of their induced guilts and their confusion is resolved within a new belief system.

It is readily apparent that coercive techniques of persuasion are seldom all or none. One can best talk about degree of coercive persuasion, perhaps ranging from the extreme of Chinese communist brainwashing to middle-range examples such as American military indoctrinations to the minimal extremes of, say, religious summer camps. Yet, techniques of coercive persuasion are but one kind of socialization procedure, and except in their most recent efforts at a more or less systematic use, are in no sense unique. Furthermore, in their most extreme form, they are highly impractical. As Somit (1968) notes:

> To be successful, it demands a uniquely structured and controlled environmental setting and an inordinate investment in time and manpower. Despite the cost entailed, its effectiveness is limited to individual subjects or, even under optimum conditions, to a small group of persons (p. 142).

Furthermore, without social support, even the few converts achieved by such extensive efforts will revert to their previous beliefs if given the option, as the history of American soldiers' experience in Korea demonstrated (Lifton, 1961).

Contemporary Claims to Brainwashing

From what we have noted above, it is apparent that techniques of coercive persuasion cannot play a major role in accounting for current concerns with alternative religious movements.

For some, the popularity of these movements have led them to assert that converts must have been brainwashed; for others, such a claim legitimates their own efforts at "deprogramming." While coercive persuasion techniques may play a role in some conversions, they clearly do not account for a majority of conversion to any new religious group. Robbins (1977) notes that such claims as "brainwashing" essentially are tools of personal rhetoric legitimating political suppression of unpopular religious groups. One's ability to withstand these methods is assumed to have been seriously damaged. Comments offered to support the disapproved stance are taken as a sign of mental aberration rather than the result of a search for meaning and significance by a competent individual. The doctrines embraced by these persons are regarded as so unacceptable by those both in the mainstream and in power that attention is focused on how these beliefs are acquired rather than on what the beliefs are. The right of persons to choose for themselves, something we venerate highly, is thus denied converts to deviant sects and cults (Robbins and Anthony, 1979).

Likewise, Shupe and Bromley (1979) note that an anti-cult movement is emerging based upon the polemical assumptions that cults are pseudoreligious movements preying upon unfortunate victims who are not freely converted and hence need to be "deprogrammed" for both their own and society's good. The anti-cult movement has gained support largely because the new religious movements disproportionately appeal to the young, who in the process of conversion to new sects or cults are abandoning the religion of their parents, at least in form if not in content. Hence, as we have already noted, interpersonal factors are an important determinant of religious commitment so that one anticipates parental/child conflict to occur both as a motivating factor for youth participation in new religious movements and as a consequence of that participation (Pilarzyk, 1978).

Partial support for this speculation is in the largely parental support for popular "deprogrammers" and legal debates emerging concerning parental authority over children who have converted to less legitimated religions (Robbins and Anthony, 1979). Paradoxically, this has led to several studies on the process of deprogramming as opposed to virtually no studies of an identifiable process of brainwashing presumably utilized by the more controversial of the new religious movements. While some have tried to sensationalize deprogramming as a new right of exorcism (Shupe, Spielman and Stigall, 1977), overall the process is less dramatic. Schein (1971) has provided the most general model of coercive persuasion. Employing this model, Kim (1979) notes that deprogramming essentially employs these well-known techniques to achieve three aims: (1) first, to motivate the person to "unfreeze" their previous commitment to the cult or sect; (2) second, to provide information that requires the reevaluation of one's previous commitment in light of the belief to which the person is to be "re-converted"; and (3) finally, a "refreezing" of the supported perspective to which the person is now recommitted.

Interestingly, one could as easily use descriptions of deprogramming to establish descriptions of some conversions in groups where control is maintained by the converting agency. However, within religious movements such control is seldom maintained, and overall it is obvious that the fervor and controversy surrounding new religious movements and their converts requires a less polemical analysis of what is a more general process rooted firmly in the history of religion.

THE REEMERGENCE OF SUDDEN CONVERSIONS

Granted that recent concern with "brainwashing" is largely polemically expressed, we ought not overlook the fact that once again a focus is upon what the classical literature refers to as sudden conversion. The overriding issue seems once again to be focusing upon two contending pathways to commitment—the gradual, progressive commitment to a faith versus the sudden, emotional acceptance of a faith. Active and passive models of conversion apply, but now the passive model is used *ipso facto* by many to delegitimate the validity of conversion. Long ago, Ames (1910) noted that the goal ought to be to prevent sudden conversion by "salvation through education." Similarly, Strickland (1924) observed that sudden conversions were less frequent in a community where gradual conversions were effectively produced through religious education and this fact was " . . . a cause for joy and not lamentation." In this sense, the current concern with brainwashing completes a full circle to the debates on sudden and gradual conversion that marked the classical period of psychological research on conversion. As Sargant (1957) claims, the success of the great revivalists in early America was linked to their ability to induce sudden conversions via processes less positively evaluated by contemporary intellectuals. These processes stressed an "assault upon the emotions" instead "of appealing to adult intelligence and reason" (Sargant, 1957, p. 95).

Yet, it must also be emphasized that while sudden and gradual conversions are often contrasted, each complements the other. For instance, as Coe (1916) also long ago noted, the persistence of religious groups who initiate members by sudden conversions risk problems of perpetuation that by definition must be maintained by other, less emotional factors. Likewise, as Coe also believed, even persons who themselves were sudden converts attempt to socialize others, especially their children, via gradual conversion processes. Perhaps there is a cyclic inevitability in both personal and cultural concerns with the classic yet still relevant distinction between sudden and gradual conversion.

In this context, one must expect controversy to surround conversions given the fact that various religious groups solicit and legitimate diverse interpretations and modes of confrontation with what persons perceive to be divine. Hence, even in the most extreme cases, we must be careful not to utilize naively and uncritically delegitimating modes of explanation (Johnson, 1979; Richardson, 1980). One is tempted to "explain away" quickly religious beliefs and practices distant from one's own. Yet, the appropriate psychological task is to illuminate psychological principles operating in conversions, whatever their nature. For instance, Kroll-Smith (1980) demonstrates how even the most private experiences of a holiness sect are influenced by social psychological factors. Similarly, White and White (1980) show how modification in Mormon theology facilitates social adaptability and the ability of Mormons to accept social change. Likewise, several studies (Lebra, 1970; Turner, 1979; Weigert, D'Antonio, and Rubel, 1971) indicate how conversion to new religious beliefs allows individuals to adapt to cultural changes. Even converts to deviant religions are often by that very process socialized to accept other dominant cultural values (Johnson, 1961). Deviant religious movements may themselves solicit converts who in different groups or other cultural contexts would otherwise be maladapted (Lewellen, 1979). Finally, one cannot underestimate the power of such variant religious bodies to reconceptualize commonly accepted social realities so that they both justify their participation in and legitimate the continuance of their groups (Festinger, Riecken, and Schachter, 1974;) Weiser, 1974).

In summary, we note that conversion is a complex process, requiring the combined efforts of social scientists for illumination. Such studies have just begun, despite the long history of scientific concern with conversion (Allison, 1966). Research is difficult not only because of the complexity of conversion processes, but because of the obvious sensitivity to diverse theologies needed whenever one attempts to illuminate individual and collective claims of confrontation with the divine.

CONVERSION AND ATTRIBUTION THEORY

Attribution theory seems to be particularly relevant to the process of conversion. We noted that many investigators conceive of conversion as a reorientation of the self, a major personality change that is often activated by a sense of sin, guilt, and unworthiness. Lofland distinguishes persons who are active religious seekers, while Paloutzian demonstrated that converts seem to gain a new sense of purpose in life.

It has been suggested that attributions are motivated by needs for meaning, control, and self-esteem. Apparently, many who undergo conversion seem to lack a sense of meaningful direction in their lives, feel themselves to be victims of circumstances over which they seem to have little or no control, and perceive themselves in a depressingly negative light. Meaning, control, and esteem are at an ebb. Conversion, whether sudden or gradual, changes this. Regardless of whether the new affiliation is with a mainline church or a fringe cult or sect, the convert has found a place in the scheme of things. New and positive meanings have been achieved along with feelings of competence and capability. One is now "saved," and being so selected gains a heightened sense of personal worth, dignity, and esteem. The entire content of attributions about the self, others, and the world has undergone a radical shift.

These changes are repeatedly illustrated in an extensive literature on conversion. Starbuck (1899) provides much material, suggesting negative self-attributions as motives leading to conversion. We read "I was thoroughly convicted of sin," "I thought myself the greatest sinner in the world," "I was very wicked. My heart was black." Although these were the most common spurs to conversion, others also were present such as "being moved by a spirit of duty," "a higher ideal of life," "awakening to a divine impulse." When conversion took place, perspectives took on a different and positive character. It was now "I felt God's forgiveness so distinctly," "I had a sense of sins forgiven," "I experienced joy almost to weeping," "I felt as if a load was lifted from my body, and I was very happy." Just as self-attributions were modified, so were those to the deity. Images of wrath and rejection were supplanted by forgiveness, love, and acceptance. Descriptions of the process, at all levels, portray an attributional pattern needing further psychological specification.

Direct research on conversion in terms of attributional changes is lacking, but would appear to have much potential for assessing the foregoing theory. Evidence is needed to understand the nature of meaning, control, and self-esteem as such may be achieved by the convert.

SUMMARY AND CONCLUSIONS

Like religious experience and mysticism, conversion was among the first topics studied a century ago by psychologists of religion. Slowly attention shifted from conversion as a totally individual phenomenon, simply defined, to one showing many possible forms and expressions. The distinction between sudden and gradual conversion has persisted with continuing recognition that the former is usually associated with psychological and spiritual problems, while the latter marks a constructive maturational development.

Originally focus was on what stimulated and followed conversion. In contrast, contemporary workers are emphasizing the *process* of conversion. Individual variation is stressed, and this is often related to the context in which the act of conversion occurs. Among the significant sociocultural factors stimulating interest in and concern with conversion is the rise of new religious movements in the past two decades. In addition to providing new impetus to research, there has been an attempt to tie this work to other knowledge from mainline psychology, namely what is known about persuasion, brainwashing, attitude change, and the like.

Modern sophisticated research designs and statistical methods have also supported the development and assessment of theory. A good example is the "conversion tree" constructed by Heirich (1972) to clarify his work on the creation of Catholic pentacostals. As presented in Table 9-3, it not only empirically points to many significant influences in this process, but literally opens doors to further research with both Catholics and others.

These developments find fruition in a model of the conversion process that takes into consideration central influences in both classical and contemporary thinking and research on conversion. Attention is afforded the sudden-gradual distinction in conversion, individual and social factors, how deprivations enter the process and resolutions are effected, and finally the complex of growth and/or deficiency feelings and motives that seem to play such a noteworthy role in conversion.

There is little doubt that attribution processes and needs are integral to conversion. The convert is likely to reveal change, possibly radical change, in his/her views of oneself and the world. Without question, these may involve great modification in life's meanings, the sense of control one has, and concomitantly, self-esteem. Here individual interpretation and cognitive-emotional factors are of prime importance, and designate research avenues that still remain to be rigorously evaluated. Even after a century of research on conversion, it can be seen that there remains much work to be done on this fascinating and significant topic in the psychology of religion.

CHAPTER TEN
SOCIAL PSYCHOLOGY
OF RELIGIOUS
ORGANIZATIONS

"The work of the church ends where knowledge of God begins" (Underhill, 1961, p. 164).

"Between you and God there stands the church" (Stobart, 1971, p. 157).

"All this perhaps could be reduced to one thing—doctrine is the way Christian identity has been formulated and understood" (Smart, 1979, p. 285).

INTRODUCTION

The process of becoming religious continues to intrigue social scientists and to foster both theoretical and empirical debate. The simple fact is that persons are not born religious, they become religious. This process of becoming religious entails numerous possibilities. Persons may be born into a family with a particular faith and be socialized to adopt that faith as their own; persons may be born into one faith and later change to another; the previously committed may fall away, suddenly or gradually; the previously faithless may convert. In this flux of individual religious change lies also the rise and fall of churches, the growth and decline of denominations, the emergence of new religious cults, and the maintenance of religious sects. Hence, not only is the process of commitment and change crucial to the psychology of religion, but to the social characteristics of the religious groups within which persons are socialized or which individuals join, or from which individuals withdraw are obviously of relevance. Our task then in this chapter is to become acquainted with some of the social psychology of religious groups. In so doing, we will confront issues that have long been of concern in the social scientific study of religion and that have recently emerged into public focus and debate. Both the rise and fall of religious collectivities and the commitments and disaffection of religious individuals cannot be expected to be discussed for long without concern and controversy.

Churches, Denominations, and Sects

While it may be true that psychologists are particularly prone to define religious commitment in individualistic terms, it remains abundantly obvious that such commitment cannot occur in a social vacuum. Most persons' religious commitment is to a faith shared with others, and having some degree of organizational control. Whitehead's (1926) insistence on great solitary figures of religious imagination—Mohammed brooding in the desert, Buddha resting under the Bodhi tree, and Christ crying out from the cross—is balanced by the fact that such solitary figures maintain their religious importance within great traditions maintained by generations of the faithful organized into churches, sects, and cults. Hence, to be religious is at least partly to be related in some fashion to a religious organization. Similarly, to change religious commitment is often related to changing religious organizations. Therefore, we need to confront a task that perennially has occupied the sociology of religion—the classification of types of religious organizations.

The Weber-Troeltsch Legacy

Early sociologists struggled with classification schemes for religious organizations. This struggle continues today with little evidence of unanimity among those most concerned with the issue of the nature and types of religious organizations. Yet it is clear that if a dominant classification scheme has emerged, it is that of the church-sect scheme initiated by Weber (1930) and perhaps given most of its initial prominence by Troeltsch (1931) and his popularization to American social scientists in the work of Niebuhr (1929).

Weber's initial distinction between church and sect primarily had to do with requirements of membership—the sect being a more restrictive membership, requiring stronger criteria of commitment for membership than the church. Troeltsch's extension of Weber's initial work focused upon the paradoxical relationships between churches and sects as forms of religious organization. While Troeltsch's distinctions were never precise and were never intended as primary classification schemes to guide empirical research, the tendency in the distinction was clear enough. As Dittes (1976) has emphasized, the religious sect is usually the claimant to a "purer" form of religious commitment, uncompromising in its faith commitment and hence likely to be intolerant of "worldly compromises." Hence, membership is more restrictive and demanding, often with criteria of significant personal experiences and sacrifice required for admittance to full membership. On the other hand, churches tend to be by their very success "contaminated" with worldly concerns. While still pure in intent, the churches' compromise with the world is perhaps most reflected in their relative lack of stringent requirements for membership, often no more than an admission of faith and participation in a ritual of acceptance demanding little in the way of personal sacrifice. Not surprisingly, sects tend to develop within churches and in opposition to them, likely leading their members to take a "holier than thou" attitude with respect to their previous but now merely "churchly" comrades in faith (Martin, 1969; Stark and Bainbridge, 1979).

Troeltsch's distinctions have set the tone for immense conceptual and empirical debate in the sociology of religion. Arguments run the gamut from emphasizing that Troelsch's distinction between church and sect were intended to apply only provincially to pre-twentieth-century Western expression of Christian faith to claims that the distinction remains essential to the sociology of religion. Numerous modifications and extensions of the distinction have been proffered. For some, the concept of "church" is less relevant to Western expressions of religion, especially in America, where church-state separation is maintained. In this sense, "denominations" replace the church with nevertheless similar churchlike characteristics—denominations tend to be relatively lacking formal criteria of membership or at least to have criteria that are fairly nonrestrictive (Knudsen, Earle, and Shriver, 1978). Furthermore, denominations tend toward social acceptability and hence tend to be politically compromised with the state (Swatos, 1975, 1976). Also, while denominations may maintain an absolutist stance within their theological expressions, politically and socially they maintain a relativistic stance of legitimacy to the diversity of political organization; the expression of which they are but one example. On the other hand, sects may develop into denominations and hence achieve "churchly" characteristics, but often their stance of absolutism is expressed as much in social and political terms as in their theology. Hence, if there is a useful common thread that runs throughout much of the history and debate on church-sect distinctions, it is precisely one of degree of tension with the social context that is conceptually most common—so much so that Johnson (1963) has argued that only this single defining distinction between church and sect be conceptually maintained. Sects reject their social, cultural milieu; churches (denominations) accept their social, cultural milieu.

Johnson's single dimension can be extended slightly to speak of degree of acceptance or rejection of the social and cultural milieu. Hence, religous organizations that tend to reject their environments are more "sect-like" and those that tend to accept their environments are more "church-like." This can be easily diagrammed as follows:

Churches (Denominations)	Sects
Acceptance of Environment	Rejection of Environment

This chart not only allows us to identify sect/church distinctions distinctively along a single continuum, but it permits quantification as well. As Bainbridge and Stark (1980) have recently argued, not only must conceptualization regarding church-sect distinctions be theoretically meaningful, they must have empirical usefulness as well. The distinction of degree of rejection of environment can be operationalized and tested by seeing if religious organizations identified as more sect-like have members who identify their organization as having tension with its environment. On the other hand, religious organizations that are more church-like should have members who identify their organization as having little tension with its environment. Bainbridge and Stark have studied the views of members of religious organizations that vary along the continuum of rejection of environment. They studied sixteen Protestant denominations ranging from clearly sect in nature to clearly church in nature. Some examples of these denominations graphed along the continuum of acceptance and rejection of the social order and hence of presumed tension with that order are as follows:

DENOMINATIONS		SECTS	
CHURCH-LIKE	LESS CHURCH-LIKE	LESS SECT-LIKE	SECT-LIKE
Methodists Disciples of Christ	Presbyterians American Baptists	Southern Baptists	Church of Christ Seventh-Day Adventists
Less tension with social order	More tension with social order		

Bainbridge and Stark tallied the responses from 2,326 different members of sixteen Protestant denominations to questions grouped into five major categories: deviant norms, deviant beliefs, deviant behaviors, conversion and defense, and social encapsulation. Note that the first three categories deal with presumed tension insofar as they refer to beliefs, behaviors, and norms deviant with respect to an assumed secular social order. The last two categories deal with specific activities that likely produce tension insofar as they serve to set the believer at odds with a secular order that favors tolerance and pluralism.

A summary of representative questions for specific sects, and sectlike groups as well as for denominations judged as low or medium in tension with the social order is presented in Table 10-1.

While Table 10-1 is relatively self-explanatory, we need to emphasize what is most important for our present discussion—the more sectlike the organization, the more its members tend to adhere to norms, behaviors, and beliefs at odds with the dominant secular environment within which they exist. Likewise, they tend to identify their own beliefs as exclusively assuring salvation and to be concerned with converting other persons to similar beliefs. Thus it would appear that tension with environment is a meaningful conceptual distinction and a continuum

TABLE 10-1 Rejection of Environment by Religious Organizations Along a Church-Sect Continuum

	PERCENT OF EACH GROUP GIVING THE INDICATED RESPONSE								
	DENOMINATIONS		SECTLIKE				SECTS		
	LOW TEN-SION (1032)	MEDIUM TEN-SION (844)	MO. LUTH. (116)	S. BAPT. (79)	C. of GOD (44)	C. of CHRIST (37)	NAZA-RENE (75)	ASSEM. of GOD (44)	SEV-ENTH DAY AD. (35)
DEVIANT NORMS									
The respondent disapproves of dancing.	1	9	28	77	77	95	96	91	100
The respondent disapproves "highly" of someone who drinks moderately.	4	6	2	38	43	57	57	57	60
DEVIANT BELIEFS									
Darwin's theory of evolution could not possibly be true.	11	29	64	72	57	78	80	91	94
It is completely true that the Devil actually exists.	14	38	77	92	73	87	91	96	97
DEVIANT BEHAVIORS									
Grace is said at all meals in the respondent's home.	16	25	41	53	66	65	69	80	77
The respondent reads the Bible at home regularly.	12	24	21	63	48	49	59	57	69

(cont)

TABLE 10-1 Rejection of Environment by Religious Organizations Along a Church-Sect Continuum

PERCENT OF EACH GROUP GIVING THE INDICATED RESPONSE

	DENOMINATIONS		SECTLIKE			SECTS			
	LOW TEN-SION (1032)	MEDIUM TEN-SION (844)	MO. LUTH. (116)	S. BAPT. (79)	C. of GOD (44)	C. of CHRIST (37)	NAZA-RENE (75)	ASSEM. of GOD (44)	SEV-ENTH DAY AD. (35)
CONVERSION/DEFENSE									
Once or more the respondent has tried to convert someone to his or her religious faith.	38	50	63	89	86	84	83	86	83
The respondent says, "I tend to distrust a person who does not believe in Jesus."	19	27	34	53	46	51	47	55	33
PARTICULARISM									
Only those who believe in Jesus Christ can go to heaven.	13	39	80	92	59	89	81	89	77
Being of the Hindu religion would definitely prevent salvation.	4	15	40	32	32	60	35	41	17

¹Adapted from Bainbridge and Stark, 1980

along which religious organizations can be empirically placed.[1] In addition, further refinement within the sect classification can be made. Sociologist Bryan Wilson (1961, 1969, 1970, 1973) has perhaps done most to clarify sect classifications. Related to tension with environment is the degree of involvement with the secular order—from more withdrawn to most involved. An example of Wilson's classification scheme is presented in Table 10-2.

Even though tension with the environment is perhaps the single most useful empirical distinction between churches and sects, further conceptual refinement is needed. Redekop (1974) has argued that while sects clearly have their origin in protest against the secular world and, indeed, often the worldliness of their initial church host, various additional factors must be considered. For instance, the nature of the particular values of society that the sects oppose is crucial. One might anticipate that sects that attack values more central to the culture—say, secular medicine—would create more tension than those that attack less crucial beliefs, such as which day is to be kept as the Sabbath. In addition, the ability of the society to absorb religious differences must be considered as well as the strategies and tactics of sects in their opposition to the environment. Obviously, a sect that espouses militant opposition to society is likely to elicit more active negative retaliation than one that merely uses persuasive techniques to argue for its opposition to society. Yet sects tend to reject the world and hence are likely to find themselves being rejected in turn. Furthermore, the fact that sects tend to emerge within churches or denominations and express opposition to their parent body assures some degree of tension between the parent organization and its "troublesome offspring" (Coser, 1954).

Conflict between and within organizations is reflected in the psychologies of their members. Hence, a model is needed that relates the psychological concerns of individual participants to the social characteristics of religious collectivities.

Individuals and Religious Collectivities

At this stage of our knowledge, models cannot be empirically derived for explaining participation of individuals in various types of religious organizations. Nevertheless, numerous conceptual schemes exist for linking individuals to participation in religious organizations, particularly as subcases of models for explaining social movements in general (Oberschall, 1973; Toch, 1965). Given so many models, the issue is not one of their empirical "truth" or "falsity" but rather one of their heuristic value for organizing existing empirical knowledge and suggesting additional study.

RELIGIOUS MOVEMENTS

Religious movements are but a specific case of the more general issue of social movements of all types. What makes religious movements perhaps more controversial is the lack of criteria by which their claims can be evaluated. In fact, it is precisely on the inability to accept universal criteria for religious truth that an

---

[1]One must cautiously interpret these data as empirical support for Bainbridge and Stark's claim to an *empirical* test that sects exhibit much tension with the social order. It is not clear in their study whether or not the criteria for ordering religious groups along the continuum of tension with the social order were independent of their respondent's indices of tension within the social order. If this is the case, the authors do not have a rigorous independent test of their thesis.

TABLE 10-2   Wilson's Sect Classification[1]

I. Introversionist
Sects of this type attempt to gain personal holiness for their members through retiring from the world. "This type is completely indifferent to social reforms, to individuals, to individual conversion and to social revolutions" (Wilson, 1969: 364–65). The European Pietist movements and their American counterparts (e.g., Old Order Amish Mennonite, Hutterian Brethren, etc.) are examples of this type of sect.

II. Utopian
The modal response of utopian sects is rather complex. They seem partly to withdraw from the world, while at the same time generating conceptual blueprints for the remaking of it (Wilson, 1969: 370). This type may be distinguished from the introversionist by the motive for withdrawal expressed by each: e.g., the introversionist sect's withdrawal constitutes a defensive reaction, whereas the utopian sect's seeming withdrawal reflects its view that a return to a communitarian life-style, and the more pervasive primary group relations that obtain therein, is the most reasonable and felicitous mode of societal life.

III. Revolutionary
The revolutionary sect embraces the echatological movements, such as the Christadelphians, which hold a belief in the imminent destruction of the world and the ultimate establishment of God's sanctified kingdom on earth. Sects of this type are normally hostile to social reform and civil authority (which they believe represent agencies of the Antichrist) (Wilson, 1969: 365).

IV. Conversionist
This type represents "the typical . . . evangelical . . . fundamentalist sect. Its reaction towards the outside world is to suggest the latter is corrupted because man is corrupted . . . This type of sect takes no interest in programmes of social reform or in the political solution of social problems and may even be actively hostile towards them . . . the Assemblies of God and other pentecostal movements . . ." are examples of this type (Wilson, 1969: 364–65).

V. Thaumaturgical
Sects of this type exhibit a rather personalistic response to the world centered around the possibility of experiencing contact with the supernatural. These groups, while somewhat secretive about their operation, usually emphasize the performance of good works related to divine-spiritual healing and the performance of "miracles." The spiritualist churches are clear examples of this type (Wilson, 1969: 368).

VI. Manipulationist
Manipulationist sects proclaim the possession of a distinctive knowledge beneficial to the attainment of all worthy cultural goals. These sects normally accept the goals of the outside world (nominally at least) and provide their members with new methods for attaining them. Christian Science represents this type of sect (Wilson, 1969: 367).

VII. Reformist
"This type of sect . . . studies the world in order to involve itself in it by good deeds. It takes unto itself the role of social conscience" (Wilson, 1969: 369). Sects of this type are exemplified by the Society of Friends and the Unitarian-Universalist Church.

---

[1]Adapted from Welch, 1977.

inexhaustible supply of fuel to fire new religious movements is assured. Our task here is less to evaluate religious movements than to describe the dynamics involved in them. Furthermore, since sects emerge within churches, we must concern ourselves with factors affecting both maintaining church commitment as well as disaffection from church commitment, whether or not for a sect alternative.

Almost by definition the precipitating condition for new sects is in the failure of existing churches to provide for or meet the needs of all their members. Given the almost infinite diversity of human wants and aspirations, such failures are inevitable. In this sense, *any organization* exists both to provide solutions for some persons while failing to provide solutions for others. Hence, we can talk about an organizational failure setting the stage for a problem situation. In this sense, at least some church members are likely to feel deprived relative to what they want from the church. This view has long been dominant in the sociology of religion. It is known as *deprivation theory*.

Deprivation Theory: Its Use and Misuse

The nearest thing modern sociology has produced to a universal theory of explaining specifically religious movements is deprivation theory. Dittes (1971) has reminded us that such an explanation is at least as old as the Old Testament, where religious commitment is rooted in exiles and is carried through in the New Testament where religion is existentially rooted in the distraught, the impoverished, and the alienated. In fact, as Dittes (1971b) correctly notes, "Among social scientists, one would be hard pressed to find any major theorists who did *not* formulate his understanding of religion as a compensation for deprivation" (p. 394). We can illustrate Dittes' point by referring to views of religion of two classic theorists, Freud and Marx. Both men are prime examples of the limits of a simple deprivation thesis.

On one hand, Freud (1964) treated religion, especially what we would call more fundamentalistic or evangelical religion, as *illusional*. Contrary to more common thought, by this Freud did not mean that such religions were false. Illusion for Freud meant that the primary motivating factor in religious belief is wish fulfillment. Hence, illusions may be either true or false, depending upon presumably objective criteria. Yet, clearly, what is psychologically important about illusions is that they take otherwise deprived states and negate them in terms of a future possible fulfillment. For instance, one's reasonable fear of death might be resolved through belief in immortality. For Freud, such a belief is an illusion, not because we know it to be false (it may or may not be) but rather because the believer would rather it be true than false. Hence, Freud is a "deprivation" theorist *par excellence* in that religious beliefs and practices resolve for the better otherwise problematic, "deprived" realities. In this sense, Freud, like James, sees religious experience as a resolution to otherwise discontented states. However, in later writings, Freud (1961) treats religion as *delusional*, implying not only serious pathological deprivation, but negating the truth claim of religion in an unwarranted methodological move. Clearly, Freud felt that strong wishes that something might be true could lead to distortions of reality such that objectively false beliefs nevertheless are perceived to be true. In Freud's (1964) own words,

> We say to ourselves: it would indeed be very nice if there was a God, who was both creator of the world and a benevolent providence, if there were a moral order and

a future life, but at the same time it is very odd that this is all just as we should wish it (p. 53).

Yet the obvious problem here is that effort to claim that religious beliefs are not "false" entails much more than psychological analysis, whether or not from Freud.

In a similar view, Marx's (1964) treatment of religion as the "spirit of a spiritless situation" and as the "opium of the masses" is sociologically illuminating and yet can be misleading. Clearly, religion can serve to alleviate and provide meaningful answers to otherwise insufferable conditions. In this sense, Marx correctly insists that religious responses are factually correct with respect to identifying objectively exploitive conditions, especially for particular social groups. However, like Freud, Marx makes the unwarranted methodological move in claiming that religion is in fact "false" and hence whatever resolutions it claims to provide in the face of such conditions are only apparent (Gabel, 1975).

Hence, as briefly noted, both Freud and Marx exemplify deprivation theory insofar as they assert for purely theoretical reasons religion to be efforts, however misguided, to resolve either psychological or sociological aspects of "deprivation." Yet most contemporary empirical research on deprivation theory has been less conceptually sophisticated and most limited. Excellent reviews of this massive research literature are readily available (Goone, 1966; Hine, 1974; Moeller and Johnson, 1975). Generally, for reasons we shall note shortly, this literature fails to find significant empirical support for deprivation theories. However, we first need to look at a purely conceptual issue since it is an essential part of the model of religious movements that we shall shortly propose.

Conceptualizing Deprivation

Our own definition of religious experience, congruent with that of James' (see Chapter Seven) notes that religious experience is a resolution to an otherwise problematic situation. Similarly, we initiate our model of religious movements by asserting the existence of a problematic situation—the failure of existing religious organizations to meet the needs of at least some persons. In this sense, religious responses are efforts, whether or not successful, at resolutions to what can be perceived as "deprived" conditions. By definition, and *for purely conceptual reasons,* all religion is seen as a response to what in the absence of this response is deprivation. For some, as we shall soon see, deprivation is perceived in advance and resolutions are actively sought. For others, only after "seeing the light" is their previous situation perceived as "deprived." Yet the error is to assume that, given our definition, one could empirically test whether or not religion is a response to deprivation. If religion is so conceived, the task is to illuminate empirically the nature and types of responses to deprivation within a religious framework, and not one of testing whether or not a religious response exists independent of deprivation. In this sense, our conceptualization meshes nicely with the relevant empirical literature.

The Empirical Literature on Deprivation

As already indicated, the empirical literature on deprivation theory is massive and well summarized. For our purpose, we can note that three major conclusions seem most warranted.

First, conceptual efforts to relate deprivation to the formation of religious movements as well as to general indices of religious commitment are numerous. The classic efforts of Freud and Marx have already been noted. Most recently, the work of the sociologist Glock (1964) has received wide attention. Not only has Glock conceived of the origin of religions as largely a response to deprivation, but he has attempted to link particular forms of religious movements to particular categories of deprivation. For instance, Glock argues that economic deprivation leads to the formation of religious sects while physiological deprivations lead to the formation of religiously rooted healing movements. While Glock's efforts are well received and his efforts to define the conceptualization of deprivation are well noted, his classifications lack any widespread empirical support.

Second, efforts to link relatively objective measures of deprivation to religious movements have notoriously failed. Argyle and Beit-Hallshmi (1975) note the wide diversity of indices of deprivation utilized by researchers, including economic, organismic, psychic, ethical, and social. While these categories are precisely those used by Glock in his classification of types of deprivation, often such indices fail to intercorrelate even positively. Furthermore, the almost ad hoc use of presumed indices of objective deprivation such as sex (Christopher, Fearon, McCoy, and Noble, 1971), are clearly unwarranted and are indicative of what Dittes (1971) has called "promiscuous empiricism" in response to much of the statistically sophisticated yet conceptually impoverished research within the deprivation tradition.

Third, recent advances in conceptualizations within deprivation reseach have been made by taking into account the more subjective factor of "felt deprivation" (Bibby and Brinkerhoff, 1973; Hoge and Carroll, 1973). Hence, research is beginning to look beyond categories of persons who can be presumed to be deprived via some objective indicator. Researchers now are using techniques to assess whether or not persons feel deprived, regardless of their objective situation. When such controls are initiated, even the relative weak relationship between objective indices of deprivation and religiosity are typically reduced to nonsignificance indicating no direct evidence for linking felt deprivation and religiosity (McNamara and George, 1978). These studies must be cautiously interpreted given the fact that no combination of variables forcefully predicts psychological well-being (Hadaway and Roof, 1978), but it nevertheless is clear that religious commitment does not make an objectively hard life easier to endure or make persons necessarily happier (Davies, 1962; Lang and Cooper, 1971; McNamara and George, 1978). Of course, this is reasonable given what we say concerning such variables as psychological health and religion as discussed in Chapter Twelve.

An illustration of the relationship between deprivation and religion emphasizing economic deprivation, one of Glock's forms is presented in Research Box 10-1.

The Role of Deprivation in Religious Movements

Given what we have said above concerning deprivation research, it is clear that no simple relationship between deprivation, objective or "felt," should relate to the origin of religious movements. What is needed is more sophisticated conceptualizations and empirical studies linked to these conceptualizations. Yet our own position suggests that deprivation is essential to religious movements and can be conceptualized in two fashions.

RESEARCH BOX 10-1.   *Sales, S. Economic Threat as a Determinant of Conversion Rates in Authoritarian and Nonauthoritarian Churches,"* Journal of Personality and Social Psychology, *1972, 23, 420–28.*

Working from the hypothesis that economic threat, a form of deprivation, stimulates authoritarianism, hence affiliation with authoritarian religious bodies, the author analyzed conversion data for the period 1920–39. Eight churches with relatively complete and accurate conversion data were selected for study; four were considered authoritarian and four were nonauthoritarian. The former were the Southern Baptist Convention, Church of Jesus Christ of Latter-day Saints, Seventh-Day Adventist, and the Roman Catholic Church. The nonauthoritarian churches were Presbyterian Church in the U.S.A., the Congregational Christian Church, the Northern Baptist Convention, and the Protestant Episcopal Church.

Data were gathered for each year on per capita disposable income and an estimated "conversion ratio" for each religious body. This was the ratio of the number of converts to the possible convert population. The results clearly indicated that affiliation with an authoritarian church increased as per capita disposable income decreased. In contrast, the opposite held true for the nonauthoritarian churches for which conversion rates increased with disposable income. Thus, the hypothesis was supported.

Using data from Seattle for the period 1960–70, it was possible to replicate the first study in its essentials. Focusing on the Roman Catholic and Presbyterian churches, it was observed that during the good years of the decade when unemployment was low, more converts were made to the Presbyterian church than to the Roman Catholic church. As theorized, the situation reversed during the high unemployment years. Again the hypothesis was supported.

Following what we said elsewhere concerning Maslow's notion of deficiency and growth motivation, we suggest that two major categories of deprivation are also implied: Growth and deprivations refer to more "sophisticated" deficiencies that one can realize following fulfillment of more basic needs. Growth deficiencies lead one to seek their fulfillment which, if religiously interpreted, can lead to religious resolution. On the other hand, more basic needs, if unfilled, produce "deficiency deprivations" leading to more basic religious solutions associated with perhaps less sophisticated types of religiosity. In either case, a problem or deficiency exists by definition. Hence, the first step in the formation of religious movements as with all social movements is some failure on the part of established organizations to fulfill or meet the needs of all persons. Inevitably, some persons are relatively deprived. However, the issue is to account for individual *susceptibility* to religious movements and requires a consideration of *felt deprivation*. Hence, in an attributional sense, only persons who perceive themselves as deprived, whether or not objectively, are susceptible to social movements aimed at resolving their problems. Furthermore, such persons need to attribute religious significance to their problems or the proffered solutions to become being susceptible to *religious* movements. Of course, with religious movements the interminable debate is centered precisely on the legitimacy of such claimed deprivations as well as their proffered solutions.

AN ATTRIBUTIONAL MODEL FOR RELIGIOUS MOVEMENTS

Given that persons must perceive themselves as deprived in terms of either growth or deficiency needs in order to be susceptible to new religious movements, we now must look at the other side of the coin. Religious movements are collective efforts to offer the solution to such difficulties or problems. Religious movements both define lacks or deprivations and propose their solutions. In this sense, as Stark and Bainbridge (1981) have recently emphasized, religious movements are a permanent aspect of societies. More particularly, when issues of "ultimate concern" such as questions of life's meaning, the limits of life as confronted in death awareness, or the question of pain and suffering (to name but a few) are aroused, religious organizations both persist and arise to offer a variety of resolutions. Hence, the rise of new sects to challenge existing denominations is assured. Our simple descriptive model then insists that equal attention be paid to *resolutions,* objective or felt, as collectively offered. Such resolutions are psychologically relevant solutions, collectively offered and supported. In this sense, religious movements are *always* at least collectively perceived solutions to problems or deprivations. Indeed, they are often perceived to be ultimate solutions to life's ultimate problems.

The reciprocal acknowledgement of both deprivations and collective resolutions can be summarized in terms of our model that was proposed in chapter nine. Here, with slight modification, it is again presented and discussed relative to the social psychology of religious organizations.

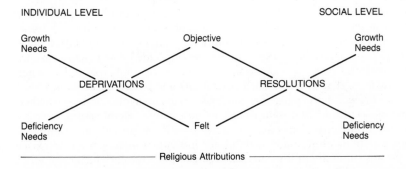

In this chart we see that the crucial factor is that both individuals and societies become susceptible to religious movements when individual deprivations, whether of growth or deficiency needs, are matched with proposed collective resolutions. At such times, both the person and society are susceptible to a new religious movement and a variety of contingencies determine whether or not any individual will participate in such a movement. Of specific concern to us is the attributional sense in which both deprivations and their resolutions are *religiously* defined. When this is done, specific religious social movements arise. However, our model is only a device to allow a gross overview of what are infinitely complex and varied movements for which social scientific data are far from complete.

Such movements vary in controversy and, as we shall see later with cults, become particularly controversial when led by a single, charismatic figure. However, whatever the type of religious movements, our model allows a gross overview that links all movements in terms of the key concepts of deprivations and collective resolutions. As we shall see shortly, scientific data relevant to the maintenance and change of faith is far from complete. Yet in a broader social-psychological sense, several factors have been empirically identified that link individuals to participation in religious groups. Not surprisingly, much of these data are provided by sociologists. Yet as we shall see, many of the major variables accounting for participation and withdrawal from religious groups are really quite prosaic. Hence, we shall refer to various identified contingencies. However, before we do, let us summarize what we have said thus far.

CHURCH-SECT AND THE ATTRIBUTIONAL MODEL

So far, we have categorized religious organizations primarily by their degree of rejection of the secular order—denominations or churches tend to accept the social order and have at least a mutual tolerance for each other's social-political validity. Sects tend to reject the social order and to take a more exclusive stance with respect to their mutual legitimacies. Yet even sects tend to accept each other's mutual social-political validity, even though they often make exclusive and very restrictive theological claims to truth. Insofar as sects tend to have emerged from denominations, a degree of hostility between sects and at least their parent denomination can be expected.

In chapter seven, we noted that religious experience can be meaningfully summarized in terms of two criteria. First, it represents a recognition of some discontent, and second, it represents a resolution in religious terms. For religious organizations, we have followed a similar view but added a social dimension. Religion in its social sense provides resolutions to deprivations that entail belief in a being or force that provides such resolutions and whose existence is effectively legitimated within the particular religious organization of concern—whether it be church or sect (Stark and Bainbridge, 1979a). Hence, membership in a religious organization can be expected to resolve or at least provide a meaningful context for questions of ultimate meaning for individual members and it exists precisely because individuals find such an organization's resolutions meaningful. As a corollary, one might anticipate that new religious organizations arise in periods of crisis precisely because new solutions to issues are needed that in fact also partly account for the existence of the crisis. In this sense, religious organizations represent collective efforts at resolutions to life's riddles, however recognized or defined. The crucial issue is whether the solution is expressed in ultimate or divine terms, or is shared among others. If so, it is religious (Stark and Bainbridge, 1981). Such a view has a long history in sociological efforts at clarification of religious collectivities. (Glock and Hammond, 1973). Yet at this level of abstraction our model sheds little light upon specific issues in new religious movements or maintenance of old religious faiths. The social psychology of such processes entails infinite diversity that must be empirically revealed. For the real or imagined solution to life's riddles is as varied and contested as the social phenomena of religion itself. And it is the social phenomena of religion that have become of immense concern to the popular press in recent years. Not surprisingly, then, social scientists have made this concern itself a matter of study, for the "California phenomenon" has indeed become a national concern.

RELIGIOUS COMMITMENT

The "California Phenomenon"

The West Coast, and especially California, seems to be the "life laboratory" for the emergence and initial social acceptability of numerous new religious movements. While this "California phenomenon" spreads nationwide, the California-based religious movements are assured of high visibility and study. Numerous excellent texts summarize research on the new religious movements, much of it centered on California studies (Glock and Bellah, 1976; Needleman and Baker, 1978; Robbins and Anthony, 1981). Yet it has become more and more apparent that California is but the often flamboyant tip of an otherwise unnoticed iceberg. Just as numerous studies were documenting the decline of traditional, mainline religion in America, the emergence of new religious movements both within and outside of the mainline denominations seemed to burst upon the American scene. Efforts to study the "counter culture" (Glock, 1976) of the 1960s wound up studying instead the emergence of new religious movements as part of the fallout of this culture. As Cox (1978) so aptly notes, real interest and concern with the new religions paralleled a process long noted with drug addictions—only when the movements began to affect the middle class directly was great concern shown. In his words:

> When the Hare Krishnas were mainly providing an alternative to the hippie dropouts in Haight Ashbury, there was one understanding of them. When they began providing an alternative lifestyle to finishing medical school, for example, then a different kind of interest emerged (pp. 124–125).

Of course, given our discussion of religious organizations, we would expect new religious movements to create controversy since, whether emerging within organized bodies or from anew, they are likely to be in tension with their surrounding environment. Hence, it is not surprising that claims about the motivational participation in new religious movements runs the gamut from an applause for a new religious awakening in America to a bemoaning of the escapism and moral unaccountability of persons participating in such movements (Bird, 1979). It would be premature and indeed naive to expect a definitive theory of the rise of these new religious movements at this time. Perhaps, as Bell (1971) notes, such movements are a genuine effort to confront a long-developing spiritual vacuum that has become intolerable to many; perhaps, as Westhues (1972) argues, such movements are a natural counter to the secularization trends that have slowly occurring; perhaps as Prichard (1976) observes, such movements are an ongoing expression of continual religious ferment that has characterized America throughout its history, or perhaps, as Tiryakian suggests, we have but recently become aware of more visible forms of a "theurgic restlessness" that lies at the heart of Western civilization (Tiryakian, 1974). Whatever the reasons, our discussion of religious commitment and withdrawal of religious conversion and apathy must be within the context of all this well-documented religious ferment. Yet this religious ferment itself is contained within the fabric of classic religious commitment expressed within the confines of the major denominations. So we shall first consider issues surrounding the growth and decline of churches and denominations.

Contingencies Accounting for Church Commitment and Participation

It was not that long ago that two major researchers in the sociology of religion, Stark and Glock, raised the issue of whether or not America was entering a post-Christian era (Stark and Glock, 1968). A major factor in their questioning was survey research documenting a decline in what they perceived to be central, core Christian beliefs—most centrally the belief in the Divinity of Christ. Their own conclusion was provokingly pessimistic for mainline Christian denominations:

> As matters now stand we can see little long-term future for the church as we know it. A remnant church can be expected to last for a long time if only to provide the psychic comforts which are currently dispensed by orthodoxy. However, eventually substitutes for even this function are likely to emerge leaving churches of the present with no effective rationale for existing (p. 210).

Associated with this view are two assumptions that can be seriously questioned. One assumption is that religious beliefs and church attendance are heavily correlated and hence changes in one can be used to infer changes in the other—people who tend to drop religious belief commitments will likely lower rates of church attendance, or persons who lower rates of church attendance probably do so because of loss of belief. Yet the most critical evaluation of the evidence relating belief and attendance indicates that these two variables are clearly not heavily correlated (Demerath, 1965). Second, evidence, largely from Gallup poll data, that church attendance is declining overall is debatable. In fact, at least one major investigator has argued that church attendance for Catholics is increasing while stated importance of belief is decreasing (Greeley, 1972). This apparently paradoxical finding is readily understandable when we realize that persons attend churches for a variety of reasons, not all related to religious beliefs. We shall soon note some of these reasons. However, before we move on, we must consider the other side to the Stark and Glock claim. That side has become known as the "Kelley thesis."

The Kelley Thesis: The Strictness Contingency

Amidst predictions of doom for traditional Christian churches, one investigator burst upon the scene with a book that has stimulated much controversy and empirical investigation (Kelley, 1972). The book *Why Conservative Churches Are Grow-*

ing uses a variety of data sources to argue that decline in church attendance such as claimed by Stark and Glock was misleading. In fact, more "liberal," "ecumenical" churches were declining in church membership while more "conservative," "fundamentalist" churches were increasing in membership.

Kelley's thesis is primarily related more to the strictness of churches in what they profess and practice than to the beliefs of churches that are varying in growth rates. It is the strict, serious churches that are growing in numbers, while the more lenient churches are decreasing in numbers. Kelley's own listing of "minimal maxims of seriousness or strictness" are noted in Table 10-3, along with a listing of religious organizations along an exclusivist-ecumenical gradients associated with Kelley's criteria of strictness.

While Kelley's thesis is strongly stated and needs continual empirical refinement, its major thrust is receiving support (Bouma, 1979; McGaw, 1980; Perry and Hoge, 1981). However, strict churches tend to increase membership not by converting members of other, more lenient denominations, but by the maintenance of their own members, especially children (Bibby, 1978; Bibby and Brinkerhoff, 1973). Therefore, strict churches effectively socialize their children and maintain their adults as members. As such, we can return now to the reasons persons attend churches.

TABLE 10-3   Kelley's Exclusivist-ecumenical Gradient

Black Muslims	Most Exclusivist
Jehovah's Witnesses	
Evangelicals and Pentecostals	
Orthodox Jews	
Churches of Christ	
Latter-day Saints (Mormons)	
Seventh-day Adventists	
Church of God	
Church of Christ, Scientist	
Southern Baptist Convention	
Lutheran Church-Missouri Synod	
American Lutheran Church	
Roman Catholic Church	
Conservative Jews	
Russian Orthodox	
Greek Orthodox	
Lutheran Church in America	
Southern Presbyterian Church	
Reformed Church in America	
Episcopal Church	
American Baptist Convention	
United Presbyterian Church	
United Methodist Church	
United Church of Christ	
Reform Jews	
Ethical Culture Society	
Unitarian-Universalists	Least Exclusivist

CHURCH COMMITMENT: FIVE MAJOR SOCIAL PSYCHOLOGICAL CONTINGENCIES

Several theories have been profferred to attempt to explain differential commitment to churches. Typically, church attendance is used as a criterion of commitment. Hence, most often the empirical issue is "What determines differential rates of church attendance?" In confronting this question, it is immediately obvious that comparisons across divergent denominations is fraught with difficulties. For instance, there is more theological pressure for Catholics to attend church regularly than for Jews to attend synagogue. Hence, most reasonable comparisons are made within compatible denominations. Even within Protestantism, one must be careful in comparing radically divergent denominations. For instance, Hadaway (1980) found that the Kelley thesis with regard to strictness may not serve to increase church growth or attendance rates within liberal Protestant denominations as it does in conservative Protestant denominations. Likewise, Bouma (1980) argues that even within conservative Protestant denominations the same factors that promote growth and attendance may also promote disaffection—for instance some members quit even conservative churches because these churches are perceived as too strict. Perhaps it will be most fruitful to discuss studies of church growth and attendance empirically in light of five major competing explanations (Hoge and Carroll, 1978; Hoge and Polk, 1980).

The Deprivation Contingency

Perhaps one of the most widely utilized theories to explain church commitment is deprivation theory. Largely associated with the empirical work of Glock and Stark, (1965; Stark, 1972) such theories generally assume that church commitment compensates in some sense for deprivations. Hence, religion is a substitute compensator for the otherwise distraught. However, as already noted, numerous empirical studies have failed to find that church attenders are more deprived on either objective or subjective criteria of deprivation (Campbell, Converse, and Rogers, 1976; Hood, 1983). In addition, supposedly objective and subjective deprivation indices may not even correlate with one another. Hence, as Dittes (1971) suggests, perhaps it is not so much that deprivation theory is wrong, but more so that it contains such a basic truth as not to relate meaningfully and differentially to church commitments.

To Dittes' comments we can only note that insofar as religious membership resolves problems or provides meaning for its members, deprivation theory in the broadest sense should prove most useful in formulating empirically identifiable factors affecting initial membership and less to factors accounting for maintenance of faith. Similarly, as already noted, our own model conceptually affirms the role of deprivation in all religious movements insofar as they are resolutions to problems, however conceived. Hence, the empirical issue in deprivation research should be to focus upon how religious organizations resolve otherwise deprived conditions. Of course, existing religious collectivities ought not to have members high on measures of deprivation, especially felt deprivation, as it is precisely their membership that overcomes or resolves their problems. Hence, in this sense, religious membership is a *solution* for persons who are thereby no longer deprived.

The Status Contingency

If deprivation theory predicts, in its most naive formulations, church commitment among the poor, the downtrodden, and the dispossessed, status theory tends to equate such claims. Various expression of status-type theories confront the social usefulness and value-enhancing status of church participation. While the empirical data remain complex and defy simple summary, nevertheless several generalizations appear reasonable. Among these generalizations is the fact that church attendance and social status tend to be positively correlated, with higher status persons attending churches more frequently than lower status persons (Goode, 1968). While this finding apparently runs counter to predictions made by deprivation theorists, in fact it need not be the case. First, as a general rule, higher status persons tend to be involved in more associational activities and voluntary organizations, and hence church attendance is simply another specific instance of this general fact. This explains Greeley's finding that Catholics who indicate that religion is less important to them nevertheless have high rates of church attendance. Simply put, the meaning of and hence reasons for religious attendance are different for higher status than lower status persons.

As a second point relating status and church participation, it is worth noting that there are strong relationships between type of religious organization and social status—with more sect-and cult-type organizations associated with lower classes and more church-type organizations associated with higher status and less orthodoxy (Demerath, 1965). This partly attenuates the relationship between church attendance and social status since, as already noted, the more strict and sect-like religious organizations also tend to facilitate higher rates of attendance and to be associated with lower status.

The Local Cosmopolitan Contingency

Closely related to status theory is *localism theory*. Within this perspective, a local-cosmopolitan dimension is utilized to predict church commitment and attendance (Roof, 1976; Roof and Perkins, 1975). Localism implies commitment to more or less well-defined and isolated community standards, while cosmopolitanism implies more urban and pluralistic standards. Also associated with localism are more communal and less hierarchically organized religious groups facilitating a greater sense of community and high rates of church attendance (Woodrum, 1978). Thus, for largely interpersonal reasons, church attendance is facilitated independent of other belief or faith commitments. Indeed, while more conservative and lower status churches tend to be more communal and hence facilitate high attendance rates, this may be changing. Nelson (1971) argues that churches, including higher status ones, tend to become more associational as society becomes more differentiated. This seems true despite the fact that more cosmopolitan cultures as a whole tend to be less church-oriented than more traditional cultures (Roof and Hoge, 1980). The overall net effect of this trend, if indeed it proves true, would be to lower differences in rates of attendance between status and class groups.

The Socialization Contingency

Broadly defined, socialization theory argues that initial socialization is a crucial factor in effecting church commitment (Nash, 1968; Nash and Berger,

1962). Under this perspective, causation is essentially dual directional. Parents with children usually attend church more, perhaps using the church as an agent to socialize their children. Likewise, children of parents who attend church also participate more frequently. Such a view is accentuated in Christian denominations where concern for childrearing is of obvious doctrinal concern. Much of socialization theory is contained in our discussion of religious development in childhood.

The Belief Contingency

Perhaps the most obvious of theories predicting church commitment is belief theory. Simply put, it argues that persons with strong religious beliefs are also more likely to be strongly church-committed. However, such an obvious view must be tempered two ways. First, only when religious commitment entails a strong belief in the necessity of a religious organization is it likely to affect church attendance. Second, the well-established empirical correlation between religious belief and church commitment may also function in a circular fashion—persons who become religiously committed may then attend church more frequently; persons who attend church more frequently, for whatever reasons, may become more religiously committed (King and Hunt, 1972). Indeed, as Hartel and Nelson (1974) have recently argued, despite variation in church attendance as indicated by Gallup poll data for 1967–68, basic religious beliefs in the same period have remained relatively constant with shifts mainly in the proportion of persons indicating disbelief. Likewise, Vernon has indicated that even persons expressing "none" with respect to religious preference may attend church frequently (Vernon, 1968). Hence, the common-sense view that religious beliefs are primary determinants of church commitment is far from accurate.

Vernon (1968) offers a perspective that is somewhat unexpected in research on religion. He turns the tables and attends to the unaffiliated, those who are not church members. This work is presented in Research Box 10-2.

LEAVING RELIGION: APOSTASY

What for many is the unquestioned decline of religious authority in many areas of life has set the tone for concern with factors affecting religious defection. On the extreme is apostasy—persons initially committed to a particular faith who now identify themselves as having no faith commitment. Yet, as expressed, the matter is too simple. For faith commitment can be identified in a variety of ways—persons might continue to identify themselves as "Catholic" or "Jew" long after they have stopped attending church or synagogue. Yet for obvious reasons of ease of measurement, most studies of apostasy rely essentially upon self-reports. Most typically, persons are asked to identify the religious commitment within which they were raised and their present commitment. The apostates are those who having had a religious commitment now state they have none. The research monograph by Caplovitz and Sherrow (1977) remains the major empirical study within this framework.

Caplovitz and Sherrow utilized data collected by the National Opinion Research Center (NORC) over a three-year period in the early 1960s. The study

RESEARCH BOX 10-2.   *Vernon, G. M. "The Religious "Nones": A Neglected Cate-gory," Journal for the Scientific Study of Religion, 1968, 7, 219–29.*

Noting that research on religion has either neglected those who do not designate a religious affiliation or combines them with persons indicating that they are either atheists or agnostics, the author distinguishes a "none" category to find out aspects of their religious beliefs.

Comparing religious "nones" with members of ten religious bodies, the "nones" believed less than the others in a personal God; however, only a quarter expressed agnostic beliefs, and another quarter could be considered atheists. Only 7 percent affirmed a strong belief in God, but some degree of belief tended to be held by 38 percent. Relative to a feeling of having been in "the presence of God," some 26 percent of the "nones" felt they were or might have been. About a quarter believed that they might have suffered punishment from God for their acts. Although these percentages were consistently less than for the members of religious groups, they clearly suggest that the "none" category shows some degree of religious belief and orientation and might be distinguished in their own right from those consider-ing themselves atheists and agnostics.

Utilizing comparisons based on nonreligiously associated variables, it was ob-served that the "nones" tend to be like the most religiously active in their rejection of ethnic prejudice. Except for Mormons, a highly committed religious group, the "nones" felt that they could face the death of a loved one as much as, if not more than, most of the religionists. In terms of marital adjustment, male "nones" appear similar to religious males, although female "nones" may be slightly less adjusted in their marriages.

Religious "nones" are most accurately perceived as simply religiously nonaffil-iated rather than rejecting of faith. They seem to reject church membership more than religion per se.

focused upon college seniors for purposes unrelated to research on religion. How-ever, fortunately for Caplovitz and Sherrow, the two crucial questions noted above were included in the NORC survey, allowing identification of apostasy. From other data collected in the survey, sophisticated statistical techniques were uti-lized to determine the origins of apostasy in this sample.

Perhaps what is most surprising is that the percentage of apostates remains small across major religious groupings—approximately 12 percent for Jews and Protestants and only half that for Catholics (Caplovitz and Sherrow, 1977). Furthermore, utilizing a distinction between two types of religious identity rooted in the work of Lenski, (1961) this research suggests that Jews more than Catholics or Protestants tend to identify with religion on that basis of group commitment while Catholics and Protestants identify with religion more on the basis of beliefs and practices. In Lenski's terms, the former is "religiosity" while the latter is "communality" or "ethnicity."

As for the minority of those who could be identified as apostates, the determinants appeared to be identical across all religious groupings. Both political radicalism and "maladjustment" appeared to be major factors in apostasy, with poor parental relations and intellectualism identified as additional, although less significant, factors. Overall, it appears that all of these factors tend to interrelate yet operate to produce apostasy only if religiosity is lost first. Simply put, loss of religiosity is produced by political radicalism, maladjustment, poor parental relations, intellectualism, or a combination of these. When this occurs, apostasy is likely to follow. In this sense, we have what appears rather obvious: Apostates are those who for a variety of reasons have lost their religiosity. This holds true whether the loss is in terms of beliefs and behaviors ("religiosity") or in terms of community identification ("communality" or "ethnicity").

While the Caplovitz and Sherrow (1977) study is far from conclusive, it remains the most ambitious empirical study to date and the one against which future research must be compared, (Perry, Davis, Doyle and Dyble, 1980). Furthermore, much of their data are congruent with research explaining apostasy in terms of three interrelated theories suggested by Caplovitz and Sherrow: secularization, alienation-rebellion, and universalism-particularism.

Secularization is a general term referring to the withdrawal of religious sanctions and interpretation of the world in favor of alternative models, rooted in scientific claims. In this view, since personal identity is rooted in legitimations provided by one's belief commitments, the loss of religious beliefs leads to alternative beliefs within which one's identity is maintained. Hence, other NORC-based research (Hadaway and Roof, 1979) indicates that religious "nones" are more "worldly" in terms of such things as seeing X-rated movies and going to bars. This is understandable in terms of the removal of religious sanctions against such activities as one adopts more secular commitments, at least with respect to personal behavior.

Similar to the secularization theory is the alienation-rebellion theory. In this view, as persons become alienated from institutions and normatively sanctioned authorities, they tend to rebel and adopt alternative life styles. For the formerly religious, this means a rejection of religious views and a seeking of support within more secular alternatives. Typical in this view is the relevance of data indicating that adolescents are likely to include a rejection of parental religious beliefs as one act of rebellion from the parents. While the Caplovitz and Sherrow study found the variable of quality of parental relationships to be a relatively minor determinant of apostasy, other studies have directly disputed this and have shown this variable to be crucially important in determining the maintenance of religious commitment (Dudley, 1978; Hunsberger, 1980).

A final theory of apostasy is that of universalism/achievement versus particularism/ascription. These rather clumsily named variables refer to what are often competing belief systems—those of classical religion seen to be rooted in particularism and ascription of status and those of modern society seen to be in terms of universalism and achievement of status. The more one is engaged in modern society, the more one is likely to adopt more universal perspectives and to be committed to achievement orientations. As such, one's religious identity tends to be undermined, especially insofar as such identity requires a particularism and a status based primarily upon ascription. Hence, research indicating less religious commitment among the "worldly successful" is readily interpreted within this perspective (Welch, 1978).

Yet, if we do not know with any adequate empirical precision the determinants of apostasy, it remains true that apostasy is not a common phenomenon. Most persons identify themselves as religious, either on the basis of beliefs and practices or community and ethnicity (Lazerwitz, 1977). Persons are typically socialized to be religious and later in life continue to identify themselves as religious. Even so, they may not adhere to the faith of their parents. When persons change religious commitment, it is usually just that, a change in religious commitment, one for another. Persons convert. What then are the factors determining religious conversion?

DENOMINATIONAL SWITCHING

As we shall see shortly, conversion is a term utilized in a variety of ways to identify a change in religious commitment. Least dramatic, but nevertheless important, is changing from one denomination to another, or what has come to be known in the scientific literature as *switching*. Clearly, denominational switching lacks dramatic appeal because a person who switches is simply moving from one socially accepted mode of religious expression to another. As we have already seen, because denominations fall along the "church" end of the tension continuum and hence outside of particular denominational concerns, switching has not become an item of concern for the popular press. However, this state of affairs is changing, partly because of the rise in social visibility and growth of the more fundamental denominations and the apparent failure of earlier scientific predictions to predict correctly the decline of more fundamentally oriented faiths.

It was Stark and Glock (1968) who most vociferously predicted that the pattern of American faith commitment was changing to a commitment away from more conservatively oriented faiths to the more liberal. While their own data were largely California-based and heavily linked with high-status Protestant denominations, their explanation for the predicted trend toward liberal denominations was based upon two factors: (1) upwardly mobile persons tend to seek out and identify with high-status denominations that are typically more liberal in orientation, and (2) liberal theologies are more compatible with an increasingly secular society. Yet, we have already confronted the "Kelley thesis" and the obvious failure of the predicted demise of more conservative religious groups. Indeed, as we shall soon see, the fervor of new religious growth and commitment is anything but rooted in liberal religiosity. Yet as Greeley (1972) has emphasized, America is a "denominational society" within which many Americans clearly use religious membership as an important factor in terms of self-identity. Hence, we might not be surprised that in a period of rapid social change and uncertainties persons seek alternate faith commitments. Within those seeking to switch denominations, three factors appear to be most important in providing explanations: social mobility, interpersonal factors, and experiential factors.

Social Mobility

Social mobility is a crucial if unclear factor in affecting denominational switching. Most typically, social mobility is associated with changes in peer-group interaction, in living location, and in a variety of factors that facilitate some degree of change. Denominational switching is but one specific instance. Nevertheless, most denominational switching is minor and clearly interdenominational. For instance, a Protestant is much more likely to switch to another closely related Protestant denomination than to become a Catholic or a Jew (Roof and Hadaway, 1979). Obviously, belief compatibility operates here. However, if people are upwardly mobile, their religious views are most likely to become liberalized as they move to denominational membership in the more liberal, higher status Protestant denominations (Roof and Hadaway, 1979). On the other hand, some evidence suggests that the downwardly mobile are likely to adopt more conservative denominational memberships. This occurs not only because denominations composed of largely lower class members tend to have less status (which is associated with theological conservatism), but also perhaps because their smaller size facilitates more communal patterns of association that tend to be conservative.

Interpersonal Factors

While the typical view of denominational switching is likely to focus upon purely personal reasons for changing church membership, scientific studies tend to support interpersonal factors as important for denominational switching. Among the most important of these is communal identification and styles of association. Numerous investigators have emphasized that much of religious commitment is less a primary concern with the specific content of religious beliefs than with the patterns of communal involvement and interpersonal styles of association made possible by church membership. Here again we have Lenski's distinction between two basic types of religious commitment noted earlier in this chapter. Yet, now we emphasize the communal factor in a variety of expressions. For instance, as already noted, several studies have shown the importance of communal or ethnic identification for some Jews, independent of a belief commitment in Judaism as a religious faith. Likewise, marriage has long been known to be a good predictor of denominational switching, even across denominations. For instance, Wallace has shown that a person married to a committed Catholic is likely to convert to Catholicism (Wallace, 1975). Likewise, Becker (1977) has emphasized the importance of peer-group relationships for religious membership. Furthermore, a significant body of literature indicates the importance of communal style in determining church commitment (Hood, 1983). Interestingly, much of this literature associates the continual growth of more conservative denominations with essentially interpersonal variables as we have seen in our discussion of the "Kelley thesis." Finally, we can note that even when children abandon the faith commitment of their parents, it is often in terms of moving to a more communal form of expression and not in terms of abandoning specific beliefs. Hence, as Wieting (1975) argues, much intergenerational change in religious membership is more in terms of forms of religious expression than in terms of the meanings attached to specific religious symbols or even in terms of the content of specific religious beliefs.

It is worth emphasizing that social mobility and communal factors are not independent. Indeed, the well-documented persistent power of the rural church is related to the fact of little mobility in rural communities, leading both to belief stability and tightly knit patterns of interpersonal association. Indeed, while beliefs are a factor in religious commitment, their independent power to predict denominational switching is largely rooted in methodological problems associated with identity belief change prior to switching, or vice versa. Yet, for our present purpose, it is sufficient to emphasize that social mobility is largely related to anticipated belief changes—both because belief change leads to activities fostering social mobility (for instance education) and because social mobility situates a person in a new context that may foster belief change (for instance a change from a rural to a city environment). Still, it is important to note a consensus among investigators that belief and community can operate in union or independently to foster differing styles of denominational commitment and switching. A useful typology employing both belief and communal (interpersonal) factors has been provided by Brinkerhoff and Burke (1980):

		DEGREE OF BELIEF COMMITMENT	
DEGREE OF		HIGH	LOW
Communal	High	Fervent followers	Ritualists
Identification	Low	Outsiders	Apostates

In this model, note that fervent followers both believe and identify with the religious community, while apostates neither believe nor identify with the religious community. However, among believers are those primarily motivated by communal identification (ritualists) and those primarily motivated by belief (outsiders).

Experiential Factors

Finally, several investigators are beginning to emphasize the role of experiential factors in denominational switching. In this context, it is important to emphasize that denominational switchers are typically likely to be more religious than nonswitchers. This holds true whether religiosity is identified in terms of church attendance (Alston, 1971) or in terms of reported religious experience (Hadaway, 1980; Nelsen and Potvin, 1980). In the latter case, it appears that high rates of reported religious experience among switchers also works in a dual fashion: Persons seeking religious experiences may do so precisely because their present denomination is found lacking. Hence, such switchers are, in Hadaway's (1978) term, "committed seekers." These persons are likely to locate within a denomination that facilitates the kind of experiences they seek as well as providing theological legitimation of such experiences. On the other hand, switchers who move to churches that emphasize the more experiential aspects of religion are likely to have these experiences elicited as part of their new commitment. Until recently, emphasis on such experiences have tended to be rooted in lower status denominations into which the lower classes are disproportionately attracted (VanRoy, Bean and Wood, 1973). However, more recently such issues have been the concern of many of the new religious movements whose attraction has been to other than the disaffected and the downtrodden. Here then the concern becomes more controversial, for the experience is more extreme and the reactions are more intense. This is especially the case where cults are concerned.

CULTS

If tension with environment is used as the single most fruitful criterion by which churches and sects are empirically distinguished, what of cults? It is obvious that the term *cult* has a pejorative connotation, more so in the recent and popular press. In one sense, the word cult appears to have become the sociological equivalent of "madness" to the popular mind. Even the sociological literature on cults tends toward the dramatic and the extreme (Eister, 1972). Yet probably the most useful comparison is that between sects and cults. As Stark and Bainbridge (1975) argue, sects tend to rise from *within* religious organizations and to move toward their own new religious grouping. Hence, sects are inherently religious protest movements. On the other hand, cults lack prior ties with religious bodies and tend to emerge afresh, often under the direction of a single charismatic leader. As such, we can anticipate that both sects and cults tend to share a rejection of their environment, with cults even more dramatic in their emergence. This occurs not only because cults are new and hence do not share many prior links to social legitimacy, but also because their leader is likely to be a solitary, powerful, and charismatic figure. Hence, the leader of a cult is likely to be as feared and rejected by non-members of the cult as he or she is revered by members of the cult. An earlier work (Barnes and Becker, 1938) on charismatic leadership notes the current concern with this issue well:

> Charismatic domination is established through the extraordinary qualities (real or supposed) of the leader. . . . Law is not the source of his authority; on the contrary, he proclaims new laws on the basis of revelation, oracular utterance, and inspiration (Vol. 1, p. 22).

Given the charismatic nature of cult leadership combined with the fact that cults, like sects, tend to be in tension with their environment, one can anticipate that explanations of both cult leaders and followers tend to be denigrating. For those outside a particular cult, activities and aspirations of the cult are likely to seem bizarre at best. Recently, Bainbridge and Stark (1979) summarized the models of cult formation in terms of social exchange theory. They identify pathological, entrepreneur, and subcultural-evolution models. Basically, their pathological and entrepreneur models are denigrating explanations of cult formation, "explaining away" what cults claim to be doing in favor of misguided or devious underlying motives, especially of the cult leader.

In terms of our own model of religious movements, it is important to note that cults, defined primarily by charismatic leadership of religious collectivities emerging afresh under conditions of tension with their environment, are especially unlikely to be well received precisely because they offer generally unacceptable alternatives to objective or felt problems, for significant numbers of persons. As such, unique explanations for cult formation are unneeded and unwarranted in the most general sense. We suggest three summary models of cult explanation, two rather identical with the efforts of Bainbridge and Stark, and one clearly different.

Pathological Models of Cult Formation

Pathological models of cult formation abound. Basically, all of these explanations assume that cult leaders are themselves suffering from serious psychopathologies for which they have found public acceptance among at least an isolated group of followers. Usually, the additional claim is made that cult members also suffer from pathologies that make them susceptible to the charismatic yet pathological characteristics of their leader. Indeed, it is often the pathology of the leader that is assumed to account for his or her charisma.

Clearly, the pathological model of cult formation is depreciative and in lay language assumes cults to be "sick." However, as noted in Chapter Twelve, the relationship between mental health and religion is complex, and while some religious cults may derive from and indeed foster illness among its members, others do not. Even recent scientific studies of the more flamboyant cults of our times, such as the People's Temple Movement, cannot be illuminated only by appeals to pathological processes (Johnson, 1979; Richardson, 1980). Furthermore, insofar as cults are *collective* objective or felt resolutions to problems, such relatively stable social processes obviously cannot be assumed explainable by unstable psychological pathologies. In a similar fashion, as more than one investigator has noted, functioning members of socially deviant groups are by definition adjusted members of those groups however "maladjusted" they may appear by other normative standards or tests (Simmonds, Richardson and Harder, 1976). Clearly, then, whatever truth there is to pathological models of cult formation, as a general theory of cult formation it is both unsatisfactory and unwarranted.

Entrepreneurial Models of Cults Formation

A second model of cult formation, often explicit in the popular press, is what Bainbridge and Stark have labeled the entrepreneurial model. Basically, this model assumes that cult leaders are primarily charismatic figures using their talents to profit from their cult members. While such leaders may be sincere, the likelihood is that they are deceitful and motivated by hopes of personal material gain. In essence, like "Elmer Gantry," their sincerity is but a ploy for the exploitation of others. However, for some entrepreneural cults the claim is that cult leaders are sincere and deem it appropriate to profit from what they can provide for others, often with justifications in explicit theological terms.

An advantage of entrepreneurial models is that they link cult formation to normal social processes in which services are provided, at a profit, for those in need. Hence, new religious movements are created, marketed, and sold in the same way as any other product or service. In terms of our own model of religious collectivities, it is again important to note that even with an entrepreneural model of cult formation, resolutions to problems are provided, however objective or felt. However, clearly entrepreneural models of cult formation also tend toward depreciation of the cult and suggest a "duping" on the part of many if not most cult members.

Veridical Models of Cult Formation

As a final model of cult formation, we propose the veridical model. Simply put, this model assumes at least the conceptual possibility that cults arise precisely for the reasons claimed by their leaders and members. Clearly, here is a claim to a legitimacy of theological beliefs that are not part of psychology or sociology *per se* but nevertheless must be taken into account. Many major investigators in the scientific study of religion have argued the wisdom of including supernatural belief assumptions in empirical work. The range of claims is as might be expected, from Berger's (1967) insistence of a "methodological atheism" through Garret's (1974) plea for a "methodological agnosticism" to Hodges' (1974) argument for what might be called an "informed theism." Clearly, what we are arguing for here is the possibility that cult leaders and their members, as with any religious collectivity, are acting on the basis of beliefs and experiences objectively "true" within the boundaries of their faith. In other words, what makes religious movements unique is not the psychological or social processes involved in their formation maintenance, but their actual relationship to a perception and experience of the divine. Little empirical research informed by this model has been done, despite persuasive arguments by O'Dea (1966) to study the specific content of religious experiences and perceptions in order to understand their process of institutionalization in particular concrete cases.

INTERRELATING MODELS OF CULT FORMATION

The three models of cult formation are not mutually exclusive. From an attributional approach, clearly differing meanings can be attached to otherwise assumed "identical" responses. Hence, even assuming pathological processes are operating in either a leader or his or her followers, such processes do not negate the possibility of religious truths. As James (1902) noted long ago, religious pathological responses are nevertheless still *religious*. As an example, a critical yet sympathetic biography of Mary Baker Eddy, founder of Christian Science, (Peel, 1966) allows for the simultaneous operation of pathological and veridical claims. Using a more dated example, many Christians certainly would not find it offensive to view historically the emergence of Christianity as a cult whose founder can be explored within a veridical model as we propose (Schillebeeck, 1981). Likewise, perhaps profit can be made from otherwise legitimately perceived religious activities. The issue here is that any evaluation of the legitimacy of religious collectivities or their leaders presumes theological criteria that themselves can be debated. The diversity of religious groups, new, old and emerging and changing, attests to this simple fact.

Extrinsic and Intrinsic Cults

Another typology of cults proposed by Campbell (1978) is rooted in the classic work of Troeltsch. Campbell speaks of "instrumental" and "illumination" cults in which the distinction parallels with our discussions of intrinsic and extrinsic religion in a number of chapters. Illumination cults are primarily rooted in a development of the true spiritual self and as such can be conceived as directed toward spiritual growth in and of itself and hence are intrinsic in our terms. While cults (as do other forms of religious collectivities) differ in how they define true spirituality, intrinsic religiosity, whether individually or collectively expressed, is in and of itself and ultimately debatable only in theological terms. In this limited sense, scientific explanations are always partial and do not speak directly to theological claims.

On the other hand, instrumental cults are directed to experiences or activities that function toward other ends—whatever they might be. Hence, such cults might have a tendency to become more secularized insofar as the ends they seek tend to become more and more "worldly" and pragmatic (Schneider, 1973).

Summary of Cult Formation

It is clearly the case that controversy is likely to surround both the formation and maintenance of cults. Not only are cults by definition in conflict with their environment, but the likelihood of their being led by a charismatic person contributes to their delegitimation. Simply put, cults are a threat to the culture insofar as they propose radical alternative solutions appealing to significant persons. Indeed, part of the effort of emerging cults is to convince otherwise contented persons that in fact they have problems that the cult can resolve. In extreme cases, claims to brainwashing can be used to delegitimate both the cult and its newly acquired members. We looked critically at such claims in Chapter Nine. Now we need simply note that cult formation is a normal process that in gross terms follows the logic of our model linking individual deprivations and collective resolutions.

SECULARIZATION THESES

As a conclusion to this chapter, we must note that a dominant theme in the scientific study of religion has been that which is covered under the phrase "secularization." While there are an almost infinite variety of these theories, they basically share a common theme in their extremes: the extinction of religion (Fenn, 1978; Martin, 1978). Perhaps most forcefully put, this theme is expressed by anthropologist A.F.C. Wallace (1966):

> . . . in starkest form, the question about the evolutionary fate of religion is a question about the fate of supernaturalism. . . . But as a cultural trait, belief in supernatural powers is doomed to die out, all over the world, as a result of the increasing adequacy and diffusion of scientific knowledge and of the realization by secular faiths that supernatural belief is not necessary to the effective use of ritual. The question of whether such a denouement will be good or bad for humanity is irrelevant to the prediction; the process is inevitable (pp. 264–265).

Like so many others, Wallace's claim, has recently been challenged by a series of studies on the relationship between traditional religiosity such as expressed in denominations and less traditional religiosity as expressed in sects and cults (Bainbridge and Stark, 1980b; Stark and Bainbridge, 1979b, 1981; Stark, Bainbridge, and Kent, 1981). What is clearly apparent from this research is a dual thesis shedding considerable doubt upon widely accepted secularization theses. First, where traditional religiosity is most dominant, sects and cults are less popular. For instance, the South has fewer sects and cults than the West, especially California. Furthermore, the South is more traditionally religious and the West less so. Second, there is a consistent inverse correlation between new sect and cult formation and the stability of more traditional religiosity across a wide variety of indices, especially denominational growth. The conclusion of this research is obvious: While particular forms of religion rise and fall, religion per se is a quite constant phenomena. Hence, rather than doomed to extinction, religion is reasonably expected to continue in an ever-changing variety of forms and expressions as alternative explanations and confrontations with ultimate issues surrounding humanity are offered. As Stark and Bainbridge (1981) state:

> . . . those confidently predicting the demise of religion are misreading superficial indicators as basic, and are incorrectly limiting their conception of religion to a specific set of contemporary organizations. We agree that the future of liberal-Protestantism, for example, seems utterly grim. Indeed, all organizations in the Christian-Judaic tradition may be fated to whither away. But we note several potent signs that, even should all these religious bodies crumble, human commitment to supernaturalism will remain (pp. 361–362).

While Stark and Bainbridge may have overstated their case a bit with respect to the Christian-Judaic tradition, material in this chapter clearly suggests the permanence of religion insofar as it represents a collective effort at resolutions of individual deprivations, however conceived. Given this, one ought to expect continual religious fervor as persons move into and out of religious collectivities as well as create new ones. Much of this is to be understood in terms of the context of more social psychological concerns, as noted in this chapter. Yet when the focus is more exclusively upon individual psychological processes involved, we confront a major topic of concern throughout the scientific study of religion—conversion.

ATTRIBUTION THEORY AND RELIGIOUS ORGANIZATIONS

As noted earlier, people make attributions when crises of meaning, control, and self-esteem occur. These are obviously concomitants of deprivation, which we have seen is a spur to the development of religious bodies. Old meanings no longer suffice; new ones are demanded. People feel that their contacts with God in the established churches may have shortcomings; hence, control through prayer and ritual is limited. Cults and sects provide greater individual involvement and thus less of a sense of powerlessness. Possibly the new group offers a more convincing argument that one is chosen or saved in a new rebirth of spiritual feeling, thus raising self-esteem to new heights. Deprivations of all types retreat into the background as the latest religious affiliation and commitment becomes increasingly salient.

As discussed earlier, both deprivations and resolutions, have attributional aspects. They involve views of both the self and the world, and religious systems can provide the justifying frameworks within which these are produced. As with conversion per se, for this is a conversion phenomenon, negative attributions toward oneself and others shift with acquisition of new religious attachments to a positive perspective. These are the individual aspects of crisis resolution.

Deprivation and resolution are rather high-level phenomena. They involve interactions between individuals and circumstances that need further specification. There are also a number of kinds of deprivations, and although Glock has defined these, the possible variety of resolutions has yet to be clarified. In other words, the process between these points remains unclear on the level of the individual. Different patterns of attributions along with probably different developmental histories require examination and designation. To date, nothing of this sort seems to have been studied. Attention needs to be directed toward understanding the characteristics and dispositions of the persons involved in these transitions, the nature of the events that move them through the process of change from one spiritual system to another, and how the resolution comes about. As we have frequently stated, this area also demands research.

SUMMARY AND CONCLUSIONS

Being religious in our society, or for that matter in any social order, invariably means affiliation with a religious group—a sect, a cult, or a church. The study of religious bodies is the central issue of the sociology of religion. That it has major psychological relevance goes without saying, for the social psychology of religious organizations is concerned primarily with the relationship between the individual and these groups. We want to know what stimulates the development of these bodies, the motivations of those who join them, the processes by which they develop, how people are socialized into them, and the "careers" of both the converts and the organizations with which they affiliate.

The distinction between sects and churches is extremely significant for it suggests that religious collectivities may be ordered along a dimension of rejection to acceptance of the social order, respectively. Those entering at the sect-cult end of the continuum are theorized to suffer from a number of possible deprivations and frustrations. These may be economic, social, political, medical, or psychological, and often some combination of these factors is operating. The religious group promises a resolution of these difficulties either by standing against society and suggesting that the adherent has found a more basic and lasting answer to his/her troubles. Still, research on deprivations has been somewhat contradictory, for such does not always stimulate religious activity relative to group life. The negative position that religion can only be aroused by shortcoming and deficiency gains much support, but considerable room is left over for deprivations of "growth" needs. In addition, researchers need to consider the concept of deprivation both objectively and subjectively.

Religious organizations represent collective efforts to resolve the "problematic situations" of life. This generalization, however, masks a complexity that has yet to be theoretically encompassed. Considerable theory building has taken place, but there are so many variations on individual–religious organization themes that we find ourselves attending to some aspects of the problem while ignoring others. Focus may be on church attendance or belief, two central issues that may be positively related, but which are far from perfectly congruent with each other. Although there is the perception that many diverse phenomena are theoretically tied together, work on affiliation with conservative churches is poorly related to questions of denominational switching. On the surface, apostasy seems quite different, but it too is associated with a search for compatible belief systems. In the background, the specter of secularization worries church people, but it is also a reality that social scientists must acknowledge to understand both attachment to cults, sects, and churches on the one hand, and their rejection on the other.

It is almost as if the concerns of chapters three through nine plus elements of Chapters Eleven and Twelve come to fruition in this chapter. We must be concerned with socialization, religious experience, conversion, moral issues, and the potential of psychopathology when we confront the groups and institutions within which people express their religion. In this latter regard, questions of personal faith orientation have remained separate from matters of affiliation, leaving open a door to further theoretical speculation and research. Attributional issues have also been untouched, and the model proposed here admits these for consideration. In the last analysis, on the level of the social psychology of religious institutions, we will have to deal with individuals in the religious organizational context and how this affects efforts to attain meaning, control, and esteem in life.

CHAPTER ELEVEN
RELIGION AND
MORALITY

There is laid in the very nature of carnal men a foundation for the torments of hell: there are those corrupt principles, in reigning power in them, and in full possession of them, that are seeds of hell fire (Jonathan Edwards in Gardiner, 1904, pp. 81–82).

If you want honour, wealth, or after death, a blissful life among the gods.
Then take good care that you observe the precepts of a moral life! (Buddhist scriptures in Conze, 1959, p. 84).

But let one set a strict guard upon himself; for if out of curiosity one offers evil the little finger, it soon takes the whole hand (Kierkegaard in Bretall, 1936).

It is forbidden to the house of Israel to rob or to snatch anything from any creature, for in all the punishments in the Law, none is more grievous than that for illegitimate gain . . . He who robs his fellow of a farthing is as though he took away his life (Montefiore and Loewe, 1963, p. 396).

These comments from Buddhist, Christian, and Jewish theologies more than amply testify to the inseparability of faith from the moral life. In a more contemporary tone, Bergson (1935) avers that

> . . . morality is coextensive with religion. It would therefore be vain to raise the objection that religious prohibitionists have not always dealt with things that strike us today as immoral or antisocial (p. 123).

To put the question of the role of religion and morality in perspective, we will first examine the extent to which religion could be related to morality and thus review the evidence for the association of religiosity to personal morality within the Judeo-Christian heritage. This examination will be followed by a survey of the relationship of religiosity to interpersonal morality. *Personal morality* primarily affects individuals and includes sexual activity and the use and abuse of drugs and alcohol. While such actions usually have interpersonal effects, the areas themselves principally involve decisions about ourselves. On the other hand, *interpersonal morality* concerns our views and responses to others—for example, prejudice, helping those in need, and crime and delinquency.

Finally, the answers that can currently be given to questions about the relationship of religion to morality are presented. We also discuss what else we need to know and how this knowledge might be obtained and used to provide better answers to these questions.

HOW MUCH CAN RELIGION BE EXPECTED TO RELATE TO MORALITY

Possible Confounding Factors

Basically, the answer to this query is, "not as much as one might think." As we have discussed throughout this book, the reasons for our frequent inability to offer conclusive data must again be acknowledged. These concern the unreliability of measures, a lack of congruence in degree of generality versus specificity between indices of religiosity and morality, and the presence of other confounding influences. Unhappily, we can always point to a lack of definitive research. Let us briefly reconsider these problems.

Reliability

No measuring instrument is perfect. Perhaps the investigator asks questions poorly, or maybe the person filling out an inventory misreads or misunderstands part of it. Serious difficulties exist in operationally defining both religiosity and morality. Technically, this means that the strongest correlations we can reasonably expect between these domains will not be as high as desired even under the best of conditions.

Lack of Congruence

Religion is usually assessed in a very general way when studied relative to morality. For example, the use of general belief scales is widespread. Many studies have even employed the simplistic question of whether or not a person is a church member. Morality, however, is evaluated on a variety of levels of generality. Some utilize questionnaires much like those that judge religiousness. Others focus on actual behaviors such as real-life helping actions of good samaritans. Whenever a general measure of religion is used, a general measure of morality should be included. When specific indices are employed, associations could be quite low and "statistically insignificant" because of the great complexity of both personal religion and morality.

Other Influences

When a moral decision is made, religion is seldom the only factor affecting the outcome. Consider the case of someone in need. Whether that person is helped by the most well-meaning of people is a function of more than just good intentions. Latane and Darley (1970) noted that we first must realize that the other individual really requires our aid. Schwartz (1968) further observed that potential helpers also must accept responsibility and be aware of the consequences of their behavior for any value system including religion. Otherwise, the two are likely to be independent of each other. Furthermore, the definition of helping that is part of the religious person's spiritual outlook needs to be congruent with that of the investigator, or their empirical correspondence could be quite chancy and difficult to interpret.

Considering these negative influences, it is not surprising that the affiliation of religion and moral activity is usually quite weak. Unfortunately, as we shall see in the rest of this chapter, few studies have met any of these conditions well; yet, despite these handicaps, religion still relates meaningfully to some moral actions.

RELIGION AND PERSONAL MORALITY

Personal morality includes the potential of physical or psychological injury to the self. It is also "personal" in the sense that people in our culture vary in whether they believe the actions in question are immoral—and so these matters are also personal decisions. Polls do, however, tell us that the overwhelming majority of Americans consider what we will discuss to be moral issues and problems. This view also occupies a central place in Jewish, Catholic, and Protestant theologies (Aquinas, 1952: Part II of the Second Part; Questions 3, 25–27, 44; Jakobovits, 1975; Tillich, 1963). From these perspectives, personal morality is a religious obligation to preserve and enhance one's bodily health and mental well-being.

Three personal morality areas have been investigated for their relationships to religion: sex, illicit drug usage, and alcohol abuse. Examination of these activities in the following pages reveals both the usual complexity of these associations plus what readers already should have come to expect—namely, a marked discrepancy between religious hopes and the way people actually express themselves.

NONMARITAL SEXUAL BEHAVIOR

The Religious Perspective

Sexual expression has always been one of the central concerns of institutionalized faith. The violation of religious sexual mores by premarital or extramarital intercourse, or by what may be viewed as "perverse sexual practices," is considered among the most serious of sinful activities. In the past, breaking these religious taboos could result in death or, at the least, social ostracism and public condemnation (Bataille, 1962).

The book of Deuteronomy in the Bible provides a number of punishments for premarital intercourse, ranging from fines to death by stoning. Saint Paul regarded the marital sexual state as being on a much lower plane than virginity and celibacy; however, Luther reversed the order of these conditions by affirming that sexual activity within marriage is the natural state of things. Early Catholicism, however, regarded even sex within marriage as incompatible with spiritual thought and action (Hunt, 1974). In one form or another, this conflict, although much muted, continues to the present day. Such conceptions of sin-associated sexual behavior constitute a burden suffered by many throughout life (Masters and Johnson, 1970).

In brief, the traditional Judeo-Christian norm for sexuality is clear: Complete sexual activity is restricted to married, heterosexual couples. Nonmarital intercourse, whether premarital or extramarital, is wrong. Therefore, one might expect evidence of greater inhibition and limitation in sexual activity on the part of the devout than their less religiously committed fellows. Although this hypothesis gains much support, it finds considerable qualification in modern America (Hopkins, 1977).

PREMARITAL SEXUAL RELATIONS

Important research on sexuality in the United States dates back to the Kinsey reports of the 1940s and 1950s (Kinsey, Pomeroy, and Martin, 1948; Kinsey, Pomeroy, Martin, and Gebhard, 1953). Very large national samples of men and women were interviewed and classified as either active or inactive Protestants, Catholics, and Jews. These and other studies have been fairly consistent in their findings, suggesting that the most religiously involved persons are least likely to engage in premarital sexual behavior (Argyle and Beit-Hallahmi, 1975; Hunt, 1974; Kinsey et al., 1948; 1953; Mahoney, 1980; Tavris and Sadd, 1975).

The results of Kinsey's work are clear. For example, 63 percent of religiously inactive Protestant females reported having premarital intercourse, whereas only 30 percent of the actives responded similarly (Kinsey et al., 1953). With age, premarital involvement increases markedly among singles of both sexes, with some evidence of a widening gap between religious and nonreligious individuals (see Table 11-1). A two-to-one ratio of nonmarital sex when comparing nonChristians to Christians is relatively typical of a number of more recent studies as well (Middleton and Putney, 1962; Reiss, 1969).

Much has been made of the probability that sexual attitudes and behavior have become more liberal in the last two decades. Glenn and Weaver (1979) examined data on a variety of sexual activities from seven national samples drawn during the 1970s and found that standards for premarital sex had relaxed greatly during this time. Differences among religious groups in approval of such behavior narrowed considerably, with the largest changes noted among Catholics (Singh, 1980). Another recent survey found no significant association between religiosity and premarital activity for either males or females (King, Abernathy, Robinson,

TABLE 11-1.   Selected Data on Religion and Pre- and Extramarital sexual activity

PREMARITAL INTERCOURSE		
PROTESTANTS[1,2]	MALES[3]	FEMALES[3]
Religiously active[4]	35.9%	19.9%
Religiously inactive	62.2	46.6

FEMALES ONLY[5]			
	PROTESTANT	CATHOLIC	JEWISH
Strongly religious			
Under 25 years old	73%	73%	40%
35 years and older	51	47	—[6]
Mildly Religious			
Under 25 years old	92	92	89
35 years and older	71	61	46
Not Religious			
Under 25 years old	94	94	94
35 years and older	79	70	56

EXTRAMARITAL INTERCOURSE		
PROTESTANTS[1,2]	MALES[3]	FEMALES[3]
Religiously active[4]	10.8%	6.4%
Religiously inactive	29.7	20.2

[1]Only Protestants were selected because of incomplete data on Catholics and Jews, especially among the males.

[2]Sources: Kinsey et al. (1948) and Kinsey et al. (1953).

[3]Males and females over sixteen years old.

[4]Because of a change in designation between 1948 and 1953, for the latter date religiously active is equivalent to devout.

[5]Source is Tavris and Sadd (1975).

[6]Not enough data.

and Balswick, 1976). A fairly representative study is presented in Research Box 11-1.

Studies using scales of moral values reflect a strong relationship between religious feeling and involvement and sexual standards. Crissman (1942) asked students to judge how wrong a set of behaviors were. Some of these behaviors were antireligious while others dealt with nonmarital sexual activity. This instru-

RESEARCH BOX 11-1.   *Herold, E. S. and Goodwin, M. S., "Adamant Virgins, Potential Nonvirgins, and Nonvirgins," Journal of Sex Research, 1981, 17, 97–113.*

Working from the theory that sexual ideology precedes sexual behavior, the idea that premarital intercourse is acceptable should precede actual premarital sexual involvement. Relative to participation in this behavior, three groups were identified. These were: (1) adamant virgins—females who had not engaged in intercourse, and who indicated that they were unlikely to do so; (2) potential nonvirgins—females who had not participated in intercourse, but who felt they were likely to do so premaritally; and (3) nonvirgins—females who had engaged in intercourse, and who felt they would continue the activity. Although many hypotheses were constructed relative to differences among these groups, the one of most significance here was that premarital intercourse would be unacceptable to adamant virgins on religious and moral grounds. Potential nonvirgins would be less likely to demonstrate such a basis.

Data were obtained from 408 college women and 106 high-school girls ranging in age from sixteen to twenty-two. Fifty-two percent had engaged in premarital intercourse. In terms of the above criteria, there were 165 adamant virgins (AVs), 70 potential nonvirgins (PNVs), and 245 nonvirgins (NVs). The rest of the sample were deemed undecided and eliminated from the study. The church-attendance pattern of the groups was as follows:

CHURCH ATTENDANCE	AVs	PNVs	NVs
Never or less than once a month	28%	64%	72%
1 to 4 times per month	30	19	19
Once a week or more	42	17	9

This pattern was highly significant and statistically showed that adamant virgins attended church significantly more than both potential nonvirgins and nonvirgins. The last two groups did not differ meaningfully from each other. Of eight factors influencing virginity status, religiosity fell into third place behind peer experience of premarital intercourse and being involved in a steady dating commitment. It was concluded that "low religiosity combined with high peer group permissiveness may set the stage for . . . anticipatory socialization" (p. 110) into premarital intercourse. Apparently, religious commitment is a powerful deterrent to such sexual involvement.

ment has been used with college students from several cultures for forty years. Recently, Gorsuch correlated the religious and sexual items, and, in keeping with the Kinsey reports, found that the association between religiosity and negative views of nonmarital sex continues to persist across peoples and decades.

Today individuals feel freer than ever before to discuss and admit to nonmarital sexual activity, yet there is still evidence that committed Christians remain only half as likely to become premaritally involved as their spiritually inactive counterparts. For example, Krejci (1980) reports that Catholic college students vary in their attitudes toward premarital sex depending on their religious self-perspective. Of those whose self-identification is with the church, only 34 percent disagree with the church's stand against premarital relations. Eighty-nine percent who were low in their identification with Catholicism felt similarly.

In the massive (100,000 women) *Redbook Report on Female Sexuality,* Tavris and Sadd (1975) also point out that religious identification inhibits premarital sex (see Table 11-1). One somewhat unexpected fact was that two-thirds of their sample had their first premarital encounters by the age of sixteen or seventeen. This was true for both strongly religious and nonreligious groups of women.

The guilt-arousing function of religion has been posited as inhibiting surrender to sexual temptation. Tavris and Sadd (1975) cite a large study of students and adults that affirms this view of the role of guilt. Apparently guilt is present for the initial sexual encounter, especially for females. However, as this behavior continues, the guilt dissipates. Similar interpretations are possible for the findings of Mahoney (1980) that religiosity is negatively correlated with seven sexual activities for females and eleven for males. These included age at first coitus, number of different coital partners, percent of self-initiated coitus, extensiveness of sexual experience, frequency of coitus, sexual responsiveness, and sexual enjoyment, among other possibilities. The same is true of Sorenson's (1973) national study of adolescent sexuality.

The role of religion as a control on premarital sexual behavior may be decreasing, but its influence is still with us and is subtly expressed. For example, the frequency of such involvement is currently less among the most devout and shows greater confinement to procedures that vary least from what is traditionally accepted in sexual relations (Hunt, 1974; Kinsey et al., 1953; Martin and Westbrook, 1973).

Extramarital Infidelity

Historically, extramarital sexual behavior has been more disapproved than its premarital counterpart. Churches and civil authorities sanction marriage, and extramarital acts are a direct challenge to religious and political institutions and their legitimizing doctrines. A strong case can also be made that such disfavor has almost everywhere, in all times, fallen most heavily on women. Females have been brutally treated with the severest penalties including death, while offending males received much lighter treatment—if any punishment at all (Lewinsohn, 1958). Despite such general negativity, extramarital sexual violations appear to have always been practiced. The involvements of noted personages are often taken for granted, yet religious prohibitions and concerns still pervade the morality of a fickle apparent "majority."

The role of religion in inhibiting sexual behavior is even more clear with extramarital contacts than with premarital relations. Kinsey and his co-workers (1948; 1953) point to a strong inverse relationship between devoutness and such involvement. They further claim that the "active incidences of extramarital coitus had been more affected by the religious backgrounds of the females in the sample than by any other factor" (Kinsey et al., 1953, p. 424). Among the most religious women, between five and seven percent had been extramaritally involved, while for nonreligious females rates were three to four times higher. By the early 1970s, according to Hunt (1974), the incidence of such activity had about doubled, but the percentages were still not high. A similar result was recently found among the readers of *Psychology Today,* who returned a survey. Seventeen percent of the "very religious" said they might cheat on their spouse, whereas 53 percent of the "not" or "anti-religious" reported they could see themselves acting thus (Hassett, 1981).

These tendencies have continued to be observed in the most current work. The numbers still remain fairly low, and religion remains "the strongest inhibiting factor" (Tavris and Sadd, 1975, p. 162).

The relationship of religion to most areas of morality is generally seen as a question of the impact of religious norms in nonreligious areas of life. Other explanations have been offered for the differences observed in nonmarital sexual activity. For example, Mol (1970) suggests that religion takes up one's time, and so less attention is given to sex. Gorsuch (1976) asserts that this and a wide variety of psychodynamic interpretations are wrong since they cannot explain one well-established fact—namely, the equivalence of intercourse rates of religious and nonreligious persons within marriage relationships (Martin and Westbrook, 1973).

Religion does appear to have a major impact in at least one area for which the Judeo-Christian tradition has a clear norm. This restriction of intercourse to marriage cuts nonmarital coitus rates greatly among the faithful while leaving marital sexuality untouched (Kinsey et al., 1948; 1953; Tavris and Sadd, 1975). However, norms do not completely determine behavior, and it is evident that virtually nothing in society has been found that does. The reduction of any set of behaviors to the degree noted here is one of the more powerful effects found by contemporary social scientists.

ILLICIT DRUG USE

Churches strongly oppose the use of illicit drugs, but how influential is their opposition? Does religiosity relate to the use of such drugs? The literature that responds to this question comes from two research traditions: (1) investigation of religion as a social control mechanism for drugs; and (2) the study of the origins of illicit drug use.

Religion as a Control on Drug Usage

Research on religion as a social control to prevent drug abuse is quite recent. The results are typified by McIntosh, Fitch, Wilson, and Nyberg (1981), who also reference most of the work in this area of study. They found religious salience, or the strength of religious belief and behavior, to be negatively correlated with the use of all categories of drugs. It was concluded that "adolescents who frequently attend church services use less marijuana and hard drugs " (p. 70), and that religious preference is less important to this finding than salience of beliefs and religious activity.

Linden and Currie (1977) report similar findings. In their study of 750 Canadian youth, religious associations and activity were also related to low teen-age drug use. These workers felt that church attendance strengthened ties to conventional persons and ideas that oppose the values of a drug subculture. In like manner, Steffanhagen, McAree, and Nixon (1972) showed that female college undergraduates who used drugs were less interested in religion and were less religiously identified than their non-drug-using classmates. Corresponding observations were made among psychiatric in-patients by Westermayer and Walzer (1975). They noted that heavy drug involvement declines as church attendance increases. Other work supports these social control views by continuing to find negative relationships between religious commitment and illicit drug usage (Rohrbaugh and Jessor, 1975; Gorsuch, 1980).

A massive study of over ten thousand youth in Minnesota further confirms the influence of religion on drug usage (Benson, Wood, Johnson, Eklin, and Mills, 1983). A wide variety of indices of religious belief and behavior related negatively to the use of many drugs such as marijuana, LSD, PCP, Quaaludes, amphetamines, etc. (see Research Box 11-2).

A review of research in this area concludes that religion

> predicts those who have *not* used an illicit drug, regardless of whether the research is conducted prospectively or retrospectively, and regardless of whether the religious variable is defined in terms of membership, active participation, religious upbringing, or the meaningfulness of religion as viewed by the person (Gorsuch and Butler, 1976b, p. 41).

Religion and the Motivation to Use Drugs

Interpretations of the relationship between religion and drug usage are still in an early stage of development. For example, Gorsuch and Butler (1976a; 1976b) regard this association as an index of the degree of socialization to a culture opposed to drug abuse. These authors further note that any comprehensive theoretical orientation to this area of study must include the fact that religion also can be an indicator of drug use. To illustrate, in the 1960s some religious groups formed around LSD employment, and American Indian utilization of peyote in religious ceremonies has a fairly long history. Within these bodies, socialization into the faith may well result in greater use of the approved drug.

The supportive belief that drug-induced ecstasy can bring one into direct contact with the supernatural or aid in the quest to reach God is well established in certain quarters. Leary (1970) claims that if the atmosphere is "right," 40 to 90 percent of those taking psychedelic drugs may report intense religious mystical experiences. The work of Smith (1970), which dealt with LSD, suggested the association of this hallucinogenic drug with radical religious beliefs and practices. Noted psychologist of religion Walter Houston Clark (1968; 1971) has long hypothesized that drugs could enhance spiritual feelings and experiences.

These findings imply that it may be more accurate to conceptualize the ef-

RESEARCH BOX 11-2.   *Benson, P. L., Wood, P. K., Johnson. A. L., Eklin, C. H., & Mills, J. E.* Report on 1983 Minnesota Survey on Drug Use and Drug-Related Activities. Minneapolis: Search Institute, 1983.

Working with the Minnesota's Governor's Office and the state departments of education and public welfare, these researchers from Search Institute, one of foremost national organizations undertaking research on religion, carried out this massive survey. Over 10,600 youth in the eighth, tenth, and twelfth grades filled out a 122-item survey on drug use and related attitudes. The students were in seventy public and thirty-three private schools, which were randomly selected to represent the entire state of Minnesota.

In addition to obtaining demographic information on a wide variety of family, community, and respondent characteristics, facts were gathered on the frequency of use of different drugs for the preceding two weeks, twelve months, and in one's lifetime. These data concerned utilization of alcohol, cigarettes, marijuana, LSD, amphetamines, Quaaludes, barbiturates, cocaine, heroin, and PCP. In addition, summary indices for the preceding month, year, and life of the student for all of the drugs, excluding alcohol and cigarettes, were computed. These scores were correlated with measures of religious importance, church attendance, and membership in church groups, among others. Summary religiosity scores were also calculated.

The obtained correlations between the religious and drug variables were consistently significant statistically in a negative sense, meaning that the more religion was a part of the student's life, the less any of the drugs were employed. The reasons for this repeatedly found pattern of relationships was not explored, hence the mechanisms for connection could involve (1) direct religious inhibition of drug activity, (2) the mediation of religious values for non-use through the home, or (3) other interactions not yet known.

fects of religion for or against illicit drug abuse in American culture as byproducts of socialization into a religious group. Unfortunately, this general theoretical position has yet to be researched.

ALCOHOL USE AND ABUSE

The use and abuse of alcohol is somewhat similar to that of illicit drugs. It is also quite different because the problem now involves a legal drug. Further, religious groups take different views of the use of alcohol. This fact can lead to some predictable results, as when an investigator asks if the respondent has taken a drink of *any* alcoholic beverage and then finds out that all active participants of a tradition that uses wine in its religious ceremonies are "drinkers."

Alcohol and Religious Groups

The past thirty years has witnessed many changes in attitudes and behavior in this realm, and what seemed so evident at an earlier time now may not be as valid. Methodists have removed traditional prohibitions against drinking and acculturation among Jews to mainstream American values regarding the use of alcohol has been proceeding at a rapid pace. Finally, the introduction of a wide variety of drugs may act as alcohol substitutes.

Typical research findings can be illustrated by a major study of a representative national sample (Cahalan, 1970; Cahalan, Cisin, and Crossley, 1969). Protestant bodies traditionally opposed to *any* use were labeled "conservative," while those whose norms allow some social drinking were defined as "liberal." Catholics were included separately. The results are shown in Table 11-2.

Once again, we see the impact of norms. Religious standards on drinking cut rates of alcohol use and abuse approximately in half. These findings remain after controls for sex, age, and social position are considered.

Among religious groups, study after study have revealed that while Jews show the least abstinence from alcohol (Skolnick, 1958), they possess extremely low rates for pathological drinking (Riley and Marden, 1959; Rose and Stub, 1955; Wechsler, Demone, Thum, and Kasey, 1970). Methodists express negative attitudes toward drinking, yet a study of a college sample showed that "more Methodist students drink to get intoxicated than any other group" (Chafetz and Demone, 1962, p. 91). Mormons hold similar views, and a smaller proportion of Mormon college men and women drink than any other religious body assessed (Straus and Bacon, 1953). Despite this, it was noted that "of the Mormons who drink, 88% had been tight, 74% drunk, and 40% had passed out" (p. 136). We also find apparent contradictions in the use of alcohol by Catholics. Irish Catholics tend to have positive attitudes toward drinking plus extremely high rates for alcoholism, while Italian Catholics rival Jews for the lowest incidence (Bales, 1962; Cahalan and Cisin, 1968; Skolnick, 1958; Trice, 1966; Wechsler et al., 1970).

Making sense out of these observations is not easy because cultural and class factors are interwoven with religious considerations. One noteworthy factor is the meaning of alcohol for different groups. It can be employed for medicinal purposes, conviviality, and in religious ritual. Rosenman (cited in Chafetz and Demone, 1962, p. 84) points out that Judaism considers alcohol a gift of God that must not be abused. Snyder (1964) presents data that show that orthodox and conservative Jews become intoxicated less than their reform or secular coreligionists. This relates to a strong normative attitude against social drinking in more traditional Jewish homes; hence, to the extent Jews identify with the values and practices of general American society, unrestrained drinking increases (Chafetz

TABLE 11-2 Alcohol Abuse in Selected Religious Traditions

TRADITION	% HEAVY USERS	% OF USERS WHO ABUSE
None	20%	25%
Catholic	19%	23%
Liberal Protestant	13%	16%
Conservative Protestant	7%	13%

Adapted from Cahalan (1970; Cahalan, Cisin, & Crossley, 1969)

and Demone, 1962). What we observe here and among Italian-Catholics is that alcohol is tightly circumscribed by its use in religious ceremonies in home, church, and synagogue.

In the mainstream of American Christianity, at least historically, alcohol has been viewed as a "tool of the Devil" and is rarely identified with religious practice. Irish Catholics show essentially no ritualistic involvement for alcohol but demonstrate a strong cultural orientation toward its use for both health and pleasure (Bales, 1962). Therefore, drinking becomes associated with both personal gratification and tension reduction.

REASONS FOR ALCOHOL USE AND ABUSE

Horton (1943) has looked at alcohol usage across cultures and claims that its consumption increases with the prevailing level of psychosocial insecurity for a people. The lack of ritualistic limitation among Irish Catholics, plus its potential for reducing anxiety, would seem to support a high rate of chronic intoxication in this group. This would not be true of either Jews or Italian Catholics.

On another level, we see that orthodoxy in belief and practice among Protestants correlates with less drinking than among those with more liberal inclinations (Moberg, 1969; Straus and Bacon, 1953). Religion seems to act as a suppressor, but what about the extreme use of alcohol among Methodist and Mormon college students? Neither of these groups face any notable adult drinking problem, and one might hypothesize that an adolescent rebellion is present that later subsides.

A number of scholars carry this idea further. Alcoholism seems to be troublesome among groups that generally take the most negative stance toward unlimited drinking (Straus and Bacon, 1953). General consumption may be high in these religious bodies, but group controls are strong. When intoxication appears, it could signify rejection of the values of the faith. Apparent exceptions, such as among Irish Catholics, may be more due to culture than to religion (Knupfer and Room, 1967). Sanctions against drinking that get into the home may have a religious origin, but they also gain support from other cultural elements. This seems to be true among Jews and Moslems, and probably exists in other groups where religion, nationality, and regional influences are operative (McGonegal, 1972; Midgley, 1971).

If we return to Table 11-2, the data in the last column call the "rebellion hypothesis" into question. Cahalan's findings rather cleanly support a counterview—namely, the stronger the religious norm is against any alcohol use, the less likely people will become heavy drinkers if they do drink. These researchers (Cahalan, Cisin, and Crossley, 1969) argue that religious norms are operating here rather than ethnicity or some other variable. Of those who attended religious services at least once a week, 10 percent were drinkers in this study. Twenty-two percent of nonattenders were heavy drinkers. This observation has been repeatedly confirmed by other studies, which report that more religious people possess norms against casual and heavy alcohol use (Goodwin, Johnson, Maher, Rappaport, and Guze, 1969; Larson and Wilson, 1980; Middleton and Putney, 1962; Moberg, 1969; Parfrey, 1976). Following this well-established finding, Burkett (1980) searched for connections between religious beliefs and nonuse of alcohol. Analyzing adolescents, he concluded that the belief that drinking is a sin is one key element in this relationship. The impressive study of Benson et al. (1983) also notes that religion seems to counter alcohol use.

Affecting beliefs about alcohol is only one way in which a religious norm might influence drinking behavior. Consumption may also be affected by the *socially normative aspect* of such attitudes. Believing that alcohol use is a sin could create a certain social climate that might inhibit those who believe that the use of alcohol is not sinful. This effect was observed by Bowers (1968), who studied the drinking values and behavior of students at colleges from several religious traditions. He noted that anti-drinking values did inhibit alcohol consumption, and he further observed rejection of alcohol in college settings where most students did drink. In addition, those who had no anti-alcohol bias, but who were in a college of students who disapproved of drinking, drank less than their peers at other colleges. This inhibiting of alcohol utilization due to a predominance of nondrinkers, beyond any effect from holding an anti-drinking position, does show a group normative effect.

If we look further into the psychology of alcohol usage, there is evidence that alcoholics, more than nonalcoholics, come from religious families (Walters, 1957; Wittman, 1939). Still, Wahl (1956) found no differences in religious training or activity between samples of heavy drinkers and teetalers, but there might have been more subtle, religion-derived influences. Wahl observed that Catholics, among whom the rate of alcoholism is highest, also feel most guilty about excessive drinking; however, this does not influence the depth or frequency of intoxication. Heavy drinking might actually work to deny and repress such guilt; hence, alcoholism is maintained. It has, however, been claimed that religious conversion can be effective in combatting alcoholism (Clark, 1971).

The verdict is far from final regarding any of these inferences. We are inclined to believe that religion may be meaningfully tied to the use of alcohol where (1) its utilization is circumscribed by religious ritual as with Jews; (2) a strong religious prohibition against alcohol is well established, as in the conservative Protestant family; and (3) where a cultural norm exists about drinking that counters religious controls, as among Irish Catholics. In all of these examples, the idea of norms, standards, and frames of reference for drinking behavior are present.

COUNTERING ALCOHOL ABUSE: POSSIBLE ROLES FOR RELIGION

There is reason to believe that religion can be employed successfully as part of a broader framework to minimize, if not completely inhibit, the use of alcohol. Alcoholics Anonymous works towards such a goal and has flourished for almost a half century. AA has been quite effective in dealing with alcoholism, and claims success with 75 percent of those who join its ranks. Outside observers consider actual figures to be in the 30 to 40 percent range—still a remarkable accomplishment (Calhoun, 1977; Geiger, 1960). Groups such as AA are basically secular; however, they recognize the strength of religious experience, practices, and institutions, and employ them in a dynamic manner (Bean, 1975). Empirical data on reasons for the success of failure of this and similar "religiously oriented" programs are, unfortunately, still sketchy. They constitute an important research task for the psychology of religion.

INTERPERSONAL MORALITY

Interpersonal morality refers to a morality of relationships. An immoral act in this area is less significant for its effect on the person engaged in the behavior than for what it portends for others. Prejudice and delinquent and criminal activities constitute the negative side of the domain, while compassion and altruistic responsivity comprise its positive aspect. Although religion has always stressed interpersonal morality, there is very good reason to ask if religious people differ from their less committed peers in these expressions.

Prejudice and Discrimination

The Judeo-Christian heritage has a central theological doctrine: "the love of neighbor as one's self." This fundamental theme states that all people should live in peace and harmony under the dominion of God and church. That life deviates markedly from this noble aspiration goes without saying. Antisemitism has a long history in Christian-dominated cultures, as does slavery and racism (Busell, 1964; Isaac, 1964). The feelings of Catholics for Protestants and vice versa have often been far from amicable, and the members of many Protestant bodies have harbored little less than considerable ill will for their co-religionists (Olson, 1963).

Research results in this area are rather surprising since a number of potentially significant variables have been shown to be independent of the association of religion and prejudice (Gorsuch and Aleshire, 1974). One of these is the kind of prejudice studied. All types of prejudice on which sufficient data exist lead to the same conclusion. This includes anti-semitism, anti-black, anti-Catholic biases among white Americans, as well as general ethnocentrism, or the tendency to make sharp, unrealistic, negative distinctions between one's own group and other "outgroups." We suspect that the same findings would hold for any country and ethnic group where prejudice against another people or nationality is part of the prevailing culture. Two other variables that were also of no consequence were the section of the country in which the measurements were made and whether college students, church members, or the general public participated in the research.

Empirical study of the relationship of religion and prejudice has employed several definitions such as the following, with each producing a different result (see Gorsuch and Aleshire, 1974, for a review and references to this work).

Church Membership and Activity

The simplest and earliest approach to defining religiosity was to denote it in terms of church membership. For example, Merton (1940) and Sanford and Levinson (1948) labeled people religious if they were members of a church. These studies invariably found that members were more prejudiced than nonmembers.

The interpretation that easily came to mind was that the church produces prejudice. This remains unsubstantiated by later studies.

Recognizing the limits of church membership as an index of religiosity and wishing to explore this realm further, Parry (1949) and Sanford (1950) used religious activity as a measure of commitment. They both came to the same conclusion, which has since been widely supported—namely, that religiously *very active* people and their nonreligious counterparts are less prejudiced than relatively *inactive* religious people (Struening, 1963). Figure 11-1 shows that the casual attender is the most prejudiced of all who go to church.

Data from studies of religious activity cannot be used to support the claim that churches create prejudice. If this were so, the most active members would be most exposed to these influences and would be the most bigoted. Instead, the highly prejudiced people are those religionists who are *least* influenced by the churches.

FIGURE 11-1. Pictorial Representation of the Relationship between Prejudice and Church Attendance

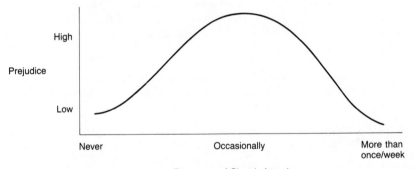

ILLUSTRATIVE DATA[1]

	PREJUDICE SCORES	
Church Attendance (Frequency/month)	Study 1	Study 2
0	14.7	14.8
1	25.0	18.4
2	26.0	18.0
3	23.8	17.6
4	22.0	16.4
5–7	19.9	15.3
8–10	16.3	15.0
11 and up	11.7	11.8
Sample size	889	943

[1]Study 1 comes from Struening (1957) and Study 2 from Struening and Lehmann (1969)

Still, we must ask, "Why are the most religious and nonreligious equivalent in their lower indications of prejudice?" Gorsuch and Aleshire (1974) suggest that this lack of prejudice is associated with a deviant value position. Classically, casual church attendance seems typical of the "American way of life." Neither a strongly religious nor a strongly nonreligious position appears to be part of the mainstream value system of Americans. To be either of these extremes implies deviance, and could be a sign that the individual is thinking through his/her personal value system. Assuming that prejudice is inherently illogical, such people should be low in prejudice. Other possibilities also exist. For example, it may be that the explanation necessary to understand the greater tolerance of the religiously active may differ from that needed to comprehend the stance of the nonreligious person.

TYPE OF RELIGIOUSNESS

It is apparent that measuring religious activity rather than simply membership changes one's interpretation of the religion-prejudice relationship. This implies that perhaps religion comes in different forms, one of which is related to love and brotherhood, another to prejudice and bigotry. This fog of somewhat conflicted understandings began to lift when Gordon Allport, a major investigator in this area, commented that

> The role of religion is paradoxical. It makes prejudice and it unmakes prejudice. While the creeds of the great religions are universalistic, all stressing brotherhood, the practice of these creeds is frequently divisive and brutal. The sublimity of religious ideals is offset by the horrors of persecution in the name of these same ideals. Some people say the only cure for prejudice is more religion; some say the only cure is to abolish religion (Allport, 1954, p. 444).

Undertaking an extensive program of research, Allport and his students soon made notable headway in solving this problem. Theory first centered about the observation that religiosity was not one thing, but many, each form resulting from different motives, perceptions, and meanings. Thus developed the concepts of intrinsic and extrinsic religion about which we have talked so much in these pages and described in detail in Chapter 1.

Studies show that persons who evidence an intrinsic faith are relatively unprejudiced, while their extrinsic counterparts, who make up the bulk of churchgoers, manifest high levels of bigotry (see Research Box 11-3). The much larger numbers of the latter managed to submerge and obscure the views of the far fewer intrinsics (Allport and Ross, 1967; Feagin, 1964; Hunt and King, 1971; Photiadis and Biggar, 1962). Allen and Spilka (1967) introduced their concepts of committed and consensual faith, which stressed cognitive inflexibility and closed-mindedness on the part of extrinsic religionists. Other workers rapidly confirmed these findings by showing that those for whom faith served as a guide to mature living rejected prejudice and discrimination (Strommen, 1967; Tisdale, 1966; Vanecko, 1966). These studies also noted more prejudiced people among fundamentalists (Gorsuch and Aleshire, 1974), but it is not known if fundamentalism attracts more consensual-extrinsic church members than do religiously orthodox or liberal groups.

RESEARCH BOX 11-3.   *Allport, G. W. and Ross. J. M. "Personal Religious Orienta-*
tion and Prejudice," Journal of Personality and Social
Psychology, *1967, 5, 432-443.*

Recognizing that a considerable body of research claims that churchgoers are more prejudiced than nonattenders, these scholars noted a somewhat contradictory finding—namely, that those who attend church most frequently tend to be low in prejudice. This suggested that there might exist different religious, orientations among churchgoers, one form being compatible with prejudice, another countering bigotry. Prior to the present study, Gordon Allport had sponsored such thinking in his concepts of interiorized and institutionalized faith (Allport, 1954) and intrinsic and extrinsic faith (Allport, 1959; 1966). Respectively, these last forms represent religion as a search for truth or as an instrumental, utilitarian value. Since prejudice seems to reflect the latter possibilities and is antithetic to the former, it was theorized that prejudice would be positively related to an extrinsic orientation and negatively related to an intrinsic outlook.

Direct and indirect measures of prejudice were used. These included items indicating prejudice against blacks, Jews, and other minorities. Statements connoting a lack of sympathy with mental patients and a generalized distrust of people (a "jungle" perspective) were also used. Scales designed to assess intrinsic and extrinsic religiosity were also constructed. These instruments were administered to 309 churchgoers from six faiths—Roman Catholic, Lutheran, Nazarene, Presbyterian, Methodist, and Baptist in five northern and southern states.

Three groups of churchgoers were distinguished: intrinsic, extrinsic, and indiscriminately pro-religious. On the indices of anti-black, anti-Jewish, anti-other, jungle, and views of mental patients, the extrinsically religious were more prejudiced than their intrinsic counterparts, while the indiscriminately pro-religious were even more prejudiced than either the extrinsic or intrinsic religionists. The indiscriminately pro-religious respondents seem to be a group that may just uncritically agree with attitude statements in general—a kind of "yea-saying" tendency. Clearly, the utilitarian, extrinsic approach also leans in the direction of prejudice, so the question is no longer how religious a person is, but how that person is religious.

Although the problem of religion and prejudice seems to be essentially solved, Batson, Naifeh, and Pate (1978) have recently challenged the foregoing results on the basis of bias in the measures employed. They suggest that people are likely to answer intrinsic religion and prejudice questions in terms of how socially desirable and approved such answers might be rather than respond to them truthfully. Indeed, there is a long history of work on such biases (Berg, 1967; Edwards, 1957), but there are also many arguments against their having truly significant effects (Block, 1965). Resolution of this question will have to await more decisive research.

In a number of studies, Batson and his students suggest the notion of religion as *quest.* They feel that this is the form that counters prejudice (Batson, 1976; Batson and Gray, 1981). Conceptually, quest faith sounds, in part, like what Allport (1959; 1966) felt intrinsic religion is. In Batson's system, it appears as a kind of open-minded struggle to resolve religious doubts rather than a personal spiritual explanation that offers constructive meaning and guidance for everyday living.

Little research has been done on the religion-prejudice connection since the Gorsuch and Aleshire review (1974). We suspect that this is because their work came at the end of an era. By the early 1970s, mainstream American culture no longer countenanced blatant prejudice. The casual church attender thus stopped admitting to bigoted outlooks, and results became nonreplicable. For example, the data published in Gorsuch and McFarland (1972) had been designed as a major study on prejudice, but was analyzed for other purposes because very few admitted to being prejudiced. Simply put, more people must state their prejudices before their other characteristics can be evaluated relative to these outlooks. This line of research can only be re-opened when another group is found for which it is socially acceptable to be negative. Then, perhaps, research can identify the role of church-related parameters, such as theology, in contrast to more culturally oriented factors.

It is clear that the weight of evidence leans in the direction of intrinsic-committed religion countering prejudice and discrimination and extrinsic-consensual faith supporting it. Most religionists apparently are more extrinsic than intrinsic, making it appear as if religion is more likely to encourage bigotry than stand as a moral bulwark against it. In many local areas, churches function as agencies advocating a prejudicial status quo, for as Johnson (1952) insightfully observed, "The church has its roots too deep in the culture to admit of radical moral crusading" (p. 132). The problem is not religion per se, but rather the kind of faith a person has which determines how he/she sees and deals with others.

RELIGION, COMPASSION AND ALTRUISM

No theme expresses the spirit of religion better than the identification of faith with humanity and community. Whether the term describing this relationship is love, justice, compassion, helping, responsibility, mercy, grace, charity, or a host of other similar sentiments and actions, the message is one of positive feeling and support for others. Niebuhr (1928) tells us that "Love is, in short, a religious attitude" (p. 45). It is the essence of interpersonal morality—a free giving of aid, of sympathy, of the self to realize the highest ethical ideals of religion. In a similar vein, Pope John XXIII (1963) wrote in his noted encyclical *Pacem in Terris* that "the social order must be a moral one" (Topical Summary, p. 2). Judaism also speaks of "the right of our neighbor and his claim upon us" (Baeck, 1948, p. 195). The Western spiritual tradition continually stresses obligations and duties to others as fundamental moral imperatives. These are the ideals. We must ask to what degree they are realized by those who profess religion to be a significant part of their lives.

Compassion

Compassion has largely been defined in research as responses to questionnaire items. These are of two types. On the one hand, a person is asked to rate a value such as "helping" on a scale of how important it is. By this criterion of compassion, religious people score high. They rate "helpful," "forgiving," and "helping others" as more important than their nonreligious peers (Rokeach, 1969a; 1969b; Christenson, 1976). In these studies, religion was defined in the same general way as compassion—i.e., people were asked to rate the significance of an item such as "salvation," or to indicate their frequency of church attendance.

Saying that helping is important is only the beginning of *being* helpful. Some scholars thus approach compassion in a second way, by using other questions as well as rating this concept itself. For example, Rokeach (1969b) asked for people's responses to situations that he felt reflected compassion. This suggested that religious helping was solely a matter of saying that one was more helpful without recognizing and responding to the actual needs that people have.

While Rokeach's study was a major effort, several problems were immediately noted. Larson (1970) and Spilka (1970) felt the value items were ambiguous. Gorsuch (1970) questioned whether the religious item "salvation" was more appropriate for conservative Christians, whereas compassion items concerned with civil-rights activities and publicly funded dental and medical care, etc., were most suitable for liberal Christians. A negative relationship between conservative religious inclinations and liberal social action is not surprising and may have confounded Rokeach's findings.

In response to the foregoing criticisms, Christenson (1976) found a relationship between church attendance and the perceived importance of helping, but also failed to replicate the results of Rokeach. To interpret this outcome, consider the nature of the variables. One was church attendance, which, unlike Rokeach's "salvation," is equally appropriate for both conservative and liberal Christians. His dependent variables were several items asking whether, for example, "unemployment" was a problem in the community, and whether one was willing to allocate public funds for job training. These measures did not relate to church attendance.

This study corrects Rokeach's work by using neither a liberal nor a conservative definition of religion, and so does not confirm his finding. Still, it cannot be considered an adequate test of a positive relationship between religion and helping because the social compassion item was still perceived as compassionate only by liberals. Conservative religionists may feel that public funds are inappropriate since each individual Christian should be helping these people. For this group, solving such problems through public money could be "a cold, detached, and ineffective method which primarily helps only the bureaucrats whose salaries are paid from the taxes of hard-working folk."

Our point here is not that either a conservative or liberal approach to helping others is better; that is an issue for theology and philosophy rather than psychology. We believe that evaluating "helpful" behaviors when the helper feels that such methods do more harm than good is not a good test of that person's aiding tendencies. A liberal Christian's helpfulness needs to be evaluated against a liberal definition of helping, and a religious conservative's aiding perspective needs to be evaluated against a conservative definition of helping. This has yet to be done.

Religious people perceive their faith as relevant to decisions involving compassion. Lehman (1971) posed a set of hypothetical situations and asked how meaningful religion was to each and what the respondent would do. The situations included two of compassion (voting for a bill to send food to the hungry and sparing the lives of enemy soldiers during war). His first conclusion was consistent with the relationship of reported religion and the rating of helping noted above: More religious people saw religion as being relevant to more situations. Also, the more one viewed faith as pertinent, the more religious sources would be consulted to decide the issue. Lehman (1969) further notes:

> It would be presumptuous of the writer to decide which course of action in each situation was the choice truly in line with the guidance traditional religion would provide . . . on a given item some respondents said they would do one thing and others reported the opposite, but both groups said their actions would be guided by traditional religion (p. 5).

Altruistic and Helping Behavior

We have been talking about questionnaire responses, which indeed tell us much, but we need to examine the final test of what people say—namely, what do they do.

It has been claimed that "Religion is the mother of philanthropy" (Andrews, 1953, p. 85), and although much of what is given to churches goes for their support, a considerable amount is donated for the many social and welfare programs to which religious institutions give aid. We are not speaking of small amounts of money, for in 1980, $22.2 billion was allocated to churches (Bureau of the Census, 1981). Insofar as faith is a factor in helping one's fellow human beings, Andrews (1953) concludes that "a very substantial portion of present giving to all causes springs from religious motivation" (p. 95).

In recent years, research on altruism and helping behavior has emphasized one-to-one situations in which persons may be called upon to provide aid for others. A few studies have looked at religion, but the results have not always been as clear as one would desire. The problem usually concerns difficulties in both the conceptualization and design of such research.

The simple administration of paper-and-pencil tests of helping behavior and religious attitudes may or may not reveal meaningful relationships (Annis, 1976; Langford and Langford, 1974; Nelson and Dynes, 1976), but the actual testing of helping in experimental situations also seems to be inconsistent in revealing the role of religion in altruistic behavior. In a study designed to assess the readiness of religious and nonreligious persons to volunteer help for a retarded child, some contradictions were present, but religious women were much more likely to offer to help than religious men, nonreligious persons, or those identifying themselves as atheists (Smith, Wheeler, and Diener, 1975).

An interesting study on helping behavior, which might bear on one's view of and trust in people, utilized what is called the "lost letter technique." Apparently, mailing a "lost letter"—one just found lying somewhere—is indicative of a willingness to help strangers (Forbes and Gromoll, 1971). The lost letters could be either stamped or unstamped. The latter method places a greater burden of responsibility on the finder, yet it has been shown that people still will mail such letters, meaning in most circumstances that the recipient will pay postage due. Forbes, TeVault, and Gromoll (1971) employed stamped and unstamped "lost letters." These were located at ten conservative, ten liberal, and five Catholic churches on Sunday morning at the time of services. Those in attendance at all three groups of churches were equal in mailing the "lost letters," with 36 to 42 percent of the letters being returned. Those who attended liberal and Catholic churches were more likely to mail stamped letters than those from conservative churches (percentages mailed were 87, 89, and 42 percent, respectively). If the letters were unstamped, there was a much greater response from the conservative churches (58 percent) as opposed to 13 percent for the liberal churches and 11 percent for the Catholics. What this means is by no means clear, but it does suggest a fair degree of willingness on the part of churchgoers to help strangers. Unfortunately, we do not know how these people compare to nonattenders.

The helping situation is, however, quite complex. Nelson and Dynes (1976) distinguish helping in emergency or disaster situations and ordinary (nonemergency) circumstances. They see religion, especially in its devotional (primarily prayer) aspects, as fostering a sympathetic identification with others. It is thus suggested that the greater one's devotional commitment, the more the person will help people in general, meaning in ordinary, nonemergency situations. Another aspect of religion is its institutional form, and traditional religious groups are usually organized to provide aid when disasters occur. It was theorized that indications of structured religious involvement would tie to helping in emergencies.

Using a very large sample of largely middle-aged persons, ordinary helping behavior was defined as the regular contribution of money or the provision of needed material goods to social welfare and service agencies. Also considered were informal services such as aiding stranded motorists, picking up hitchhikers, and helping bereaved individuals. Emergency helping was distinguished by the donation of funds to relief organizations and the offering of goods and services following a disaster. In this work, information was available on aid after a tornado.

Although there was some overlap between devotionalism and church attendance relative to providing help in ordinary situations, the basic hypotheses of the study were supported. Devotionalism predicted ordinary helping behavior but not that required in disaster circumstances. Emergency aid was favorably influenced by formal church activities such as attendance and congregational affiliation.

As we have frequently seen, form of personal faith is often quite important when religious attitudes and feelings are translated into behavior. Benson and his co-workers (1980), for example, found that opportunities to help strangers appeal more to persons who are intrinsically religious.

In a series of experimental efforts, Batson and his associates (Darley and Batson, 1973; Batson, 1976; Batson and Gray, 1981) examined relationships between altruistic responses and faith orientations. Darley and Batson (1973) observed whether the participants, seminary students, would stop to help an individual who was slumped over in a doorway and whose distress was indicated by coughs and groans. Previously, the students were exposed to instructions and materials that either dealt with the ministerial vocational career (termed task-relevant condition) or the parable of the good samaritan (the helping-relevant condition). Following this experience, situations were created so that some of the participants believed they had to hurry to a nearby building. The remaining students were not subject to this instruction. The basic questions for this research were whether the "hurry–no hurry" task or helping conditions had an effect relative to intrinsic, extrinsic, or quest religious orientations. No comparison of religious versus nonreligious people was attempted.

The task-helping message circumstances had no effect on helping behavior, but those in a hurry were less inclined to offer aid than those not in a hurry. In addition, the quest religious tendency was the only one involved in offering help. Neither the intrinsic or extrinsic measures tied to helping. An interesting phenomenon concerned whether the helper was willing to take the word of the victim that he was alright or persisted in trying to provide aid. Persisting helpers showed greater intrinsic and doctrinally orthodox tendencies, whereas those apparently responding most to the victim's own interpretations of his situation were more quest oriented (Batson, 1976).

In a follow-up study, Blackford et al. (1983) found that reading the parable of the good samaritan did increase subsequent helping behavior, but the hurry condition did not demonstrate the effect noted by Darley and Batson (1973). The discrepancies between these two studies suggest a need for further research. Paloutzian and Wilhelm (1983) further found no relationship between the quest orientation and altruism as indicated by active participation in voluntary helping organizations.

In a third study, Batson and Gray (1981) followed up this question of whether the helper was responding to his/her own needs or to those of the victim (see Research Box 11-4).

The role of religion in sponsoring help to those less fortunate is not clear, but the evidence does suggest that, in one form or another, whether by personal action or through formal church organizations, religion is a spur to providing aid individually and collectively. The details of these relationships still need to be spelled out. Apparently, both the religious and helping aspects of this equation are much more complex than was initially believed.

RELIGION, CRIME, DELINQUENCY, AND DISHONESTY

There are serious problems in assessing the role of religion in crime and delinquency. Before this can be accomplished, the criminal and delinquent must be identified and there is reason to believe that crime statistics are extremely unreliable. Definitions vary by jurisdictions for the same acts; data are collected by many different agencies—local, state, and federal—and their definitions also vary. Much crime never comes to light, or if it does, it may not be formally recorded (Taft and England, 1964).

Independent investigations with anonymous informers also show marked discrepancies between official reports and victim information. In one Philadelphia study, 80 percent of serious crimes were apparently never reported to the police (Mauss, 1975). In another study, 99 percent of a sample of almost 1,700 persons admitted the commission of felonies and/or misdemeanors that would draw sentences of one year or more in New York State (Wallerstein and Wyle, 1947). One implication of this work is that most, if not all, of the respondents would be considered "law abiding citizens." The mean number of offenses for a male was eighteen and for a woman eleven. Religion was included indirectly as a variable

RESEARCH BOX 11-4   *Batson, C. D. and Gray, R.A. "Religious Orientation and Help-ing Behavior: Responding to One's Own or to the Victim's Needs?"* Journal of Personality and Social Psychology, 1981, 40, 511-20.

Sixty female undergraduates with a "moderate" interest in religion were separated into four groups of fifteen each. The two conditions on which this breakdown was based concerned whether the victim wanted or did not want help, and whether or not such aid was socially appropriate. All completed scales of intrinsic, extrinsic, and quest faith. The research situation concerned a get-acquainted conversation be-tween the participants and a fictitious young lady, Janet Armstrong. This "conver-sation" was carried on through notes transmitted in sealed envelopes by the experimenters. A situation was constructed in which the notes indicated that Janet was lonely and lost in this university far from home and seemed either desirous of being helped (high helping situation) or felt she could work through her problem by herself (low helping situation). In what is defined as a high social appropriate-ness condition, "Janet" indicated she uses prayer to deal with her difficulties. In a low social appropriateness condition, she reported that she usually becomes intoxi-cated when under stress. More help was proffered by listeners for the high appro-priate condition whether or not "Janet" desired such.

To the degree a participant reported she felt she was helpful, there was a tenden-cy to embrace the intrinsic kind of faith, which also related to helping whether or not such aid was desired. Quest religion was affiliated with offering help when it was wanted and not making an offer when it was not wanted. It was concluded that an intrinsic orientation means an aiding response because of an internal need on the part of the helper rather than in reaction to the needs of the person to be sup-ported. In contrast, Batson and Gray feel the quest religious outlook is "primarily a response to the expressed needs of the victim" (p. 518), and is therefore more adequate and appropriate.

through knowledge of occupation. It was determined that ministers had the lowest number of offenses, an average of 8.2. And this is what was admitted!

Religion has usually been viewed as an antidote to crime. Pictured as reposi-tories of conforming morality, church and synagogue reserve their harshest indict-ments for the wrongdoer. Popular theory states that the criminal and delinquent have rejected religious faith and are therefore not in the fellowship of worship and belief. This view is, however, false.

Lying and Deception-Dishonest Behavior

If we look at the honesty aspect of morality, we can start with the massive investigations of Hartshorne and May (1928; 1929; 1930) in which some 11,000 school children participated. No real association of churchgoing behavior and honesty was demonstrated. Those who enrolled in Protestant Sunday schools cheated less than those not in these schools, but this reflected higher class levels for the former rather than any religious influence. Another unhappy sign was that the more one attended Sunday school, the less likely that person would be cooperative and helpful, hardly an indication of the constructive role of spiritual involvement.

Other work shows similar results. Hightower (cited in Raab and Selznick, 1964) studied some 3,000 children and found no relationship between amount of biblical information and tendencies to lie and cheat. This observation parallels work on college students that revealed no association between religion and cheating on examinations (Parker, 1971). More noteworthy is the disclosure in one study that 92 percent of religious students affirmed that it was morally wrong to cheat, yet 87 percent of this same group agreed with the statement, "If everyone else cheats, why shouldn't I?" (Goldsen, Rosenberg, Williams, and Suchman, 1960). In line with this finding, a recent investigation revealed that 72 percent of a group of highly religious college students admitted that they had cheated on examinations (Spilka and Loffredo, 1982). Those who were intrinsically religious either cheated less or admitted less to such behavior than their extrinsically oriented peers.

In a somewhat less religiously selective study, Paloutzian and Wilhelm (1983) experimentally assessed cheating tendencies and also observed them to be negatively associated with intrinsic faith. Batson's quest orientation was unrelated to the cheating.

There is good reason to believe that the person who violates moral prescriptions by lying and cheating feels that he/she will not be caught. In other words, no one will even suspect their dishonesty. Where such an outlook prevails, Wright (1967) claims that religion doesn't affect one's resistance to temptation, but it may intensify guilt. The separation of feelings and behavior remains a problem that religious educators have yet to overcome. If, however, immoral activity is likely to be visible to others, Wright (1967) further points out that religion does exercise a restraining influence. The issue is not right or wrong, but "what will others think?" Conformity in the public eye is apparently more important than private compliance with moral standards. In a rather candid manner, 52 percent of a sample of delinquents admitted that their religious views did not impede them from violating the law (Cortes and Gatti, 1972).

Criminal and Delinquent Behavior

These findings become of even greater significance when we examine the relationship between religious activity and crime and delinquency. Studies involving thousands of offenders throughout the nation show, as one scholar has put it, "a higher proportion of delinquents and criminals report religious affiliation and activity than the rest of the population" (Falk, 1961, p. 160). It has also been claimed that "the . . . proportion of religious affiliates is at least 50 percent higher among prisoners than the general population" (Barnes and Teeters, 1959, p. 615). To illustrate, Kvaraceus (1949) found that 92 percent of a group of delinquents claimed religious affiliations and 54 percent were attending church regularly. Wattenberg (1950) obtained like results in his work on over 2,100 juvenile law breakers in Detroit. Forty-four percent attended church regularly and 26 percent occasionally. Only 14 percent never went to church. The difference between repeaters and nonrepeaters was not large, with 46 percent of the latter being regular attenders and 39 percent of the former responding similarly. These findings also hold for adult criminals (Taft and England, 1964).

A number of studies show that delinquents and criminals express more favorable attitudes toward Sunday observance, the Bible, and the role of religion in countering misconduct than their law-abiding peers (Middleton and Fay, 1941; Smith, 1956). Chances are that incarcerated law breakers are especially desirous of providing positive views of themselves to others—hence, they respond to questionnaries with answers designed to gain social approval (Swickard and Spilka, 1961).

Some research claims no observable ties between religious attitudes, church participation, and tendencies to violate civil and social norms (Middleton and Putney, 1962; Scholl and Beker, 1964). There are, of course, also studies that confirm the hoped-for aspiration that faith will counter illegal activities (Jensen and Erickson, 1979).

Once again we encounter contradictory observations. One of the continuing problems in this research concerns the fact that religion is usually treated simplistically (Knudten and Knudten, 1971). Other factors such as ethnic group and class level are frequently ignored, and their contribution to the designation of someone as delinquent or criminal is well known.

Despite these shortcomings, most studies show that conventional religion is not an effective force for moral behavior or against criminal activity. Church attendance and the usual verbalized beliefs may either indicate a superficial faith or reflect something deeper.

When the researcher looks beneath the surface of what is commonly taken as religion, another picture begins to emerge. Gannon (1967) studied 150 Catholic delinquents and concluded first that "What matters to these boys, when it comes to action, is what their friends say and not what their church teaches" (p. 6). He then adds, "entirely missing from their religious experience is any personal sense of involvement with God" (p. 6).

Another recent investigation casts additional light on these possibilities. Cortes and Gatti (1972) conducted an in-depth examination of 100 Catholic delinquents. They attended services and took part in regular religious rituals, but this did not mean that their faith was a truly internalized guide to living. It proved to be a superficial habitual observance and little more. The researchers concluded that not one of their delinquents showed a deep religious commitment, although an outside observer might classify them as religious. Allen and Sandhu (1967) also showed that church affiliation and attendance had no bearing on delinquency, but strength of religious commitment did work to enhance personal controls. These few studies stand in relative isolation, but they are highly suggestive of the importance of religion with regard to delinquent behavior. The qualification is that faith must be treated as a many-faceted phenomenon, not a simple concept.

MORALITY AND FORM OF PERSONAL FAITH

Despite the great outpouring of research on the dimensions of faith during the last decade and a half, personal morality has been studied independently of these considerations. In radical contrast, interpersonal morality has been extensively investigated in relation to intrinsic-committed and extrinsic-consensual orientations. In fact, these forms were initially developed in research on religion and prejudice. The few studies done on helping behavior do include different spiritual outlooks. Where such have been introduced in work on crime and delinquency, they tend to be treated indirectly.

It would be quite easy and also erroneous to generalize findings from research on religion and interpersonal morality to the personal domain, but obviously making such inferences would be scientifically untenable. We require research, and it is apparent that the entire realm of personal morality is virgin territory for investigation. Much still remains to be done in the interpersonal area, particularly on deception, crime, and delinquency.

The introduction of Batson's quest orientation and his work on the influence of social desirability response sets necessitates further examination of the religious correlates of prejudice and helping behavior. Despite Batson's significant contribution and challenging questions, the evidence is still overwhelming that intrinsic-committed faith counters prejudice and extrinsic-consensual religion supports it. With respect to helping behavior, the picture is less clear. Quest faith seems to be most responsive to the wishes of "victims," but the desire to help is still very much affiliated with intrinsic spiritual leanings. More work is obviously required to clarify these associations. Research on cheating, lying, crime, and delinquency relative to form of personal faith has just begun. The need for further specifications and detailing of factors involved in these relationships does not belie the conclusion of Hassett (1981) from his own work that "religious commitment was easily the best predictor of institutional morality" (p. 49). Unhappily, he also adds that very little work is being conducted on these issues.

RELIGION, ATTRIBUTION, AND MORAL BEHAVIOR

Kelley (1971) offers a fundamental point of relevance to our discussion—namely, that "the attributor is not only an agent of control in relation to his own immediate interests, but is also an agent of moral control, and this fact is reflected in his attributional biases and tendencies" (p. 24). This raises the basic question of the nature of the explanations or attributions used by wrongdoers to rationalize their behavior. Our concern is, of course, with the place of religion in this reasoning.

The first and most obvious possibility is that, despite personal protestations of religious commitment, spiritual considerations may be irrelevant. Herberg's (1960) cryptic observation that "a majority of . . . Americans who had testified that they regarded religion as something "very important" answered that their religious beliefs had no real effect on their ideas or conduct . . . in everyday life" (p. 73). Although this remark related specifically to politics and business, it appears easily generalizable far beyond these limits. Attributions regarding what is relevant are made to other factors than religion.

In other words, religion, whether it be personal faith and principle or a conception of the role of God, may not be considered pertinent to situations in which immoral activity occurs.

Recent work does suggest that people vary their religious attributions (perceptions of the role of God and one's own faith) in accordance with the nature of the situation in which they find themselves (Spilka and Schmidt, 1983). Denial of religious considerations when such might limit personal gratification is suggestive of extrinsic-consensual opportunism. Persons holding such a perspective are also less likely than their intrinsic-committed peers to utilize spiritual reference when explaining their own actions and those of others.

As a rule, people have to explain both to themselves and others why they act as they do, and these explanations may include religious attributions. If these do enter the picture, an excuse that "the Devil got into me" or "made me do it" will probably find acceptance in very few places in modern America. There are, however, instances where moral violations are viewed this way, especially in very conservative groups. The sinner, with appropriate signs of penitence, prayer, confession, and promises of future moral purity, is usually accepted back into the fold. It should be noted that making an attribution to the Devil reduces one's own complicity in the immoral behavior. It also permits others to attribute similar problems to this outside cause. These attributions are, in essence, meanings that salvage one's self-esteem by removing the blame from the wrongdoer and others who bear a similarity to him/her.

Just as "the Devil" may be invoked to explain one's behavior, the same is true of the concept of God. One possibility may permit people to act immorally without concern. For example, a study of God concepts held by religious-prejudiced people and their unprejudiced counterparts showed that the former held views of a deity that was abstract, distant, impersonal, and uninvolved in human affairs (Spilka and Reynolds, 1965). This deistic perspective allows a person to do whatever is desired with impunity. Religious bigots can thus attribute disinterest to their God.

In contrast, religious-unprejudiced individuals tended to make one of two different God attributions. Those of an intrinsic-committed nature perceived God as warm, close, and personal, very much a part of daily life. Identification with such an image seems to include a responsibility to act in a similar moral manner.

A second portrayal of God held by some religious-unprejudiced persons might be seen as conflicted. Here the deity is represented as real, close, and personal, but also as punitive and threatening. An individual may thus deny and/or avoid prejudice because he/she is accountable. The attribution is to a judgmental God who expects compliance with moral precepts.

Both loving and controlling God concepts have a scriptural basis and are taught to children at home and in church settings. Attributions of a vengeful, awe-inspiring, wrathful being can easily stimulate fear and feelings of guilt for the slightest deviation from what is regarded as good and right. Thoughts of "hellfire and damnation" have probably kept many people in line, and also have created much unhappiness, dread, and ineffective behavior. Masters and Johnson (1970) indict this kind of faith for its destructive influence on sexual expression. It can reduce nonmarital activity, but at what cost to intimacy within marriage.

Perceiving the deity as integral to human life may have desirable or undesirable implications. Hammond (1982) and Kopplin (1976) have both measured ideas of what the former calls an "interventionist" God. Possessing such an outlook can counter one form of personal immorality—namely, drug abuse. Hammond (1982) comments that addicts "who affirmed a radically interventionist God for the most part reported a low difficulty in kicking drugs" (p. 41). This was not true of those who held a deistic perspective.

There is rather graphic evidence that modification of one's religious stance, and thus its attributions, can change behavior to an extreme degree. Alcoholics become teetotalers; addicts campaign vehemently against drug use; sexual license is supplanted by puritanical abstinence; and criminal activity yields to a demanding code of self-control. These may be the outcome of conversion, and this literature is replete with instances of such fundamental transformations in life style.

Illustrations of these effects pervade the recent phenomenal proliferation of cults in American life. Whether the adherents to these groups are termed "Jesus freaks," "born-agains," or join organizations such as the Unification Church, Hare Krishna, or The Children of God among other possibilities, they have in common a high probability of previously being residents of criminal or drug sub-cultures. During their preconversion lives, indications are that religious attributions were either of no consequence or were negative. Religious faith was essentially nonexistent, or, if we can generalize from the work of Benson and Spilka (1972), done in quite a different setting, self-hatred may have paralleled unfavorable God attributions.

Then came conversion to a religious system that did not permit drugs. This had been the lot of 75 percent or more of the converts. Now usage was rigidly proscribed (Judah, 1974, 1977; Mauss and Peterson, 1973; Snelling and Whitley, 1974). Problems were solved; the immoral was replaced by a devout attachment to the highest popular morality. As Mauss and Peterson (1973) put it, these people are on their way to respectability. Attributions were often to a God who in forgiveness and loving kindness had benevolently touched their lives, giving them the strength to resist temptation. They could also attribute to themselves self-blame for their earlier immorality and self-control for their current one. Moral praise-worthiness was substituted for moral culpability (Shaver, 1975), and self-esteem and self-control are enhanced.

Changes as radical as these can be interpreted as a shift to an intrinsic-committed faith from whatever outlook existed prior to the conversion experience. This further implies a change in the attributions a person makes for oneself and others. People who hold an extrinsic-consensual orientation are much more likely than their intrinsic-committed fellows to see life's occurrences in terms of chance and fate. They are also more ready to see events as determined by powerful persons. God is accorded a very minor role at most. In other words, the individual tends to view him/herself as a victim of the whims of fortune and others (Spilka, Schmidt, and Loffredo, 1982). If one's destiny is thus determined, there is hardly a need to be concerned with morality. Life is a matter of luck and what one can get away with.

Acknowledging an active and major role for the deity can lead either to a fear-motivated conformity or to a sense of peace and security with extremely favorable moral implications. Such would work to enhance identification of the intrinsic-committed religionist with that supernatural being to whom is attributed a loving, forgiving nature. Error could be perceived as personal shortcoming to be rectified within a framework of tolerance and understanding. Morality would then be a desirable goal. If ethical action is motivated by fear of punishment, self-images may be quite negative and we might hypothesize that such individuals will behave morally, but not beyond the utilitarian minimum required in any situation.

In relatively recent work, Dienstbier and his colleagues (Dienstbier, Hillman,

Lehnhoff, Hillman, and Valkenaar, 1975; Dienstbier, 1978) have been applying attribution ideas to the domain of moral development and behavior. Thus far, religion has not been a part of this research. One possible link, however, is provided by Spilka and Loffredo (1982), who studied cheating among religious students. The rather high rate of cheating reported (72 percent) was justified by reference to situational factors and other people. Cheaters did not make negative attributions to themselves, but, to instructors, the nature of tests, a need to cheat in order to pass examinations, and the perception that cheating was really well-accepted behavior. Intrinsic-committed respondents not only admitted to cheating less than extrinsic-consensualists, but tended to deny supportive rationalizations. As Dienstbier (1978) notes, "Specific attributions that people make about potential moral dilemmas determine whether moral values . . . are relevant to one's moral choices" (p. 186). In our work, most of the religious students did not consider their faith as relevant. Where it was so considered, it appeared to exert a noteworthy effect.

Other attributional connections with potential for understanding relationships between religion and morality are also available. Embree (1983) is in the process of developing an attributional framework concerned with sexual morality. Forsyth (1981) distinguishes four types of ethical ideologies and ideologists. These can be inferred easily to kinds of religionists. They are: (1) *situationist*—a highly relativistic, situation-based morality, not greatly different from the theological position of Joseph Fletcher (1966) which he advocated in his *Situation Ethics;* (2) *subjectivist*—also a relativistic position, but premised on personal values, a stance often found in liberal and intellectual orientations to faith; (3) *absolutist*—reference is to universal moral rules in a nonrelativistic sense, an outlook congenial to both highly orthodox and fundamentalistic persons; and (4) *exceptionist*—an absolutist moral position, but one tempered by pragmatics, a posture descriptive of most Americans. Forsyth has utilized this system attributionally relative to understanding moral responsibility, but has not yet explicitly associated it with religion.

Sophisticated research tying religion and moral behavior together by means of attributional considerations is obviously in its infancy. What has been done thus far does indeed look productive.

SUMMARY AND CONCLUSIONS

It should be abundantly evident that religion is a factor influencing moral behavior; however, the relationship is extremely complex and probably varies with the kind of personal or interpersonal morality being studied. We are still in a position to offer some tentative conclusions. These are:

1. Traditionally religious people appear to be more personally moral than their non-religious peers. By this, we mean that they are less likely to engage in nonmarital sexual activity, tend to avoid illicit drugs, and abuse alcohol infrequently. These effects are reasonably strong with the rates of these behaviors among the devout often being half of those of nonreligious persons.

2. The relationship of religion to interpersonal morality is far from simple. Truly intrinsic and committed religious people are among the most tolerant in our society,

but so are the nonreligious. A problem arises with those who take their faith casually. Altruistic and helping behavior has been difficult to evaluate because the definition of helping has been highly variable on an operational level. Philosophical and theological interpretations also enter the picture. Even with these serious considerations, those who are strongly committed and others who are struggling to resolve basic spiritual questions seem to be the most helpful. Delinquency and crime rates among religious and nonreligious persons tend to be similar, but there are indications that an intrinsic-committed faith counters such antisocial behavior.

3. Since most research on religion and morality has been associational in nature, the issue of the causes of the observed relationships has not been addressed. Strictly speaking, we cannot conclude that religious groups and degrees of activity have produced differences in moral behavior. People might simply affiliate with groups, the members of which behave as they do. In all probability, we feel that the groups and the extent of commitment probably are responsible for what has been found.

4. Most of the research is too old or too naively done to be considered ''state of the art.'' There is relatively little work that breaks religion into components and takes into account the generality/specificity of religious predictors and that which is to be understood and/or predicted. In addition, few studies have been seriously concerned with the reliability of the measures used, or other variables known to moderate ties between religious values and behavior. Better research treating the complexity of people on the level they should be regarded may well find much stronger associations than noted thus far. Nevertheless, despite the grossness of the initial work already carried out, many of the findings must be viewed as quite impressive.

5. Given the foregoing considerations, a research program that would systematically explore the attributions of people who engage in immoral activities, especially those who claim to be religious, would greatly increase our understanding of faith in this complex.

There is a fundamental hypothesis underlying much of what we have discussed in this chapter—namely, *the behavior of religious people differs from that of the nonreligious when religious norms differ from those of their society.* Stated differently, we suggest that when religion clearly articulates a norm not widely held in the social order, then being active in that spiritual body means the norm is likely to be followed and active religionists will deviate from the way societal conformists behave. Much of what we have presented in this chapter supports this view.

But how can our hypothesis be consistent with the fact that religious people have the same delinquency and crime rates in general as nonreligious persons? It is consistent because religious people, in general, do not have a norm distinctively different from that of society on crime and delinquency. All of our populace (excepting, of course, possibly those on the other side of the law) is opposed to crime. Differences, however, do emerge when we get more deeply into the nature of one's faith. There we find that the possibly much stronger anti-crime norm among intrinsic-committed persons may not only reflect a quantitative difference, but possibly a qualitative one—hence, their norm is indeed a truly different one.

A final inference can thus be drawn from this hypothetical position. If a religious group wishes its adherents to follow a norm of society more closely than do other members of that same society, it must build that norm into a new and higher place. This higher norm must be explicitly held as a norm for the religious group. Only then will a distinctive life be found among the faithful.

CHAPTER TWELVE
RELIGION AND MENTAL DISORDER

God should be brought forth to meet Satan and then Satan could go and teach the people the right . . . It was my job to start it and to get the spirit working . . . I am the true spirit of God and the product of the earliest stages of man after it was evolved from the seas. When I was in the rage there was something telling me that I was the true spirit of Christ (Boisen, 1936, pp. 168–69).

She wore a crown of thorns. She scarred her face with pepper so no man would find her attractive. Someone had the bad taste to praise her hands, so she dipped them into lye. She set up housekeeping in a hut in the family garden and ate no food except the most meager and unappetizing (McGinley, 1969, p. 129).

I was carried outside my body. Time, body and space seemed to recede. I had nothing to do with them. My spirit rose to such fearful heights that I should have died if the experience had lasted longer. I saw God . . . and about four hours later I came back to earth (Clark, 1929, p. 131).

These illustrations refer to people and events that appear to be truly different, and when someone like those exemplified above just "doesn't fit in," contemporary society favors a psychological-psychiatric interpretation of what is wrong. Individual deviation, regardless of its expression, is most often viewed as mental illness or a problem of adjustment.

It was not always this way, for each historical period seems to prefer a certain kind of explanation of life's problems. For many centuries, understanding was sought in religion and the churches offered absolute and definitive answers. When the question concerned unusual or unacceptable thinking and behavior, the reason lay first with God. The book of Deuteronomy states that the penalty for not obeying the commandments and statutes is that "The Lord shall smite thee with madness. . . ." (Deuteronomy 28:28). An abnormal mental condition was the result of willful failure to behave properly. The cure was also divinely provided in the image of Christ driving devils from a distressed man into a herd of swine (Mark 5:12–13). These scriptural citations were the basis of much popular and ecclesiastical knowledge about mental disorder even into the twentieth century (Rotenberg, 1978). Sin and wrongdoing are still perceived as causes of disturbed behavior and may actually play a role in bringing about such abnormalities (Mowrer, 1961; Ramsey and Seipp, 1948; Rotenberg, 1978).

The relationship between religion and mental disorder is, however, a complex one with a long history. Our purpose in this chapter will be to show these intricate connections. We will first overview some of this mixed and troubled past in order to see where we are today. Second, an understanding of the function of religion relative to coping and adjustment will be offered. Here it is necessary to recognize the many roles religion may perform for the individual. For example, it can be: (1) an expression of mental disorder; (2) a socializing and suppressing force to maintain normality; (3) a haven for disturbed persons; (4) a therapy to help troubled people; or, in a sense, "hazardous to your mental health" and contribute to the strain and tension that brings on abnormality. Next, we will approach religion from the viewpoint of some well-known forms of mental deviance and see what research tells us about the place of religion in these conditions. This should provide some insight into the relationship of faith to personality adequacy, neurosis, and psychosis. Finally, possible ties between different forms of personal religion and mental disorder will be examined. In keeping with our theme of attributional processes in religion, we will note the nature of the attributions that associate religion with mental disorder. These considerations will be summarized as we conclude the chapter. There are few topics in the psychology of religion that are more involved and controversial than this relationship of faith and abnormality. It is a realm that demands more rigorous study than has yet been afforded it.

A BRIEF LOOK AT HISTORY

A Troubled and Confused Past

Relative to its understanding and treatment of mental aberration, the Judeo-Christian tradition exhibits a very checkered past. Kindness and compassion existed side-by-side with cruelty and punishment. The former, however, dominated in the early church when humane methods and prayer were employed to restore mental well-being (McNeil, 1953). At first, shrines in which tolerance and sympathy prevailed were established (Zilboorg and Henry, 1941); however, a growing concern with sin plus needs to enhance church power and political conformity shifted the emphasis of ecclesiastical authorities to confession and repentence. Renaissance, Reformation, and the era of the Enlightenment brought new threats to the power of the church and mental disorder often became identified with witchcraft. Literally hundreds of thousands of disturbed persons met their deaths because of such views (Bromberg, 1937; Brown, 1940).

We know today of the role of socioeconomic status in the definition of mental disorder, and a case can be made that subtle awareness of the influence of wealth and power were also present during those difficult times when witches and warlocks were regarded as a common danger. When the labels of saint and witch were applied, the former tended to be assigned to those of upper-class origin (George and George, 1966); those of more modest means had a much greater likelihood of being designated witches (Deutsch, 1946; Mackay, 1869; Zilboorg and Henry, 1941). It does not take much reading to conclude that abnormal thinking and behavior, probably of similar variety, may have been present among many members of both groups.

With the rapid development of medicine during the Renaissance, the church established asylums, one of the more famous being the monastery of St. Mary of Bethlehem in London, better known as Bedlam. Unhappily, it developed a very poor reputation for care of the mentally disturbed. In many other instances, religiously sponsored institutions represented the best of which an uninformed humanity was capable.

There was little conflict between the church and mental specialists until the beginning of the twentieth century. In 1910, Freud claimed that religious and neurotic behavior had much in common (Brill, 1938). Statements such as "religion is comparable to a childhood neurosis . . . mankind will overcome this neurotic phase, just as so many children grow out of their similar neuroses" (Freud, 1957; p. 96) further separated the faithful from psychoanalytic thinking and practice. Finally, assertions that "psychoanalysis leads to . . . the denial of God" appeared to make this widening breach irreparable (Freud, 1957; p. 63–64).

During this period, and with psychoanalysis as a guiding theoretical force, medical control of the mentally disordered was passing into the hands of a psychoanalytically based psychiatry. Asylums became hospitals and lunatics were now termed patients. Custodial care of the "mentally ill" was instituted until they regained their "mental health." Despite the presence of religion in the guise of hospital chaplains, its role continued to be both peripheral and minimal.

In recent years, the antagonism between clinicians and religionists has been replaced by mutual concern and cooperation. A noted religious educator affirms that "the concept of mental health is essentially that of wholeness or the salvation of souls." He further adds that "mind, body, and spirit are . . . a unity" (Maves, 1953; p. vii). Rollo May, whose training bridges both psychology and religion, further claims that "people suffer personality breakdowns because they do not have meaning in their lives" (May, 1940; p. 13).

Symbolizing this rapproachment, which has primarily involved professionals who deal with mental disturbance, the Academy of Religion and Mental Health (more recently named the Institutes of Religion and Health) was formed. Its first director defined the goal of the academy as "a search for meaning in human existence" (Anderson, 1960; p. 5). Concurrently, the rapid growth of the pastoral psychology and counseling movement further testifies to the utility of coordination between psychiatry, psychology, and religion relative to work with the mentally distressed.

Just as many social scientists have felt that religion can be psychologically explained, we now have the contrary viewpoint that treats "psychology as a theological discipline internal to theology itself" (Hiltner, 1961; p. 251). Thus, we have come full circle to the realization that cooperation between these fields is essential in the fullest sense of the term.

SOME CONCERNS AND CAUTIONS

Before examining the research and thinking that relates religion and mental disorders, we must recognize that there is good reason for caution and reticence when undertaking this task. Serious shortcomings exist in all aspects of this work, and these must be kept in mind when interpreting various studies. In fact, an in-depth treatment of this realm is likely to be more productive of defining research needs than of offering substantive answers.

Problems of Definition

Research relating religion, personality, and abnormality spans almost a century. During the last four decades, when the lion's share of scientific work has been undertaken, many changes have taken place in both the definition and understanding of both mental disorder and religion. The American Psychiatric Association has attempted three times to develop standard classifications of abnormality. Most empirical students of the clinical area accept such diagnostic labels as reasonably well-established facts, but their application is likely to be considerably less precise than is desirable from either applied or research perspectives. In other words, much inconsistency may be present in work involving clinical categories. Caution must therefore be exercised when reading about schizophrenics, neurotics, or other psychological-psychiatric groupings.

One cannot feel more secure when overviewing the religious facets of these research efforts. Not uncommon are studies, mostly over twenty years old, that simply designated religious groups as Catholic, Protestant and Jewish (Hollingshead and Redlich, 1958; Rose, 1955; Srole et al., 1962). As a rule, little or no attention was afforded degree of religious involvement or commitment, or such confounding factors as socioeconomic class or ethnic group, both of which affect incidence of mental disorder. It should be noted further that these classifications, especially that of Protestant, are likely to be so socially broad as to define no meaningful body of people. When the *Yearbook of American and Canadian Churches* lists about 260 religious bodies of which approximately 220 are said to be Protestant, the futility of conducting research with such designations is obvious.

Earlier we discussed the multidimensional nature of religion and suggested that the dichotomy of intrinsic-committed and extrinsic-consensual forms of faith might be useful; however, virtually no study associating religion and mental disorder goes beyond some loose breakdown of religiosity based on frequency of church attendance or a distinction of individuals as orthodox, fundamentalistic, or low, moderate, or strong in religiousness. In sum, simplistic indicators of religion suggest poor understanding of this highly complex realm by many researchers. Still, all may not be lost, for consistency over studies is likely to speak to reliable findings. In addition, there are many investigations that merit consideration, if only for their stimulation of further research.

FUNCTIONS OF RELIGION RELATIVE TO MENTAL DISORDER

In earlier work, it was proposed that religion and mental disturbance might be related in four different ways (Spilka and Werme, 1971).[1] These are: (1) Religion may allow or sponsor the expression of psychological abnormality. Bizarre, unusual, or deviant thinking and behavior are sometimes considered acceptable when they take place within the framework of a religious system. Although the person may be regarded as "different," the label of mental disorder is not openly applied. (2) Religion can act as a control, a socializing agency that restricts and suppresses pathological behavior and thought. To the extent a disturbed person is capable of controlling abnormal responses, others within the religious group, or the rules of the institution may direct that individual's actions into approved channels. (3) A religious system may also serve as a protection, a refuge, or a haven from the strains and difficulties of coping with life. Relatively isolated communities such as the Amish, Hutterites, various sects or cults, or convents and monasteries may provide an ordered, controlled daily existence that permits reasonably acceptable adjustment to these conditions. (4) Finally, religion may be therapeutically useful by providing directions for more effective interaction with the world. It can, through the offices of clergy, pastoral counselors, or the judicious use of doctrine, improve one's outlook, understanding, and controls, and thus enhance personal capability.

To complete the possible pattern of religion-abnormality relationships, it is necessary to add a fifth alternative—namely, religion can be a stressor that may either exacerbate existing weaknesses of personality or even bring on maladjustment. The demands of a spiritual system may simply be more than certain people can handle. In addition, a religious body might also create conditions that require or reinforce deviant and pathological thinking and behavior.

These possibilities are not necessarily independent of each other. Suppression and therapy could overlap and take place within a bounded religious community. Related factors such as economic forces, education, and ethnic background may further complicate matters. We will therefore attempt to point out many of the qualifying and confounding issues that make this area both fascinating and troubling. Let us now examine the various functions of religion in greater depth relative to the way people cope with what Thomas Szasz (1960) terms "problems of living."

[1]The authors are deeply indebted to Dr. James E. Dittes for this conceptual framework.

RELIGION AS AN EXPRESSION OF MENTAL DISORDER

Mystical Experience

Some of the most graphic expressions of mental aberration have been religious. Among the most noteworthy are symptomatic forms of intense or extreme spiritual experience. These have often been termed mystical. A full understanding of these manifestations may be found in Chapter Eight. It should first be recognized that the incidence of self-defined religious mystical experience is quite high and apparently rather normal (Greeley, 1975; Hay and Morisy, 1978; Tisdale, 1975). Still, it is commonly acknowledged that "some mystics are badly disoriented personalities" (Greeley, 1974; p. 81) and that their experiences may, in form and content, reflect abnormal states of mind.

In a very definitive paper, sociologist Rodney Stark (1965) presented a classification of religious experiences, some of which illustrate the presence of pathology. For example, his *salvational* type is said to be motivated by a sense of "sin and guilt" (p. 102). Of a more serious nature, with considerable potential for underlying mental disturbance, is what Stark calls the *revelational* experience. It is the least common and the most deviant form usually including visual and auditory hallucinations that are regarded as messages from the Divine, angels, or Satan. This view gains some confirmation from a recent study that shows that religious mystical experiences in which intense, unpleasant physical-emotional reactions and/or hallucinations are present along with signs of psychological distress (Jackson and Spilka, 1980). Anton Boisen (1952) studied mystical identifications in cases of severe mental disorder and suggested that these represent extreme personality conflicts.

Glossolalia

Sometimes associated with mystical experience is *glossolalia,* the phenomenon of "speaking in tongues." Again the evidence is that most tongue-speakers are quite normal, solid citizens; however, this behavior also reflects personality tendencies that could be viewed as deviant. Kildahl (1972) perceived these people as suggestible, passive, submissive, and dependent on spiritual authority figures. Psychiatrist Mansell Pattison (1968) went further and claimed that such individuals demonstrate "overt psychopathology of a sociopathic, hysterical, or hypochondriacal nature" (p. 76). This certainly implies serious disorder. Kildahl (1972) cites one researcher, Paul Qualben, to the effect that "more than 85 percent of tongue-speakers had experienced a clearly defined anxiety crisis preceding their speaking in tongues" (p. 57). Kildahl concluded that "preoccupation with internal psychological factors seemed to create the necessary atmosphere in which a person was ready to speak in tongues" (p. 58). Although glossolalia reflects an altered state of consciousness, it may also be a manifestation of personal turmoil and, in some instances, of severe mental aberration (Goodman, 1972; Richardson, 1973).

Conversion

Intense religious experience and glossolalia have frequently been associated with religious conversion. Although most conversions are not indicative of abnormality, they may mirror psychological problems. The early and noteworthy study by E. D. Starbuck (1899) illustrates some of these considerations. High among the motives he observed to be present at conversion were "fear of Death or Hell," and "Remorse, Conviction for Sin, etc." (p. 52). The most common emotional states were "depression, sadness, pensiveness" with "restlessness, anxiety, uncertainty" (p. 63) following closely.

In another classic study of over 2,000 persons, E. T. Clark's *Psychology of Religious Awakening* (1929), three kinds of "religious awakening" were identified: the definite crisis awakening, the emotional stimulus awakening, and the gradual awakening. The first two, which account for about one-third of Clark's sample, seem to have the highest potential of expressing abnormal mental processes. Most commonly cited is an overwhelming sense of sin, guilt, and depression, frequently of a sexual nature. More recently, Christenson (1963) described similar examples.

Clark's research suggested a distinction between a radical, sudden conversion and one of a gradual nature. Early scholars, such as William James and J. B. Pratt, had offered like ideas. It has also been observed that persons who experience sudden conversions often seem rather unstable emotionally and might even have repeated conversion experiences with frequent lapses in religious commitment. Lutoslawski (1923) denotes these as superficial conversions, which are commonly found in revival situations. A followup of persons who made such "decisions" during a Billy Graham crusade in Great Britain showed that about half had lapsed during the first year (Argyle, 1959). Another investigation revealed that 87 percent reverted within six months to their former religious habits (Argyle, 1959). Evidence was present that almost one-third of these people had converted at least twice and some up to six times (Argyle, 1959). These sudden, apparently superficial conversions represent what psychiatrist Leon Salzman (1953, 1969) calls the "regressive-pathological" type that is said to result from conflicts with authority, notably one's father.

Other work on the sudden-gradual conversion distinction has consistently shown that the rapid form is associated with higher anxiety, neurotic tendencies, and poorer adjustment than is true of those who acquire their faith over an extended period (Kildahl, 1965; Roberts, 1965; Spellman, Baskett, and Byrne, 1971). In some instances, severe depression with the likelihood of suicide is a component in these conversions (Cavenar and Spaulding, 1977).

Sudden conversion resulting from underlying mental disturbance is relatively infrequent. Clark (1929) claimed that only 6.7 percent of his large sample could be so classified. Starbuck's (1899) research suggested an incidence of only seven percent. Most conversions are positive and constructive occurrences, but the rapid acquisition of religious faith may reflect difficulties in coping with one's impulses and relations with the world.

Scrupulosity

Another religious manifestation of psychological disturbance has been termed *the scrupulosity syndrome* (Mora, 1969). O'Doherty (1978) refers to it as "an agony of doubt and uncertainty about sin or guilt, a meticulous care for and observance of the law" (p. 46). Mailloux (Overholser, 1963) discusses two forms of scrupulosity. The first involves verbalization "in terms of fear: fear of sin, of doing the wrong thing . . . they appeal to their priests whenever they have to make any moral decision, and they usually anticipate such decisions" (p. 101). The second emphasizes compulsive doubt. These persons are less anxious than the others, but are always seeking reassurance. An overwhelming obsession with sin drives these people to a compulsive, ritualistic observance in order to gain a sense of purification, something that is never obtained. The condition is considered neurotic in nature and likely to originate early in life (Strauss, 1960; Weisner and Riffel, 1960). Attributionally, it involves a sense of the self as bad and an image of the deity as tolerating no variation from the most extreme adherence to whatever rules may be imagined.

Religion in Mental Disorder

If religion is an expression of emotional problems, one might expect it to deviate in a number of ways from an enriching, constructive faith, and this seems to be true. Argyle (1959) observed that religiously inclined mental patients express their faith in troubled and bizarre ways. Oates (1955) found that psychotics who felt religion played a role in their disorder distorted the nature of faith in their early lives. Reifsnyder and Campbell (960) further claimed that the religion of psychiatric patients was often inconsistent, shallow, and confused. Like Hardt (1963), these researchers noted that those suffering from serious psychological problems perceived a vindictive, controlling, and unforgiving deity who was punishing them for being sinful. Such disturbed persons attribute to themselves violations of religious proscriptions. These causes of their difficulties are mediated through a threatening and punitive God.

Paranoid religious ideas, while not overly common, are quite impressive when encountered, and a number of clinical workers have reported delusions of grandeur, suspicion, and persecution among religious patients (Bennett, 1964; Brightwell, 1962; Lowe and Braaten, 1966; Rokeach, 1964). Apparently, the religion of disturbed persons has a high probability of also being deviant and inadequate. Research Box 12-1 illustrates these tendencies.

Disorder Among the Clergy

Another expression of mental disorder through religion is noted in Finch's (1965) significant comment that "personality disorder combined with circumstances can lead a person to believe that he has a vocation to the ministry" (p. 26). A rather massive literature has developed to support this assertion (Menges and Dittes, 1965). Clerical rates for mental disorder well above those for the general population have repeatedly been reported (Kelley, 1958; 1961; Malzberg, 1959; Moore, 1936; 1944). In addition, the incidence of serious psychiatric problems among seminarians and active clergy seems distressingly high. Masserman and Palmer (1961) rejected 21 percent of ministerial candidates for psychological problems. McAllister (1965) observed a group of hospitalized priests and suggested that 77 percent had emotional difficulties of great severity while they were in seminary. Kennedy et al. (1977) identified 65 percent of a sample of Catholic priests as either maldeveloped or underdeveloped sociopsychologically. Studying alcoholism among Catholic and Episcopal clergy, Sorenson (1973) indicated that it appears to correlate with a need for personal power.

Questions may be raised about the rigor with which investigations of this nature have been carried out. Morgan's (1958) study is a case in point. In an attempt to determine the incidence of severe mental disorder among clergy and

RESEARCH BOX 12-1.   *Lowe, C. M. and Braaten, R. O. "Differences in Religious At-*
titudes in Mental Illness," Journal for the Scientific Study of
Religion, *1966, 5, 435–445.*

Theory suggests that "religious concern and conflict characterizes patients in psychiatric hospitals" (p. 435); however, the evidence supporting this view has often been anecdotal and contradictory. The purpose of this study was simply to determine objectively the religious attitudes of hospitalized mental patients. A 27-item religion questionnaire was constructed; 18 of the items were directed at the respondent's perception of some aspect of religion as relating to his/her abnormal condition. Data were gathered on 508 psychiatric patients in a Veteran's Administration hospital.

No differences were found in the religious attitudes of any of the diagnostic categories or other classifications of the mental patients. The longer one was in the hospital, the less that individual was certain of or concerned about the existence of God. In addition, those in the hospital seven or more years felt most unloved by God and that God was of little help to them. The tendency was for increasing length of hospitalization to associate with a shift from religious interest to concern about oneself. Still, those longest in the hospital felt that religion could help bring about personal improvement, and they tended to pray most when unhappiness was greatest. Despite this potential for religion, it is felt that loss of investment in religion was part of a general pattern of withdrawal from the world as psychiatric conditions worsened.

other professionals, he used hospital chaplains as a source of information. Of 156 canvassed, only 22 percent provided useful data. Crude population estimates for the professionals were made, and it was concluded that clergy tended to be underrepresented in mental hospitals. There can be little doubt that these findings and inferences are overgeneralizations from small, biased samples, and that much basic information on diagnosis, class level, age, ethnic group, etc., were lacking.

Although we lack solid data comparing clergy and other professionals, and even with the general population, psychological difficulties can motivate disturbed persons to seek the clerical life as an outlet for their emotional problems.

RELIGION AS A SOCIALIZING AND SUPPRESSING AGENT

Just as religion may function as an expression of disorder, it also may operate to reduce mental disturbance through the way it controls and channels behavior into acceptable avenues. Churchgoers are likely to be more socially conservative, conforming, and acquiescent than their less religious counterparts (Adorno et al., 1950; Fisher, 1964; Glock and Stark, 1965; 1966; Herberg, 1960; Photiadis, 1965). There is also evidence that being reared in a religious home means that undesirable emotional expressions will be suppressed, particularly if these involve anger and aggression (Bateman and Jensen, 1958).

Religion as an Environment of Social Control

The foregoing tendencies actually describe many characteristics of a religious environment. Church members and religionists represent the conventional mainstream of American life. Persons who are mentally deviant, through their contacts and associations with conforming viewpoints, may come to accept these outlooks and respond accordingly. Social disapproval is a strong shaper of thinking and behavior, and one's family, friends, and neighbors can offer both the affectional support and interpersonal directions and controls that aid persons to "fit in," be "one of the folks," and not "rock the boat."

In other words, the religious community offers a learning environment that can direct abnormal thinking and actions into acceptable channels. Although one's fellows are the socializing and suppressing agents through which approved social values and responses are mediated, the doctrines and tenets of religious systems function similarly. These could be the factors underlying the findings of Rohrbaugh and Jessor (1975) that the more religious a person is, the greater the likelihood he/she will possess good impulse controls. Concurrently, there was less probability of evidencing either deviant behavior or tendencies.

Recent work by McDonald and Luckett (1983) suggests that the forms of maladaptive behavior demonstrated by mainline Protestants could reflect the strong socialization tendencies that might be expected in this core American group. These homes may impart overly strong and repressive personal controls to their members, forcing them to reference themselves to ideal expectations rather than the necessities of coping with reality. There are implications this may also be true for cult members. Ross (1983) found that the adjustment of Hare Krishna members improved the longer they were associated with this group, implying the possibility that the social controls exercised by this cult constitute a constructive learning environment for its adherents.

There are also indications that the environment of a socioreligious group can suppress undesirable behavior, especially relative to drinking and alcoholism. Among Jews, as one goes from reform to orthodox groups, intoxication reduces (Snyder, 1962). The more orthodox and traditional a Jewish home is, the more the time and place for drinking alcohol is circumscribed by religious ritual (Bales, 1962). As might be expected, social drinking increases to the extent Jews identify with the values of modern American society (Snyder, 1964).

A similar social control view has been advanced by Linden and Currie (1977) to account for their observation that adolescent and young adult drug usage declines as religious activity increases. They perceive the important inhibiting influence to be association with conventional, church-oriented persons.

The Control Functions of Religious Doctrine

Disturbed persons may find much satisfaction within religious institutions and their doctrines. Pruyser (1971) cites Freud to the effect that religion is "a perennial form of wish fulfillment and need gratification. . . (it) is not strict enough in demanding renunciation of infantile wishes; on the contrary, it condones them by symbolic satisfactions" (p. 79). Thus, deviance may gain support and find an outlet through socially admissable channels.

Institutionalized religion lives by rules—formal and informal ones. The Ten Commandments, the Golden Rule, various creeds and doctrinal regulations defining the qualities of a "good Jew" or a "good Christian" exert pressure for conformity in thought and behavior. Backed by images of God's love, mercy, or vengeance, they can be taken very seriously, even by disordered individuals. When internalized, or even if looked upon as external restraints, they may act as very effective suppressors and socializing forces.

The argument has been advanced that even in severe disorder, religiosity may prevent worse things from occurring. In one instance, we read, "occasional religiosity in paranoid schizophrenia might itself be a mechanism to control underlying hostility and aggressive behavior" (McDonald and Luckett, p. 33).

No clearer example of the role of doctrine can be found than the relationship between suicide, and the negativity with which such actions are regarded by Western churches. Dublin (1963) claims "suicide . . . is infrequent where the guidance and authority of religion are accepted without question, where the church forms the background of communal life, and where duties are rigidly prescribed" (p. 74). The faith usually alluded to in this work is Roman Catholicism, although Greek Orthodoxy and orthodox Judaism hold a similar position. Countries in which these religions dominate tend to show the lowest suicide rates (Dublin, 1963; Durkheim, 1951). The incidence of suicide for Protestants has usually been two to three times higher than that observed for Jews and Catholics (Argyle, 1959).

Gibbs (1966) implies that other social factors influence variation in the suicide rates of various religious groups. We might further suggest that a religious climate which regards suicide with extreme disapproval is likely to produce civil authorities and physicians who are unwilling to define a death as suicide unless the evidence is unquestionable.

There are both historical and contemporary examples of religious control that raise questions about the extremes to which such groups may go. Most might lament the mass suicide at Masada in 73 A.D., when a group of Zealots in their quest for freedom left only their deaths to greet the Roman conquerors. The situation seems radically different with the mass suicide of those in the Jim Jones' People's Temple Movement, where social-religious control appears to have resulted from the megalomania of its leader (Levi, 1982).

Religious Role Models

Research reveals the importance of exemplars of desired behavior (Bandura, 1971; 1972; 1977). One learns by observing others; others serve as "models" both from what we observe in daily life and symbolically through communications about their performance. Ministers, priests, rabbis, biblical heroes and heroines, Jesus and his apostles, religious martyrs and other significant spiritual figures stand as sanctified models to be admired and emulated. They may therefore serve as influential referents for some mentally disturbed persons. As Bandura (1977) affirms, "models . . . teach novel styles of thought and conduct. Modeling influences can strengthen or weaken inhibitions over behavior" (p. 49).

The Complexity of Religious Control Relationships

Generally, religious activity is associated with fewer expressions of deviant behavior. Stark (1971) shows that mentally disturbed persons who reside in a community assign less personal importance to religion and are also less likely to be religiously active than a comparable group of ordinary citizens. He also feels that "psychopathology seems to *impede* the manifestation of conventional religious beliefs and activities" (p. 175). This is one interpretation; however, it can be argued that these deviants may be so disturbed that they tend to be rejected by most congregants. They might also attribute to themselves such negative qualities that they cannot accept the sympathetic views that religious doctrines promulgate (Benson and Spilka, 1973).

Self-concept theory suggests that one's views of the self correspond to similar outlooks toward the world; hence, negative self-attributions should affiliate with negative images of the deity, and there is support for this expectation (Benson and Spilka, 1973). Since unfavorable self-attributions are commonly associated with psychological problems, parallel antithetic feelings toward religion might in some instances prevent these persons from benefiting from the positive control aspects of institutionalized faith. In other cases, negative, threatening, punitive God images might serve to restrict many very undesirable expressions of abnormality.

This double role for the self overlaps with the multiform causation perspective of Jensen and Erickson (1979) who note reductions of drug use and delinquency with an increase in church participation. These researchers point to the strictness of denominational attitudes along with the models and controls set by co-religionists and clergy as factors mitigating these forms of deviance.

From a number of vantage points, religious systems and their adherents can suppress abnormal thinking and behavior and aid disturbed persons to become better integrated into the larger social community and also enhance their own internal organization. The fundamental consideration here is that adherence to mainline religion means adherence to the dominant values and norms of our culture, and therefore less deviance and abnormality. A poignant example of this is shown in Research Box 12-2

RELIGION AS A HAVEN

Religion may provide disturbed individuals with a refuge from the *sturm and drang* of life, a safe harbor from the turmoil of living. This can take place in three ways: First, daily existence may be directed and controlled; second, social acceptance into a religious group might alleviate fears of isolation and rejection; and third, strong identification with one's faith endows that person with the perceived security of divine protection.

Deviant Groups and Practices

In terms of social inclusion into a body of spiritually like-minded people, Kildahl (1972) refers to the fellowship of glossolalics he studied as exhibiting "a tremendous openness, concern, and care for one another . . . they bore each

RESEARCH BOX 12-2: *Stark, R., "Psychopathology and Religious Commitment,"* Journal for the Scientific Study of Religion, *1971, 12, 165–176*

Utilizing the theory that conventional religious commitment is necessarily opposed to unconventional, deviant thinking and behavior, the author hypothesized a negative relationship between the two variables. In other words, low psychopathology should relate to high religious commitment. One hundred mentally disturbed persons were carefully matched with 100 normal controls and compared on a number of religious indicators. The results were as follows:

	MENTALLY ILL	MATCHED CONTROLS
Percent claiming no religious affiliation	16	3
Percent saying "religion not important at all"	16	4
Percent not belonging to a church	54	40
Percent never attending church	21	5

In all instances, the hypothesis was confirmed as the mentally disturbed persons showed significantly less conventional religious involvement than did the normal controls. In another aspect of this study, indices of psychic inadequacy and neurotic distrust were constructed. Comparisons of Protestant and Catholics in a national sample revealed that those low in these undesirable characteristics were significantly more likely to be religiously orthodox and frequent church attenders than those with high scores. Conventional religiousness is therefore opposed to mental disturbance.

other's burdens . . . were with each other in spirit and in physical presence'' (p. 84). Such an atmosphere must be extremely gratifying to the person who knows his or her deviant behavior and thinking might result in social ostracism.

One study of Jehovah's Witnesses concluded that their rate of schizophrenia was three to four times higher than that for the general population (Spencer, 1975). This is a conservative religious group with a long history. It exists on the fringes of mainline American religion and may appeal to disturbed persons desiring to participate in an ultra-traditional spiritual community with an extremely strict moral code. Such controls may offer some protection to the member from the stresses and temptations of life.

Deviant religious movements frequently attract mentally alienated and distressed persons. Deutsch (1980) observes that the tenacity of attachment to a cult leader can reflect emotional immaturity and child-like dependency needs. The bizarre behavior of some of the founders of these groups may fascinate individuals whose reality contacts are weak. One study of the Unification Church, "the Moonies," revealed that about four in ten members admitted severe mental difficulties prior to joining the church. Thirty percent sought professional help and six percent had been hospitalized (Galanter, Rabkin, Rabkin, and Deutsch, 1979).

Among the more common forms of deviance manifested prior to membership in these groups are severe drug problems, alcoholism, prostitution, and criminal activity (Galanter et al., 1979; Judah, 1974; Snelling and Whitley, 1974). In Judah's study of Hare Krishna devotees, 85 percent had employed LSD and 17 percent had used heroin prior to their entering the movement (Judah, 1974).

The search for a spiritual haven is not easy. Especially among the cults and sects, mentally deviant persons are likely to move easily from one such group to another; hence, affiliation tends to be unstable (Judah, 1977; Kanter, 1972). There is some indication that shifts in commitment increase with severity of neurotic distress (Galanter et al., 1979).

Although we cite evidence on the correlation of abnormality with membership in "fringe" religious groups, it is necessary to qualify this position. Most members of these bodies are psychologically quite normal, and such factors as social circumstances and economic status influence the probability of joining these movements (Clark, 1949; McLoughlin, 1978; Sasaki, 1979; Wood, 1965).

Religious Communities

Earlier we noted Finch's view that disturbed persons might feel they belong in a religious vocation (Finch, 1965). This view is confirmed by Kelley (1958), who concludes that the religious life attracts candidates liable to have psychiatric difficulties rather than causing such problems. Although she felt that Catholic nuns in teaching orders are under much stress, her work (Kelley, 1961) demonstrated that teaching nuns had lower rates for mental hospitalization than cloistered sisters. The incidence among nuns who performed domestic functions was over seven times higher than for teachers. Psychosis affected some 80 percent of those confined to mental institutions, 65 percent of whom were diagnosed as schizophrenic. Depressive symptoms were, however, quite common. Kelley hypothesized that the highly structured life of these religious communities of women may lead to feelings of failure to live up to the demands of their circumstances. These in turn generate a sense of inadequacy and guilt that results in depression.

Jahreiss (1942) and Kurth (1961) also observed high rates of severe disturbance among nuns, and again more abnormality was found in the cloistered orders than in the active ones. Kurth suggests two factors produce this situation. First, "many mentally ill individuals seek to enter religious life. Such neurotic and pre-psychotic individuals are especially attracted to cloistered life which, by its nature, caters to the needs of schizoid individuals" (p. 20). Second, Kurth claims "that too many Superiors of convents in the United States think that all their candidates are psychologically sound and enjoy good mental health" (p. 23). As we will shortly see, seeking such a haven often exacerbates the problem of mental disorder among the vulnerable.

The Hutterites

One of the most significant studies on religion and mental disorder was carried out by Eaton and Weil (1955), who studied the Hutterites. This is a relatively isolated Anabaptist sect whose communities are scattered throughout the Dakotas, Montana, and adjacent Canadian provinces. Originating in central Europe in the sixteenth-century and primarily of German and Swiss extraction, these people came to North America in the 1870s. Their Bible-centered faith stresses brotherly love and communal ownership of property. Life is tightly circumscribed at every turn from birth to death. The question is asked if such a supportive, controlling atmosphere into which members are born rather than converted will evidence low rates of neurosis and psychosis. Even if a person shows signs of disturbance, the community provides a loving and therapeutic climate in the hope of returning the individual to a productive life.

The expectations of Eaton and Weil for low rates of abnormality were only partially borne out. The incidence of the lesser neurotic conditions does appear quite low, but for the more severe psychotic disorders the opposite is true. It is theorized that the protective social milieu reduces extreme antisocial or aggressive symptoms while stimulating guilt and depression because of failure to live up to expectations. One could argue that four centuries of relative isolation may have increased the potential of organic and genetic bases for the more severe mental conditions. The stress of meeting the demands of such a structured life could also aggravate underlying psychotic pathology, while channeling neurotic forms into acceptable expressions. These communities seem to perform better as refuges for the less seriously distressed than their more seriously affected co-religionists.

Churches and religious communities may offer disturbed persons some degree of security and safety in a threatening world. The effectiveness of such shelter is highly variable and often not very effective. In many instances, the system may act as a shield for a limited time. Some abnormal individuals may even be able to match their condition with the requirements of their spiritual circumstances.

RELIGION AS THERAPY

The suppression-socialization functions of religion may well work to improve the individual's mental state; however, a number of religious activities can be *actively* therapeutic and result in major benefits to troubled people. Among these possibilities are intense religious experience, glossolalia, conversion, and prayer.

Intense Religious Experience

Anton Boisen, whose life was a mixture of deep religious experiences and profound mental disorder, makes the point that "a psychotic experience in itself is a religious experience" (Overholser, 1963; p. 100). He further claims that mystical experiences are attempts to deal with threats to the integrity of the personality and usually follow times of intense distress. The outcome is often a constructive reorganization of the self and attitudes toward the world (Boisen, 1952). Maslow (1964) talks similarly of mystical encounters as "peak-experiences" in which "the world . . . is seen only as beautiful, good, desirable, worthwhile, etc., and is never experienced as evil or undesirable" (p. 63). This enthusiasm strongly overstates the case, for there are many tales of mystical encounters that are terrifying and distressing (Brown, Spilka, and Cassidy, 1978; Greeley, 1974; Leuba, 1925; Stark, 1965).

The overall view is that these experiences are beneficial, and that good and bad experiences may be distinguishable on the basis of their components. Initial evidence suggests that instances in which feelings of joy, peace, enlightenment, and unity prevail seem to have favorable outcomes (Greeley, 1974; 1975; Jackson and Spilka, 1980).

The therapeutic effects of mystical experience run the gamut from simple expressions of well-being to radical changes in outlook and behavior. Trew (1971) points to reductions in guilt feelings, and a heightened sense of security and belonging. Hartocollis (1976) regards these occurrences as efforts to control one's aggressive tendencies. Since the turning in of such impulses has been claimed by clinicians to be a cause of suicide, it is not surprising that mystical happenings have been regarded as preventives for suicide and loneliness (Horton, 1973).

Drug-induced religious experience also seems to have beneficial effects with alcoholics, narcotic addicts, neurotics, and terminal cancer patients (Clark, 1968; Pahnke, 1969). Clark (1968) feels these effects are enhanced when the experience is defined by the person as having a religious character. Hine (1969) suggests that the encouragement of extreme mystical experiences in Pentecostal sects generally aids adjustment and may help integrate these people into their group and provide a more supportive social environment.

Glossolalia

Glossolalia also appears to act therapeutically. Kildahl (1972) reports a heightened sense of well-being, improved social sensitivity and concern, and a religious maturing following a tongue-speaking experience. Hutch (1980) similarly speaks of "a deepening of the spiritual dimension of human existence" from glossolalia (p. 265). More to the psychological state of the person, Kelsey (1968) sees tongue-speaking as an effort to resolve neurotic conflicts. The research of Lovekin and Malony (1977) failed to support any of these claims, suggesting a need for further study.

Overviewing the area, Pattison (1968) examines glossolalia from a number of perspectives, a major one of which is as a therapeutic way of reducing anxiety and tension. Obviously definitive answers are not yet available, but the weight of thinking and data affirm glossolalia as beneficial to its practitioners.

Conversion

The therapeutic qualities of religious conversion have been eulogized for centuries. Descriptive phrases such as "new birth," "the unification of character, the achievement of a new self" (Pratt, 1920; p. 123) speak to hopes of personal growth and betterment. These are the goals of therapy, and the stories of converts glow in the replacement of grief and unhappiness with joy and peace.

When we discussed conversion as an expression of mental disorder, emphasis was placed upon the radical, sudden, and often superficial conversion. In this section, we emphasize what Pratt (1920) called *volitional* conversion Clark (1929), *the gradual awakening,* and what Salzman (1953; 1969) identified as *progressive* or *maturational*. Most converts appear to have had this kind of experience.

Potentially constructive conversion is seen as an active striving "to create and maintain orderliness and meaningfulness" (Strauss, 1979; p. 161). It is also often regarded a collective process in which the seeker is allied with others of similar outlook. The image of a passive individual waiting for divine intervention is rejected as the careers of converts attest to their deep involvement in religious-social interactions.

A major difficulty in research on conversion is that information is gathered after the conversion has taken place. In some instances, objective data are available for the time prior to the conversion, but this is more the exception than the rule. People distort memories to keep them in line with present feelings (Bem and McConnell, 1970). In other words, if a person has converted, the tendency would be to contrast pre- and post-conversion times, usually to make the earlier period appear negative in the light of current outlooks.

A number of scholars working with mentally disturbed persons who have had conversion experiences point out that these may have good or bad repercussions (Bergman, 1953; Gallemore et al., 1969). The latter are usually rigid, inadequate, and bizarre spiritual expressions that reflect fear, confusion, guilt, and depression among other possibilities. On the positive side, there are indications of increased openness, extravertive tendencies, emotional responsivity, improved health and greater happiness, conflict resolution, and productive identity formation (Bragan, 1977; Gallemore et al., 1963; Gordon, 1964; Johnson, 1959; Shaver, Lenauer, and Sadd, 1980). Greater control of abnormal sexual impulses has also been reported (Cesarman, 1957). Conversion among Mexican-Americans from Catholicism to Protestantism has been associated with a shift in values toward success and achievement through the avenues approved in mainstream American society (Bronson, 1966).

Conversion can clearly exercise a therapeutic effect on those who undergo this experience. The gradual, progressive-maturational form is apparently most likely to demonstrate the improvement in personal behavior that one hopes will result from effective therapy.

A final note is in order. The foregoing therapeutic effects of conversion are not restricted to entry into a religious body associated with the mainstream of the Judeo-Christian tradition. They have also been found to hold true for sects such as the Unification Church and the Hare Krishna (Galanter, 1982; Ross, 1983). An example of this may be seen in Research Box 12-3.

Prayer

In a 1978 national sample, 89 percent of the respondents indicated that they pray (Gallup and Poling, 1980); over half admit to daily prayer (Greeley, 1979). If practice is premised on belief, it is apparent that most Americans attribute efficacy to prayer. Heiler (1932) views it as the most personal of religious acts, suggesting that its underlying motive is "to fortify, to reinforce, to enhance one's life" (p. 355). Such a widespread and deeply meaningful behavior may have considerable therapeutic potential. It is therefore surprising that extremely little research has been undertaken to assess this likelihood. The point is well made, however, by Clark (1958) who sees it "as an inexpensive substitute for the psychiatrist's couch" (p. 324).

The fundamental element in prayer is that the person believes he/she has a direct line to the deity, and that God is likely to notice this supplication, allegiance and praise, and will respond accordingly. The hoped-for result is often protection and forgiveness, but subjective well-being and a sense of personal control and strength are important concomitants.

According to psychiatrist Kenneth Appel (1959), prayer performs a personality-integrative role. Kidorf (1966) notes that the Shiva, a collective Jewish

RESEARCH BOX 12-3:   *Galanter, M.; Rabkin, R.; Rabkin, J.; and Deutsch, A. "The 'Moonies': A Psychological Study of Conversion and Membership in a Contemporary Religious Sect," American Journal of Psychiatry, 1979, 136, 165–170.*

The purpose of this study was to understand the mental state of members of a charismatic religious group relative to their conversion and continuation of membership. The sample consisted of 237 members of the Unification Church and 305 comparison persons from a national sample who had taken one of the measures. A 216-item questionnaire provided demographic information plus scores for neurotic distress, general well-being, and intensity of religious commitment.

There were strong indications that the converts tended to experience psychological problems prior to joining the church, and over a third either sought help or were hospitalized (36 percent). Following conversion, there was a noteworthy decline in neurotic distress. This related to marked increases in religiosity. General well-being and a lessening of symptoms was associated with increases in religiosity. Despite these changes, the converts scored lower in general well-being than the comparison group. Continued membership was also affiliated with apparent improvement in religiosity and personal outlooks. This study suggests the benefits of conversion, even to religious groups outside of the mainstream of American religion.

mourning ceremony, should be regarded as a form of group therapy. Johnson (1953) suggests that loneliness and conflict tend to be reduced, especially if prayer occurs in a public situation where others are similarly involved.

Although prayer is probably most significant for its role in crisis, its utilization during times of stress varies widely by religious group. In one study, 78 percent of Baptists acknowledged its use while only one percent of Jews acted similarly (McCann, 1962). Welford (1947a, 1947b) noted an increase in prayer with frustration and regarded it as an effort to cope with a trying situation rather than an attempt to escape reality.

The idea that there are "no atheists in foxholes" implies that danger in battle will arouse religious feelings. Soldiers have reported that they felt that praying was beneficial in these circumstances (Stouffer et al., 1949). Generally in death-related situations, there is also evidence that the incidence of prayer increases and helps the bereaved cope with loss (Loveland, 1968).

Prayer clearly operates as therapy for many people. It is noteworthy that praying for help is considered quite appropriate from childhood on; however, the belief that these efforts are objectively efficacious seems to reduce regularly with increasing age (Brown, 1966; 1968).

Other Therapeutic Possibilities in Religion

Oates (1970) claims that religious practice and activities in a mental institution aid the therapeutic process by enhancing communication and reducing separation and isolation among the patients and staff. Stoudenmire (1976) discusses the utility of religion and clergy to counter guilt and depression in housewives.

Propst (1980) employed a religious imagery technique with fairly religious, mildly depressed persons and found that it increased group interaction, a necessary adjunct to lessening a depressive outlook. Many similar illustrations can be offered where a person's religious commitment can be employed in pastoral counseling to aid that individual to cope successfuly with reality and improve adjustment skills.

A final comment might be made about a practice that is widespread in various groups—namely, confession. Both private and public confession can be used to gain a sense of forgiveness and to make a commitment for constructive behavioral change (Boisen, 1958; Mowrer, 1961). The basic idea is that one may acquire considerable internal strength from identification with a spiritual framework. In other chapters, it is also shown how religion may contribute to the mental well-being of the individual.

RELIGION AS A HAZARD

Unhappily, all is not psychologically sound and beneficial in our religious institutions and their doctrines, and Chesen (1972) says so bluntly in his book, *Religion May Be Hazardous To Your Health.* Pruyser (1977), in like manner, refers to "The seamy side of current religious beliefs." The message is simply that religion contains elements that can adversely affect the mental well-being of its adherents.

Religion as a Source of Abnormal Mental Content

Pathological religious mental content can seriously inhibit the efforts of therapists to deal with the real causes of mental disorder. Identification with "higher powers" aids rejection of reality and potential helpers may be regarded as "lesser beings." Southard (1956) illustrates these possibilities in his examples of persons "possessed by the Holy Ghost," or, who receive "messages from God." In another case, the singing of religious hymns appears to have helped a patient keep out of contact with reality. Spiritual expressions, because of their deep roots in our cultural order, can effectively inhibit therapeutic intervention.

Some religious activities may become substitutes for dealing with life. Some years ago, a sign was frequently attached to taxicabs and buses in many cities. Its advice was "Go to church and leave your troubles there." Recourse to prayer may indeed be very personally gratifying, but if it replaces appropriate and necessary action, its spiritual function has been distorted and may constitute a serious psychological problem. In like manner, the meanings attached to religious symbols can reflect magical thinking suggestive of mental pathology. Obviously, religion can supply a fair amount of content for use by disturbed people, and thus may support deviance.

Religion as a Source of Abnormal Motives

O'Connell (1961) asks, "Is mental illness a result of sin?" He concludes that it is not. The situation is, however, far more complex than a simple yes or no can convey. The sense of guilt promulgated by various faiths acts as a very powerful motive for disordered thinking and behavior. Obsession with sin is to be expected when a system emphasizes moral perfection (Miller, 1973). Personal attempts to assuage feelings of wrongdoing or to make up for religiously disapproved thoughts and actions have been associated with disturbed forms of mysticism, conversion, prayer, confession, bizarre rituals, self-denial, and torture (Clark, 1958; Cutten, 1908; James, 1902).

The admiration usually afforded saints must pale at the sin-countering efforts of some of these heroic figures. McGinley (1969) cites examples of brutal and painful masochism that abound in this literature. The expungement of sin with its concomitant reduction in guilt are extremely significant religious motives. Unhappily, the potential of serious pathology resulting from these needs may be considerable.

A powerful church that claims subservience to the domination of God has to foster dependency in its followers. Individual variation and innovation is a threat to the institution and is likely to be suppressed by the authorities. Among the devices still used to keep people in line are tales of "God's wrath," Job's misery and affliction, and threats of ultimate punishment. The arousal of unquestioning allegiance requires a suspension of critical reasoning and the substitution of what Pruyser (1977) calls "unbridled and untutored fantasy" (p. 333-34). Primitive thinking plus the arousal of "infantile wishes" are seen by those of psychoanalytic inclination as central themes in all religion. "Blind faith" clearly demands an almost childish lack of realism for its maintenance. The desire for an obedient followership is also likely to stimulate immature, unrealistic thinking. The outcome may be as tragic as the mass suicide of the People's Temple group in Guyana.

Religious institutions and their adherents benefit from what Pruyser (1977) terms "sacrifice of intellect" (p. 332). The simplification of complex issues and the sponsorship of polarized thinking into an either-or framework permits the psychological mechanism of denial to operate more easily. Awareness of reality is reduced and elemental phrases such as "God works in mysterious ways" find a ready audience. Authoritarian pronouncements are taken at face value and piety may become so personally restricted that social sensitivity is dulled. Humanitarian sentiments are opposed by a stress on personal devotion. Crime, evil, wrongdoing, and misery tend to be ignored, and faith becomes socially blind. In a troubled world, this could reflect a disordered intellect.

There is much potential in religion for creating mental aberration. The attachment of religious doctrines and symbols to movements such as the Inquisition of the Middle Ages or contemporary hate groups such as the Ku Klux Klan further show how easily faith can be deformed. In such instances, the dividing line between individual pathology and normality may become quite tenuous.

RELIGION AND SPECIFIC FORMS OF MENTAL DISORDER

We have seen that religion can express, suppress, produce, hide, and counter psychological disturbance. In addition, since most research has looked at specific forms of abnormality and the place of religion in their dynamics, additional insights may be gained by examining some of these findings.

A CAUTION ON CONFOUNDING FACTORS: THE "HIDDEN" INFLUENCE OF SOCIOECONOMIC STATUS

First, more words of caution need to be offered. In studies relating religion and mental disorder, other factors of considerable importance may be hidden behind the scenes. One of the most frequent of these "hidden" variables is socioeconomic status, and we will now use it to illustrate the possible influence of such factors in the research with which we are concerned.

The sociology of religion tells us that American religious groups are not socioeconomically equivalent. Episcopalians, Presbyterians, and Jews tend to be rather high on the class ladder. Catholics, Pentecostal sects, and Baptist bodies group toward the lower end of the economic distribution (Chalfant, Beckley, and Palmer, 1981; Demerath, 1965; Lazerwitz, 1964; Pope, 1948; Schneider, 1964; Stark and Glock, 1968). We also know that church attendance and religiosity vary with class level and tend to increase as one goes up in class status (Demerath, 1965). Recent national polls show that this trend may be present for only some churches (Chalfant, Beckley, and Palmer, 1981).

Relating these facts to rates for mental disorder is very difficult, as much of the research distinguishes samples by religion in the crudest way (Hollingshead and Redlich, 1958; Malzberg, 1973; Roberts and Myers, 1954; Rose and Stub, 1955; Srole et al., 1962). An illustration is provided by Malzberg (1973) in which first admissions for mental disorders are classified religiously for Protestants, Roman Catholics, Jews, and Other. With the category of "Other" totally undefined, we may be less informed with this "information" than without it.

The plot thickens further when we observe that the incidence of serious disorder decreases as one goes up the class ladder (Dohrenwend and Dohrenwend, 1969; Hollinghead and Redlich, 1958; Srole et al., 1962). This finding is rapidly complicated by evidence that clinicians assign more severe diagnoses the lower the class level of the patient (Hollingshead and Redlich, 1958). In addition, some groups such as Jews are more sensitive to the meaning of mental disturbance and seek aid faster than members of other religious bodies. It is also likely that persons from religions in the upper economic classes will not show up in reports on mental pathology, because they often resort to private practitioners, and outpatient therapy. In all of this work, very little is known about the degree of religious commitment of those affected.

Research on religion and abnormality frequently employs psychological tests to establish diagnoses. Unhappily, many of these instruments are biased so that deviation from a middle-class background increases the probability of giving abnormal responses (Auld, 1952). This is especially true for religious persons from lower-class backgrounds. Such may also be implied by the tendency of people to respond to psychological tests with socially approved and desirable answers rather than the truth (Berg, 1967; Edwards, 1957). The more conventional and conforming a person is, the more that individual may avoid giving responses considered deviant by middle-class standards. Crandall (1966) even found that the more religious children are, the greater their tendency to respond in a socially desirable manner. A similar finding was reported by Mayo, Puryear, and Richek

(1969) for religious males only, who seemed quite concerned with presenting socially approved images of themselves.

We need to ask if this may be the reason that Catholics express more externally directed hostility than Protestants (Brown, 1965) on a measure shown
to possess possible class bias (Roberts and Jessor, 1958). A recent study also reveals
that the greater the religious involvement, the less likely one will report emotional
difficulties (Ness and Wintrob, 1980). We might also ask if clerics who break down
are of the same class level as those who do not show signs of abnormality. Since
Mexican-American Catholics who convert to Protestantism possess views in line
with American middle-class values (Bronson, 1966; Bronson and Meadow, 1968),
this might imply that such converts react better to personality tests than their
counterparts who remain Catholic.

Religion as suppression and socialization seems to reflect middle-class leanings, so people who control deviant tendencies and remain in religious settings
are possibly more middle-class in outlook than those who cannot make such adjust-
ments. In contrast, religion as an expression of mental disorder or as a haven
and refuge could be more the lot of lower economic status persons.

Socioeconomic factors may lie behind the scenes in much work relating
religion and mental disorder. Other factors such as sex, age, and ethnic group
can also act as unstudied and unanalyzed variables in much of this research. Consider these possibilities in a critical way when you read the research discussed
in this volume.

Religion and Personality Adequacy

Psychologists try to comprehend factors in the background of the individual
which predispose one to later difficulties and possibly severe breakdown. Attention is usually first directed at environmental influences—home, community, social
life, etc. One weakness of this work is that the reseach examines the process of
coping and adjustment when it is often well along, and often after a disorder has
developed. Although many problems plague this literature, some insight may be
gained on the place of religion in this process plus some of the shortcomings and
needs of this work.

There are no nice, clean dividing lines that distinguish persons whose coping effectiveness and personalities may be said to be truly outstanding, the great
majority who are described as normal, and those regarded as emotionally
disordered people. The problem is still troublesome when distinctions are made
between the severely afflicted and normals, in part because many of the former
show their disturbed thinking and behavior in some but not all situations.

The real problem concerns a gradual shading of essentially normal
ineffectiveness and inadequacy into the conditions defined as neuroses. Here we
are dealing with chronic maladjustments, difficulties involving anxiety, feelings
of inferiority, and efforts to escape the ordinary habitual frustrations of life with
which most people cope successfully. They are usually not severe enough to prevent the person from living and working outside of a mental-care facility, but
are enough of a problem to keep those affected from being personally integrated,
effective, and happy.

Estimates of the number of such people vary widely. One source suggests
the United States has twenty million neurotics (Coleman, Butcher and Carson,

1980). A noted research project (Srole et al., 1962) claimed that only 18.5 percent of a New York sample could be called well. Some 58 percent were classified as having mild to moderate symptoms of disorder, while 23 percent demonstrated severe impairment. For our purposes, we will consider together mild and moderate adjustment and coping problems and also include under this rubric indications of neuroticism.

Personality Adequacy and the Religious Context

The principal contemporary position on personality disorder emphasizes the social circumstances within which it develops. A well-known source of stress for the individual occurs when that person or his/her group exists in a setting dominated by peoples with different expectations and values. Rosenberg (1962) refers to this as contextual dissonance. He observes that children who are reared in a dissonant religious content—meaning that their faith is not that of the dominant community—are likely to evidence low self-esteem, anxiety, depressive outlooks, and emotional disturbance. One could infer that this situation is crucial to the extent that religion is an important part of the cultural context. If it is of little consequence, its effect should be minimal.

Probably the major instance of a religious minority in the Western world is the case of the Jews. Victims of persecution for almost 2,000 years, if a group has ever lived in a dissonant religious context, it is this people. Rosenberg's findings of the association of disturbance and such dissonance should be evident with this group, and there are signs that it is. Fernando (1975) studied the backgrounds of Jewish and Protestant depressives and found that religiosity was correlated with depression among the Jews but not among the Protestants. He concludes that the marginal position of Jews is a mental stressor that contributes to the development of emotional problems. Argyle (1959) and Srole and Langner (1962) confirm a higher incidence of neuroticism among Jews than Christians, but less serious impairment. Long conditioning to bigotry and discrimination could also act as an immunizing force against severe abnormality—hence, the lower rates of extreme mental conditions for Jews (Becker, 1971; Srole and Langner, 1962).

Studies are not clear on whether distressed persons seek out deviant and minority religious groups or develop their problems as a result of contextual dissonance. Probably both factors enter the process; however, when the individual has been a life-long participant in such a faith and then develops a disorder, dissonance might be a contributor. When affiliation occurs in adolescence or adulthood, the new religion may be expressive of pre-existing emotional turmoil. There is, however, also evidence that conversion may aid adjustment (Srole et al., 1962).

Personality Adequacy and Religion in the Home

One of the great research gaps in the literature on religion and mental disorder concerns the nature of faith in the family setting and the development of emotional difficulties. Although an immense amount of writing and research has been offered on early home environment and mental pathology, religion rarely enters the picture.

General theory regarding disorder suggests that emotional deprivation in childhood or the presence of mentally deviant parents is likely to result in abnormality in children (Benda, 1969; Mishler and Waxler, 1968). In other words, non-normal, child-parent interactions may be the culprit. McAllister (1969) supports such a conclusion in an isolated study of the disturbed members of religious communities. Among these troubled clergy, he found sexual confusion from possibly too much identification with the parent of the opposite sex. Furthermore, mothers were the dominant figures in 91 percent of these homes and in 86 percent, one parent demonstrated psychiatric symptoms.

The higher rates for the less severe conditions found among Jews also provides some support for the emotional deprivation hypothesis. A noted study on child-rearing practices by Sears, Maccoby, and Levin (157) claimed that Jewish working-class mothers tend to be emotionally colder than their Christian counterparts. The combination of lower status and lack of warmth would fit in with expectations regarding the development of coping and adjustment difficulties.

Kurokawa (1969), who worked with traditional and acculturating Mennonite families, also offers some information on potential disorder and emotional deprivation and conflict. Feelings of adequacy and freedom were present in these children to the extent that their mothers might be said to be progressive rather than traditional and authoritarian.

Another study on Catholic, Protestant, and Jewish children's expressions of aggression in fantasy claimed that the restrictive socialization practices of Catholic parents result in a "defensive avoidance of aggression in fantasy among these children (Lesser, 1959; p. 67). Higher anxiety was also present in the Catholic sample. Unfortunately, no direct investigation of how these observations relate to actual parental practices was undertaken, nor were such distinctively associated with religion. The likelihood of ethnic and class factors influencing this work might be considerable.

There are a few studies that assess the view people have of their families in relation to religion, and the results suggest a beneficial effect. Believers perceive their parents as more accepting and holding positive values. These families are characterized as happier and as interacting better than are those of nonreligious individuals (Brown and Lowe, 1951; Johnson, 1973).

As noted, research relating religion, home environment, and personality adequacy or mental disorder is extremely sparse and often anecdotal. For example, we read that many theological students desire to become ministers because of shortcomings in their early relationships with parents. They are said to seek a protective, loving father, something implied as lacking in their childhood (Academy of Religion and Mental Health, 1960). Positive God-images are, however, said to result from a happy early home life, but objective data regarding these inferences is lacking. The fundamental elements of theory are present, and a few timorous steps toward a research understanding have been made (Stewart, 1967). It is not an understatement to say that this area constitutes one of the great unexplored regions in the psychology of religion.

Religion and Personality: Correlative Studies

Although we lack research on casual relationships between religion and personality, there is no dearth of efforts to find correlates of religious beliefs and behavior. In many instances, a relationship is evident, but we are unable to say if the religious elements observed cause what was found or vice versa.

Considering first some of the negative findings, Dreger (1952) observed that conservative religious attitudes are found in conjunction with personality rigidity, feelings of guilt over moral transgression, emotional immaturity, and dependency needs. In another study, a sample of "healthy" Mennonites displayed similar tendencies, especially inclinations toward being guilt-ridden relative to community responsibilities plus inflexibility toward authority (Thiessen, Wright and Sisler, 1969). Primarily for Catholics, Keene (1967) sees a rigid orthodoxy and a stress on rituals to be correlates of neuroticism. Rokeach's (1960) significant research program suggests that a general concomitant of formal religious affiliation and commitment is anxiety and tension. This is in keeping with other reports of religiosity tying to less self-acceptance, more dependency, constriction, and less spontaneity of response (Graff and Ladd, 1971).

Turning over the coin of research, there are many indications that religion is related to constructive personality trends. Greater involvement in religion seems to counter feelings of powerlessness and normlessness, while concomitantly enhancing social integration (Dean, 1968; Dean and Reeves, 1962; Gladding, 1977; Lee and Clyde, 1971). Brown and Lowe (1951) also showed believers to be more optimistic, to be extroverted, and to relate better to their families than nonbelievers. Although Thiessen, Wright, and Sisler (1969) found Mennonites to be guilt-ridden, they observed that members of this body possessed a considerable sense of social responsibility to others. Wright's (1959) affirmation of an association between religion and sociability speaks to a similar regard for people, but it should be noted that this was most prevalent among liberal religious men who could admit doubt into their religious system.

A number of studies agree that religion is of definite benefit to older persons. Moberg (1956) and O'Reilly (1958), respectively including institutionalized Protestant and Catholic geriatric patients, reported that past and current religious activity was affiliated with present adjustment. Testing the hypothesis that involvement in social organizations should also relate to life satisfaction in the elderly, Cutler (1976) observed such an association only for membership in church-affiliated groups. Acuff and Gorman (1967) studied older professors and found that religious activity mitigated the distress of retirement and was generally correlated with improved adjustment.

Looking at other aspects of personal faith than activity, Funk (1955) found that religious doubt was associated with anxiety, and guilt about not living up to spiritual ideals. Flakoll (1974) focused on images of God held by a sample of junior high school students. Those who maintain loving God images show higher self-esteem and fewer signs of maladjustment, personality problems, and neurosis than their peers whose concepts of God were controlling, vindictive, distant, and stern. This work confirmed that of Benson and Spilka (1973), which attempted to determine which came first, self-esteem or God images. They concluded that self-esteem is a major contributor to the concepts of God held by religious persons. High self-esteem goes with a loving, kindly, accepting God and low self-esteem affiliates with images of an omnipotent, stern, controlling, vindictive deity. Note that these attributions have appeared a number of times in this chapter and may be central in understanding connections between religion and coping behavior. The research of Flakoll, which is presented in Research Box 12-4 illustrates both the correlational approach and self-esteem relative to God images.

RESEARCH BOX 12-4   *Flakoll, D., "Self-esteem, Psychological Adjustment and Images of God." Paper presented at the Convention of the Society for the Scientific Study of Religion, Washington, D.C., October 1974.*

The significance of self-esteem as one aspect of adjustment prompted this investigation of ties between this dimension of personality and the kind of God-images held by religious Lutheran youth. One hundred and forty male and female junior high school students in attendance at a Lutheran camp were administered an extensive battery of psychological measures to assess self-esteem and perspectives on God.

Generally, images of a loving God were affiliated with high self-esteem, while perceptions of God as stern or controlling reflected low self-esteem. In addition, signs of maladjustment, personality disorder, and even psychosis related to the holding of controlling, stern, and impersonal concepts of God. In contrast, a loving God-image opposes these tendencies.

Among religious individuals, the images of God that are held may be sensitive indicators of current or incipient mental problems. Flakoll points out how low self-esteem counters religious ideals. It can also be an expression of certain traditional negative Christian God images that may have unfortunate implications for persons whose adjustment and self-esteem is low.

We have now seen that religion relates almost equally well with evidence of both positive and negative adjustment for persons of all ages. The tale does not end here, however, for we can add the further confusion of studies that reveal no relationship between religion and personal effectiveness. For example, Hanawalt (1963) studied samples of Jewish, Catholic, and Protestant women and found that feelings of security and self-esteem were unrelated to religious beliefs. In like manner, other workers also report no meaningful relationships between religion and signs of disorder (Gurin, Veroff, and Feld, 1960; Lantz, 1949; Ranck, 1955).

Apparently, every possibility has been found relative to associations between measures of religiousness and personality adequacy. What is the real state of affairs? We submit that all of these seemingly contradictory findings may be true, as we will see when we again consider the multidimensional nature of personal faith, regarding it as more than a single and simple phenomenon.

Religion and Psychosis

There is no evidence that religious persons become psychotic more or less frequently than those considered nonreligious. While degree of spiritual commitment is unrelated to the prevalence of severe mental disorder, there are indications that religious thinking among disturbed persons is different from that of normals (Argyle, 1959; Hardt, 1963; Lowe, 1955; Reifsnyder and Campbell, 1960; Rutledge, 1951; Schofield and Balian, 1959). In pathology, religious ideas are said to be shallow, confused, and inconsistent (Reifsnyder and Campbell, 1960). Religious disorganization may be part of a broader breakdown in integration.

A number of researchers have looked at the God images of severely disturbed persons and these also appear to deviate from what is held by most people. Attributions to an unforgiving, punitive, threatening, revengeful God are commonly noted (Hardt, 1963). Very childish, immature images with parallels to one's parents have also been reported. In some instances, heterosexual or homosexual attachments to God are pictured (Matsuhashi in Summerlin, 1980; Rutledge, 1951).

As part of a massive research program on correspondences between God images and those of parents (Tamayo and St.-Arnaud, 1980) point out that schizophrenics have usually experienced abnormal relationships with their parents during childhood. The God images of these seriously disturbed people are also inconsistent and contradictory. A confused pattern of maternal and paternal elements are found with God symbolization being more maternal than paternal. These findings seem to be in line with McAllister's (1969) earlier noted conclusions about troubled cross-sex, child-parent identifications among disturbed clergy. The above observations suggest that God concepts may offer a sensitive indication of either actual or impending serious mental disorder.

In line with this view, Lowe and Braaten (1966) discovered that as certainty of belief in God increased, length of hospitalization reduced. This might suggest that resolution of emotional turmoil and a lessening of religious conflict go together. Campbell (1958) had earlier shown psychotics reveal a much higher level of religious conflict than hospitalized normals, so it is possible that severe anxiety involving religious doubts and concerns may be a contributing factor to the onset of severe mental disorder.

Estimates of the frequency of religious content in serious psychological disturbance vary widely (Argyle and Beit-Hallahmi, 1975), but the actual incidence probably ranges from 10 to 20 percent. When these elements are present, they tend to stress self-critical, guilt-ridden depression or paranoid delusions of grandeur and persecution. Where hallucinations are found they commonly take the form of messages from God, angels, or the devil, exhorting the person to carry out grandiose missions or to change one's sinful ways (Group for the Advancement of Psychiatry, 1968). A noteworthy example of these tendencies has been termed "Mennonite psychosis," which is characterized by a disturbance in reality contact, considerable emotion, and depressive and paranoid symptoms. Here the person is the victim of much self-blame, strong feelings of guilt, and paranoid delusions (Thiessen, Wright, and Sisler, 1969).

We have cited studies that show that intense religious experiences, conversion, and glossolalia may be related to severe mental disorder, but in most instances, this is not true. In addition, much work claims inordinate amounts of breakdown and extreme pathology among clergy and renowned historical religious figures, but an overview of this literature shows that the majority of clerics and saints either are or were, in their own time, quite normal, if not exceptional in a positive sense. A good illustration is provided by Argyle and Beit-Hallahmi (1975), who note:

> Joan of Arc has been diagnosed as Lesbian, transvestite, schizophrenic, paranoid, creative psychopath, hysteric and epileptic. Kenyon (1971) discusses these theories but concludes that she was basically normal, "a simple, pious girl, immature, suggestible, and she overidentified with (the) saints" (p. 136).

Rather than religion being a prime cause of mental disorder, a stronger case suggests that it makes a contribution in relatively few cases. In all likelihood, whatever the bases for disorder are, spiritual content seems to be a convenient vehicle for its expression.

As a stressor for some, especially in depression, religion can add to feelings of worthlessness, self-blame, and guilt (Andreason, 1972). Schizophrenic withdrawal from reality is also supported by much in religion, such as stories of miracles, extraordinary feats of endurance, prophetic foresight, and occurrences such as the Flood, the Tower of Babel, the destruction of Sodom and Gomorrah, and the fall of the walls of Jericho. The stuff of extreme fantasy is present for whatever selection the already disturbed person may desire to make. In most instances, the real causes of emotional breakdown appear to lie elsewhere.

MENTAL DISORDER AND FORM OF PERSONAL FAITH

When we discussed intrinsic-committed and extrinsic-consensual forms of personal faith, it was evident that the first type represents the spiritual orientation that theologians, clergy, and religious educators have valued for centuries. In contrast, the expedient, utilitarian approach of the extrinsic-consensualist runs counter to religious ideals. Research has further shown that a pattern of desirable personal and social characteristics are the lot of those who tend to be intrinsic and committed in outlook. The individual attributes of extrinsic and consensual perspectives, however, leave much to be desired. It is therefore a small theoretical step to hypothesizing that personality adequacy and mental well-being may well tie to intrinsic-committed faith, while signs of psychological distress and disorder are more likely to accompany extrinsic-consensual tendencies. The little research attempting to evaluate these possibilities clearly points in such a direction.

Considering personality adequacy along a number of dimensions, Pargament, Steele and Tyler (1979) claim that:

> Intrinsic religious motivation appears to have positive and comprehensive significance for the church/synagogue's member's self-attitudes, world-attitudes and coping skills . . . less intrinsically motivated church/synagogue members reflect a less favorable set of psychosocial competence characteristics (p. 417).

In specific, these researchers found that an intrinsic orientation related to a greater sense of control over one's life and a higher level of interpersonal trust. Working along similar lines, Wiebe and Fleck (1980) found that intrinsics demonstrated greater superego strength (stronger conscience) and emotional sensitivity than their extrinsic counterparts. In addition, feelings of powerlessness are countered by intrinsic-committed tendencies while a sense of helplessness correlates with extrinsic-consensual leanings (Minton and Spilka, 1976).

Underlying these more favorable qualities may be a spiritual dimension of religious integration and meaning which intrinsically committed persons possess. Soderstrom and Wright (1977) noted such for a large sample of college students with this orientation. They demonstrated a greater sense of purpose in their lives than the extrinsics. Others who carried out almost identical investigations also reported intrinsic religionists to be more self-actualized and better adjusted social-ly (K. B. Brown; J. F. Burke, and C. A. Rice in Summerlin, 1980).

In contrast, extrinsic-consensual people turn to religion when things go wrong; it is a support when trouble appears, otherwise their faith lacks personal relevance. Using an index of psychopathology, one group of researchers observed that it is affiliated with prayer only during times of crisis, something we would particularly expect of extrinsics. A parallel decline in church attendance also sug-gests an extrinsic-consensual outlook (Lindenthal, Myers, Pepper, and Stern, 1970).

Work with psychiatric patients and form of personal faith is extremely sparse, but one study did reveal that such persons were more extrinsically religious than a comparison sample of normals (VanderPlate, 1973).

What little research is available on personal religious orientation and men-tal disorder appears to be consistently in line with suggestions that a faith which provides an open-minded, competent guide for everyday living is found in conjunc-tion with good adjustment and effective coping behavior. A shallow, externalized religion that is needed when things aren't what one desires is more likely to be a correlate of shortcomings in personality and social interaction.

The data already cited on religion as an expression of psychopathology reveal a shallow, confused religion which merits the label extrinsic and consensual. Ob-jective verification of such a possibility awaits further research, but our expec-tation is that this kind of religion is not a strength for these disturbed people.

Where personal faith either performs therapeutically or acts as a socializing force for the distressed individual, there should be signs of growth from an extrinsic-consensual orientation to an intrinsic-committed perspective.

Those who find in their faith a haven from the strife of normal existence would seem to embrace an ineffective religion, and again extrinsic-consensual elements probably dominate. It is a fending off of the world and the realities of normal living.

Similar influences may be present when religion performs as a hazard and exacerbates weaknesses in personality. Here fantasy might support withdrawal from a threatening world or exaggeration of a sense of guilt and sin, possible marks of an extrinsic-consensual faith.

RELIGION, MENTAL DISORDER, AND THE ATTRIBUTIONAL PROCESS

We have noted that attribution is a significant part of religion and how it helps people achieve meaning and a sense of control, and can act to maintain and enhance self-esteem. The mentally disordered person is, in this regard, no dif-ferent from normals in desiring these goals, and for many, faith performs these roles in a very convincing manner.

A good place to begin our search has been suggested by the noted nineteenth-century American cleric, Henry Martyn Dexter, who stated that "the demand of the human understanding for causation requires but the one old and only answer, God" (Edwards, Catrevas and Edwards, 1955, p. 220). Here we encounter two possibilities for those who are disturbed—namely, unclear and confused God images (McAllister, 1969; Tamayo and St.-Arnaud, 1980) and threatening, punitive, and vindictive concepts of the deity (Benson and Spilka, 1973; Flakoll, 1974; Hardt, 1963). In the first instance, disorganized, bewildering notions of God could reflect a like quality of the distressed person's thinking processes. Such shallow and disjointed ideas suggest: (1) the probability of high levels of meaninglessness and normlessness, (2) a sense of powerlessness and incapability, and (3) low self-esteem. In the first instance, inconsistent and bewildering God concepts on the part of abnormal religious persons should parallel feelings that events are not clear and understandable, nor might behavior seem ordered and regulated by norms and standards. This has been found in a number of studies of mental disturbance (Dunhan, 1964; McClosky and Schaar, 1965; Oken, 1973). In like manner, the strength and clarity of religious commitment is associated with psychosocial integration (Dean and Reeves, 1962; Gladding, 1977; Stack, 1981). In other words, an incongruent, shallow faith might imply attributions of social undesirability or ineptitude to oneself for possible social isolation and loneliness. Relative to religion, the attribution may be of being forsaken by God or not knowing what God wants of the person.

Meaninglessness and normlessness are associated with feelings of hopelessness and powerlessness (Dean, 1961; Josephson and Josephson, 1973; Spilka, 1970), while the latter variable is positively affiliated with an extrinsic-consensual faith and negatively with its intrinsic-committed counterpart (Minton and Spilka, 1976). On the basis of both theory and research, we hypothesized that the religious orientation of disturbed persons was likely to be extrinsic and consensual. We know that such a faith is superficial and utilitarian; hence, personal attributions of powerlessness should correlate with vague and unclear God images. Needless to say, poor self-esteem should follow since it is consonant with extrinsic-consensual religion and antithetic to intrinsic-committed faith (Benson and Spilka, 1973; Spilka, 1976).

The prevalence of depression among members of religious communities has been noted by a number of researchers (Eaton and Weil, 1955; Kelley, 1961). Seligman and his associates (Seligman, 1975; Seligman, Abramson, Semmel, and Von Baeyer, 1979) claim that this state results from attributions of self-blame and helplessness.

In religious settings, the depressed person probably views the demands and requirements of the spiritual life as correct and appropriate. An attribution of rectitude to the system is combined with definitions of the self as seriously deficient in required ability and morality.

Behind the rules and regulations of the group, there is also a likelihood of emphasizing the punitive, unmerciful, and even revenge-seeking attributes of the deity. A sense of worthlessness, sin, and guilt becomes one's lot. There is compulsion to do penance and a growing scrupulosity can deepen the depressive mood so that the individual foresees only a downward spiral of ever-worsening outcomes. A suicidal potential is not a farfetched possibility under such circumstances, particularly when the person attributes less and less efficacy to prayer and ritualistic observance. There is also the possibility of making attributions to oneself as having alienated God in an unredeemable way.

Still, there may be a way out of the pit through that intense, mystical encounter that endows the struggling seeker with the feeling of having been touched by divine forgiveness. Helplessness is transformed into hope, futility into a renewed faith, and the "way" becomes clear. The self to which a state of unmodifiable error and blame has been attributed has now been changed by the being that can set all things right. Former attributions to a threatening and demanding deity are now replaced by new attributions to a merciful, forgiving God.

In like manner, conversion experiences that aid personality integration could involve a shift of God images from either being confused or menacing to ones stressing love and forgiveness. Here may be the probability of growth and maturation both mentally and spiritually by acquisition of an intrinsic-committed faith. When these self-enhancing attributions occur in the context of an accepting social body—a fellowship of believers—new supportive social affiliations can develop. Galanter et al. (1979) imply that this is one avenue for entrance into deviant religious groups such as the Unification Church. Judah (1974; 1977) agrees with this view for both "The Moonies" and Hare Krishna.

Intense religious experiences and conversion involve radical shifts in the nature of religious attributions. New meanings have been acquired, and these imply heightened control over one's life and possibly worldly events through the establishment of a direct line to the deity. Concomitantly, self-esteem is greatly raised.

In the last analysis, the attributional approach requires an analysis of individual behavior as a function of many specifics—situations, events, dispositions. Drawing generalizations is very chancy, and we are able to offer very few of these hence this is an area ripe for theory construction and the inference of factors which relate religion and psychopathology.

When religion and mental disorder are found together, attributions to one's self, to faith, and to God must be understood in their relationships. In some instances sin and guilt may be the issues; in others, self-glorification as a divine messenger could round out the paranoid picture. We advance the proposition that the constructive and positive images of self and God that encompass the life of the intrinsic-committed person may counter abnormality by endowing such people with a protective inner strength. Lacking such, the extrinsic-consensualist could develop the distorted religious themes found among the emotionally disturbed. To date, we lack the research to assess this theoretical stance; it is, however, an avenue meriting examination.

SUMMARY AND CONCLUSIONS

In all probability, since the origin of religion in prehistoric times, a close, complex, and meaningful relationship has existed between religion and mental deviance. The centuries have witnessed radical changes in the interpretation of abnormality and its treatment by church authorities until its redefinition as a form of illness shifted control to the medical establishment. Still, in contemporary life, for the individual and society, faith has not been fully divorced from the realm of mental disorder. We have noted the continuing existence of a variety of functions that religion performs both for the alleviation of psychological distress and also for its creation and maintenance. From the standpoint of the person, however, vulnerability to mental disorder may be expressed by the kind of faith the individual embraces. Intrinsic-committed religion could either be a bulwark against breakdown and/or develop out of personal effectiveness in coping with the world. In contrast, an extrinsic-consensual perspective might dispose the person to respond in an inefficient and inadequate manner. Difficulties in adjustment may also be reflected in the adoption of such a spiritual mode.

Despite the fact that a great deal of research on religion and mental disorder has been published, it is apparent that this work generally tends to be scattered, poorly conceived and carried out, and frequently lacks any coherent theoretical organization. Clearly, this is a fruitful area needing much more rigorous examination. It is our feeling that an attributional approach might provide the desired integration, especially if this is coordinated with recognition of the multiform nature of individual religion. A few initial efforts are starting to appear in the scientific psychological literature, and we are hopeful these will soon expand and prove helpful.

CHAPTER THIRTEEN
PSYCHOLOGY, PSYCHOLOGISTS, AND RELIGION: PRESENT REALITIES AND FUTURE TRENDS

The empirical psychology of religion is literally as old as scientific psychology itself. For its first thirty years, it was at the heart of the profession. The next forty years witnessed its decline and movement to the periphery of the field. The last thirty years have seen a rejuvenation of interest in the psychological study of religion, in both its empirical and applied aspects. Recognition of the significance of faith in the psychological life of the individual is increasing at a rapid pace, as has been illustrated throughout this volume. More than ever before, we are at a crossroads requiring consideration of our strengths and weaknesses and the direction in which this field is going.

The problems we need to contemplate are basically twofold in nature: (1) those relating directly to the scientific study of religious belief, experience, and behavior; and (2) the relationship of religion and psychology—the fundamental underlying questions that concern both religionists and psychologists regarding the association of these spheres. This is our immediate task.

RESEARCH IN THE PSYCHOLOGY OF RELIGION

The Current State of the Field

In this book, we have attempted an overview of the psychology of religion. Without question, it is incomplete. As already noted, our history is long, and writing and research have been prodigious. Our emphasis has been with the empirical approach—thus, pastoral work has not been surveyed and evaluated. In like manner, phenomenologically, humanistically, and psychoanalytically oriented scholars may also feel slighted. Our intent was to provide an appreciation of many of the issues relating religion and the individual to which psychological research and understanding are relevant. These issues are summarized below.

Problems of Theory

It is necessary to recognize that all the great classical problems of the psychology of religion that were formulated fifty to one hundred years ago are still with us. These have often been redefined, and sometimes rephrased in a new language, if not fractionated into subproblems and issues that seem distant from their original focus. New research methods and sophisticated procedures have been directed toward their solution. Unhappily, psychometric strengths, complex and abstruse statistical techniques, and the use of high-speed computers are no substitute for an organizing theory, and here is the basic weakness. Theoretically, the psychology of religion is poorly organized. Dittes (1969) noted a decade and a half ago that the main problem of the psychology of religion is a lack of theoretical specification. This problem is still very much with us.

In Chapter One, we spoke of what might be termed broad metatheoretical traditions: an instinct tradition, a defensive-protective tradition, a growth-realization tradition, a habit tradition. As a rule, these traditions have been too loosely framed to be research-productive. In like manner, the potential richness of psychoanalytic and phenomenological thought has only been realized in a very limited way. Those so oriented have preferred intellectual discussion or case-history reference that does not meet the criteria of science and operationalization. These have been treated in Chapter Two.

Lack of directive theory to guide research has, in large part, stemmed from the fact that those working in the psychology of religion have only recently begun to place this field in the context of mainstream psychology. The last two decades have witnessed the beginnings of such coordination, and like that mainstream, the psychology of religion lacks "grand," overriding theories that cross many areas. Hypothetical frameworks tend to be confined to specific problems. We saw how Piaget's cognitive views dominate our understanding of childhood faith. Social psychology appears to have much potential, and a few pioneering efforts have utilized cognitive dissonance theory (Brock, 1961–62; Feather, 1964; Festinger, Riecken, and Schachter, 1964). Batson and Ventis (1982) suggest that social comparison theory is relevant to religion, but research along these lines has yet to be undertaken. Our own reliance on attribution theory derives from contemporary social psychology, and as noted, is currently stimulating a number of studies in the psychology of religion. We would argue that substantive progress cannot take place until research is firmly theoretically based. Note, for example, especially in the chapters on religious experience, mysticism, and conversion, the consistent effort to conceptualize the problems of these areas.

In addition to guidance from general-psychological theory, Dittes (1969) suggests that one may look within religion itself as a source of theory. In this respect, theology has been discussed as a possibly fruitful basis for theory (Hodges, 1974; Spilka, 1970) and has generated some research (Spilka, 1976), but again this was not developed to any extent. We will come back to the basic question that this kind of work raises—namely, to what degree can theological concepts gain status in the psychology of religion? Psychological ideas appear to have gained acceptance within current theology (Homans, 1968).

Making Data Meaningful

Obviously, there is no paucity of research findings in the psychology of religion. Unfortunately, all too often these findings tend to be widely scattered and remain uncoordinated. What are termed *meta-analyses* may be a very significant means of pulling this material together in a coordinated and constructive manner. Recent work has attempted such analyses relative to religiosity and mental health (Bergin, 1983), intrinsic and extrinsic religiousness (Donahue, 1983), and religion, personality, and lifestyle (Donahue and Bergin, 1983). In 1971, Hunt and King undertook this kind of effort for the intrinsic-extrinsic distinction, pointing to the fact that this dichotomous formulation had then firmly established itself in the field. Simple notions of a single generalized form of religiosity must be rejected as in error.

Behind the scenes, there are serious questions about the samples used in much of the cited research. The subject of expedient choice—the college student—prevails. Although the results of this work are probably valid and generalizable, they do need checking, especially with older respondents who function religiously within church and synagogue settings. Sociologists have examined institutional frameworks, but understandably without concern for the interests of psychologists. Pargament and his associates are, however, engaged in social-psychological investigations of individuals relative to congregation development and the strengths and weaknesses of local churches and synagogues (Pargament, Silverman, Johnson, Echemendia, and Snyder, 1982; Pargament, Pargament, Shack, Shack, and Echemendia, 1983). Attention has also been afforded relationships between religious institutions as support systems and the psychosocial competence and mental status of church members (Pargament, 1977, 1982; Pargament, Steele, and Tyler, 1979a, 1979b). Overlapping considerations with frameworks for such research are discussed in the chapter on the social psychology of religious organizations.

Pargament's work points up a major weakness in the psychology of religion. Only a few scholars, of whom he is one, have actually developed organized and coherent research programs. Other noteworthy efforts are Hood's work on religious experience (see the chapters on religious experience and mysticism); Batson's studies of the Quest religious orientation (Batson and Ventis, 1982), and the massive and varied large-scale investigations of Strommen and his associates, primarily on youth (Strommen, 1963; Strommen, Brekke, Underwager, and Johnson, 1972; Schuller, Strommen, and Brekke, 1980). In contrast to these undertakings, most published research represents a one-time labor, commonly publications of theses or dissertations. Fruitful possibilities are therefore stillborn unless they appeal to other workers. The literature thus often reads like a random collection of isolated efforts and essentially untried measures.

This lack of programmatic research is combined easily with the use of very sophisticated multivariate statistical procedures such as factor analysis. Usually employed to construct objective measures or to demonstrate the multidimensional nature of various phenomena, such studies may degenerate into a complex mindless multidimensionality without a theoretical framework to make sense out of what has been found. All too clearly, this points up the fact that the computer has become a mixed blessing. The ease with which data may be submitted for analysis permits one to utilize esoteric methods with a minimal understanding of their implications.

Subjectivity versus Objectivity

If there is a fundamental dilemma underlying the psychology of religion, it is the issue of whether subjective reports or objective measurement should be employed in religious research. In mainstream psychology, the terms *idiographic* and *nomothetic* have been employed. The former claims to emphasize reflective, intuitive individuality and purports to focus on the qualitative and descriptive. Historically, it has been associated with phenomenological and psychoanalytic psychologies. In contrast, the nomothetic approach stresses objective methodologies, reliable measures, and may resort to mathematical-statistical statements. Terms like *empirical* and *positivistic* are assigned to this approach. Although both of these positions have their vociferous advocates, the distinction is, in large part, extreme, naive, and unrealistic.

A rapprochement is, however, in process, although its conditions are not always satisfactory to the partisans of these stances. Hanford (1975, 1976) has proposed a "synoptic" solution which blends the strengths of these positions, and utilizes both survey and case-study methods. Malony (1977) discusses $N = 1$ methodology, namely the rigorous experimental study of individuals. This approach has a definite following in mainstream psychology (Davidson and Costello, 1969), but has yet to be applied substantively in the psychology of religion. Tageson (1982) refers to a functional phenomenology that wants to establish mathematical relationships among subjective variables. This rather "objective phenomenology" seems rather close to the "subjective behaviorism" of Miller, Galanter, and Pribham (1960). Embracing this middle position, we accept the qualitative richness of individual religious experience and feeling, but feel that they may be most fruitfully viewed as providing an entre for collecting data that are public and reproducible. In this way, the subjective is a theoretical avenue to the objective.

Naturalistic versus Experimental Research

Religion is a phenomenon of living and not easily subjected to experimental manipulation, although some enterprising efforts in this direction have been reported throughout this volume. One example is the demonstration by Orsachuk and Tatz (1973) that belief in afterlife could be influenced by increasing a person's death anxiety. The work of Batson and Gray (1981), Hood (1978), and Pahnke (1963) further illustrates variations on the experimental method. Still, it is relatively rarely utilized in our field. The issue of experimentation in the psychology of religion is a complex one and has been discussed in depth elsewhere (Batson, 1977, 1979; Yeatts and Asher, 1979).

Much classical work in psychology and religion has employed what might be thought of as naturalistic methods. Reliance was, and remains, on some form of naturalistic observation of individual and collective religious experience, belief, and behavior. This has taken three forms: (1) observation of religious activity; (2) verbal statements of one's beliefs, actions, or experiences; and (3) the completion of questionnaires regarding same. These last two approaches may most accurately be considered approximations to true naturalistic research. Unfortunately, the process of soliciting statements and the application of objective measures does influence the responses of people. Many factors, such as the characteristics of the interviewer, nonreligious tendencies of respondents, the nature of the questionnaires utilized, the way queries are phrased, the evaluative or testing content, etc., cloud the picture, but it is hoped that any effects can be determined, minimized, and understood to provide the kinds of data rigorous research demands.

What we call "naturalistic" research, particularly that employing procedures (2) and (3), usually eventuates in correlational data—namely, information on relationships among two or more observations, test scores, and the like. The reviews of the literature on intrinsic and extrinsic religion by Donahue (1983) and Hunt and King (1971) show how often researchers have simply correlated scores on these scales with similar scores on other objective measures. Much information can be gained this way, but it is limited. Although statistical techniques leading to causal inferences may be applied to such data, they can never result in the solidity of causal explanation provided by experimental research. Correlation does not mean causation.

There is, however, another set of procedures known as *quasi-experimental designs* (Campbell and Stanley, 1966; Cook and Campbell, 1979). These are to be employed when one cannot randomly assign people to research groups or fully exercise experimental control as is usually true of research on religion, particularly when such research is undertaken in naturalistic settings. A fair amount of research in the psychology of religion could be considered as quasi-experimental, but it is doubted that those who carried out these studies always considered their work as employing these designs. Detailed discussion of such approaches is beyond what we can accomplish here; however, interested readers may benefit from studying the above references since Batson and Ventis (1982) see a considerable potential for these procedures in the psychology of religion.

Regardless of research design, statistical methodology, or whether one employs subjective or objective approaches, in the last analysis, data can only be made meaningful by reference to a conceptual framework. Data never speak for themselves; they require interpretation, and this is premised upon ideas already constructed by thoughtful and creative researchers. The old adage that seeing is believing becomes, in reality, believing is seeing. What we believe and theorize tells us what the data mean.

MAINSTREAM PSYCHOLOGY, PSYCHOLOGISTS, AND THE PSYCHOLOGY OF RELIGION

The Place of the Psychology of Religion

We have commented that there has been an amazingly rapid growth in research in the psychology of religion in the past quarter of a century and that this area has been formally recognized as worthy of a being a division of the

American Psychological Association. Despite these significant signs of recognition, it must be acknowledged that the field is still peripheral to mainstream psychology. Studies of introductory psychology texts show that 40 percent of those published in the 1950s included something about religion, but this number dropped to 27.5 percent for texts issued in the 1970s. Still, the treatment of this material became significantly more objective and less negative over this time period (Spilka, Comp, and Goldsmith, 1981). It is to be noted that the massive increase in publications in the psychology of religion is apparently not brought to the attention of beginning psychology students. In addition, citation is mostly to classic figures such as William James, Freud, and Jung plus philosophers or theologians. Research is generally overlooked. Andrews (1979) suggests that introductory texts perform a "gate-keeping" function for selecting potential initiates into the field of psychology. These volumes therefore stress the objective, scientific nature of psychology, and exclude religion. In other words, there is no place for a discussion of psychology and religion, when a narrow definition of psychology as a science holds sway.

When advanced psychology texts are examined, religion is referenced much more often (Spilka, Amaro, Wright, and Davis, 1981). Citation is found in 75 percent of social psychology texts, 42 percent of those concerned with childhood and adolescence, and 64 percent that deal with personality. Although psychologists come in for the majority of attention, sociologists, anthropologists, theologians, and philosophers are extensively cited. Discussion preempts research and a very few studies are repeatedly mentioned. Again, there is little evidence that textbook writers or psychology editors for the various publishers are aware of recent work in the psychology of religion. Hunsberger (1980) places the blame both on psychology in general and the psychology of religion for this state of affairs. In addition to biases against religion in mainstream psychology, he sees scientific shortcomings such as a lack of focus and direction plus poor empirical and theoretical work in the psychology of religion. The problem is not as simple as it might appear on the surface.

There is still little doubt that religion is not generally viewed in a congenial and accepting manner by psychologists (Clement, 1978; Ragan, Malony, Beit-Hallahmi, 1980; Struening, 1963). In itself, this could account for the paucity of recognition of research in mainstream texts, but there are noteworthy exceptions to this rule. To explain the position of psychologists and other academic disciplines relative to religion, Lehman and Shriver (1968) proposed a "scholarly distance hypothesis" that asserts the more an academic discipline considers religion a legitimate area of study, the less likely its members will be religious. In other words, low scholarly distance implies a scientific, analytic view of religion. Here one would find the social sciences and psychology. In contrast, high scholarly distance fields such as chemistry and physics that do not study religion should contain members more positive and less questioning about religion. This view has been supported in comparisons among academic disciplines for both faculty and students (Beit-Hallahmi, 1977; Hoge, 1974; Lehman and Shriver, 1968). Ragan, Malony, and Beit-Hallahmi (1980) theorize that this might also be true among psychological specialties with those not studying or being involved with religion (e.g., industrial or experimental psychology) revealing higher levels of religiosity among their members than subfields dealing with religion (e.g., social or clinical psychology). No support was found for this hypothesis.

But who are those psychologists who work in the psychology of religion? Here the evidence suggests that psychologists who study religion tend to be more religious than those not concerned with these matters (Beit-Hallahmi, 1977; Ragan, Malony, and Beit-Hallahmi, 1980). In any event, Andrews's (1979) judgment that "The psychology of religion has been the troublesome outsider knocking at the gates of the city of general psychology" (p. 37) is still basically true. A case, however, has been made in these pages that the situation is changing, but it is clear that progress is slow.

RELATIONSHIPS BETWEEN PSYCHOLOGY AND THEOLOGY

A wag described the development of psychology in interesting terms when he claimed, "Psychology first lost its soul, then its mind, then consciousness, but strangely enough it still behaves" (Baker, 1963, p. 1). This seems to encapsulate the long historical trek of psychology from religion and theology through philosophy to behaviorism. It also speaks to what Vande Kemp (1982a, 1982b) posits as "the tension between psychology and theology" (1982a, p. 105). Despite the variety of coordinating and cooperating organizations such as the Academy of Religion and Health, the Society for the Scientific Study of Religion, the Religious Research Association, and others that more directly tie Christianity and Judaism to psychology, religious and psychological barriers exist between these domains. They can be expected to continue, because there are many basic premises underlying psychology and theology that are unlikely to be resolved in the forseeable future (Thomas, 1962). Needless to say, just as there is not one psychology, there are also many theologies, and disagreements among both psychologists and theologians are also likely to persist for a long time to come. Still, both fields focus on the human individual and have many concerns in common. There is thus a basis for a meaningful and fruitful dialogue. This has been well stated by Novak (1968):

> . . . the astute reader of theological discourse will soon discover that every sentence in such discourse, however, obliquely, refers to human actions, or dispositions, or programs . . . The "Kingdom of God" . . . has an other-worldly, apocalyptic concomitant; yet, in its own right, it is a concrete this-worldly ideal. Theology studies ultimate visions of communal relationships and personal identity insofar as these affect actual human experience (p.52).

Little doubt exists that there is considerable motivation for communication between theology and psychology. More religionists are represented in these endeavors than psychologists. *The Journal of Psychology and Theology* is, however, ample testimony to contemporary interest, but a large number of articles and books also speak to the potential of exchange and integration (Carter, 1977; Collins, 1980, 1981; Homans, 1968; Narramore, 1980). Among other possibilities, we read of Christian and Jewish psychologies (Fleck and Carter, 1981; Kaplan, 1967), biblical psychology (Thomas, 1962), and theological psychology (Spilka, 1976). The general pattern of the first three of these efforts seems to be the incorporation of psychological information about humans into various theologies along with designation of the boundaries between the fields. As noted earlier, the last work suggests that theology might be employed as a theoretical basis for research in the psychology of religion..Others have sounded similar themes (Marvin, 1980). The utilization of theology within psychology for research purposes has been very limited (Spilka, 1976). Its main application has been to pastoral care and counseling (Aden, 1969; Collins, 1977), topics that are left to other students of the psychology of religion. Further explorations of the possibilities inherent in psychology-theology interchanges would seem warranted. Just as the values and techniques of psychology have proven meaningful to many religionists, it is probable that the values and perspectives of various theologies might be theoretically and empirically compatible to a good number of psychologists.

A CONCLUDING NOTE

A massive amount of information has been presented in these pages. Without question, it is difficult to digest, but this is the nature of the psychology of religion. Although this information may seem scattered and diverse, and indeed it is, we would like to emphasize that there is a basic psychological theme underlying our treatment of religion. At times, it has not been extensively developed, for it is only now that it is gaining widespread acceptance within the field. This is the theme of attribution. Psychologically, much of religion is an attributional phenomenon. This assumes that religion provides: (1) a set of meanings for the individual that permits one to make sense out of much, if not most, of what happens in life, especially when naturalistic explanations appear inadequate; (2) the wherewithal to feel that one has some control over the course of events through the holding of various beliefs and engaging in certain practices and behaviors; and (3) a sense of personal worth, dignity, and esteem—a feeling that one is a special product of creation and continues to occupy a privileged place in the "scheme of things." The task now is to understand these motives for religious action when religion means many different things and takes many different forms.

REFERENCES

AARSON, B., and OSMOND, H. *Psychedelics*. Garden City, N.Y.: Doubleday, 1970.

Academy of Religion and Mental Health, *Religion in the Developing Personality*. Proceedings of the second academy symposium 1958, New York: New York University Press, 1960.

ACOCK, A. C., and BENGSTON, V. L. "On the Relative Influence of Mothers and Fathers: A Covariance Analysis of Political and Religious Socialization. *Journal of Marriage and the Family*, 1978, *40*, 519–30.

ACUFF, G. and GORMAN, B. "Emeritus Professors: The Effect of Professional Activity and Religion on 'Meaning,' " *Sociological Quarterly*, 1967, *9*, 112–115.

ADEN, L. "Pastoral Counseling as Christian Perspective," in P. Homans (ed.), *The Dialogue Between Theology and Psychology*. Chicago: University of Chicago Press, 1968, pp. 163–81.

ADLER, A. *Social Interest: A Challenge to Mankind*. New York: Capricorn, 1964.

———. *Superiority and Social Interest*, 3rd ed., revised. New York: Norton, 1979.

ADORNO, T. W.; FRENKEL-BRUNSWIK, E.; LEVINSON, D.J.; and SANFORD, R. N. *The Authoritarian Personality*. New York: Harper, 1950.

AL-ISSA, I. "Social and Cultural Aspects of Hallucinations," *Psychological Reports*, 1977, *84*, 570–87.

ALLEGRO, J. M. *The Sacred Mushroom and the Cross*. New York: Bantam, 1971.

ALLEN, D. E. and SANDHU, H. S. "Alienation, Hedonism, and Life-vision of Delinquents," *Journal of Criminal Law, Criminology and Police Science*, 1967, *58*, 325–29.

ALLEN, R. O. and SPILKA, B. "Committed and Consensual Religion: A Specification of Religion-Prejudice Relationships," *Journal for the Scientific Study of Religion*. 1967, *6*, 191–206.

ALLISON, J.   "Recent Empirical Studies of Religious Conversion Experience," *Pastoral Psychology,* 1966, *14,* 21–33.

ALLMAN, L. R., and JAFFE, D. T. (eds.).   *Readings in Adult Psychology: Contemporary Perspectives.* New York: Harper and Row, 1977.

ALLPORT, G. W.   *The Nature of Prejudice.* Cambridge, Mass.: Addison-Wesley, 1954.

————.   "The Religious Context of Prejudice." *Journal for the Scientific Study of Religion,* 1966, *5,* 447–57.

————.   "Religion and Prejudice," *The Crane Review,* 1959, *2,* 1–10.

———— and KRAMER, P. M.   "Some Roots of Prejudice." *Journal of Psychology,* 22, 9–39.

———— and ROSS, J. M.   "Personal Religious Orientation and Prejudice." *Journal of Personality and Social Psychology,* 1967, *5,* 432–443.

————; VERNON, P. E.; and LINDZEY, G.   *Manual for the Study of Values, 3rd Edition,* Boston: Houghton Mifflin, 1960.

ALSTON, J.   "Religious Mobility and Socio-economic Status," *Sociological Analysis,* 1971, *32,* 140–48.

AMES, E. S.   *The Psychology of Religious Experience.* Boston; Houghton Mifflin, 1910.

ANDERSON, D. E.   "Survey Indicates Blacks Most Religious Subgroup." *The Denver Post,* June 4, 1982, p. 4E.

ANDERSON, G. C.   "Current conditions and trends in relations between religion and mental health. "Address opening the first annual meeting of the Academy of Religion and Mental Health, New York, January 14, 1960.

ANDREASON, N. J. C.   "The Role of Religion in Depression," *Journal of Religion and Health,* 1972, *11,* 153–66.

ANDREWS, A. R.   "Religion, Psychology, and Science: Steps Toward a Wider Psychology of Religion," *Journal of Psychology and Theology,* 1979, *7,* 31–38.

ANDREWS, F. E.   *Attitudes toward Giving.* New York: Russell Sage, 1953.

ANGYAL, A.   *Foundations for a Science of Personality.* New York: Viking, 1972.

ANNIS, L. V.   "Emergency Helping and Religious Behavior," *Psychological Reports,* 1976, *39,* 151–58.

APPEL, K. E.   "Religion," in Silvano Arieti (ed.), *American Handbook of Psychiatry. Vol. II,* New York: Basic Books, 1959.

AQUINAS, ST. THOMAS.   *Summa Theologica,* Vol. II. Chicago: Encyclopedia Britannica (Great Books of the Western World, Vol. 20), 1952.

ARGYLE, M.   *Religious Behavior.* Glencoe, Ill.: The Free Press, 1959.

———— and BEIT-HALLAHMI, B.   *The Social Psychology of Religion.* London: Routledge and Kegan Paul, 1975.

AULD, F., JR.   "Influence of Social Class on Personality Test Responses," *Psychological Bulletin,* 1952, *49,* 318–32.

BACH, G. R. and WYDEN, P.   *The Intimate Enemy.* New York: William Morrow, 1969.

BACK, K. W. and BOURQUE, L. B.   "Can Feelings Be Enumerated?" *Behavioral Science,* 1970, *15,* 487–96.

BAECK, L.   *The Essence of Judaism,* rev. ed. New York: Schocken, 1948.

BAER, H. A.   "The Levites of Utah," *Review of Religious Research,* 1978, *19,* 279–84.

BAILEY, R. W.   *The Minister and Grief.* New York: Hawthorn, 1976.

BAINBRIDGE, W. S. and STARK, R.   "Cult Formation: Three Compatible Models," *Sociological Analysis,* 1979, *40,* 283–95.

————.   "Sectarian Tension," *Review of Religious Research,* 1980a, *22,* 105–23.

————.   "Client and Audience Cults in America," *Sociological Analysis,* 1980b, *41,* 199–214.

BAKER, R. A. (ed.)   *Psychology in the Wry.* Princeton, N.J.: D. Van Nostrand, 1963.

BALES, R. F.   "Attitudes Toward Drinking in the Irish Culture," in *Society, Culture, and Drinking Patterns* by D. J. Pittman and C. R. Snyder (eds.). New York: Wiley, 1962, 157–87.

BANDURA, A. (ed.), *Psychological Modeling.* Chicago: Aldine-Atherton, 1971.
————. *Social Learning Theory.* New York: General Learning Press, 1972.
————. *Social Learning Theory.* Englewood Cliffs, N.J.: Prentice-Hall, 1977.
BANE, J. B.; KUTSCHER, A. H.; NEALE, R. E.; and REEVES, R. B. (eds). *Death and Ministry.* New York: Seabury, 1975.
BARBER, T. X. *LSD, Marijuana, Yoga, and Hypnosis.* Chicago: Aldine, 1970.
BARNES, H. E. and BECKER, H. *Social Thought from Lore to Science,* Vol. 1. Boston: Heath, 1938.
BARNES, H. R. and TEETERS, N. K. *Horizons in Criminology,* 3rd ed. New York: Prentice-Hall, Inc., 1959.
BARR, H. L.; LANGS, R. J.: HOLT, R. R.; GOLDBERGER, L.; and KLEIN, G. S. *LSD, Personality, and Experience.* New York: Wiley, 1972.
BATAILLE, G. *Death and Sensuality.* New York: Ballantine, 1962.
BATEMAN, M. M., and JENSEN, J. S. "The Effect of Religious Background on Modes of Handling Anger." *J. soc. psychol.,* 1958, *47,* 133–41.
BATSON, C. D., "Religion as Prosocial Agent or Double Agent," *Journal for the Scientific Study of Religion,* 1976, *15,* 29–45.
————. "Experimentation in Psychology of Religion: An Impossible Dream," *Journal for the Scientific Study of Religion, 16,* 412–18.
————. "Experimentation in the Psychology of Religion: Living with or in a Dream," *Journal for the Scientific Study of Religion,* 1979, *18,* 90–93.
———— and GRAY, R. A., "Religious Orientation and Helping Behavior: Responding to One's Own or to the Victim's Needs?" *Journal for the Scientific Study of Religion,* 1981, *40,* 511–20.
————, NAIFEH, S. J. and PATE, S., "Social Desirability, Religious Orientation, and Racial Prejudice," *Journal for the Scientific Study of Religion,* 1978, *17,* 31–41.
———— and VENTIS, W. L., *The Religious Experience.* New York: Oxford University Press, 1982.
BEAN, M., "Anonymous Alcoholics," AA and religion. *Psychiatric Annals,* 1975, *5,* 36–37, 40–42.
BECKER, E. *The Denial of Death.* New York: Free Press, 1973.
BECKER, L. B. "Predictors of Change in Religious Beliefs and Behaviors during College," *Sociological Analysis,* 1977, *38,* 65–74.
BECKER, R. J. "Religion and Psychological Health," in M. B. Strommen (ed.), *Research on Religious Development: A Comprehensive Handbook.* New York: Hawthorn, 1971, 391–421.
BEIT-HALLAHMI, B. "Curiosity, Doubt and Devotion: The Beliefs of Psychologists and the Psychology of Religion," in H. N. Malony (ed.), *Current Perspectives in the Psychology of Religion.* Grand Rapids, Mich.: Eerdmans, 1977, pp. 381–91.
BELL, D. "Interpretations of American Politics," in D. Bell (ed.), *The Radical Right.* Garden City, N.Y.: Doubleday, 1963, p. 47–73.
————. "Religion in the Sixties," *Social Research,* 1971, *38,* 447–97.
BELLAH, R. "Civil Religion in America." *Daedalus,* 1967, *96,* No. 1, 1–21.
BEM, D. and McCONNELL, H. K. "Testing the Self-perception Explanation of Dissonance Phenomena: On the Salience of Premanipulation Attitudes," *Journal of Personality and Social Psychology,* 1970, *14,* 23–31.
BENDA, C. E. "The Existential Approach to Religion," in E. M. Pattison (ed.) *Clinical Psychiatry and Religion,* Boston: Little, Brown, 1969, 37–48.
BENDIKSEN, R., HEWITT, M., and VINGE, D. "Cancer Residency for Clergy: A Preliminary Evaluation of an Institutional Response to Clergy Involvement in Cancer management." Paper presented at the Convention of the Society for the Scientific Study of Religion, San Antonio, Texas, October 27, 1979.

BENHAM, W. G. (ed.).   *Putnam's Complete Book of Quotations.* New York: G. P. Putnam's Sons, 1927.

BENNETT, G. F.   "Religious Activity and the Suspicious Person," *Journal of Pastoral Care,* 1964, *18,* 140–47.

BENSON, P. H.   *Religion in Contemporary Culture.* New York: Harper, 1960.

BENSON, P. L.   "God Is Alive in the U.S. Congress, But not Always Voting against Civil Liberties and for Military Spending." *Psychology Today,* December 1981, *15,* (12) 47–57.

———— and SPILKA, B.   "God Image as a Function of Self-Esteem and Locus of Control," *Journal for the Scientific Study of Religion.* 1973, *13,* 297–310.

————; DEHORTY, J.; GARMAN, L.; HANSON, E.; HOCHSWENDER, M.; LEBOLD, C., ROHR, R., and SULLIVAN, J.   "Intrapersonal Correlates of Nonspontaneous Helping Behavior," *Journal of Social Psychology,* 1980, *110,* 87–95.

———— and WILLIAMS, D. L.   *Religion on Capitol Hill: Myths and Realities.* New York: Harper and Row, 1982.

————; WOOD, P. K.; JOHNSON, A. L.; EKLIN, C. H.; and MILLS, J. E.   Report on 1983 *Minnesota Survey on Drug Use and Drug-Related Attitudes.* Minneapolis: Search Institute, 1983.

BERG, I. A.   *Reponse Set in Personality Assessment.* Chicago: Aldine, 1967.

BERGER, P.   *The Precarious Vision.* Garden City, N.Y.: Doubleday, 1967.

———— and LUCKMANN, T.   *The Social Construction of Reality.* Garden City, N.Y.: Doubleday, 1967.

BERGIN, A. E.   "Psychology as a Science of Inner Experience," *Journal of Humanistic Psychology,* 1964, *4,* 95–103.

————.   "Religiosity and Mental Health: A Critical Reevaluation and Meta-analysis," *Professional Psychology,* 1983, *14,* 170–184.

BERGSON, H.   *The Two Sources of Morality and Religion.* Garden City, NY: Doubleday, 1935.

BERKOWITZ, L.   "Social Motivation." In G. Lindzey and E. Aronson (eds.), *The Handbook of Social Psychology,* 2nd ed., Vol. 3. Reading, MA: Addison-Wesley, 1969, 50–135.

BERLYNE, D. E.   *Conflict, Arousal, and Curiosity.* New York: McGraw-Hill, 1960.

BERMAN, A. L.   "Belief in Afterlife, Religion, Religiosity and Life-Threatening Experiences," *Omega,* 1974, *5,* 127–35.

BERMAN, A. and HAYS, J.   "Relationship between Death Anxiety, Belief in an Afterlife, and Locus of Control," *Journal of Consulting and Clinical Psychology,* 1973, *41,* 318.

BERMAN, L. A.   *Jews and Intermarriage.* New York: Thomas Yoseloff, 1968.

BERGMAN, P.   "A Religious Conversion in the Course of Psychotherapy," *American Journal of Psychotherapy,* 1953, *7,* 41–58.

BERNARD, L. L.   *Instinct.* New York: Henry Holt, 1924.

BERNSTEIN, B.   "Aspects of Language and Learning in the Genesis of the Social Process. In D. Hymes (ed.), *Language in Culture and Society.* New York: Harper and Row, 1964, p. 251–263.

BERTOCCI, P. A.   *Religion as Creative Insecurity.* New York: Association Press, 1958.

BETTELHEIM, B.   *The Uses of Enchantment.* New York: Knopf, 1976.

———— and JANOWITZ, M.   *Dynamics of Prejudice.* New York: Harper, 1950.

BETTY, L. S.   "Towards a Reconciliation of Mysticism and Dualism," *Religious Studies,* 1977, *14,* 291–303.

BIBBY, R. W.   "Why Conservative Churches Are Growing: Kelley Revisited," *Journal for the Scientific Study of Religion,* 1978, *17,* 129–37.

————, and BRINKERHOFF, M. B.   "The Circulation of the Saints: A Study of People Who Join Conservative Churches," *Journal for the Scientific Study of Religion,* 1973, *12,* 273–83.

BIERCE, A.   *The Enlarged Devil's Dictionary.* Garden City, N.Y.: Doubleday, 1967.

BINDRA, D.   *Motivation: A Systematic Reinterpretation.* New York: Ronald, 1959.

BIRD, F.   "The Pursuit of Innocence: New Religious Movements and Moral Accountability," *Sociological Analysis,* 1979, *40,* 335–46.

BLACKFORD, R.; PORCH, T.; RADANT, N.; SHABHAZ, P.; and BUTMAN, R. E.   *From Jerusalem to Jericho Revisited: A Study in Helping Behavior.* Paper presented at the meeting of the American Psychological Association, Anaheim, Calif., August 1983.

BLACKNEY, R. B.   *Meister Eckhart: A Modern Translation.* New York: Harper, 1941.

BLACKWOOD, L.   "Social Change and Commitment to the Work Ethic," in R. Wuthnow (ed.), *The Religious Dimension: New Directions in Quantitative Research.* New York: Academic, 1979, 241–56.

BLOCK, J.   *The Challenge of Response Sets.* New York: Appleton-Century-Crofts, 1965.

BOCK, G. D.   "The Jewish Schooling of American Jews: A Study of Non-Cognitive Educational Effects." *Dissertation Abstracts International,* A37, 1977, p. 4628.

BOISEN, A. T.   *Exploration of the Inner World.* Chicago: Willett, Clark, 1936.

————.   "The General Significance of Mystical Identification in Cases of Mental Disorder," *Psychiatry,* 1952, *15,* 287–96.

————.   "Religious Experience and Psychological Conflict," *American Psychologist,* 1958, *13,* 568–70.

BORTNER, R. W. and HULTSCH, D. C.   "A Multivariate Analysis of Correlates of Life Satisfaction in Adulthood," *Journal of Gerontology,* 1970, *25,* 41–47.

BOSWELL, J.   *Life of Samuel Johnson, LLD.* Chicago: Encyclopedia Britannica, 1952.

BOTWINICK, J.; WEST, R.; and STORANDT, M.   "Predicting Death from Behavioral Test Performance," *Journal of Gerontology,* 1978, *33,* 755–62.

BOUMA, G. D.   "The Real Reason One Conservative Church Grew," *Review of Religious Research,* 1979, *20,* 127–37.

————.   "Keeping the Faithful: Patterns of Membership Retention in the Christian Reformed Church," *Sociological Analysis,* 1980, *3* 259–64.

BOURQUE, L. B.   "Social Correlates of Transcendental Experiences," *Sociological Analysis,* 1969, *30,* 151–63.

———— and BACK, K W.   "Values and Transcendental experiences," *Social Forces,* 1968, *47,* 34–48.

———— and BACK, K. W.   "Language, Society, and Subjective experience," *Sociometry,* 1974, *34,* 1–21.

BOWERS, W. J.   "Normative Constraints on Deviant Behavior in the College Context," *Sociometry* 1968, *31,* 370–85.

BOWKER, J.   *The Sense of God.* Oxford: Clarendon Press, 1973.

BOYAR, J. I.   "The Construction and Partial Validation of a Scale for the Measurement of the Fear of Death." Unpublished doctoral dissertation, University of Rochester. *Dissertation Abstracts,* 1964, *25,* 2041.

BRAGAN, K.   "The Psychological Gains and Losses of Religious Conversion," *British Journal of Medical Psychology,* 1977, *50,* 177–80.

BRESSLER, M. and WESTOFF, C. F.   "Catholic Education, Economic Values and Achievement." *American Journal of Sociology,* 1963, *69,* 225–33.

BRETALL, R. (ed.),   *A Kierkegaard Anthology.* New York: Princeton University Press, 1936.

BRIGHTWELL, L. E.   "A Study of Religious Delusions," *Bulletin of the Tulane Medical Society,* 1962, *21,* 159–72.

BRILL, A. A. (ed.)   *The Basic Writings of Sigmund Freud.* New York: Modern Library, 1938.

BRITTON, J. H., and BRITTON, J. O.   *Personality Changes in Aging.* New York: Springer, 1972.

BROCK, T. C.   "Implications of Conversion and Magnitude of Cognitive Dissonance," *Journal for the Scientific Study of Religion,* 1961-62, *1,* 198–203.

BROEN, W. E., JR.   "A Factor-Analytic Study of Religious Attitudes." *Journal of Abnormal and Social Psychology,* 54, 176–79.

BROMBERG, W.   *The Mind of Man.* New York: Harper, 1937.

BRONSON, L. and MEADOW, A. "The Need Achievement Orientation of Catholic and Protestant Mexican-Americans," *Revista Interamericana de Psicologia*, 1968, *2*, 159–68.

_____. "Changes in Personality Needs and Values Following Conversion to Protestantism in a Traditionally Roman Catholic Ethnic Group," Ph.D. dissertation, University of Arizona, 1966.

BROWN, D. G. and LOWE, W. L. "Religious Beliefs and Personality Characteristics of College Students," *Journal of Social Psychology*, 1951, *33*, 103–29.

BROWN, G. A.; SPILKA, B; and CASSIDY, S. "The Structure of Mystical Experience and its Pre- and Post-lifestyle Correlates," Paper presented at the Convention of the Rocky Mountain Psychological Association, Denver, Colorado, April 8, 1978.

BROWN, J. F. *The Psychodynamics of Abnormal Behavior*. New York: McGraw-Hill, 1940.

BROWN, L. B. "A Study of Religious Belief." *British Journal of Psychology, 53,* 259–72.

_____. "Aggression and Denominational Membership," *British Journal of Social and Clinical Psychology*, 1965, *4*, 175–78.

_____. "The Structure of Religious Belief." *Journal for the Scientific Study of Religion, 5,* 259–72.

_____. "Ego-centric Thought in Petitionary Prayer: A Cross-cultural Study," *Journal of Social Psychology*, 1966, *68*, 197–210.

_____. "Some Attitudes Underlying Petitionary Prayer," in A. Godin (ed.), *From Cry to Word: Contributions to a Psychology of Prayer*. Brussels, Belgium: Lumen Vitae Press, 1968, 65–84.

BROWNING, D. S. *Generative Man: Psychoanalytic Perspectives*. New York: Dell, 1975.

BRUDER, E. E. "Clinical Pastoral Training in Preparation for the Pastoral Ministry," *Journal of Pastoral Care*, 1962, *16*, 25–34.

BRYER, K. B. "The Amish Way of Death: A Study of Family Support Systems." *American Psychologist*, 1979, *34*, 255–61.

BUBER, M. *Between Man and Man*. New York: Macmillan, 1965.

BULL, N. J. *Moral Judgment from Childhood to Adolescence*. Beverly Hills, CA, 1969.

BULMAN, R. J. and WORTMAN, C. B. "Attributions of Blame and Coping in the 'Real World': Severe Accident Victims React to Their Lot." *Journal of Personality and Social Psychology*, 1977, *35*, 351–63.

BUMPASS, L. "The Trend of Interfaith Marriage in the United States." *Social Biology*, 1970, *17*, 253–59.

_____ and SWEET, J. "Differentials in Marital Instability." *American Sociological Review*, 1972, *37*, 754–66.

Bureau of the Census, *Statistical Abstract of the United States 1981. 102nd Edition*. Washington, DC: U.S. Department of Commerce, 1981.

BURGESS, E. W. and COTTRELL, L. S. *Predicting Success or Failure in Marriage*. New York: Prentice-Hall, 1939.

BURKETT, S. R. "Religiosity, Beliefs, Normative Standards and Adolescent Drinking," *Journal of Studies on Alcohol*, 1980, *41*, 662–71.

BUSSELL, H. O. III. *Slavery, Segregation, and Scripture*. Grand Rapids, Mich.: Eerdmans, 1964.

BYRNE, D. "Repression-Sensitization as a Dimension of Personality," in B. A. Maher (ed.), *Progress in Experimental Personality research*. Vol. 1. New York: Academic, 1964, pp. 169–220.

BYU Today, "How to Cope with the ERA Challenge?" May 1980, 34(3).

CAHALAN, D. *Problem Drinkers*. San Francisco: Jossey-Bass, 1970.

_____ and CISIN, I. H. "American Drinking Practices: Summary of Findings from a National Probability Sample I: Extent of Drinking by Population Subgroups. *Quarterly Journal of Studies on Alcohol*, 1968, *29*, 130–51.

_____; CISIN, I. H; and CROSSLEY, H. M., *American Drinking Practice: A National Study of Drinking Behavior and Attitudes*. New Brunswick, N. J.: Rutgers Center of Alcohol studies, 1969.

CALHOUN, J. F.   *Abnormal Psychology: Current Perspectives,* 2nd ed. New York: CRM/Random House, 1977.

CAMPBELL, A.   *The Sense of Well-Being in America.* New York: McGraw-Hill, 1981.

———, CONVERSE, P. E. and RODGERS, W. L.   *The Quality of American Life.* New York: Russell Sage, 1976.

CAMPBELL, B.   "A Typology of Cults," *Sociological Analysis.* 1978, *39,* 228–40.

CAMPBELL, D. T. and STANLEY, J. C.   *Experimental and Quasi-Experimental Designs for Research.* Chicago: Rand McNally, 1966.

CAMPBELL, E. I.   "A Study of Religious Conflict in Hospitalized Psychotics and Hospitalized Normals," Unpub. Ph.D. Dissertation, University of Pittsburg, 1958.

CANNON, L.   Reagan's recruitment of God in His Campaign, *The Denver Post* February 14, 1984, p. 21A.

CARDWELL, J.D.   On Keeping the Sabbath Day Holy: Perceived Powerlessness and Church Attendance of Mormon Males and Females," in J. D. Cardwell (ed.), *The Social Context of Religiosity.* Lanham, MD: University Press of America, 1980, 145–156.

CANTRIL, H.   *The Psychology of Social Movements.* New York: Wiley, 1941.

CAPLOVITZ, D. and SHERROW, F.   *The Religious Dropouts.* Beverly Hills: Sage, 1977.

CAREY, R. G.   "Weathering Widowhood: Problems and Adjustment of the Widowed during the First Year," *Omega,* 1979–80, *10,* 163–74.

——— and POSAVAC, E. J.   "Attitudes of Physicians on Disclosing Information To and Maintaining Life for Terminal Patients" *Omega,* 1978, *9,* 67–77.

CARROLL, J. B.   (ed.) *Language, Thought and Reality: Selected Writings of Benjamin Lee Whorf.* New York: Wiley, 1956.

CARTER, J. D.   "Secular and Sacred Models of Psychology and Religion," *Journal of Psychology and Theology,* 1977, *5,* 197–208.

CAVAN, R. S. et al. *Personal Adjustment in Old Age.* Chicago: Science Research Associates, 1949.

CAVENAR, J. O. and SPAULDING, J. G.   "Depressive Disorders and Religious Conversions," *Journal of Nervous and Mental Disease,* 1977, *165,* 200–212.

CECIL, D.   *Melbourne.* Indianapolis: Bobbs-Merrill, 1939.

CERNY, L. J. II   "Christian Faith and Thanatophobia," *Journal of Psychology and Theology,* 1975, *3,* 202–209.

CERNY, L. J. II, and CARTER, J. D.   "Death Perspectives and Religious Orientation as a Function of Christian Faith." Paper presented at the 1977 Convention of the Society for the Scientific Study of Religion, Chicago, Illinois.

CESARMAN, F. C.   "Religious Conversion of Sex Offenders," *Journal of Pastoral Care,* 1957, *11,* 25–35.

CHAFETZ, E. and DEMONE, H. E. JR.   *Alcoholism and Society.* New York: Oxford University Press, 1962.

CHALFANT, H. P.; BECKLEY, R. E.; and PALMER, C. E.   *Religion in Contemporary American Society.* Sherman Oaks, Ca.: Alfred, 1981.

CHAVE, E. J.   *Measure Religion: Fifty-two Experimental Forms.* Chicago: University of Chicago Press, 1939.

CHESEN, E. S.   *Religion May Be Hazardous to Your Health.* New York: Macmillan, 1972.

CHRISTENSEN, H. T., and CANNON, K. L.   "The Fundamentalist Emphasis at Brigham Young University: 1935–1973." *Journal for the Scientific Study of Religion,* 1978, *17,* 53–57.

CHRISTENSON, J. A.   "Religious Involvement, Values and Social Compassion." *Sociological Analysis,* 1976, *37,* 218–27.

CHRISTIANSEN, C. W.   "Religious Conversion," *Archives of General Psychiatry,* 1963, *9,* 207–216.

CHRISTOPHER, S.; FEARON, J.; McCOY, J.; and NOBLE, C.   "Social Deprivation and Religiosity," *Journal for the Scientific Study of Religion,* 1971, *10,* 385–92.

CLARK, E. T.   *The Psychology of Religious Awakening.* New York: Macmillan, 1929.

_____. *The Small Sects in America.* New York: Abingdon, 1949.

CLARK, S. L, and CARTER, J. D.   "Death Perspectives: Fear of Death, Guilt and Hope as Functions of Christian Faith." Paper presented at the 1978 Convention of the Western Association of Christians for Psychological Studies, Malibu, California, June 15-17, 1978.

CLARK, W. H.   *The Psychology of Religion.* New York: Macmillan, 1958.

_____.   "The Relationship Between Drugs and Religious Experience," *Catholic Psychological Record,* 1968a, *6,* 146-55.

_____.   *Chemical Ecstasy: Psychedelic Drugs and Religion.* New York: Sheed and Ward, 1969.

_____.   "Intense Religious Experience," in Strommen, M. P. (ed.), *Research on Religious Experience: A Comprehensive Handbook.* New York: Hawthorn, 1971, 521-50.

CLAYTON, R. R.   "5-D or 1?" *Journal for the Scientific Study of Religion, 10,* 37-40.

CLEMENT, P. W.   "Getting Religion," *APA Monitor,* June 1978, pp. 2, 19.

CLINE, V. B., and RICHARDS, J. M. JR.   "A Factor-Analytic Study of Religious Belief and Behavior." *Journal of Personality and Social Psychology,* 1965, *1,* 569-78.

COE, G. A.   *The Psychology of Religion.* Chicago: University of Chicago Press, 1916.

_____.   *The Spiritual Life.* New York: Abingdon, 1922.

COLEMAN, J. C.; BUTCHER, J. N.; and CARSON, R. C.   *Abnormal Psychology and Modern Life,* 6th ed. Glenview, Illinois: Scott, Foresman, 1980.

COLLINS, G. R.   *The Rebuilding of Psychology: An Integration of Psychology and Christianity.* Wheaton, Ill.: Tyndale, 1977.

_____.   "Integrating Psychology and Theology: Some Reflections on the State of the Art," *Journal of Psychology and Theology,* 1980, *8,* 72-79.

_____.   *Psychology and Theology.* Nashville: Abingdon, 1981.

COMSTOCK, G. W. and PARTRIDGE, K. B.   "Church Attendance and Health." *Journal of Chronic Diseases,* 1972, *25,* 665-72.

CONZE, E. (ed.).   *Buddhist Scriptures.* Baltimore, Md.: Penguin, 1959.

COOK, T. D. and CAMPBELL, D. T.   *Quasi-experimentation: Design and Analysis Issues for Field Settings.* Chicago: Rand McNally, 1979.

CORNWALL, M.; OLSEN, J; and WEED, S.   "The Influence of Parents on Youth Religiosity." Paper presented at the annual meeting of the Religious Research Association, San Antonio, TX, 1979.

CORSSAN, J. D.   *The Dark Interval.* Niles, Ill.: Argus Communications, 1975.

CORTES, J. B. and GATTI, F. M.   *Delinquency and Crime.* New York: Seminar Press, 1972.

COSER, L.   "Sect and Sectarians," *Dissent,* 1954, *1,* 360-69.

COX, H.   "Deep Structures in the study of the new religions," in J. Needleman and G. Baker (eds.), *Understanding the New Religions.* New York: Seabury, 1978, pp. 122-30.

CRANDALL, V. C., and GOZALI, J.   "The Social Desirability Responses of Children of Four Religious Cultural Groups," *Child Development,* 1969, *40,* 751-62.

CRISSMAN, P.   "Temporal Change and Sexual Differences in Moral Judgment," *Journal of Social Psychology,* 1942, *16,* 218-27.

CRUMBAUGH, J. C., and MAHOLICK, L. T.   *The Purpose in Life Test.* Munster, Ind.: Psychometric Affiliates, 1969.

CUTLER, S.   "Sources of Age Differences in Attitudes about Euthanasia." Paper presented at the 1979 meetings of the Gerontological Society, Washington, D. C., November 25-29, 1979.

CUTLER, S. J.   "Membership in Different Types of Voluntary Associations and Psychological Well-being," *Gerontologist,* 1976, *16,* 335-39.

CUTTEN, G. B.   *The Psychological Phenomena of Christianity.* New York: Charles Scribner's Sons, 1908.

_____.   *Speaking with Tongues.* New Haven, Conn.: Yale University Press, 1927.

DARLEY, J. M. and BATSON, C. D.   "From Jerusalem to Jericho: A Study of Situational and Dispositional Variables in Helping Behavior," *Journal of Personality and Social Psychology*, 1973, *27*, 100–108.

DASHEFSKY, A, and SHAPIRO, H. M.   *Ethnic Identification among American Jews*. Lexington, MA.: D. C. Health, 1974.

DATTA, L. E.   "Family Religious Background and Early Scientific Creativity." *American Sociological Review*, 1967, *32*, 626–35.

DAVIDS, A.   "Alienation, Social Apperception, and Ego Structure," *Journal of Consulting Psychology*, 1955, *19*, 21–27.

DAVIDSON, J. D.   "Glock's Model of Religious Commitment: Assessing Some Different Approaches and Results. *Review of Religious Research*, 1975, *16*, 83–93.

DAVIDSON, P. O. and COSTELLO, C. G. (eds.).   *N = 1: Experimental Studies of Single Cases*. New York: Van Nostrand Reinhold, 1969.

DAVIES, J. C.   "Toward a Theory of Revolution," *American Sociological Review*, 1962, *27*, 5–19.

DEAN, D. G.   "Alienation: Its Meaning and Measurement," *American Sociological Review*, 1961, *26*, 753–58.

_____.   "Anomie, Powerlessness and Religious Participation," *Journal for the Scientific Study of Religion*, 1968, *7,*151–54.

_____ and REEVES, J. A.   "Anomie: A Comparison of a Catholic and a Protestant Sample," *Sociometry*, 1962, *25*, 209–212.

DECONCHY, J. P.   "The Idea of God: Its Emergence between Seven and Sixteen Years," in A. Godin (ed.), *From Religious Experience to a Religious Attitude*. Brussels: Lumen Vitae Press 1964; pp. 111–22.

DEMERATH, N. J. III.   *Social Class in American Protestantism*. Chicago: Rand McNally, 1965.

_____ and HAMMOND, P. E.   *Religion in Social Context*. New York: Random House, 1969.

DEUTSCH, A.,   *The Mentally Ill in America*. New York: Columbia University Press, 1946.

_____.   "Tenacity of Attachment to a Cult Leader: A Psychiatric Perspective," *American Journal of Psychiatry*, 1980, *137*, 1569–73.

DEWEY, J.   *The Quest for Certainty*.   New York: Minton, Balch, 1929.

DICKSTEIN, L.   "Death Concern: Measurement and Correlates," *Psychological Reports*, 1972, *30, *563–571.

DIENSTBIER, R. A.   "Attribution, Socialization, and Moral Decision Making," in J. H. Harvey, W. J. Ickes, and R. F. Kidd (eds.), *New Directions in Attribution Research, Vol. 2*. Hillsdale, N.J.: Erlbaum, 1978, pp. 181–206.

_____.   "Emotion-Attribution Theory: Establishing Roots and Exploring Future Perspectives," in R. A. Dienstbier (ed)., *Nebraska Symposium on Motivation, 1978*. Lincoln: University of Nebraska Press, 1979, 237–306.

_____, HILLMAN, D.; LEHNHOFF, J.; HILLMAN, J.; and VALKENAAR, M. C.,   "An Emotion-Attribution Approach to Moral Behavior: Interfacing Cognitive and Avoidance Theories of Moral Development," *Psychological Review*, 1975, *82*, 229–315.

DIGGORY, J. C. and ROTHMAN, D. C.   "Values Destroyed by Death," *Journal of Abnormal and Social Psychology*, 1961, *63*, 205–10.

DITTES, J. E.   "Psychology and Religion," in G. Lindzey and E. Aronson (eds), *The Handbook of Social Psychology*. 2nd ed., Vol. 5. Reading, Mass.: Addison-Wesley, 1969, pp. 602–59.

_____.   "Typing the Typologies: Some Parallels in the Career of Church-sect and Extrinsic-intrinsic," *Journal for the Scientific Study of Religion*, 1971a, *10*, 375–83.

————. "Conceptual Deprivation and Statistical Rigor," *Journal for the Scientific Study of Religion*, 1971b, *10*, 393–95.

DIXON, R.D., and KINLAW, B.J.R.   "Belief in the Existence and Nature of Life after Death: A Research Note," 1982–83, *Omega, 13*, 287–93.

DOHRENWEND, B. P. and DOHRENWEND, B. S.,   *Social Status and Psychological Disorder.* New York: Wiley-Interscience, 1969.

DOLMATCH, T. B. (ed.)   *Information Please Almanac 1982*, (36th edition) New York: Simon and Schuster, 1981.

DONAHUE, M. J.   *Intrinsic Versus Extrinsic Religiousness: A Meta-Analysis.* Unpublished manuscript.

————— and BERGIN, A. E.   *Religion, Personality, and Lifestyle: A Review and Meta-analysis.* Paper presented at the Convention of the American Psychological Association, Anaheim, California, August, 1983.

DOWNING, J. J. and WYGANT, W., JR.   "Psychedelic Experience and Religious Belief," in R. Blum (ed.), *Utopiates: The Use and Users of LSD-25.* New York: Atherton, 1964, pp. 187–98.

DOWNTON, J. V. JR.   "An Evolutionary Theory of Spiritual Conversion and Commitment: The Case of the Divine Light Mission," *Journal for the Scientific Study of Religion*, 1980, *19*, 381–96.

DREGER, R. M.   "Some Personality Correlates of Religious Attitudes," *Psychological Monographs, 1952, 66*, No. 3.

DRESSER, H. W.   *Outlines of the Psychology of Religion.* New York: Thomas Y. Crowell, 1929.

DUBLIN, L. I.   *Suicide.* New York: Ronald, 1963.

DUCASSE, C. J.   *A Critical Examination of the Belief in a Life after Death.* Springfield, Ill.: C. C. Thomas, 1961.

DUDLEY, R. L.   "Alienation from Religion in Adolescents from Fundamentalist Religious Homes," *Journal for the Scientific Study of Religion*, 1978, *17*, 389–99.

DUKE, E. H.   "Meaning in Life and Acceptance of Death in Terminally Ill Patients." Unpublished Ph.D. dissertation, Northwestern University, 1977.

DUNHAM, H. W.   "Anomie and Mental Disorder, in M. B. Clinard (ed.), *Anomie and Deviant Behavior.* New York: Free Press of Glencoe, 1964, 128–57.

DURKHEIM, E.   *Suicide.* New York: The Free Press, 1951.

DYER, T. and LUCKEY, E. B.   "Religious Affiliation and Selected Personality Scores as They Relate to Marital Happiness of a Minnesota College Sample." *Marriage and Family Living*, 1961, *23*, 46–47.

DYNES, R. R.   "Church-sect Typology and Socio-Economic Status." *American Sociological Review*, 1955, *20*, 555–60.

EATON, J. W. and WEIL, R. J.   *Culture and Mental Disorders.* Glencoe, Ill.: The Free Press, 1955.

EDWARDS, A. L.   *The Social Desirability Variable in Personality Assessment and Research.* New York: Dryden, 1957.

EDWARDS, J. N. and KLEMMACK, D. L.   "Correlates of Life Satisfaction: A Reexamination," *Journal of Gerontology*, 1973, *28*, 497–502.

EDWARDS, K. J. and WESSEL, S. J.   "Relationship of Psychosocial Maturity to Intrapersonal, and Spiritual Functioning." Paper presented at the 1980 Convention of the American Psychological Association, Montreal, Canada: September 5, 1980.

EDWARDS, T., CATREVAS, C. N. and EDWARDS, J.   *The New Dictionary of Thoughts.* New York: Standard Book Co., 1955.

EINSTEIN, A.   "Religion and Science," in A. M. Drummond and R. H. Wagner (eds.), *Problems and Opinions.* New York: Century, 1931, pp. 355–58.

EISTER, A. W. "An Outline of a Structural Theory of Cults," *Journal for the Scientific Study of Religion,* 1972, *11,* 319–30.

ELKIND, D. "The Child's Concept of His Religious Denomination, I: The Jewish Child." *Journal of Genetic Psychology,* 1961, *99,* 209–55.

_____. "The Child's Concept of His Religious Denomination, II: The Catholic Child, *Journal of Genetic Psychology,* 1962, *101,* 185–93.

_____. "The Child's Concept of His Religious Denomination, III: The Protestant Child." *Journal of Genetic Psychology,* 1963, *103,* 291–304.

_____. "Piaget's Semi-clinical Interview and the Study of Spontaneous Religion." *Journal for the Scientific Study of Religion,* 1964, *4,* 40–47.

_____. "The Origins of Religion in the Child." *Review of Religious Research,* 1970, *12,* 35–42.

_____. "The Development of Religious Understanding in Children and Adolescents," in M. Strommen (ed.), *Research on Religious Development.* New York: Hawthorn Books, 1971; pp. 655–85.

ELLMAN, I. "Jewish Intermarriage in the United States of America," in B. Schlesinger (ed.), *The Jewish Family.* Toronto, Canada: University of Toronto Press, 1971, 25–62.

ELLWOOD, C. A. *The Reconstruction of Religion.* New York: Macmillan, 1922.

ELLWOOD, R. S., JR. *Mysticism and Religion.* Englewood Cliffs, N.J.: Prentice-Hall, Inc., 1980.

ELMORE, T.M. *The Development of a Scale to Measure Psychological Anomie.* Unpublished doctoral dissertation, Ohio State University, 1962.

EMBREE, R. A. "Attribution: An Experimental Application: The Effects of Religious Norm and Sexual Orientation on Judgments about Sexual Morality." Paper presented at the 26th annual meeting of SSSS, Chicago, Ill., November 1983.

ERICKSON, D. "Differential Effects of Public and Sectarian Schooling on the Religiousness of the Child." Unpublished doctoral dissertation, University of Chicago, 1962.

ETHERIDGE, F. M, and FEAGIN, J. R. "Varieties of Fundamentalism: A Conceptual and Empirical Analysis of Two Protestant Denominations." *The Sociological Quarterly,* 1979, *20,* 37–48.

FAIRCHILD, R. W. "Delayed Gratification: A Psychological and Religious Analysis." In M. P. Strommen (ed.), *Research on Religious Development.* New York: Hawthorn, pp. 155–210.

FALK, G. J."Religion, Personal Integration and Criminality," *Journal of Educational Sociology,* 1961, *35,* 159–61.

FAULKNER, J. E., and DEJONG, G. F. "Religiosity in 5-D: An Empirical Analysis." *Social Forces,* 1966, *45,* 246–54.

FAUNCE, W. A. and FULTON, R. L. "The sociology of Death: A Neglected Area of Research," *Social Forces,* 1958, *36,* 205–209.

FEAGIN, J. R. "Prejudice and Religious Types: A Focused Study of Southern Fundamentalists." *Journal for the Scientific Study of Religion,* 1964, *4,* 3–13.

FEATHER, N. T. "Acceptance and Rejection of Arguments in Relation to Attitude Strength, Critical Ability, and Intolerance of Inconsistency," *Journal of Abnormal and Social Psychology,* 1964, *69,* 127–36.

FEIFEL, H. "Religious Conviction and Fear of Death among the Healthy and the Terminally Ill," *Journal for the Scientific Study of Religion,* 1974, *13,* 353–60.

_____ and BRANSCOMB, A. B. "Who's Afraid of Death?" *Journal of Abnormal Psychology,* 1973, *81,* 282–88.

FELDMAN, K. A. "Change and Stability of Religious Orientations during College." *Review of Religious Research,* 1969, *11,* 40–60 and 103–128.

FENN, R. K.   *Toward a Theory of Secularization*, Society for the Scientific Study of Religion, Monograph Series, No. 1, 1978.

FERGUSON, L. W.   "Primary Social Attitudes." *Journal of Psychology*, 1939, *8*, 217–23.

———.   "The Stability of the Primary Social Attitudes. I: Religionism and Humanitarianism." *Journal of Social Psychology*, 1941, *12*, 283–88.

———.   "A Revision of the Primary Attitude Scales." *Journal of Psychology*, 1944, *17*, 229–41.

———.   "The Sociological Validity of Primary Social Attitude Scale No. 1: Religionism." *Journal of Social Psychology*, 1946, *23*, 197–20.

FERNANDO, S. J. M.   "A Cross-cultural Study of Some Familial and Social Factors in Depressive Illness," *British Journal of Psychiatry*, 1975, *127*, 46–53.

FESTINGER, L.; RIECKEN, H. W.; and SCHACHTER, S.   *When Prophecy Fails*. New York: Harper and Row, 1964.

FEUER, L. S.   *The Scientific Intellectual*. New York: Basic Books, 1963.

FICHTER, J. H.   *Religion and Pain*. New York: Crossroad, 1981.

——— (ed.).   *Alternatives to American Mainline Churches*. New York: Rose of Sharon Press, 1983.

FINCH, J. G.   "Motivations for the Ministry—A Pathological View," *Insight,* Summer 1965, *4*, No. 1, 26–31.

FISCHER, S.   "Acquiescence and Religiosity," *Psychological Reports*, 1964, *15*, 784.

FLAKOLL, D. A.   "Self-esteem, Psychological Adjustment, and Images of God," Paper presented at the 1974 convention of the Society for the Scientific Study of Religion, Washington, D.C., October 26, 1974.

FLECK, J. R. and CARTER, J. D. (eds.)   *Psychology and Christianity*. Nashville: Abingdon, 1981.

FLETCHER, J.   *Situation Ethics: The New Morality*. Philadelphia: Westminster, 1966.

FLORIAN, V. and HAR-EVEN, D.   "Fear of Personal Death: The effects of Sex and Religious Belief," 1983-84, *Omega, 14,* 83–91.

FORBES, G. B. and GROMOLL, H. F.   "The Lost Letter Technique as a Measure of Social Variables," *Social Forces*, 1971, *50*, 113–15.

———; TEVAULT, R. K.; and GROMOLL, H. F.,   "Willingness to Help Strangers as a Function of Liberal, Conservative or Catholic Church Membership: XI. A Field Study with the Lost-Letter Technique," *Psychological Reports*, 1971, *28*, 947–49.

FORSYTH, D. R.   "Moral Judgment: The Influence of Ethical Ideology," *Personality and Social Psychology Bulletin, 7,* 218–33.

FOWLER, J. W.   *Stages of Faith: The Psychology of Human Development and the Quest for Meaning*. San Francisco: Harper and Row, 1981.

FRANKL, V. E.   *Man's Search for Meaning*. New York: Washington Square, 1963.

FRANZBLAU, A.   "Conversion to Judaism: Psychologically Speaking," in D. M. Eichhorn (ed.), *Conversion to Judaism*. New York: Ktav, 1965, 189–207.

FREUD, S.   *Civilization and its Discontents*. New York: Norton, 1961.

———.   *The Future of an Illusion*. Garden City, N. Y.: Doubleday, 1964.

FROMM, E.   *Psychoanalysis and Religion*. New Haven, CN.: Yale, 1950.

FUKUYAMA, Y.   "The Major Dimensions of Church Membership." *Review of Religious Research*, 1961, *2*, 154–61.

FULTON, R. L., and GEIS, G.   "Social Change and the Funeral Director," *Sociological Symposium*, 1968, *1*, 1–9.

FUNK, R. A.   "A Survey of Religious Attitudes and Manifest Anxiety in a College Population," Unpublished Ph.D. Dissertation, Purdue University, 1955.

FURNHAM, A. F.   "Locus of Control and Theological Beliefs." *Journal of Psychology and Theology*, 1982, *10*, 130–36.

FURST, P. T.   *Hallucinogens and Culture.* San Francisco: Chandler and Sharp, 1976.

GABEL, J.   *False Consciousness.* New York: Harper and Row, 1975.

GALANTER, M.   "Charismatic Religious Sects and Psychiatry: An Overview." *American Journal of Psychiatry,* 1982, *139,* 1539–48.

_____; RABKIN, R.; RABKIN, J.; and DEUTSCH, A.   "The Moonies: A Psychological Study of Conversion and Membership in a Contemporary Religious Sect," *American Journal of Psychiatry,* 1979, *136,* 165–69.

GALLEMORE, J. L. JR.; WILSON, W. P.; and RHOADS, J. M.   "The Religious Life of Patients with Affective Disorders," *Diseases of the Nervous System,* 1969, *30,* 483–87.

GALLUP, G.   "Taking of One's Life Opposed by 51 Pct. on Moral Grounds," *The Denver Post,* May 4, 1975, p. 17.

_____.   "Views on Religion Relevance Level Out after '74 Decline," *The Denver Post,* March 27, 1981, p. 5F.

_____.   *Adventures in Immortality.* New York: McGraw-Hill, 1982.

_____ and POLING, D.   *The Search for America's Faith.* Nashville: Abingdon, 1980.

GANNON, T. M.   "Religious Control and Delinquent Behavior," *Sociology and Social Research,* 1967, *51,* 418–31 (as abstracted and quoted in "The Religious Delinquent," *Trans-action,* 1967, *5,* (2), p. 6).

GANS, H. J.   *The Levittowners.* New York: Random House, 1967.

GARDINER, H. N. (ed.).   *Selected Sermons of Johnathan Edwards.* New York: Macmillan, 1904.

GARDNER, H.   "What We Know (and Don't Know) About the Two Halves of the Brain," *Harvard Magazine,* 1978, *80,* 24–27.

GARDNER, J. W.   *Morale.* New York: Norton, 1978.

GARRETT, W. R.   "Troublesome Transcendence: The Supernatural in the Scientific Study of Religion," *Sociological Analysis,* 1974, *35,* 167–80.

GARRITY, T. F. and WYSS, J.   "Death, Funeral and Bereavement Practices in Appalachian and non-Appalachian Kentucky," *Omega,* 1976, *7,* 209–28.

GAZZANIGA, M. S. and LeDOUX, J. E.   *The Integrated Mind.* New York: Plenum, 1978.

GEIGER, H. J.   "Anonymous Struggle for Twenty-five Years," *New York Times Magazine,* June 5, 1960, pp. 26, 74–76.

GEORGE, K. and GEORGE, C. H.   "Roman Catholic Sainthood and Social Status," in Bendix, R. and Lipset, S. M. (eds.), *Class, Status and Power, Second Edition,* New York: The Free Press, 1966, 394–401.

GERNER H.L.   "A Study of the Freedom Riders with Particular Emphasis upon Three Dimensions: Dogmatism, Value-Orientation, and Religiosity." Paper presented at the convention of the Religious Research Assn., Columbus, OH, June 18, 1965.

GERRARD, N. L. and GERRARD, L. B.   *Scrabble Creek Folks: Mental Health, Part II.* Unpublished Report, Department of Sociology, Morris Harvey College, West Virginia, 1966.

GERSON, G. S.   "The Psychology of Grief and Mourning in Judaism," *Journal of Religion and Health,* 1977, *16,* 260–74

GEYER, A. F.   *Piety and Politics.* Richmond, Va.: John Knox Press, 1963.

GIBBS, H. W. and ACHTERBERG-LAWLIS, J.   "Spiritual Values and Death Anxiety: Implications for Counseling with Terminal Cancer Patients," *Journal of Counseling Psychology,* 1978, *25,* 563–69.

GIBBS, J. P.   "Suicide," in R. K. Merton and R. A. Nisbet (eds.), *Contemporary Social Problems. Second Edition,* New York: Harcourt, Brace and World, 1966, 281–321.

GIBRAN, K.   *The Prophet.* New York: Alfred A. Knopf, 1923.

GLADDING, S. T.   "Psychological Anomie and Religious Identity in Two Adolescent Populations," *Psychological Reports,* 1977, *41,* 419–24.

GLENN, N. D. and WEAVER, C. N.   "Attitudes toward Premarital, Extramarital and Homosexual Practices in the U.S. in the 1970s," *Journal of Sex Research,* 1979, *15,* 108–18.

GLICK, I. O.; WEISS, R. S.; and PARKES, C. M.   *The First Year of Bereavement.* New York: Wiley, 1974.

GLOCK, C. Y.   "On the Study of Religious Commitment." *Religious Education Research Supplement,* 1962, *57*(4), 98–110.

_____.   "On the Origin and Evolution of Religious Groups," in R. Lee and Marty, M. E. (eds.), *Religion and Social Conflict.* New York: Oxford University Press, 1944, pp. 24–36.

_____.   "Consciousness among Contemporary Youth: An Interpretation," in Glock, C. Y. and Bellah, R. N. (eds.), *The New Religious Consciousness.* Berkeley, Calif.: University of California Press, 1976, pp. 333–66.

_____ and BELLAH, R. N. (eds.).   *The New Religious Consciousness.* Berkeley, Calif.: University of California Press, 1976.

_____ and HAMMOND, P. E. (eds.).   *Beyond the classics.* New York: Harper and Row, 1973.

_____ and STARK, R.   *Christian Beliefs and Anti-semitism.* New York: Harper, 1966.

_____ and STARK, R.   *Religion and Society in Tension.* Chicago: Rand McNally, 1963.

GODIN, A.   "Some Developmental Tasks in Christian Education," in M. P. Strommen (ed.), *Research on Religious Development.* New York: Hawthorn, 1971, pp. 109–54.

GOLDEN, H.   *Carl Sandburg.* New York: Fawcett, 1961.

GOLDMAN, R.   *Religious Thinking from Childhood to Adolescence.* London: Routledge, 1964.

GOLDSEN, R. K.; ROSENBERG, M.; WILLIAMS, R. M. JR.; and SUCHMAN, E. A.   *What College Students Think.* Princeton, N.J.: D. Van Nostrand, 1960.

GOLDSTEIN, S. and GOLDSCHEIDER, G.   *Jewish Americans.* Englewood Cliffs, NJ: Prentice-Hall, 1968.

GOLEMAN, D.   *The Varieties of Meditative Experience.* New York: Dutton, 1977.

_____ and DAVIDSON, R. J. (eds.).   *Consciousness: Brain, States of Awareness and Mysticism.* New York: Harper and Row, 1969.

GOODE, E.   "Social Class and Church Participation," *American Journal of Sociology,* 1966, *72,* 102–11.

_____.   "Class Styles of Religious Sociation," *British Journal of Sociology,* 1968, *19,* 1–16.

GOODENOUGH, E. R.   *Toward a Mature Faith.* New Haven, CN: Yale University Press, 1955.

GOODMAN, F. D.   "Phonetic Analysis of Glossolalia in Four Cultural Settings," *Journal for the Scientific Study of Religion,* 1969, *8,* 227–39.

_____.   *Speaking in Tongues: A Cross Cultural Study of Glossolalia.* Chicago: University of Chicago Press, 1972.

GOODWIN, D. W.; JOHNSON, J.; MAHER, C.; RAPPAPORT, A.; and GUZE, S. B.   "Why People Do Not Drink: A Study of Teetotalers," *Comprehensive Psychiatry,* 1969, *10,* 209–14.

GORDON, A.   *Intermarriage.* Boston: Beacon, 1964.

GORDON, S.   "Personality and Attitude Correlates of Religious Conversion," *Journal for the Scientific Study of Religion,* 1964, *4,* 60–63.

GORER, G.   *Death, Grief and Mourning.* New York: Doubleday, 1965.

GORSUCH, R. L.   "Identifying the Religiously Committed Person." Paper presented at the meeting of the American Association for the Advancement of Science, Dallas, Texas, December 1968.

_____.   "Value Conflict in the School Setting." Final report. George Peabody College for Teachers, Project #9-0427, Office of Education, Department of Health, Education and Welfare. ERIC Document (ED 057 410), August 1971.

_____.   "Rokeach's Approach to Value Systems and Social Compassion," *Review of Religious Research,* 1970, *11,* 139–42.

———. "Religion as a Significant Predictor of Important Human Behavior," in W. J. Donaldson Jr. (ed.), *Research in Mental Health and Religious Behavior.* Atlanta, Ga.: Psychological Studies Institute, 1976, 206–21.

———. "An Interactive, Multiple Model Approach to Illicit Drug Use," in D. J. Lettieri (ed.). *Theories of Drug Use.* Washington, D.C.: National Institute on Drug Abuse, 1980, 18–23, 383–85.

———. "Review of Milton Rokeach's *Understanding Human Values.*" *Journal for the Scientific Study of Religion,* 1980, *19*(3), 316.

———. *Factor Analysis,* 2nd ed. Hillsdale, NJ: Lawrence E. Erlbaum, 1983.

———. "Measurement: The Boon and Bane of Investigating Religion. *American Psychologist,* 1984, *39,* 228–36.

——— and ALESHIRE, D.   "Christian Faith and Ethnic Prejudice: A Review and Interpretation of Research," *Journal for the Scientific Study of Religion,* 1974, *13,* 281–307.

——— and BARNES, M. L.   "Stages of Ethical Reasoning and Moral Norms of Carib Youth." *Journal of Cross-Cultural Psychology,* 1971, *4,* 283–301.

——— and BUTLER, M.   "Initial Drug Abuse: A Review of Predisposing Social Psychological Factors," *Psychological Bulletin,* 1976a, *81,* 120–37.

——— and BUTLER, M.   "Toward Developmental Models of Non-medical Drug Use," in S. B. Sells and D. D. Simpson (eds.), *The Effectiveness of Drug Abuse Treatment,* Vol. 5. Cambridge, Mass.: Ballinger, 1976b, pp. 1–186.

——— and MALONY, H. N.   *The Nature of Man's Social Psychological Perspective: The Third John G. Finch Symposium on Psychology and Religion.* Springfield, Illinois: Charles C. Thomas, 1976.

——— and MCFARLAND, S.   "Single vs. Multiple-Choice Item Scales for Measuring Religious Values," *Journal for the Scientific Study of Religion,* 1972, *11,* 53–64.

———, O'CONNOR; J., and GHAMSAVARI, F.   "Important Issues: An Approach to Measuring Stages of Moral Judgment and Evaluating the Nature of the Stages." Unpublished paper, 1973.

——— and SMITH, C. S.   *Sanctioning and Causal Attributions to God: A Function of Theological Position and Actor's Characteristics.* Unpublished paper, 1983a.

——— and SMITH, C. S.   "Attributions of Responsibility to God: An Interaction of Religious Beliefs and Outcomes." *Journal for the Scientific Study of Religion,* 1983, *22,* 340–52.

GRAFF, R. W. and LADD, C. E.   "POI Correlates of a Religious Commitment Inventory," *Journal of Clinical Psychology,* 1971, *27,* 502–4.

GRANEY, M. J.   "Happiness and Social Participation in Aging," *Journal of Gerontology,* 1975, *30,* 701–706.

GRAY, D. B.   "Measuring Attitudes toward the Church." *Journal for the Scientific Study of Religion,* 1970, *9,* 293–97.

GREELEY, A. M.   "Influence of the 'Religious Factor' on Career Plans and Occupational Values of College Graduates." *American Journal of Sociology,* 1963, *68,* 658–71.

———. *The Denominational Society,* Glenview, Ill.: Scott Foresman, 1972.

———. *Ecstasy: A Way of Knowing.* Englewood Cliffs, N.J.: Prentice-Hall, 1974.

———. *The Sociology of the Paranormal,* Beverly Hills, CA: Sage, 1975.

———. *Death and Beyond.* Chicago: Thomas More, 1976.

———. "Ethnic Variations in Religious Commitment," in R. Wuthnow (ed.), *The Religious Dimension: New Directions in Quantitative Research.* New York: Academic, 1979, 113–34.

——— and GOCKEL, G. L.   "The Religious Effects of Parochial Education," in M. P. Strommen (ed.), *Research on Religious Development.* New York: Hawthorn, 1971, pp. 264–301.

——— and ROSSI, P. H.   *The Education of Catholic Americans.* Chicago: Aldine, 1966.

GREEN, R. W. (ed.)   *Protestantism and Capitalism.* Boston: D. C. Heath, 1959.

GREIL, A. L. "Previous Disposition and Conversion to Perspectives of Social and Religious Movements," *Sociological Analysis,* 1977, *38,* 115–25.

Group for the Advancement of Psychiatry, *The Psychic Function of Religion in Mental Illness and Health.* January, 1968, *VI,* Report No. 67.

GURIN, G.; VEROFF, J.; and FELD, S., *Americans View Their Mental Health.* Joint Commission on Mental Illness and Health. Monograph Ser. No. 4, New York: Basic Books, 1960.

GUTMANN, D. "The Cross-Cultural Perspective: Notes toward a Comparative Psychology of Aging," in Birren, J. E. and Schaie, K. W. (eds.) *Handbook of the Psychology of Aging.* New York: Van Nostrand Reinhold, *1977,* 302–26.

HADAWAY, C. K. "Conservative and Social Strength in a Liberal Congregation," *Review of Religious Research,* 1980, *21,* 302–14.

_____. "Denominational Switching and Religiosity," *Review of Religious Research,* 1980, *21,* 451–61.

_____ and ROOF, W. C. "Religious Commitment and the Quality of Life in American Society," *Review of Religious Research,* 1978, *19,* 295–307.

_____ and ROOF, W. C. "Those Who Stay Religious "Nones" and Those Who Don't: A Research Note," *Journal for the Scientific Study of Religion,* 1979, *18,* 194–200.

HADDEN, J. K. *The Gathering Storm in the Churches.* Garden City, N.Y. Doubleday, 1969.

HALL, C. S., and LINDZEY, G. *Theories of Personality,* 3rd. ed. New York: Wiley, 1978.

HALL, G. S. "The Moral and Religious Training of Children and Adolescents." *Pedagogical Seminary,* 1891, *1,* 196–210.

_____. *Adolescence,* 2 vols. New York: D. Appleton, 1904.

HAMMARSKJOLD, D. *Markings.* New York: Knopf, 1964.

HAMMOND, B. "The Interventionism Variable in the God-Concept and Its Relationship to the Treatment of Drug Abuse." Unpublished thesis for the Master of Divinity degree, Iliff School of Theology, March 1982.

HANAWALT, N. G. "Feelings of Security and of Self-Esteem in Relation to Religious Beliefs," *Journal of Social Psychology,* 1963, *59,* 347–53.

HANFORD, J. T. "A Synoptic Approach: Resolving Problems in Empirical and Phenomenological Approaches to the Psychology of Religion," *Journal for the Scientific Study of Religion,* 1975, *14,* 219–27.

_____. *Study Strategies Derived from a Synoptic View of Psychology of Religion.* Unpublished manuscript.

HARDT, D. V. *Death: The Final Frontier.* Englewood Cliffs, N. J.: Prentice-Hall, 1979.

HARDT, H. D. "Mental Health Status and Religious Attitudes of Hospitalized Veterans," Unpub. Ph.D. Dissertation, University of Texas, 1963.

HARDY, A. *The Spiritual Nature of Man.* Oxford: Clarendon Press, 1979.

HARMS, E. "The Development of Religious Experience in Children." *American Journal of Sociology,* 1944, *50,* 112–22.

HARNER, M. J. (ed.). *Hallucinogens and Shamanism.* New York: Oxford University Press, 1973.

HARRELL, S. "Modes of Belief in Chinese Folk Religion." *Journal for the Scientific Study of Religion,* 1977, *16,* 55–65.

HARRISON, M. I. "Sources of Recruitment to Catholic Pentacostalism," *Journal for the Scientific Study of Religion,* 1974, *13,* 49–64.

_____ and MANIHA, J. K. "Dynamics of Dissenting Movements within Established Organizations: Two Cases and a Theoretical Interpretation," *Journal for the Scientific Study of Religion,* 1978, *17,* 207–44.

HARMS, E. "The Development of Religious Experience in Children." *Journal of Sociology.* 1944, *50,* 112–22.

HARTOCOLLIS, P. "Aggression and Mysticism," *Contemporary Psychoanalysis,* 1976, *12,* 214–26.

HARTSHORNE, H. and MAY, M. A.   *Studies in the Nature of Character: Vol. I: Studies in Deceit.* New York: Macmillan, 1928.

_____ and MAY, M. A.,   *Studies in the Nature of Character. Vol. II. Studies in Service and Self-Control.* New York: Macmillan, 1929.

_____; MAY, M. A.; and SHUTTLEWORTH, F. K.,   *Studies in the Nature of Character. Vol. III: Studies in the Organization of Character.* New York: Macmillan, 1930.

HARVEY, J. H., and WEARY, C.   *Perspectives on Attributional Processes.* Dubuque, IA: William C. Brown, 1981.

HASSETT, J.   " 'But That Would Be Wrong. . .': *Psychology Today's* Report on Cheating, Lying, and Bending the Rules in Everyday Life," *Psychology Today,* November 1981, 34–50.

HAUN, D. L.   "Perception of the Bereaved, Clergy, and Funeral Directors Concerning Bereavement," *Dissertation Abstracts International,* A37, 1977, p. 6791.

HAY, D. and MORISY, A.   "Reports of Ecstatic, Paranormal, or Religious Experience in Great Britain and the United States—A Comparison of Trends." *Journal for the Scientific Study of Religion,* 1978, *17,* 255–68.

HEILER, F.,   *Prayer.* New York: Oxford University Press, 1932.

HEIRICH, M.   "Change of Heart: A Test of Some Widely Held Theories about Religious Conversion," *American Journal of Sociology,* 1977, *83,* 653–80.

HERBERG, W.   *Protestant, Catholic, Jew.* Garden City, N.Y.: Doubleday, 1960.

HERBERT, F.   *The Dune.* New York: Berkeley, 1965.

HEROLD, E. S. and GOODWIN, M. S.   "Adamant Virgins, Potential Nonvirgins, and Nonvirgins," *Journal of Sex Research,* 1981, *17,* 97–113.

HERTEL, B. R.   "Inconsistency of Beliefs in the Existence of Heaven and Afterlife," *Review of Religious Research,* 1980, *21,* 171–83.

HESCHEL, A. J.   *Man Is Not Alone.* New York: Jewish Publication Society, 1951.

HILL, C. M. (ed.)   *The World's Great Religious Poetry.* New York: Macmillan, 1924.

HILTNER, S.   "Conclusion: The Dialogue on Man's Nature," in Simon Doniger (ed.), *The Nature of Man.* New York: Harper, 1961, 237–61.

HIMMELFARB, H. S.   "The Interaction Effects of Parents, Spouse and Schooling: Comparing the Impact of Jewish and Catholic Schools." *The Sociological Quarterly,* 1977, *18,* 464–77.

HINE, V. H.   "The Deprivation and Disorganization Theories of Social Movements," in I. Zaretsky and M. Leone (eds.), *Religious Movements in Contemporary America.* Princeton, N.J.: Princeton University, 1965, pp. 646–64.

HINE, V. H.   "Pentecostal Glossolalia: Toward a Functional Interpretation," *Journal for the Scientific Study of Religion,* 1969, *8,* 211–26.

HIRCH, E. G.   *My Religion.* New York: Macmillan, 1925.

HOBHOUSE, L. T.   *Morals in Evolution.* New York: Henry Holt, 1906.

HODGES, D. L.   "Breaking a Scientific Taboo: Putting Assumptions about the Supernatural into Scientific Theories of Religion," *Journal for the Scientific Study of Religion,* 1974, *13,* 393–408.

HOELTER, J. W.   "Religiosity, Fear of Death and Suicide Acceptability," *Suicide and Life-Threatening Behavior,* 1979, *9,* 163–72.

_____ and EPLEY, R. J.   "Religious Correlates of Fear of Death," *Journal for the Scientific Study of Religion,* 1979, *18,* 404–11.

HOFFER, E.   *The True Believer.* New York: Harper, 1951.

HOFFMAN, E.   *The Way of Splendour.* Boulder, Colo.: Shambala, 1981.

HOGE, D. R.   "A Test of Theories of Denominational Growth and Decline," in D. R. Hoge and D. A. Roozen (eds.), *Understanding Church Growth and Decline.* Philadelphia: Pilgrim Press, 1979.

HOGE, D. R. and CARROLL, J. W.   "Religiosity and Prejudice in Northern and Southern Churches," *Journal for the Scientific Study of Religion,* 1973, *12,* 181–97.

_____. *Commitment on Campus: Changes in Religion and Values Over Five Decades.* Philadelphia: Westminster, 1974.

_____ and CARROLL, J. W. "Determinants of Commitment and Participation in Suburban Protestant Churches," *Journal for the Scientific Study of Religion,* 1978, *17,* 107-27.

_____ and KEETER, L. "Determinants of college teachers' religious beliefs and participation." *Journal for the Scientific Study of Religion,* 1976, *15,* 221-35.

_____. and G. H. PETRILLO, "Development of Religious Thinking in Adolescence: A Test of Goldman's Thinking." *Journal for the Scientific Study of Religion,* 1978, *17,* 139-54.

_____ and PETRILLO, G. H. "Determinants of Church Participation and Attitudes among High School Youth." *Journal for the Scientific Study of Religion,* 1978, *17,* 359-79.

_____ and POLK, D. T. "A Test of Theories of Protestant Church Participation and Commitment," *Review of Religious Research,* 1980, *21,* 315-29.

HOGGATT, L. and SPILKA, B. "The Nurse and the Terminally Ill Patient: Some Perspectives and Projected Actions," *Omega,* 1978, *9,* 255-66.

HOGGE, J. H., and FRIEDMAN, S. T. "The Scriptural Literalism Scale: A Preliminary Report." *Journal of Psychology,* 1967, *66,* 275-79.

HOLE, G. "Some Comparisons among Guilt-Feelings, Religion and Suicidal Tendencies in Depressed Patients," *Suicide and Life-Threatening Behavior,* 1971, *1,* 138-42.

HOLLINGSHEAD, A. B. and REDLICH, F. C. *Social Class and Mental Illness.* New York: Wiley, 1958.

HOLMES, U. T. *A History of Christian Spirituality.* New York: Seabury, 1980.

HOLT, R. R. "Imagery: The Return of the Ostracized," *American Psychologist,* 1964, *19,* 254-64.

HOMANS, P. (ed.) *The Dialogue Between Theology and Psychology.* Chicago: University of Chicago Press.

HONIGMANN, J. J. *The World of Man.* New York: Harper and Row, 1959.

HOOD, R. W., JR. "Religious Orientation and the Report of Religious Experience," *Journal for the Scientific Study of Religion,* 1970, *9,* 285-91.

_____. "A Comparison of the Allport and Feagin Scoring Procedures for Intrinsic/Extrinsic Religious Orientation," *Journal for the Scientific Study of Religion,* 1971, *10,* 370-74.

_____. "Normative and Motivational Determinants of Reported Religious Experience in Two Baptist Samples." *Review of Religious Research,* 1972, *13,* 192-96.

_____. "Religious Orientation and the Experience of Transcendence," *Journal for the Scientific Study of Religion,* 1973a, *12,* 441-48.

_____. "Forms of Religious Commitment and Intense Religious Experience," *Review of Religious Research,* 1973b, *15,* 29-36.

_____. "Hypnotic Suggestibility and Reported Religious Experience," *Psychological Reports,* 1973c, *33,* 549-50.

_____. "Psychological Strength and the Report of Intense Religious Experience," *Journal for the Scientific Study of Religion,* 1974, *13,* 65-71.

_____. "The Construction and Preliminary Validation of a Measure of Reported Mystical Experience," *Journal for the Scientific Study of Religion,* 1975, *14,* 29-41.

_____. "Mystical Experience as Related to Present and Anticipated Future Church Participation," *Psychological Reports,* 1976, *39,* 1127-36.

_____. "Eliciting Mystical States of Consciousness with Semistructured Nature Experiences," *Journal for the Scientific Study of Religion,* 1977, *16,* 155-63.

_____. "Differential Triggering of Mystical Experience as a Function of Self-Actualization," *Review of Religious Research,* 1977a, *18,* 264-70.

_____. "The Usefulness of the Indiscriminately Pro and Anti Categories of Religious Orientation." *Journal for the Scientific Study of Religion,* 1978, *17,* 419-31.

————. "Anticipatory Set and Setting: Stress Incongruities as Elicitors of Mystical Experience in Solitary Nature Situations," *Journal for the Scientific Study of Religion,* 1978, *17,* 279–87.

————. "Social Psychology and Religious Fundamentalism," in A. W. Childs and G. B. Melton (eds.), *Rural Psychology.* New York: Plenum, 1983, pp. 169–98.

————. "Social Legitimacy, Dogmatism, and the Evaluation of Intense Experience," *Review of Religious Research,* 1980, *21,* 184–94. (See Hood, R. W., Jr. "A Typology for the Empirical Study of Mysticism." Paper presented at annual meeting of American Psychological Association, Los Angeles, California, 1981).

————., and HALL, J. R. "Comparison of Reported Religious Experience in Caucasion, American Indian, and Mexican American Samples," *Psychological Reports,* 1977, *41,* 657–58.

————; HALL, J. R.; WATSON, P. J.; and BIDERMAN, M. "Personality Correlates of the Report of Mystical Experience. *Psychological Reports,* 1979, *44,* 804–806.

———— and HALL, J. R. "Gender Differences in the Description of Erotic and Mystical Experiences," *Review of Religious Research,* 1980, *21,* 195–207.

———— and MORRIS, R. J. "Knowledge and Experience Criteria in the Report of Mystical Experience," *Review of Religious Research,* 1981, *23,* 76–84.

———— and MORRIS, R. "Sensory Isolation and the Differential Elicitation of Religious Imagery in Intrinsic and Extrinsic Persons," *Journal for the Scientific Study of Religion,* 1981, *20,* 261–73.

HOOPER, T. "Some Meanings and Correlates of Future Time and Death among College Students." Unpublished Ph.D. dissertation, University of Denver, 1962.

———— and SPILKA, B. "Some Meanings and Correlates of Future Time and Death among College Students," *Omega,* 1970, *1,* 49–56.

HOPKINS, J. R. "Sexual Behavior in Adolescence," *Journal of Social Issues,* 1977, *33*(2), 67–85.

HOWES, D. H. "One the Relationship between the Intelligibility and Frequency of Occurrence of English Words." *Journal of the Acoustical Society of America,* 1957, *29,* 296–305.

HORTON, D. "The Functions of Alcohol in Primitive Society: A Cross-Cultural Study," *Quarterly Journal of Studies on Alcohol,* 1943, *4,* 199–320.

HORTON, P. C. "The Mystical Experience as a Suicide Preventive," *American Journal of Psychiatry,* 1973, *130,* 294–96.

———— and R. L. SOLOMON. "Visual Duration Threshold as a Function of Word Probability." *Journal of Experimental Psychology,* 1951, *41,* 401–410.

HSU, F. L. K. *Religion, Science and Human Crises.* London: Routledge and Kegan Paul, 1952.

HULME, W. E. *Pastoral Care Comes of Age.* Nashville: Abingdon, 1970.

Information Please, *Information Please Almanac, Atlas and Yearbook,* 1979. New York: Information Please, 1978.

HUNSBERGER, B. "Background Religious Denomination, Parental Emphasis, and the Religious Orientation of University Students." *Journal for the Scientific Study of Religion,* 1976, *15,* 251–55.

————. "Problems and Promise in the Psychology of Religion: An Emerging Social Psychology of Religion," *Canadian Journal of Behavior Science,* 1980, *12,* 64–77.

————. "The Religiosity of College Students: Stability and Change over Years at University." *Journal for the Scientific Study of Religion,* 1978, *17,* 159–64.

————. *Religion and Attribution Theory: A Test of the Actor-Observer Bias.* Paper presented at the Convention of the Society for the Scientific Study of Religion, Knoxville, Tennessee, November, 1983.

————. "A reexamination of the Antecedents of Apostasy," *Review of Religious Research,* 1980, *21,* 158–70.

HUNT, M.   *Sexual Behavior in the 1970s.* Chicago: Playboy Press, 1974.

HUNT, R. A.   "The Interpretation of the Religious Scale of the Allport-Verron-Lindzey Study of Values." *Journal for the Scientific Study of Religion,* 1968, *7,* 65–77.

———.   "Mythological-Symbolic Religious Commitment: The LAM Scales." *Journal for the Scientific Study of Religion,* 1972, *11,* 42–52.

——— and KING, M. B.   "The Intrinsic-Extrinsic Concept: A Review and Evaluation," *Journal for the Scientific Study of Religion,* 1971, *10,* 339–56.

HUNTER, E.   *Brainwashing in Red China.* New York: Vanguard, 1951.

HUTCH, R. A.,   "The Personal Ritual of Glossolalia," *Journal for the Scientific Study of Religion,* 1980, *19,* 255–66.

HUXLEY, A.   *The Doors of Perception and Heaven and Hell.* New York: Harper and Row, 1963.

ICKES, W., and LAYDEN, M. A.   "Attributional styles," in J. H. Harvey, W. Ickes, and R. F. Kidd (eds.), *New directions in Attributional Research,* Vol. 2, Hillsdale, NJ: Lawrence Erlbaum Associates, 1978, 119–52.

ISAAC, J.   *The Teaching of Contempt.* New York: Holt, Rinehart and Winston, 1964.

JACKSON, C. W., JR., and KELLEY, E. L.   "Influence of Suggestion and Subject's Prior Knowledge in Research on Sensory Deprivation," *Science,* 1962, *132,* 211–212.

JACKSON, E. N.   "Resources for Facing New Horizons," in a symposium on *Cathastrophic Illness: Impact on Families, Challenges to the Professions.* New York: Cancer Care Inc. of the National Cancer Foundation, 1967, 26–36.

———.   *Understanding Grief.* New York: Abingdon, 1957.

JACKSON, J. J.   "Aged Negroes: Their Cultural Departure from Statistical Stereotypes and Urban-Rural Differences." *Gerontologist,* 1970, *10,* 140–65.

JACKSON, L. A.   "Call Us Ishmael: Suicide in Contemporary Society." *Christianity and Crisis,* November 27, 1972, 259–63.

JACKSON, N. J. and SPILKA, B.   "Correlates of Religious Mystical Experience: A Selective Study. Paper presented at the 1980 Convention of the Rocky Mountain Psychological Association, Tucson, Arizona, April 10, 1980.

JAHRREISS, W. O.   "Some Influences of Catholic Education and Creed upon Psychotic Reactions," *Diseases of the Nervous System,* 1942, *3,* 377–81.

JAKOBOVITS, I.   *Jewish Medical Ethics.* New York: Bloch, 1975.

JAMES, W.   *Habit.* New York: Henry Holt, 1890.

———.   *Varieties of Religious Experience.* New York: Longmans, Green, 1902.

JANSSEN, S. G. and HAUSER, R. M.   "Religion, Socialization and Fertility. *CDE Working Paper 80-5,* Center for Demography and Ecology, University of Wisconsin-Madison, May 1980.

JAYNES, J.   *The Origin of Consciousness in the Breakdown of the Bicameral Mind.* Boston: Houghton Mifflin, 1976.

JEEVES, M. A.   "Contribution on Prejudice and Religion and General Statement on Nature and Purpose of Religious Psychology." *Proceedings of the 15th International Congress of Psychology,* Brussels, 1957.

JEFFERS, F. C., NICHOLS, C. R., EISDORFER, C.   "Attitudes of Older Persons Toward Death: A Preliminary Study," *Journal of Gerontology,* 1961, *61,* 53–56.

JENSEN, G. F. and ERICKSON, M. L.   "The Religious Factor and Delinquency," in R. Wuthnow (ed.), *The Religious Dimension: New Directions in Quantitative Research.* New York: Academic, 1979, 157–77.

JOHNSON, B.   "Critical Appraisal of the Church-Sect Typology," *American Sociological Review,* 1957, *22,* 88–92.

———.   "Do Holiness Sects Socialize in Dominant Values?" *Social Forces, 1961, 39,* 309–17.

———.   "On Church and Sect," *American Sociological Review,* 1963, *28,* 539–49.

_____. "Church and Sect Revisited," *Journal for the Scientific Study of Religion*, 1971, *10*, 124–37.

JOHNSON, C. L. and WEIGERT, A. J. "An Emerging Faith Style: A Research Note on the Catholic Charismatic Renewal," *Sociological Analysis*, 1978, *39*, 166–72.

JOHNSON, D. P. "Dilemmas of Charismatic Leadership: The Case of the People's Temple," *Sociological Analysis*, 1979, *40*, 315–23.

JOHNSON, F. E. "Do Churches Exert Significant Influence on Public Morality?" *The Annals of the American Academy of Political and Social Science*, March 1952, *280*, 125–32.

JOHNSON, M. A. "Family Life and Religious Commitment," *Review of Religious Research*, 1973, *14*, 144–50.

_____. *The Relationship between Religious Knowledge and Selected Cognitive and Personality Variables*. Unpublished doctoral dissertation, Temple University, Philadelphia, Penn., 1974.

JOHNSON, P. E. "A Psychological Understanding of Prayer," *Pastoral Psychology*, 1953, *4*, 33–39.

_____. *Psychology of Religion* (rev. ed.). New York: Abingdon, 1959.

_____. "Conversion," *Pastoral Psychology*, 1959, *10*, 51–56.

_____, *Person and Counselor*. New York: Abingdon, 1967.

JOHNSON, W. *The Search for Transcendence*. New York: Harper and Row, 1974.

JOHNSTON, W. *Silent Music*. New York: Harper and Row, 1974.

JOHNSTONE, R. *The Effectiveness of Lutheran Elementary and Secondary Schools as Agents of Christian Education*. St. Louis: Concordia Seminary, 1966.

JONES, E. E. and NISBETT, R. E. "The Actor and the Observer: Divergent Perceptions of the Causes of Behavior," in E. G. Jones, D. E. Kanouse, H. H. Kelley, R. E. Nisbett, S. Valins, and B. Weiner (eds.), *Attribution: Perceiving the Causes of Behavior*. Morristown, NJ: General Learning Press, 1971, pp. 79–94.

_____, Kanouse, D. E., Kelley, H. H., Nisbett, R. E., Valins, S., and B. Weiner, *Attribution: The Causes of Behavior*. Morristown, NJ: General Learning Press, 1972.

JOSEPHSON, E. and JOSEPHSON, M. R. "Alienation: Contemporary Sociological Approaches, in F. Johnson (ed.), *Alienation: Concept, Term, and Meanings*. New York: Seminar Press, 1973, 163–81.

JUDAH, J. S., *Hare Krishna and the Counterculture*. New York: Wiley, 1974.

_____. "Attitudinal Changes Among Members of the Unification Church." Paper presented at the 1977 Convention of the American Association for the Advancement of Science, Denver, Colorado, February 22, 1977.

JUNG, C. G. *Psychology and Religion*. New Haven, Conn.: Yale University Press, 1938.

_____. *Modern Man in Search of a Soul*. New York: Harcourt, Brace and World, 1962.

KAHOE, R. D. "Comment on Thompson's Openmindedness and Indiscriminate Anti-Religious Orientation," *Journal for the Scientific Study of Religion*, 1976, *15*, 91–93.

_____. "Personality and Achievement Correlates of Intrinsic and Extrinsic Dimensions: A Value Base for Evaluating Religious Behavior," in W. J. Donaldson (ed.), *Research in Mental Health and Religious Behavior*. Atlanta, GA: Psychological Studies Institute, 1976, 178–90.

_____ and DUNN, R. F. "The Fear of Death and Religious Attitudes and Behavior." *Journal for the Scientific Study of Religion*, 1975, *14*, 379–382.

KALISH, R. A. "Some Variables in Death Attitudes," *Journal of Social Psychology*, 1963, *59*, 137–45.

_____. "Experiences of Persons Reprieved from Death," in A. H. Kutscher (ed.), *Death and Bereavement*. Springfield, Ill.: Charles C. Thomas, 1969, 84–96.

KALISH, R. A. and DUNN, L. "Death and Dying: A Survey of Credit Offerings in Theological Schools and Some Possible Implications," *Review of Religious Research*, 1976, *17*, 134–40.

_____ and REYNOLDS, D. K.   *Death and Ethnicity.* Los Angeles: University of Southern California, 1976.

KANTER, R. M.   *Commitment and Community: Communes and Utopias in Social Perspective.* Cambridge, Mass.: Harvard University Press, 1972.

KAPLAN, M. M.   *Judaism as a Civilization.* New York: Schocken, 1967.

KASTENBAUM, R. J.   *Death, Society, and Human Experience.* St. Louis: C. V. Mosby, 1981.

KATZ, S. T.   "Language, Epistemology, and Mysticism," in S. T. Katz (ed.), *Mysticism and Philosophical Analysis.* New York: Oxford University Press, 1978, pp. 22-74.

KAWAMURA, W. I., and WRIGHTMAN, L. S. Jr.   "The Viability of Religious Belief: A Factorial Study of Religious Attitudes, Values, and Personality." Paper presented at the Southeastern Regional Convention of the Society for the Scientific Study of Religion, Atlanta, Georgia, January 1969.

KAZANTZAKIS, N.   *Report to Greco.* New York: Simon and Schuster, 1961.

KEENE, J. J.   "Baha'i World Faith: Redefinition of Religion." *Journal for the Scientific Study of Religion,* 1967, *6,* 221-35.

KEENE, J. J.   "Religious Behavior and Neuroticism, Spontaneity and Worldmindedness, *Sociometry,* 1967, *30,* 137-57.

KEESING, R. M. and KESSING, F. M.   *New Perspectives in Cultural Anthropology.* New York: Holt, Rinehart and Winston, 1971.

KELLEY, D. M.   *Why Conservative Churches Are Growing.* New York: Harper and Row, 1972.

KELLEY, H. H.   "Attribution Theory in Social Psychology," in D. Levine (ed.), *Nebraska Symposium on Motivation,* 1967, No. 15. Lincoln: University of Nebraska Press, 1967, 192-238.

_____.   *Attribution in Social Interaction.* Morristown, NJ: General Learning Corporation, 1971.

KELLEY, J. R.   "Relativism and Institutional Religion." *Journal for the Scientific Study of Religion,* 1970, *9,* 281-294.

KELLEY, Sr., M. W.   "The Incidence of Hospitalized Mental Illness Among Religious Sisters in the United States," *American Journal of Psychiatry,* 1958, *115,* 72-75.

_____.   "Depression in the Psychosis of Members of Religious Communities of Women," *American Journal of Psychiatry,* 1961, *118,* 423-25.

KELSEY, M. T.   *Tongue Speaking: An experiment in Spiritual Experience.* Garden City, N.Y.: Doubleday, 1964.

KENKEL, W. F.   *The Family in Perspective,* 2d ed. New York: Appleton-Century-Crofts, 1966.

KENNEDY, E. C.; HECKLER, V. J.; KOBLER, F. J.; and WALKER, R. E.   "Clinical Assessment of a Profession: Roman Catholic Clergymen," *Journal of Clinical Psychology,* 1977, *33,* (Supplement), 120-28.

KENYON, F. E.   "The Life and Health of Joan of Arc." *Practitioner,* 1971, *207,* 835-42.

KIDORF, I. W.   "The Shiva: A Form of Group Psychotherapy," *Journal of Religion and Health,* 1966, *5,* 43-46.

KILDAHL, J. P.   "The Personalities of Sudden Religious Converts," *Pastoral Psychology,* 1965, *16,* 37-44.

_____.   *The Psychology of Speaking in Tongues.* New York: Harper and Row, 1972.

KIELY, M. C. and DUDEK, S. Z.   "Attitudes Toward Death in Aged Persons," *Psychiatric Journal of the University of Ottawa,* 1977, *2,* 181-84.

KIM, B.   "Religious Deprogramming and Subjective Reality," *Sociological Analysis,* 1979, *40,* 197-207.

KIM, H. C.   "The Relationship of Protestant Ethic Beliefs and Values to Achievement." Journal for the Scientific Study of Religion, 1977, *16,* 255-62.

KIMBALL, S. W.   *Faith Precedes the Miracle.* Salt Lake City, Utah: Deseret, 1975.

KING, K., ABERNATHY, T. J., ROBINSON, I. E., and BALSWICK, J. O., "Religiosity and Sexual Attitudes and Behavior among College Students," *Adolescence,* 1976, *11,* 535–39.

KING, M. B. "Measuring the Religious Variable: Nine Proposed Dimensions." *Journal for the Scientific Study of Religion,* 1967, *6,* 173–90.

―――― and HUNT, R. A. "Measuring the Religious Variable: Amended Findings." *Journal for the Scientific Study of Religion,* 1969, *8,* 321–323.

―――― and HUNT, R. A. *Measuring Religious Dimensions: Studies in Congregational Involvement.* Dallas, TX: Southern Methodist University Press, 1972a.

―――― and HUNT, R. A. "Measuring the Religious Variable: Replication." *Journal for the Scientific Study of Religion,* 1972b, *11,* 240–51.

―――― and HUNT, R. A. "Measuring the Religious Variable: National Replication," *Journal for the Scientific Study of Religion,* 1975, *14,* 13–22.

KING, S. H. and FUNKENSTEIN, D. "Religious Practice and Cardiovascular Reactions during Stress." *Journal of Abnormal and Social Psychology,* 1957, *55,* 135–37.

KINSEY, A. C.; POMEROY, W. B; and MARTIN, C. E., *Sexual Behavior in the Human Male.* Philadelphia: Saunders, 1948.

――――; POMEROY, W. B.; MARTIN, C. E.; and GEBHARD, P. H., *Sexual Behavior in the Human Female,* New York: Pocket Books, 1965.

KIRKPATRICK, C. "Religion and Humanitarianism: A Study of Institutional Implications." *Psychological Monographs,* 1949, *63,* No.9.

KIVETT, V. R.; WATSON, J. A.; and BUSCH, J. C. "The Relative Importance of Physical, Psychological, and Social Variables to Locus of Control Orientation in Middle Age." *Journal of Gerontology,* 1977, *32,* 203–10.

KLINGER, E. *Structure and Functions of Fantasy.* New York: Wiley, 1971.

KLOPFER, F. J. and PRICE, W. F. "Euthanasia Acceptance as Related to Afterlife Belief and Other Attitudes," 1979, *Omega, 9,* 245–53.

KLUEGEL, J. R. "Denominational Mobility." *Journal for the Scientific Study of Religion,* 1980, *19,* 2639.

KNUDSEN, D. D.; EARLE, J. R.; and SHRIVER, D. W. Jr. "The Concept of Sectarian Religion: An Effort at Clarification," *Review of Religious Research,* 1978, *20,* 44–60.

KNUDTEN, R. D. and KNUDTEN, M. S. "Juvenile Delinquency, Crime, and Religion," *Review of Religious Research,* 1971, *12,* 130–152.

KNUPFER, G. and ROOM, R. "Drinking Patterns and Attitudes of Irish, Jewish, and White Protestant American Men," *Quarterly Journal of Studies on Alcohol,* 1967, *28,* 676–69.

KOHLBERG, L. "Stage and Sequence: The Cognitive-Developmental Approach to Socialization," in D. A. Goslin (ed.), *Handbook of Socialization Theory and Research.* Chicago: Rand McNally, 1969, pp. 347–480.

KOPPLIN, D., "Religious Orientations of College Students and Related Personality Characteristics." Paper presented at the Convention of the American Psychological Association, Washington, D.C., 1976.

KREJCI, J. "Attitudes toward Church Teachings on Abortion, Birth Control, and Premarital Sex." Paper presented at the 1980 Convention of the Society for the Scientific Study of Religion, Cincinatti, Ohio, October 31, 1980.

KRIS, E. *Psychoanalytic Explorations in Art.* New York: International Universities Press, 1952.

KROLL-SMITH, J. S. "The Testimony as Performance: The Relationship of an expressive event to the belief System of a Holiness sect. *Journal for the Scientific Study of Religion.* 1980, *19,* 16–25.

KRUGLANSKI, A. W.; HAMEL, I. Z.; MAIDES, S. A.; and SCHWARTZ, J. M. "Attribution theory as a Special Case of Lay Epistemology," in J. H. Harvey, W. Ickes, and R. F. Kidd (eds.), *New Directions in Attribution Research, Vol. 2.* Hillsdale NJ: Lawrence E. Erlbaum, 1978, 299-333.

KRUTCH, J. W.   *Samuel Johnson.* New York: Henry Holt, 1944.

KUBLER-ROSS, E.   "The Dying Patient's Point of View," in Brim, O. G., Jr.; Freeman, H. E.; Levine, S.; and Scotch, N. A. (eds.). *The Dying Patient.* New York: Russell Sage, 1970, 156-70.

KUHRE, B. E.   "The Religious Involvement of the College Student from a Multi-dimensional Perspective," *Sociological Analysis,* 1971, *32,* 61-69.

KUNG, H.   *Freud and the Problem of God.* New Haven, CN: Yale University Press, 1979.

KUROKAWA, M.   "Acculturation and Mental Health of Mennonite Children," *Child Development,* 1969, *40,* 689-705.

KURTH, C. J.   "Psychiatric and Psychological Selection of Candidates for the Sisterhood," *Guild of Catholic Psychiatrists Bulletin,* 1961, *8,* 19-25.

KUTSCHER, A. H. and KUTSCHER, A. H., Jr.   "Results of a Survey: Opinions of Clergy Widows and Widowers," in Kutscher, A. H. and Kutscher, L. G. (eds.) *Religion and Bereavement.* New York: Health Sciences Publishing Corp., 1972, 199-212.

_____ and KUTSCHER, L. G. (eds.). *Religion and Bereavement.* New York: Health Sciences Publishing Corp., 1972.

KVARACEUS, C.   "Delinquent Behavior and Church Attendance," *Sociology and Social Research,* 1949, *34,* 284-89.

LABARRE, W.   *They Shall Take Up Serpents.* New York: Schocken, 1969.

_____.   "Hallucinogens and the Shamantic Origins of Religion," in P. T. Furst (ed.), *Flesh of the Gods.* New York: Praeger, 1972, pp. 261-78.

_____.   *The Peyote Cult,* rev. ed., Hampden, Conn.: Shoestring Press, 1974.

LAFFAL, J.; MONAHAN, J. and RICHMAN, P.   "Communication of Meaning in Glossolalia," *Journal of Social Psychology,* 1974, *92,* 277-91.

LAING, R. D. and COOPER, D. G.   *Reason and Violence.* New York: Random House, 1971.

LANDIS, J. T.   "Religiousness, Family Relationships, and Family Values in Protestant, Catholic and Jewish Families." *Marriage and Family Living,* 1960, *22,* 341-47.

LANE, R. E.   *Political Thinking and Consciousness.* Chicago, Markham, 1969.

LANGFORD, B. and LANGFORD, C.   "Church Attendance and Self-Perceived Altruism," *Journal for the Scientific Study of Religion,* 1974, *13,* 221-22.

LANTZ, H.   "Religious Participation and Social Orientation of 1,000 University Students," *Sociology and Social Research,* 1949, *33,* 285-90.

LARSEN, S.   *The Shaman's Doorway.* New York: Harper and Row, 1976.

LARSON, D. B. and WILSON, W. P.   "Religious Life of Alcoholics," *Southern Medical Journal,* 1980, *73,* 723-27.

LARSON, D. N.   "Rokeach in Linguistic Perspective," *Review of Religious Research,* 1970, *11,* 146-48.

LASKI, M. *Ecstasy.* Bloomington, Ind.: University of Indiana Press, 1961.

LATANE, B. and DARLEY, J. M.   *The Unresponsive Bystander.* New York: Appleton-Century-Crofts, 1970.

LAZERWITZ, B.   "The Community Variable in Jewish Identification," *Journal for the Scientific Study of Religion,* 1977, *16,* 361-69.

_____.   "Religion and Social Structure in the United States, in L. Schneider (ed.), *Religion, Culture and Society.* New York: Wiley, 1964, 426-39.

LEARY, T.   "The Religious Experience: Its Production and Interpretation," *Psychedelic Review,* 1964, *1,* 324-46.

LEBON, G.   *The Crowd.* London: T. Fisher Unwin, 1903.

LEBRA, T. S.   "Religious Conversion as a Breakthrough for Transculturation: A Japanese Sect in Hawaii," *Journal for the Scientific Study of Religion,* 1970, *9,* 181-96.

LEE, G. R. and CLYDE, R. W.   "Patterned Sources of Variation in Anomie: A Study of the Effects of Socio-economic and Religious Variables." Paper presented at the Convention of the Society for the Scientific Study of Religion, Chicago; Oct. 1971.

LEE, R. R.   *Theological Belief as a Dimension of Personality.* Unpublished doctoral dissertation, Northwestern University, Evanston, Illinois, 1965.

LEFCOURT, H. M.   "Internal versus External Control of Reinforcement: A Review. *Psychological Bulletin,* 1966, *65,* 206–20.

LEHMAN, E. C. Jr.   "On Perceiving the Relevance of Traditional Religion to Contemporary Issues," *Review of Religious Research,* 1971, *13,* 34–41.

————.   *Traditional Religion and Ethical Decision-making: An Empirical Note.* Unpublished manuscript, 1969.

———— and SHRIVER, D. W.   "Academic Discipline as Predictive of Faculty Religiosity," *Social Forces,* 1968, *47,* 171–82.

Leming, M. R.   "The Effects of Personal and Institutionalized Religion upon Death Attitudes." Paper presented at the Convention of the Society for the Scientific Study of Religion, San Antonio, Texas, October 27, 1979.

————.   "Religion and Death: A Test of Homans' Thesis," *Omega,* 1980, *10,* 347–64.

LENSKI, G.   *The Religious Factor.* Garden City, N.Y.: Doubleday, 1961.

LEONARD, W. M. II.   "Sociological and Social-Psychological Correlates of Anomia among a Random Sample of Aged," *Journal of Gerontology,* 1977, *32,* 303–10.

LERNER, M.   *America as a Civilization.* New York: Simon and Schuster, 1957.

LERNER, M. J.   "The Justice Motive in Social Behavior." *Journal of Social Issues,* 1975, *31,* 1–19.

LESSER, G. S.   "Religion and the Defensive Responses in Children's Fantasy," *Journal of Projective Techniques,* 1959, *23,* 64–68.

LESTER, D.   "Experimental and Correlational Studies of the Fear of Death," *Psychological Bulletin,* 1967, *67,* 27–36.

————.   "Religious Behaviors and Attitudes Toward Death," in Godin, A. (ed.) *Death and Presence.* Brussels, Belgium: Lumen Vitae, 1972, 107–124.

LEUBA, J. H.   *A Psychological Study of Religion.* New York: Macmillan, 1912.

————.   *The Psychology of Religious Mysticism.* New York: Harcourt Brace, 1925.

————.   "Studies in the Psychology of Religious Phenomena," *American Journal of Psychology,* 1896, *7,* 309–85.

LEVENSON, H.   "Multidimensional Locus of Control in Psychiatric Patients." *Journal of Consulting and Clinical Psychology,* 1973a, 41, 397–404.

————.   "Perceived Parental Antecedents of Internal, Powerful Others, and Chance Locus of Control Orientations." *Developmental Psychology,* 1973b, 9, 268–74.

————.   "Activism and Powerful Others: Distinctions within the Concept of Internal-External Control." *Journal of Personality Assessment,* 1974, 38, 377–83.

LEVI, K.   *Violence and Religious Commitment: Implications of Jim Jones People's Temple Movement.* University Park, Pa.: Pennsylvania State University Press, 1982.

LEVIN, M.   *Classic Hassidic Tales.* New York: Citadel, 1966.

LEVITAN, T.   *The Laureates: Jewish Winners of the Nobel Prize.* New York: Twayne, 1960.

LEWELLEN, T. C.   "Deviant Religion and Cultural Evolution: The Aymara Case," *Journal for the Scientific Study of Religion,* 1979, *18,* 243–51.

LEWINSOHN, R.   *A History of Sexual Customs.* New York: Harper and Row, 1958.

LEWIS, I. M.   *Ecstatic Religion: An Anthropological Study of Spirit Possession and Shamanism.* Middlesex, England: Penguin, 1971.

LIEBERMAN, M. A.   "Psychological Correlates of Impending Death: Some Preliminary Observations," *Journal of Gerontology,* 20, 181–90.

LIFTON, R. J.   *Thought Reform and the Psychology of Totalism.* New York: Norton, 1961.

LILLY, J. C.   "Mental Effects of Reduction of Ordinary Levels of Physical Stimuli on Intact Healthy Persons," *Psychiatric Research Reports,* 1956, *5,* 1–9.

————.   *The Deep Self.* New York: Warner, 1977.

———— and LILLY, A.   *The Dyadic Cyclone.* New York: Simon and Schuster, 1976.

LINDEN, R. and CURRIE, R.   "Religiosity and Drug Use: A Test of Social Control Theory," *Canadian Journal of Criminology and Corrections,* 1977, *19,* 346–55.

LINDENTHAL, J. J.; MYERS, J. K.; PEPPER, M. P.; and STERN, M. S.   "Mental Status and Religious Behavior," *Journal for the Scientific Study of Religion,* 1970, *9,* 143–49.

LIPSET, S. M.   "Religion and Politics in the American Past and Present," in R. Lee and M. E. Marty (eds.), *Religion and Social Conflict.* New York: Oxford, 1964, 69–126.

LOFLAND, J.   *Doomsday Cult.* Englewood Cliffs, N.J.: Prentice-Hall, 1966.

————.   "Becoming a World-Saver Revisited," *American Behavioral Scientist,* 1977, *20,* 805–18.

———— and SKONOUD, N.   "Conversion Motifs," *Journal for the Scientific Study of Religion,* 1981, *20,* 373–85.

———— and STARK, R.   "Becoming a World Saver: A Theory of Conversion to a Deviant Perspective," *American Sociological Review,* 1965, *30,* 862–74.

LONG, D.; ELKIND, D.; and SPILKA, B.   "The Child's Conception of Prayer." *Journal for the Scientific Study of Religion,* 1967, *6,* 101–109.

LOVEKIN, A. and MALONY, H. N.   "Religious Glossolalia: A Longitudinal Study of Personality Changes," *Journal for the Scientific Study of Religion,* 1977, *16,* 383–93.

LOVELAND, G. G.   "The Effects of Bereavement on Certain Religious Attitudes," *Sociological Symposium,* 1968, *1,* 17–27.

LOWE, W. L.   "Religious Beliefs and Religious Delusions," *American Journal of Psychotherapy,* 1955, *9,* 54–61.

————. and BRAATEN, R. O.   "Religious Attitudes in Mental Illness," *Journal for the Scientific Study of Religion,* 1966, *5,* 435–45.

LURIE, W. A.   "A Study of Spranger's Value-Types by the Method of Factor Analysis." *Journal of Social Psychology,* 1937, *8,* 17–38.

LUTOSLAWSKI, W.   "The Conversion of a Psychologist," *Hibbert Journal,* 1923, *21,* 697–710.

MACDONALD, A., Jr.   "Birth Order and Religious Affiliation." *Developmental Psychology,* 1969, *1,* 628.

MACDONALD, C. B. and LUCKETT, J. B.   "Religious Affliliation and Psychiatric Diagnoses," *Journal for the Scientific Study of Religion,* 1983, *22,* 15–37.

MACKAY, C.   *Memoirs of Extraordinary Popular Delusions and the Madness of Crowds.* London: George Routledge and Sons, 1869.

MACKIE, A.   *The Gift of Tongues.* New York: George H. Doran, 1921.

MADGE, V.   *Children in Search of Meaning.* New York: Morehouse-Barlow, 1966.

MACHALEK, R.   "Definitional Strategies in the Study of Religion." *Journal for the Scientific Study of Religion,* 1977, *16,* 395–401.

MADSEN, G. E., and VERNON, G. M.   "Maintaining the Faith during College: A Study of Campus Religious Group Participation. *Review of Religious Research,* 1983, *25,* 127–41.

MAGNI, K. G.   The Fear of Death: Studies of Its Character and Concomitants," in A. Godin (Ed.), *Death and Presence.* Brussels, Belgium: International Center for Studies in Religious Education, 1972, 129–42.

————.   "Reactions to Death Stimuli among Theology Students," *Journal for the Scientific Study of Religion.* 1970, *9,* 247–48.

MAGNUSSON, D.   "Wanted: A Psychology of Situations," in D. Magnusson (ed.). *Toward a Psychology of Situations.* Hillsdale, NJ: Lawrence Erlbaum Associates, 1981, pp. 9–32.

MAHONEY, E. R.   "Religiosity and Sexual Behavior among Heterosexual College Students," *Journal of Sex Research* 1980, *16,* 97–113.

MALINOWSKI, B.   "The Role of Magic and Religion," in Lessa, W. A. and Vogt, E. Z. (eds.), *A Reader in Comparative Religion.* New York: Harper and Row, 1965, 63–72.

MALONY, H. N.   "N = 1 Methodology in the Psychology of Religion," in H. N.

Malony (ed.), *Current Perspectives in the Psychology of Religion.* Grand Rapids, Mich.: Eerdmans, 1977, pp. 352–67.

MALZBERG, B. "Important Statistical Data About Mental Illness, in S. Arieti (ed.), *American Handbook of Psychiatry.* Vol. I, New York: Basic Books, 1959, 161–74.

———— "The Distribution of Mental Disease According to Religious Affiliation in New York State, 1949–1951," in A. Shiloh and I. C. Cohen (eds.), *Ethnic Groups of America: Their Morbidity, Mortality and Behavior Disorders.* Vol. I. *The Jews.* Springfield, IL: C. C. Thomas, 1973, 284–95.

MARANELL, G. M. *Responses to Religion.* Lawrence: University Press of Kansas, 1974.

MARGENAU, H. "On Interpretations and Misinterpretations of Operationalism. *Scientific Monthly,* 1954, *79,* 209–10.

MARSHALL, E., and S. HAMPLE, (eds.). *Children's Letters to God.* New York: Simon and Schuster, 1966.

———— and S. HAMPLE, (eds.) *More Children's Letters to God.* New York: Simon and Shuster, 1967.

MARTIN, D. *A General Theory of Secularization.* New York: Harper and Row, 1978.

———— and WRIGHTSMAN, L. S. "Religion and Fears about Death: A Critical Review of Research," *Religious Education,* 1964, *59,* 174–76.

———— and WRIGHTSMAN, L. S. The Relationship between Religious Behavior and Concern about Death," *Journal of Social Psychology,* 1965, *65,* 317–23.

MARTIN, J. and WESTBROOK, M. "Religion and Sex in a University Sample: Data Bearing on Mol's Hypothesis," *Australian Journal of Psychology,* 1973, *25,* 71–79.

MARTY, M. E. *The New Shape of American Religion.* New York: Harper, 1959.

————; ROSENBERG, S. E.; and GREELEY, A. M. *What Do We Believe?* New York: Meredith, 1968.

MARVIN, M. L. "Social Modeling: A Psychological-theological Perspective," *Journal of Psychology and Theology,* 1980, *8,* 211–21.

MARX, K. "Contributions to the Critique of Hegel's Philosophy of Right," in R. Niebuhr (ed.), *Marx and Engels on Religion.* New York: Schocken, 1964, pp. 41–58.

MASLOW, A. H. *Religions, Values, and Peak Experiences.* Columbus, Ohio: Ohio State University Press, 1964.

————. "Deficiency Motivation and Growth Motivation," in M. R. Jones (ed.), *Nebraska Symposium on Motivation, 1955.* Lincoln, Nebr.: Nebraska University Press, pp. 1–30.

————. *Motivation and Personality* (2nd ed.). New York: Harper and Row, 1970.

————. *Toward a Psychology of Being.* New York: D. Van Nostrand, 1962.

MASSERMAN, J. H. and PALMER, R. T. "Psychiatric and Psychologic Tests for Ministerial Personnel," *Pastoral Psychology,* 1961, *12* (112), 24–33.

MASTERS, R. E. L. and HOUSTON, J. *The Varieties of Psychedelic Experience.* New York: Delta, 1966.

MASTERS, W. H. and JOHNSON, V. E. *Human Sexual Inadequacy.* Boston: Little, Brown, 1970.

MAUSS, A. L. *Social Problems as Social Movements.* New York: J. B. Lippincott, 1975.

———— and PETERSON, D. M. "Prodigals as Preachers: Jesus Freaks and the Return to Respectability." Paper presented at 1973 Convention of the Society for the Scientific Study of Religion, San Francisco, October 25, 1973.

MAVES, P. B. (ed.). *The Church and Mental Health.* New York: Scribner's, 1953.

————. "Religious Development in Adulthood," in M. B. Strommen (ed.). *Research on Religious Development: A Comprehensive Handbook.* New York: Hawthorn, 1971, 777–97.

MAY, C. L. "A Survey of Glossolalia and Related Phenomena in Non-Christian Religions," *American Anthropologist,* 1956, *58,* 75–96.

MAY, R. *The Springs of Creative Living.* New York: Abingdon-Cokesbury, 1940.

MAYO, C. C.; PURYEAR, H. B.; and RICHEK, H. G. "MMPI Correlates of Religiousness in Late Adolescent College Students," *Journal of Nervous and Mental Disease*, 1969, *149*, 381–85.

MCALLISTER, R. J. "The Emotional Health of the Clergy," *Journal of Religion and Health*, 1965, *4*, 333–36.

————. "The Mental Health of Members of Religious Communities," in E. M. Pattison (ed.), *Clinical Psychiatry and Religion*, Boston: Little, Brown, 1969, 211–22.

MCCANN, R. V., *The Churches and Mental Health*. Joint Commission on Mental Illness and Health, Monogr. Ser. No. 8. New York: Basic Books, 1962.

MCCLELLAND, D. C. *The Achieving Society*. Princeton, NJ: D. Van Nostrand, 1961.

————; ATKINSON, J. W.; CLARK, R. A.; LOWELL, E. L. *The Achievement Motive*. New York: Appleton-Century-Crofts, 1953.

————. "Some Social Consequences of Achievement Motivation," in Marshall R. Jones (ed.), *Nebraska Symposium on Motivation*, 1955, Lincoln, NB: University of Nebraska Press, 1955, 41–65.

————. RINDLISBACHER, A.; and DECHARMS, R. "Religious and Other Sources of Parental Attitudes Toward Independence Training," in D. C. McClelland (ed.), *Studies in Motivation*. New York: Appleton-Century-Crofts, 1955, 389–97.

MCCLOSKY, H. and SCHAAR, J. H. "Psychological Dimensions of Anomy," *American Sociological Review*, 1965, *30*, 14–40.

MCCONAHAY, J. B., and J. C. HOUGH, JR. "Love and Guilt-Oriented Dimensions of Christian Belief." *Journal for the Scientific Study of Religion*, 1973, *12*, 53–64.

MCDOUGALL, W. *An Introduction to Social Psychology* (2nd ed.). Boston: J. W. Luce, 1909.

MCGINLEY, P. *Saint-Watching*. New York: Viking, 1969.

MCGONEGAL, J. "The Role of Sanction in Drinking Behavior," *Quarterly Journal of Studies on Alcohol*, 1972, *33*, 692–97.

MCGUIRE, M. B. "Towards a Sociological Interpretation of the Catholic Pentecostal Movement," *Review of Religious Research*, 1975, *16*, 94–104.

————. *Religion: The Social Context*. Belmont, Ca: Wadsworth, 1981.

MCINTOSH, W. A.; FITCH, S. D.; WILSON, J. B.; and NYBERG, K. L. "The Effect of Mainstream Religious Social Controls on Adolescent Drug Use in Rural Areas," *Review of Religious Research*, 1981, *23*, 54–75.

MCKEE, B. *The Seasons of a Man's Life*. New York: Knopf, 1978.

MCKEON, R. (ed.). *The Basic Writings of Aristotle*. New York: Random House, 1941.

MCLEAN, M. D. "Religious World Views." *Motive*, 1952, *12*(5), 22–26.

MCLOUGHLIN, W. F. *Revivals, Awakenings and Reform*. Chicago: University of Chicago Press, 1978.

MCNAMARA, P. H. and GEORGE, A. S. "Blessed Are the Downtrodden: An Empirical Test," *Sociological Analysis*, 1978, *39*, 303–20.

MCNEILL, J. T. "Religious Healing of Soul and Body: An Historical Survey," in P. B. Maves (ed.), *The Church and Mental Health*. New York: Scribner's, 1953, 43–60.

MEISSNER, W. W. "Affective Responses to Psychoanalytic Death Symbols," *Journal of Abnormal and Social Psychology*, 1958, *56*, 295–99.

MELCHERT, N. "Mystical Experience and Ontological Claims," *Philosophy and Phenomenological Research*, 1977, *37*, 445–63.

MENGES, R. J. and DITTES, J. E. (eds.). *Psychological Studies of Clergymen*. New York: Thomas Nelson, 1965.

MERTON, R. K. "Facts and Factitiousness in Ethnic Opinionnaires," *American Sociological Review*, 1940, *5*, 13–28.

MERTON, T. *Mystics and Zen Masters*. New York: Delta, 1961.

METALSKY, G. I., L. Y., ABRAMSON, M. E. P., SELIGMAN, A., SEMMEL, and C. PETERSON. "Attributional Styles and Life Events in the Classroom: Vulnerability and Invulnerability to Depressive Mood Reactions." *Journal of Personality and Social Psychology*, 1982, *43*, 612–17.

————— and L. Y. ABRAMSON."Attributional Styles: Toward a Framework for Conceptualization and Assessment," in P. C. Kendall and S. D. Hollon (eds.), *Assessment Strategies for Cognitive Behavioral Interventions.* New York: Academic, 1980, 13–58.

MIDDLETON, R., and PUTNEY, S. "Religion, Normative Standards, and Behavior," *Sociometry,* 1962, *25,* 141–52.

MIDDLETON, W. C. and FAY, P. J. "Attitudes of Delinquent and Nondelinquent Girls toward Sunday Observance, the Bible, and War," *Journal of Educational Psychology,* 1941. *32.* 555–58.

MIDGLEY, J. "Drinking and Attitudes toward Drinking in a Muslim Community," *Quarterly Journal of Studies on Alcohol,* 1971, *32,* 148–58.

MILLER, D. T., and M. ROSS. "Self-Serving Biases in the Attribution of Causality: Fact or Fiction?" *Psychological Bulletin,* 1975, *82,* 213–225.

MILLER, G. A.; GALANTER, E. H.; and PRIBHAM, K. *Plans and The Structure of Behavior.* New York: Holt, 1960.

MILLER, W., *Why Do Christians Break Down?* Minneapolis: Augsburg, 1973.

MINDELL, C. H. and VAUGHAN, C. E. "A Multidimensional Approach to Religiosity and Disengagement." *Journal of Gerontology,* 1978, *33,* 103–8.

MINEAR, J. D. and BRUSH, L. R. "The Correlations of Attitudes toward Suicide with Death Anxiety, Religiosity, and Personal Closeness to Suicide," 1980–81, *Omega, 11,* 317–24.

MINTON, B. and SPILKA B. "Perspectives on Death in Relation to Powerlessness and Form of Personal Religion." *Omega,* 1976, *7,* 261–68.

MISHLER, E. G. and WAXLER, N. E. *Interaction in Families: An Experimental Study of Family Processes and Schizophrenia.* New York: Wiley, 1968.

MOBERG, D. "Religious Activities and Personal Adjustment in Old Age," *Journal of Social Psychology,* 1956, *43,* 261–67.

—————. "Religiosity in Old Age," *Gerontologist,* 1965, *5,* 78–87.

—————. "Theological Self-Classification and Ascetic Moral Views of Students," *Review of Religious Research,* 1969, *10,* 100–107.

—————. "Religious Practices," in M. B. Strommen (ed.). *Research on Religious Development: A Comprehensive Handbook.* New York: Hawthorn, 1971, 551–98.

MOL, H. "Religion and Sex in Australia," *Australian Journal of Psychology,* 1970, *22,* 105–14.

MONAGHAN, R. R. "Three Faces of the True Believer: Motivations for Attending a Fundamentalist Church." *Journal for the Scientific Study of Religion,* 1967, *6,* 236–45.

MONTEFIORE, C. G. and LOEWE, H. (eds.). *A Rabbinic Anthology.* New York: Meridian, 1963.

MOODY, R. *Life after Death.* New York: Bantam, 1976.

MOORE, P. "Mystical Eminence, Mystical Doctrine, Mystical Technique," in S. T. Katz (ed.), *Mysticism and Philosophical Analysis.* New York: Oxford University Press, 1978, pp. 101–131.

MOORE, T. V. "Insanity in Priests and Religions," *Ecclesiastical Review,* 1936, *95,* 485–98.

—————. *The Nature and Treatment of Mental Disorders.* New York: Grune & Stratton, 1944.

MORA, G. "The Scrupulosity Syndrome," in Pattison, E. M. (ed.), *Clinical Psychiatry and Religion,* Boston: Little, Brown, 1969, 163–74.

MORGAN, L. JR., "Mental Illness Among the Clergy," *Pastoral Psychology, 9(84),* 1958, 29–36.

MORRIS, R. J. and HOOD, R. W. JR. "Religious and Unity Criteria of Baptists and Nones in Reports of Mystical Experience," *Psychological Reports,* 1980, *46,* 728–30.

MOWRER, O. H. *The Crisis in Psychiatry and Religion.* Princeton, NJ: D. Van Nostrand, 1961.

MUELLER, C. W. and JOHNSON, W. T. "Socioeconomic Status and Religious Participation," *American Sociological Review,* 1975, *40,* 785–800.

MUGGERIDGE, M.   *A Third Testament.* Boston: Little, Brown, 1976.

MÜLLER, M.   *Natural Religion.* New York: Longmans, Green, 1889.

NAGI, M. H., PUGH, M. D. and LAZERINE, N. G.   "Attitudes of Catholic and Protestant Clergy toward Euthanasia," 1977-78, *Omega, 8,* 153-64.

NARANJO, C. and ORNSTEIN, R. O.   *On the Psychology of Meditation.* New York: Viking, 1971.

NARRAMORE, B.   "Perspectives on the Integration of Psychology and Theology," *Journal of Psychology and Theology,* 1973, *1,* 3-18.

NASH, D.   "A Little Child Shall Lead Them: A Statistical Test of an Hypothesis that Children Were the Source of the American Religious Revival," *Journal for the Scientific Study of Religion,* 1968, *7,* 238-40.

_____ and BERGER, P.   "The Child, the Family, and the Religious Revival in the Suburbs," *Journal for the Scientific Study of Religion,* 1962, *2,* 85-93.

NEEDLEMAN, J. and BAKER, G. (eds.).   *Understanding the New Religions.* New York: Seabury, 1978.

NELSEN, H. M.   "Gender Differences in the Effects of Parental Discord on Preadolescent Religiousness." *Journal for the Scientific Study of Religion,* 1981, 351-60.

_____; EVERETT, R. F.; P. D. MADER, and W. C. HAMBY.   "A Test of Yinger's Measure of Non-doctrinal Religion: Implications for Invisible Religion as a Belief System." *Journal for the Scientific Study of Religion,* 1976, *15,* 263-67.

_____ and HERTEL, B. R.   "Are We Entering a post-Christian Era: Religious Belief and Attendance in America, 1957-1968," *Journal for the Scientific Study of Religion,* 1974, *13,* 409-19.

_____ and POTVIN, R. H.   "Toward Disestablishment: New Patterns of Social Class, Denomination, and Religiosity among American Youth," *Review of Religious Research,* 1980, *22,* 137-154.

NELSON, F. I.   "Religiosity and Self-Destructive Crises in the Institutionalized Elderly," *Suicide and Life-Threatening Behavior,* 1977, 7, 67-74.

NELSON, G. K.   "Communal and Associational Churches," *Review of Religious Research,* 1971, *12,* 102-110.

NELSON, L. D. and DYNES, R. R.,   "The Impact of Devotionalism and Attendance on Ordinary and Emergency Helping Behavior," *Journal for the Scientific Study of Religion,* 1976. *15,* 47-59.

NESS, R. C. and WINTROB, R. M.   "The Emotional Impact of Fundamentalist Religious Participation: An Empirical Study of Intragroup Variation," *American Journal of Orthopsychiatry,* 1980, *50,* 302-15.

NEUGARTEN, B. L.   *Middle Age and Aging.* Chicago: University of Chicago Press, 1968.

NEUMANN F.   "Anxiety and Politics," in M. R. Stein, A. J. Vidich, and D. M. White (eds.), *Identity and Anxiety.* New York: Free Press, 1960, 269-90.

NICHOLSON, H. C., and EDWARDS, K.   "A Comparison of Four Statistical Methods for Assessing Similarity of God Concept to Parental Images." Paper presented at the annual meeting of the Society for the Scientific Study of Religion, 1979.

NIEBUHR, H. R.   *The Social Sources of Denominationalism.* New York: Holt, 1929.

NIEBUHR, R.   *Does Civilization need Religion?* New York: Macmillan, 1928.

NOLAN, T.   "Ritual and Therapy," in Schoenberg, B., Carr, A. C., Kutscher, A. H., Peretz, D., and Goldberg, I. K. (eds.). *Anticipatory Grief.* New York: Columbia University Press, 1974, 358-64.

NOVAK, M.   "Secular saints," *The Center Magazine,* May 1968, *1*(4), 51-59.

NUDELMAN, A. E.   "Stress and Illness Behavior among Christian Scientists and Others." Paper presented at the Convention of the Society for the Scientific Study of Religion, Cincinnati, Ohio, 1980.

NUNN, C. Z.   "Child-Control through a 'Coalition with God.' " *Child Development,* 1964, *35,* 417-432.

OATES, W.   *Religious Factors in Mental Illness.* New York: Association, 1955.
_____.   *When Religion Gets Sick.* Philadelphia: Westminister, 1970.
OBERSCHALL, A.   *Social Conflict and Social Movements.* Englewood Cliffs, N.J.: Prentice-Hall, 1973.
O'BRIEN, E.   *Varieties of Mystical Experience.* New York: New American Library, 1964.
O'BRIEN, M. E.   "Religious Faith and Adjustment to Long-Term Hemodialysis." *Journal of Religion and Health,* 1982, *21,* 68-80.
O'CONNELL, D. C.   "Is Mental Illness a Result of Sin?" in A. Godin (ed.), *Child and Adult Before God.* Brussels, Belgium: Lumen Vitae Press, 1961, 55-64.
O'DEA, T. F.   "Five Dilemmas in the Institutionalization of Religion." *Journal for the Scientific Study of Religion,* 1961, *1,* 30-39.
_____.   "Sects and Cults," in D. Shills (ed.), *International Encyclopedia of the Social Sciences.* Vol. 14. New York: Macmillan, 1965, pp. 130-36.
_____.   *The Sociology of Religion.* Englewood Cliffs, N.J.: Prentice-Hall, 1966.
ODEN, T. C.   *Should Treatment be Terminated?* New York: Harper and Row, 1976.
O'DOHERTY, E. F.   *Religion and Psychology.* New York: Alba House, 1978.
OKEN, D.   "Alienation and Identity: Some Comments on Adolescence, The Counter-culture, and Contemporary Adaptations, in F. Johnson (ed.), *Alienation: Concept, Term, and Meanings.* New York: Seminar Press, 1973, 83-110.
OLSON, B. E.   *Faith and Prejudice.* New Haven, Conn.: Yale, 1963.
ORBACH, H. L.   "Aging and Religion: A Study of Church Attendance in the Detroit Metropolitan Area." *Geriatrics,* 1961, *16,* 530-40.
O'REILLY, C. T.   "Religious Practice and Personal Adjustment," *Sociology and Social Research,* 1958, *42,* 119-21.
ORNSTEIN, R. O.   *The Psychology of Human Consciousness.* 2nd ed. New York: Harcourt, Brace, Jovanovich, 1977.
OSARCHUK, M. and TATZ, S. J.   "Effect of Induced Fear of Death on Belief in an Afterlife," *Journal of Personality and Social Psychology,* 1973, *27,* 256-60.
OSIS, K. and HARALDSON, E.   *At the hour of death.* New York: Avon, 1977.
OSTOW, M., and SCHARFSTEIN, B. A.   *The Need to Believe.* New York: International Universities Press, 1954.
OTTO, R.   *The Idea of the Holy.* New York: Oxford University Press, 1923.
_____.   *Mysticism East and West.* New York: Macmillan, 1932.
OVERHOLSER, W.   "Psychopathology in Religious Experience," in the Proceedings of the Fifth Academy Symposium, 1961, of the Academy of Religion and Mental Health, *Research in Religion and Mental Health.* New York: Fordham University Press, 1963, 100-116.
PAHNKE, W. N.   *An Analysis of the Relationship between Psychedelic Drugs and the Mystical Consciousness.* Unpublished Ph.D. dissertation, Harvard University, 1963.
_____.   "Drugs and Mysticism," *International Journal of Parapsychology,* 1966, *8,* 295-320.
_____.   "Psychedelic Drugs and Mystical Experience," in E. M. Pattison (ed.), *Clinical Psychiatry and Religion.* Boston: Little, Brown, 1969, 149-62.
_____ and RICHARDS, W. A.   "Implications of LSD and Experimental Mysticism," *Journal of Religion and Health,* 1966, *5,* 175-208.
PAINE, T.   *The Political Works of Thomas Paine.* Chicago: Donohue Brothers, 1897.
PALMORE, E. and JEFFERS, F. C. (eds.).   *Prediction of Life-span.* Lexington, Mass.: Heath, 1971.
_____.   "The Effects of Aging on Activities and Attitudes." *Gerontologist,* 1968, *8,* 259-63.
PALOUTZIAN, R. F.   "Purpose in Life and Value Changes Following Conversion," *Journal of Personality and Social Psychology,* 1981, *41,* 1153-60.
_____ and WILHELM, R.   "Faith and Works? A Behavioral Study of Religion, Cheating, and Altruism." Paper presented at the meeting of the American Psychological Association, Anaheim, Calif., August 1983.

PARFREY, P. S.   "The Effect of Religious Factors on Intoxicant Use," *Scandinavian Journal of Social Medicine*, 1976, *4*, 135–40.

PARGAMENT, K. I.   *The Relationship Between the Church/Synagogue as an Organization, the Fit of the Member with the Church/Synagogue and the Psychosocial Effectiveness of the Member.* Unpublished doctoral dissertation, University of Maryland, 1977.

_____; TYLER, F. B.; and STEELE, R. E.   "Is Fit It? The Relationship Between the Church/Synagogue Member Fit and the Psychosocial Competence of the Member," *Journal of Community Psychology*, 1979, *7*, 243–52.

_____.   "The Interface Among Religion, Religious Support Systems and Mental Health," in D. Biegel and A. Naperstak (eds.), *Community Support Systems.* New York: Springer, 1982.

_____; PARGAMENT, A. S.; SHACK, M.; SHACK, T.; and ECHEMENDIA, R. J.   *Assessing the Strengths and Weaknesses of a Synagogue: A Case Study.* Paper presented at the Convention of the Society for the Scientific Study of Religion, Knoxville, Tennessee, 1983.

_____; SILVERMAN, W.; JOHNSON, S.; ECHEMENDIA, R. J.; and SNYDER, S.   *The Congregation Development Program: A Data-based Method of Evaluation of Churches and Synagogues.* Paper presented at the Convention of the Society for the Scientific Study of Religion, Providence, Rhode Island, October 1982.

_____; STEELE, R. E.; and TYLER, F. B.   "Religious Participation, Religious Motivation and Psychosocial Competence," *Journal for the Scientific Study of Religion*, 1979, *18*, 412–19.

_____; TYLER, F. B.; and STEELE, R. E.   "The Church/Synagogue and the Psychosocial Competence of the Member: An Initial Inquiry into a Neglected Dimension," *Journal of Community Psychology*, 1979, *7*, 649–64.

PARKER, C. A.,   "Changes in Religious Beliefs of College Students," in Strommen, M. P. (ed.), *Research on Religious Development.* New York: Hawthorn, 1971, 724–76.

PARKES, C. M.   *Bereavement: Studies of Grief in Later Life.* New York: International Universities Press, 1972.

PARRY, H. J.   "Protestants, Catholics and Prejudice," *International Journal of Opinion and Attitude Research*, 1949, *3*, 205–13.

PARRUCCI, D. J.   "Religious Conversion: A Theory of Deviant Behavior," *Sociological Analysis*, 1968, *29*, 144–54.

PATTISON, E. M.   "Behavioral Science Research on The Nature of Glossolalia," *Journal of the American Scientific Affiliation*, 1968, *20*, 73–86.

PEATLING, J. H.   "Cognitive Development in Pupils in Grades Four through Twelve: The Incidence of Concrete and Abstract-Religious Thinking." *Character Potential*, 1974, *7*, 52–61.

_____ and C. W. LABBS,   "Cognitive Development of Pupils in Grades Four through Twelve: A Comparative Study of Lutheran and Episcopalian Children and Youth." *Character Potential*, 1975, *7*, 107–115.

PECK, R. F., and HAVIGHURST, R. J.   *The Psychology of Character Development.* New York: Wiley, 1960.

PEEL, R.   *Mary Baker Eddy.* New York: Holt, Rinehart, and Winston, 1966.

PELLETIER, K. R. and GARFIELD, C.   *Consciousness: East and West.* New York: Harper and Row, 1976.

PENFIELD, W.   *The Mystery of the Mind.* Princeton, N.J.: Princeton University Press, 1975.

PERRY, E. L. and HOGE, D. R.   "Faith Priorities of Pastor and Laity as a Factor in the Growth and Decline of Presbyterian Congregations," *Review of Religious Research*, 1981, *22*, 221–41.

_____, DAVIS, J. H., DOYLE, R. T., and DYBLE, J. E.   "Toward a Typology of Unchurched Protestants," *Review of Religious Research*, 1980, *21*, 388–404.

PETER, L. J. (ed.).   *Peter's Quotations.* New York: Bantam, 1977.

PHARES, E. J.   *Locus of Control in Personality,* Morristown, NJ: General Learning Press, 1976.

PHOTIADIS, J. D. and BIGGAR, J.   "Religiosity, Education, and Ethnic Distance," *American Journal of Sociology,* 1962, *67,* 666–72.

———.   "Overt Conformity to Church Teaching as A Function of Religious Belief and Group Participation," *American Journal of Sociology,* 1965, *70,* 423–28.

PIAGET, J.   *The Moral Judgment of the Child.* New York: Free Press, 1932; reprint 1965 (trans. M. Gabain).

———.   *The Child and Reality.* Paris: Editions Denol, 1972 (translated to English, 1972; New York: Viking Press, 1974).

PILARZYK, K. T.   "The Origin, Development, and Decline of a Youth Culture Movement: An Application of Sectarianization Theory. *Review of Religious Research,* 1978, *20,* 23–43.

PLATO.   *The Dialogues of Plato* (B. Jowett, trans.). Chicago: Encyclopedia Britannica, 1952.

PLUTCHIK, R. and AX, A. F.   "A Critique of 'Determinants of emotional state' by Schachter and Singer (1962)," *Psychophysiology,* 1967, *4,* 79–82.

PODLESNY, J. A. and RASKIN, D. C.   "Physiological Measures and the Detection of Deception," *Psychological Bulletin,* 1977, *84,* 782–90.

POLANYI, M. and PROSCH, H.   *Meaning.* Chicago: Univ. of Chicago Press, 1975.

POLYTHRESS, N. G.   "Literal, Antiliteral, and Mythological Religious Orientations." *Journal for the Scientific Study of Religion,* 1975, *14,* 271–84.

PONTIER, R.   "The Right of Conscience." *Event,* September 1971, 24–27.

POPE JOHN XXIII.   *Pacem in Terris.* New York: American Press, 1963.

POPE, L.   "Religion and The Class Structure," *The Annals of the American Academy of Political and Social Science,* March, 1948, 84–91.

PRATT, J. B.   *The Religious Consciousness.* New York: Macmillan, 1920.

———.   *Matter and Spirit.* New York: Macmillan, 1922.

PRESTON, C. E. and HORTON, J.   "Attitudes among Clergy and Lawyers toward Euthanasia," *Journal of Pastoral Care,* 1972, *26,* 108–15.

PRICE, R. H. and LYNN, S. J.   *Abnormal Psychology in the Human Context.* Homewood, Ill.: Dorsey, 1981.

PRICHARD, L. K.   "Religious Change in Nineteenth Century America," in C. Y. Glock and R. N. Bellah (eds.), *The New Religious Consciousness.* Berkeley, Calif.: University of California Press, 1976, p. 297–330.

Princeton Religion Research Center. *Religion in America 1979–80.* Princeton, N.J., 1980.

PROPST, R. L.   "A Comparison of The Cognitive Restructuring Psychotherapy Paradigm and Several Spiritual Approaches to Mental Health," *Journal of Psychology and Theology,* 1980, *8,* 107–14.

PROUDFOOT, W. and SHAVER, P.   "Attribution Theory and the Psychology of Religion," *Journal for the Scientific Study of Religion,* 1975, *14,* 317–30.

PRUYSER, P. A.   *Dynamic Psychology of Religion.* New York: Harper, 1968.

PRUYSER, P. W.   "A Psychological View of Religion in The 1970s," *Bulletin of the Menninger Clinic,* 1971, *35,* 77–97.

———.   "The Seamy Side of Current Religious Beliefs," *Bulletin of the Menninger Clinic,* 1977, *41,* 329–48.

QUINLEY, H. E.   *The Prophetic Clergy.* New York: Wiley, 1974.

RAAB, E. and SELZNICK, C. J.   *Major Social Problems,* 2nd ed. New York: Harper and Row, 1964.

RAGAN, C.; MAHONY, H. N.; and BEIT-HALLAHMI, B.   "Psychologists and Religion: Professional Factors and Personal Belief," *Review of Religious Research,* 1980, *21,* 208–17.

RAMBO, L. R. "Current Research in Religious Conversion," *Religious Studies Review*, 1982, *8*, 146–59.

RAMSEY, G. V. and SEIPP, M. "Public Opinions and Information Concerning Mental Health," *Journal of Clinical Psychology*, 1948, *4*, 397–406.

RAMSEY, P. *The Patient as Person*. New Haven, Conn.: Yale University Press, 1970.

RANCK, J. G. "Some Personality Correlates of Religious Attitude and Belief," *Dissertation Abstracts*, 1955, *15*, 878–79.

RANDALL, T. M., and DESROSIERS M. "Measurement of Supernatural Belief: Sex Differences and Locus of Control." *Journal of Personality Assessment*, 1980, *44*, 493–498.

REA, M. P. GREENSPOON, S. and SPILKA, B. "Physicians and the Terminal Patient: Some Selected Attitudes and Behavior," 1975, *Omega*, *6*, 291–302.

REDEKOP, C. "A New Look at Sect Development," *Journal for the Scientific Study of Religion*, 1974, *13*, 345–52.

REIFSNYDER, W. E. and CAMPBELL, E. I. "Religious Attitudes of Male Neuropsychiatric Patients: I. Most Frequently Expressed Attitudes," *Journal of Pastoral Care*, 1960, *14*, 92–97.

REISS, I. L. "Premarital Sex Permissiveness among Negroes and Whites," *American Sociological Review*, 1969, *29*, 688–98.

_____. *Family Systems in America*. New York: Holt, Rinehart and Winston, 1976.

REYNOLDS, D. K. and NELSON, F. L. "Personality Life Situation and Life Expectancy," *Suicide and Life-Threatening Behavior*, 1981, *11*, 99–110.

RICHARDSON, A. H. "Social and Medical Correlates of Survival among Octogenarians: United Automobile Worker Retirees and Spanish-American War Veterans," *Journal of Gerontology*, 1973, *28*, 207–15.

RICHARDSON, J. T. "Psychological Interpretations of Glossolalia: A Reexamination of Research," *Journal for the Scientific Study of Religion*, 1973, *12*, 99–207.

_____. "People's Temple and Jonestown: A Corrective Comparison and Critique," *Journal for the Scientific Study of Religion*, 1980, *19*, 239–55.

_____ and FOX, S. W. "Religious Affiliation as a Predictor of Voting Behavior in Abortion Reform Legislation. *Journal for the Scientific Study of Religion*, 1972, *11*, 347–59.

_____ and STEWART, M. "Conversion Process Models and the Jesus Movement," *American Behavioral Scientist*, 1977, *20*, 819–38.

_____, STEWART, M., and SIMMONDS, R. B. *Organized Miracles: A Study of a Contemporary Youth, Communal, Fundamentalist Organization*. New Brunswick, N.J.: Transaction Books, 1979.

RILEY, J. JR. and MARDEN, C. F., "Who, What and How Often?" in R. G. McCarthy (ed.), *Drinking and Intoxication*. Glencoe, Ill.: The Free Press, 1959, 182–89.

RING, K. *Life at Death*. New York: Coward, McCann and Geoghegan, 1980.

RITZEMA, R. J. "Attribution to Supernatural Causation: An Important Component of Religious Commitment." *Journal of Psychology and Theology*, 1979, *7*, 286–93.

ROBACK, A. A. "The Jew in Modern Science," in D. D. Runes (ed.), *The Hebrew Impact on Western Civilization*, abridged ed. New York: Philosophical Library, 1951, 62–193.

ROBERTS, A. H. and JESSOR, R. "Authoritarianism, Punitiveness, and Perceived Social Status," *Journal of Abnormal and Social Psychology*, 1958, *56*, 311–14.

ROBERTS, B. H. and MYERS, J. K. "Religion, National Origin, Immigration, and Mental Illness," *American Journal of Psychiatry*, 1954, *110*, 759–64.

ROBERTS, F. J. "Some Psychological Factors in Religious Conversion, *British Journal of Social and Clinical Psychology*, 1965, *4*, 185–87.

ROBERTSON, R. "On the Analysis of Mysticism: Pre-Weberian, Weberian, and Post-Weberian Perspectives," *Sociological Analysis*, 1975, *36*, 241–66.

ROBBINS, T. "Even a Moonie Has Civil Rights," *The Nation*, February 26, 1977, 233–42.

_____ and ANTHONY, D.   "Cults, Brainwashing, and Countersubversion. *Annals of the American Academy of Political and Social Science,* 1979, *446,* 78–90.

_____ and ANTHONY, D. (eds.).   *In Gods We Trust.* New Brunswick, N.J.: Transaction Books, 1981.

ROHRBAUGH, J. and JESSOR, R.   "Religiosity in Youth: A Personal Control Against Deviant Behavior," *Journal of Personality,* 1975, *43,* 136–55.

ROKEACH, M.   *The Open and Closed Mind.* New York: Basic, 1960.

_____.   *The Three Christs of Ypsilanti.* New York: Knopf, 1964.

_____.   "Value Systems and Religion," Part I of the H. Paul Douglass Lecture to the Religious Research Association, June 19, 1969(a).

_____.   "Religious Values and Social Compassion," Part II of the H. Paul Douglass Lecture to the Religious Research Association. June 20, 1969(b).

_____.   *The Nature of Human Values.* New York: Free Press, 1973.

ROOF, W. C.   "Traditional Religion in Contemporary Society: A Theory of Local-Cosmopolitan Plausibility," *American Sociological Review,* 1976, *41,* 195–208.

_____, HADAWAY, C. K.; HEWITT, M. L.; MCGAW, D.; and MORSE, R.   "Yinger's Measure of Non-doctrinal Religion: A Northeastern Test." *Journal for the Scientific Study of Religion,* 1977, *19,* 403–408.

_____ and HADAWAY, C. K.   "Shifts in Religious Preference—the Mid-seventies," *Journal for the Scientific Study of Religion,* 1977, *16,* 409–12.

_____ and HADAWAY, C. K.   "Denominational Switching in the Seventies: Going Beyond Stark and Glock," *Journal for the Scientific Study of Religion,* 1979, *18,* 363–77.

ROOF, W. C. and HOGE, D. R.   "Church Participation in America: Social Factors Affecting Membership and Participation," *Review of Religious Research,* 1980, *21,* 405–26.

ROOF, W. C. and PERKINS, R. B.   "On conceptualizing Salience in Religious Commitment," *Journal for the Scientific Study of Religion,* 1975, *14,* 111–28.

ROOZEN, D. A.   *The Churched and the Unchurched in America.* Washington, D. C.: Glenmary Research Center, 1978.

ROSE, A. M. (ed.).   *Mental Health and Mental Disorder.* New York: Norton, 1955.

ROSE, A. M. and STUB, H. R.   "Summary of Studies on the Incidence of Mental Disorders," in A. M. Rose (ed.), *Mental Health and Mental Disorder: A Sociological Approach.* New York: Norton, 1955, 87–116.

ROSEGRANT, J.   "The Impact of Set and Setting on Religious Experience in Nature," *Journal for the Scientific Study of Religion,* 1976, *15,* 301–10.

ROSEN, B. C.   "Race, Ethnicity, and the Achievement Syndrome." *American Sociological Review,* 1959, *24,* 47–60.

ROSEN, B. C.   *Adolescence and Religion.* Cambridge, MA: Schenkman, 1965.

ROSEN, G.   "History," in S. Perlin (ed.). *A Handbook for the Study of Suicide.* New York: Oxford, 1975, 3–30.

ROSENBERG, M.   "The Dissonant Religious Context and Emotional Disturbance," *American Journal of Sociology,* 1962, *68,* 1–10.

ROSENTHAL, E.   "Studies of Jewish Intermarriage in the United States." Reprinted as a separate from the *1963 American Jewish Yearbook* by the American Jewish committee (53 pages).

ROSS, M. W.,   "Clinical Profiles of Hare Krishna Devotees," *American Journal of Psychiatry,* 1983, *140,* 416–20.

ROSSI, A. M., STURROCK, J. B., and SOLOMON, P.   "Suggestion Effects on Reported Imagery in Sensory Deprivation," *Perceptual and Motor Skills,* 1963, *16,* 39–45.

ROSTEN, L. (ed.).   *Religions of America.* New York: Simon and Schuster, 1975.

ROSZAK, T.   *The Making of a Counter Culture.* Garden City, N.Y.: Doubleday, 1969.

_____.   *The Unfinished Animal.* New York: Harper and Row, 1975.

ROTENBERG, M.   *Damnation and Deviance.* New York: Free Press, 1978.

ROTTER, J. B. "Generalized Expectancies for Internal Versus External Control of Reinforcement." *Psychological Monographs,* 1966, 80, No. 1, Whole No. 609, pp. 1-28.

ROYCE, J. *The Sources of Religious Insight.* New York: Charles Scribner's Sons, 1912.

RUBIN, Z. *Liking and Loving.* New York: Holt, Rinehart and Winston, 1973.

RUBIN, Z., and PEPLAU, A. "Belief in a Just World and Reactions to Another's Lot: A Study of Participants in the National Draft Lottery." *Journal of Social Issues,* 1973, 73-93.

RUSSELL, B. *Mysticism, Logic and Other Essays.* London: Longmans, Green, 1921.

RUSSELL, G. W. "The View of Religions from Religious and Non-Religious Perspectives," *Journal for the Scientific Study of Religion,* 1975, *14,* 129-38.

RUSSELL, O. R. *Freedom to Die.* New York: Human Sciences Press, 1975.

RUTLEDGE, A. L. "Concepts of God Among The Emotionally Upset," *Pastoral Psychology,* 1951, *2,* 22-27.

SALMAN, L. "The Psychology of Religious and Ideological Conversion," *Psychiatry,* 1953, *16,* 177-87.

―――. "Religious Conversion," in E. M. Pattison (ed.), *Clinical Psychiatry and Religion,* Boston: Little, Brown, 1969, 175-88.

SAMARIN, W. J. *Tongues of Men and Angels.* New York; Macmillan, 1972.

SANFORD, R. N. "Ethnocentrism in Relation to Some Religious Attitudes and Practices," in T. W. Adorno, E. Frenkel-Brunswik, D. J. Levinson, and R. N. Sanford (eds.), *The Authoritarian Personality.* New York: Harper, 1950, 208-21.

―――― and LEVINSON, D. J. "Ethnocentrism in Relation to Some Religious Attitudes and Practices," *American Psychologist,* 1948, *3,* 350-51.

SARGANT, W. *Battle for the Mind.* London: Heinemann, 1957.

SASAKI, M. A. "Status Inconsistency and Religious Commitment, in R. Wuthnow (ed.), *The Religious Dimension: New Directions in Quantitative Research,* New York: Academic, 1979, 135-56.

SCHACHTEL, E. *Metamorphosis: On the Development of Affect, Perception, Attention and Memory.* New York: Basic Books, 1959.

SCHACHTER, S. "The Interaction of Cognitive and Physiological Determinants of Emotional States," in L. Berkowitz (ed.), *Advances in Experimental Social Psychology,* Vol. 1. New York: Academic, 1964, 49-80.

―――. *Emotion, Obesity, and Crime.* New York: Academic, 1971.

―――― and SINGER, J. E. "Cognitive, Social, and Physiological Determinants of Emotional State," *Psychological Review,* 1962, *69,* 379-99.

SCHARFSTEIN, B. *Mystical Experience.* Indianapolis: Bobbs-Merrill, 1973.

SCHEIN, E. *Coercive Persuasion.* New York: Norton, 1971.

SCHNEIDER, H. W. *Religion in 20th Century America.* New York: Atheneum, 1964.

SCHNEIDER, L. The Dilemma of Instrumentalism," in O'Dea, T. F. and O'Dea, J. (eds.), *Readings on the Sociology of Religion.* Englewood Cliffs, N.J.: Prentice-Hall, 1973, pp. 192-208.

SCHILLEBEECK, E. *Jesus.* New York: Random House, 1981.

SCHOENBERG, B.; CARR, A. C.; KUTSCHER, A. H.; PERETZ, D.; and GOLDBERG, I. K. (eds.). *Anticipatory Grief.* New York: Columbia University Press, 1974.

SCHOFIELD, W. and BALIAN, L. "A Comparative Study of The Personal Histories of Schizophrenic and Nonpsychiatric Patients, *Journal of Abnormal and Social Psychology,* 1959, *59,* 216-25.

SCHOLL, M. E. and BEKER, J. "A Comparison of the Religious Beliefs of Delinquent and Non-delinquent Protestant Adolescent Boys," *Religious Education,* 1964, *59,* 250-53.

SCHUMAN, H. "The Religious Factor in Detroit: Review, Replication, and Reanalysis." *American Sociological Review,* 1971, *36,* 30-48.

SCHWARTZ, S. H. "Words, Deeds, and the Perception of Consequences and Responsibility in Action Situations," *Journal of Personality and Social Psychology,* 1968, *10,* 232–42.

SCOBIE, G. E. W.   "Types of Religious Conversion," *Journal of Behavioral Science,* 1973, *1,* 265–71.

_____. *Psychology of Religion.* New York: Wiley, 1975.

SCOTT, W. A.   *Values and Organizations: A Study of Fraternities and Sororities.* Chicago: Rand McNally, 1965.

_____. *Measuring Religious Beliefs as Values.* Unpublished manuscript, 1969.

SEARS, R. R., MACCOBY, E. E. and LEVIN, H.   *Patterns of Child Rearing.* New York: Harper and Row, 1957

SEEMAN, M.   "The Meaning of Alienation." *American Sociological Review,* 1959, *24,* 783–90.

SEGGAR, J. and KUNZ, P.   "Conversion: Evaluation of a Step-like Process for Problem-solving," *Review of Religious Research,* 1972, *13,* 178–84.

SELIGMAN, M. E. P.; ABRAMSON, L. Y.; SEMMEL, A.; and VON BAEYER, C.   "Depressive Attributional Style," *Journal of Abnormal Psychology,* 1979, *88,* 242–47.

_____. *Helplessness: On Depression, Development, and Death.* San Francisco: Freeman, 1975.

SHAH, I.   *Caravan of Dreams.* Baltimore: Penguin, 1972.

SHAPIRO, H. M. and DASHEFSKY, A.   "Religious Education and Ethnic Identification: Implications for Ethnic Pluralism." *Review of Religious Research,* 1974, *15,* 93–102.

SHAVER, K. G.   *An Introduction to Attribution Processes.* Cambridge, Mass.: Winthrop, 1975.

SHAVER, P.; LENAUER, M.; and SADD, S.   "Religiousness, Conversion, and Subjective Well-Being: The "Healthy-Minded" Religion of Modern American Women. *American Journal of Psychiatry,* 1980, *137,* 1563–68.

SHEPARD, R. N.   "The Mental Image," *American Psychologist,* 1978, *33,* 125–37.

SHEPHERD, W. G.   "Religion and the Counter Culture—A New Religiosity," in P. H. MacNamara (ed.), *Religion American Style.* New York: Harper and Row, 1974, pp. 348–58.

SHOEMAKER, S., and GORSUCH, R.   "Training in Awareness of Consequences." Unpublished manuscript, 1982.

SHRAUGER, J. S. and R. E. SILVERMAN.   The Relationship of Religious Background and Participation to Locus of Control." *Journal for the Scientific Study of Religion,* 1971, *10,* 11, 16.

SHUPE, A. D. JR. and BROMLEY, D. G.   "The Moonies and the Anti-Cultists: Movement and Countermovement in Conflict," *Sociological Analysis,* 1979, *40,* 325–34.

_____; SPIELMAN, R.; and STIGALL, S.   "Deprogramming," *American Behavioral Scientist,* 1977, *20,* 941–56.

SILVERMAN, W.   "Bibliography of Measurement Techniques Used in the Social Scientific Study of Religion." *Psychological Documents,* 1983, *13,* 1 (ms. no. 2539).

SILVESTRI, P. J.   "Locus of Control and God Dependence." *Psychological Reports,* 1979, *45,* 89–90.

SIMMONDS, R. B.; RICHARDSON, J. T.; and HARDER, M. W.   "A Jesus Movement Group: An Adjective Check List Assessment," *Journal for the Scientific Study of Religion,* 1976, *15,* 323–37.

_____. "Conversion or Addiction?" *American Behavioral Scientist,* 1977, *20,* 909–24.

SINGER, J. L.   *Daydreaming: An Introduction to the Experimental Study of Inner Experience.* New York: Random House, 1966.

SINGER, M.   "The Use of Folklore in Religious Conversion: The Chassidic Case," *Review of Religious Research,* 1980. *22,* 170–85.

SINGH, B. K.   "Trends in Attitudes toward Premarital Sexual Relations," *Journal of Marriage and the Family,* 1980, *42,* 387–93.

SKLARE, M.   *America's Jews.* New York: Random House, 1971.

SKOLNICK, J. H.   "Religious Affiliation and Drinking Behavior," *Quarterly Journal of Studies of Alcohol,* 1958, *19,* 452-70.

SMART, N.   *In Search of Christianity.* New York: Harper and Row, 1979.

SMITH, D. E.   "LSD, Violence and Radical Religious Beliefs," *Journal of Psychedelic Drugs,* 1970, *3,* 38-40.

SMITH, H.   "Do Drugs Have Religious Import?" *Journal of Philosophy,* 1964. *61,* 517-30.

————.   *Forgotten Truth.* New York: Harper and Row, 1976.

SMITH, M.   "Prisoner's Attitudes toward Organized Religion," *Religious Education,* 1956, *51,* 462-64.

SMITH, R. E.; WHEELER, G.; and DIENER, E.   "Faith without Works: Jesus People, Resistance to Temptation and Altruism," *Journal of Applied Social Psychology,* 1975, *5,* 320-30.

SNELLING, C. H. and WHITLEY, O. R.   "Problem-solving Behavior in Religious and Parareligious Groups: An Initial Report," in A. W. Eister (ed.), *Changing Perspectives in the Scientific Study of Religion,* New York: Wiley, 1974, 315-334.

SNOW, D. A. and PHILLIPS, C. L.   "The Lofland-Stark Conversion Model: A Critical Reassessment," *Social Problems,* 1980, *27,* 430-47.

SNYDER, C. R.   "Culture and Jewish Sobriety: The Ingroup-outgroup Factor," *Society, Culture and Drinking Patterns,* in D. J. Pittman and C. R. Snyder (eds.), New York: Wiley, 1962, 188-225.

————.   "Inebriety, Alcoholism, and Anomie. in M. B. Clinard (Ed.) *Anomie and deviant behavior.* New York: The Free Press of Glencoe, 1964, pp. 189-212.

SNYDER, M. L.; STEPHAN, W. G.; and D. ROSENFIELD.   "Attributional Egotism," in J. H. Harvey, W. Ickes, and R. F. Kidd (eds.), *New Directions in Attribution Research,* Vol. 2. Hillsdale, N J: Lawrence Erlbaum Associates, 1978, 5-34.

SODERSTROM, D. and WRIGHT, W. E.   "Religious Orientation and Meaning in Life," *Journal of Clinical Psychology,* 1977, *33,* (Supplement), 65-68.

SOMIT, A.   "Brainwashing," in D. Solls (ed.), *International Encyclopedia of the Social Sciences,* Vol. 2. New York: Macmillan, 1968, pp. 138-43.

SORENSON, A. A.   "Need for Power Among Alcoholic and Nonalcoholic Clergy," *Journal for the Scientific Study of Religion, 1973, 12,* 101-8.

SORENSON, R. C.   *Adolescent Sexuality in Contemporary America.* New York: World, 1973.

SOUTHARD, S.   "Religious Concern in the Psychoses," *Journal of Pastoral Care,* 1956, *10,* 226-33.

SPELLMAN, C. M.; BASKETT, G. D.; and BYRNE, D.,   "Manifest Anxiety as A Contributing Factor in Religious Conversion," *Journal of Consulting and Clinical Psychology,* 1971, *36,* 245-47.

SPENCER, J.   "The Mental Health of Jehovah's Witnesses," *British Journal of Psychiatry,* 1975, *126,* 556-59.

SPIEGEL, Y.   *The Grief Process: Analysis and Counseling.* Nashville: Abingdon, 1977.

SPILKA, B.   "Alienation and Achievement Among Oglala Sioux Secondary School Students," *Final Report Project MH 11232,* National Institute of Mental Health, Washington, D. C., 1970.

————.   "Images of Man and Dimensions of Personal Religion: Values for an Empirical Psychology of Religion," *Review of Religious Research,* 1970, *11,* 171-82.

————.   "Religious Values and Social Compassion: A Problem in Theory and Measurement. *Review of Religious Research, 1970, 11,* 149-51.

————.   "The 'Compleat' Person: Some Theoretical Views and Research Findings for a Theological-psychology of Religion," *Journal of Psychology and Theology,* 1976, *4,* 15-24.

————.   "The Current State of the Psychology of Religion," *Bulletin of the Council for the Study of Religion,* 1977, *9,* 96-99.

————.   "Utilitarianism and Personal Faith." *Journal of Psychology and Theology,* 1977, *5,* 226-33.

_____. *Toward a Psychosocial Theory of Religious Mysticism with Empirical Reference.* Paper presented at the convention of the Rocky Mountain Psychological Association, Tucson, Arizona, April 11, 1980.

_____; ADDISON, J.; and ROSENSOHN, M. "Parents, Self, and God: A Test of Competing Theories of Individual-Religion Relationships." *Review of Religious Research,* 1975, *16,* 154–65.

_____; AMARO, A.; WRIGHT, G.; and DAVIS, J. *The Treatment of Religion in Current Psychology Texts.* Paper presented at the Convention of the American Psychological Association, Los Angeles, California, August 1981.

_____, ARMATAS, F. and NUSSBAUM, J. "The Concept of God: A Factor Analytic Approach." *Review of Religious Research.* 1964, *6,* 28–36.

_____; COMP, G.; and GOLDSMITH, W. M. "Faith and Behavior: Religion in Introductory Psychology Texts of the 1950's and 1970's," *Teaching of Psychology,* 1981, *8,* 158–60.

_____ and LOFFREDO, L. "Classroom Cheating among Religious Students: Some Factors Affecting Perspectives, Actions and Justifications." Paper presented at the 1982 Convention of the Rocky Mountain Psychological Association, Albuquerque, New Mexico, April 30, 1982.

_____ and MULLIN, M. "Personal Religion and Psychosocial Schemata: A Research Approach to a Theological-Psychology of Religion." *Character Potential,* 1977, *8,* 57–66.

_____; PELLEGRINI, R. J.; and DAILEY, K. "Religion, American Values and Death Perspectives." *Sociological Symposium.* 1968, *I,* 57–66.

_____; READ, S.; ALLEN, R. O.; and DAILEY, K. A. "Specificity and Generality: The Criterion Problem in Religious Measurement." Paper presented at the 1968 Convention of the American Association for the Advancement of Science, Dallas, Texas, December 31, 1968.

_____ and REYNOLDS, J. F. "Religion and Prejudice: A Factor-Analytic Study," *Review of Religious Research,* 1965, *6,* 163–68.

_____ and SCHMIDT, G. "Attributions as a Function of Personal Faith and Locus of Control." Paper presented at the convention of the Rocky Mountain Psychological Association, Albuquerque, New Mexico, April 30, 1982.

_____ and SCHMIDT, G. "General Attribution Theory for the Psychology of Religion: The Influence of Event-Character on Attributions to God. *Journal for the Scientific Study of Religion,* 1963, *22,* 326–39.

_____; SCHMIDT, G.; and LOFFREDO, L. "General Attributions Theory for the Psychology of Religion: A Formulation and Its Initial Test." Paper presented at the 1982 Convention of the Society for the Scientific Study of Religion, Providence, Rhode Island, October 24, 1982.

_____, SHAVER, P.; and KIRKPATRICK, L. *General Attribution Theory for the Psychology of Religion.* Journal for the Scientific Study of Religion, 1985.

_____; STOUT, L.; MINTON, B.; and SIZEMORE, D. "Death and Personal Faith: A Psychometric Investigation." *Journal for the Scientific Study of Religion,* 1977, *16,* 169–178.

_____ and SPANGLER, J. D. "Spiritual Support in Life-Threatening Illness." Paper presented at the Convention of the Society for the Scientific Study of Religion, San Antonio, Texas, October 31, 1979.

_____, SPANGLER, J. D.; and NELSON, C. B. "Spiritual Support in Life-Threatening Illness," *Journal of Religion and Health,* 1983, *22,* 98–104.

_____; SPANGLER, J. D.; and REA, M. P. "The Role of Theology in Pastoral Care for the Dying," *Theology Today,* 1981, *38,* 16–29.

_____ and WERME, P. "Religion and Mental Disorder: A Research Perspective," in M. P. Strommen (ed.), *Research on Religious Development: A Comprehensive Handbook,* New York: Hawthorn, 1971, 161–81.

SPRANGER, E. *Types of Men.* New York: Johnson, 1928.

SPRINGER, S. P. and DEUTSCH, G.   *Left Brain, Right Brain.* San Francisco: Freeman, 1981.

SROLE, L. and LANGNER, T. S.   "Religious Origin," in Srole, L., Thomas, A. C. and Langner, T. S. (eds.) *Mental Health in the Metropolis* New York: McGraw-Hill, 1962, Chapter 16.

_____; LANGNER, T. S.; MICHAEL, S. T.; OPLER, M. K.; and RENNIE, T. A. C.   *Mental Health in the Metropolis.* New York: McGraw-Hill, 1962.

STAAL, F.   *Exploring Mysticism.* Berkeley, Calif.: Berkeley Center for South and Southeast Asian Studies, University of California.

STACE, W. T.   *Mysticism and Philosophy.* New York: Macmillan, 1960.

_____. "Man against Darkness," in C. Muscatine and M. Griffith (eds.), *The Borzoi College Reader.* New York: Knopf, 1966, 540-50.

STACK, W.   "Religion and Anomia in America," *Journal of Social Psychology,* 1981, *114,* ·299-300.

STARBUCK, E. D.   *The Psychology of Religion.* New York: Charles Scribner's Sons, 1899.

STARK, R.   "Class, Radicalism, and Religious Involvement in Great Britain." *American Sociological Review,* 1964, *29,* 698-706.

_____.   "A Taxonomy of Religious Experience," *Journal for the Scientific Study of Religion.* 1965, 5, 97-116.

_____.   "Psychopathology and Religious Commitment," *Review of Religious Research,* 1971, *12,* 165-76.

_____.   "The Economics of Piety: Religious Commitment and Social Class," in G. Thielbar and S. Feldman (eds.), *Issues in Social Inequality.* Boston: Little, Brown, 1972, pp. 483-503.

_____ and BAINBRIDGE, W. S.   "Of Churches, Sects, and Cults: Preliminary Concepts for a Theory of Religious Movements," *Journal for the Scientific Study of Religion,* 1979a, *18,* 117-33.

_____ and BAINBRIDGE, W. S.   "Cults of America: A Reconnaissance in Space and Time," *Sociological Analysis,* 1979b, *40,* 347-59.

_____ and BAINBRIDGE, W. S.   "Secularization and Cult Formation in the Jazz Age," *Journal for the Scientific Study of Religion,* 1981, *20,* 360-73.

_____; BAINBRIDGE, W. S.; and KENT, L.   "Cult Membership in the Roaring Twenties: Assessing Local Receptivity," *Sociological Analysis,* 1981, *42,* 137-61.

_____; DOYLE, D. P.; and RUSHING, J. L.   "Beyond Durkheim: Religion and Suicide," *Journal for the Scientific Study of Religion,* 1983, *22,* 120-31.

_____, FOSTER, B. D.; GLOCK, C. Y.; and QUINLEY, H.   "Sounds of Silence," *Psychology Today,* April 1970, *3,* (11), 38-41, 60-61.

_____ and GLOCK, C. Y.   *American Piety: The Nature of Religous Commitment.* Berkeley, Calif.: University of California Press, 1968.

STEFFENHAGEN, R. A.; McAREE, C. P.; and NIXON, H. L. II   "Drug Use among College Females: Sociodemographic and Social Psychological Correlates. *International Journal of the Addictions,* 1972, *7,* 285-303.

STENGEL, E.   *Suicide and Attempted Suicide.* Baltimore: Penguin, 1964.

STEWART, C. W.   *Adolescent Religion.* Nashville: Abingdon, 1967.

STEWART, D. W.   "Religious Correlates of the Fear of Death," *Journal of Thanatology,* 1975, *3,* 161-64.

STEWART, L., and STEWART, M.   "The Fundamentals: A Testimony to the Truth." Los Angeles: Privately distributed, 12 pamphlets, 1910.

STOBART, ST. CLAIR.   *Torchbearers of Spiritualism.* New York: Kennikat, 1971.

STONES, C. R.   "The Jesus People: Fundamentalism and Changes in Factors Associated with Conservatism," *Journal for the Scientific Study of Religion,* 1978, *17,* 155-58.

STOUDENMIRE, J.,   "The Role of Religion in The Depressed Housewife," *Journal of Religion and Health,* 1976, *15,* 62-67.

STOUFFER, S. A.   et al., *The American Soldier. II. Combat and Its Aftermath*. Princeton, N.J.: Princeton University Press, 1949.

STRAUS, E. B.   "Magic and Scruples," *Catholic World*, 1960, *199*, 205–11.

STRAUSS, R. and BACON, S. D.   *Drinking in College*. New Haven: Yale University Press, 1953.

STRAUSS, R. A.   "Religious Conversion as a Personal and Collective Accomplishment," *Sociological Analysis*, 1979, *40*, 158–65.

STRICKLAND, B. R., and SHAFFER, S.   "I-E, I-E, and F." *Journal for the Scientific Study of Religion*, 1971, *10*, 366–69.

STRICKLAND, F. L.   *Psychology of Religious Experience*. New York: Abingdon, 1924.

STROMMEN, M. P.   *Profiles of Church Youth*. St. Louis: Concordia, 1963.

STROMMEN, M. P.   "Religious Education and the Problem of Prejudice," *Religious Education*, 1967, *62*, 52–58.

_____; BREKKE, M. L.; UNDERWAGER, R. C.; and JOHNSON, A. L.   *A Study of Generations*. Minneapolis: Augsburg, 1972.

STRUENING, E. L.   *The Dimensions, Distribution, and Correlates of Authoritarianism in a Midwestern University Faculty Population*. Unpublished doctoral dissertation, Purdue University, West Lafayette, Indiana, 1957.

STRUENING, E. L.   "Anti-demoncratic Attitudes in Midwest University," in H. H. Remmers (ed.)., *Anti-democratic Attitudes in American Schools*. Evanston, Ill.: Northwestern University Press, 1963, pp. 210–58.

_____ and LEHMANN, S.   "Authoritarianism and Prejudiced Attitudes of University Faculty Members," in R. Perrucci and J. E. Gerstl (eds.). *The Engineers and the Social System* New York: Wiley, 1969, p. 161–99.

SUEDFELD, P.   "The Benefits of Boredom: Sensory Deprivation Reconsidered," *American Scientist*, 1975, *63*, 60–69.

SUEDFELD, P. and VERNON, J.   "Visual Hallucinations in Sensory Deprivation: A Problem of Criteria," *Science*, 1964, *145*, 412–13.

SUMMERLIN, F. A.   (ed.). *Religion and Mental Health: A Bibliography*. Rockville, MD: National Institutes of Mental Health, U. S. Department of Health and Human Services, 1980.

SUZUKI, D. T.   *Mysticism: Christian and Buddhist*. New York: Harper and Row, 1957.

SWARTZ, P. and SEGINER, L.   "Response to Body Rotation and Tendency to Mystical Experience," *Perceptual and Motor Skills*, 1981, *53*, 683–88.

SWATOS, W. H. Jr.   "Monopolism, Pluralism, Acceptance and Rejection: An Integrated Model for Church-Sect Theory," *Review of Religious Research*, 1975, *18*, 174–85.

SWATOS, W. H. Jr.   "Weber or Troeltsch: Methodology, Syndrome, and the Development of Church-Sect Theory," *Journal for the Scientific Study of Religion*, 1976, *15*, 129–44.

SWENSON, W. M.   "Attitudes Toward Death in an Aged Population," *Journal of Gerontology*, 1961, *16*, 49–52.

SWICKARD, D. L., and SPILKA, B.   "Hostility Expression among Majority and Minority Group Delinquents," *Journal of Consulting Psychology*, 1961, *25*, 216–20.

SZASZ, T. S.   "The Myth of Mental Illness," *American Psychologist*, 1960, *15*, 113–18.

TAFT, D. R. and ENGLAND, R. W. JR.   *Criminology*, 4th ed. New York: Macmillan, 1964.

TAFT, R.   "Peak Experiences and Ego Permissiveness: An Exploratory Factor Study of Their Dimensions in a Normal Person," *Acta Psychologica*, 1969, *29*, 35–64.

_____.   "The Measurement of the Dimensions of Ego Permissiveness," *Personality: An International Journal*, 1970, *1*, 163–84.

TAGESON, C. W.   *Humanistic Psychology: A Synthesis*. Homewood, Ill.: Dorsey, 1982.

TAMAYO, A. and ST.-ARNAUD, P.   "The Parental Figures and The Representation of God of Schizophrenics and Delinquents," in A. Vergote and A. Tamayo (eds.),

The Parental Figures and the Representation of God: A Psychological and Cross-Cultural Study, The Hague: Mouton Publishers and Leuven University Press, 1980, 145–68.

TAPP, R. B.   "Dimensions of Religiosity in a Post-traditional Group." *Journal for the Scientific Study of Religion,* 1971, *10,* 41–47.

TART, C. T.   "Science, States of Consciousness, and Spiritual Experiences: The Need for Specific Sciences," in C. T. Tart (ed.), *Transpersonal Psychologies.* New York: Harper and Row, 1960, pp. 11–58.

TAWNEY, R. H.   *Religion and the Rise of Capitalism.* New York: Harcourt, Brace, 1926.

TAVRIS, C. and SADD, S.   *The Redbook Report on Female Sexuality.* New York: Dell, 1975.

TAYLOR, S. E.   "Adjustment to Threatening Events: A Theory of Cognitive Adaptation." *American Psychologist,* 1983, *38,* 1161–73.

TEMPLER, D. I.   "The Construction and Validation of a Death Anxiety Scale," *Journal of General Psychology,* 1970, *82,* 165–77.

————.   "Death Anxiety in Religiously Very Involved Persons," *Psychological Reports,* 1972, *31,* 361–62.

———— and DOTSON, E.   "Religious Correlates of Death Anxiety," *Psychological Reports,* 1970, *26,* 895–97.

———— and RUFF, C. F.   "The Relationship between Death Anxiety and Religion in Psychiatric Patients," *Journal of Thanatology,* 1975, *3,* 165–68.

———— and VELEBER, D. M.   "Suicide rate and religion within the United States," *Psychological Reports,* 1980, *47,* 898.

TEYLER, T. J. (ed.).   *Altered States of Awareness.* San Francisco: Freeman, 1972.

THIESSEN, I.; WRIGHT, M. W.; and SISLER, G. C.   "A Comparison of Personality Characteristics of Mennonites with Non-mennonites," *Mental Health Digest,* October 1969, *1*(1), 37–38.

THOMAS, L. E. and COOPER, P. E.   "Measurement and Incidence of Mystical Experience: An Exploratory Study," *Journal for the Scientific Study of Religion,* 1978, *17,* 433–37.

THOMAS, O. C.   "Psychology and Theology on the Nature of Man," *Pastoral Psychology,* February 1962, *13,* No. 121, 41–46.

THOMPSON, A. D.   "Open-mindedness and Indiscriminate Antireligious Orientation." *Journal for the Scientific Study of Religion,* 1974, *13,* 471–78.

THOMPSON, S. C.   "Will It Hurt Less If I Can Control It? A Complex Answer to a Simple Question." *Psychological Bulletin,* 90, 1981, 89–101.

THURSTONE, L. L., and CHAVE, E. J.   *The Measurement of Attitude.* Chicago: University of Chicago Press, 1929.

TILLICH, P.   *The Courage to Be.* New Haven, Conn.: Yale, 1952.

————.   *Systematic Theology, Vol. III.* Chicago: University of Chicago, 1963.

————.   *Dynamics of Faith.* New York: Harper and Row, 1957.

TIPTON, R. M., HARRISON, B. M., and J. MAHONEY.   "Faith and Locus of Control." *Psychological Reports,* 1980, *46,* 1151–54.

TIRYAKIAN, E. A. (ed.).   *On the Margin of the Invisible.* New York: Wiley, 1974.

TISDALE, J. R.   "Mystical Experience: Normal and Normative," *Religion in Life,* 1975, *5,* 370–74.

TISDALE, J. R.   "Selected Correlates of Extrinsic Religious Values," *Review of Religious Research,* 1966, *7,* 78–84.

TOCH, H.   *The Social Psychology of Social Movements.* New York: Bobbs-Merrill, 1965.

TRAVISANO, R. V.   "Alteration and Conversion as Qualitatively Different Transformations," in G. P. Stone and H. A. Farberman (eds.), *Social Psychology through Symbolic Interaction.* Waltham, Mass.: Ginn-Blaisdell, 1970, pp. 594–606.

TREW, A.   "The Religious Factor in Mental Illness," *Pastoral Psychology,* 1971, *22,* 21–28.

TRICE, H. M.   *Alcoholism in America.* New York: McGraw-Hill, 1966.

TROELTSCH, E.   *The Social Teachings of the Christian Churches.* New York: Macmillan, 1931.

TROTTER, W.   *Instincts of the Herd in Peace and War.* New York: Macmillan, 1919.

TURNER, P. R.   "Religious Conversion and Community Development," *Journal for the Scientific Study of Religion,* 1979, *18,* 252–60.

TURNER, R. and KILLIAN, L.   *Collective Behavior.* Englewood Cliffs, N. J.: Prentice-Hall, 1957.

UEBERSAX, J.   "The Quantitative Study of Mystical Phenomena." Paper presented at the annual meeting of the Society for the Scientific Study of Religion, San Antonio, Texas, 1979.

ULANOV, B.   *Religion and the Unconscious.* Philadelphia: Westminster, 1975.

UNAMUNO, M. DE.   *The Tragic Sense of Life.* New York: Dover, 1954.

UNDERHILL, E.   *Mysticism.* New York: Dutton, 1961.

VALINS, S., and NISBETT, R. E.   *Attribution Processes in the Development and Treatment of Emotional Disorders.* General Learning Press, 1971, 14 pp.

VANDEKEMP, H.   "The Tension Between Psychology and Theology: An Anthropological Solution," *Journal of Psychology and Theology,* 1982, *10,* 205–11.

VANDERPLATE, C.   "Religious Orientation in Psychiatric Patients and Normals," *Proceedings of the 20th Annual Convention of the Christian Association for Psychological Studies,* Grand Rapids, Mich., 1973.

VANECKO, J. J.   "Religious Behavior and Prejudice: Some Dimensions and Specifications of the Relationship," *Review of Religious Research,* 1966, *8,* 27–37.

VAN ROY, R. F.; BEAN, F. D.; and WOOD, J. R.   "Social Mobility and Doctrinal Orthodoxy," *Journal for the Scientific Study of Religion,* 1973, *12,* 427–39.

VENABLE, D. and GORSUCH, R. L.   "I and E in Developmental Perspective." Submitted for publication, 1983.

VERBIT, M. F.   "The Components and Dimensions of Religious Behavior: Toward a Reconceptualization of Religiosity," in P. E. Hammond and B. Johnson (eds.), *American Mosaic.* New York: Random House, 1970, 24–39.

VERGOTE, A. and TAMAYO, A.   *The Parental Figures and the Representation of God.* The Hague: Mouton, 1980.

VERNON, G. M.   "Measuring Religion: Two Methods Compared." *Review of Religious Research,* 1962, *3,* 159–65.

_____.   *Sociology of Religion.* New York: McGraw-Hill, 1962.

_____.   "Marital Characteristics of Religious Independents." *Review of Religious Research,* 1968, *9,* 162–70.

_____.   "The Religious Nones: A Neglected Category," *Journal for the Scientific Study of Religion,* 1968, *7,* 219–29.

VERNON, G. M. and WADDELL, C. E.   "Dying as Social Behavior," *Omega,* 1974, *5,* 199–206.

VOLKEN, L.   *Visions, Revelations, and the Church.* New York: P. J. Kennedy and Sons, 1961.

WAHL, C. W.   "Some Antecedent Factors in the Family Histories of 109 Alcoholics," *Quarterly Journal of Studies of Alcohol,* 1956, *17,* 643–54.

WALBERG, H. J.   "Denominational and Socio-Economic Correlates of Professional Self-Concept. Reprint from the *International Yearbook for the Sociology of Religion,* 1967, 153–64.

WALLACE, A. F. C.   *Religion: An Anthropological View.* New York: Randon House, 1966.

WALLACE, R. A.   "A Model of Change in Religious Affiliation," *Journal for the Scientific Study of Religion,* 1975, *14,* 345–55.

WALLERSTEIN, J. S. and WYLE, J. C.   "Our Law-Abiding Law Breakers," *Probation,* 1947, *25,* 107–12.

WALLIN, T., and CLARK, A.   "Religiosity, Sexual Gratification, and Marital Satisfaction in the Middle Year of Marriage. *Social Forces,* 1964, *42,* 303–9.

WALSTER, E. and WALSTER, G. W.   *A New Look at Love*. Reading, Mass.: Addison-Wesley, 1978.

WALTERS, A., and BRADLEY, R.   "Motivation and Religious Behavior," in M. Strommen (ed.). *Research on Religious Development: A Comprehensive Handbook*. New York: Hawthorn, 1971, p. 599-651.

WALTERS, O. S.   "The Religious Background of Fifty Alcoholics," *Quarterly Journal of Studies of Alcohol*, 1957. *18*, 405-16.

WARNER, W. L., MEEKER, MARCIA, and EELLS, K.   *Social Class in America*. New York: Harper and Row, 1960.

WATKINS, M. M.   *Waking Dreams*. New York: Harper and Row, 1976.

WATTS, A.   *The Joyous Cosmology*. New York: Pantheon, 1962.

WATTENBERG, W. W.   "Church Attendance and Juvenile Misconduct," *Sociology and Social Research*, 1950, *34*, 195-202.

WEBER, M.   *The Protestant Ethnic and the Spirit of Capitalism*. New York: Scribner's, 1930.

WECHSLER, H., DEMONE, H. W., THUM, D., and KASEY, E. H.   "Religious-ethnic Differences in Alcohol Consumption," *Journal of Health and Social Behavior*, 1970, *11*, 21-29.

WEIBE, K. F. and FLECK, J. R.   "Personality Correlates of Intrinsic, Extrinsic and Non-religious Orientations," *Journal of Psychology*, 1980, *105*, 181-87.

WEIGERT, A. J. and THOMAS, D. L.   Religiosity in 5-D: A critical note. *Social Forces*, 1969, *48*, 260-263.

_____; D'ANTONIO, W. V.; and RUBEL, A. J.   "Protestantism and Assimilation among Mexican Americans: An Exploratory Study of Minister's Reports," *Journal for the Scientific Study of Religion*. 1971, *10*, 219-32.

WEISER, N.   "The Effect of Prophetic Disconfirmation of the Committee," *Review of Religious Research*, 1974, *16*, 19-30.

WEISNER, W. M. and RIFFEL, P. A.   "Scrupulosity: Religion and Obsessive Compulsive Behavior in Children," *American Journal of Psychiatry*, 1960, *117*, 314-18.

WEISSMAN, A. D.   *On Dying and Denying*. New York: Behavioral Publications, 1972.

WESTBERG, G. E.   *Good Grief*. Philadelphia: Fortress, 1962.

WELCH, M. R.   "Analyzing Religious Sects: An Empirical Examination of Wilson's Sect Typology," *Journal for the Scientific Study of Religion*, 1977, *16*, 125-41.

WELCH, M. R.   "Religious Non-Affiliates and Worldly Success," *Journal for the Scientific Study of Religion*, 1978, *17*, 59-61.

WELFORD, A. T.   "A Psychological Footnote to Prayer," *Theology Today*, 1947a, *3*, 498-501.

_____.   "Is Religious Behavior Dependent Upon Affect or Frustration?" *Journal of Abnormal and Social Psychology*, 1947b, *42*, 310-19.

WEST, L. J. (ed.).   *Hallucinations*. New York: Grune and Stratton, 1962.

WESTERMAYER, J. and WALZER, V.   "Drug Usage: An Alternative to Religion," *Diseases of the Nervous System*, 1975, *36*, 492-495.

WESTHUES, K. (ed.).   *Society's Shadow: Studies in the Sociology of Countercultures*. Toronto, Canada: McGraw-Hill, 1972.

WHITE, O. K. JR. and WHITE, D.   "Abandoning an Unpopular Policy: An Analysis of the Decision Granting Mormon Priesthood to Blacks," *Sociological Analysis*, 1980, *41*, 231-45.

WHITE, V.   *God and the Unconscious*. New York: Meridian, 1961.

WHITEHEAD, A. N.   *Religion in the Making*. New York: Macmillan, 1926.

WIEMAN, H. N., and WESTCOTT-WIEMAN. R.   *Normative Psychology of Religion*. New York: Crowell, 1935.

WIETING, S. G.   "An Examination of Intergenerational Patterns of Religious Belief and Practice," *Sociological Analysis*, 1975. *36*, 137-49.

WILLIAMS, J. P.   "The Nature of Religion." *Journal for the Scientific Study of Religion*, 1962, *2*, 3-14.

WILSON, B. R. (ed.).   *The Social Impact of New Religious Movements.* New York: Rose of Sharon Press, 1981.

WILSON, B. R.   *Sects and Society.* London: Heinemann, 1961.

_____.   "A Typology of Sect," in R. Robertson (ed.), *Sociology of Religion.* Baltimore: Penguin, 1969, pp. 361-83.

_____.   *Religious Sects.* New York: McGraw-Hill, 1970.

_____.   *Magic and the Millenium.* New York: Harper and Row, 1973.

WILSON, J.   *Religion in American Society: The Effective Presence.* Englewood Cliffs, NJ: Prentice-Hall, 1978.

WILSON, W. C.   "Extrinsic Religious Values and Prejudice." *Journal of Abnormal and Social Psychology,* 1960, *60,* 286-88.

WIMBERLY, R. C.   "Dimensions of Commitment: Generalizing from Religion to Politics." *Journal for the Scientific Study of Religion,* 1978, *17,* 225-40.

WITTKOWSKI, J. and BAUMGARTNER, I.   "Religiosity and Attitude Toward Death and Dying in Old Persons," *Zeitschrift fur Gerontologie,* ,1977, *10,* 61-68.

WITTMAN, P.   "Developmental Characteristics and Personalities of Chronic Alcoholics, *Journal of Abnormal and Social Psychology,* 1939, *34,* 361-77.

WONG, P. T. P.   "Frustration, Exploration, and Learning." *Canadian Psychological Review,* 1979, *20,* 133-44.

WONG, P. T. P. and B. WEINER.   "When People Ask "Why" Questions, and the Heuristics of Attributional Search." *Journal of Personality and Social Psychology, 40,* 1981, 650-63.

WOODWARD, K. L.   "How America Lives with Death," *Time,* April 6, 1970, 81-88.

WOODWARD, K. L. and SALHOLZ, E. "The Rights New Bogeyman," *Newsweek,* July 6, 1981, 48-50.

WOOD, W. W.   *Culture and Personality Aspects of the Pentacostal Holiness Religion.* The Hague: Mouton and Company, 1965.

WORCHEL, S. and ANDREOLI V.   "Escape to Freedom: The Relationship between Attribution of Causality and Psychological Reactance," in J. H. Harvey, W. J. Ickes, and R. F. Kidd (eds.), *New Directions in Attributional Research. Vol. I.* Hillsdale, N.J.: Lawrence E. Erlbaum, 1976, pp. 249-269.

WORTMAN, C. B. "Causal Attributions and Perceived Control," in J. H. Harvey, W. Ickes, and R. F. Kidd (eds.), *New directions in Attributional Research. Vol. I,* 1976, pp. 23-52.

WRIGHT, D.   "Morality and Religion: A Review of Empirical Studies," *Rationalist Annual,* 1967, 26-36.

WRIGHT, J. C.   "Personal Adjustment and Its Relationships to Religious Attitudes and Certainty," *Religious Education,* 1959, *54,* 521-23.

WRIGHT, S. A., and D'ANTONIO, W. V.   "A Research Note on Yinger's Study of the Substructure of Religion." Paper presented at the meeting of the Society for the Scientific Study of Religion, San Antonio, Texas, October 1979.

WULF, J., PRENTICE, D., HANSUM, D., FERRAR, A., and SPILKA, B.   "Religiosity and Sexual Attitudes and Behavior among Evangelical Christian Singles." *Review of Religious Research,* 1984, *26,* 119-31.

WUTHNOW, R.   *Experimentation in American Religion.* Berkeley, Calif.: University of California Press, 1978.

YAFFE, J.   *The American Jews.* New York: Random House, 1968.

YEATTS, J. R. and ASHER, W.   "Can We Afford Not To Do True Experiments in Psychology of Religion? A Reply to Batson," *Journal for the Scientific Study of Religion,* 1979, *18,* 86-89.

YINGER, J. M.   "Pluralism, Religion, and Secularism." *Journal for the Scientific Study of Religion,* 1967, *6,* 17-28.

_____.   "A Research Note on Interfaith Marriage Statistics. *Journal for the Scientific Study of Religion,* 1968a, *7,* 97-103.

————. "On the Definition of Interfaith Marriage." *Journal for the Scientific Study of Religion*, 1968b, *7*, 104–7.

————. "A Structural Examination of Religion." *Journal for the Scientific Study of Religion*, 1969, *8*, 88–100.

————. *The Scientific Study of Religion*. New York: MacMillan, 1970.

————. " A Comparative Study of the Substructures of Religion." *Journal for the Scientific Study of Religion, 16*, 1977, 67–86.

ZAEHNER, R. C. *Mysticism: Sacred and Profane*. New York: Oxford University Press, 1961.

ZILBOORG, G. and HENRY, G. W. *A History of Medical Psychology*. New York: Norton, 1941.

ZUBECK, J. P. (ed.). *Sensory Deprivation: Fifteen Years of Research*. New York: Appleton-Century-Crofts, 1969.

Author Index

SUBJECT INDEX